STREI

Wiltshire and Swindon

rst published 2002 by

ilip's, a division of
ctopus Publishing Group Ltd
-4 Heron Quays, London E14 4JP

rst colour edition 2002
rst impression 2002

BN 0-540-08112-4

Printed and bound in Spain
by Cayfosa-Quebecor

Contents

III **Key to map symbols**

IV **Key to map pages**

VI **Route planning**

VIII **Administrative and Postcode boundaries**

1 **Street maps** at 2½ inches to 1 mile

163 **Street maps** at 1¼ inches to 1 mile

213 **Street maps** at 2½ inches to 1 mile

218 **Town maps** of Andover and Frome

219 **Town map of** Bath at 5 inches to 1 mile

220 **Index** of towns and villages

223 **Index** of streets, hospitals, industrial estates, railway stations, schools, shopping centres, universities and places of interest

Digital Data

The exceptionally high-quality mapping found in this atlas is available as digital data in TIFF format, which is easily convertible to other bit mapped (raster) image formats.

The index is also available in digital form as a standard database table. It contains all the details found in the printed index together with the National Grid reference for the map square in which each entry is named.

For further information and to discuss your requirements, please contact Philip's on 020 7531 8439 or george.philip@philips-maps.co.uk

Key to map symbols

22a	**Motorway** with junction number
	Primary route – dual/single carriageway
	A road – dual/single carriageway
	B road – dual/single carriageway
	Minor road – dual/single carriageway
	Other minor road – dual/single carriageway
	Road under construction
	Pedestrianised area
DY7	**Postcode boundaries**
	County and unitary authority boundaries
	Railway
	Railway under construction
	Tramway, miniature railway
	Rural track, private road or narrow road in urban area
	Gate or obstruction to traffic (restrictions may not apply at all times or to all vehicles)
	Path, bridleway, byway open to all traffic, road used as a public path
	The representation in this atlas of a road, track or path is no evidence of the existence of a right of way
214 168 72	**Adjoining page indicators** (The colour of the arrow indicates the scale of the adjoining page - see scales below)
217	**The map area within the blue band is shown at a larger scale on the page, indicated by the blue block and arrow**

Walsall	**Railway station**
	Private railway station
	Bus, coach station
	Ambulance station
	Coastguard station
	Fire station
	Police station
	Accident and Emergency entrance to hospital
H	**Hospital**
	Place of worship
i	**Information Centre** (open all year)
P	**Parking**
P&R	**Park and Ride**
PO	**Post Office**
	Camping site
	Caravan site
	Golf course
	Picnic site
Prim Sch	**Important buildings, schools, colleges, universities and hospitals**
River Medway	**Water name**
	River, stream
	Lock, weir
	Water
	Tidal water
	Woods
	Houses
Church	**Non-Roman antiquity**
ROMAN FORT	**Roman antiquity**

Abbreviation	Meaning	Abbreviation	Meaning
Acad	**Academy**	Mkt	**Market**
Allot Gdns	**Allotments**	Meml	**Memorial**
Cemy	**Cemetery**	Mon	**Monument**
C Ctr	**Civic Centre**	Mus	**Museum**
CH	**Club House**	Obsy	**Observatory**
Coll	**College**	Pal	**Royal Palace**
Crem	**Crematorium**	PH	**Public House**
Ent	**Enterprise**	Recn Gd	**Recreation Ground**
Ex H	**Exhibition Hall**	Resr	**Reservoir**
Ind Est	**Industrial Estate**	Ret Pk	**Retail Park**
IRB Sta	**Inshore Rescue Boat Station**	Sch	**School**
Inst	**Institute**	Sh Ctr	**Shopping Centre**
Ct	**Law Court**	TH	**Town Hall/House**
L Ctr	**Leisure Centre**	Trad Est	**Trading Estate**
LC	**Level Crossing**	Univ	**University**
Liby	**Library**	Wks	**Works**
		YH	**Youth Hostel**

■ The small numbers around the edges of the maps identify the 1 kilometre National Grid lines ■ The dark grey border on the inside edge of some pages indicates that the mapping does not continue onto the adjacent page

The scale of the maps on the pages numbered in blue is 3.92 cm to 1 km • 2½ inches to 1 mile • 1: 25344

0 – ¼ – ½ – ¾ – 1 mile
0 – 250 m – 500 m – 750 m – 1 kilometre

The scale of the maps on pages numbered in green is 1.96 cm to 1 km • 1¼ inches to 1 mile • 1: 50688

0 – ¼ – ½ – ¾ – 1 mile
0 – 250m – 500m – 750m – 1kilometre

The scale of the maps on pages numbered in red is 7.84 cm to 1 km • 5 inches to 1 mile • 1: 12672

0 – 220 yards – 440 yards – 660 yards – ½ mile
0 – 125 m – 250 m – 375 m – ½ kilometre

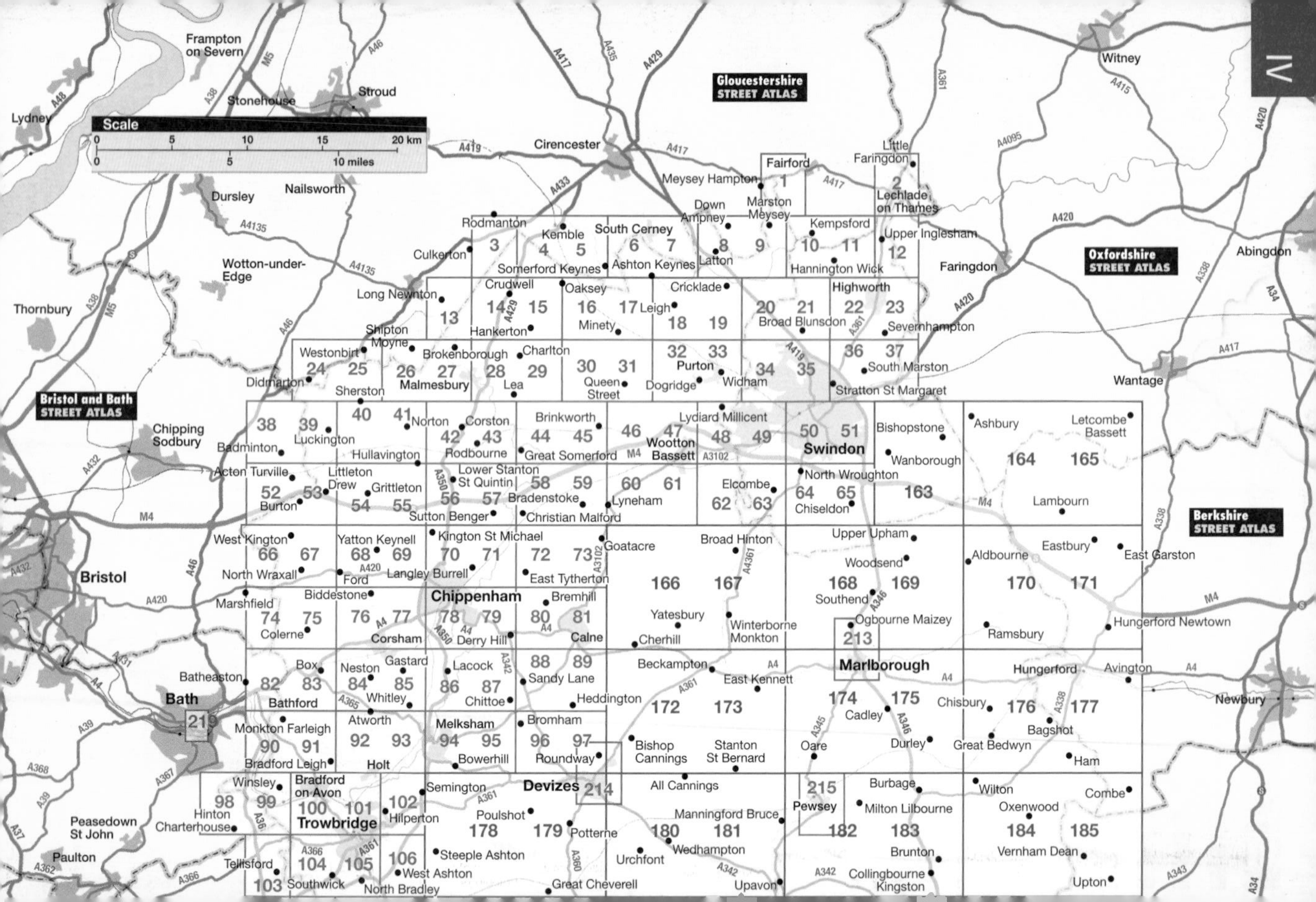
Scale
0 5 10 15 20 km
0 5 10 miles
Gloucestershire STREET ATLAS
Oxfordshire STREET ATLAS
Berkshire STREET ATLAS
Bristol and Bath STREET ATLAS
Lydney
Frampton on Severn
Stonehouse
Stroud
Witney
Cirencester
Dursley
Nailsworth
Wotton-under-Edge
Thornbury
Chipping Sodbury
Bristol
Bath
Abingdon
Faringdon
Wantage
Newbury
Peasedown St John
Paulton
Fairford
Little Faringdon
Lechlade on Thames
Meysey Hampton
Down Ampney
Marston Meysey
Rodmanton
Kemble
South Cerney
Kempsford
Upper Inglesham
Culkerton
Somerford Keynes
Ashton Keynes
Latton
Hannington Wick
Crudwell
Oaksey
Cricklade
Highworth
Long Newnton
Hankerton
Minety
Leigh
Broad Blunsdon
Severnhampton
Shipton Moyne
Westonbirt
Brokenborough
Charlton
Purton
South Marston
Didmarton
Sherston
Malmesbury
Lea
Queen Street
Dogridge
Widham
Stratton St Margaret
Badminton
Luckington
Norton
Corston
Brinkworth
Lydiard Millicent
Wootton Bassett
Swindon
Bishopstone
Ashbury
Letcombe Bassett
Hullavington
Rodbourne
Great Somerford
Wanborough
Acton Turville
Littleton Drew
Grittleton
Lower Stanton St Quintin
Bradenstoke
Lyneham
Elcombe
North Wroughton
Chiseldon
Lambourn
Burton
Sutton Benger
Christian Malford
West Kington
Yatton Keynell
Kington St Michael
Goatacre
Broad Hinton
Upper Upham
Aldbourne
Eastbury
East Garston
North Wraxall
Ford
Langley Burrell
East Tytherton
Woodsend
Marshfield
Biddestone
Chippenham
Bremhill
Southend
Yatesbury
Winterborne Monkton
Ogbourne Maizey
Ramsbury
Hungerford Newtown
Colerne
Corsham
Derry Hill
Calne
Cherhill
Batheaston
Box
Neston
Gastard
Lacock
Sandy Lane
Beckampton
East Kennett
Marlborough
Hungerford
Avington
Bathford
Whitley
Chittoe
Heddington
Cadley
Chisbury
Bagshot
Monkton Farleigh
Atworth
Melksham
Bromham
Bishop Cannings
Stanton St Bernard
Oare
Durley
Great Bedwyn
Ham
Bradford Leigh
Holt
Bowerhill
Roundway
Winsley
Bradford on Avon
Semington
Devizes
All Cannings
Burbage
Wilton
Combe
Hinton Charterhouse
Trowbridge
Hilperton
Poulshot
Potterne
Manningford Bruce
Pewsey
Milton Lilbourne
Oxenwood
Wedhampton
Urchfont
Steeple Ashton
Tellisford
Southwick
West Ashton
North Bradley
Great Cheverell
Upavon
Brunton
Collingbourne Kingston
Vernham Dean
Upton
A48 A38 M5 A46 A417 A435 A429 A419 A433 A4135 A361 A4095 A415 A420 A338 A34 A432 M4 A350 A3102 A4361 A346 A4 A342 A345 A365 A366 A363 A3102 A360 A367 A368 A39 A37 A362 A343 A36
1 2 3 4 5 6 7 8 9 10 11 12 13 14 15 16 17 18 19 20 21 22 23 24 25 26 27 28 29 30 31 32 33 34 35 36 37 38 39 40 41 42 43 44 45 46 47 48 49 50 51 52 53 54 55 56 57 58 59 60 61 62 63 64 65 66 67 68 69 70 71 72 73 74 75 76 77 78 79 80 81 82 83 84 85 86 87 88 89 90 91 92 93 94 95 96 97 98 99 100 101 102 103 104 105 106 163 164 165 166 167 168 169 170 171 172 173 174 175 176 177 178 179 180 181 182 183 184 185 213 214 215 219

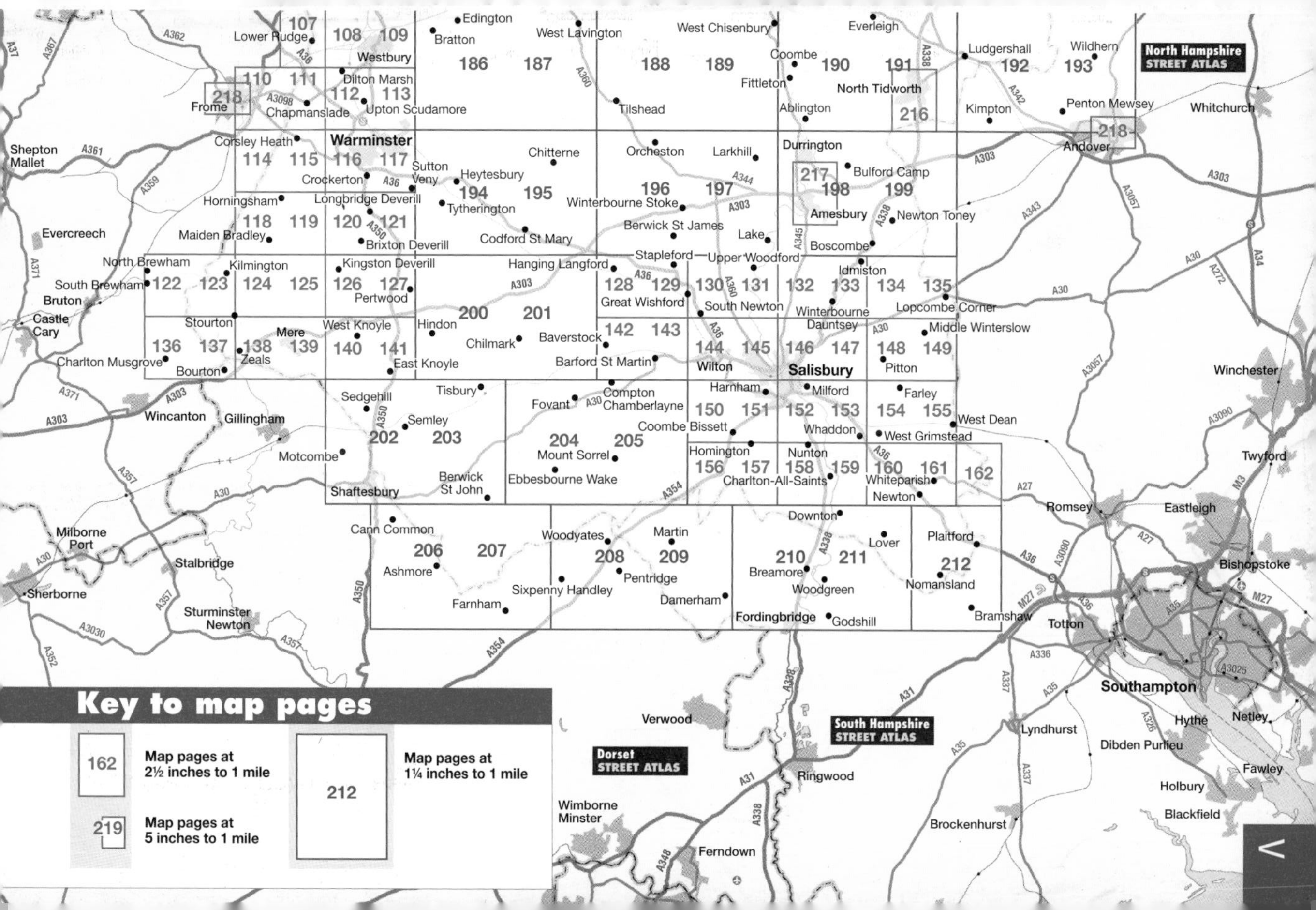

Key to map pages
162 Map pages at 2½ inches to 1 mile
219 Map pages at 5 inches to 1 mile
212 Map pages at 1¼ inches to 1 mile
North Hampshire STREET ATLAS
South Hampshire STREET ATLAS
Dorset STREET ATLAS
V
Lower Rudge
Westbury
Edington
Bratton
West Lavington
West Chisenbury
Everleigh
Ludgershall
Wildhern
Whitchurch
Frome
Dilton Marsh
Chapmanslade
Upton Scudamore
Tilshead
Coombe
Fittleton
Ablington
North Tidworth
Kimpton
Penton Mewsey
Andover
Shepton Mallet
Corsley Heath
Warminster
Sutton Veny
Crockerton
Heytesbury
Chitterne
Orcheston
Larkhill
Durrington
Bulford Camp
Horningsham
Longbridge Deverill
Tytherington
Winterbourne Stoke
Amesbury
Newton Toney
Evercreech
Maiden Bradley
Brixton Deverill
Codford St Mary
Berwick St James
Lake
Boscombe
North Brewham
Kilmington
Kingston Deverill
Hanging Langford
Stapleford
Upper Woodford
Idmiston
South Brewham
Bruton
Pertwood
Great Wishford
South Newton
Winterbourne Dauntsey
Lopcombe Corner
Castle Cary
Stourton
Mere
West Knoyle
Hindon
Chilmark
Baverstock
Middle Winterslow
Charlton Musgrove
Zeals
Bourton
East Knoyle
Barford St Martin
Wilton
Salisbury
Pitton
Winchester
Sedgehill
Tisbury
Fovant
Compton Chamberlayne
Harnham
Milford
Farley
Wincanton
Gillingham
Semley
Coombe Bissett
Whaddon
West Dean
West Grimstead
Motcombe
Homington
Nunton
Twyford
Shaftesbury
Berwick St John
Mount Sorrel
Ebbesbourne Wake
Charlton-All-Saints
Whiteparish
Newton
Romsey
Eastleigh
Cann Common
Downton
Milborne Port
Ashmore
Woodyates
Martin
Lover
Plaitford
Stalbridge
Breamore
Pentridge
Sixpenny Handley
Woodgreen
Nomansland
Bishopstoke
Sherborne
Farnham
Damerham
Sturminster Newton
Fordingbridge
Godshill
Bramshaw
Totton
Southampton
Verwood
Lyndhurst
Netley
Hythe
Dibden Purlieu
Fawley
Ringwood
Holbury
Wimborne Minster
Brockenhurst
Blackfield
Ferndown

Route planning

VII
Wiltshire
Hampshire
Somerset
Dorset
SALISBURY PLAIN
VALE OF WARDOUR
CRANBORNE CHASE
BLACKMOOR VALE
Salisbury
Southampton
SOUTHAMPTON
EASTLEIGH
Winchester
Andover
Amesbury
Durrington
Tidworth
Warminster
Westbury
Frome
Radstock
Midsomer Norton
Bruton
Castle Cary
Wincanton
Mere
Gillingham
Shaftesbury
Sherborne
Stalbridge
Sturminster Newton
Blandford Forum
Wimborne Minster
Ferndown
Verwood
Fordingbridge
Ringwood
Romsey
Totton
Lyndhurst
Brockenhurst
Hythe
Wilton
Evercreech

Administrative and Postcode boundaries

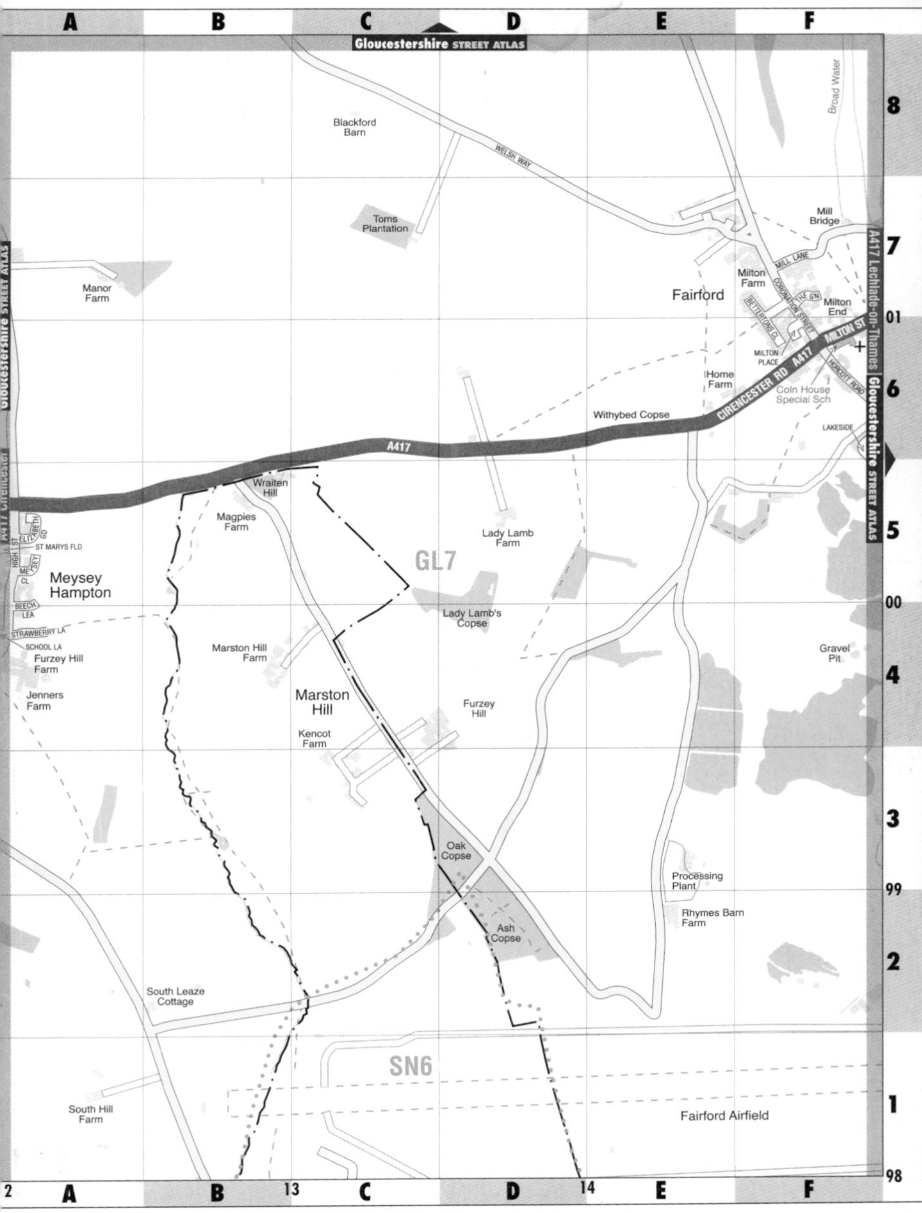
Gloucestershire STREET ATLAS
Blackford Barn
WELSH WAY
Toms Plantation
Broad Water
Mill Bridge
MILL LANE
Milton Farm
Fairford
CORONATION STREET
THE GN
Milton End
BETTERTONS CL
MILTON ST
MILTON PLACE
A417
CIRENCESTER RD
HORCOTT ROAD
Home Farm
Coln House Special Sch
Withybed Copse
LAKESIDE
A417 Lechlade-on-Thames
Gloucestershire STREET ATLAS
Manor Farm
A417 Cirencester
Wraiten Hill
Magpies Farm
Lady Lamb Farm
GL7
ST MARYS FLD
Meysey Hampton
Lady Lamb's Copse
STRAWBERRY LA
SCHOOL LA
Furzey Hill Farm
Marston Hill Farm
Gravel Pit
Jenners Farm
Marston Hill
Furzey Hill
Kencot Farm
Oak Copse
Processing Plant
Rhymes Barn Farm
Ash Copse
South Leaze Cottage
SN6
South Hill Farm
Fairford Airfield
A B C D E F
8 7 01 6 5 00 4 3 99 2 1 98
2 13 14

9
10

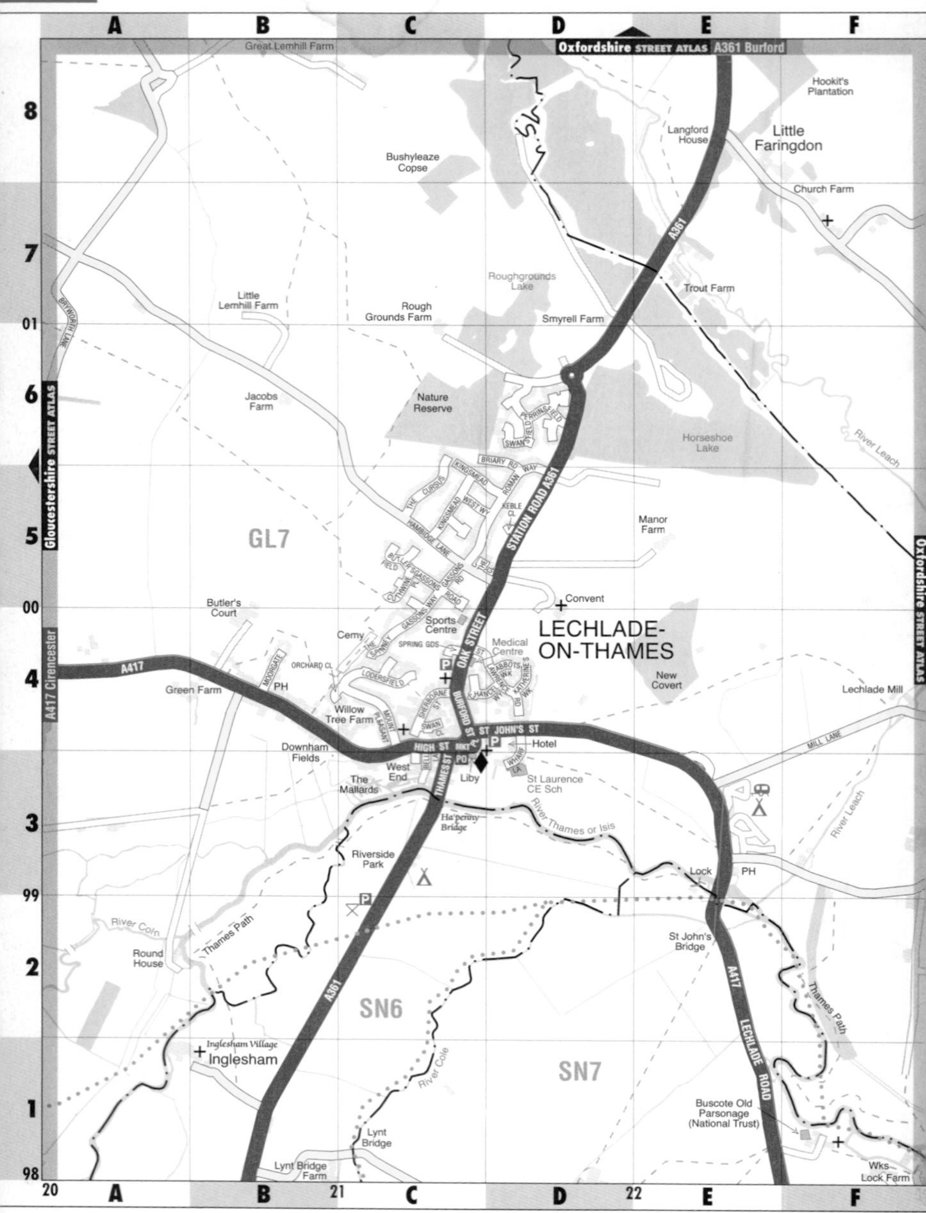

A B C D E F
Oxfordshire STREET ATLAS A361 Burford
Great Lemhill Farm
Hookit's Plantation
Langford House
Little Faringdon
Bushyleaze Copse
Church Farm
A361
Roughgrounds Lake
Trout Farm
Little Lemhill Farm
Rough Grounds Farm
Smyrell Farm
BRYWORTH LANE
Jacobs Farm
Nature Reserve
PERRINSFIELD
SWANFIELD
Horseshoe Lake
River Leach
Gloucestershire STREET ATLAS
BRIARY RD
KINGSMEAD
ROMAN WAY
THE CURSUS
WEST WY
KEBLE CL
STATION ROAD A361
GL7
HAMBIDGE LANE
Manor Farm
BUTLER'S FIELD
GASSONS RD
THWAITE PL
GASSONS WAY
GASSONS ROAD
Oxfordshire STREET ATLAS
Butler's Court
Convent
Sports Centre
OAK STREET
LECHLADE-ON-THAMES
Cemy
THE SPINNEY
SPRING GDS
Medical Centre
A417 Cirencester
A417
MOORGATE
ORCHARD CL
LODERSFIELD
ABBOTS WK
ST KATHERINE'S WK
New Covert
Green Farm
PH
SHERBORNE ST
HANCE
Lechlade Mill
Willow Tree Farm
PLEASANT
SWAN CL
BURFORD ST
ST JOHN'S ST
MILL LANE
Downham Fields
HIGH ST
MKT
Hotel
WHARF LA
West End
THAMES ST
PO
Liby
The Mallards
St Laurence CE Sch
Ha'penny Bridge
River Thames or Isis
River Leach
Riverside Park
Lock
PH
River Coln
Thames Path
St John's Bridge
Round House
A361
A417
Thames Path
SN6
Inglesham Village
Inglesham
SN7
LECHLADE ROAD
River Cole
Buscote Old Parsonage (National Trust)
Lynt Bridge
Lynt Bridge Farm
Wks
Lock Farm
8 7 01 6 5 00 4 3 99 2 1 98
20 21 22

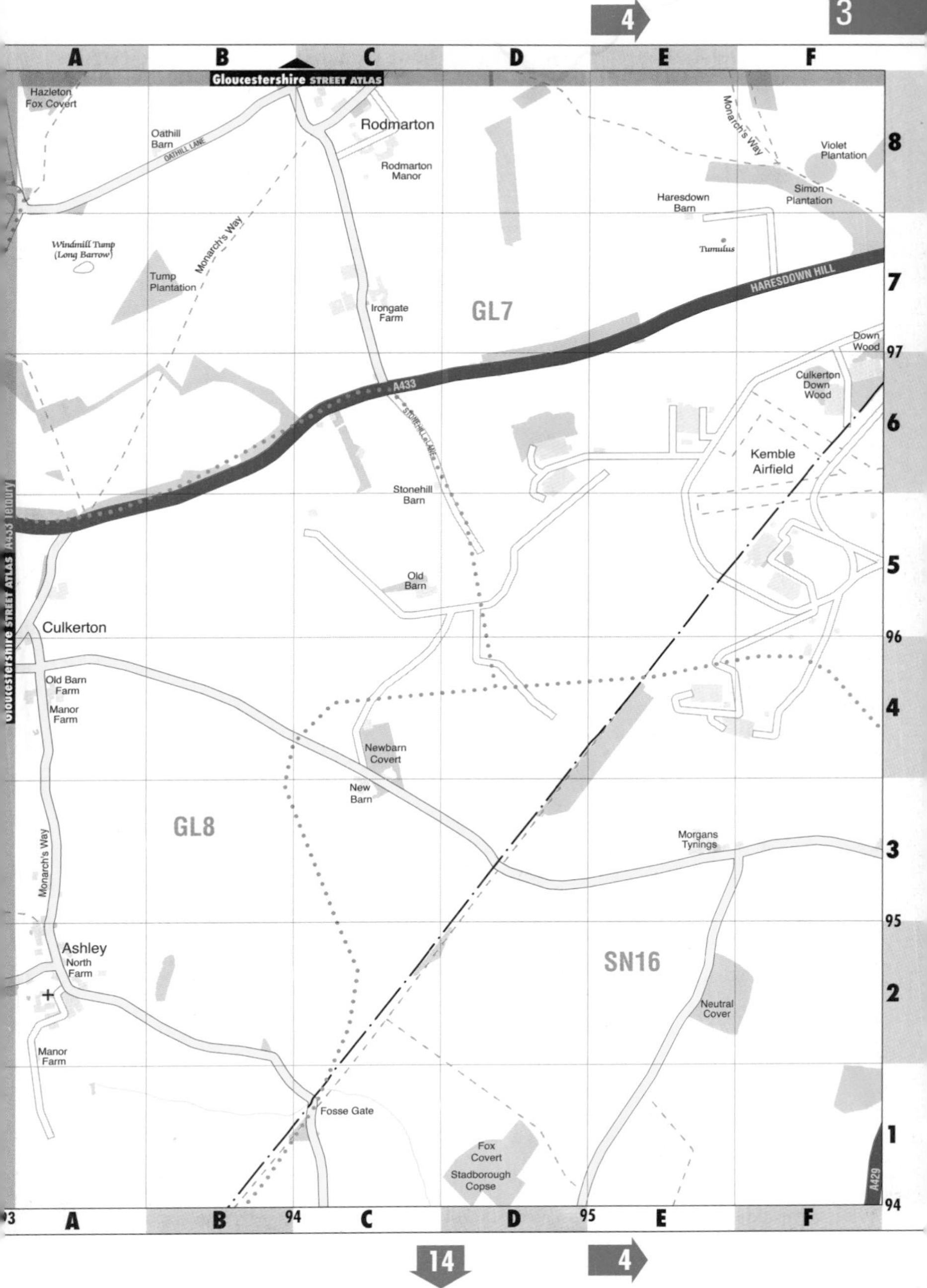
Gloucestershire STREET ATLAS
A
B
C
D
E
F
8
7
97
6
5
96
4
3
95
2
1
94
Hazleton Fox Covert
Oathill Barn
OATHILL LANE
Rodmarton
Rodmarton Manor
Monarch's Way
Violet Plantation
Simon Plantation
Haresdown Barn
Tumulus
Windmill Tump (Long Barrow)
Tump Plantation
Irongate Farm
GL7
HARESDOWN HILL
Down Wood
Culkerton Down Wood
A433
STONEHILL LANE
Kemble Airfield
Stonehill Barn
Gloucestershire STREET ATLAS
A433 Tetbury
Old Barn
Culkerton
Old Barn Farm
Manor Farm
Newbarn Covert
New Barn
GL8
Morgans Tynings
Ashley
North Farm
SN16
Neutral Cover
Manor Farm
Fosse Gate
Fox Covert
Stadborough Copse
A429
93
94
95

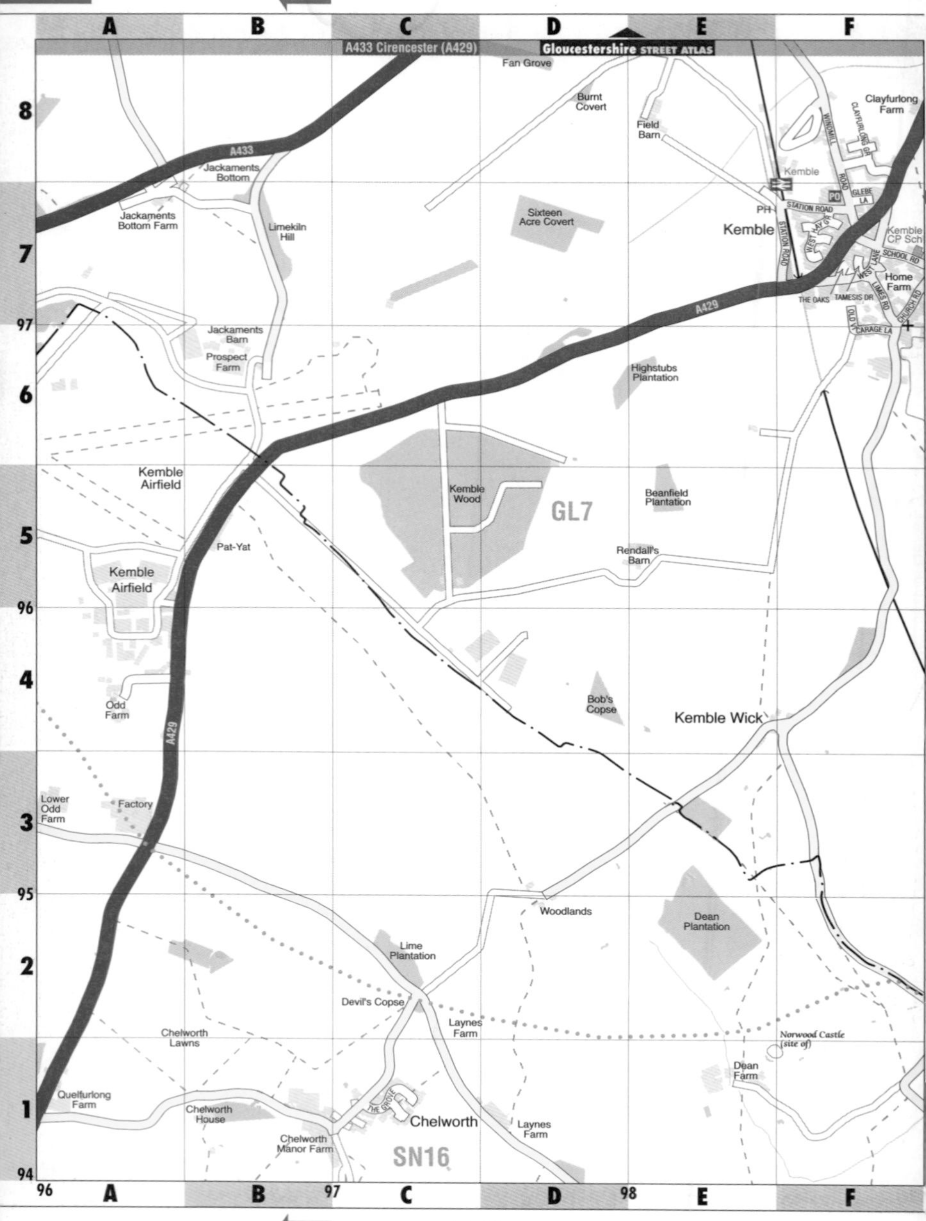
A433 Cirencester (A429)
Gloucestershire STREET ATLAS
A
B
C
D
E
F
8
7
97
6
5
96
4
3
95
2
1
94
96
97
98
Fan Grove
Burnt Covert
Field Barn
Clayfurlong Farm
A433
Jackaments Bottom
Jackaments Bottom Farm
Limekiln Hill
Sixteen Acre Covert
Kemble
PH
STATION ROAD
PO
GLEBE LA
Kemble CP Sch
SCHOOL RD
Home Farm
WINDMILL ROAD
CLAYFURLONG GR
WEST HAY GR
WEST LANE
LIMES RD
CHURCH RD
THE OAKS
TAMESIS DR
OLD YD
GARAGE LA
A429
Jackaments Barn
Prospect Farm
Highstubs Plantation
Kemble Airfield
Kemble Wood
GL7
Beanfield Plantation
Pat-Yat
Rendall's Barn
Kemble Airfield
Odd Farm
Bob's Copse
Kemble Wick
Lower Odd Farm
Factory
Woodlands
Dean Plantation
Lime Plantation
Devil's Copse
Laynes Farm
Chelworth Lawns
Norwood Castle (site of)
Dean Farm
Quelfurlong Farm
Chelworth House
THE GROVE
Chelworth
Laynes Farm
Chelworth Manor Farm
SN16

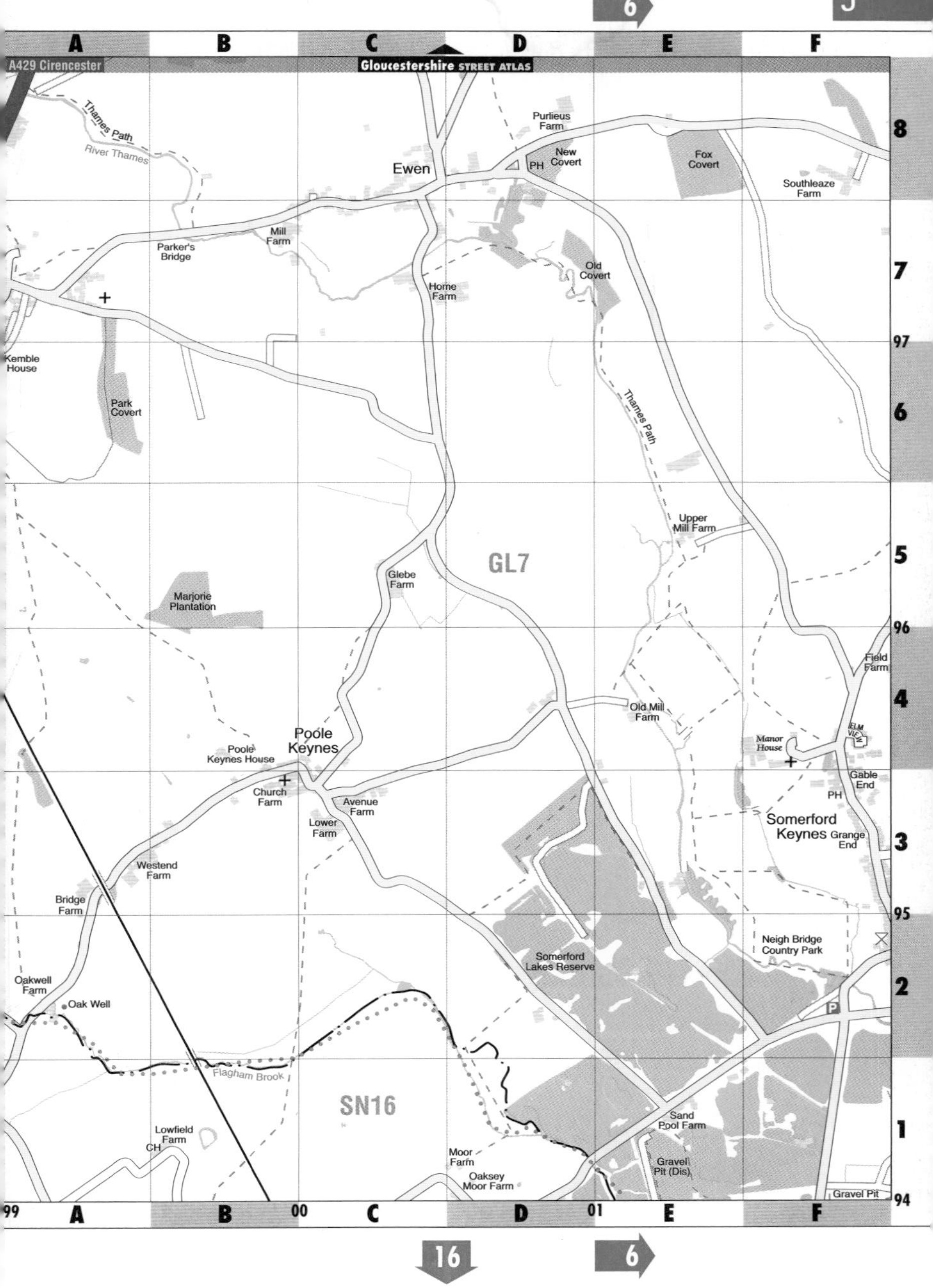
A B C D E F
A429 Cirencester
Gloucestershire STREET ATLAS
8
7
97
6
5
96
4
3
95
2
1
94
99 A B 00 C D 01 E F
Thames Path
River Thames
Ewen
Purlieus Farm
PH
New Covert
Fox Covert
Southleaze Farm
Mill Farm
Parker's Bridge
Home Farm
Old Covert
Kemble House
Park Covert
Thames Path
Upper Mill Farm
GL7
Glebe Farm
Marjorie Plantation
Field Farm
Old Mill Farm
Poole Keynes
Poole Keynes House
Church Farm
Manor House
ELM VIEW
Gable End
PH
Avenue Farm
Lower Farm
Somerford Keynes
Grange End
Westend Farm
Bridge Farm
Neigh Bridge Country Park
Somerford Lakes Reserve
Oakwell Farm
Oak Well
P
Flagham Brook
SN16
Lowfield Farm
CH
Sand Pool Farm
Moor Farm
Oaksey Moor Farm
Gravel Pit (Dis)
Gravel Pit

5

Gloucestershire STREET ATLAS
A
B
C
D
E
F
8
7
97
6
5
96
4
3
95
2
1
94
02
03
04
Hillview Farm
NORTHMOOR LANE
Dryleaze Covert
Camperdown
Castle
Berry Farm
ASHTON ROAD
Ash Copse
PH
SILVER STREET
CHURCH LA
SCHOOL LA
PO
Gravel Pit
Sewage Works
RIVER WAY
CHURN CL
Cross Roads Farm
MEADOW WAY
LANGET
JUBILEE GD
PH
HIGH STREET
Upper Up
Langet End
HAM LANE
BERKELEY CL
SUDELEY DR
Manor Farm
Shorncote
Glebe Farm
Old Manor Farm
GL7
Downs Farm
Ann Edwards Sch
BERKELEY CLOSE
OAK WY
THE LEAZE
Refuse/Slag Heap
Keynes Country Park
Ashton Down
Sewage Works
P
SPRATSGATE LANE
Cotswold Community
Cotswold Water Park
Works
Yacht Club
Millennium Park Centre
WHITEFRIARS LANE
P
Bag End
North End Farm
North End
Macks Farm
Clayhill Copse
SPINE ROAD WEST
SN6
B4696
Mill End
Furze Brake
Manor Farm
Old Manor Farm
Bell Copse
COX'S HILL
Ring and Bailey
Lower Mill Farm
Thames Path
Church Farm
Ashton Keynes
PH
BACK STREET
THE LEAZE
Moat
CHURCH WK
RICHMOND CT
PO
Manor House
Brook End
HIGH ROAD
FORE STREET
Gravel Pit
Freeth's Wood
PARK PL
EASTFIELD

5
17

8

A
B
C
D
E
F
Gloucestershire STREET ATLAS A419 Cirencester
Sisters Farm
Fosse Farm
Old Downs
Dukes Brake
Ashton Lodge Farm
Rainbows End
BOW WOW
Wildmoorway Lock (disused)
CIRENCESTER ROAD
River Churn
THE LENNARDS
MILL CT
BOXBUSH ROAD
FIELD CL
ROBERT FRANKLIN WY
LAKESIDE
ROBERT FRANKLIN WY
THE LENNARDS
Box Bush Farm
WILDMOORWAY LANE
HUXLEY CT
STATION ROAD
South Cerney
GL7
B4696
A419
CERNEY WICK LANE
Weir
Bakers Farm
Cerney Wick
BROADWAY LANE
PH
Stones Farm
Cerneywick Farm
SPINE ROAD (EAST)
B4696
WICKWATER LANE
Galegoes
Rosemary
Cerneywick Copse
Wickwater Farm
FRIDAYS HAM LANE
SN6
Cleveland Farm
New Covert
Wheatleys Barn Farm
Sewage Works
Works
Kent End Farm
Kent End
Rixon Gate
Gravel Pit
Thames Path
Witts End
KENT END
HARRIS RD
FRIDAYS HAM LANE
Sports Ground
Guest Farm
Rixon Farm
8
97
6
5
96
4
3
95
2
1
94
05
06
07

18

8

7

Gloucestershire STREET ATLAS

7

19

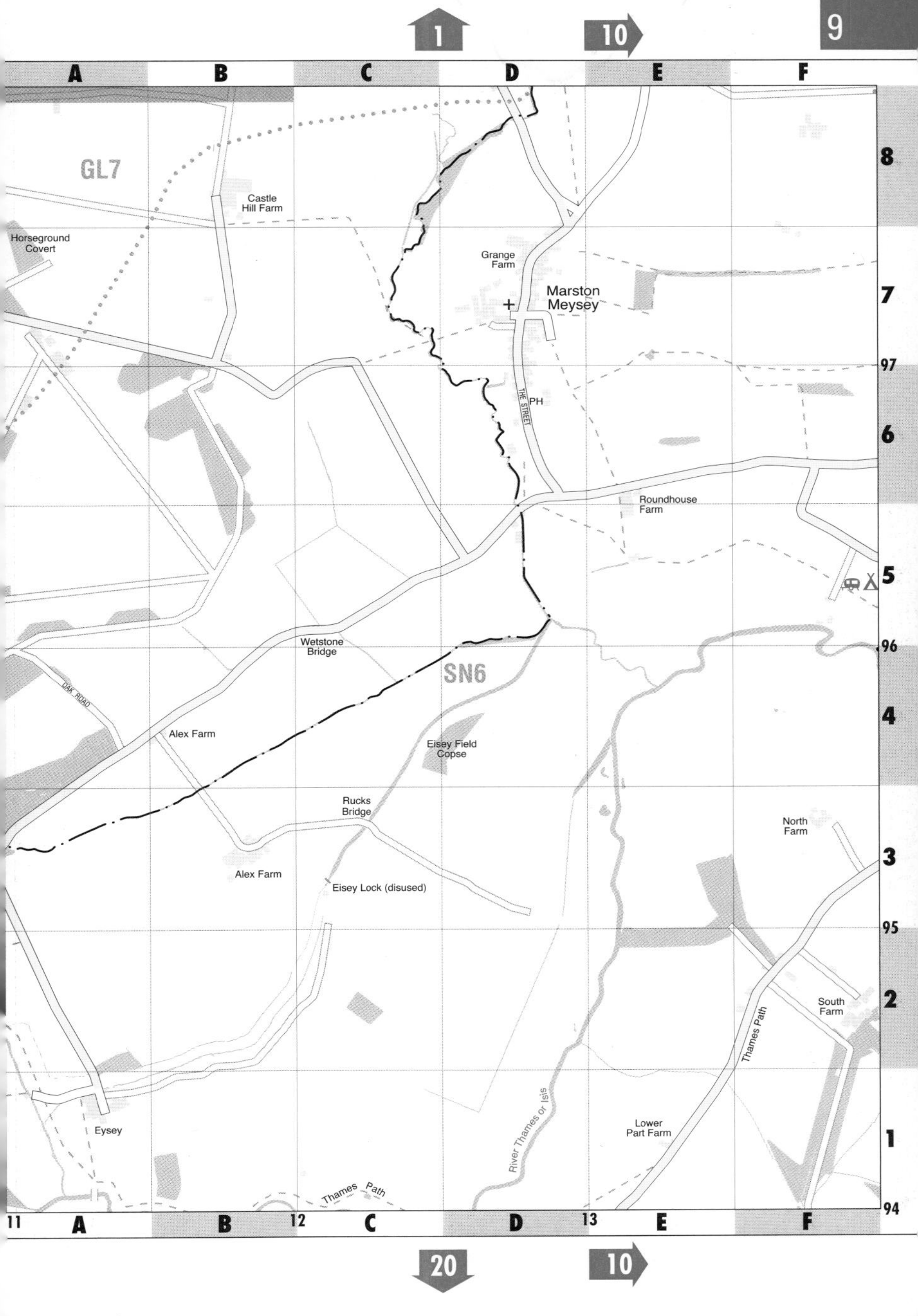
1
10
A
B
C
D
E
F
GL7
Castle
Hill Farm
Horseground
Covert
Grange
Farm
Marston
Meysey
THE STREET
PH
Roundhouse
Farm
Wetstone
Bridge
SN6
OAK ROAD
Alex Farm
Eisey Field
Copse
Rucks
Bridge
Alex Farm
Eisey Lock (disused)
North
Farm
South
Farm
Thames Path
River Thames or Isis
Lower
Part Farm
Eysey
Thames Path
8
7
97
6
5
96
4
3
95
2
1
94
11
12
13
20
10

1
9

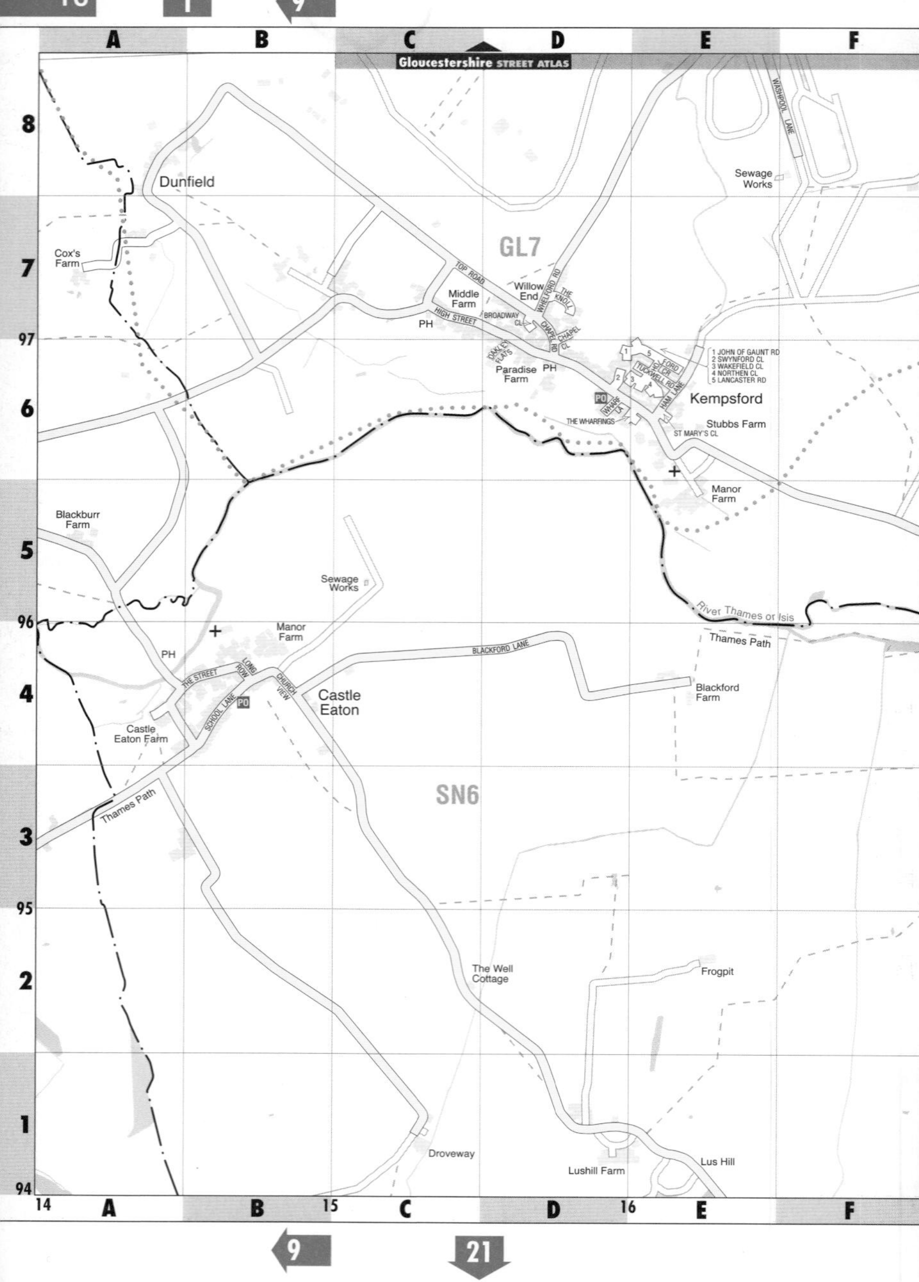
A
B
C
D
E
F
Gloucestershire STREET ATLAS
8
7
97
6
5
96
4
3
95
2
1
94
14
15
16
Dunfield
Cox's Farm
GL7
TOP ROAD
Middle Farm
Willow End
WHELFORD RD
THE KNOLL
HIGH STREET
BROADWAY CL
CHAPEL RD
CHAPEL CL
PH
OAKLEY FLATS
Paradise Farm
PH
1 JOHN OF GAUNT RD
2 SWYNFORD CL
3 WAKEFIELD CL
4 NORTHEN CL
5 LANCASTER RD
FORD CR
TUCKWELL RD
HAM LANE
Kempsford
PO
WHARF LA
THE WHARFINGS
Stubbs Farm
ST MARY'S CL
Manor Farm
WASHPOOL LANE
Sewage Works
Blackburr Farm
Sewage Works
River Thames or Isis
Thames Path
Manor Farm
PH
THE STREET
LONG ROW
CHURCH VIEW
BLACKFORD LANE
Castle Eaton
SCHOOL LANE
PO
Blackford Farm
Castle Eaton Farm
Thames Path
SN6
The Well Cottage
Frogpit
Droveway
Lushill Farm
Lus Hill

9
21

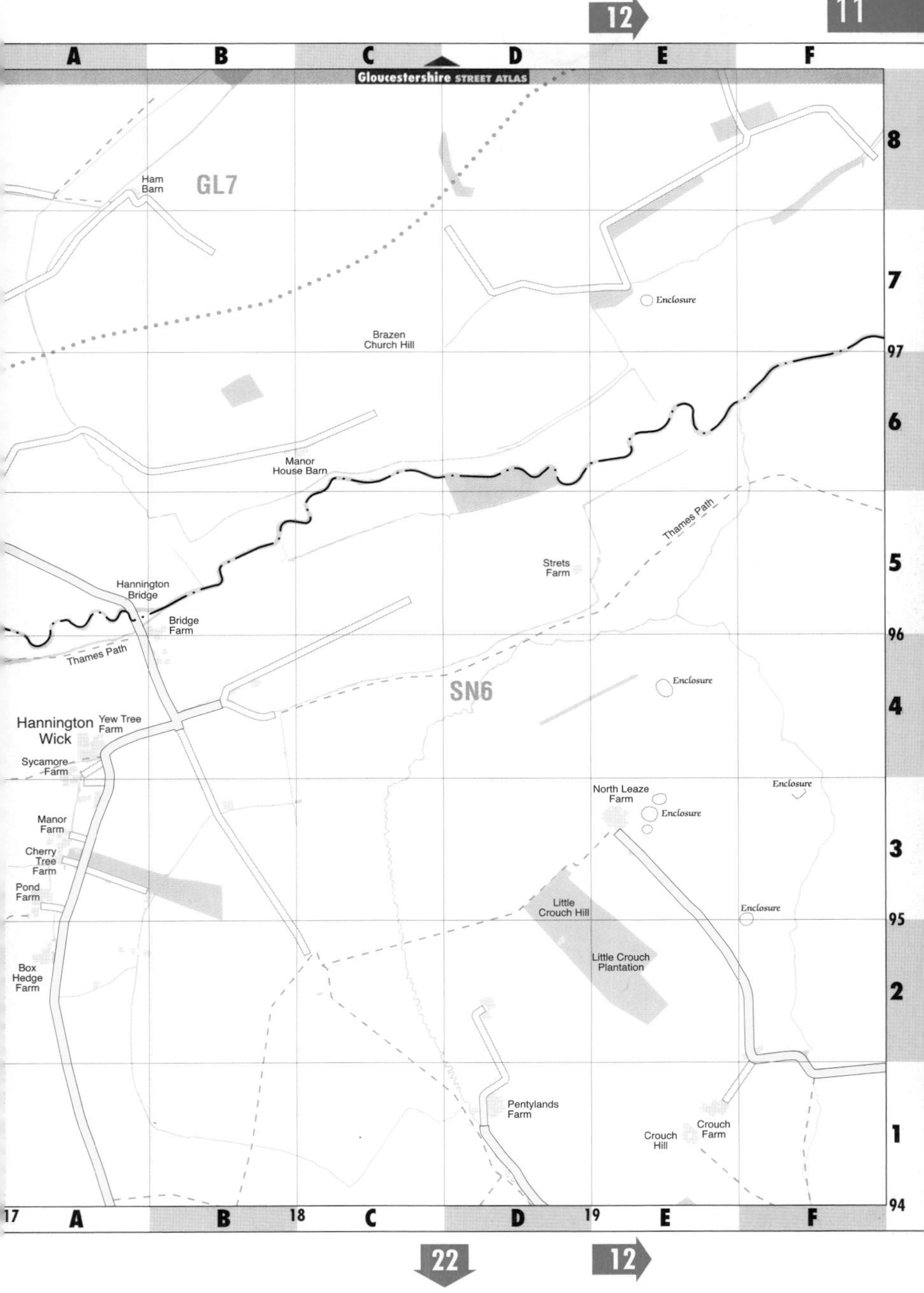
A
B
C
D
E
F
Gloucestershire STREET ATLAS
8
Ham Barn
GL7
7
Enclosure
Brazen Church Hill
97
6
Manor House Barn
Thames Path
5
Strets Farm
Hannington Bridge
Bridge Farm
96
Thames Path
Enclosure
SN6
4
Hannington Wick
Yew Tree Farm
Sycamore Farm
North Leaze Farm
Enclosure
Enclosure
Manor Farm
3
Cherry Tree Farm
Pond Farm
Little Crouch Hill
Enclosure
95
Box Hedge Farm
Little Crouch Plantation
2
Pentylands Farm
Crouch Farm
Crouch Hill
1
94
17
18
19

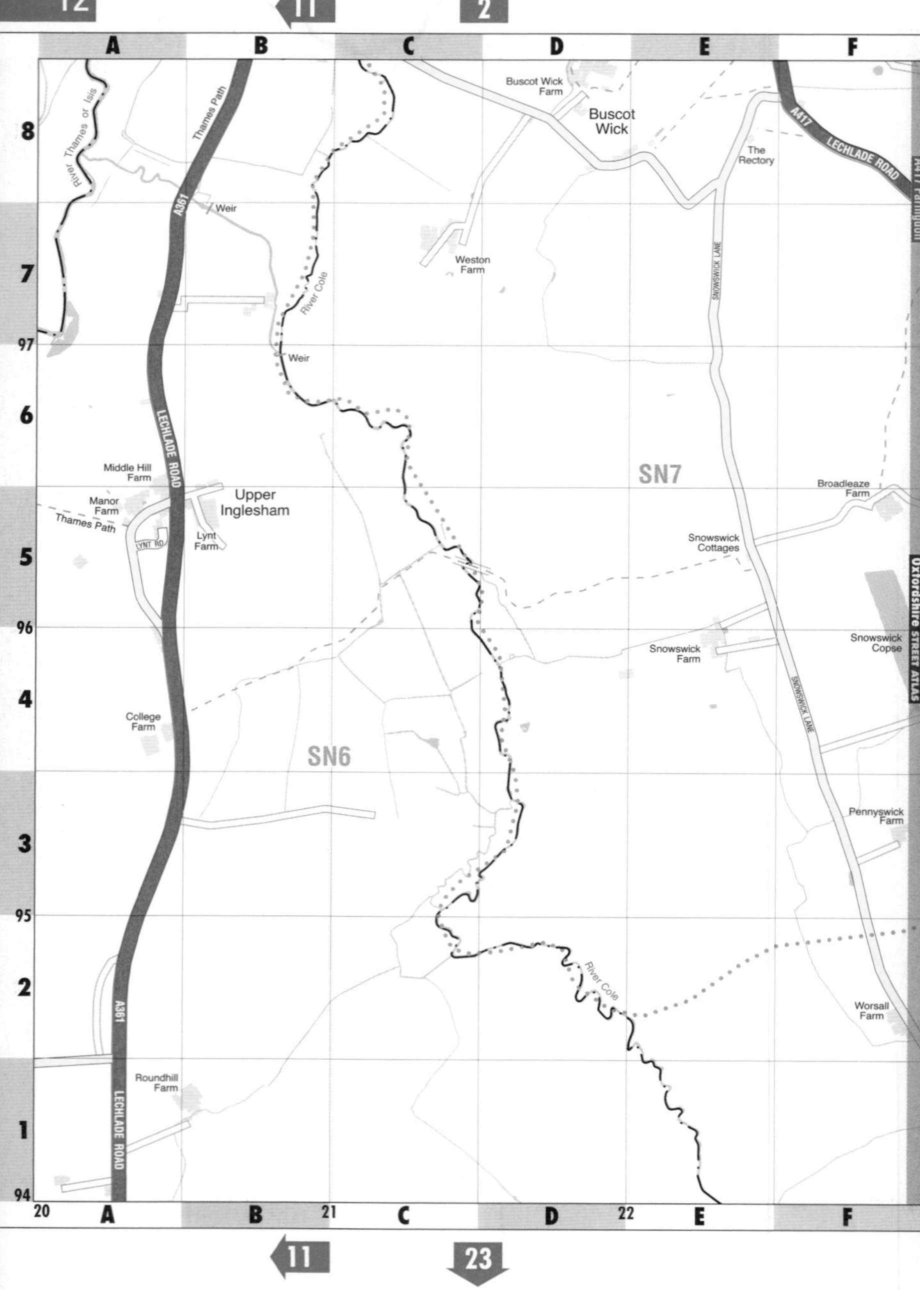
11
2
A
B
C
D
E
F
8
7
97
6
5
96
4
3
95
2
1
94
20
21
22
River Thames or Isis
Thames Path
A361
Weir
Buscot Wick Farm
Buscot Wick
A417
LECHLADE ROAD
The Rectory
A417 Faringdon
Weston Farm
River Cole
SNOWSWICK LANE
Weir
LECHLADE ROAD
Middle Hill Farm
Manor Farm
Thames Path
Upper Inglesham
LYNT RD
Lynt Farm
SN7
Broadleaze Farm
Snowswick Cottages
Oxfordshire STREET ATLAS
Snowswick Farm
Snowswick Copse
College Farm
SN6
Pennyswick Farm
River Cole
Worsall Farm
A361
Roundhill Farm
LECHLADE ROAD
11
23

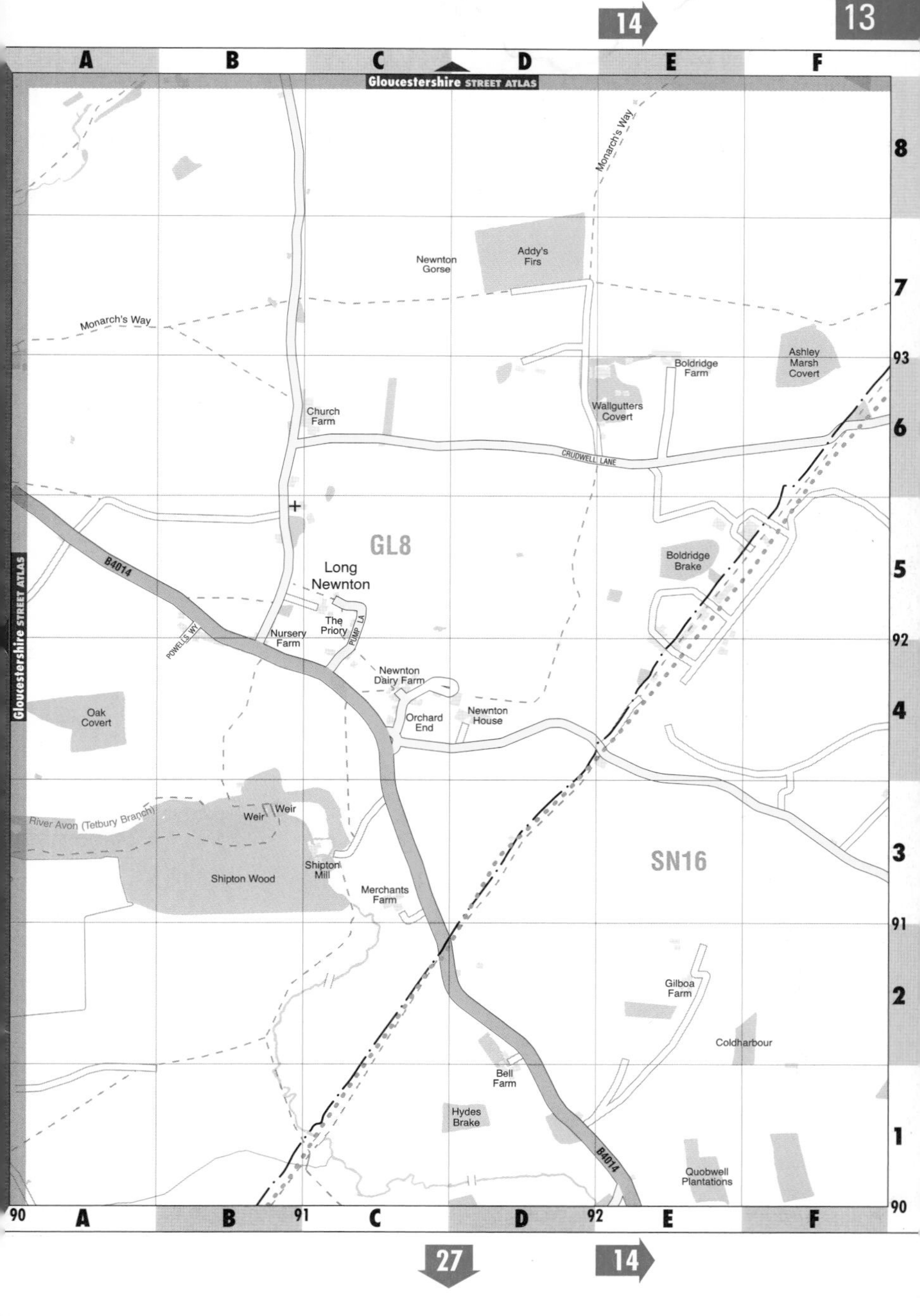
14
A
B
C
D
E
F
Gloucestershire STREET ATLAS
8
Monarch's Way
Newnton Gorse
Addy's Firs
7
Monarch's Way
93
Boldridge Farm
Ashley Marsh Covert
Church Farm
Wallgutters Covert
6
CRUDWELL LANE
GL8
Boldridge Brake
5
Long Newnton
B4014
The Priory
PUMP LA
Nursery Farm
POWELLS WY
92
Newnton Dairy Farm
Oak Covert
Orchard End
Newnton House
4
Weir
Weir
River Avon (Tetbury Branch)
3
Shipton Wood
Shipton Mill
SN16
Merchants Farm
91
Gilboa Farm
2
Coldharbour
Bell Farm
Hydes Brake
1
B4014
Quobwell Plantations
90
90
A
B
91
C
D
92
E
F
27
14
Gloucestershire STREET ATLAS

13
3

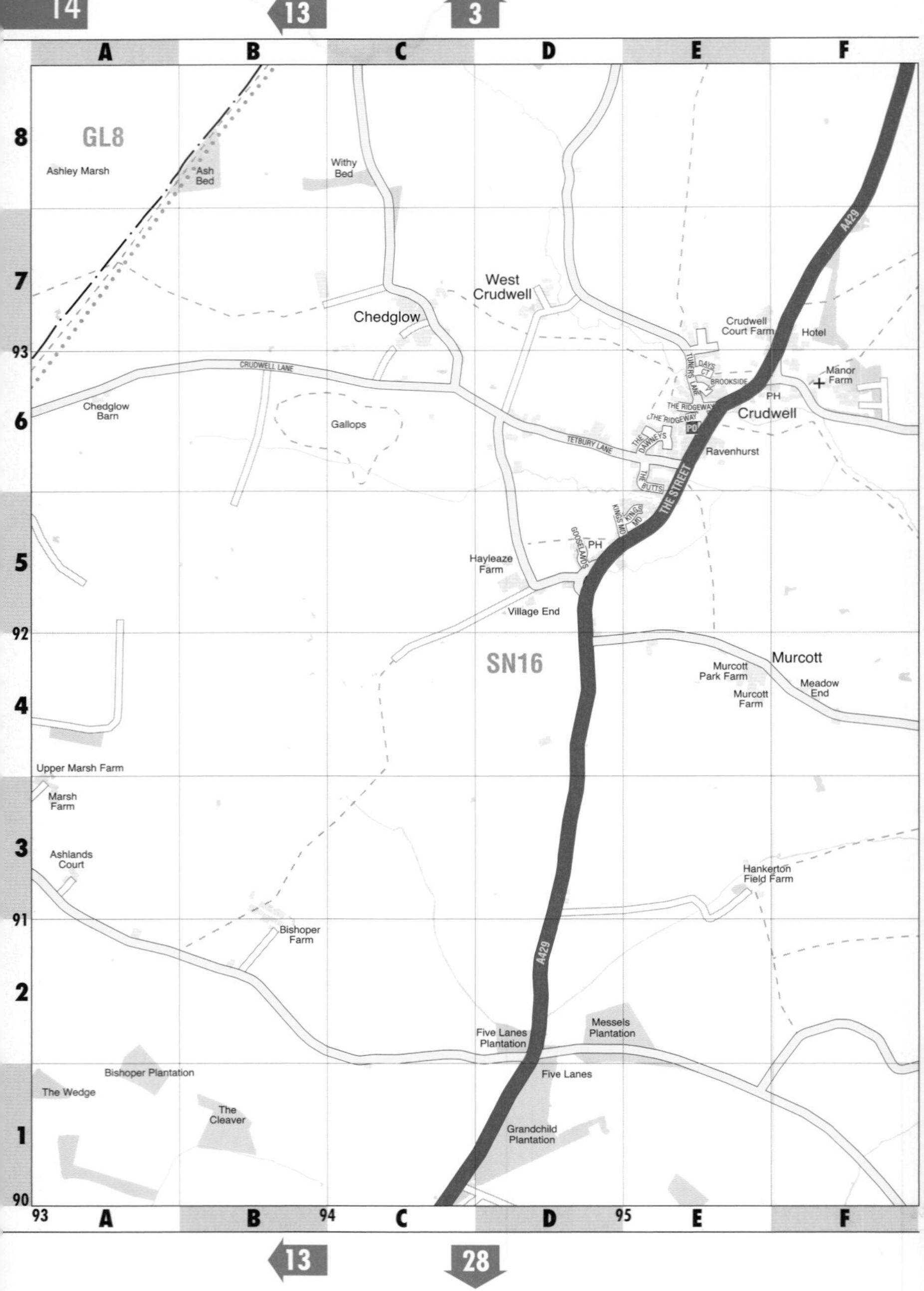
A
B
C
D
E
F
8
7
93
6
5
92
4
3
91
2
1
90
93
94
95
GL8
Ashley Marsh
Ash Bed
Withy Bed
West Crudwell
Chedglow
Crudwell Court Farm
Hotel
Manor Farm
CRUDWELL LANE
TUNERS LANE
DAYS CT
BROOKSIDE
THE RIDGEWAY
PH
Crudwell
Chedglow Barn
Gallops
THE DAWNEYS
PO
TETBURY LANE
Ravenhurst
THE BUTTS
THE STREET
KINGS MD
GOOSELANDS
Hayleaze Farm
Village End
SN16
Murcott
Murcott Park Farm
Meadow End
Murcott Farm
A429
Upper Marsh Farm
Marsh Farm
Ashlands Court
Hankerton Field Farm
Bishoper Farm
Five Lanes Plantation
Messels Plantation
Bishoper Plantation
Five Lanes
The Wedge
The Cleaver
Grandchild Plantation

13
28

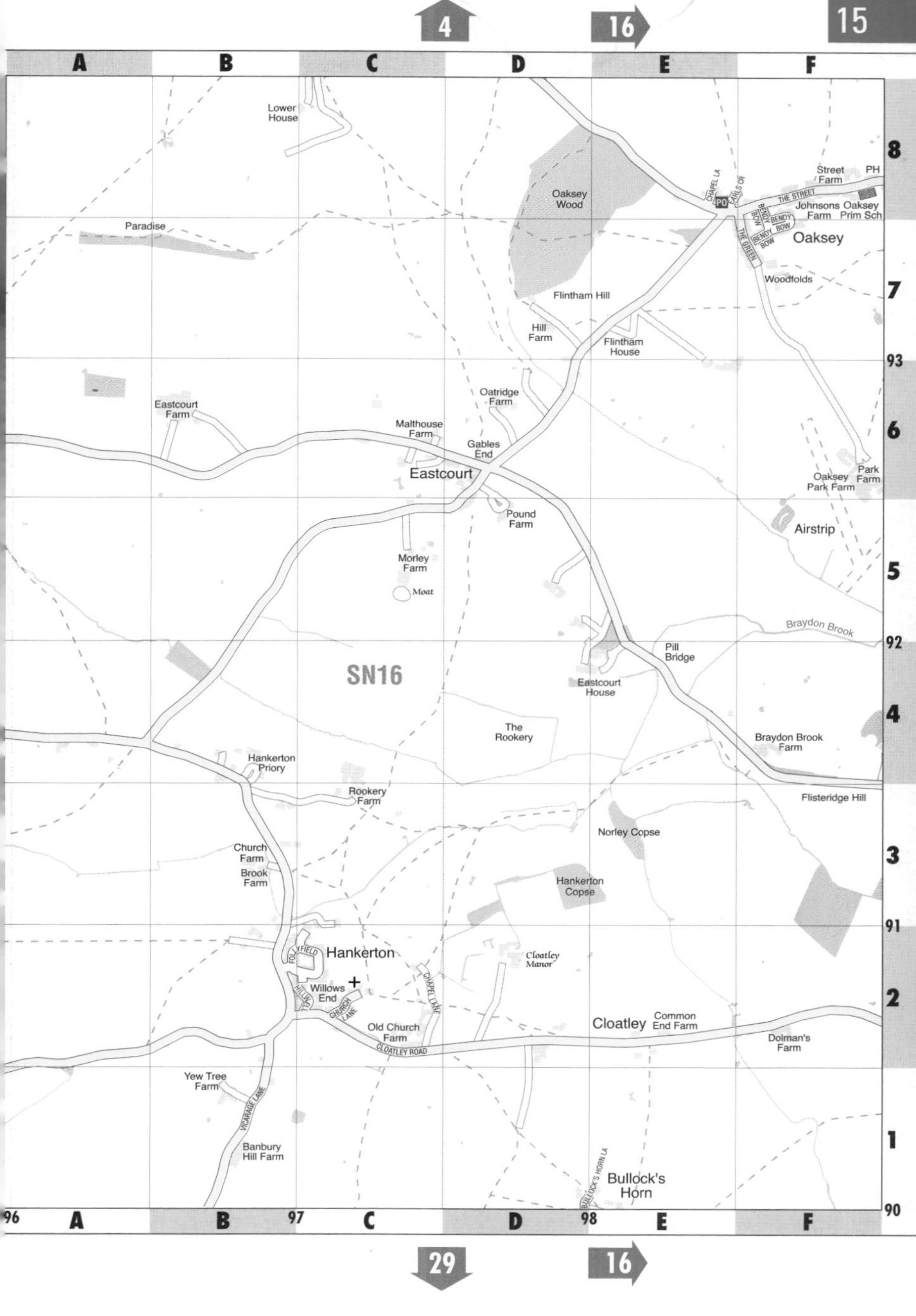
4
16
A
B
C
D
E
F
8
7
93
6
5
92
4
3
91
2
1
90
96
97
98
Lower House
Paradise
Oaksey Wood
CHAPEL LA
PO
EARLS CR
THE STREET
Street Farm
PH
Johnsons Farm
Oaksey Prim Sch
BENDY BOW
THE GREEN
Oaksey
Woodfolds
Flintham Hill
Hill Farm
Flintham House
Oatridge Farm
Eastcourt Farm
Malthouse Farm
Gables End
Eastcourt
Park Farm
Oaksey Park Farm
Pound Farm
Airstrip
Morley Farm
Moat
Braydon Brook
Pill Bridge
SN16
Eastcourt House
The Rookery
Braydon Brook Farm
Hankerton Priory
Rookery Farm
Flisteridge Hill
Norley Copse
Church Farm
Brook Farm
Hankerton Copse
FOLLYFIELD
Hankerton
Cloatley Manor
Willows End
HILLWELL
CHURCH LANE
CHAPEL LANE
Old Church Farm
Cloatley
Common End Farm
CLOATLEY ROAD
Dolman's Farm
Yew Tree Farm
VICARAGE LANE
Banbury Hill Farm
BULLOCK'S HORN LA
Bullock's Horn
29
16

15
5

A
B
C
D
E
F
8
7
93
6
5
92
4
3
91
2
1
90
99
00
01
Oaksey
PH
WICK ROAD
THE STREET
COURT FARM
Court Farm
Oaksey Bridge
Lower Moor Farm
Gravel Pit
Mallard Lake
SN16
Clattinger Farm
Swillbrook Bridge
Lower Swillbrook Farm
MINETY LANE
Oaksey Ford Bridge
Swill Brook
Park Farm
Stert Farm
Airstrip
Cooles Farm
Barn Cooles Farm
RIGSBY'S LA
Lyngrove Farm
TIDLING CORNER
Oaksey Nursery
Ash Bed
Upper Lyngrove
Brandiers Farm
LC
Field End
Flisteridge Wood
Oakwood Farm
Row Ash Farm
OAKSEY ROAD
Mansells Farm
Flistridge Farm
Maskelyne's Copse
Upper Minety
TELLINGS DR
ST LEONARDS CL
FLISTERIDGE ROAD
PH
PO
ST LEONARD'S
Osbourne Farm
Thistledown
Cowleaze Farm
Home Farm
Wellfield Farm
Mill Farm
Cockrode Farm
Laurel Farm
Alsperes Farm
Cloatley End Farm
HANKERTON ROAD
Elms Farm
The Elms
Brookside Farm
Buxwell Farm
Cloatley End
Fairholme Farm
DOG TRAP LANE
Brownockhill Plantation
Woodward Farm

15
30

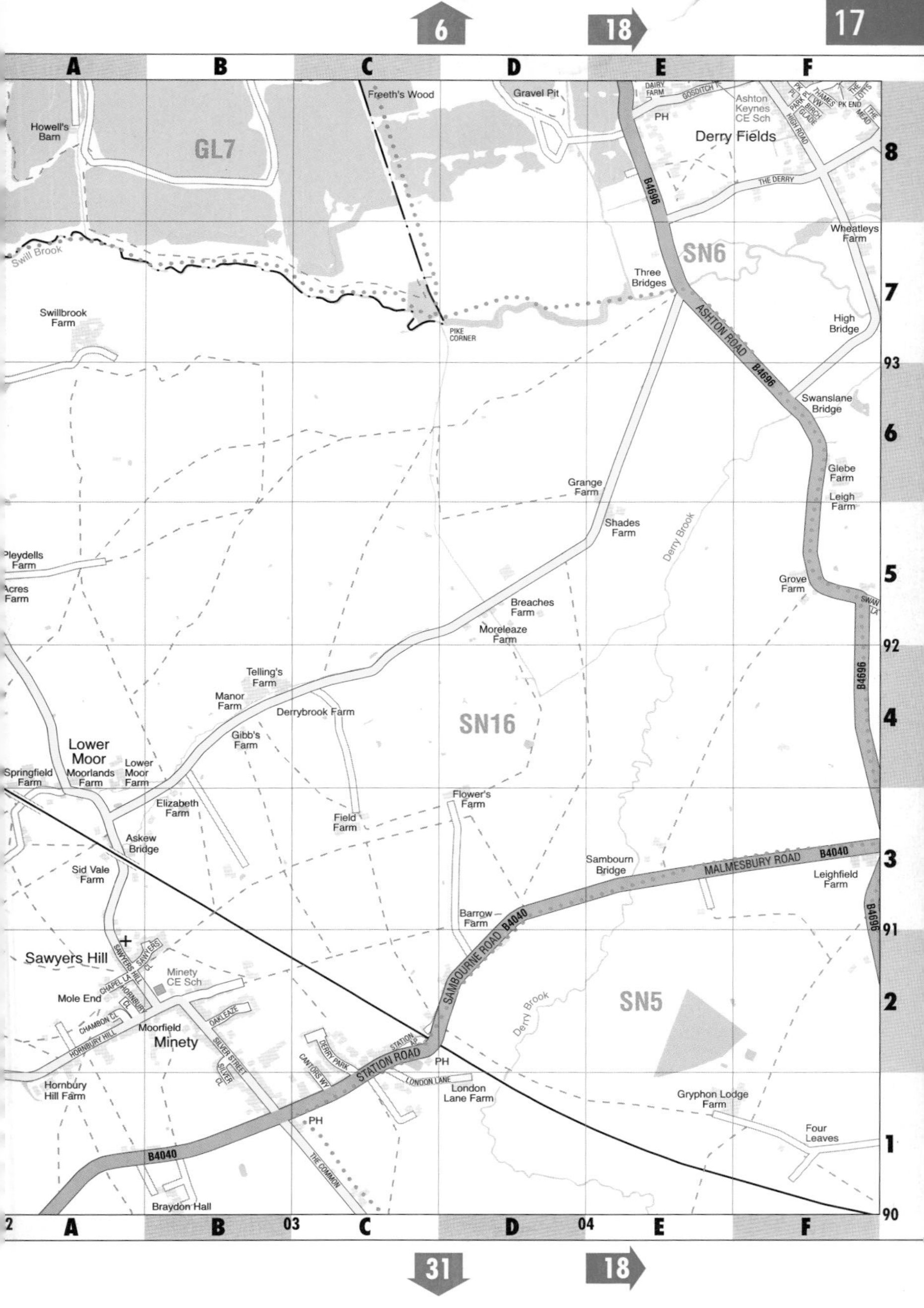
6
18
A
B
C
D
E
F
Howell's Barn
GL7
Freeth's Wood
Gravel Pit
DAIRY FARM
GOSDITCH
PH
Ashton Keynes CE Sch
Derry Fields
HIGH ROAD
THE DERRY
B4696
8
Swill Brook
SN6
Wheatleys Farm
Three Bridges
7
Swillbrook Farm
PIKE CORNER
ASHTON ROAD
High Bridge
93
Swanslane Bridge
6
Glebe Farm
Grange Farm
Leigh Farm
Shades Farm
Derry Brook
Pleydells Farm
Acres Farm
Grove Farm
5
Breaches Farm
Moreleaze Farm
92
Telling's Farm
Manor Farm
Derrybrook Farm
SN16
4
Gibb's Farm
Lower Moor
Springfield Farm
Moorlands Farm
Lower Moor Farm
Elizabeth Farm
Flower's Farm
Field Farm
Askew Bridge
Sambourn Bridge
MALMESBURY ROAD
B4040
3
Sid Vale Farm
Leighfield Farm
Barrow Farm
91
Sawyers Hill
SAWYERS HILL
SAWYERS CL
SAMBOURNE ROAD
Minety CE Sch
Mole End
CHAPEL LA
HORNBURY CL
SN5
2
CHAMBON CL
Moorfield
OAKLEAZE
HORNBURY HILL
Minety
SILVER STREET
SILVER CL
DERRY PARK
CANTORS WY
STATION AP
STATION ROAD
PH
LONDON LANE
London Lane Farm
Hornbury Hill Farm
Gryphon Lodge Farm
PH
Four Leaves
1
B4040
THE COMMON
Braydon Hall
90
2
03
04
31
18

17
7
A
B
C
D
E
F
FOUR ACRE CL
Westfields Farm
Thames Path
Gravel Pit
Manorbrook Lake
Thames Path
River Thames or Isis
Brook Farm
P
Waterhay Bridge
Waterhay Farm
Sewage Works
Waterhay
Manor Farm
Johnnys Farm
Bournelake Farm
BOURNE LAKE PK
Crossroads Farm
Upper Waterhay Farm
Archer's Farm
MALMESBURY ROAD
Cross Lanes Farm
SN6
Meliot Farm
Cove House Farm
Home Farm
Brookside Farm
SWAN LANE
HILLSIDE
Stocks Farm
Leigh CE Sch
Leigh
Leigh Hall Farm
Knapp Farm
Bowood Angus Farm
PH
BRAYDON LANE
Purley Farm
Mast
MALMESBURY ROAD
B4040
Greenacres
Blakehill Farm
Southleigh Farm
Leighfield Lodge Farm
Hardings Farm
Cox Hill
Stoke Common Farm
B4696
Bury Hill
Bridge Farm
Lower Farm
SN5
Bury Hill (Settlement)
8
7
93
6
5
92
4
3
91
2
1
90
05
06
07
17
32

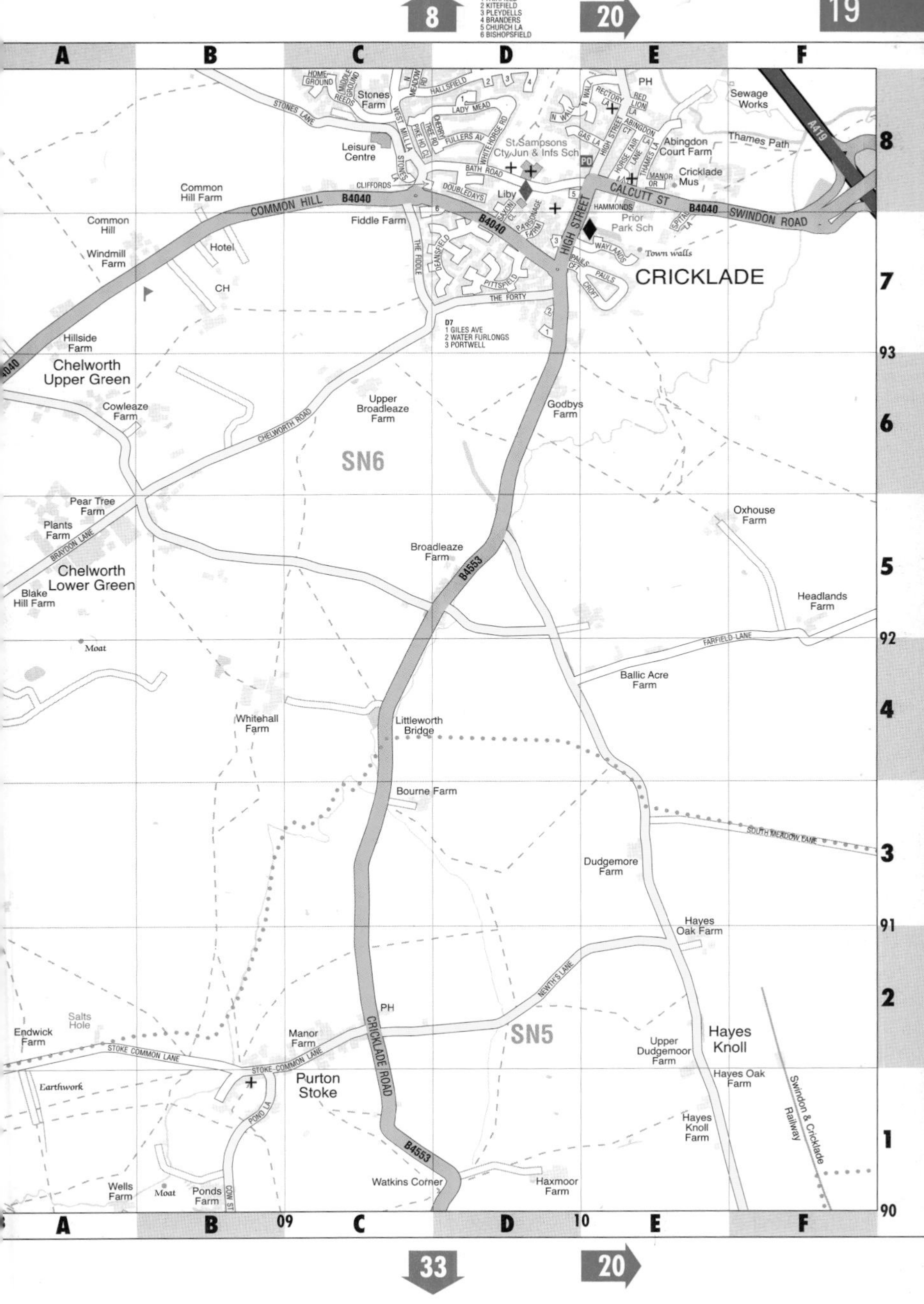
8
20
D8
1 FAIRFIELD
2 KITEFIELD
3 PLEYDELLS
4 BRANDERS
5 CHURCH LA
6 BISHOPSFIELD
A
B
C
D
E
F
CRICKLADE
Stones Farm
Leisure Centre
St Sampsons Cty Jun & Infs Sch
Abingdon Court Farm
Cricklade Mus
Sewage Works
Thames Path
Common Hill Farm
Common Hill
Windmill Farm
Hotel
CH
Fiddle Farm
Prior Park Sch
Town walls
COMMON HILL
B4040
CALCUTT ST
SWINDON ROAD
HIGH STREET
A419
D7
1 GILES AVE
2 WATER FURLONGS
3 PORTWELL
Hillside Farm
Chelworth Upper Green
Cowleaze Farm
Upper Broadleaze Farm
Godbys Farm
SN6
CHELWORTH ROAD
Pear Tree Farm
Plants Farm
BRAYDON LANE
Chelworth Lower Green
Blake Hill Farm
Broadleaze Farm
B4553
Oxhouse Farm
Headlands Farm
FARFIELD LANE
Moat
Ballic Acre Farm
Whitehall Farm
Littleworth Bridge
Bourne Farm
SOUTH MEADOW LANE
Dudgemore Farm
Hayes Oak Farm
NEWTH'S LANE
PH
Salts Hole
Endwick Farm
Manor Farm
SN5
Upper Dudgemoor Farm
Hayes Knoll
STOKE COMMON LANE
Earthwork
Purton Stoke
CRICKLADE ROAD
Hayes Oak Farm
Hayes Knoll Farm
Swindon & Cricklade Railway
POND LA
Wells Farm
Moat
Ponds Farm
COW ST
Watkins Corner
Haxmoor Farm
8
7
93
6
5
92
4
3
91
2
1
90
09
10
33
20

19
9

A
B
C
D
E
F
8
7
93
6
5
92
4
3
91
2
1
90
11
12
13
Thames Path
River Thames or Isis
Water
Eaton
House
Thames Path
Manor
Farm
Calcutt
Calcutt Ct
Farm
Calcutt
Farm
Manor Farm
Cottages
Port
Farm
Enclosures
SN6
A419
Seven Bridges
Bridge
Seven
Bridges
Farm
Kingshill
Farm
ROMAN BUILDING
(site of)
LITTLE ROSE LANE
Farfield
Farm
FARFIELD
LA
Lower Widhill
Farm
A419
Newlands
Farm
SOUTH MEADOW LANE
Weir
Chapel
Farm
SN26
ERMIN STREET
SN5
River Ray
Gravel
Pit
Blunsdon
Hill
Upper Widhill
Farm
Shepherd's
Copse
Upper
Widhill
Copse
Grove
Farm
SN25
SN25

19
34

10
22
A
B
C
D
E
F
8
7
93
6
5
92
4
3
91
2
1
90
14
15
16
35
22
Lus Hill
Share Ditch
QUEENS ROAD
Water
Eaton Copse
Botany
Bay
Gore
Farm
SN6
Crabtree
Copse
Ashmead
Brake
Pope's
Copse
Enclosure
Enclosure
Enclosures
Enclosures
Grains
Farm
FRONT LANE
Longfield
Farm
Lower
Burytown
Farm
Sewage
Works
Upper
Burytown
Farm
St Leonards
Farm
Fowlers
Farm
Staplers
Farm
SN26
Castle
Hill (Fort)
BACK LANE
Oxleaze
Farm
Lower
Blunsdon
BURYTOWN
LANE
Newmeadow
Copse
IVY LANE
WEST HILL
CHURCHWAY
MANOR CL
BURYTOWN LANE
HUNTS HILL
MALTHOUSE
CL
AKERS CT
Stubbs
Hill
Cemy
BERTON CL
Broad
Blunsdon
THE RIDGE
CHAPEL HL
Ash
Covert
Hotel
HIGH STREET
HATCHER'S
CR
PONTING'S
CL
HOLDCROFT
CL
CHURCHILL AV
1 LINLEY RD
2 LONSDALE CL
Stubbs
Hill Farm
B4019
PH
WIDHILL
LANE
HILLSIDE WY
St Andrews
Sch
SUTTON PK
SAMS LANE
SUTTON PK
BEECH LEA
Owls'
Copse
Broadbush
Mast
LADY LANE
A419
PH
Sheepslaight
Plantation

21
11

Lower Farm
Nell Farm
Sewage Works
Hannington
Manor Farm
PH
Hall
Florence Copse
Quarters Copse
Bydemill Farm
Bydemill Copse
Bydemill Brook
SN6
Sewage Works
Westrop Sch
Hampton Hill
Hampton
Hampton Farm
Hampton Copse
Cemy
CRICKLADE ROAD
B4019
Botany Farm
Highworth Rec Ctr
CH
Jubilee Copse
Snell Bridge
PH
Swanborough
Highworth Golf Club
Redlands
Stanton Water Bridge
Oxleaze Farm
TRENCHARD ROAD
Red Down
SWINDON ROAD
Red Down Farm
Red Down Hill
SN26
Red Down
A361
Enclosures
Stanton Fitzwarren
Mill Copse
Pickett's Copse
Queenlaines Farm
HIGHWORTH ROAD
Hotel
Sheepslaight Plantation

21
36

12

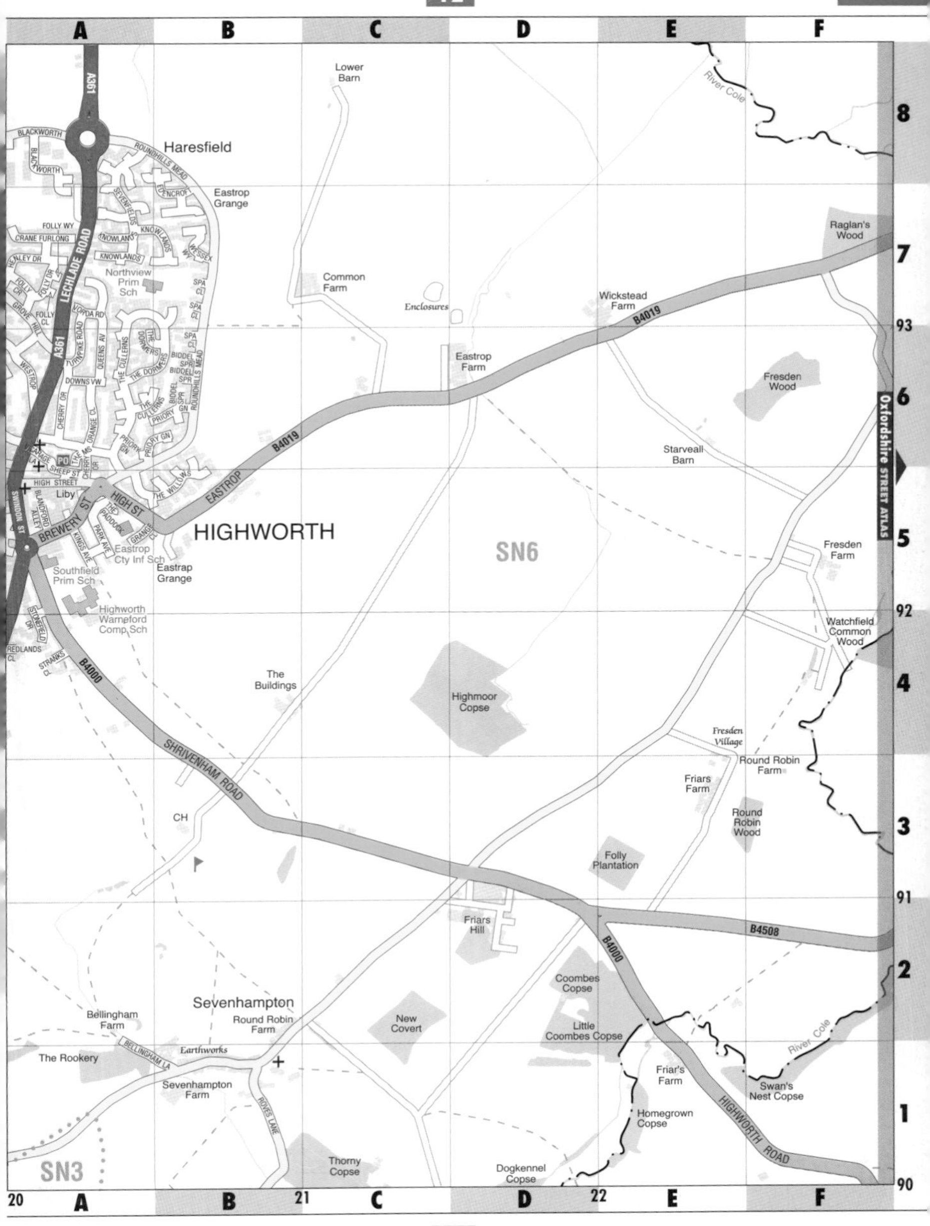
A
B
C
D
E
F
Lower Barn
River Cole
Haresfield
Eastrop Grange
Raglan's Wood
Common Farm
Enclosures
Wickstead Farm
B4019
Northview Prim Sch
LECHLADE ROAD
A361
Eastrop Farm
Fresden Wood
Oxfordshire STREET ATLAS
Starveall Barn
Liby
HIGH STREET
HIGH ST
BREWERY ST
EASTROP
HIGHWORTH
SN6
Fresden Farm
Eastrop Cty Inf Sch
Eastrap Grange
Southfield Prim Sch
Highworth Warneford Comp Sch
Watchfield Common Wood
B4000
The Buildings
Highmoor Copse
Fresden Village
Round Robin Farm
Friars Farm
SHRIVENHAM ROAD
CH
Round Robin Wood
Folly Plantation
Friars Hill
B4508
Coombes Copse
Sevenhampton
Bellingham Farm
Round Robin Farm
New Covert
Little Coombes Copse
River Cole
The Rookery
BELLINGHAM LA
Earthworks
Friar's Farm
Swan's Nest Copse
Sevenhampton Farm
ROVES LANE
Homegrown Copse
HIGHWORTH ROAD
Thorny Copse
Dogkennel Copse
SN3
8
7
93
6
5
92
4
3
91
2
1
90
20
21
22

37

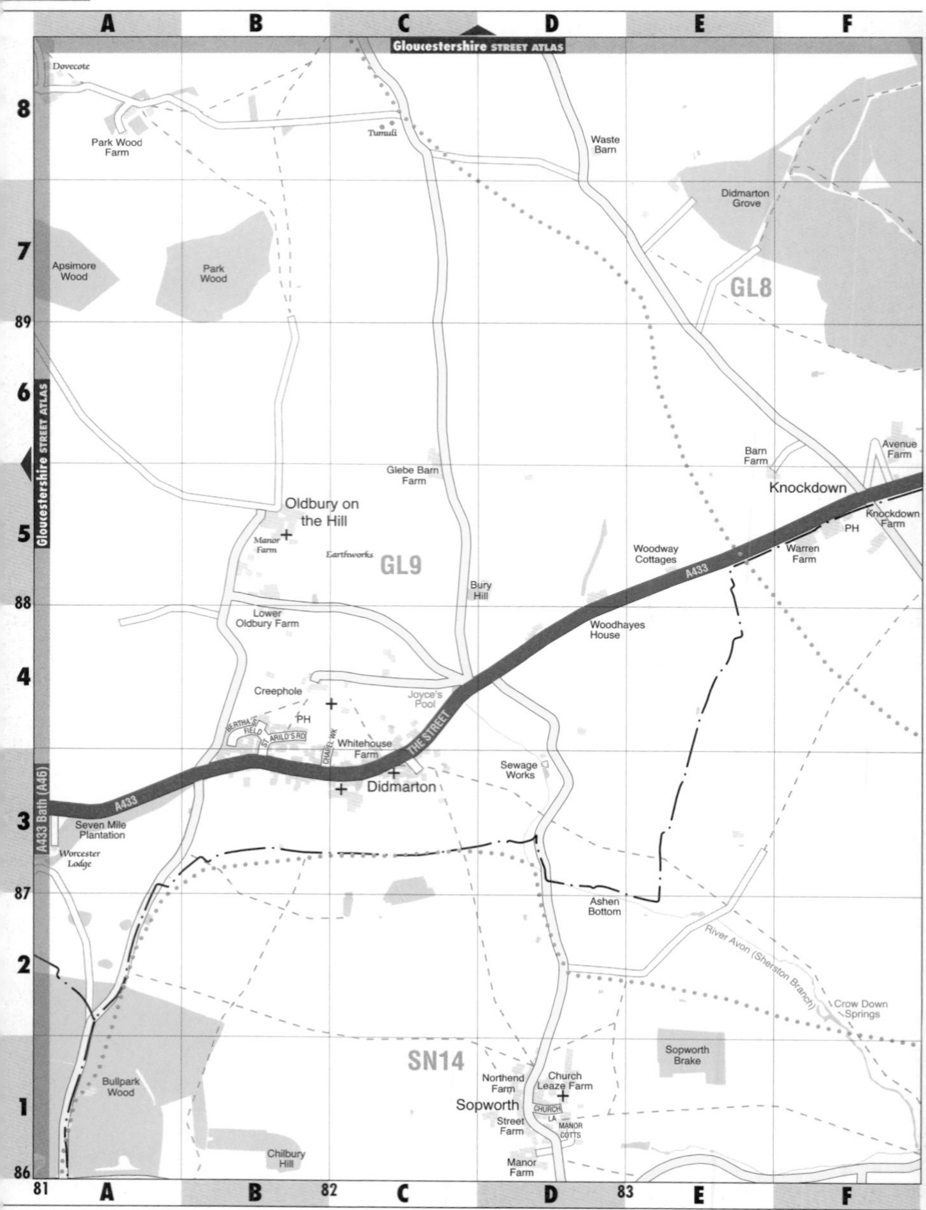
A
B
C
D
E
F
Gloucestershire STREET ATLAS
Dovecote
Park Wood Farm
Tumuli
Waste Barn
Didmarton Grove
Apsimore Wood
Park Wood
GL8
Glebe Barn Farm
Barn Farm
Avenue Farm
Knockdown
Knockdown Farm
PH
Oldbury on the Hill
Manor Farm
Earthworks
GL9
Woodway Cottages
Warren Farm
A433
Bury Hill
Lower Oldbury Farm
Woodhayes House
Creephole
Joyce's Pool
PH
BERTHA'S FIELD
ST ARILD'S RD
CHAPEL WK
Whitehouse Farm
THE STREET
Didmarton
Sewage Works
A433 Bath (A46)
Seven Mile Plantation
Worcester Lodge
Ashen Bottom
River Avon (Sherston Branch)
Crow Down Springs
Sopworth Brake
SN14
Bullpark Wood
Northend Farm
Church Leaze Farm
Sopworth
CHURCH LA
Street Farm
MANOR COTTS
Chilbury Hill
Manor Farm
8
7
89
6
5
88
4
3
87
2
1
86
81
82
83

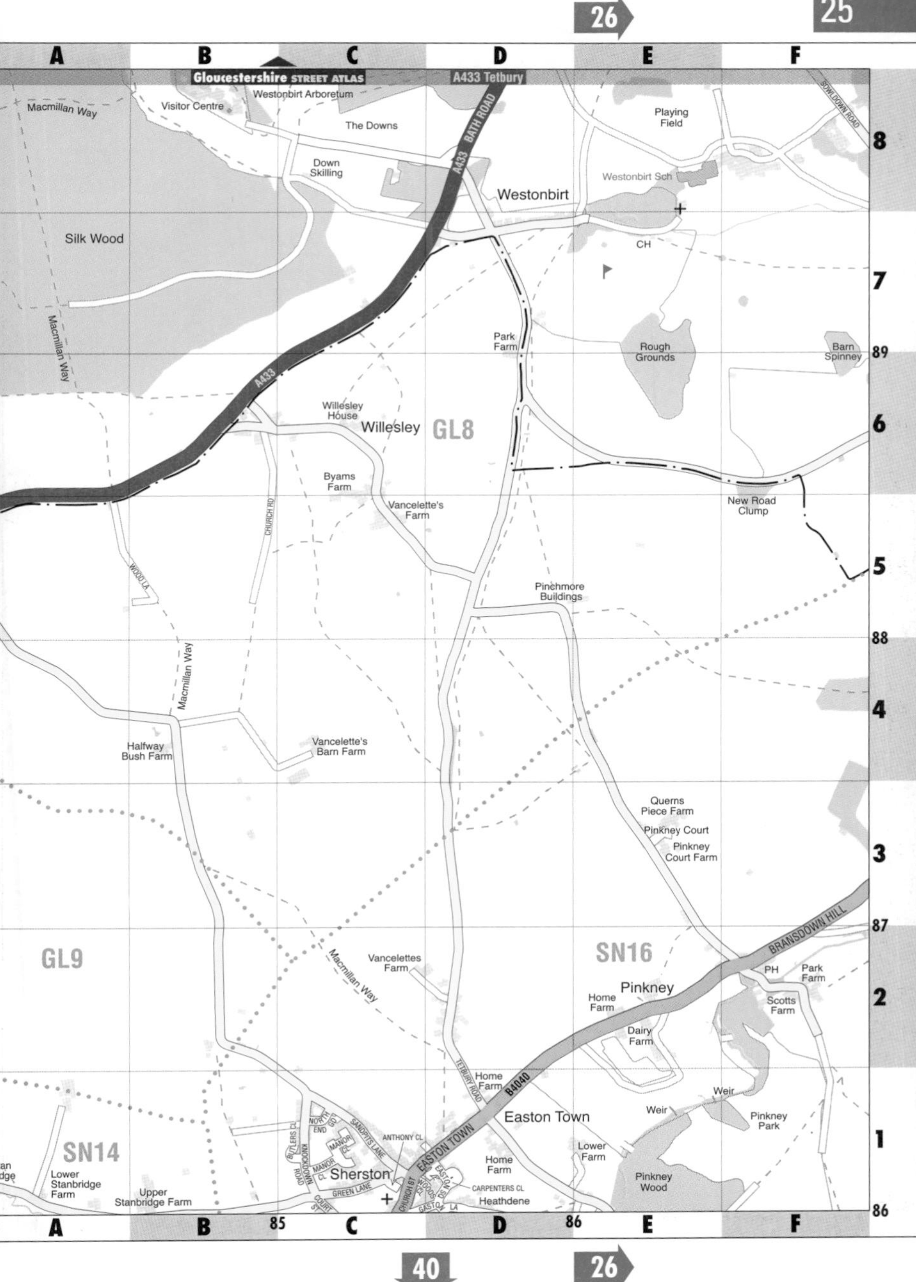
Gloucestershire STREET ATLAS
A433 Tetbury
Westonbirt Arboretum
Macmillan Way
Visitor Centre
The Downs
Playing Field
Down Skilling
Westonbirt Sch
Westonbirt
Silk Wood
CH
Park Farm
Rough Grounds
Barn Spinney
Willesley House
Willesley
GL8
Byams Farm
Vancelette's Farm
New Road Clump
Pinchmore Buildings
Macmillan Way
Halfway Bush Farm
Vancelette's Barn Farm
Querns Piece Farm
Pinkney Court
Pinkney Court Farm
GL9
SN16
Vancelettes Farm
Macmillan Way
Pinkney
Home Farm
PH
Park Farm
Scotts Farm
Dairy Farm
Home Farm
Weir
Weir
Easton Town
Pinkney Park
SN14
Lower Farm
Home Farm
Sherston
Pinkney Wood
Lower Stanbridge Farm
Upper Stanbridge Farm
Heathdene
A B C D E F
8 7 89 6 5 88 4 3 87 2 1 86
85 86

25

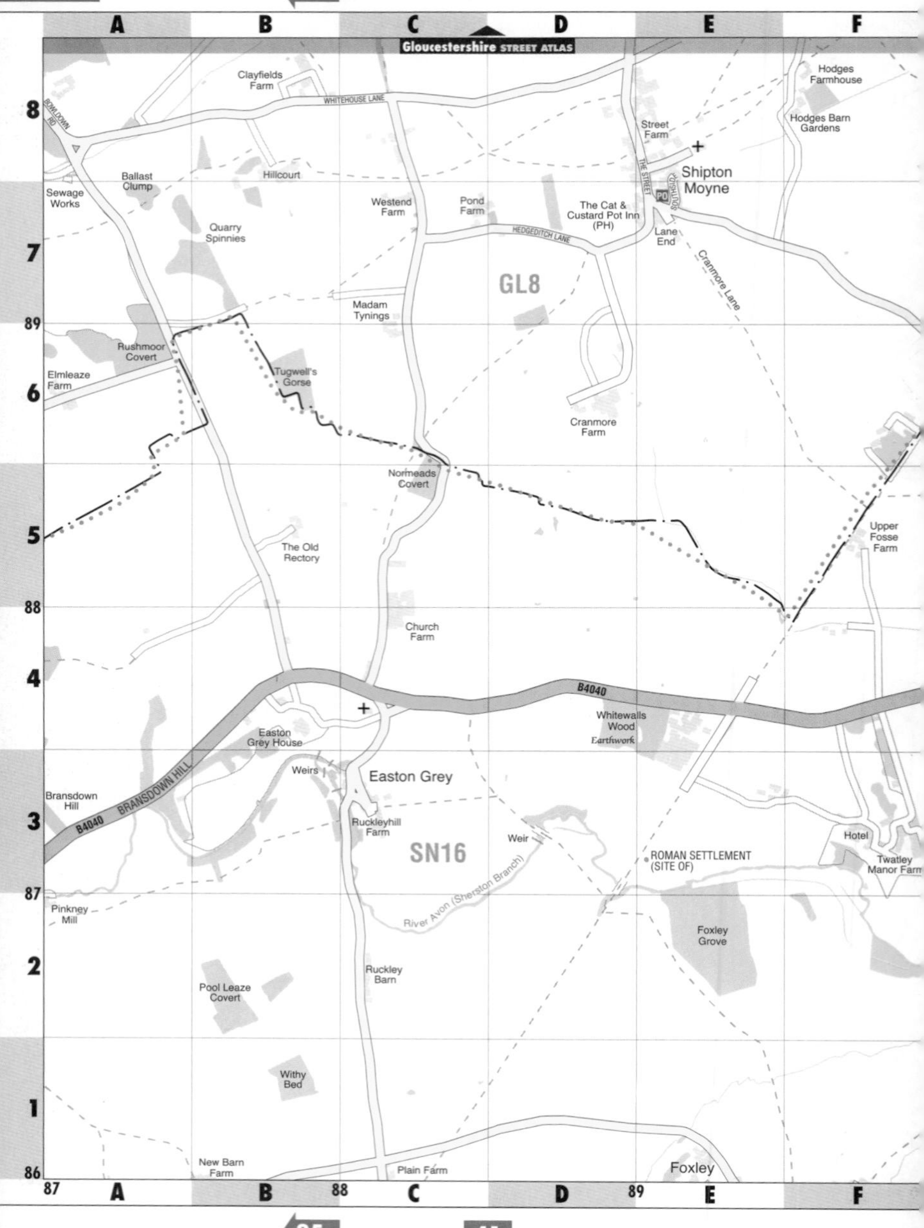

Gloucestershire STREET ATLAS
A
B
C
D
E
F
8
7
89
6
5
88
4
3
87
2
1
86
87
88
89
Clayfields Farm
WHITEHOUSE LANE
BOWLDOWN RD
Hodges Farmhouse
Hodges Barn Gardens
Street Farm
Shipton Moyne
THE STREET
SOUTHSIDE
PO
Ballast Clump
Hillcourt
Sewage Works
Westend Farm
Pond Farm
The Cat & Custard Pot Inn (PH)
Lane End
HEDGEDITCH LANE
Quarry Spinnies
Cranmore Lane
GL8
Madam Tynings
Rushmoor Covert
Elmleaze Farm
Tugwell's Gorse
Cranmore Farm
Normeads Covert
Upper Fosse Farm
The Old Rectory
Church Farm
B4040
Whitewalls Wood
Earthwork
Easton Grey House
Weirs
Easton Grey
BRANSDOWN HILL
Bransdown Hill
Ruckleyhill Farm
Weir
SN16
ROMAN SETTLEMENT (SITE OF)
Hotel
Twatley Manor Farm
River Avon (Sherston Branch)
Pinkney Mill
Foxley Grove
Ruckley Barn
Pool Leaze Covert
Withy Bed
New Barn Farm
Plain Farm
Foxley

25

41

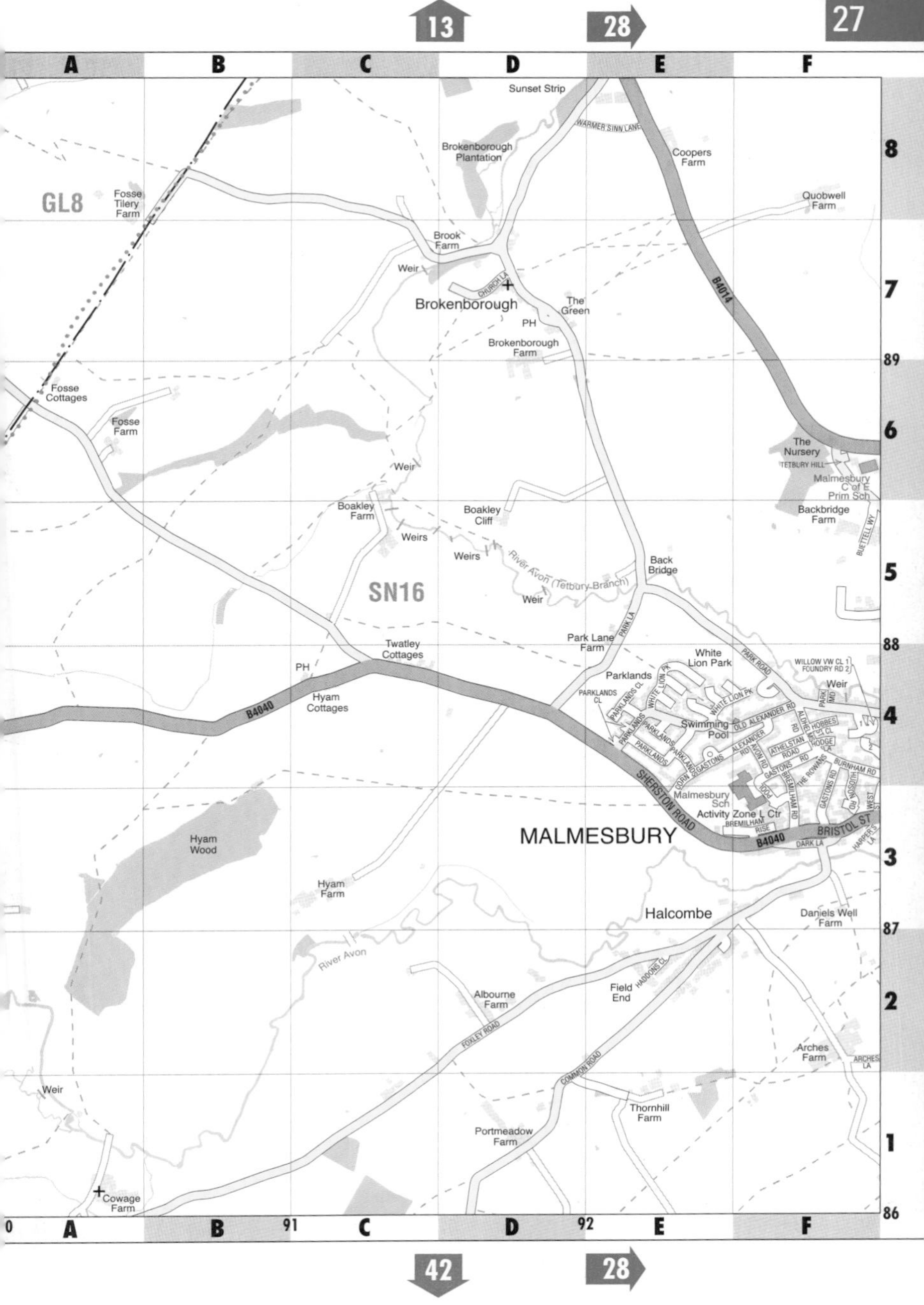
13
28
A
B
C
D
E
F
Sunset Strip
WARMER SINN LANE
Brokenborough Plantation
Coopers Farm
8
GL8
Fosse Tilery Farm
Quobwell Farm
Brook Farm
Weir
CHURCH LA
Brokenborough
The Green
PH
B4014
7
Brokenborough Farm
89
Fosse Cottages
Fosse Farm
6
The Nursery
TETBURY HILL
Malmesbury C of E Prim Sch
Weir
Boakley Farm
Boakley Cliff
Backbridge Farm
BUETTELL WY
Weirs
Weirs
River Avon (Tetbury Branch)
Back Bridge
5
SN16
Weir
PARK LA
Park Lane Farm
88
Twatley Cottages
PH
White Lion Park
PARK ROAD
WILLOW VW CL 1
FOUNDRY RD 2
Parklands
Weir
Hyam Cottages
B4040
PARKLANDS CL
Swimming Pool
4
OLD ALEXANDER RD
ALEXANDER RD
ATHELSTAN ROAD
HOBBES CL
HODGE LA
BURNHAM RD
GASTONS RD
THE ROWANS
BREMILHAM RD
HUDSON RD
SHERSTON ROAD
Malmesbury Sch
Activity Zone L Ctr
BREMILHAM RISE
BRISTOL ST
WEST ST
Hyam Wood
MALMESBURY
B4040
DARK LA
HARPER'S LA
3
Hyam Farm
Halcombe
Daniels Well Farm
87
River Avon
HADDONS CL
Field End
Albourne Farm
2
FOXLEY ROAD
Arches Farm
ARCHES LA
COMMON ROAD
Weir
Thornhill Farm
Portmeadow Farm
1
Cowage Farm
86
0
91
92
42
28

A5
1 JOHN BETJEMAN CL
2 COOPERS CL
3 MICHAEL PYM'S RD
4 WYCHURCH RD
5 LELAND CL
6 AUBREY RI
27
14
A
B
C
D
E
F
8
7
89
6
5
88
4
3
87
2
1
86
93
94
95
The Roughett
Kennels Plantation
Andover's Belt
Griffins Barn Farm
Home Farm
Gardens Plantation
Quobwell Copse
Charlton Park
PO
A429
White Lodge Farm
Filands Farm
Wycurch Marsh Bridge
Marsh Copse
B4014
Filands
THE OLD ORCHARD
PH
Marsh Farm
Long Wood
Muriel Plantation
Noah's Ark
CHARLTON ROAD
Charlton Bridge
B4040
SN16
CHUBB CL
TETBURY HILL
HANKS CL
MICHAEL PYM'S RD
ORWELL CL
WORTHEYS CL
NIEBULL CL
WEBBS
BONNERS CL
ELMER CL
MOFFAT RI
POWELL RI
LACEMAKERS RD
Cemetery Lodge
REEDS FARM RD
Sch
Whitchurch Farm
Garsdon Mill
Lily Bank Farm
Manor Farm
MILBOURNE LANE
Firs Farm
Tanner's Bridge
GLOUCESTER RD
PARK RD
Malmesbury Cricket Club
B4040
Blick's Hill
MILBOURNE PK
MONKS PK
Milbourne
Milbourne Farm
LOVER'S LA
BLICKS HILL
KATIFER LA
PO
Holloway Bridge
ABBOTS GD
MILL LANE
ABBEY ROW
BURNIVALE
Abbey
HOLLOWAY
HIGH ST
OXFORD ST
CROSS HAYES
Liby
MALMESBURY
Daniel's Well
Athelstan Mus
P
PO
KING'S WALL
INGRAM ST
SILVER ST
ST JOHN'S ST
Sewage Works
B4014
Avon Mills
Almshouses
River Avon
St John's Bridge
Southfield Farm
LT BADMINTON LA
LITTLE BADMINTON LA
MANOR VW
BARLEY CL
ORCHARD CL
ARCHES LANE
ARCHES LA
Burton Hill
Cowbridge Farm
HILLCREST
KEMBLES CL
COWBRIDGE CRES
Wks
Weir
Crabmill Farm
Street Farm
OLD BAKERY CL
THE STREET
Lea
PO
Malmesbury Community
Burton Hill Sch
SCHOOL CL
B4042
CRAB MILL LANE
PEMBROKE GN
PH
Coombe Green
Cow Bridge
Manor Farm
CRESSWELL LANE
Brillscote Farm
Foxmead Farm
Lea House
A3
1 ST MARY'S ST
2 ST MARYS LA
3 BRISTOL ST
4 MARKET ST
5 OLIVER'S LA
6 GRIFFIN ALLEY
7 ST DENNIS RD
A4
1 OLD RAILWAY CL
2 SHIPTON HL
3 FOUNDRY RD
4 BURNHAM RD
27
43

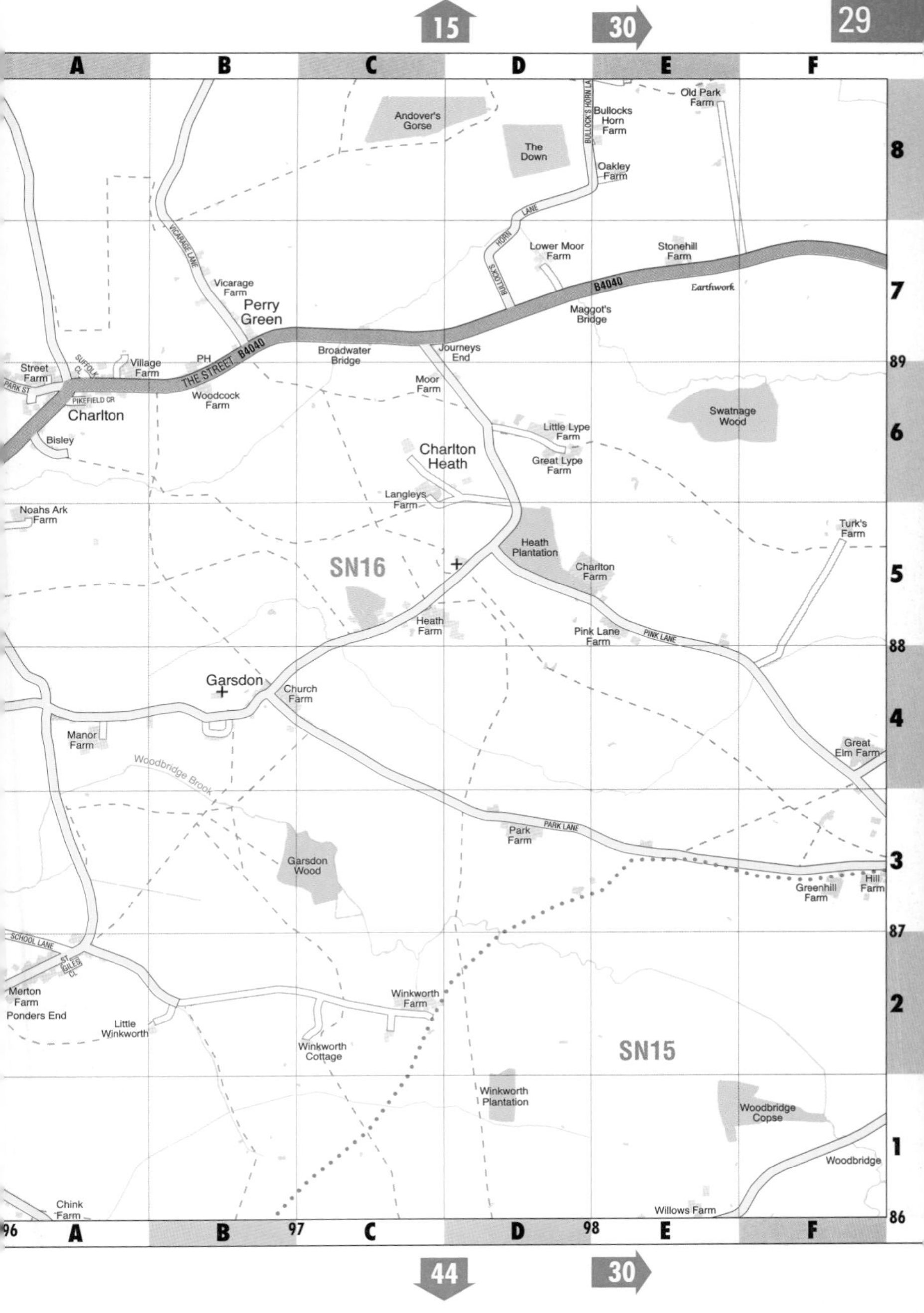
15
30
A
B
C
D
E
F
Andover's Gorse
The Down
Bullocks Horn Farm
BULLOCK'S HORN LA
Old Park Farm
Oakley Farm
HORN LANE
BULLOCK'S
Lower Moor Farm
Stonehill Farm
B4040
Earthwork
VICARAGE LANE
Vicarage Farm
Perry Green
Maggot's Bridge
Broadwater Bridge
Journeys End
PH
THE STREET
Street Farm
SUFFOLK CL
Village Farm
PARK ST
PIKEFIELD CR
Woodcock Farm
Moor Farm
Charlton
Bisley
Swatnage Wood
Little Lype Farm
Charlton Heath
Great Lype Farm
Langleys Farm
Noahs Ark Farm
Turk's Farm
Heath Plantation
SN16
Charlton Farm
Heath Farm
Pink Lane Farm
PINK LANE
Garsdon
Church Farm
Manor Farm
Great Elm Farm
Woodbridge Brook
Park Farm
PARK LANE
Garsdon Wood
Greenhill Farm
Hill Farm
SCHOOL LANE
ST GILES CL
Merton Farm
Ponders End
Little Winkworth
Winkworth Farm
Winkworth Cottage
SN15
Winkworth Plantation
Woodbridge Copse
Woodbridge
Chink Farm
Willows Farm
8
7
89
6
5
88
4
3
87
2
1
86
96
97
98
44
30

29
16

A
B
C
D
E
F
8
7
89
6
5
88
4
3
87
2
1
86
99
00
01
Park Copse
Square Plantation
Woodward Farm
Perlieu Plantation
DOG TRAP LANE
Kemble's Farm
B4040
Stone Hill
Stonehill Wood
Purlieus Farm
Cockroost Farm
Summer House Farm
Bick Farm Cottages
SN16
Water Twr
Cocked Hat Wood
Bicks Farm
Pond Hill Farm
Long Wood
Nineteen Acre Wood
Pond Farm
Braydon Wood
Great Withy Wood
Braydon Pond
Pond Lodge
Worthy Hill Farm
Braydon Wood
Braydon Wood
PINK LANE
New House Farm
PARK LANE
Woodhill Farm
Milbourne Common Wood
Somerford Farm
Sundays Hill
Fernhill Farm
Wood Hill
Tanglin Farm
SN15
Horsells Farm
Rouselands Farm
Dollaker's Green
Sundey Hill Farm

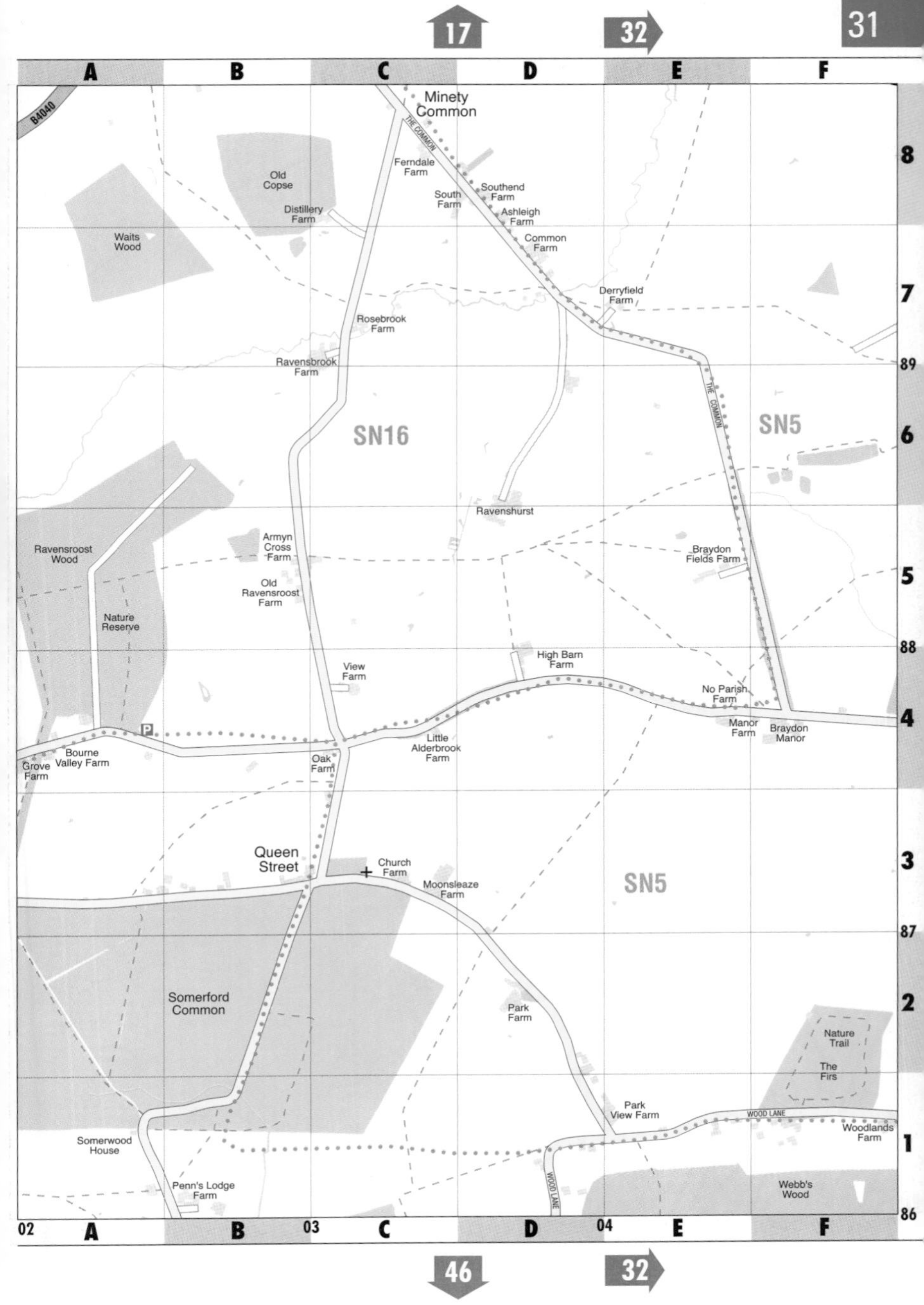
17
32
A
B
C
D
E
F
B4040
Minety
Common
THE COMMON
Old
Copse
Ferndale
Farm
Southend
Farm
South
Farm
Distillery
Farm
Ashleigh
Farm
Waits
Wood
Common
Farm
Derryfield
Farm
Rosebrook
Farm
Ravensbrook
Farm
THE COMMON
SN16
SN5
Ravenshurst
Ravensroost
Wood
Armyn
Cross
Farm
Braydon
Fields Farm
Old
Ravensroost
Farm
Nature
Reserve
High Barn
Farm
View
Farm
No Parish
Farm
P
Manor
Farm
Braydon
Manor
Little
Alderbrook
Farm
Bourne
Valley Farm
Grove
Farm
Oak
Farm
Queen
Street
Church
Farm
Moonsleaze
Farm
SN5
Somerford
Common
Park
Farm
Nature
Trail
The
Firs
Park
View Farm
WOOD LANE
Woodlands
Farm
Somerwood
House
WOOD LANE
Penn's Lodge
Farm
Webb's
Wood
8
7
89
6
5
88
4
3
87
2
1
86
02
03
04
46
32

31
18

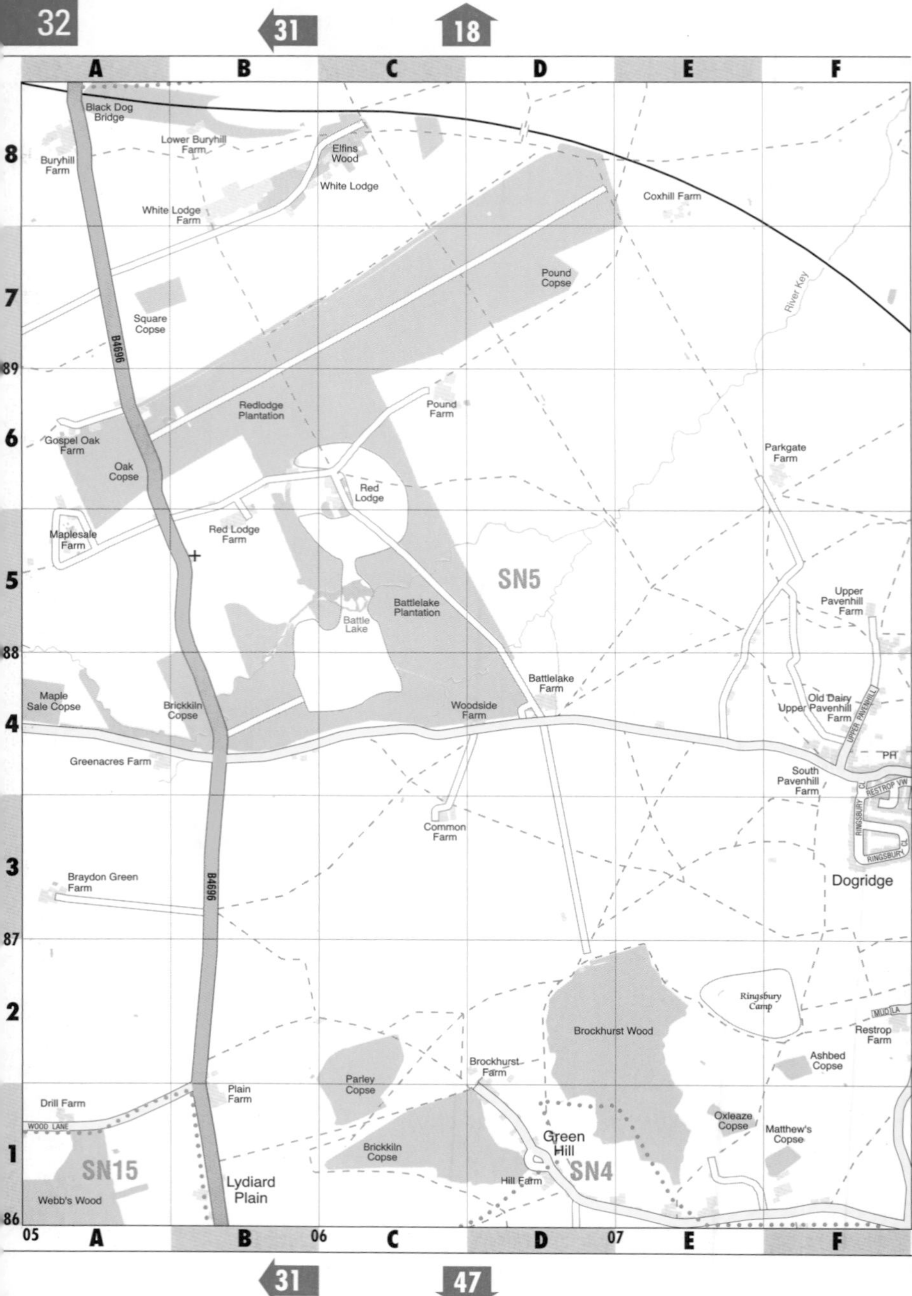
A
B
C
D
E
F
Black Dog Bridge
Lower Buryhill Farm
Buryhill Farm
Elfins Wood
White Lodge
White Lodge Farm
Coxhill Farm
Pound Copse
River Key
Square Copse
B4696
89
Redlodge Plantation
Pound Farm
Gospel Oak Farm
Oak Copse
Parkgate Farm
Red Lodge
Maplesale Farm
Red Lodge Farm
SN5
Battlelake Plantation
Battle Lake
Upper Pavenhill Farm
88
Maple Sale Copse
Brickkiln Copse
Battlelake Farm
Woodside Farm
Old Dairy
Upper Pavenhill Farm
UPPER PAVENHILL
Greenacres Farm
PH
South Pavenhill Farm
RESTROP VW
RINGSBURY CL
Common Farm
Braydon Green Farm
Dogridge
87
Ringsbury Camp
MUD LA
Brockhurst Wood
Restrop Farm
Ashbed Copse
Brockhurst Farm
Parley Copse
Plain Farm
Drill Farm
WOOD LANE
Oxleaze Copse
Matthew's Copse
Green Hill
Brickkiln Copse
SN15
SN4
Hill Farm
Lydiard Plain
Webb's Wood
86
05
06
07
8
7
6
5
4
3
2
1

31
47

19
34
A
B
C
D
E
F
Bentham Farm
BENTHAM LA
POND LA
COW STREET
Bentham House Farm
Bentham House
BENTHAM LA
Old Dairy Farm
B4553
CRICKLADE ROAD
Hurstead Farm
PACKHORSE LANE
B4553
Swindon & Cricklade Railway
Crosslanes Farm
TADPOLE LANE
Woodwards Bridge Farm
8
New Farm
Park House Farm
Folly Down Farm
Down Farm
7
West Marsh
Sewage Works
MOPES LANE
CRICKLADE ROAD
Pound Farm
Hansells Farm
SN5
Downfield Farm
89
Pry Farm
6
LC
Pen Farm
CLARDON LANE
PH
NEW ROAD
Widham Bridge
LOCKS LA
Widham Grove
WITFIELD CL
WITTS LANE
GLEVUM CL
COLLINS LANE
Purton Common
Diana Lodge
LC
5
HOGGS LA
Malthouse Farm
VASTERNE CL
VASTERNE CL
PEARTREE CL
STATION ROAD
Widham
B4553
88
Paven Hill
HOGGS LANE
WAITE MEADS CL
WILLOWBROOK
Purton Liby & Museum
HYDE LA
PO
Purton
HOGGS LANE
PAVEN CL
HOOKS HL
HIGH STREET
LONG ACRE
COLLEGE RD
PLAY CL
PH
THE HYDE
Quarry Farm
THE HYDE
Gallops Farm
4
RESTROP VW
PAVENHILL
THE MASONS
HIGHRIDGE CL
DOGRIDGE
ORCHARD GD
WATER FIELD
RESTROP ROAD
BATTLEWELL
WILLIS WY
REID'S PIECE
PIECE
REID'S PIECE
REID'S
THE PEAK
THE PEAK
CHURCH ST
St Marys Sch
THE HYDE
Bradon Forest Comp Sch
The Fox
Mill Farm
PROUD CL
KIBBLEWHITE CL
Manor Farm
Manor House
Purton House
Church End
3
Fox Mill Farm
87
Restrop
MUD LA
Bagbury Lane Farm
PH
Common Platt
THE CRESCENT
2
Manor Hill Farm
Bagbury Green Farm
Bagbury Farm
STONE LANE
Keycroft Copse
RUSSLEY CL
1
THE BEECHES
Lydiard House Farm
Manor House
Church Farm
Manor Farm
CHURCH PL
BURY FIELDS
CHESTNUT SPRINGS
Lydiard Millicent
F1
1 MARDALE CL
2 DALEFOOT CL
3 BERRY COPSE
4 KEYCROFT COPSE
86
08
A
B
09
C
D
10
E
F
48
34

34
33
20
F6
1 NEWSTEAD CL
2 SCOTNEY CRES
3 GRAYTHWAITE CL
4 SYON CL CL
5 HEPWORTH RD
A
B
C
D
E
F
8
7
89
6
5
88
4
3
87
2
1
86
11
12
13
Tadpole Farm
TADPOLE LANE
Lower Tadpole Farm
Blunsdon St Andrew
Blunsdon Abbey
NOLAN CL 1
RUBENS CL 2
SOUTHEY CL 3
LYALL CL
LADY LANE
LANDOR RD
B4534
SCARLET CL
GAMEKEEPERS CL
GREENSAND CL
MINSTER CL
SANDSTONE RD
EBOR CL
PENNINE
VIKING CL
TARKA CL
ELSTREE WY
River Ray
SN25
SN5
SN2
Grange Farm
Superstore
HAYDON END LANE
SHEPPERTON WY
WOBURN CL
Haydon End
E5
1 SPEEDWELL CL
2 MEADOWSWEET CL
HATFIELD CL
CAPESTHORNE DR
LADY LA
WESTFIELD WAY
Catherine Waite Prim Sch
BRAMDEAN CL
CHATSWORTH ROAD
Grange Farm
Haydon
HONEYSUCKLE CL 1
SNOWDROP CL 2
CORNFLOWER RD 3
MARJORAM CL 4
WESTFIELD WY
B4534
FURLONG CL
POPE CL
AUDEN CL
DOYLE CL
GLENMORE RD
BORDER CL
DICKENSON RD
Haydonleigh Sch
Superstore
POND ST
SNOWSHILL CL
NOYES CL
HAYDON CT DR
AVENUE
PADDOCK CL
ROTHER CL
SEATON CL
CALDER CL
Haydon Wick
FRANCOMES
HIGH ST
HIGH STREET
TWEED CL
THAMES AVENUE
ASHDOWN WY
SOUTHERNWOOD DR
WESTFIELD WAY B4534
BRYONY WAY
HYLDER CL
COMFREY CL
HOLMLEIGH DR
WHEATLAND
HAYDONLEIGH DR
THE BROW
CHURCHFIELD
VALLEY AV
GREEN MDW AV
TORRIDGE CL
HAMBLE RD
FROME RD
Mouldon Hill
CAYENNE PARK
TARRAGON CL
CARAWAY
CHIVES WAY
MINT
BRYONY WY
BUCKTHORN
CLOVER PARK
VENTNOR CL
SHANKLIN RD
SHERFORD RD
HELMSDALE
CATHERINE WAYTE CL
AVONMEAD
THRUSHEL
BOSCOMBE ROAD
PERIWINKLE CL 1
PURSLAKE CL 2
DAISY CL 3
ROAD
DOWNLAND RD
JASMINE CL
BASIL CL
CATMINT CL
BARTON ROAD
ABBEY
HARBOUR CL
ELDER CL
CHICORY CL
PURTON RD
COPPICE CL
LYNWOOD GR
MOREDON PK
Liby
PURTON
PURTON RD
PURTON ROAD
Moredon
BRANKSOME RD
LULWORTH RD
CHEDDAR ROAD
CHARLBURY CL
WICKDOWN AVE
COOMBE RD
CHURCH WALK
Elborough Bridge
JUBILEE RD
ELBOROUGH
FERNHAM RD
PEMBROKE GD
MOREDON ROAD
Ridgeway Farm
Herod Prim Sch
Moredon Junior Sch
CHANTRY RD
RIDGEWAY CL
MONTROSE CL
LEAZE CL
CHURCH WALK SOUTH
B4587
AKERS WAY
BOLINGBROKE RD
YARDLEY CL
GREENHILL RD
BOURNE ROAD
MANOR CR
BOTLEY COPSE 1
STOCKBRIDGE COPSE 2
FRITH COPSE 3
JACK THORNE CL 4
PURTON RD
B4553
GAIRLOCH
CL
SPARCELLS DR
B4553
THE WILLOWS
LINDEN WY
MEAD WAY
HODDS
PEAKS DN
SOUND COP
TOWER RD
WEBBS WOOD
Moredon Jun Sch
B4587
AKERS WAY
STENNESS
PORTMORE CL
Sports Ground
HARVEY GR
CHENEY MANOR
HOOK CL
SHEARWOOD
PEPPERBOX HL
MIDWINTER
SPARCELLS DRV
MORIE CL
Sparcells
DARBY CLOSE
LYNTON RD
MANOR GD
BROOKLANDS
SWINLEY DR
Roughmoor
RINSDALE CL
SN5
DARBY CL
B4006
Peatmoor Community Woodland
MEAD WAY
B4534
Refuse Tip
Cheney Manor Industrial Estate
Allot Gdns
PEATMOOR WAY
SOMERSET RD
BESSEMER RD W
PEATMOOR
RADCOT CL
CORRAL
ROUGHMOOR WY
HILLMEAD DR
LANGLEY RD
MEAD WY
Refuse Tip
DARBY CLOSE
BRINDLEY
KILN LANE
CHENEY MANOR RD
WHITBY GR
A1
1 SANDACRE RD
2 BISHOPDALE CL
3 NIGHTWOOD COPSE
B2
1 NESS CL
2 LOWES CL
3 FYNE CL
4 RANNOCH CL
5 KISHORN CL
33
C4
1 EXMOOR CL
2 WATERDOWN CL
3 CHERVIL CL
4 ANISE CL
49
D4
1 BROOKLIME CL
2 MALLOW CL
3 LICHEN CL
4 HIGHWOOD CL
5 LOVEAGE CL
6 ANGELICA CL
7 NUTMEG CL
E3
1 LOCKSGREEN
2 SAFFRON CL

A6
1 TIMANDRA CL
2 EXBURY CL
3 HONEYLIGHT VW
C5
1 HILMARTON AVE
2 WARMINSTER AVE
3 POTTERDOWN RD
21
36
A B C D E
LADY LA
B4534
Abbey Stadium
Sports Ground
1 DOBSON CL
2 RENOIR CL
3 NASH CL
SN26
Northington Poultry Farm
Brook Farm
KINGSDOWN LANE
Home Farm
Works
A419
TURNPIKE RD
Hyde Farm
7
THAMESDOWN DRIVE
THAMESDOWN DR
Abbeymeads Community Prim Sch
1 HOLDEN GARSON RD
2 PICKFORD WAY
3 STEWART CL
Groundwell Farm
CRICKLADE ROAD
A4311
Hyde
SN2
89
C6
1 TISBURY CL
2 STAVERTON WY
3 WOODFORD CL
4 AMESBURY CL
ARKWRIGHT ROAD
HARGREAVES ROAD
6
Sports Ground
Penhill Jun Sch
Penhill
St Lukes Sch
5
PH
B4141 KINGSDOWN ROAD
Kingsdown Sch
Kingsdown
BEECHCROFT RD
Liby
88
Playing Field
Seven Fields Jun & Inf Sch
Greenmeadow
Recreation Ground
SN2
BEECHCROFT ROAD
4
Ruskin Cty Junior Sch
Greenmeadow Prim Sch
SN25
Beechcroft Inf Sch
Upper Stratton
Cemy
B4006
Pinehurst
3
Rodbourne Cheney CP Sch
WHITWORTH ROAD
Headlands Comp Sch
Playing Field
Pinehurst Youth & Sports Centre
RADWAY ROAD
87
Pinehurst Jun Sch
Pinehurst Infs Sch
Rodbourne Cheney
Works
Crowdys Hill Sch
SN3
2
Kembrey Business Park
Gorse Hill
SWINDON
Rodbourne
SN2
1
Recreation Ground
St Marys RC Prim Sch
Playing Field
Gorse Hill Jun Sch
B4143 BRIDGE END RD
86
4 A B 15 C D 16 E F

50
36

35
22
B
C
D
E
F
Beech Farm
HIGHWORTH RD
SN6
SN26
The Cottage Park Farm
Park Farm
Sports Ground
South Field Copse
Great Wood
HIGHWORTH ROAD
Hunt's Copse
South Marston Park
BROADMOOR RD
7
A361
STIRLING ROAD
HUNTS RISE
WOODSIDE ROAD
BROADMOOR ROAD
WOODSIDE RD
Broadmoor Copse
Marston Copse
Kingsdown Crem
89
SN2
South Marston Park Industrial Estate
STIRLING ROAD
LANCASTER PL
LANCASTER MS
Burton Grove Farm
B4141
STIRLING ROAD
VISCOUNT WAY
6
KINGSDOWN ROAD
HIGHWORTH RD
SN25
Kingsdown Farm
HIGHWORTH ROAD
1 BROCKLEY RI
2 HORNSEY GD
3 CHOBHAM CL
4 WALWAYNE FLD
5
SN2
HIGHWORTH RD
Motor Works
Quarry Farm
QUARRYBROOK CLOSE
South Marston
BYRON COURT
CHAPEL
PO
GREENFIELDS
PH
88
Kingsdown
A361
SN3
Sewage Works
CHURCH FARM LN
NIGHTINGALE LANE
Sevor Farm
Yew Tree Farm
Downderry
A419
YEW TREE GD
4
A419
HIGHWORTH ROAD
St Julians Farm
RAWLINGS CL
MANOR PK
ASH GD
Hotel
Playing Field
Pigeon House Farm
ERMIN STREET
St Margarets
Sewage Works
South Marston Arms & Leisure Club
BELMONT CL
DELAMERE DRIVE
Stratton St Margaret
B4006
GIFFORD ROAD
SWINDON
A419
Works
Manor Farm
PARSONAGE ROAD
Grange Inf Sch
3
HOBLEY DR
ERMIN ST
GODWIN ROAD
CARMAN CL
Works
Oxleaze Farm
PIGEON HOUSE LANE
RADWAY ROAD
AZURIN CT
RAINER CL
Cemy
South Marston Farm
B4006
SWINDON RD
PARKSIDE
HEDGES CL
SHENTON CL
KENWIN CL
CHURCH WAY
87
BRIDGEMAN CL
Priory Farm
WATERMEAD
Lower Stratton
Grange Junior Sch
Works
CHAMBERLAIN RD
BLAKE CRES
ERMIN STREET
Marston Farm
2
CASSON RD
SWINDON ROAD
BUNCE RD
OVERTON GD
BOURTON AV
PARK ST
Home Farm
TILLEY'S LA
MARSHFIELD WY
RUCKLEY GD
TUDOR CR
GRANGE DRIVE
YIEWSLEY CRES
HATHERHALL CL
Hotel
A420
BIRCHWOOD RD
CRAWLEY AV
GRIFFITHS CLOSE
St Margarets Retail Park
HARROW CL
DAY'S CL
WEND RD
HARDIE CL
B4006
BUCKLEBURY CL
JOHN HERRING CR
FRILFORD DR
HIGHNAM CL
ERMIN ST
SN4
SANDGATE
PO
OXFORD ROAD
HILL VIEW ROAD
WANBOROUGH ROAD
CAMERON CL
1
WINCHESTER CL
WHILSTONE WY
CASTLE VW
CULLERNE ROAD
B4143
BURGESS CL
A4312
NYTHE ROAD
MERLIN WY A420
HILL VIEW ROAD
OXFORD RD
SWINDON RD
B4006
SLADE DR
COLEBROOK ROAD
WAVERLEY RD
TRAJAN ROAD
CAPITOL
86
17
A
B
18
C
D
19
E
F
A2
1 STRATTON OR
2 CALLAGHAN CL
3 GOULDING CL
4 SHAPLANDS
5 THE PADDOCKS
B2
1 ST MARGARET'S GN
2 FRANKTON GD
35
51
B3
1 BROWNING CL
2 WARNER CL
3 COTTARS CL
4 BARON CL
5 BOWMAN CL
6 CRISPIN CL
7 CHURCH WAY
8 FRANK WARMAN CT

23

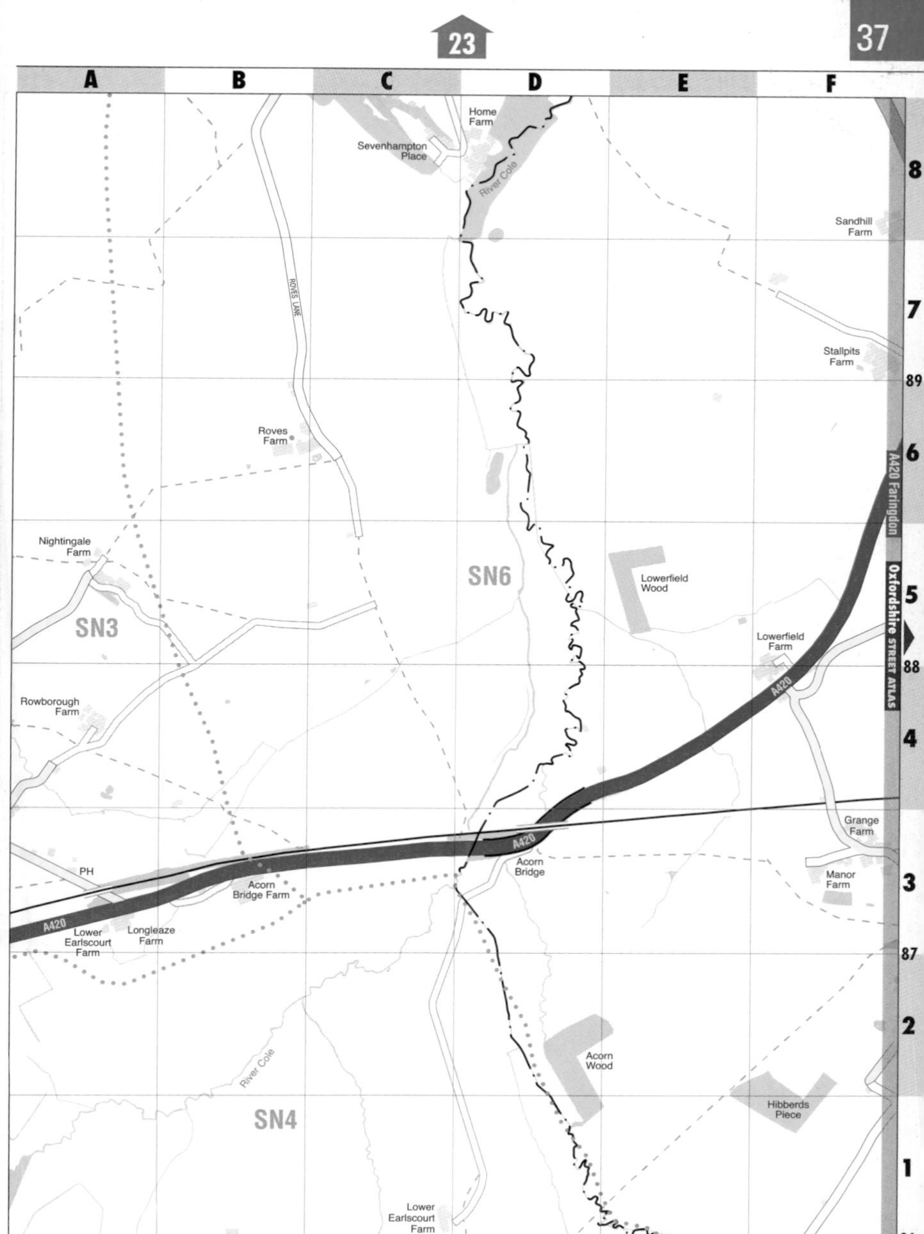
A
B
C
D
E
F
Home Farm
Sevenhampton Place
River Cole
8
Sandhill Farm
ROVES LANE
7
Stallpits Farm
89
Roves Farm
6
A420 Faringdon
Nightingale Farm
SN6
Lowerfield Wood
5
SN3
Oxfordshire STREET ATLAS
Lowerfield Farm
88
Rowborough Farm
A420
4
Grange Farm
A420
PH
Acorn Bridge
Acorn Bridge Farm
Manor Farm
3
A420
Lower Earlscourt Farm
Longleaze Farm
87
2
Acorn Wood
River Cole
Hibberds Piece
SN4
1
Lower Earlscourt Farm
86
20
21
22

163

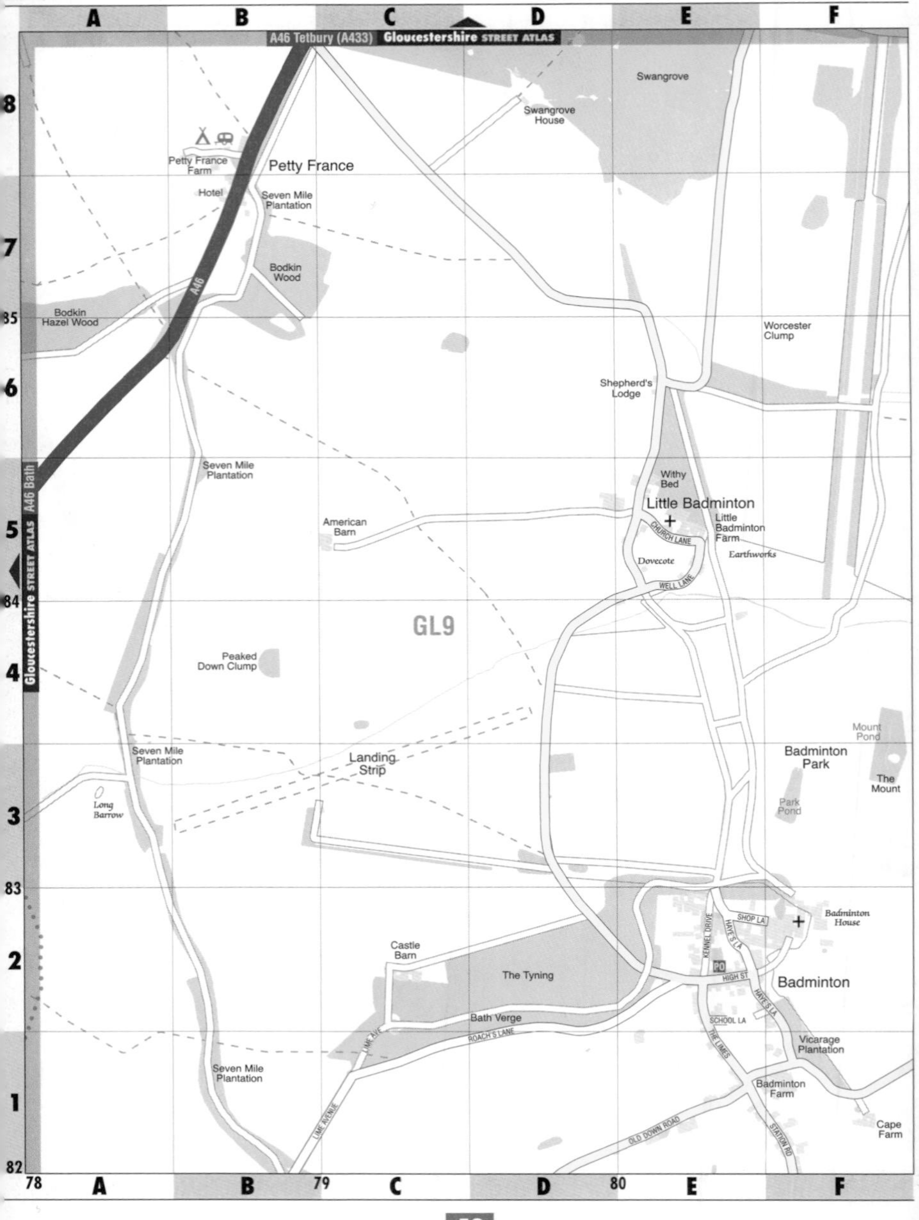
A
B
C
D
E
F
A46 Tetbury (A433)
Gloucestershire STREET ATLAS
Swangrove
Swangrove House
Petty France Farm
Petty France
Hotel
Seven Mile Plantation
Bodkin Wood
Bodkin Hazel Wood
A46
Worcester Clump
Shepherd's Lodge
Seven Mile Plantation
Withy Bed
Little Badminton
Little Badminton Farm
American Barn
CHURCH LANE
Dovecote
Earthworks
WELL LANE
A46 Bath
Gloucestershire STREET ATLAS
GL9
Peaked Down Clump
Mount Pond
Badminton Park
Seven Mile Plantation
Landing Strip
The Mount
Long Barrow
Park Pond
SHOP LA
Badminton House
KENNEL DRIVE
HAYE'S LA
Castle Barn
PO
The Tyning
HIGH ST
Badminton
HAYE'S LA
Bath Verge
SCHOOL LA
LIME AVE
ROACH'S LANE
THE LIMES
Vicarage Plantation
Seven Mile Plantation
Badminton Farm
LIME AVENUE
OLD DOWN ROAD
STATION RD
Cape Farm
8
7
85
6
5
84
4
3
83
2
1
82
78
79
80

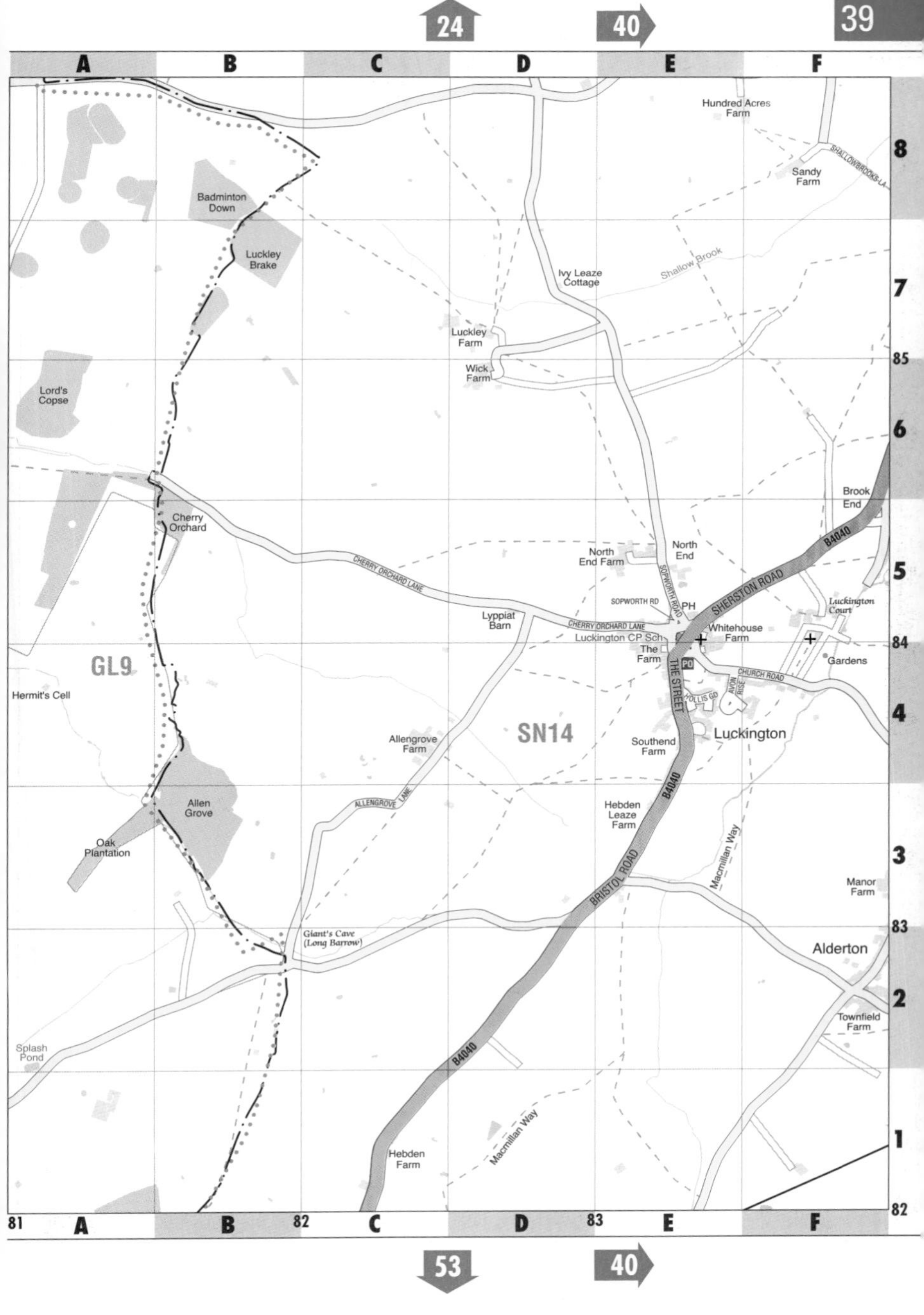
24
40
A
B
C
D
E
F
Hundred Acres Farm
SHALLOWBROOKS LA
Sandy Farm
Badminton Down
Luckley Brake
Shallow Brook
Ivy Leaze Cottage
Luckley Farm
Wick Farm
Lord's Copse
Cherry Orchard
Brook End
North End Farm
North End
B4040
SHERSTON ROAD
CHERRY ORCHARD LANE
SOPWORTH ROAD
SOPWORTH RD
PH
Luckington Court
Lyppiat Barn
CHERRY ORCHARD LANE
Whitehouse Farm
Luckington CP Sch
The Farm
PO
Gardens
GL9
CHURCH ROAD
THE STREET
HOLLIS GD
AVON RISE
Hermit's Cell
SN14
Luckington
Allengrove Farm
Southend Farm
ALLENGROVE LANE
Hebden Leaze Farm
Allen Grove
B4040
Oak Plantation
Macmillan Way
BRISTOL ROAD
Manor Farm
Giant's Cave (Long Barrow)
Alderton
Townfield Farm
Splash Pond
B4040
Macmillan Way
Hebden Farm
8
7
85
6
5
84
4
3
83
2
1
82
81
82
83
53
40

39
25

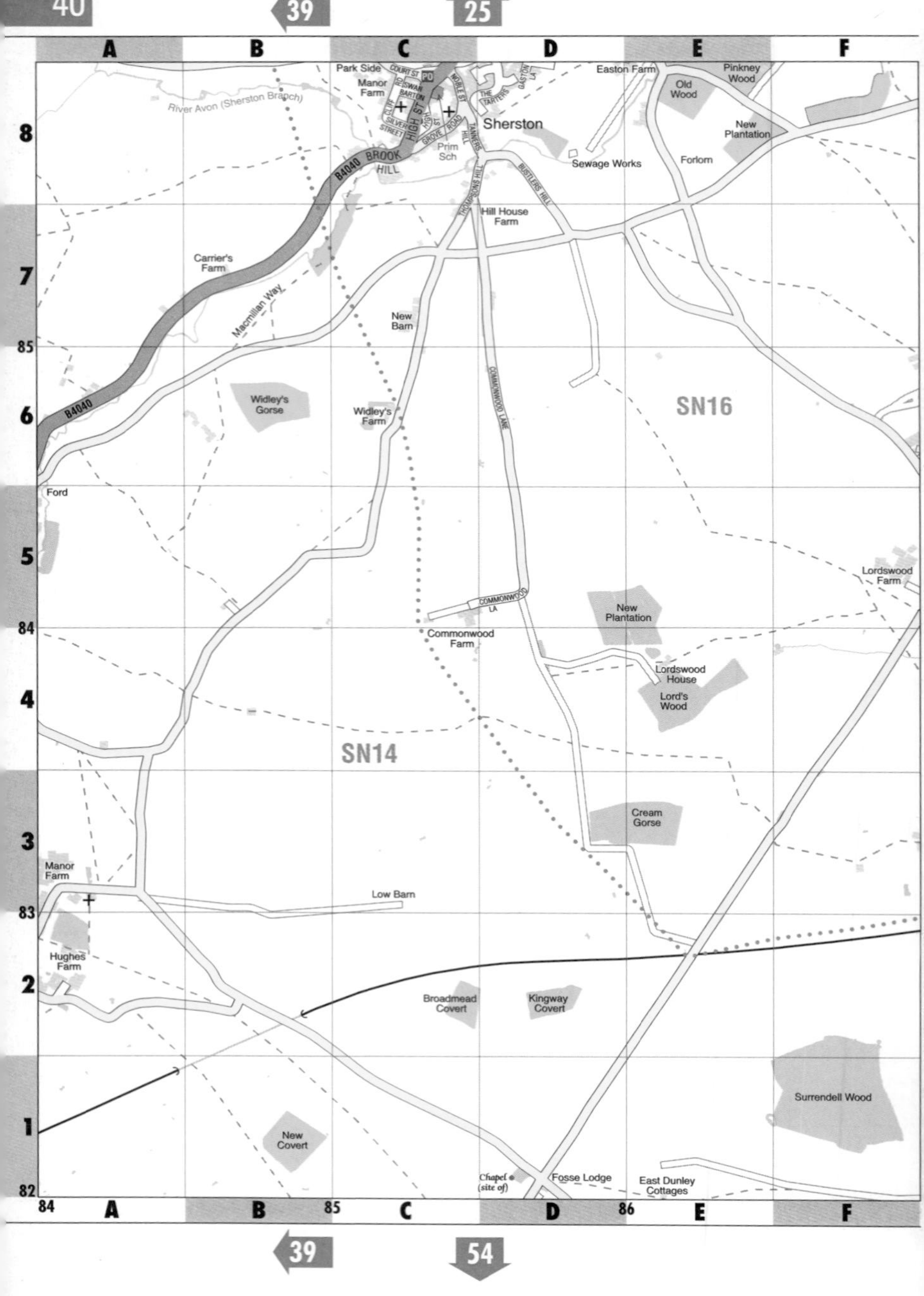
A
B
C
D
E
F
Park Side
Court St
PO
Manor Farm
Swan Barton
Cliff Rd
Silver Street
High St
Noble St
The Tarters
Gaston La
Easton Farm
Pinkney Wood
Old Wood
New Plantation
River Avon (Sherston Branch)
Sherston
Grove Road
Tanners Hill
Prim Sch
B4040 Brook Hill
Sewage Works
Forlorn
Bustlers Hill
Thompsons Hill
Hill House Farm
Carrier's Farm
Macmillan Way
New Barn
Commonwood Lane
SN16
Widley's Gorse
Widley's Farm
B4040
Ford
Lordswood Farm
Commonwood La
New Plantation
Commonwood Farm
Lordswood House
Lord's Wood
SN14
Cream Gorse
Manor Farm
Low Barn
Hughes Farm
Broadmead Covert
Kingway Covert
Surrendell Wood
New Covert
Chapel (site of)
Fosse Lodge
East Dunley Cottages
8
7
85
6
5
84
4
3
83
2
1
82
84
85
86

39
54

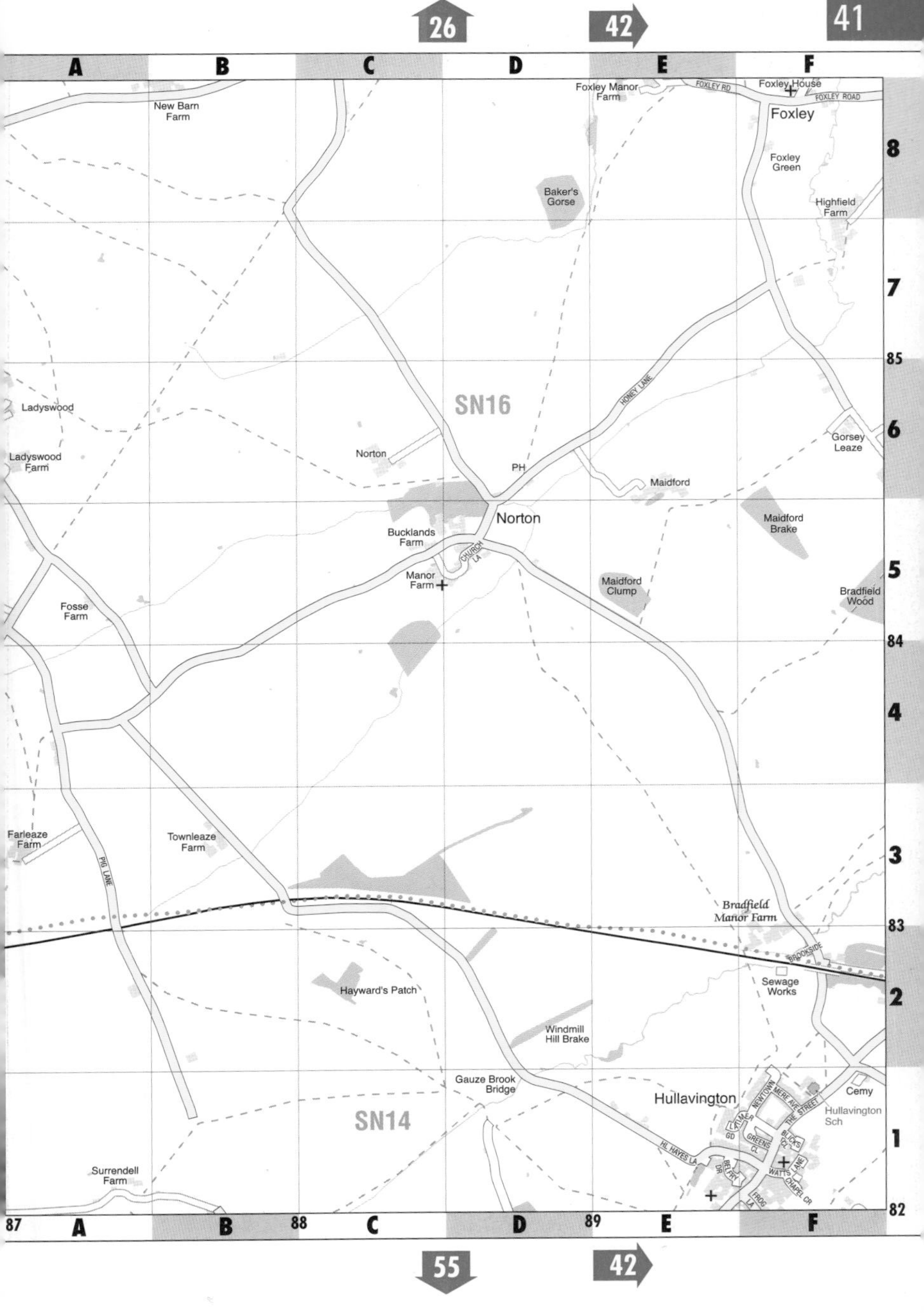
26
42
41
A
B
C
D
E
F
New Barn Farm
Foxley Manor Farm
FOXLEY RD
Foxley House
FOXLEY ROAD
Foxley
Foxley Green
Highfield Farm
Baker's Gorse
8
7
85
6
5
84
4
3
83
2
1
82
SN16
HONEY LANE
Ladyswood
Ladyswood Farm
Norton
PH
Maidford
Gorsey Leaze
Norton
Bucklands Farm
CHURCH LA
Manor Farm
Maidford Brake
Maidford Clump
Bradfield Wood
Fosse Farm
Farleaze Farm
Townleaze Farm
PIG LANE
Bradfield Manor Farm
BROOKSIDE
Sewage Works
Hayward's Patch
Windmill Hill Brake
Gauze Brook Bridge
Hullavington
NEWTOWN
MERE AVE
THE STREET
Cemy
Hullavington Sch
SN14
HL HAYES LA
LATIMER
GD
GREENS CL
BLICKS CL
BELFRY DR
WATTS LANE
CHAPEL CR
FROG LA
Surrendell Farm
87
88
89
55
42

41
27

FOXLEY ROAD
Cowage Gorse
Cowage Grove
COMMON ROAD
Burnt Heath Farm
Malmesbury Common
Whiteheath Farm
Lower West Park Farm
West Park Farm
West Park Wood
West Park
MILL LA
SN16
Bradfield Wood
Corston
Newlands Farm
Manor Farm
Firs Farm
RADNOR PK
RODBOURNE RD
BARTON WAY
KINGWAY VIEW
A429 MAIN ROAD
Gauze Brook
Kingway Nursery
A429
Court Farm
Kingway Barn
Bincombe Wood
SN14
A
B
C
D
E
F
8
7
85
6
5
84
4
3
83
2
1
82
90
91
92
41
56

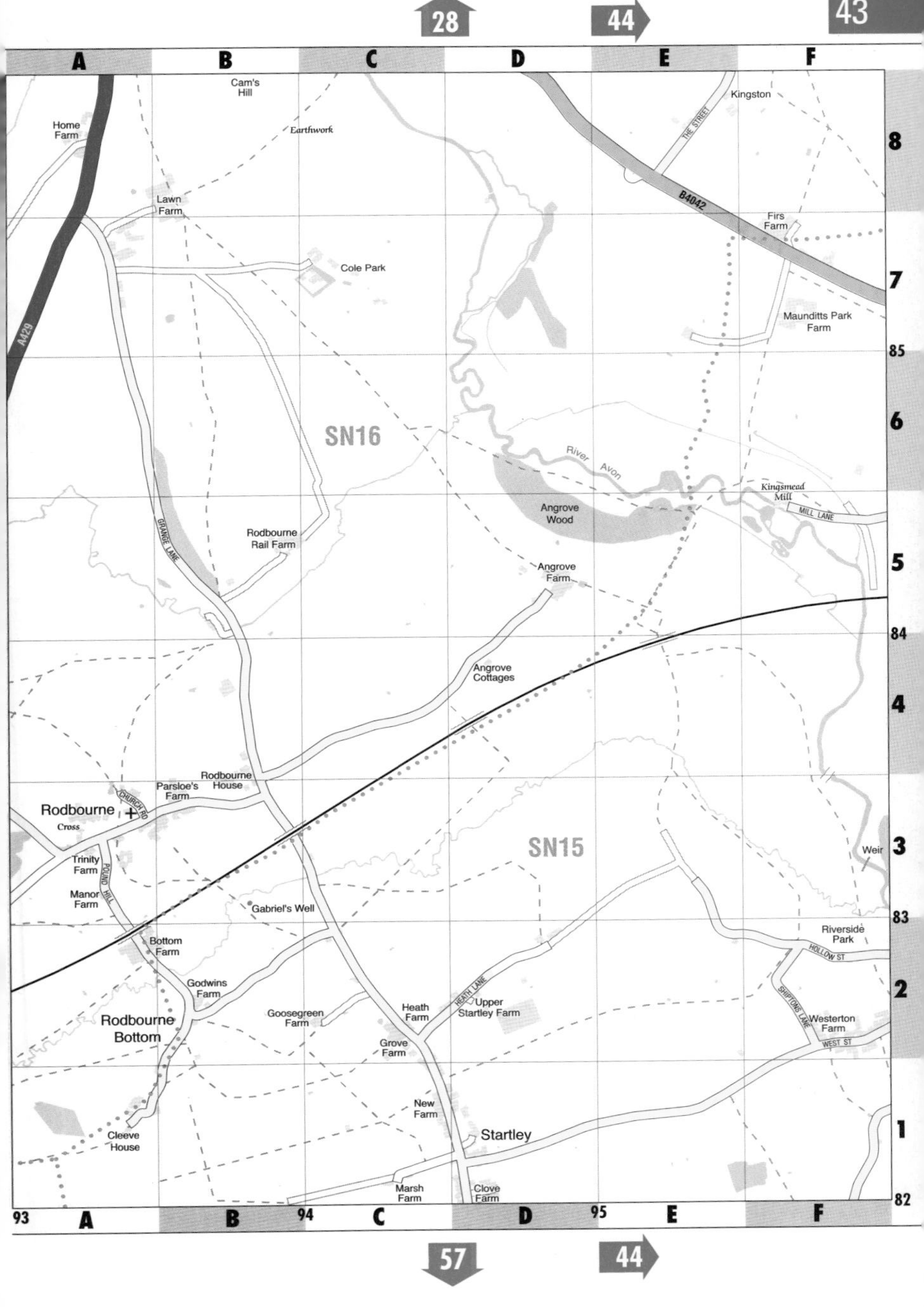
28
44
A
B
C
D
E
F
Cam's Hill
Earthwork
Home Farm
Kingston
THE STREET
8
Lawn Farm
B4042
Firs Farm
Cole Park
7
A429
Maunditts Park Farm
85
SN16
6
River Avon
Kingsmead Mill
MILL LANE
Angrove Wood
Rodbourne Rail Farm
GRANGE LANE
5
Angrove Farm
84
Angrove Cottages
4
Rodbourne House
Parsloe's Farm
Rodbourne
Cross
CHURCH RD
SN15
Weir
3
Trinity Farm
POUND HILL
Manor Farm
Gabriel's Well
83
Riverside Park
HOLLOW ST
Bottom Farm
Godwins Farm
2
HEATH LANE
Upper Startley Farm
Heath Farm
Goosegreen Farm
Rodbourne Bottom
SHIPTONS LANE
Westerton Farm
WEST ST
Grove Farm
New Farm
1
Startley
Cleeve House
Marsh Farm
Clove Farm
82
93
94
95
57
44

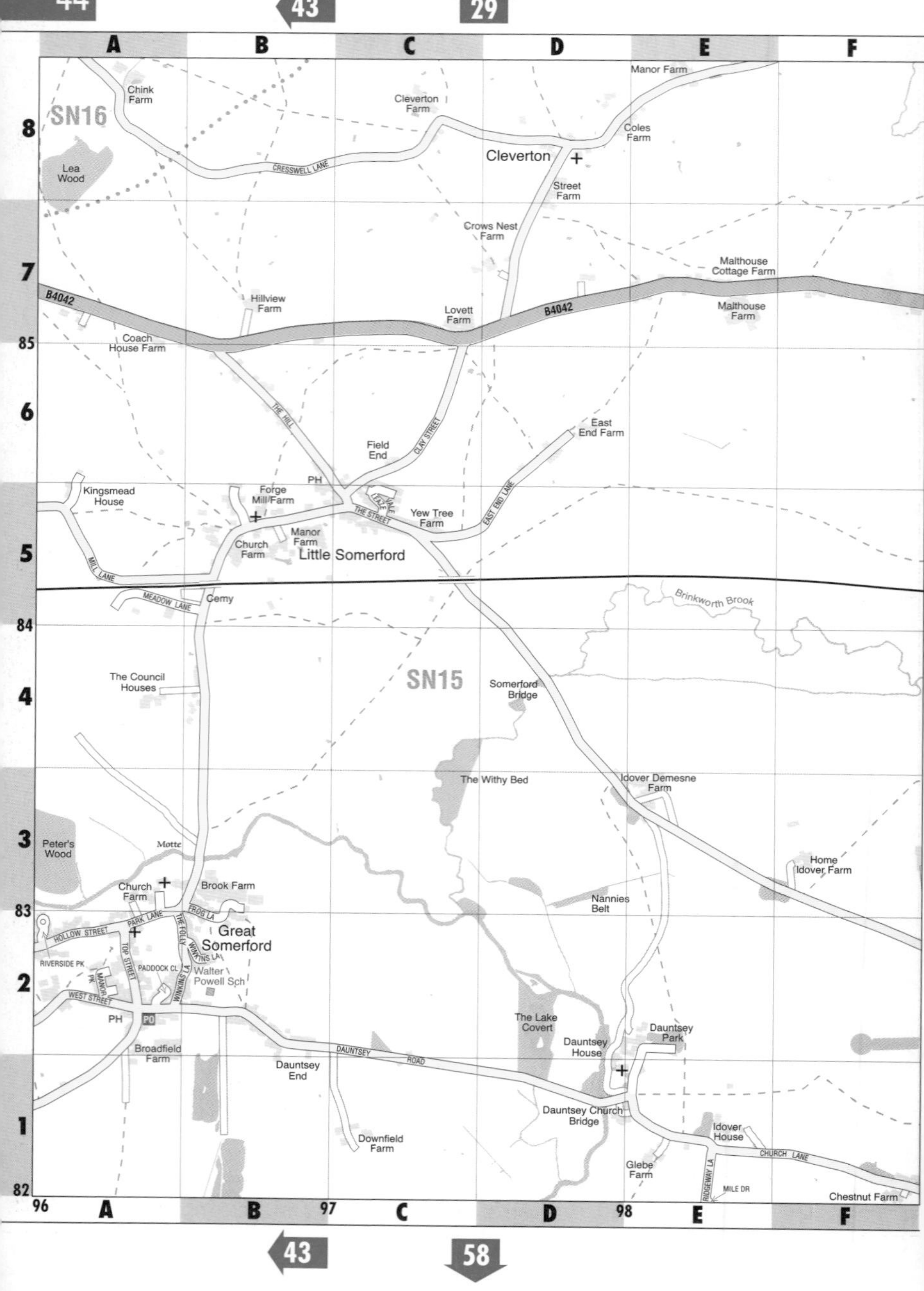
43
29
A
B
C
D
E
F
8
7
85
6
5
84
4
3
83
2
1
82
96
97
98
SN16
SN15
Chink Farm
Lea Wood
Cleverton Farm
Manor Farm
Coles Farm
Cleverton
Street Farm
CRESSWELL LANE
Crows Nest Farm
Malthouse Cottage Farm
Malthouse Farm
B4042
Hillview Farm
Lovett Farm
Coach House Farm
THE HILL
CLAY STREET
Field End
East End Farm
PH
Kingsmead House
Forge Mill Farm
Yew Tree Farm
EAST END LANE
THE STREET
VALE LEAZE
Church Farm
Manor Farm
Little Somerford
MILL LANE
MEADOW LANE
Cemy
Brinkworth Brook
The Council Houses
Somerford Bridge
The Withy Bed
Idover Demesne Farm
Peter's Wood
Motte
Home Idover Farm
Church Farm
Brook Farm
Nannies Belt
FROG LA
PARK LANE
HOLLOW STREET
THE FOLLY
Great Somerford
WINKINS LA
RIVERSIDE PK
TOP STREET
PADDOCK CL
MANOR PK
Walter Powell Sch
WEST STREET
PH
PO
The Lake Covert
Dauntsey Park
Dauntsey House
Broadfield Farm
DAUNTSEY ROAD
Dauntsey End
Dauntsey Church Bridge
Idover House
Downfield Farm
Glebe Farm
CHURCH LANE
RIDGEWAY LA
MILE DR
Chestnut Farm
43
58

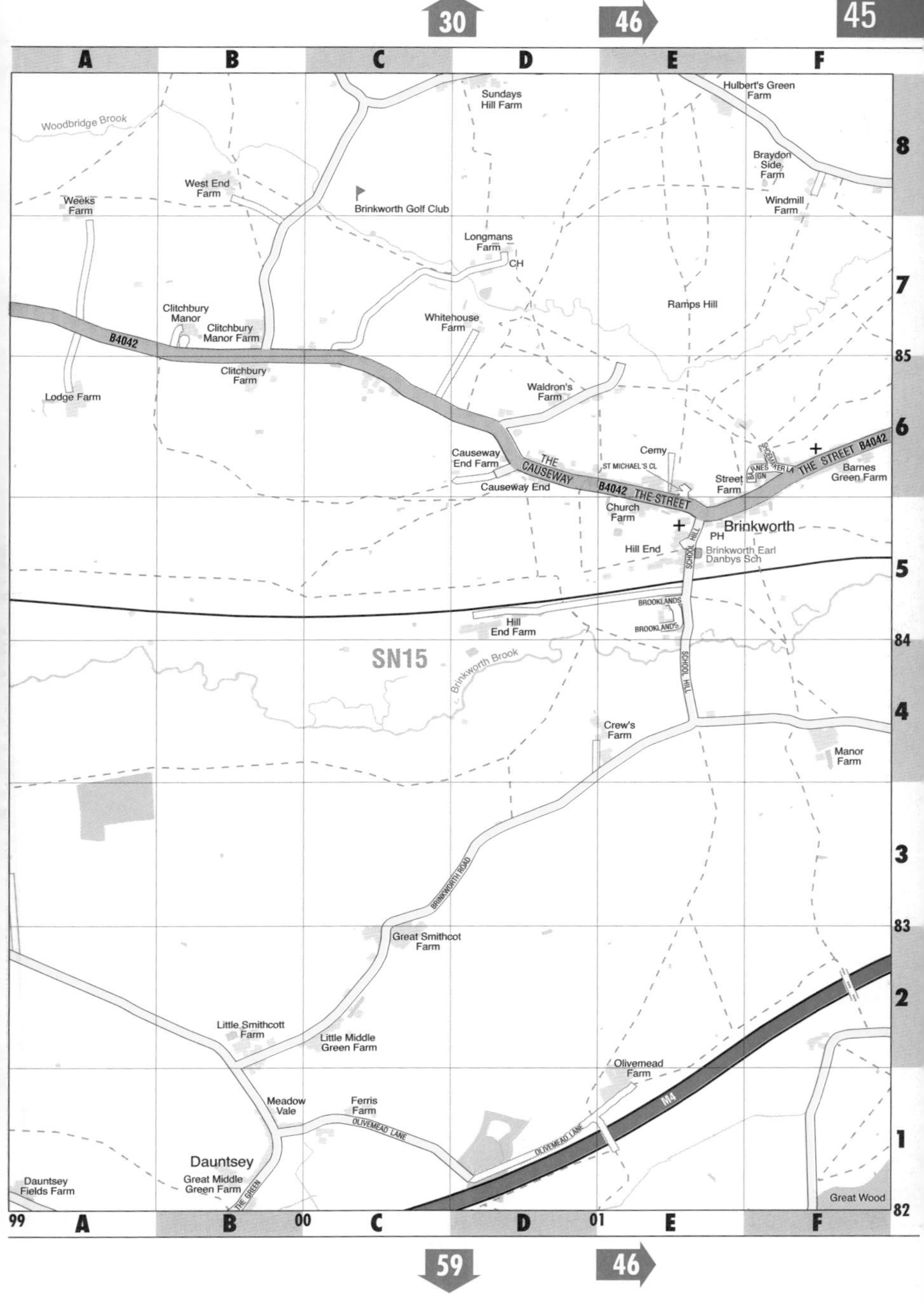
30
46
A
B
C
D
E
F
Woodbridge Brook
Sundays Hill Farm
Hulbert's Green Farm
Braydon Side Farm
Windmill Farm
West End Farm
Weeks Farm
Brinkworth Golf Club
Longmans Farm
CH
Ramps Hill
Clitchbury Manor
Clitchbury Manor Farm
Whitehouse Farm
B4042
Clitchbury Farm
Lodge Farm
Waldron's Farm
Cemy
Causeway End Farm
THE CAUSEWAY
ST MICHAEL'S CL
Causeway End
B4042 THE STREET
Street Farm
THE STREET B4042
Barnes Green Farm
Church Farm
Brinkworth
PH
Hill End
SCHOOL HILL
Brinkworth Earl Danbys Sch
BROOKLANDS
Hill End Farm
SN15
Brinkworth Brook
Crew's Farm
Manor Farm
BRINKWORTH ROAD
Great Smithcot Farm
Little Smithcott Farm
Little Middle Green Farm
Olivemead Farm
M4
Meadow Vale
Ferris Farm
OLIVEMEAD LANE
Dauntsey
Great Middle Green Farm
THE GREEN
Dauntsey Fields Farm
Great Wood
8
7
85
6
5
84
4
3
83
2
1
82
99
00
01
59
46

45
31

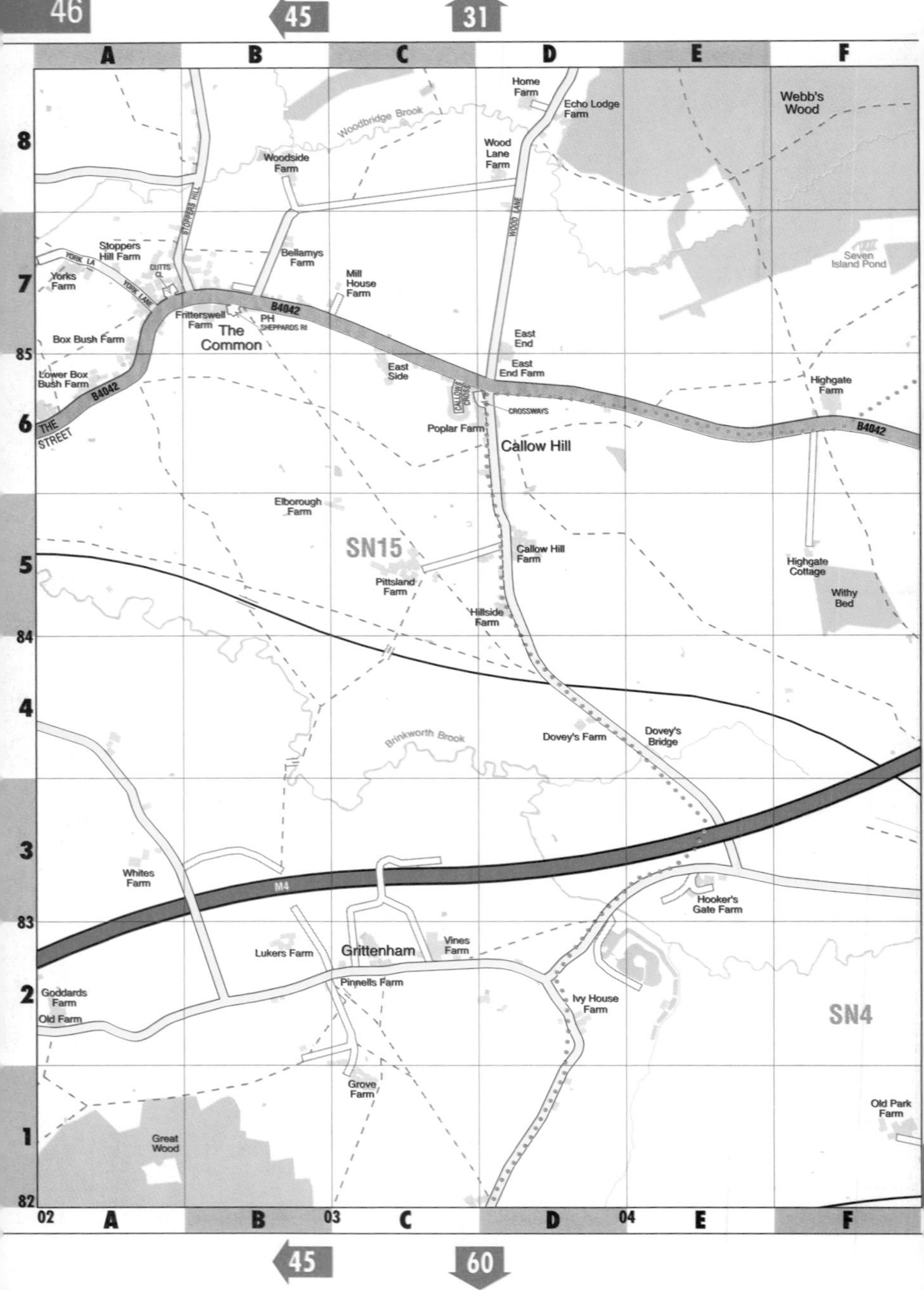
A
B
C
D
E
F
8
7
85
6
5
84
4
3
83
2
1
82
02
03
04
Home Farm
Echo Lodge Farm
Webb's Wood
Woodbridge Brook
Woodside Farm
Wood Lane Farm
STOPPERS HILL
WOOD LANE
Stoppers Hill Farm
YORK LA
YORK LANE
CUTTS CL
Yorks Farm
Bellamys Farm
Mill House Farm
Seven Island Pond
B4042
Fritterswell Farm
The Common
PH
SHEPPARDS RI
Box Bush Farm
East End
East Side
East End Farm
Lower Box Bush Farm
CALLOWS CROSS
CROSSWAYS
Highgate Farm
THE STREET
Poplar Farm
Callow Hill
Elborough Farm
SN15
Callow Hill Farm
Pittsland Farm
Highgate Cottage
Withy Bed
Hillside Farm
Brinkworth Brook
Dovey's Farm
Dovey's Bridge
Whites Farm
M4
Hooker's Gate Farm
Lukers Farm
Grittenham
Vines Farm
Pinnells Farm
Goddards Farm
Old Farm
Ivy House Farm
SN4
Grove Farm
Old Park Farm
Great Wood

45
60

32
48

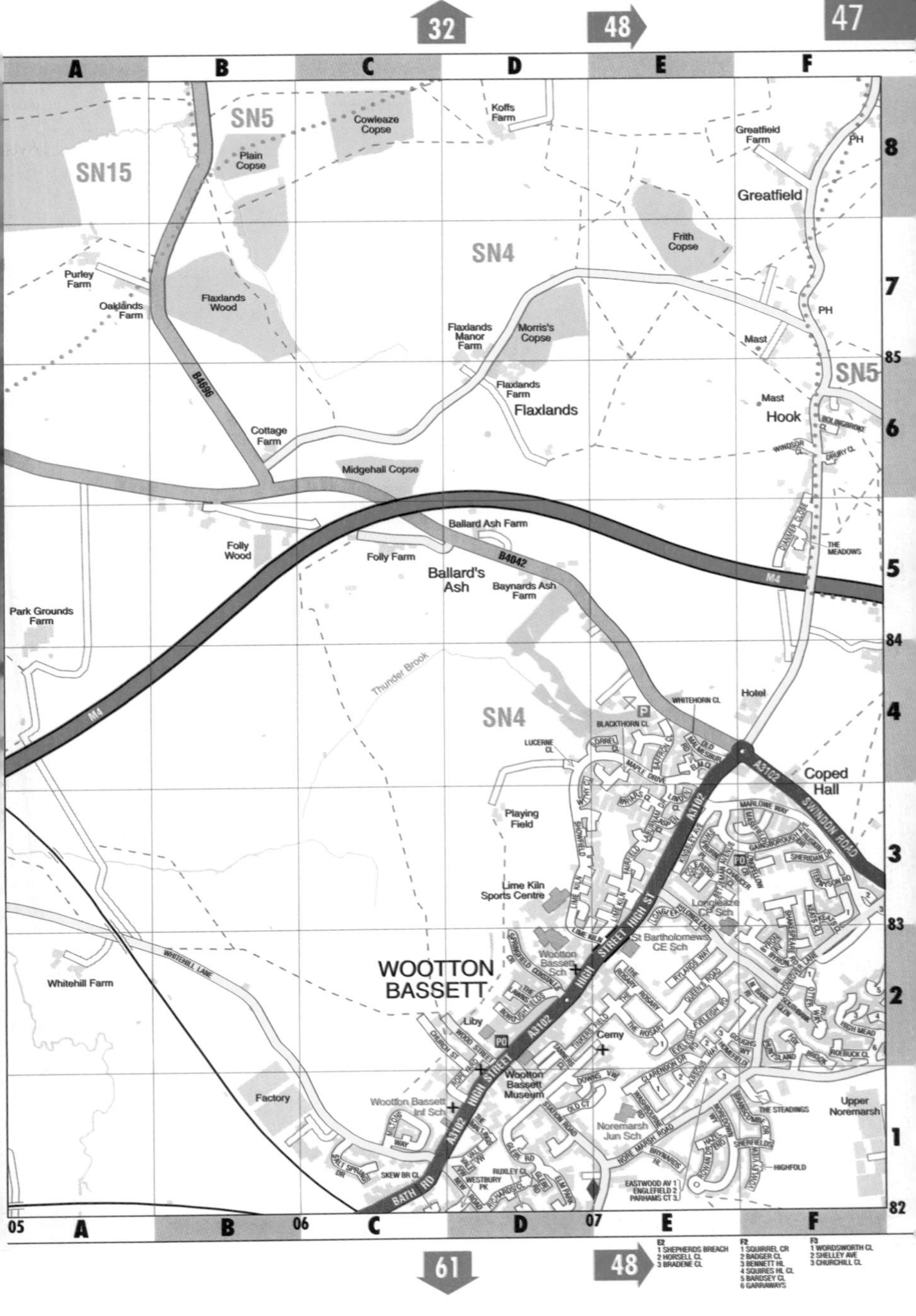

61
48

E2
1 SHEPHERDS BREACH
2 HORSELL CL
3 BRADENE CL

F2
1 SQUIRREL CR
2 BADGER CL
3 BENNETT HL
4 SQUIRES HL CL
5 BARDSEY CL
6 GARRAWAYS

F3
1 WORDSWORTH CL
2 SHELLEY AVE
3 CHURCHILL CL

47
33

F8
1 KINGSCOTE CL
2 BRAYBROOKE CL
3 SANDACRE RD
4 GRANARY CL
5 ASKERTON CL
6 STARING CL
7 HARVESTER CL
8 FENLAND CL
9 MALDWYN CL
10 LUCERNE CL
11 ALBA CL
12 LAMORA CL
13 CHEVALIER CL

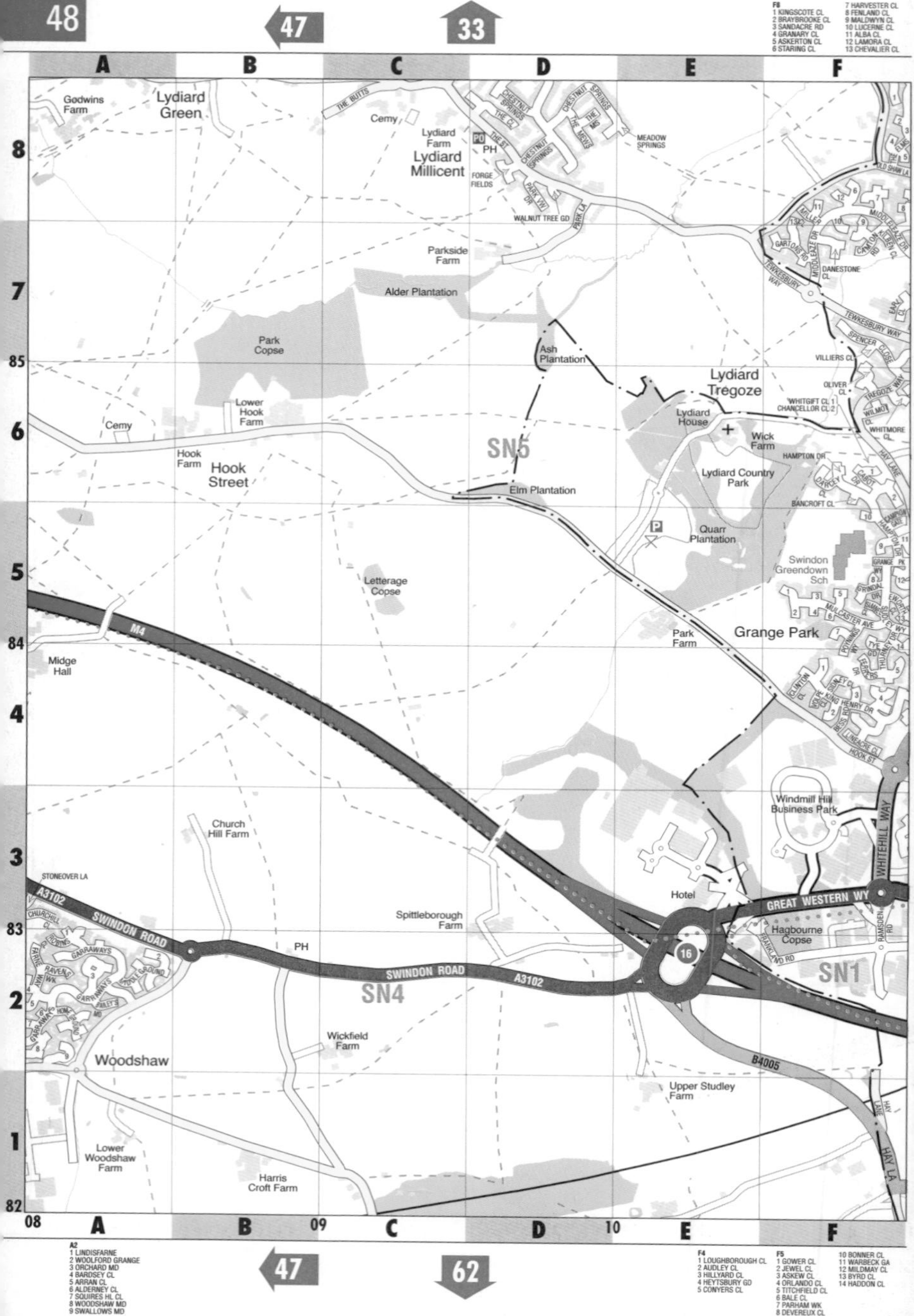

A2
1 LINDISFARNE
2 WOOLFORD GRANGE
3 ORCHARD MD
4 BARDSEY CL
5 ARRAN CL
6 ALDERNEY CL
7 SQUIRES HL CL
8 WOODSHAW MD
9 SWALLOWS MD

47
62

F4
1 LOUGHBOROUGH CL
2 AUDLEY CL
3 HILLYARD CL
4 HEYTSBURY GD
5 CONYERS CL

F5
1 GOWER CL
2 JEWEL CL
3 ASKEW CL
4 ORLANDO CL
5 TITCHFIELD CL
6 BALE CL
7 PARHAM WK
8 DEVEREUX CL
9 BABINGTON PK
10 BONNER CL
11 WARBECK GA
12 MILDMAY CL
13 BYRD CL
14 HADDON CL

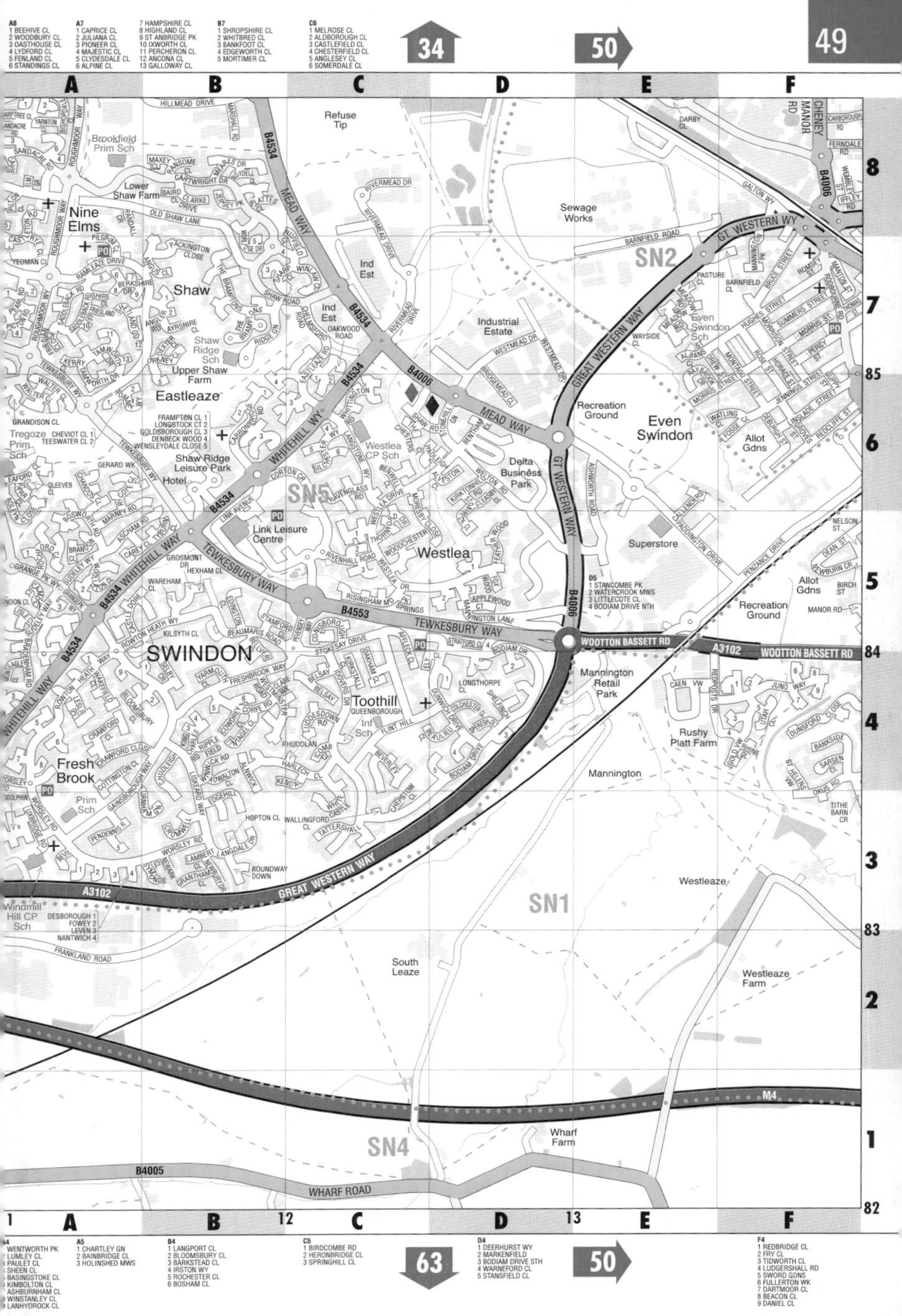

A8
1 BEEHIVE CL
2 WOODBURY CL
3 OASTHOUSE CL
4 LYDFORD CL
5 FENLAND CL
6 STANDINGS CL
A7
1 CAPRICE CL
2 JULIANA CL
3 PIONEER CL
4 MAJESTIC CL
5 CLYDESDALE CL
6 ALPINE CL
7 HAMPSHIRE CL
8 HIGHLAND CL
9 ST ANBRIDGE PK
10 IXWORTH CL
11 PERCHERON CL
12 ANCONA CL
13 GALLOWAY CL
B7
1 SHROPSHIRE CL
2 WHITBRED CL
3 BANKFOOT CL
4 EDGEWORTH CL
5 MORTIMER CL
C6
1 MELROSE CL
2 ALDBOROUGH CL
3 CASTLEFIELD CL
4 CHESTERFIELD CL
5 ANGLESEY CL
6 SOMERDALE CL
34
50
49
A B C D E F
8 7 85 6 5 84 4 3 83 2 1 82
Refuse Tip
HILLMEAD DRIVE
Brookfield Prim Sch
Nine Elms
Lower Shaw Farm
Shaw
Shaw Ridge Sch
Upper Shaw Farm
Eastleaze
Tregoze Prim Sch
FRAMPTON CL 1
LONGSTOCK CT 2
GOLDSBOROUGH CL 3
DENBECK WOOD 4
WENSLEYDALE CLOSE 5
CHEVIOT CL 1
TEESWATER CL 2
Shaw Ridge Leisure Park
Hotel
MEAD WAY
B4534
B4006
Ind Est
Industrial Estate
Sewage Works
BARNFIELD ROAD
SN2
GT WESTERN WY
GREAT WESTERN WAY
Even Swindon Sch
Even Swindon
Recreation Ground
Allot Gdns
Westlea CP Sch
Delta Business Park
SN5
Link Leisure Centre
Westlea
Superstore
D5
1 STANCOMBE PK
2 WATERCROOK MWS
3 LITTLECOTE CL
4 BODIAM DRIVE NTH
WHITEHILL WAY
TEWKESBURY WAY
B4553
SWINDON
WOOTTON BASSETT RD
A3102
Mannington Retail Park
Toothill
Inf Sch
Rushy Platt Farm
Mannington
Fresh Brook
Prim Sch
Westleaze
SN1
Windmill Hill CP Sch
DESBOROUGH 1
FOWEY 2
LEVEN 3
NANTWICH 4
FRANKLAND ROAD
South Leaze
Westleaze Farm
M4
Wharf Farm
SN4
B4005
WHARF ROAD
12
13
A4
WENTWORTH PK
LUMLEY CL
PAULET CL
SHEEN CL
BASINGSTOKE CL
KIMBOLTON CL
ASHBURNHAM CL
WINSTANLEY CL
LANHYDROCK CL
A5
1 CHARTLEY GN
2 BAINBRIDGE CL
3 HOLINSHED MWS
B4
1 LANGPORT CL
2 BLOOMSBURY CL
3 BARKSTEAD CL
4 IRSTON WY
5 ROCHESTER CL
6 BOSHAM CL
C5
1 BIRDCOMBE RD
2 HERONBRIDGE CL
3 SPRINGHILL CL
63
D4
1 DEERHURST WY
2 MARKENFIELD
3 BODIAM DRIVE STH
4 WARNEFORD CL
5 STANSFIELD CL
50
F4
1 REDBRIDGE CL
2 FRY CL
3 TIDWORTH CL
4 LUDGERSHALL RD
5 SWORD GDNS
6 FULLERTON WK
7 DARTMOOR CL
8 BEACON CL
9 DANIEL CL

49
C5
1 ROLLESTON ST
2 DUMBARTON TERR
3 BYRON ST
4 PRINCES ST
5 EASTCOTT HILL
6 REGENT ST
35
C6
1 CARFAX CL
2 MERTON ST
3 SANFORD ST
4 GORDON GDNS
5 GORDON RD
C7
1 ALEXANDRA RD
2 ARMSTRONG ST
3 LAGOS ST
4 NEWBRIDGE CL
SN2
SN1
SN3
SN4
SWINDON
Swindon
Kingshill
Okus
Old Town
New Town
Walcot West
Walcot East
Lawn
GREAT WESTERN WAY
CIRENCESTER WAY
OCOTAL WAY
COUNTY ROAD
QUEEN'S DR
QUEEN'S DRIVE
DROVE RD
CRICKLADE ST
HIGH ST
MARLBOROUGH RD
KINGSHILL ROAD
BATH RD
DEVIZES RD
CROFT ROAD
PIPERS WAY
MARLBOROUGH ROAD
M4
Swindon Town Football Club
Oasis Leisure Ctr
Steam Museum of G.W.R.
Designer Outlet
Brunel Parade
Swindon Mus & Art Gallery
Swindon Arts Centre
Holy Rood Church
Great Copse
Westlecott Farm
Burmah House
Sewage Works
Croft Wood
Recreation Ground
Roman Well
A5
1 CLARENDON LA
2 ERIN CT
3 SHIRE CT
4 ANDOVER ST
5 JOSEPH ST
6 MARLBOROUGH ST
7 COURTSKNAP CT
8 JOLLIFFE ST
B6
1 HENRY ST
2 FARINGDON RD
3 KING ST
4 RTEADING ST
5 CATHERINE ST
HARDING ST 6
49
64
D6
1 LOGAN CL
2 BROMLEY CL
3 SIDNEY CL
4 SELDON CL
E6
1 NORFOLK CL
2 STUART CL
3 MELVILLE CL
4 HERTFORD CL
5 DOUGLAS RD
6 BEDFORD RD
F4
1 KINGSWAY CL
2 CAXTON CL
3 BLAKESLEY CL
4 MONMOUTH CL
5 WALTON CL
6 BROUGHTON GRANGE
7 GEORGE GAY GDNS
8 KELHAM CL

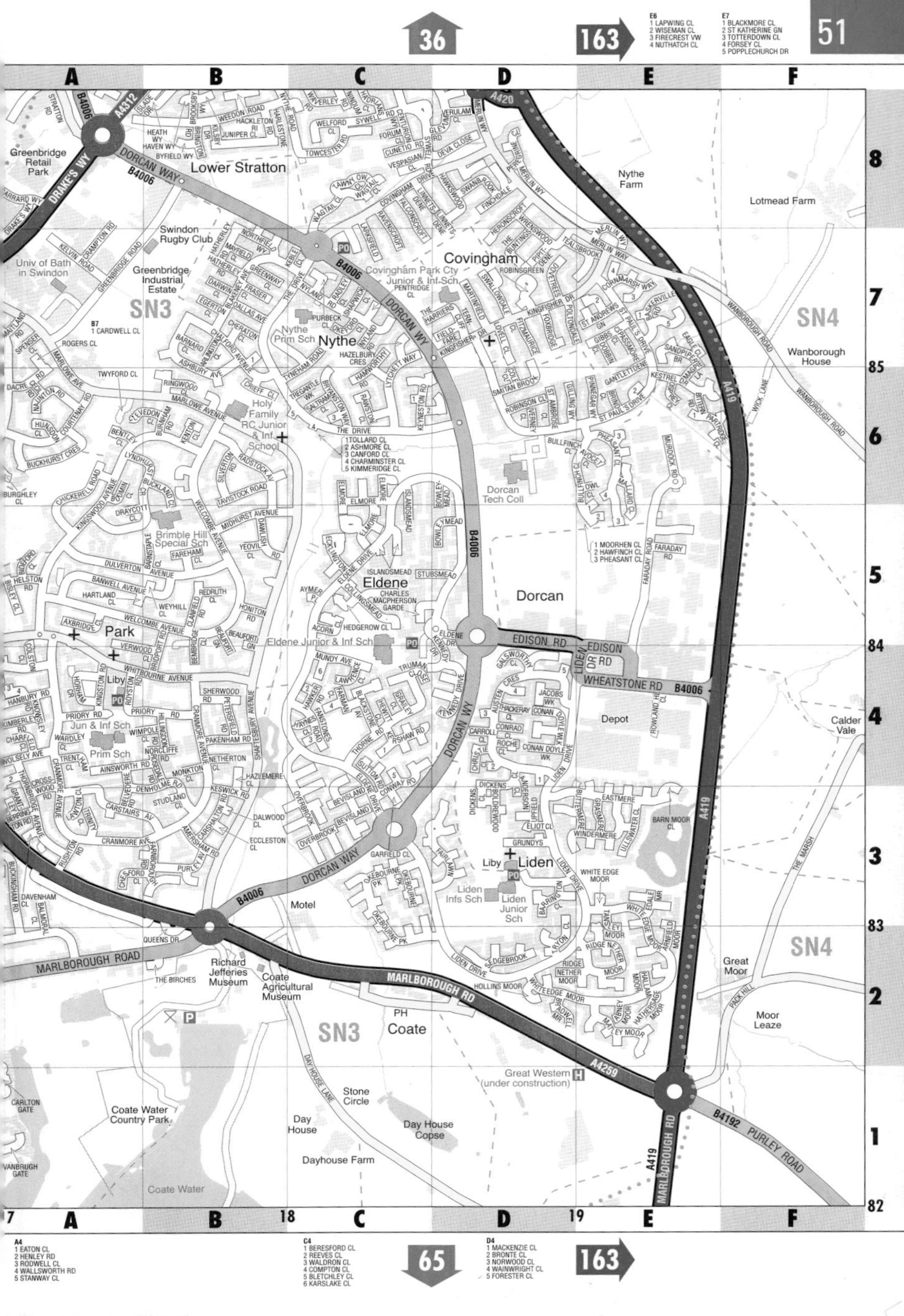

36
163
E6
1 LAPWING CL
2 WISEMAN CL
3 FIRECREST VW
4 NUTHATCH CL
E7
1 BLACKMORE CL
2 ST KATHERINE GN
3 TOTTERDOWN CL
4 FORSEY CL
5 POPPLECHURCH DR
51
A
B
C
D
E
F
8
7
85
6
5
84
4
3
83
2
1
82
7
18
19
Greenbridge Retail Park
Lower Stratton
DORCAN WAY
B4006
DRAKES WY
A4312
A420
Nythe Farm
Lotmead Farm
Swindon Rugby Club
Univ of Bath in Swindon
Greenbridge Industrial Estate
SN3
B7
1 CARDWELL CL
Covingham
Covingham Park Cty Junior & Inf Sch
Nythe Prim Sch
Nythe
SN4
Wanborough House
WANBOROUGH ROAD
A419
Holy Family RC Junior & Inf School
THE DRIVE
1 TOLLARD CL
2 ASHMORE CL
3 CANFORD CL
4 CHARMINSTER CL
5 KIMMERIDGE CL
Dorcan Tech Coll
1 MOORHEN CL
2 HAWFINCH CL
3 PHEASANT CL
FARADAY ROAD
Brimble Hill Special Sch
Eldene
Dorcan
Park
Eldene Junior & Inf Sch
EDISON RD
WHEATSTONE RD
Depot
Calder Vale
Liby
Jun & Inf Sch
Prim Sch
Motel
Liden
Liden Infs Sch
Liden Junior Sch
BARN MOOR CL
THE MARSH
Richard Jefferies Museum
Coate Agricultural Museum
MARLBOROUGH ROAD
MARLBOROUGH RD
A4259
Great Moor
Moor Leaze
PH
Coate
Great Western (under construction)
Coate Water Country Park
Stone Circle
Day House
Day House Copse
Dayhouse Farm
Coate Water
B4192
PURLEY ROAD
A4
1 EATON CL
2 HENLEY RD
3 RODWELL CL
4 WALLSWORTH RD
5 STANWAY CL
C4
1 BERESFORD CL
2 REEVES CL
3 WALDRON CL
4 COMPTON CL
5 BLETCHLEY CL
6 KARSLAKE CL
D4
1 MACKENZIE CL
2 BRONTE CL
3 NORWOOD CL
4 WAINWRIGHT CL
5 FORESTER CL
65
163

38

A
B
C
D
E
F
8
7
81
6
5
80
4
3
79
2
1
78
Lyegrove Wood
Seven Mile Plantation
LIME AVENUE
OLD DOWN ROAD
Egg Clump
Withy Moor
STATION ROAD
Sodbury Tunnel
Acton Turville
Newhouse Farm
B4040
B4039
Church Farm
PO
PH
BURTON ROAD
TORMARTON ROAD
GL9
OAKES LANE
Vicarage Cottage
Warren Barn
Fagot Pile
Pike Cottage
Old Warren
M4
Wall Leaze Wood
Parks Farm
Brotton Hill Wood
Warren Gorse
Westfield Farm
SN14
Phyldornick
Little Westfield
Tumulus
Fox Covert
79
80
Gloucestershire STREET ATLAS
M4 Bristol (M32)

66

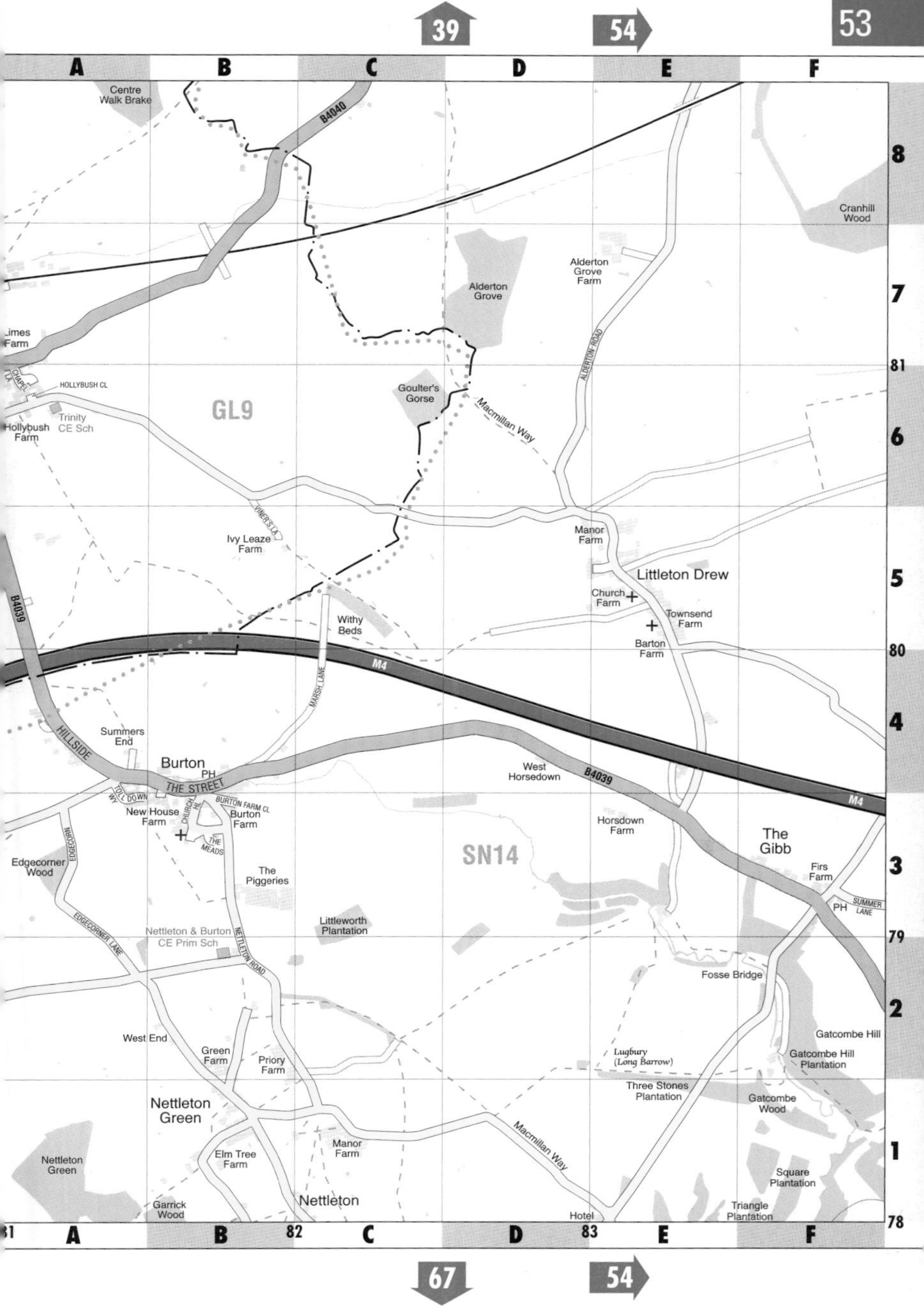
39
54
A
B
C
D
E
F
Centre
Walk Brake
B4040
8
Cranhill
Wood
Alderton
Grove
Farm
Alderton
Grove
7
Limes
Farm
CHAPEL LA
HOLLYBUSH CL
81
Goulter's
Gorse
ALDERTON ROAD
GL9
Macmillan Way
Hollybush
Farm
Trinity
CE Sch
6
VINER'S LA
Manor
Farm
Ivy Leaze
Farm
Littleton Drew
5
Church
Farm
Townsend
Farm
B4039
Withy
Beds
Barton
Farm
80
M4
MARSH LANE
4
Summers
End
HILLSIDE
Burton
PH
THE STREET
West
Horsedown
B4039
TOLL DOWN WY
BURTON FARM CL
M4
New House
Farm
CHURCH HL
Burton
Farm
Horsdown
Farm
The
Gibb
EDGECORN
THE MEADS
SN14
Edgecorner
Wood
The
Piggeries
3
Firs
Farm
SUMMER LANE
PH
EDGECORNER LANE
Littleworth
Plantation
Nettleton & Burton
CE Prim Sch
NETTLETON ROAD
79
Fosse Bridge
2
West End
Gatcombe Hill
Green
Farm
Priory
Farm
Lugbury
(Long Barrow)
Gatcombe Hill
Plantation
Three Stones
Plantation
Nettleton
Green
Gatcombe
Wood
Macmillan Way
1
Nettleton
Green
Elm Tree
Farm
Manor
Farm
Square
Plantation
Garrick
Wood
Nettleton
Hotel
Triangle
Plantation
78
81
82
83
67
54

53
40

A
B
C
D
E
F
8
7
81
6
5
80
4
3
79
2
1
78
84
85
86
Cranhill Wood
Dunley Gorse
East Dunley Farm
Little Worth Wood
Clapcote Brake
West Dunley Farm
Dunley
Dunley Wood
Dunley Wood
Dunley Wood
Dunley Wood
Ford
Brimsol Spring
FOSSE WAY
Ash Bed
Newlands Farm
Oldlands Wood
High Elms Covert
ALDERTON ROAD
SCHOOL LA
PH
Grittleton
Manor Farm
THE STREET
Limekiln Cottage
Grittleton House Sch
Sewage Works
SN14
Fosse Gate
Old Mead Covert
Foscote
M4
Ryley's Farm
Fields Plantation
Thorngove Cottage
West Foscote Farm
SUMMER LANE
Lucknow Plantation
Rat Hill
East Sevington Farm
Woodbury Hill Plantation
Rathill Plantation
B4039
Delhi Plantation
West Sevington Farm
White Gate Plantation

53
68

41
56

A
B
C
D
E
F
Pillow Mound
Surrendell Cottage
Prior's Corner
Hullavington
PH
PO
FROG LA
GIBBS LA
ROYAL FIELD CL
THE PARKLANDS
PARKLANDS DR
THE STREET
THE GARDNERS
GARDNERS DR
Wellington Place
Gardners Farm
Barnfield Farm
8
7
81
Roberts Berry Farm
Stock Wood
6
Clapcote Cottages
Hollybush Farm
Deadhill Plantation
Deadhill Wood
5
Woodbarn Farm
80
East Foscote Farm
Crowdown
SN14
Stanton Park
4
Stanton Park Cottages
Sevington Covert
Manor Farm
Leigh Delamere
3
Leigh Delamere Wood
Motel
M4
79
Leigh Delamere Service Area
Sevington
2
Moorshall Farm
Broomfield
New Buildings
Little Spinney
1
New Priory Stud Farm
HONEY KNOB HL
Easton Wood
78
87
88
89

69
56

55
42
A
B
C
D
E
F
8
7
81
6
5
80
4
3
79
2
1
78
A429
Hanger Farm
Rowden Wood
Hullavington Airfield
ANSON PLACE
Barracks
Lower Stanton Farm
BLENHEIM GD
A429
NEWBOURNE GD
SEAGRY ROAD
COOKS CL
SEAGRY RD
Glebe Farm
AVIL'S LANE
Lower Stanton St Quintin
Churchill Farm
Moat
CHURCH LANE
SN14
VALLETTA GARDENS
VALLETTA GD
VALLETTA GD
BOUVERIE PARK
RECTORY CL
Manor Farm
Prim Sch
Dovecote
Hotel
Stanton St Quintin
COURT GD
KINGTON LANE
Leaze Farm
Clanville
Long Plantation
17
M4
M4
B4122
Upper Swinley Farm
Westbrook Farm
Springfield Farm
Lower Swinley Farm
A350
SN15
Whitelands Farm
DAY'S LANE
Ford
Southsea Farm
Draycot Cerne
STANTON LA
90
91
92
55
70

43
58

A
B
C
D
E
F
8
7
81
6
5
80
4
3
79
2
1
78
94
95
Startley Farm
Seagry Heath
Honey Acre Farm
New Leaze Farm
Seagry Wood
Upper Farm
Albany Farm
AVIL'S LANE
Avil's Farm
Lower Seagry Farm
Lower Seagry
Trinity Farm
CHURCH ACRE
Vicarage Cottages
Seagry House
Five Thorn Farm
FIVE THORN LANE
Upper Seagry
HENN LANE
BROADLEAZE
Church Farm
Tithe Barn
Upper Seagry Sch
Moat
Manor Farm
Nables Farm
Woodman Croft Covert
Greenfields Farm
Ell Wood
Mill House
Weir
SCOTLAND HILL
North Draycot Park Farm
Hardinge
SN15
River Avon
M4
Long Plantation
The Cottage
Brookside
SEAGRY HILL
Summerlands Farm
Malford Farm
Weirs
AVONWEIR LA
MAIN ROAD
B4069
Christian Malford
SEAGRY RD
WILLOWBROOK END
Church Farm
BARRETT LA
CHURCH PIECE
Sutton Benger
MANOR FARM DR
PO
PARK LA
PH
HIGH STREET
BELL LA
Draycott Park Farm
Draycot House
CHESTNUT ROAD
Hotel
SUTTON LA
Sutton Benger CE Sch
QUEENS CL
Arms Farm
PH
GREGORY CL
COWLEY WAY
LEE CR
NEVILLE TR
Recreation Ground
Sewage Works
CORONATION CL
Weir
B4122
WESTLAKE PL
SUTTON LANE
B4069
The Old Rectory
B4069

71
58

57
44

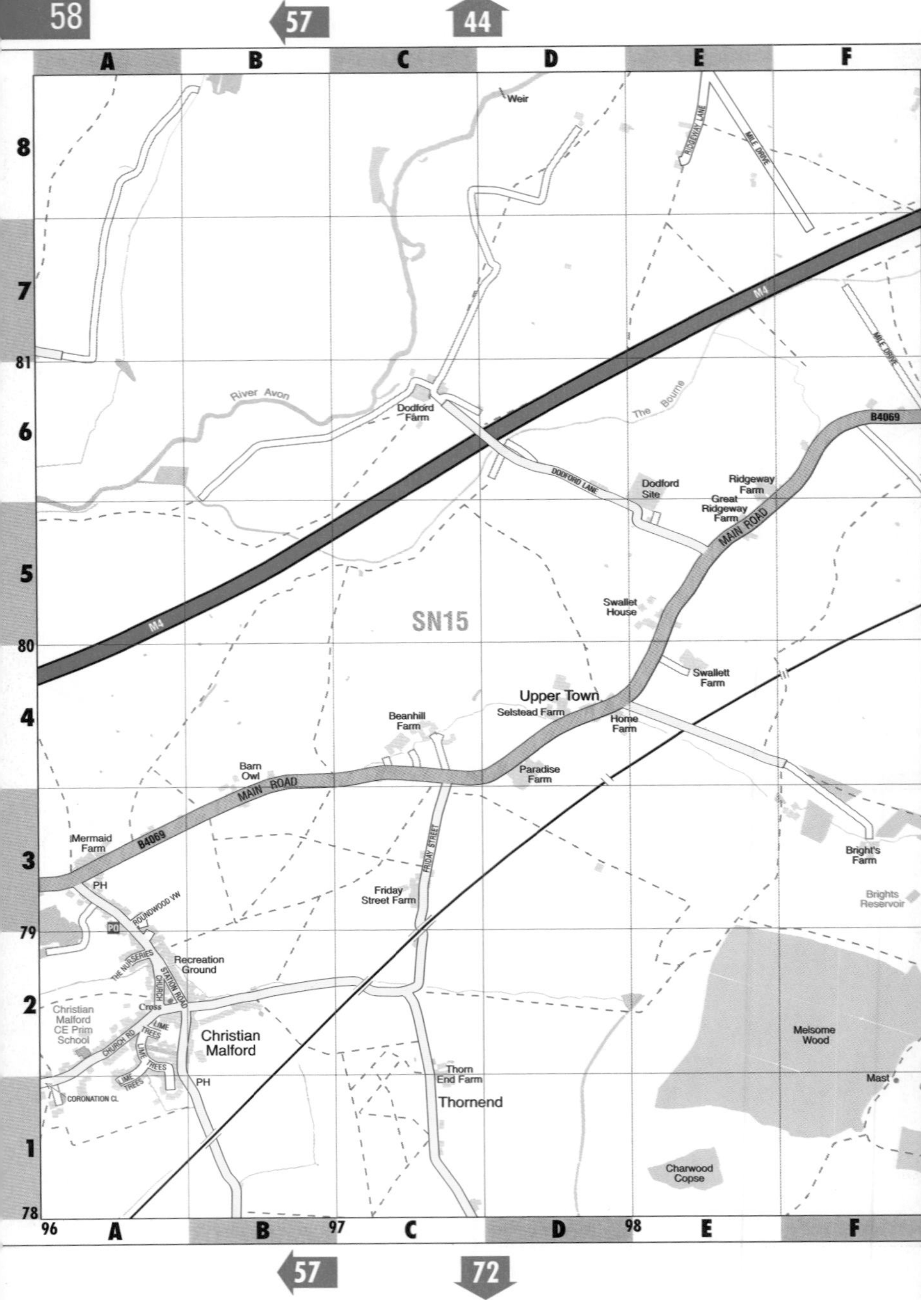
A
B
C
D
E
F
8
7
81
6
5
80
4
3
79
2
1
78
96
97
98
Weir
RIDGEWAY LANE
MILE DRIVE
M4
River Avon
Dodford Farm
The Bourne
B4069
DODFORD LANE
Dodford Site
Ridgeway Farm
Great Ridgeway Farm
MAIN ROAD
Swallet House
SN15
Swallett Farm
Upper Town
Selstead Farm
Home Farm
Beanhill Farm
Barn Owl
Paradise Farm
Mermaid Farm
Bright's Farm
FRIDAY STREET
Friday Street Farm
Brights Reservoir
PH
PO
ROUNDWOOD VW
Recreation Ground
THE NURSERIES
STATION ROAD
CHURCH
Cross
Christian Malford CE Prim School
LIME TREES
CHURCH RD
Christian Malford
Melsome Wood
Thorn End Farm
Thornend
Mast
CORONATION CL
Charwood Copse

57
72

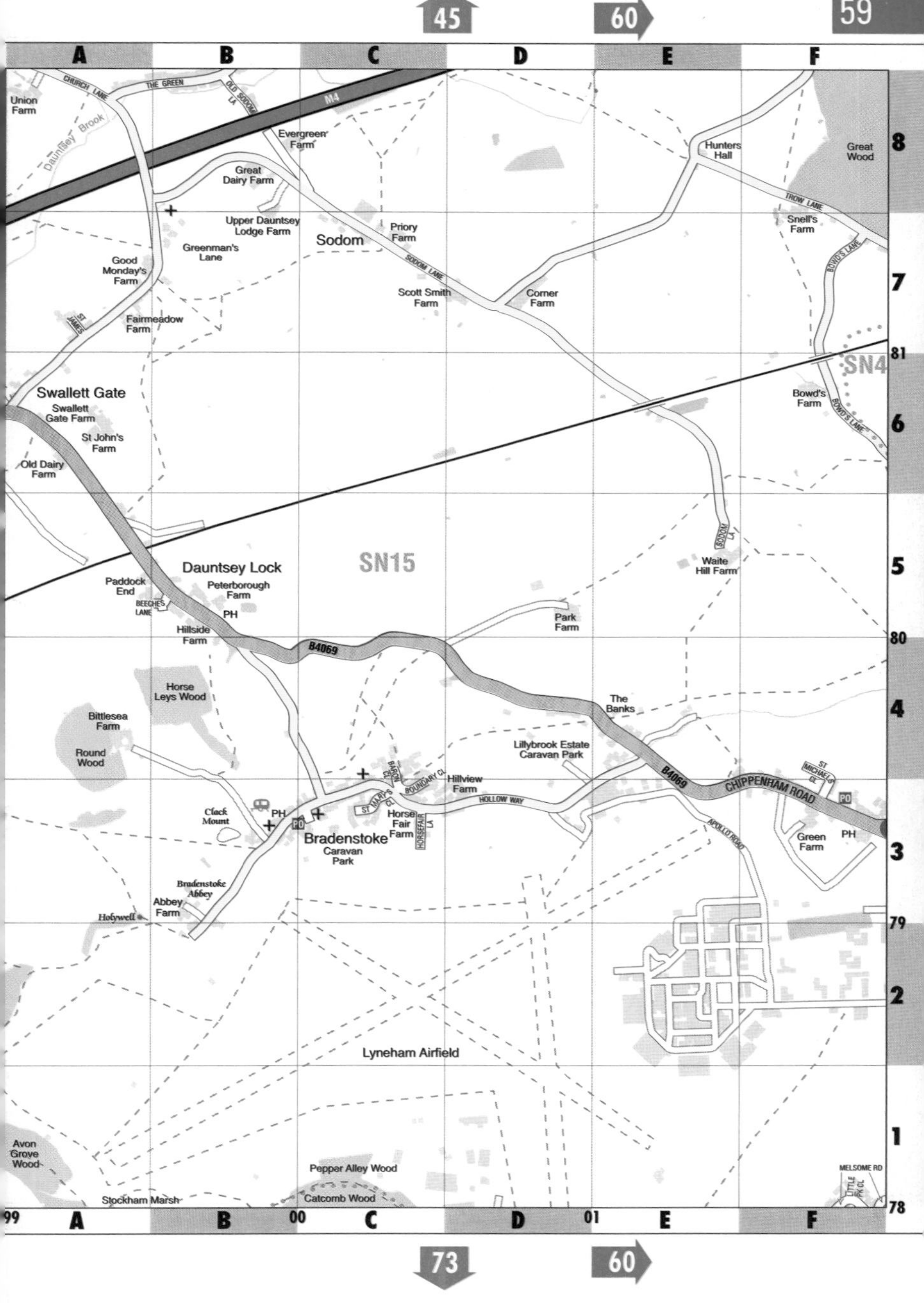
45
60
A
B
C
D
E
F
8
7
81
6
5
80
4
3
79
2
1
78
99
00
01
Union Farm
CHURCH LANE
THE GREEN
OLD SODOM LA
M4
Dauntsey Brook
Evergreen Farm
Hunters Hall
Great Wood
Great Dairy Farm
TROW LANE
Upper Dauntsey Lodge Farm
Priory Farm
Snell's Farm
Sodom
Good Monday's Farm
Greenman's Lane
SODOM LANE
BOWD'S LANE
Scott Smith Farm
Corner Farm
ST JAMES
Fairmeadow Farm
SN4
Swallett Gate
Swallett Gate Farm
Bowd's Farm
St John's Farm
Old Dairy Farm
SODOM LA
SN15
Waite Hill Farm
Dauntsey Lock
Paddock End
Peterborough Farm
BEECHES LANE
PH
Park Farm
Hillside Farm
B4069
Horse Leys Wood
The Banks
Bittlesea Farm
Round Wood
Lillybrook Estate Caravan Park
BARON CL
BOUNDARY CL
Hillview Farm
ST MICHAELS CL
ST MARY'S CL
HOLLOW WAY
CHIPPENHAM ROAD
Clack Mount
PH
PO
Horse Fair Farm
HORSEFAIR LA
APOLLO ROAD
PO
Bradenstoke
Caravan Park
Green Farm
PH
Bradenstoke Abbey
Abbey Farm
Holywell
Lyneham Airfield
Avon Grove Wood
Pepper Alley Wood
MELSOME RD
LITTLE PK CL
Stockham Marsh
Catcomb Wood
73
60

59
46

A
B
C
D
E
F
8
7
81
6
5
80
4
3
79
2
1
78
02
03
04
Great Wood
SN15
Manor House
Hart Farm
Vastern
Vastern Wood
Old Park Farm
Cheeseley Hill Farm
Greatwood Farm
Trow Lane Farm
TROW LANE
West Close Copse
Manor House
Tockenham Wick
Wiltshire Bassett Golf Club
A3102
Teagles Copse
Hillocks Wood
Tockenham Reservoir
TOCKENHAM CORNER
PRIMROSE HILL
BOYD'S LA
THE HILLOCKS
Tockenham Manor Farm
Shaw Farm
SN4
Rowley Copse
Brickkiln Copse
THE GREEN
SN15
Shaw Farm
Queen Court Farm
Court Farm
Beckett's Copse
Moat
Tockenham Farm
Tockenham
Cowleaze Copse
Manorhouse Farm
POUND CL
WEBBS CT
PH
HOCKETT'S CL
BAKERS FIELD
CALNE RD
Lyneham
LANCASTER SQUARE
HARROW GROVE
HASTINGS DRIVE
Church Farm
Church End
CHURCH LA
Tockenham Court Farm
Greenway Farm
GREENWAY
BELFAST MEAD
Middlehill Farm
ARALHEM
YORK RD
LIME CL
Jun Sch
RAF Lyneham
COMET CL
CROSS
PO
SYCAMORE CL
BRITANNIA CRES
ASH CL
ELM CL
VICTORIA DRIVE
ARGOSY RD
TEAL AVENUE
MUSCOVEY CL
SHELD DR
PINTAIL CT
EIDER AVE
EIDER AV
MALLARD AVE
PINTAIL COURT
EIDER AV
PRESTON LANE
CALNE ROAD
SLESSOR RD
TRENCHARD RD
DICKSON RD
SLESSOR RD
PORTAL PL
MELSOME RD
Preston
Preston End Farm
Preston East Farm
Thickthorn Farm

59
166

47
62

A
B
C
D
E
F
Wootton
Bassett
SKEW BR CL
WESTBURY PARK
MORSTONE RD
ELM PK
STATION RD
NEW ROAD
PIPERS CL
DUNNINGTON RD
GLENVILLE CL
TEMPLAR'S FIRS
Skew
Bridge
Knights
Farm
HUNTS MILL ROAD
VASTERN WHARF
A3102
Huntsmill
Farm
Brinkworth Brook
Brynard's
Hill
MARLBOROUGH ROAD
CH
Greenhill Common
Farm
Lanes
Farm
Kendricks
Farm
Meadow
Farm
Meux Farm
Ashdown
Farm
Wootton
Fields Farm
BROADTOWN LA
Vale
Farm
Little Park
Farm
Lower
Greenhill Farm
SN4
Barn
Hill Farm
BREACH LANE
Upper Greenhill
Farm
Lower
Ham Farm
Hambrook
Farm
The
Barton
Clyffe Pypard
Wood
Upper Ham
Farm
Common Farm
Parsonage
Farm
New House
South
Farm
Manor
Farm
Thornhill
North
Farm
WITHY BED
WOOD STREET
Wood Street
Farm
SN15
8
7
81
6
5
80
4
3
79
2
1
78
05
06
07

166
62

61
48

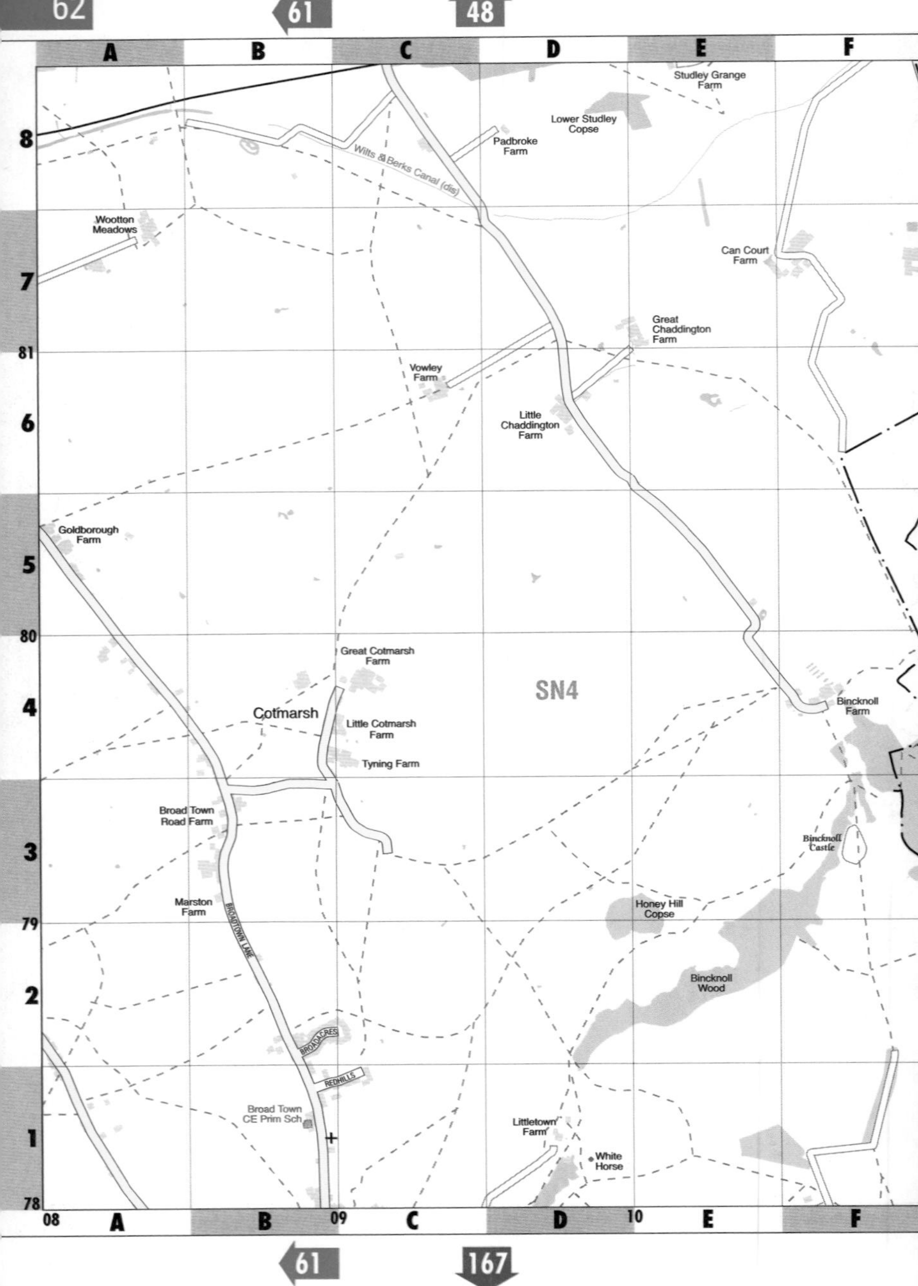
A
B
C
D
E
F
8
7
81
6
5
80
4
3
79
2
1
78
08
09
10
Studley Grange Farm
Lower Studley Copse
Padbroke Farm
Wilts & Berks Canal (dis)
Wootton Meadows
Can Court Farm
Great Chaddington Farm
Vowley Farm
Little Chaddington Farm
Goldborough Farm
Great Cotmarsh Farm
SN4
Cotmarsh
Little Cotmarsh Farm
Binckoll Farm
Tyning Farm
Broad Town Road Farm
Binckoll Castle
Marston Farm
BROADTOWN LANE
Honey Hill Copse
Binckoll Wood
BROADACRES
REDHILLS
Broad Town CE Prim Sch
Littletown Farm
White Horse

61
167

49
64
A
B
C
D
E
F
Whitehouse Farm
Common Farm
Glebe Farm
Costow Farm
Berrywood Farm
Nuttery Copse
B4005
8
WHARF ROAD
SUMMERHOUSE RD
SAVILL CR
MAUNSELL WAY
CROSS RD
VICTORIA
KELLSBOROUGH RD
ELLINGDON RD
ASHEN COPSE RD
MASKELEYNE WY
BALDEN CL
WHALLEY CR
ELCOMBE AV
COWLEAZE CR
PH
Elcombe House Farm
Hurst Copse
Horseshoe Copse
HAY LANE
7
81
6
Lower Basset Down Farm
Elcombe
Cowleaze Farm
Wroughton House
CHURCH HL
5
Salthrop House
Chilton Farm
Elcombe Hall
Salthrop Wood
80
Basset Down Farm
Basset Down Wood
SN4
Beech Copse
Nature Trail
4
Quidhampton Wood
Salthrop Farm
Clouts Wood
Markham Bottom
Science Museum Outstation
Red Barn
3
A4361
79
Wroughton Airfield
2
1
1
A
B
12
C
D
13
E
F
78
167
64

A6
1 EDGAR ROW CL
2 WHALLEY CR
3 ELCOMBE AVE
4 COWLEAZE CR

63
50

63
168

51
163
A
B
C
D
E
F
8
7
81
6
5
80
4
3
79
2
1
78
17
18
19
Badbury Farm
Badbury Wick
SN3
SN4
Burderop Wood
BROOME MANOR LA
M4
A419
B4192
MARLBOROUGH ROAD
DAY HOUSE LANE
Green Hill
MEADOW WY
Medbourne Farm
Long Copse
Crook's Copse
Taylor's Copse
15
BERICOT LANE
PH
West Farm
Badbury
Lansdown
Badbury House Farm
Sewage Works
Pinkcombe Wood
Hodson
B4005
BUTTS ROAD
Chiseldon Prim Sch
HODSON ROAD
CHURCH ST
WINDMILL PIECE
DEWEY CL
VIEW ROAD
DOWNS RD
SCHOOL CL
STATION ROAD
CASTLE VIEW ROAD
CANNEY CLOSE
HIGH ST
STROUD HILL
MAY'S LA
UPPER LA
PO
TURNBALL
BALDWIN CL
WELL CL
CHISELDON CT
Liby
Recreation Ground
THE CURNICKS
CARISBROOK TR
NORRIS CLOSE
NEW ROAD
A346
Bush House
Chiseldon
THE CR
DRAYCOT ROAD
P
New Farm
THE RIDGEWAY
LADYSMITH ROAD
CAMBRAI RD
AISNE RD
SAMBRE ROAD
168
163

52

A
B
C
D
E
F
8
7
77
6
5
76
4
3
75
2
1
74
78
79
80
Long Barrow
Tumulus
Fox Covert
Kington Down Farm
Kington Down
HOLLOWAY HILL
Down Farm
West Kington
Brook Farm
DRIFTON HILL
Latimer Farm
Elm Creek
SHIRE HILL
Hazel Grove
Bridgemead Brook
Harcombe Wood
Shirehill Farm
Lower Shirehill Farm
Gunning's Wood
SN14
New House Farm
Mountain Bower
Hillcrest Farm
Maggs Farm
Plough Farm
New Homestead Farm
The Crest
Rushmead Farm
Highfield Cottages
RUSHMEAD LANE
Downthornes Farm
TORMARTON ROAD
NORTHFIELD LA
Martor Ind Est
Culverslade
DOWN ROAD
Upper Wraxall
The Moorings
Home Farm
Laurels Farm
Upper Farm
Hillcrest Farm
Fairfield Farm
PH
A420
The Shoe
Marshfield Cemetery
Green View Farm
Northfield House
Gloucestershire STREET ATLAS

74

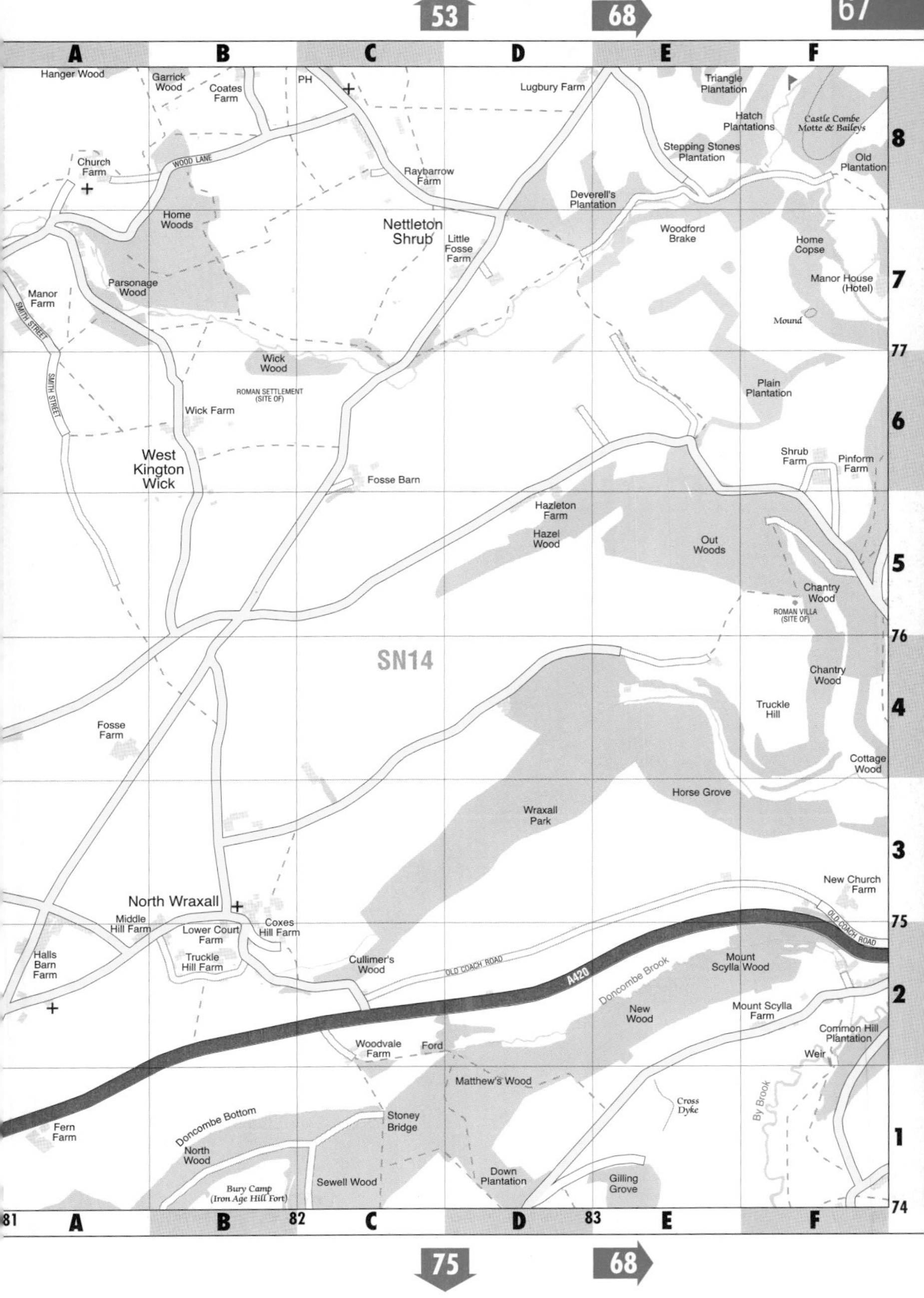
53
68
A
B
C
D
E
F
Hanger Wood
Garrick Wood
Coates Farm
PH
Lugbury Farm
Triangle Plantation
Hatch Plantations
Castle Combe Motte & Baileys
Stepping Stones Plantation
Old Plantation
Church Farm
WOOD LANE
Raybarrow Farm
Deverell's Plantation
Home Woods
Nettleton Shrub
Little Fosse Farm
Woodford Brake
Home Copse
Manor Farm
SMITH STREET
Parsonage Wood
Manor House (Hotel)
Mound
Wick Wood
Plain Plantation
ROMAN SETTLEMENT (SITE OF)
Wick Farm
West Kington Wick
Fosse Barn
Shrub Farm
Pinform Farm
Hazleton Farm
Hazel Wood
Out Woods
Chantry Wood
ROMAN VILLA (SITE OF)
SN14
Truckle Hill
Fosse Farm
Cottage Wood
Horse Grove
Wraxall Park
New Church Farm
North Wraxall
Middle Hill Farm
Lower Court Farm
Coxes Hill Farm
OLD COACH ROAD
Halls Barn Farm
Truckle Hill Farm
Cullimer's Wood
A420
Doncombe Brook
Mount Scylla Wood
New Wood
Mount Scylla Farm
Common Hill Plantation
Woodvale Farm
Ford
Weir
Matthew's Wood
Cross Dyke
By Brook
Doncombe Bottom
Stoney Bridge
Fern Farm
North Wood
Sewell Wood
Down Plantation
Gilling Grove
Bury Camp (Iron Age Hill Fort)
8
7
77
6
5
76
4
3
75
2
1
74
81
82
83
75
68

67
54

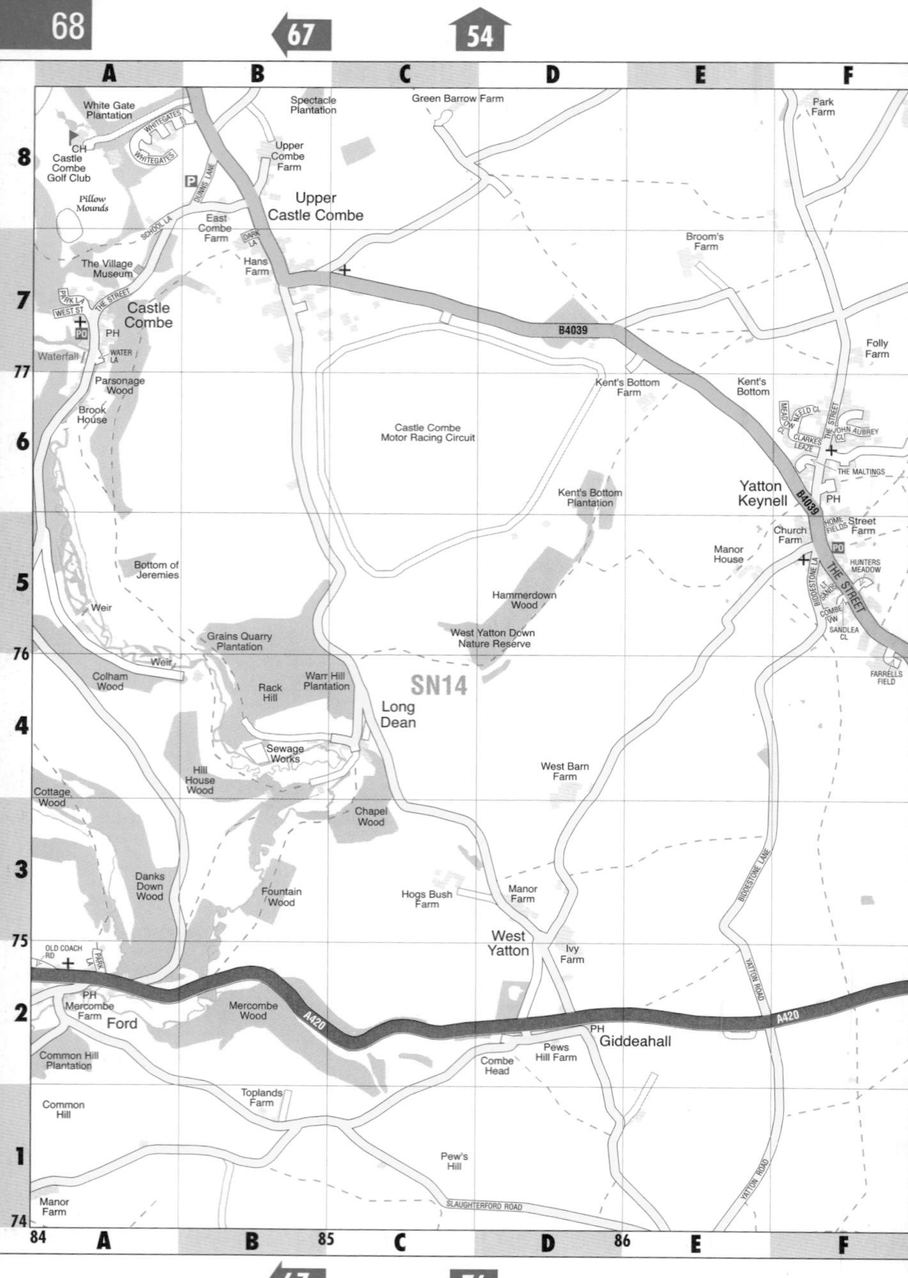
White Gate Plantation
CH
Castle Combe Golf Club
Pillow Mounds
WHITEGATES
Spectacle Plantation
Green Barrow Farm
Park Farm
Upper Combe Farm
Upper Castle Combe
DUNNS LANE
SCHOOL LA
East Combe Farm
DARK LA
Hans Farm
Broom's Farm
The Village Museum
PARK LA
WEST ST
THE STREET
Castle Combe
PO
PH
Waterfall
WATER LA
B4039
Folly Farm
Parsonage Wood
Kent's Bottom Farm
Kent's Bottom
Brook House
Castle Combe Motor Racing Circuit
MEADOW CL
NEELD CL
CLARKES LEAZE
JOHN AUBREY CL
THE MALTINGS
Yatton Keynell
Kent's Bottom Plantation
HOME FIELDS
Street Farm
Church Farm
Manor House
Bottom of Jeremies
HUNTERS MEADOW
Hammerdown Wood
BIDDESTONE LA
LT SANDS
COMBE VW
SANDLEA CL
Weir
Grains Quarry Plantation
West Yatton Down Nature Reserve
Colham Wood
Warr Hill Plantation
Rack Hill
SN14
FARRELLS FIELD
Long Dean
Sewage Works
Hill House Wood
West Barn Farm
Cottage Wood
Chapel Wood
Danks Down Wood
Fountain Wood
Hogs Bush Farm
Manor Farm
BIDDESTONE LANE
West Yatton
Ivy Farm
OLD COACH RD
YATTON ROAD
Mercombe Farm
Ford
Mercombe Wood
A420
Giddeahall
Pews Hill Farm
Common Hill Plantation
Combe Head
Toplands Farm
Common Hill
Pew's Hill
Manor Farm
SLAUGHTERFORD ROAD
A B C D E F
8 7 77 6 5 76 4 3 75 2 1 74
84 85 86

67
76

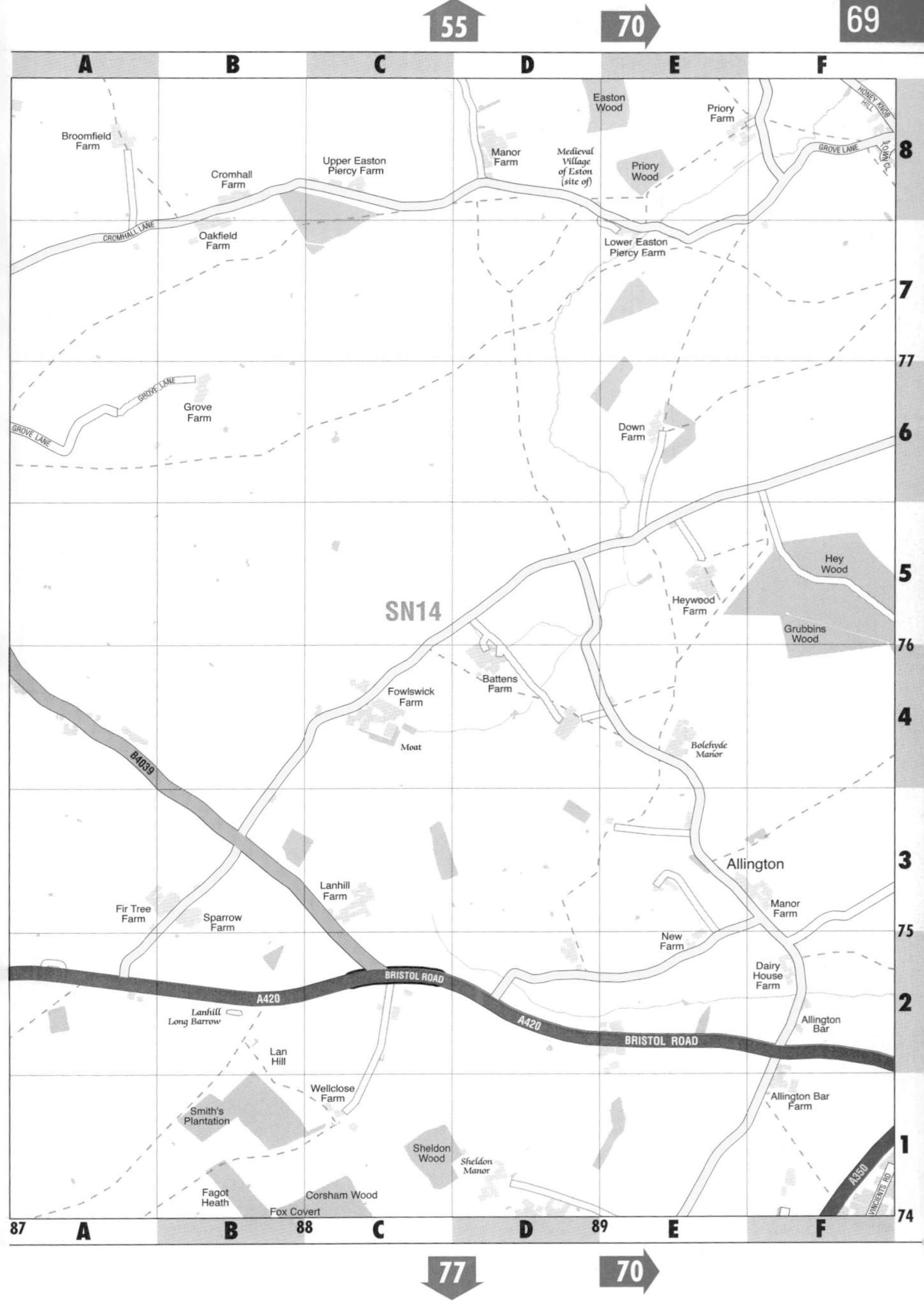
55
70
A
B
C
D
E
F
Broomfield Farm
Cromhall Farm
Upper Easton Piercy Farm
Manor Farm
Medieval Village of Eston (site of)
Easton Wood
Priory Wood
Priory Farm
HONEY KNOB HILL
GROVE LANE
TOWN CL
8
CROMHALL LANE
Oakfield Farm
Lower Easton Piercy Farm
7
77
GROVE LANE
Grove Farm
GROVE LANE
Down Farm
6
SN14
Hey Wood
5
Heywood Farm
Grubbins Wood
76
Fowlswick Farm
Battens Farm
4
Moat
Bolehyde Manor
B4039
Allington
3
Lanhill Farm
Fir Tree Farm
Sparrow Farm
Manor Farm
75
New Farm
BRISTOL ROAD
Dairy House Farm
A420
2
Lanhill Long Barrow
A420
Allington Bar
BRISTOL ROAD
Lan Hill
Wellclose Farm
Allington Bar Farm
Smith's Plantation
Sheldon Wood
Sheldon Manor
1
A350
VINCIENTS RD
Fagot Heath
Corsham Wood
Fox Covert
74
87
A
B
88
C
D
89
E
F
77
70

A1
1 LONGSTONE RD
2 ALLINGTON WY
3 THE BATTENS
4 BARKEN RD
5 PIPSMORE RD

57
72

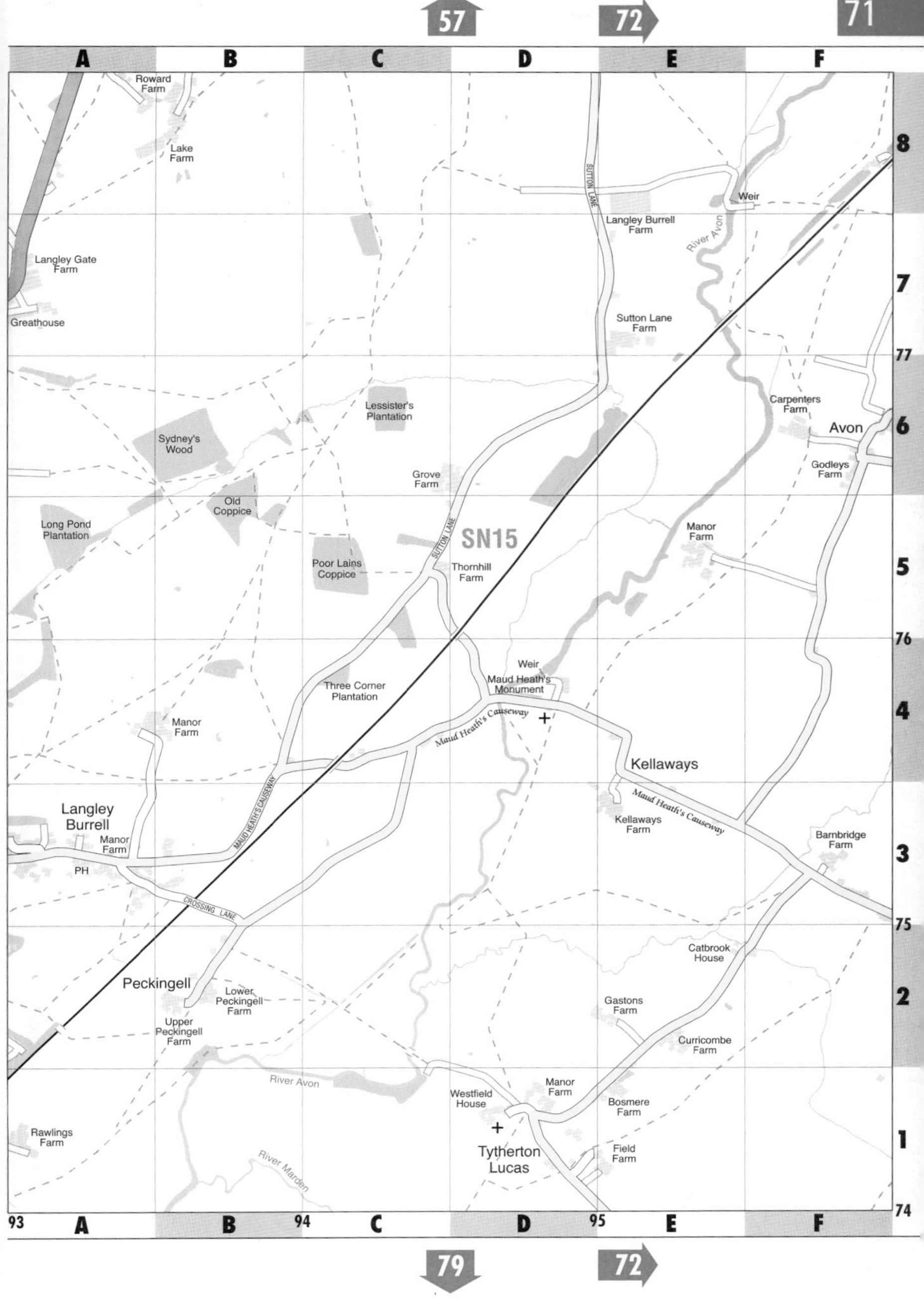
A
B
C
D
E
F
Roward Farm
Lake Farm
SUTTON LANE
Weir
Langley Burrell Farm
River Avon
Langley Gate Farm
Greathouse
Sutton Lane Farm
Lessister's Plantation
Carpenters Farm
Avon
Sydney's Wood
Godleys Farm
Grove Farm
Old Coppice
Long Pond Plantation
SN15
Manor Farm
Poor Lains Coppice
Thornhill Farm
Weir
Maud Heath's Monument
Three Corner Plantation
Maud Heath's Causeway
Manor Farm
Kellaways
Langley Burrell
MAUD HEATH'S CAUSEWAY
Kellaways Farm
Maud Heath's Causeway
Manor Farm
PH
Barnbridge Farm
CROSSING LANE
Catbrook House
Peckingell
Lower Peckingell Farm
Gastons Farm
Upper Peckingell Farm
Curricombe Farm
River Avon
Westfield House
Manor Farm
Bosmere Farm
Rawlings Farm
Tytherton Lucas
Field Farm
River Marden
8
7
77
6
5
76
4
3
75
2
1
74
93
94
95

79
72

71
58

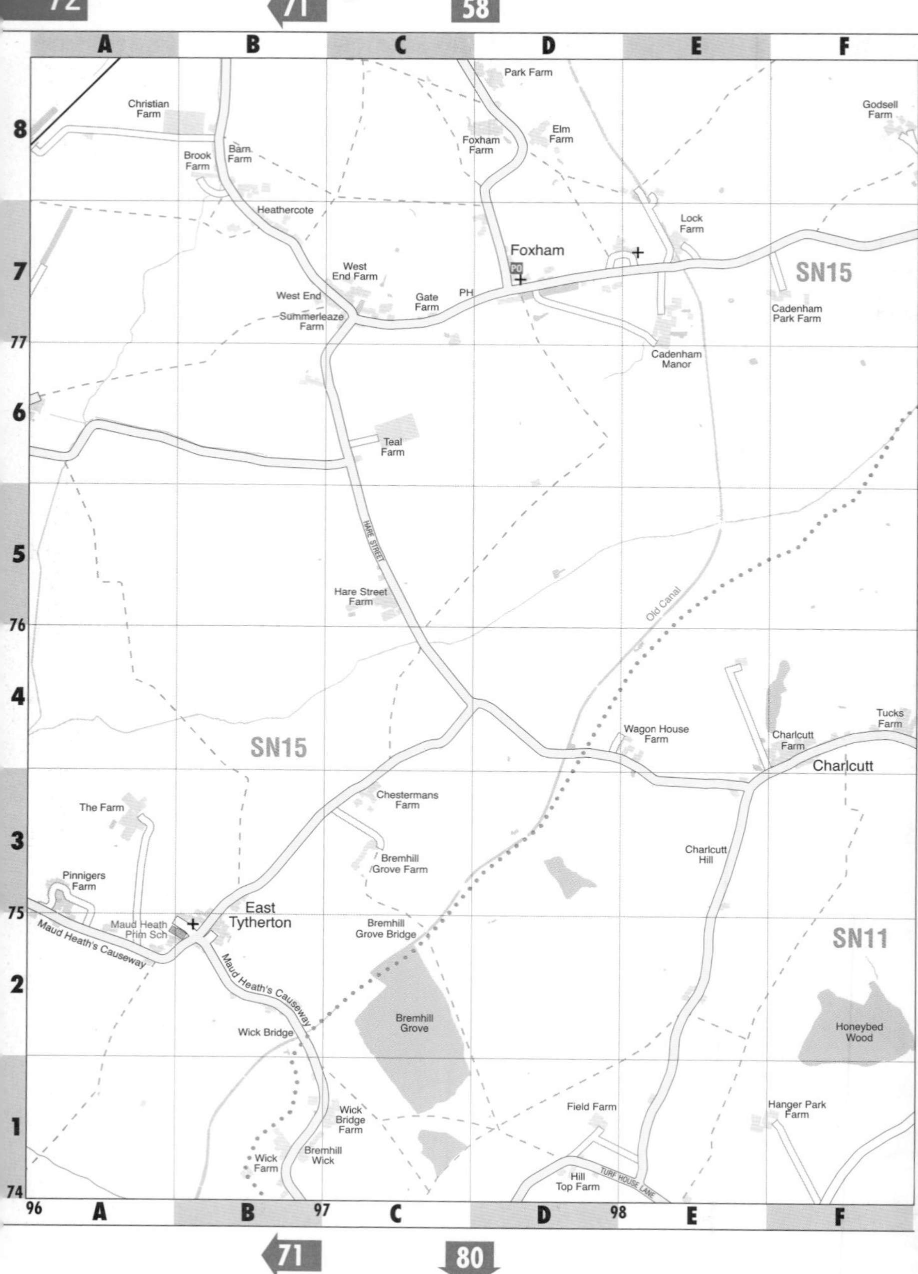
A
B
C
D
E
F
8
7
77
6
5
76
4
3
75
2
1
74
96
97
98
Park Farm
Christian Farm
Godsell Farm
Elm Farm
Foxham Farm
Brook Farm
Barn Farm
Heathercote
Lock Farm
Foxham
PO
West End Farm
SN15
West End
Gate Farm
PH
Summerleaze Farm
Cadenham Park Farm
Cadenham Manor
Teal Farm
HARE STREET
Hare Street Farm
Old Canal
Tucks Farm
Wagon House Farm
Charlcutt Farm
Charlcutt
The Farm
Chestermans Farm
Charlcutt Hill
Bremhill Grove Farm
Pinnigers Farm
East Tytherton
Maud Heath Prim Sch
Bremhill Grove Bridge
SN11
Maud Heath's Causeway
Bremhill Grove
Honeybed Wood
Wick Bridge
Wick Bridge Farm
Field Farm
Hanger Park Farm
Wick Farm
Bremhill Wick
Hill Top Farm
TURF HOUSE LANE

71
80

59
166
A
B
C
D
E
F
Avon Grove Wood
Catcomb Wood
Lyneham Airfield
SN15
GREENWAY DR
FREEGROVE RD
WHITCOMBE CL
MELSOME ROAD
8
Catcomb Old Farm
Mast
Godsell Cottages
VICTORIA CL
New Zealand Farm
A3102
Wood Farm
Lyneham Farm
7
New Zealand
Goatacre
QUAKERS WALK
GOATACRE LANE
ILES CT
Stockham Marsh Farm
77
Court Farm
Catcomb Farm
COMBE LANE
Haygrove Wood
6
Catcomb
Catcomb House Farm
SWINDON HILL
SN11
Beacon Hill
5
Beacon Hill Farm
Spirthill Farm
Siderow Farm
76
Leekshedge Farm
4
Spirthill
CHURCH RD
PH
SWINDON ROAD
3
COMPTON RD
75
Jubilee Plantation
Turnham Wood
2
Nine Acre Wood
Hilmarton Manor
Manor Park Farm
Cowage Brook
A3102
Bremhill House
Cowick Farm
Lower Penn Farm
1
Cowage Wood
74
99
A
B
00
C
D
01
E
F
81
166

66

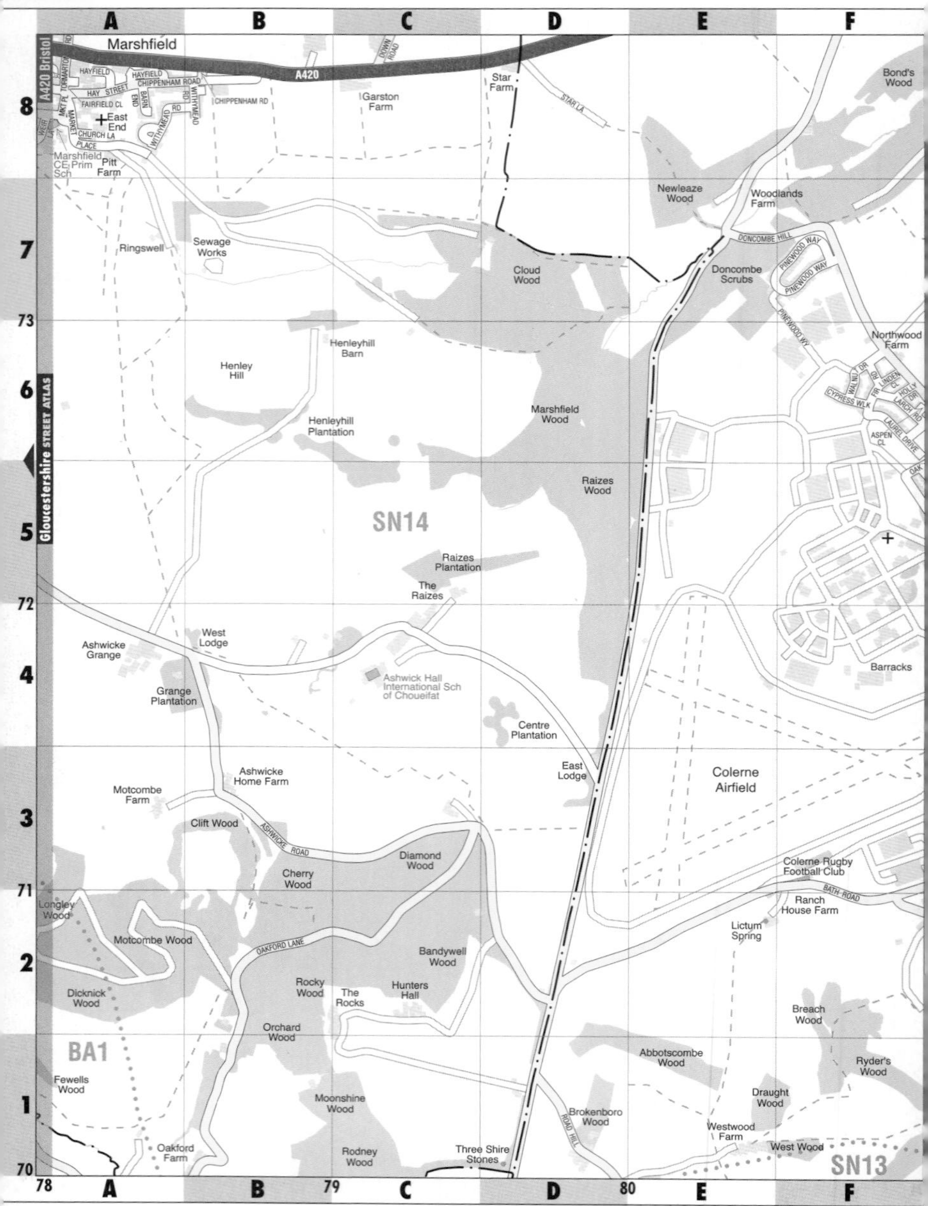
A B C D E F
Marshfield
A420 Bristol
A420
HAYFIELD
HAY STREET
CHIPPENHAM ROAD
FAIRFIELD CL
CHIPPENHAM RD
WITHYMEAD RD
East End
CHURCH LA
MARKET PLACE
Marshfield CE Prim Sch
Pitt Farm
DOWN ROAD
Garston Farm
Star Farm
STAR LA
Bond's Wood
Newleaze Wood
Woodlands Farm
Ringswell
Sewage Works
Cloud Wood
DONCOMBE HILL
Doncombe Scrubs
PINEWOOD WAY
PINEWOOD WY
Northwood Farm
Henleyhill Barn
Henley Hill
Henleyhill Plantation
Marshfield Wood
WALNUT DR
FIR
LINDEN CL
HOLLY DR
LARCH RD
CYPRESS WLK
LAUREL DRIVE
ASPEN CL
Raizes Wood
SN14
Raizes Plantation
The Raizes
West Lodge
Ashwicke Grange
Grange Plantation
Ashwick Hall International Sch of Choueifat
Barracks
Centre Plantation
East Lodge
Colerne Airfield
Ashwicke Home Farm
Motcombe Farm
Clift Wood
ASHWICKE ROAD
Diamond Wood
Cherry Wood
Colerne Rugby Football Club
BATH ROAD
Ranch House Farm
Longley Wood
Motcombe Wood
OAKFORD LANE
Lictum Spring
Bandywell Wood
Rocky Wood
The Rocks
Hunters Hall
Dicknick Wood
Breach Wood
Orchard Wood
BA1
Abbotscombe Wood
Ryder's Wood
Fewells Wood
Moonshine Wood
Draught Wood
Brokenboro Wood
ROAD HILL
Westwood Farm
Oakford Farm
Rodney Wood
Three Shire Stones
West Wood
SN13
Gloucestershire STREET ATLAS
8 7 73 6 5 72 4 3 71 2 1 70
78 79 80

67
76
A
B
C
D
E
F
Bury Camp
(Iron Age Hill Fort)
Down
Plantation
Gilling
Grove
Doncombe
Bottom
North
Wood
8
Colerne
Down
Sewell Wood
Coombs Wood
Fox Corner
Farm
Tumulus
7
Hall
Farm
73
Studs
Farm
Lucknam
Park
Home
Farm
Knowle
Hill Farm
St Martins
Farm
Park
Farm
Colerne
Park
6
By Brook
HILLCREST
FAIRVIEW
VALLEY WAY
WOODLEA
THICKWOOD LANE
Thickwood
DONCOMBE LANE
PALM RD
ROWAN CL
CHERRY RD
HAZEL WAY
ELM ROAD
POPLAR WAY
The
Groves
5
SN14
Euridge
Manor
Farm
Monk's
Wood
REDWOOD WAY
BEECH RD
Weavern
Wood
72
Eastrip
Farm
Eastrip
Lower
Eastrip Farm
4
EASTRIP LANE
Tilley's
Wood
Colerne
CE Prim Sch
Hungerford
Wood
TOTTS LANE
HITCHINGS
SKILLING
QUARRY LANE
MARTINS CFT
MARTINS CFT
FORRESTER GN
3
NURSERY RD
ROUND BARROW CL
SILVER STREET
FOSSEWAY CL
GROCYN CL
TRIMNELLS
VICARAGE LANE
MARKET PLACE
MULLING CL
EAVES AV
GREEN LA
ROCKFIELD
MOON CT
HIGH ST
OSBOURNE
CHAPEL PATH
TUTTON HILL
THE BANK
WATERGATES
PO
Widdenham
Farm
71
PH
BOX VW
WASHMERES
Washmere
Farm
SN13
2
Brown's
Wood
Medleys
Wood
Sewage
Works
Sewage
Works
By Brook
Folly
Farm
Lidbrooks
Bottom
1
Stowell Wood
SN13
70
81
82
83
83
76

B1
1 SOUTHCROFT RD
2 NORTHCROFT RD
3 PRESTLY WOOD
4 TRENCHARD AV
5 SANDY LEA AV
6 PRIESTLY WOOD RD
7 WEIR HAYES AV

E1
1 EDRIDGE PL
2 TROPENELL CL
3 BELLOT DR

Chapscroft Wood
Fox Covert
Corsham Wood
Sheldon Farm
Sheldon Corner
FROGWELL
Southernwood Farm
Starveall Farm
CHIPPENHAM LANE
Priors Copse
WEST CEPEN WAY
A350
Nature Trail
Chiverlins House
Holy Well
Middlehill Cottage
SN14
CHIPPENHAM
Stowell Farm
Beckhill Wood
Jubilee Wood
Briary Wood
Chequers Farm
Mynte Farm
Chequers Hill Plantation
A4
BATH ROAD
BATH RD
Superstore
The Folly
Mynte Wood
PH
Cross Keys
SN13
EASTON LANE
Pheasant Covert
Corsham Park
Easton Farm
Corsham Court
The Heywood Preparatory Sch
Bath Academy Of Art
Easton
Easton Court Farm
Corsham Lake
Westrop Plantation
Park Farm
Westrop
Thingley Court Farm
Corsham Town Football Club
LACOCK ROAD
LADBROOK LANE
St Patricks RC Sch
Corsham Sports & Cricket Club
Corsham CP Sch
Thingley Farm
Thingley
SN15
B3353
A B C D E F
88 89
8 7 73 6 5 72 4 3 71 2 1 70

77
70

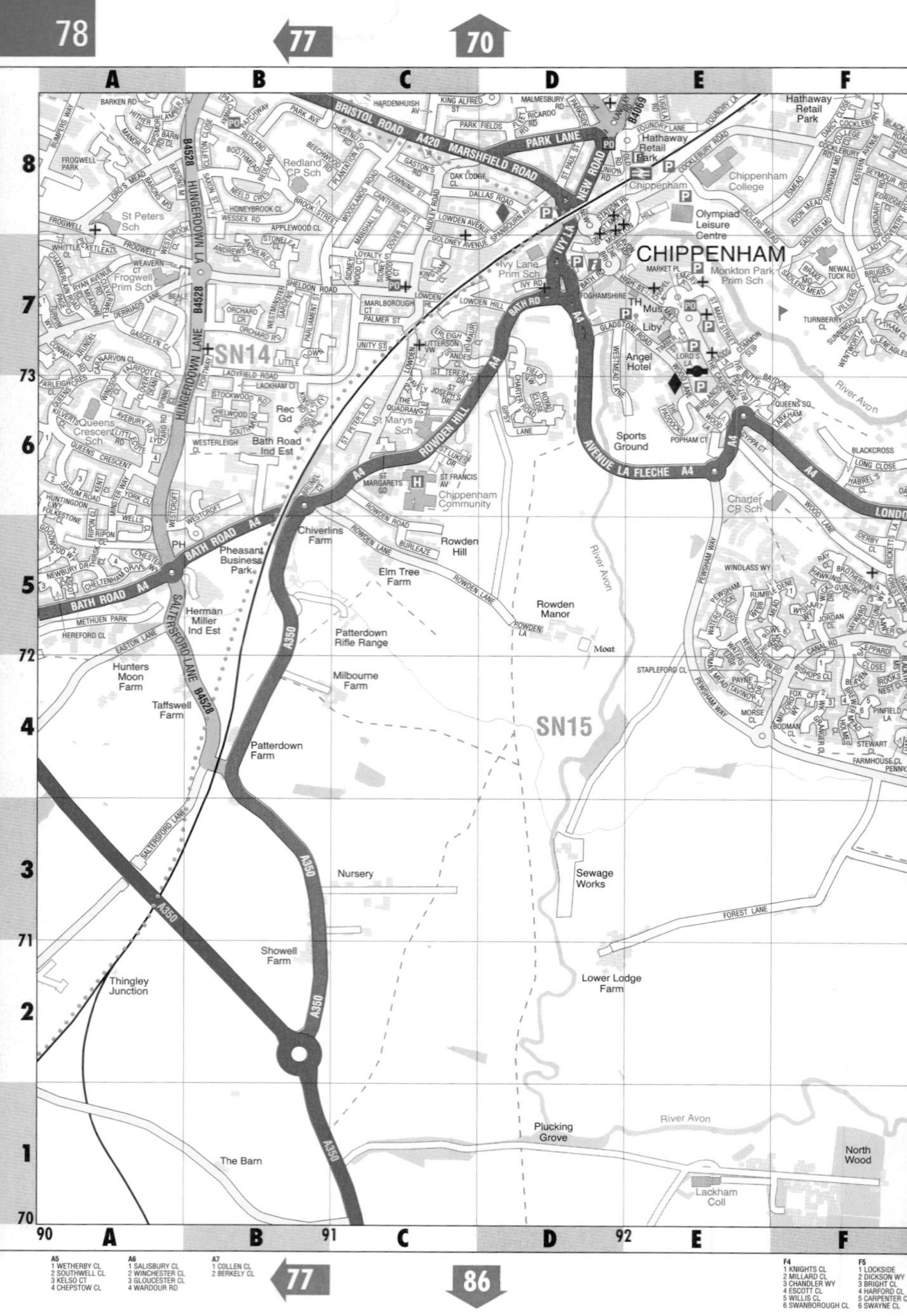

A5
1 WETHERBY CL
2 SOUTHWELL CL
3 KELSO CT
4 CHEPSTOW CL

A6
1 SALISBURY CL
2 WINCHESTER CL
3 GLOUCESTER CL
4 WARDOUR RD

A7
1 COLLEN CL
2 BERKELY CL

77
86

F4
1 KNIGHTS CL
2 MILLARD CL
3 CHANDLER WY
4 ESCOTT CL
5 WILLIS CL
6 SWANBOROUGH CL

F5
1 LOCKSIDE
2 DICKSON WY
3 BRIGHT CL
4 HARFORD CL
5 CARPENTER CL
6 SWAYNE CL

71
80
A
B
C
D
E
F
8
7
73
6
5
72
4
3
71
2
1
70
River Marden
River Avon
New Leaze Farm
Scotts Mill
Penrose
Harden's Farm
Stanley Bridge Farm
Stanley Bridge
Hither Farm
Riverside Farm
STANLEY LANE
Middle Farm
Pound Farm
HARDENS MEAD
LONDON RD
ROAD
Cemy
Gate Farm
COLBORNE CL
Jay's Farm
SN15
Studley Bridge
New Farm
LEGATE CL
Wedmore Farm
A4
Green Lane Farm
LONDON ROAD
Forest Farm
Forest Gate Farm
Close Wood
Derry Woods
PH
Middle Lodge Farm
NEW ROAD
Derry Hill
Great Lodge Farm
Gable End
A342
OLD DERRY HILL
Pewsham House
Six Acre Plantation
Derryhill Farm
Cocklemore Brook
SN11
FITZMAURICE CL
Queenwood Plantation
Golden Gates
Hannah's Wood
Nocketts Farm
DEVIZES ROAD
Derry Hill Plantation
Horse Copse
Pigsty Copse
Sherwood Moor
93
94
95
87
80

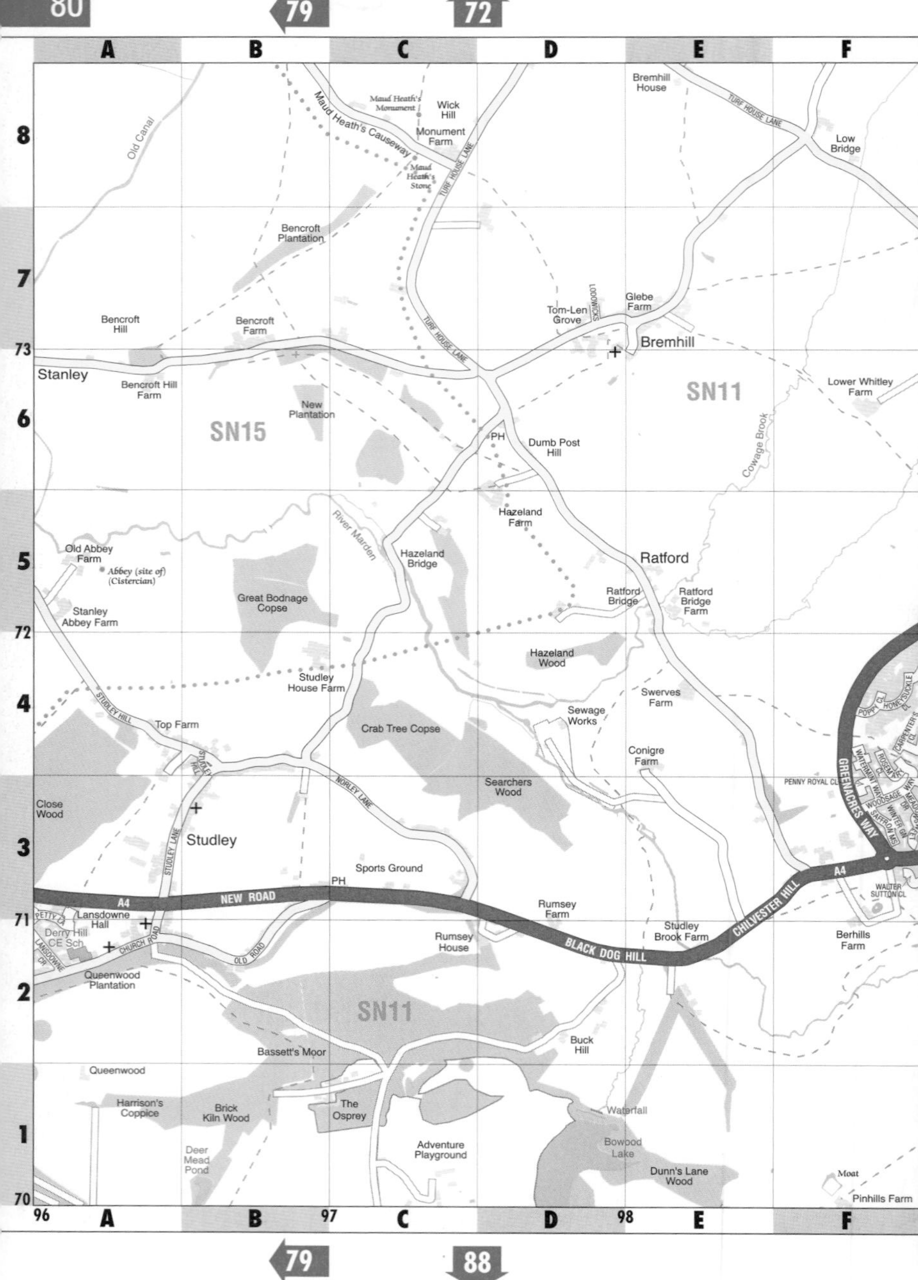
79
72
A
B
C
D
E
F
8
7
73
6
5
72
4
3
71
2
1
70
96
97
98
Old Canal
Maud Heath's Monument
Wick Hill
Maud Heath's Causeway
Monument Farm
Maud Heath's Stone
TURF HOUSE LANE
Bremhill House
TURF HOUSE LANE
Low Bridge
Bencroft Plantation
Bencroft Hill
Bencroft Farm
Tom-Len Grove
LOOSWICKS
Glebe Farm
Bremhill
Stanley
Bencroft Hill Farm
New Plantation
SN15
SN11
Lower Whitley Farm
Cowage Brook
PH
Dumb Post Hill
River Marden
Hazeland Farm
Old Abbey Farm
Abbey (site of) (Cistercian)
Hazeland Bridge
Ratford
Great Bodnage Copse
Ratford Bridge
Ratford Bridge Farm
Stanley Abbey Farm
Hazeland Wood
Studley House Farm
Swerves Farm
STUDLEY HILL
Top Farm
Sewage Works
Crab Tree Copse
Conigre Farm
STUDLEY HILL
NORLEY LANE
Searchers Wood
PENNY ROYAL CL
GREENACRES WAY
POPPY CL
HONEYSUCKLE CL
CARPENTER'S CL
ROSEMARY CL
WOODSAGE WAY
WINTER GN
SAFFRON MS
Close Wood
Studley
STUDLEY LANE
Sports Ground
PH
A4
NEW ROAD
Rumsey Farm
CHILVESTER HILL
A4
WALTER SUTTON CL
PETTY LA
Lansdowne Hall
Derry Hill CE Sch
CHURCH ROAD
LANSDOWNE CR
OLD ROAD
Rumsey House
BLACK DOG HILL
Studley Brook Farm
Berhills Farm
Queenwood Plantation
SN11
Buck Hill
Bassett's Moor
Queenwood
Harrison's Coppice
Brick Kiln Wood
The Osprey
Waterfall
Adventure Playground
Bowood Lake
Deer Mead Pond
Dunn's Lane Wood
Moat
Pinhills Farm
79
88

73
166

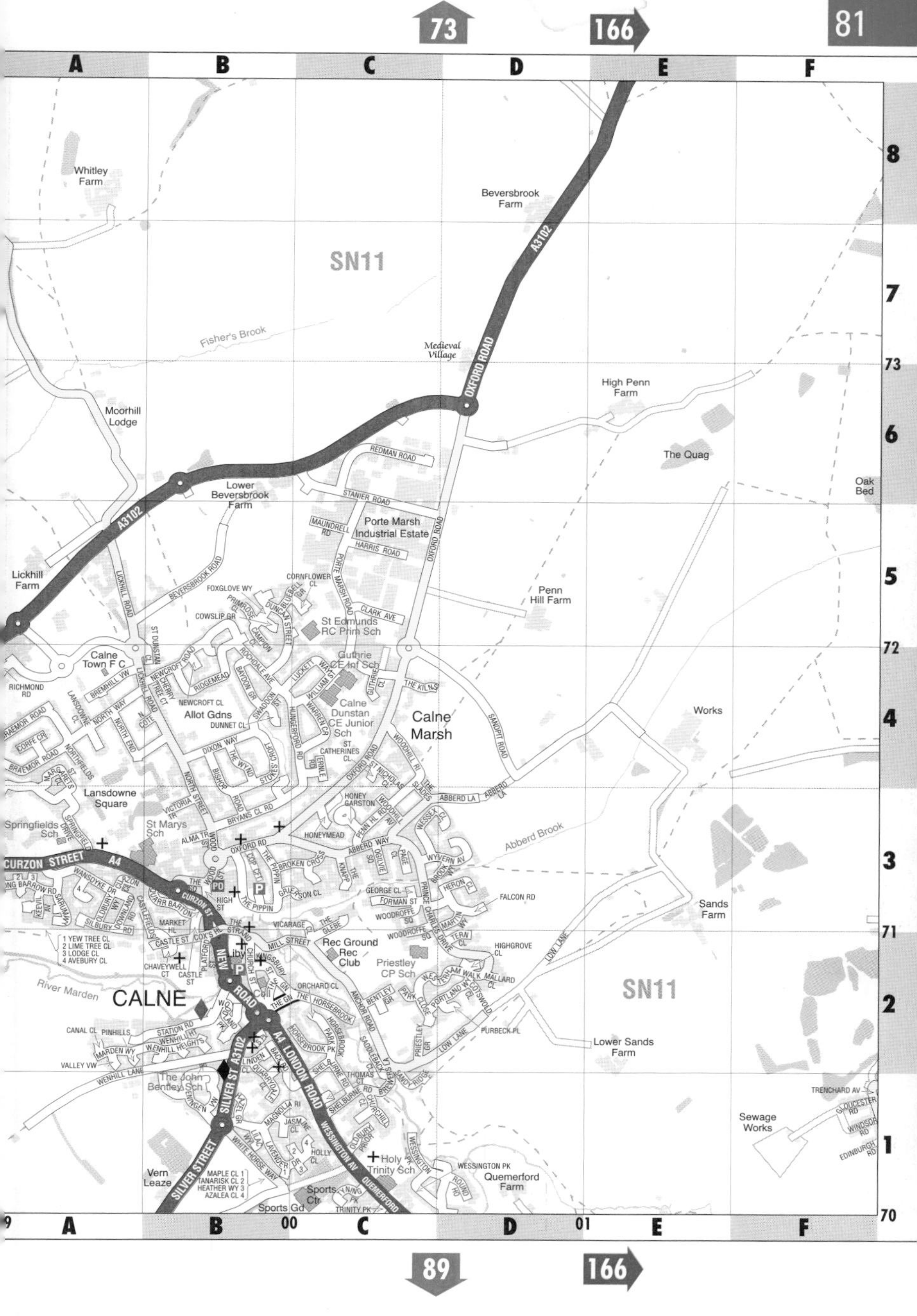
Whitley Farm
Beversbrook Farm
SN11
A3102
Fisher's Brook
Medieval Village
OXFORD ROAD
High Penn Farm
Moorhill Lodge
The Quag
Oak Bed
Lower Beversbrook Farm
REDMAN ROAD
STANIER ROAD
Porte Marsh Industrial Estate
HARRIS ROAD
Lickhill Farm
Penn Hill Farm
St Edmunds RC Prim Sch
Calne Town F C
Guthrie CE Inf Sch
Calne Dunstan CE Junior Sch
Calne Marsh
Works
Allot Gdns
Lansdowne Square
St Marys Sch
Springfields Sch
CURZON STREET
Abberd Brook
Sands Farm
Rec Ground
Rec Club
Priestley CP Sch
River Marden
CALNE
SN11
Lower Sands Farm
The John Bentley Sch
Sewage Works
Holy Trinity Sch
Vern Leaze
Sports Ctr
Sports Gd
Quemerford Farm
SILVER STREET
A4 LONDON ROAD
1 YEW TREE CL
2 LIME TREE CL
3 LODGE CL
4 AVEBURY CL
MAPLE CL 1
TANARISK CL 2
HEATHER WY 3
AZALEA CL 4

89
166

74

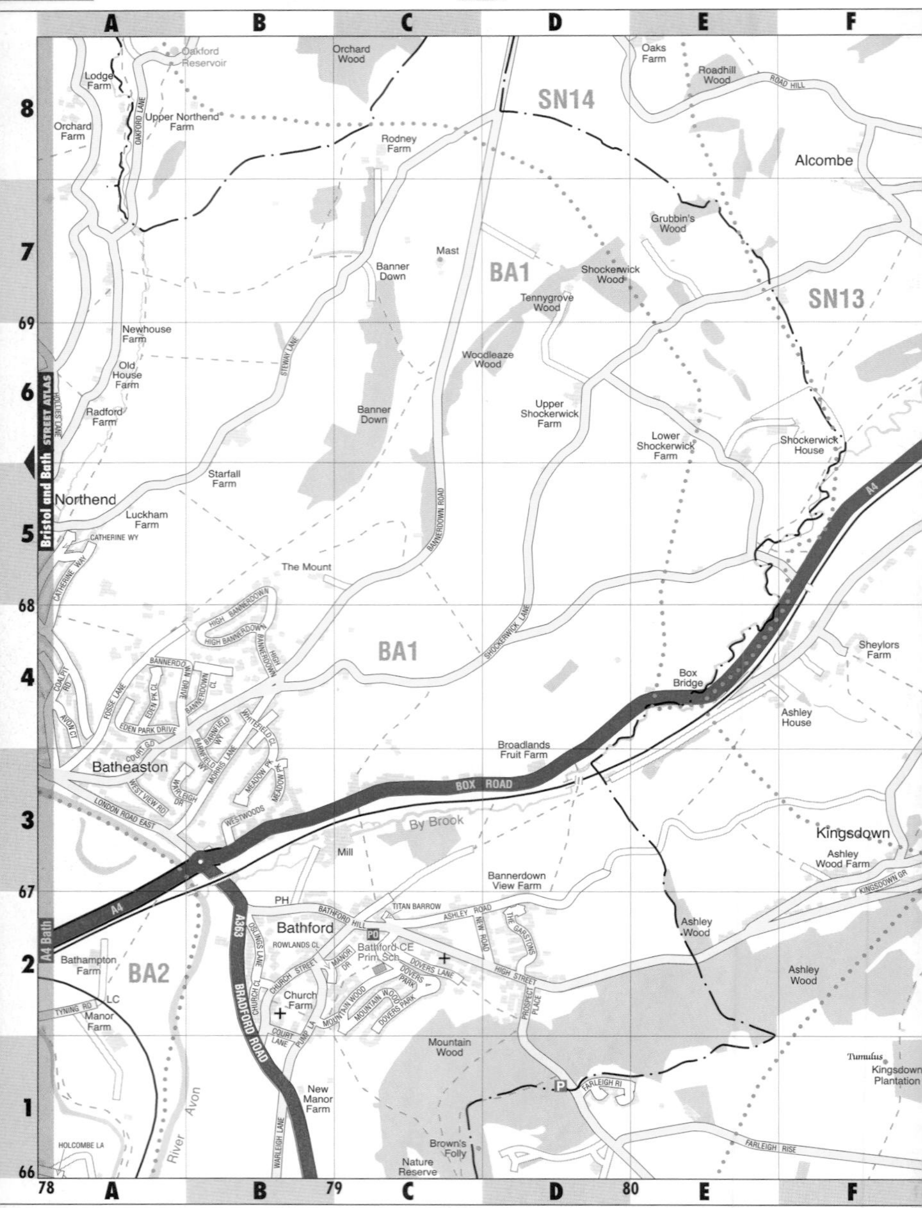

A
B
C
D
E
F
8
7
69
6
5
68
4
3
67
2
1
66
78
79
80
Orchard Wood
Oakford Reservoir
Lodge Farm
Oaks Farm
Roadhill Wood
ROAD HILL
SN14
Orchard Farm
OAKFORD LANE
Upper Northend Farm
Rodney Farm
Alcombe
Grubbin's Wood
Mast
Banner Down
BA1
Shockerwick Wood
Tennygrove Wood
SN13
Newhouse Farm
STEWAY LANE
Woodleaze Wood
Old House Farm
HOLCIES LANE
Radford Farm
Banner Down
Upper Shockerwick Farm
Lower Shockerwick Farm
Shockerwick House
Bristol and Bath STREET ATLAS
Starfall Farm
Northend
Luckham Farm
BANNERDOWN ROAD
A4
CATHERINE WY
CATHERINE WAY
The Mount
HIGH BANNERDOWN
BA1
SHOCKERWICK LANE
Sheylors Farm
COALPIT RD
BANNERDOWN
Box Bridge
FOSSE LANE
EDEN PK CL
WAR DRIVE
BANNERDOWN CL
AVON CT
EDEN PARK DRIVE
BARNFIELD WY
WHITEFIELD CL
Ashley House
COURT GD
MORRIS LANE
Broadlands Fruit Farm
Batheaston
MEADOW PK
WARLEIGH DR
WEST VIEW RD
BOX ROAD
LONDON ROAD EAST
WESTWOODS
By Brook
Kingsdown
Mill
Ashley Wood Farm
Bannerdown View Farm
KINGSDOWN GR
PH
A4
TITAN BARROW
ASHLEY ROAD
BATHFORD HILL
A363
NEW ROAD
THE GARSTONS
Bathford
OSLINGS LANE
ROWLANDS CL
Bathford CE Prim Sch
Ashley Wood
A4 Bath
Bathampton Farm
BA2
MANOR DR
DOVERS LANE
HIGH STREET
CHURCH STREET
DOVERS PARK
Ashley Wood
LC
CHURCH CL
Church Farm
MOUNTAIN WOOD
TYNING RD
Manor Farm
COURT LANE
PUMP LA
BRADFORD ROAD
PROSPECT PLACE
Mountain Wood
Tumulus
Kingsdown Plantation
FARLEIGH RI
River Avon
New Manor Farm
HOLCOMBE LA
WARLEIGH LANE
Brown's Folly
FARLEIGH RISE
Nature Reserve

90

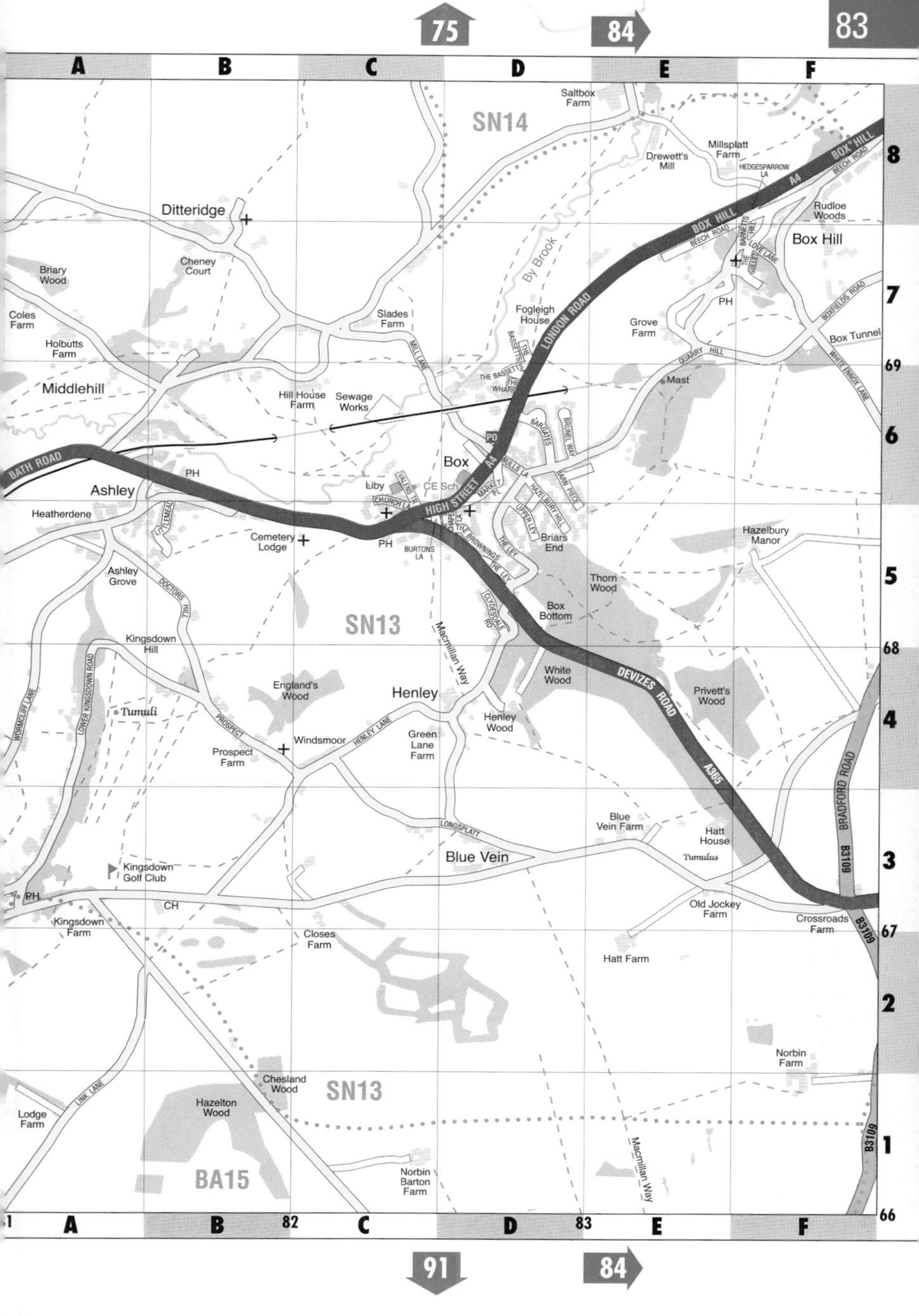
75
84
A
B
C
D
E
F
8
7
69
6
5
68
4
3
67
2
1
66
82
83
SN14
SN13
SN13
BA15
Saltbox Farm
Drewett's Mill
Millsplatt Farm
HEDGESPARROW LA
BOX HILL
A4
BEECH ROAD
Rudloe Woods
Box Hill
THE BARNETTS HILL
LOVE LANE
THE GULLEY
BOXFIELDS ROAD
Box Tunnel
WHITE ENNOX LANE
PH
Grove Farm
QUARRY HILL
Mast
Ditteridge
Cheney Court
Briary Wood
Coles Farm
Holbutts Farm
Middlehill
Slades Farm
MILL LANE
Fogleigh House
By Brook
LONDON ROAD
THE BASSETTS
THE WHARF
Hill House Farm
Sewage Works
BARGATES
BRUNEL WAY
PO
Box
BULLS LA
BARN PIECE
BATH ROAD
PH
Ashley
Heatherdene
LEMEAD
Liby
VALENS TR
CE Sch
CHURCH LA
HIGH STREET
MARKET PL
HAZELBURY HILL
UPPER LEY
CHAPEL LA
THE BROWNINGS
THE LEY
Briars End
Cemetery Lodge
PH
BURTONS LA
Hazelbury Manor
Ashley Grove
DOCTORS HILL
CLYDESDALE RD
Thorn Wood
Box Bottom
Macmillan Way
Kingsdown Hill
White Wood
DEVIZES ROAD
Privett's Wood
England's Wood
Henley
WORMCLIFF LANE
LOWER KINGSDOWN ROAD
Tumuli
PROSPECT
Windsmoor
HENLEY LANE
Green Lane Farm
Henley Wood
Prospect Farm
A365
BRADFORD ROAD
LONGSPLATT
Blue Vein Farm
Hatt House
Tumulus
Blue Vein
B3109
Kingsdown Golf Club
PH
CH
Old Jockey Farm
Kingsdown Farm
Crossroads Farm
Closes Farm
Hatt Farm
Norbin Farm
Chesland Wood
Hazelton Wood
LINK LANE
Lodge Farm
Macmillan Way
Norbin Barton Farm
91
84

83
76
A
B
C
D
E
F
8
7
69
6
5
68
4
3
67
2
1
66
84
85
86
BOX HILL
TRENCHARD AV
PARK AVENUE
KIDSTON
HIGHLANDS
PORTAL AVE
DOWDING AV
BROADWOOD AV
WESTWOOD RD
TOGHILL CR
B3109
LEYLANDS RD
WATERS BANK RD
BRADFORD ROAD
Box Highlands Sch
LEAFY LANE
SPRINGFIELD CL
CLIFT CL
Rudloe
THE LINKS
BOXFIELDS ROAD
Hawthorn
TROUT LANE
PO
ALLEN ROAD
PEEL CIR
PEEL CL
SHEFFIELD LA
BARBARA'S RD
PADDOCK LA
HUDSWELL LANE
PARK LANE
SPRING LA
Hudswell
Pockeredge Farm
SAVERNAKE ROAD
POCKEREDGE DRIVE
BASIL HILL ROAD
SPRING LANE
TASKER CL
BELLOT DR
SYON CL
FULLER AV
ABNEY CL
COTTLE MD
SPACKMAN LA
PENLEIGH CL
VALLEY ROAD
CRESWELLS
BRAKSPEAR DR
HARDHAM RI
FURZEHILL
OATHILLS
CHARLWOOD RD
SOUTHERWICKS
HITHER SPR
THE KNOWLE
POUND MEAD
WASTFIELD
TELCROFT CL
POCKERIDGE ROAD
POTLEY LANE
Potley Farm
UPPER LANE
UPPER POTLEY
CURLEW
CROFT RD
SHEARWATER WY
EDINBURGH WY
Leafield
LEAFIELD WY
Box Tunnel
Ennox Wood
RAF Rudloe Manor
WESTWELLS ROAD
OLD SHAFT ROAD
Westwells
WESTWELLS
SHEPHERDS
Leafield Ind Est
Great Lypiatt Farm
LYPIATT
New Grove Farm
ELLEY GREEN
WHITE ENNOX LA
WEST ENNOX LANE
MOOR PARK
DUDLEY PK
MOOR BARTON
NESTON CR
LEAFIELD ROAD
FLEETWOOD CL
POOL GREEN
Moor Green
Overmoor Farm
Neston
Sands Farm
Round Wood
HMS Royal Arthur
SN13
JAGGARDS LANE
PITTS CFT
CHURCH RI
Neston Prim Sch
Kingsmoor Wood
ROUGH STREET
DAWY GN
BROOKLEAZE
CHAPEL LANE
ATWORTH LANE
Chapel Plaister
Wadswick Farm
Manor Farm
Wadswick
Gallop End
WADSWICK LANE
New Wood
Neston Park
A365
Wormwood Farm
Beech Plantation
Park Farm
Botleaze Wood
Cottles Wood
BATH ROAD
Denleys Farm
Parsonage Coppice
Grove Mead Plantation
SN12
Hobbs Bottom Farm
GODWINS CL
MEAD PK
83
92

77
86

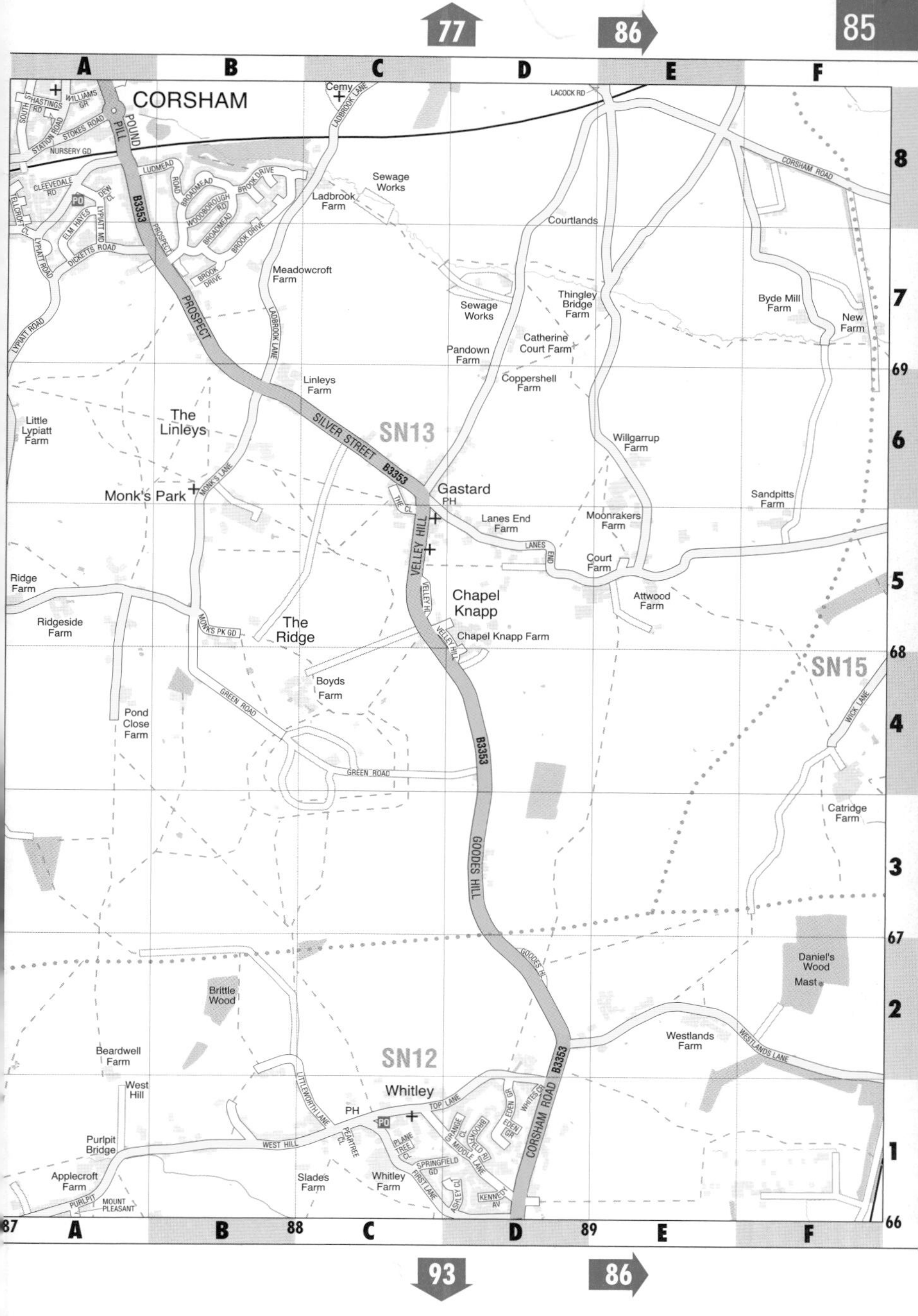
A
B
C
D
E
F
8
7
69
6
5
68
4
3
67
2
1
66
87
88
89
CORSHAM
HASTINGS RD
WILLIAMS GR
SOUTH RD
STATION ROAD
STOKES ROAD
NURSERY GD
POUND PILL
Cemy
LADBROOK LANE
LACOCK RD
CORSHAM ROAD
LUDMEAD ROAD
BROADMEAD
WOODBOROUGH RD
BROOK DRIVE
CLEEVEDALE RD
DEW CL
PO
ELLCROFT CL
ELM HAYES
LYPIATT MD
DICKETTS ROAD
LYPIATT ROAD
B3353
PROSPECT
Sewage Works
Ladbrook Farm
Courtlands
Meadowcroft Farm
Sewage Works
Thingley Bridge Farm
Byde Mill Farm
New Farm
Catherine Court Farm
Pandown Farm
Coppershell Farm
Linleys Farm
SN13
SILVER STREET
Little Lypiatt Farm
The Linleys
Willgarrup Farm
Monk's Park
MONK'S LANE
Gastard
PH
THE CL
Lanes End Farm
Moonrakers Farm
Sandpitts Farm
VELLEY HILL
LANES END
Court Farm
Ridge Farm
Chapel Knapp
Attwood Farm
Ridgeside Farm
MONK'S PK GD
The Ridge
Chapel Knapp Farm
Boyds Farm
SN15
GREEN ROAD
Pond Close Farm
WICK LANE
Catridge Farm
GOODES HILL
Daniel's Wood
Mast
Brittle Wood
Westlands Farm
WESTLANDS LANE
Beardwell Farm
SN12
West Hill
Whitley
LITTLEWORTH LANE
TOP LANE
WHITES CR
CORSHAM ROAD
Purlpit Bridge
WEST HILL
PEARTREE CL
PLANE TREE CL
GRANGE CL
EDEN GR
MIDDLE LANE
SPRINGFIELD GD
Applecroft Farm
Slades Farm
Whitley Farm
FIRST LANE
ASHLEY CL
KENNEDY AV
PURLPIT
MOUNT PLEASANT

93
86

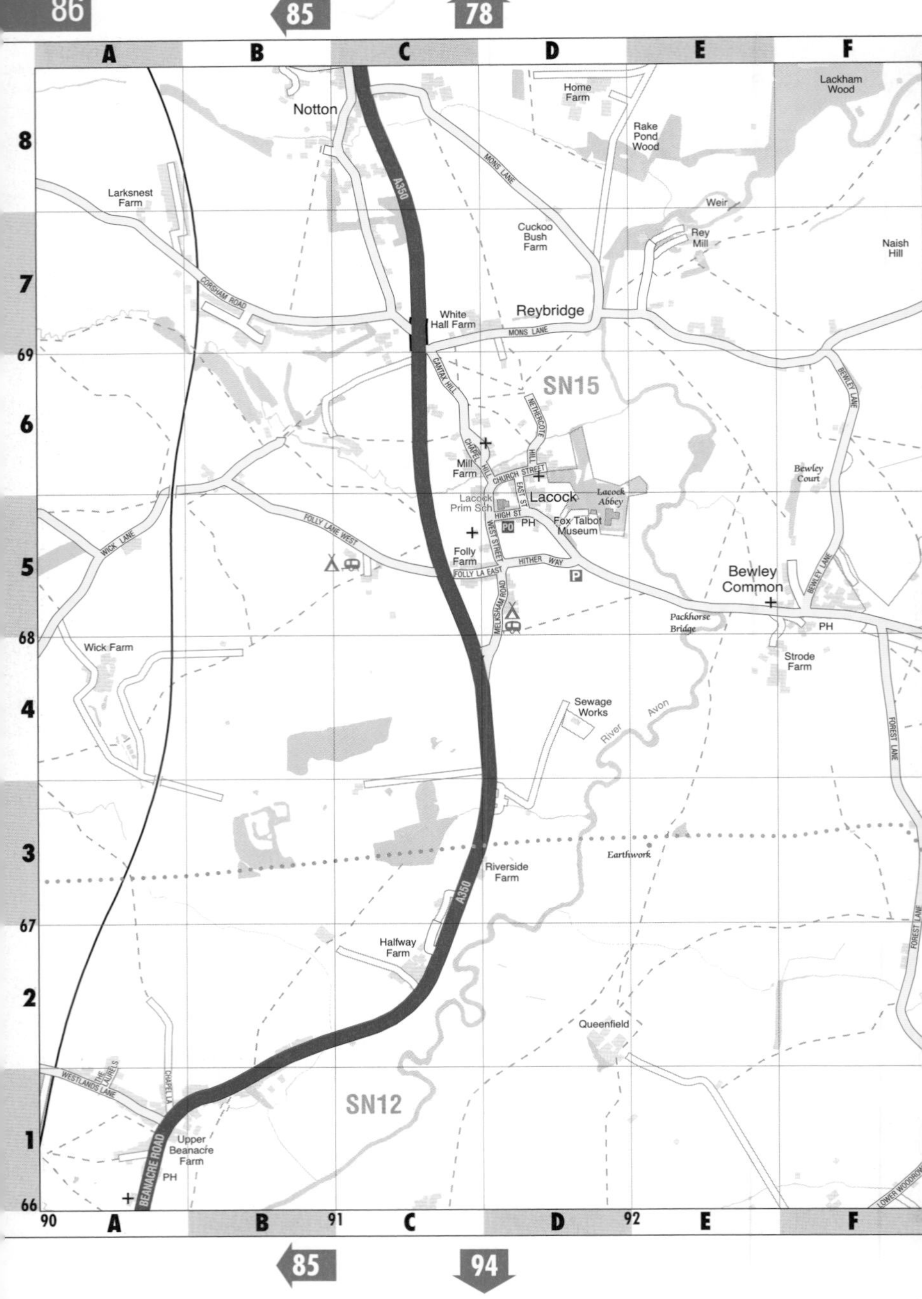
85
78
A
B
C
D
E
F
Notton
Home Farm
Lackham Wood
Rake Pond Wood
8
MONS LANE
A350
Larksnest Farm
Weir
Cuckoo Bush Farm
Rey Mill
Naish Hill
7
CORSHAM ROAD
White Hall Farm
Reybridge
MONS LANE
69
CANTAX HILL
SN15
BEWLEY LANE
NETHERCOTE HILL
6
CHAPEL HILL
Mill Farm
CHURCH STREET
Bewley Court
EAST ST
Lacock
Lacock Abbey
Lacock Prim Sch
HIGH ST
PO
PH
Fox Talbot Museum
FOLLY LANE WEST
WICK LANE
WEST STREET
Folly Farm
5
HITHER WAY
BEWLEY LANE
Bewley Common
FOLLY LA EAST
P
MELKSHAM ROAD
Packhorse Bridge
PH
68
Wick Farm
Strode Farm
Sewage Works
4
River Avon
FOREST LANE
3
Earthwork
Riverside Farm
A350
67
FOREST LANE
Halfway Farm
2
Queenfield
THE LAURELS
WESTLANDS LANE
CHAPEL LA
SN12
1
BEANACRE ROAD
Upper Beanacre Farm
PH
LOWER WOODROW
66
90
91
92

79
88

A
B
C
D
E
F
Sherwood Moor
Nocketts Hill
Horse Copse
Pigsty Copse
Loxwell Farm
Wheeler's Wood
Hazel Copse
Tacklemore Wood
Raspberry Copse
SN11
A342
DEVIZES ROAD
8
Naish Hill Farm
Fort
Ash Hill Farm
Nethermore Farm
Great Wood
Kilima Farm
Ash Grove
7
Bowden Park Farm
69
Long Copse
Nethermore Wood
Pitter's Wood
Pitter's Farm
Niehills Plantation
Mast
6
Masts
Bowden Park
SN15
The Warren
5
Briary Wood
Wheelers Wood
Home Farm
68
PH
Bowden Hill
The Coppice
National Trust
The Griffin Farm
Powney's Wood
Spye Park
4
Griffin's Wood
Bowden Hill House
Foxbury Wood
Spye Park House
3
Upper Selves Wood
Dairy Farm
67
Pond Moor
Scutts Copse
Old House Copse
Chittoe
Vicarage Plantation
2
Lower Selves Wood
Silverstreet Wood
SN12
Silverstreet Wood
SILVER STREET LANE
Kidneybean Copse
SILVER ST LA
Broadoak Wood
Frogditch Farm
Raines Copse
1
New Plantation
Reynolds Hill Farm
Oakley Farm
Colwell Copse
Rhotteridge Farm
Prickmoor Wood
66
3
94
95

95
88

87
80

A
B
C
D
E
F
Bowood Park
Bowood House
Bowood Gardens
Pinhills Farm
Home Farm
CH
Bowood Golf & Country Club
8
Bowood Lake
Monk's Hill Wood
Wash Way Wood
Pilpot Wood
Clark's Hill
Hill-top Plantation
7
Pilpot Wood
Coombe Grove
69
Great Wood
Cuff's Corner
Holland's Moor
6
SN11
A342
Mile End Farm
ROMAN VILLA (SITE OF)
PH
5
Nuthills Farm
Home Wood
Whetham Wood
Whetham
68
Leigh Wood
Pillow Mound
Sandy Lane
Whetham Farm
Stable Moor
New Moor Copse
Hopyard Copse
Weavers Bridge
St Edith's Leigh Wood
Leech Pool
4
Wans House
BACK LANE
A3102
DEVIZES ROAD
Deepet's Wood Copse
Broads Green Farm
Broad's Green
SN15
Hayfield Copse
3
Pond Moor
Bell Farm
Marsh End Farm
67
Wick Farm
Common Farm
Chittoe Heath Plantation
Chittoe Heath
Heddington Wick
2
CHITTOE HEATH
Manor Farm
Gore Farm
Gable End
Turnpike Farm
1
A3102
WESTBROOK ROAD
A342
Wyatts Lake Farm
66
96
A
B
97
C
D
98
E
F

87
96

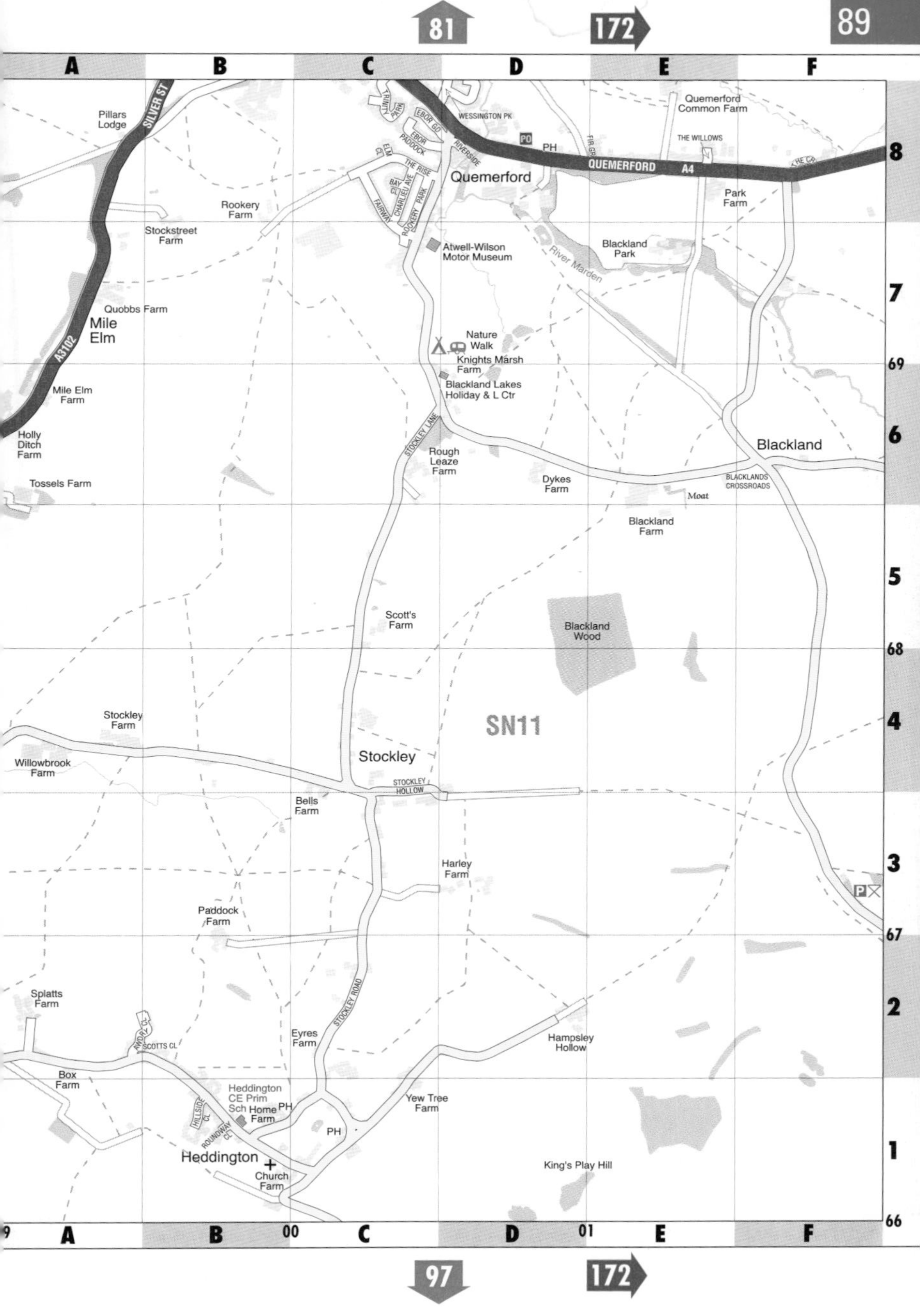

81
172
A
B
C
D
E
F
8
7
69
6
5
68
4
3
67
2
1
66
00
01
Pillars Lodge
SILVER ST
TRINITY PARK
EBOR GD
EBOR PADDOCK
ELM CL
WESSINGTON PK
RIVERSIDE
THE RISE
BAY CL
CHARLIEU AVE
FAIRWAY
ROOKERY PARK
PO
PH
FIR GR
Quemerford Common Farm
THE WILLOWS
QUEMERFORD
A4
THE CR
Quemerford
Rookery Farm
Park Farm
Stockstreet Farm
Atwell-Wilson Motor Museum
Blackland Park
River Marden
Quobbs Farm
Mile Elm
A3102
Nature Walk
Knights Marsh Farm
Blackland Lakes Holiday & L Ctr
Mile Elm Farm
Holly Ditch Farm
STOCKLEY LANE
Blackland
Rough Leaze Farm
Dykes Farm
BLACKLANDS CROSSROADS
Moat
Tossels Farm
Blackland Farm
Scott's Farm
Blackland Wood
Stockley Farm
SN11
Willowbrook Farm
Stockley
STOCKLEY HOLLOW
Bells Farm
Harley Farm
P
Paddock Farm
Splatts Farm
STOCKLEY ROAD
AMORY CL
SCOTTS CL
Eyres Farm
Hampsley Hollow
Box Farm
Heddington CE Prim Sch
Home Farm
PH
Yew Tree Farm
HILLSIDE CL
ROUNDWAY CL
PH
Heddington
Church Farm
King's Play Hill
97
172

82

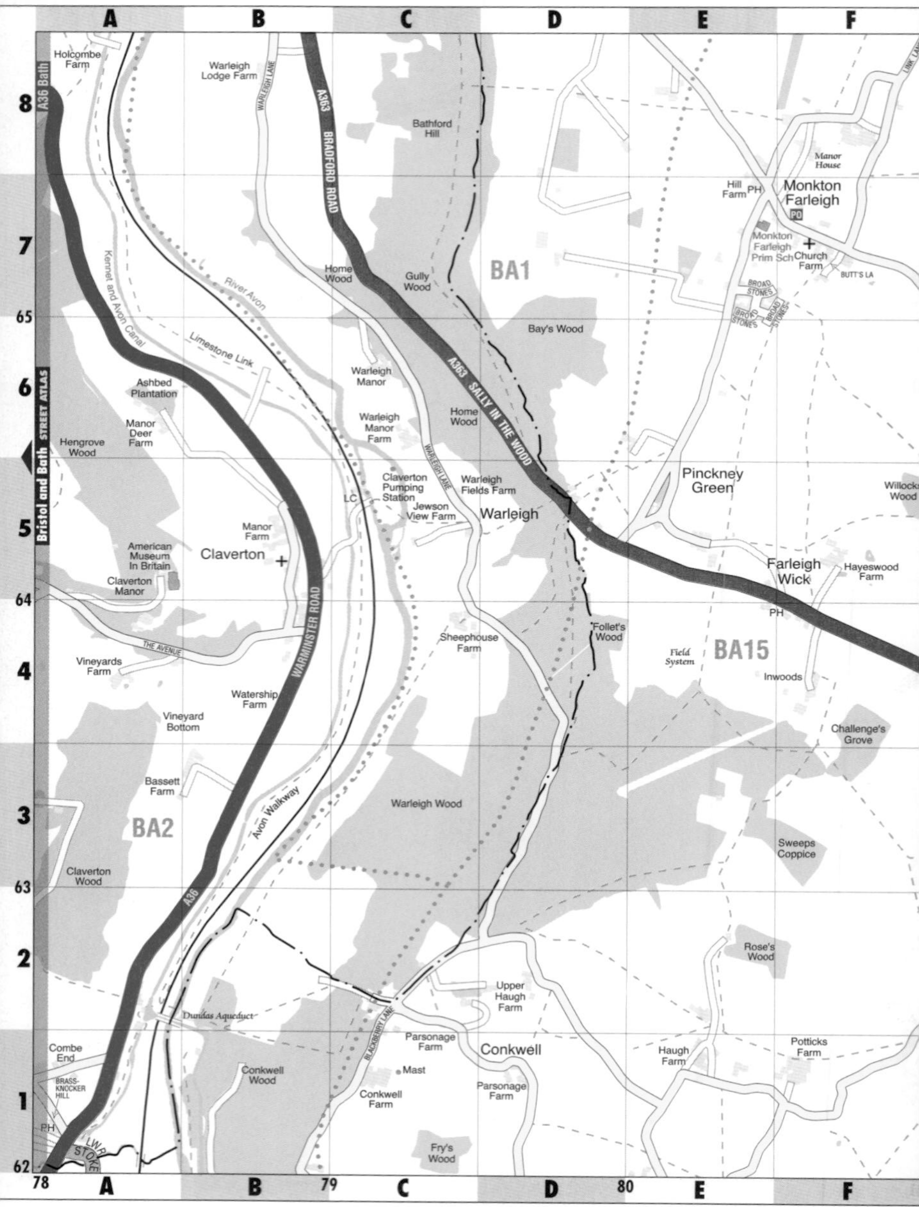
A
B
C
D
E
F
8
7
65
6
5
64
4
3
63
2
1
62
78
79
80
Holcombe Farm
A36 Bath
Warleigh Lodge Farm
WARLEIGH LANE
A363 BRADFORD ROAD
Bathford Hill
Manor House
Hill Farm
PH
Monkton Farleigh
PO
Monkton Farleigh Prim Sch
Church Farm
BUTT'S LA
BROAD STONES
Home Wood
Gully Wood
BA1
Kennet and Avon Canal
River Avon
Limestone Link
Bay's Wood
Warleigh Manor
A363 SALLY IN THE WOOD
Ashbed Plantation
Home Wood
Warleigh Manor Farm
Manor Deer Farm
Hengrove Wood
Bristol and Bath STREET ATLAS
Claverton Pumping Station
Warleigh Fields Farm
Pinckney Green
Willocks Wood
LC
Jewson View Farm
Warleigh
Manor Farm
American Museum In Britain
Claverton
Farleigh Wick
Hayeswood Farm
Claverton Manor
WARMINSTER ROAD
PH
Follet's Wood
Sheephouse Farm
THE AVENUE
Field System
BA15
Vineyards Farm
Inwoods
Watership Farm
Vineyard Bottom
Challenge's Grove
Bassett Farm
Warleigh Wood
Avon Walkway
BA2
Sweeps Coppice
Claverton Wood
A36
Rose's Wood
Upper Haugh Farm
Dundas Aqueduct
BLACKBERRY LANE
Combe End
Parsonage Farm
Conkwell
Haugh Farm
Potticks Farm
BRASS-KNOCKER HILL
Conkwell Wood
Mast
Conkwell Farm
Parsonage Farm
PH
LWR STOKE
Fry's Wood

99

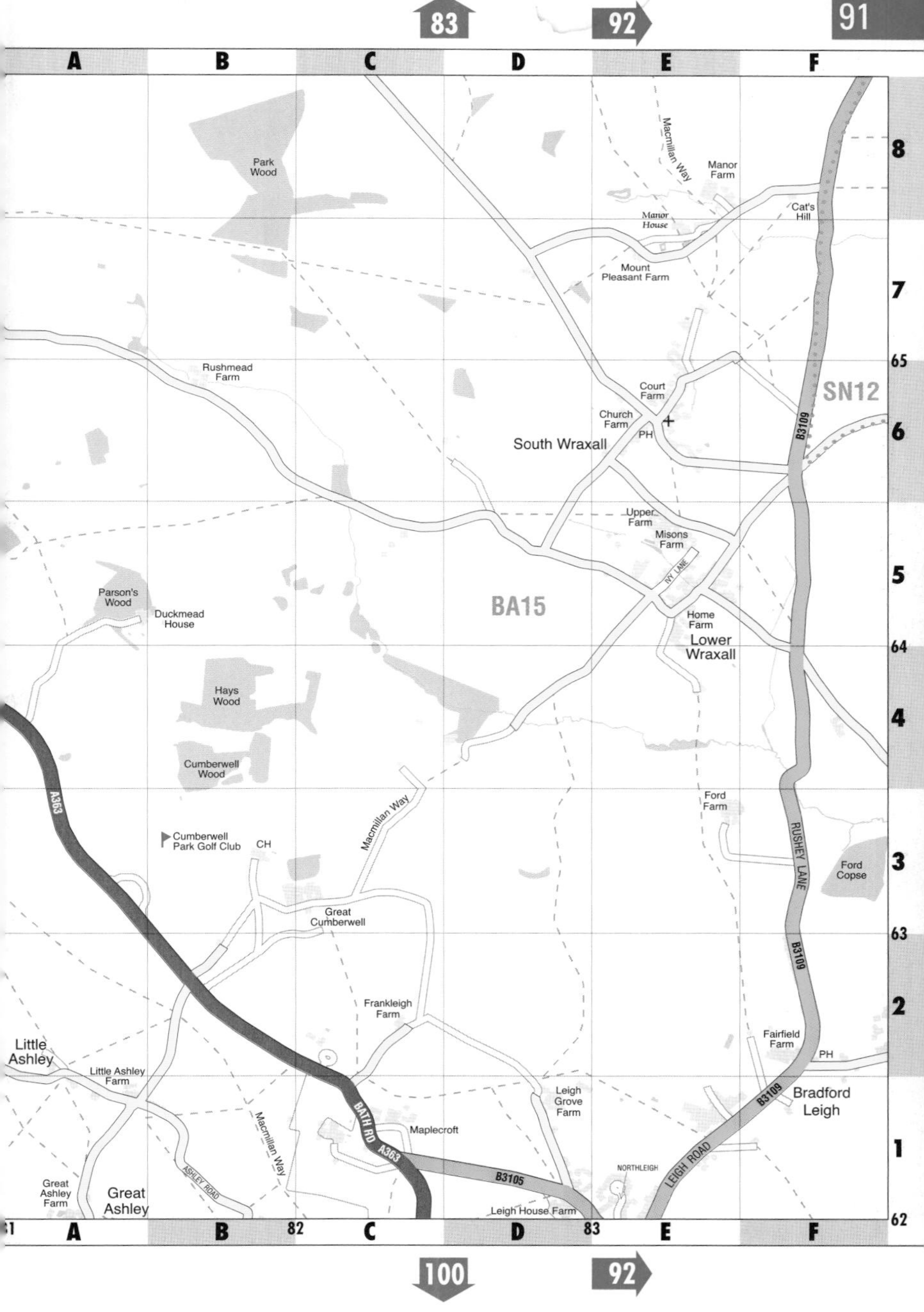
A
B
C
D
E
F
Park Wood
Macmillan Way
Manor Farm
Manor House
Cat's Hill
Mount Pleasant Farm
Rushmead Farm
Court Farm
Church Farm
PH
South Wraxall
SN12
B3109
Upper Farm
Misons Farm
IVY LANE
Parson's Wood
Duckmead House
BA15
Home Farm
Lower Wraxall
Hays Wood
Cumberwell Wood
A363
Macmillan Way
Ford Farm
Cumberwell Park Golf Club
CH
RUSHEY LANE
Ford Copse
Great Cumberwell
B3109
Frankleigh Farm
Fairfield Farm
PH
Little Ashley
Little Ashley Farm
Leigh Grove Farm
Bradford Leigh
B3109
BATH RD
Maplecroft
Macmillan Way
A363
LEIGH ROAD
NORTHLEIGH
B3105
ASHLEY ROAD
Great Ashley Farm
Great Ashley
Leigh House Farm
8
7
65
6
5
64
4
3
63
2
1
62
81
82
83

91
84

A
B
C
D
E
F
8
7
65
6
5
64
4
3
63
2
1
62
84
85
86
Hobb's Bottom Farm
Cottles Farm
PH
Poplar Farm
PO
PH
CORONATION RD
NURSERY CL
CHAPEL RI
MEAD PARK
GREENLAND CL
CHURCH ST
Atworth CP Sch
Atworth
Church Farm
Manor Farm
Stonar Sch
Withy Bed
COOMBE LANE
BRADFORD ROAD
Cock Road Plantation
Studley Farm
Lynch Bottom
Ganbrook Farm
SN12
COOMBE LANE
Newhouse Farm
Lenton Farm
BA15
Little Chalfield
Great Chalfield
Moat
Great Chalfield Manor House (NT)
Lady's Coppice
BA14
Holt Manor
Mirkens Farm
Blackacre Farm
LEIGH ROAD
GIPSY LANE
Holt
THE COMMON
GT PARKS
LT PARKS
The Midlands Ind Est
HAWCROFT
STATION RD
THE MIDLANDS
THE ELMS
B3107
THE GRAVE
CRANDON LEA
Holt Prim Sch
BRADLEY LA

91
101

85
94

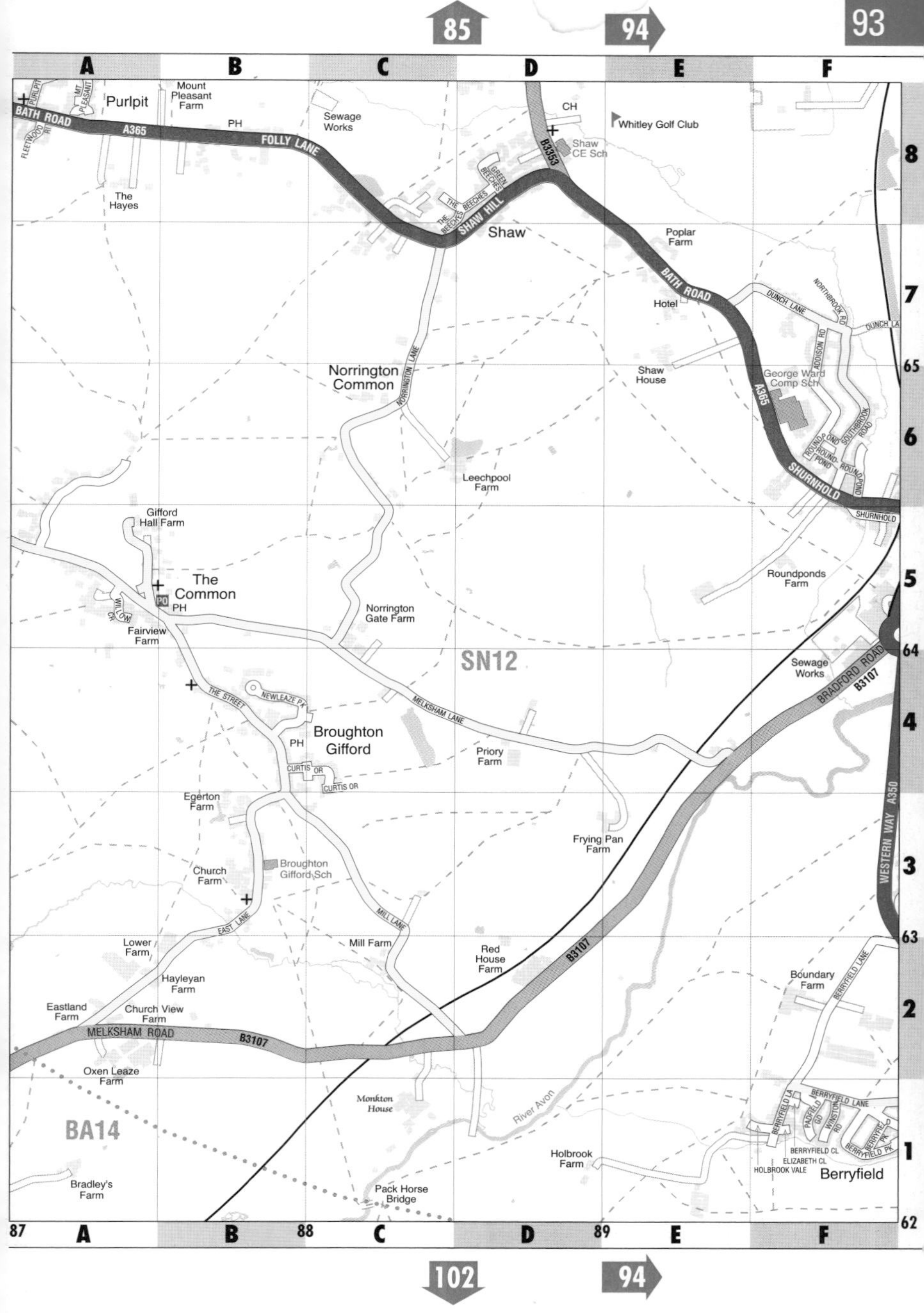
Purlpit
Mount Pleasant Farm
BATH ROAD
A365
FOLLY LANE
PH
Sewage Works
CH
Whitley Golf Club
B3353
Shaw CE Sch
The Hayes
GREEN BEECHES
THE BEECHES
SHAW HILL
Shaw
Poplar Farm
BATH ROAD
Hotel
DUNCH LANE
NORTHBROOK RD
DUNCH LA
ADDISON RD
Norrington Common
NORRINGTON LANE
Shaw House
George Ward Comp Sch
A365
SOUTHBROOK ROAD
ROUND POND
SHURNHOLD
Leechpool Farm
Gifford Hall Farm
The Common
PO
PH
WILLOW CR
Fairview Farm
Norrington Gate Farm
Roundponds Farm
SN12
Sewage Works
BRADFORD ROAD
B3107
THE STREET
NEWLEAZE PK
Broughton Gifford
MELKSHAM LANE
Priory Farm
CURTIS OR
Egerton Farm
Frying Pan Farm
WESTERN WAY
A350
Church Farm
Broughton Gifford Sch
EAST LANE
MILL LANE
Lower Farm
Mill Farm
Red House Farm
B3107
Hayleyan Farm
Boundary Farm
BERRYFIELD LANE
Eastland Farm
Church View Farm
MELKSHAM ROAD
Oxen Leaze Farm
Monkton House
River Avon
BERRYFIELD LA
PADFIELD GD
WINSTON RD
BERRYFIELD PK
BERRYFIELD CL
ELIZABETH CL
HOLBROOK VALE
Berryfield
Holbrook Farm
BA14
Bradley's Farm
Pack Horse Bridge
A B C D E F
8 7 65 6 5 64 4 3 63 2 1 62
87 88 89

102
94

93
86

A
B
C
D
E
F
8
7
65
6
5
64
4
3
63
2
1
62
90
91
92
Bezzells Farm
Lower Beanacre Farm
Beanacre Manor
Beanacre
Beechfield House (Hotel)
A350
BEANACRE ROAD
Forest Farm
LOWER WOODROW
Oakley Farm
Woodrow Farm
WOODROW
River Avon
DUNCH LA
NEW ROAD
Withybed Copse
Forty Acre Copse
MEADOW RD
LINCOLN GN
WOODROW ROAD
METHUEN AVENUE
GLENSIDE
TAMAR RD
TRENT CR
AVON ROAD
THAMES
SPENCER CL
SEVERN RD
GRANVILLE RD
PORTMAN ROAD
RIVERSIDE DR
SCOTLAND ROAD
BEANACRE RD
SAVERNAKE AVENUE
ASHDOWN DR
Melksham Forest
SAVERNAKE AV
SHERWOOD AVE
LEAZE RD
EPPING DR
Manor Farm
New Road Farm
Melksham
Works
MELKSHAM
Lowbourne Sch
SN12
MURRAY WK
FOREST ROAD
CHURCH LANE
CHURCHILL AV
LANSDOWN CL
BREAM CL
ARDEN CL
MAPLE CL
TALBOT CL
BURNSTON CL
A3102
SANDRIDGE COMMON
Blackmore Farm
Sandridge Sch
SANDRIDGE ROAD
BATH RD
THE CITY
PO
A3102
BATH ROAD
Weir
Avonside Enterprise Park
WEAVERS CROFTS
BRADFORD ROAD
NEW BROUGHTON RD
P
Liby
UNION STREET
LOWBOURNE
BATH ROAD
SANDRIDGE RD
HAMPSHIRE PL
DEVONSHIRE PL
TOWER RD
INGRAM ROAD
SNARLTON LANE
MALVERN CL
PENNINE CL
St Michaels CE Prim Sch
GLOUCESTER SQ
FORESTERS PK ROAD
BRECON CLOSE
QUANTOCK CL
Snarlton Farm
CANNON SQ
CHURCH WK
CHURCH ST
STRATTONS WK
HIGH ST
PLACE RD
LAMBOURNE CR
THACKERAY CR
RUSKIN AVENUE
PEMBROKE ROAD
QUEENSWAY
COTSWOLD CL
CHILTERN CL
Assembly Hall
Football Club
SHELLEY GD
SANGSTER AV
MILTON AV
CORONATION RD
CORNWALL CR
DORSET CRESCENT
PRIMROSE DR
CEDAR CL
THORNBANK
CHESTNUT MS
ORCHARD GD
CONIGRE CL
KINGSBURY SQ
B3112
SPA ROAD
WESSEX CL
SOMERSET CR
MARTIGNY RD
RUTLAND CL
DAISY CL
HEATHER AV
MARIGOLD CL
Bowerhill Lodge Farm
KING STREET
LARCH CL
WILLOW
LIME AV
HAZELWOOD RD
BEECH AVE
Aloeric GM Prim Sch
ST MICHAEL'S RD
B3104
WAVERLEY GD
KENILWORTH GARDENS
WOODSTOCK GD
Melksham Community
H
WILTSHIRE CR
LONG LEAZE LA
SNOWBERRY LANE
FOXGLOVE CL
LAVENDER CL
ROSEBROCK GD
HORNBEAM CR
PINE CL
GREENWOOD RD
ROWAN CT
LABURNUM DR
SEMINGTON ROAD
FARLEIGH AV
SARUM AVE
WINDSOR AVE
CARISBROOK RD
PENNYCRESS DR
CAMPION DR
SPA RD
WESTERN WAY
LONGFORD ROAD
BERKELEY CL
CONWAY CRESCENT
SPEEDWELL CLOSE
Townsend Farm
TOWNSEND FARM
A365
WESTERN WAY
The Spa
Lonsdale Farm
Wiltshire Sch of Gymnastics
Bowerhill Farm
Woolmore Farm
PH
BERRYFIELD LA
BERRYFIELD PK
MERLIN WAY
ELM CLOSE
BIRCH GR
WELLINGTON DR
ANSON GR
HAMPTON CL
MARTLET CL
OSPREY CL
FULMAR CL
KINGFISHER DR
GRASMERE
Loves Farm
Sewage Works
Christie Miller Sports Centre
LANCASTER ROAD
LYSANDER RD
AVRO WY
HALIFAX ROAD
DOWDING WAY
HURRICANE RD
GIBSON CL
BEVERLEY CL
LINCOLN GR
Bowerhill CP Sch
FALCON WAY
MAGISTER RD
HARVARD CL
Bowerhill
BOWERHILL LANE
Old Loves Farm
SEMINGTON ROAD
A2
1 ASH GR
2 LINDEN GR
3 RADNOR PL
4 WARDOUR PL

93
178

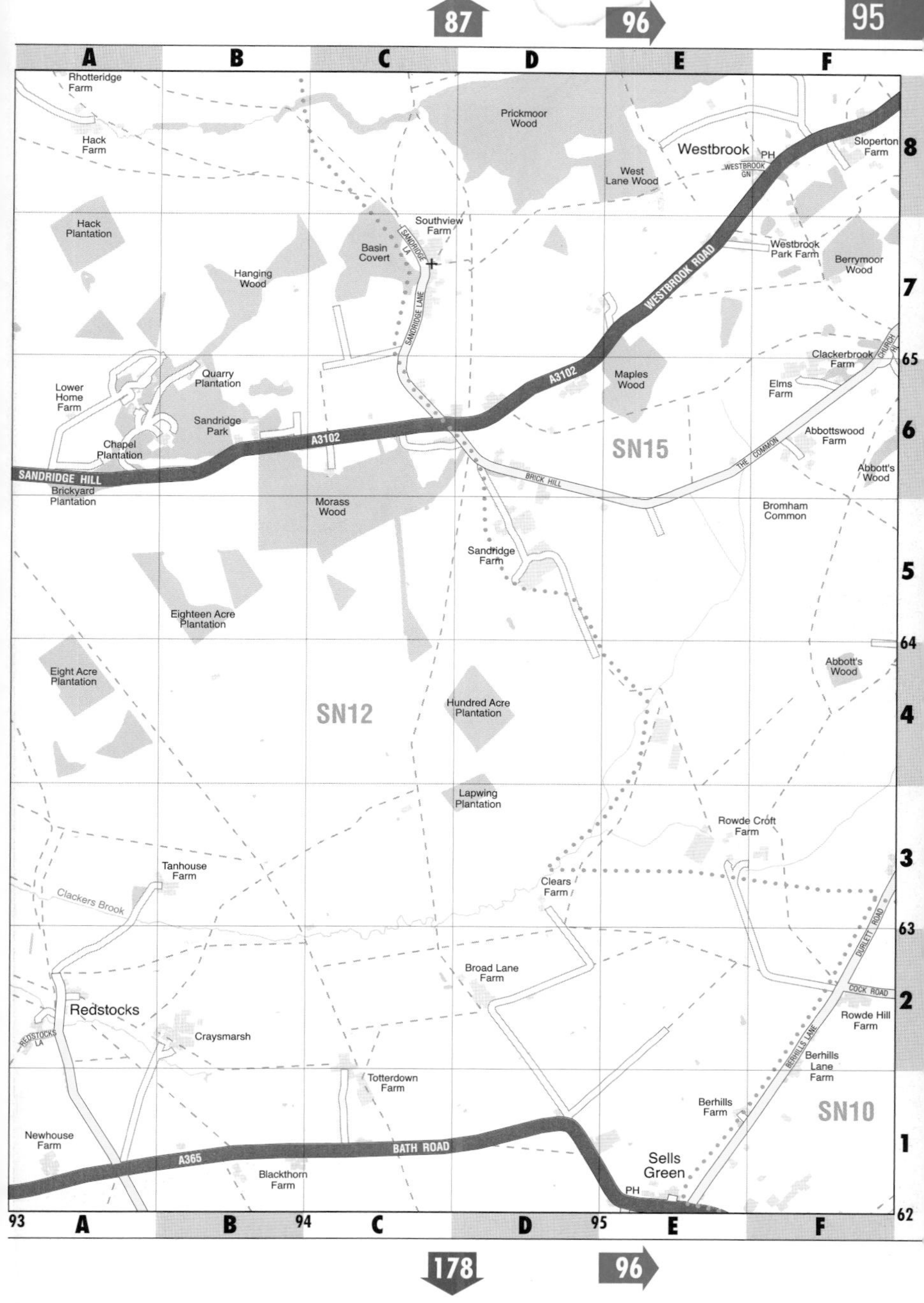
87
96
A
B
C
D
E
F
Rhotteridge Farm
Hack Farm
Prickmoor Wood
Westbrook
PH
WESTBROOK GN
Sloperton Farm
West Lane Wood
Hack Plantation
Southview Farm
Basin Covert
SANDRIDGE LA
Hanging Wood
Westbrook Park Farm
Berrymoor Wood
WESTBROOK ROAD
SANDRIDGE LANE
Clackerbrook Farm
CHURCH HL
Lower Home Farm
Quarry Plantation
A3102
Maples Wood
Elms Farm
Sandridge Park
Abbottswood Farm
Chapel Plantation
SN15
THE COMMON
SANDRIDGE HILL
BRICK HILL
Abbott's Wood
Brickyard Plantation
Morass Wood
Bromham Common
Sandridge Farm
Eighteen Acre Plantation
Abbott's Wood
Eight Acre Plantation
Hundred Acre Plantation
SN12
Lapwing Plantation
Rowde Croft Farm
Tanhouse Farm
Clears Farm
Clackers Brook
DURLETT ROAD
Broad Lane Farm
COCK ROAD
Redstocks
Rowde Hill Farm
REDSTOCKS LA
Craysmarsh
BERHILLS LANE
Berhills Lane Farm
Totterdown Farm
Berhills Farm
SN10
Newhouse Farm
A365
BATH ROAD
Sells Green
Blackthorn Farm
PH
8
7
65
6
5
64
4
3
63
2
1
62
93
94
95
178
96

95
88

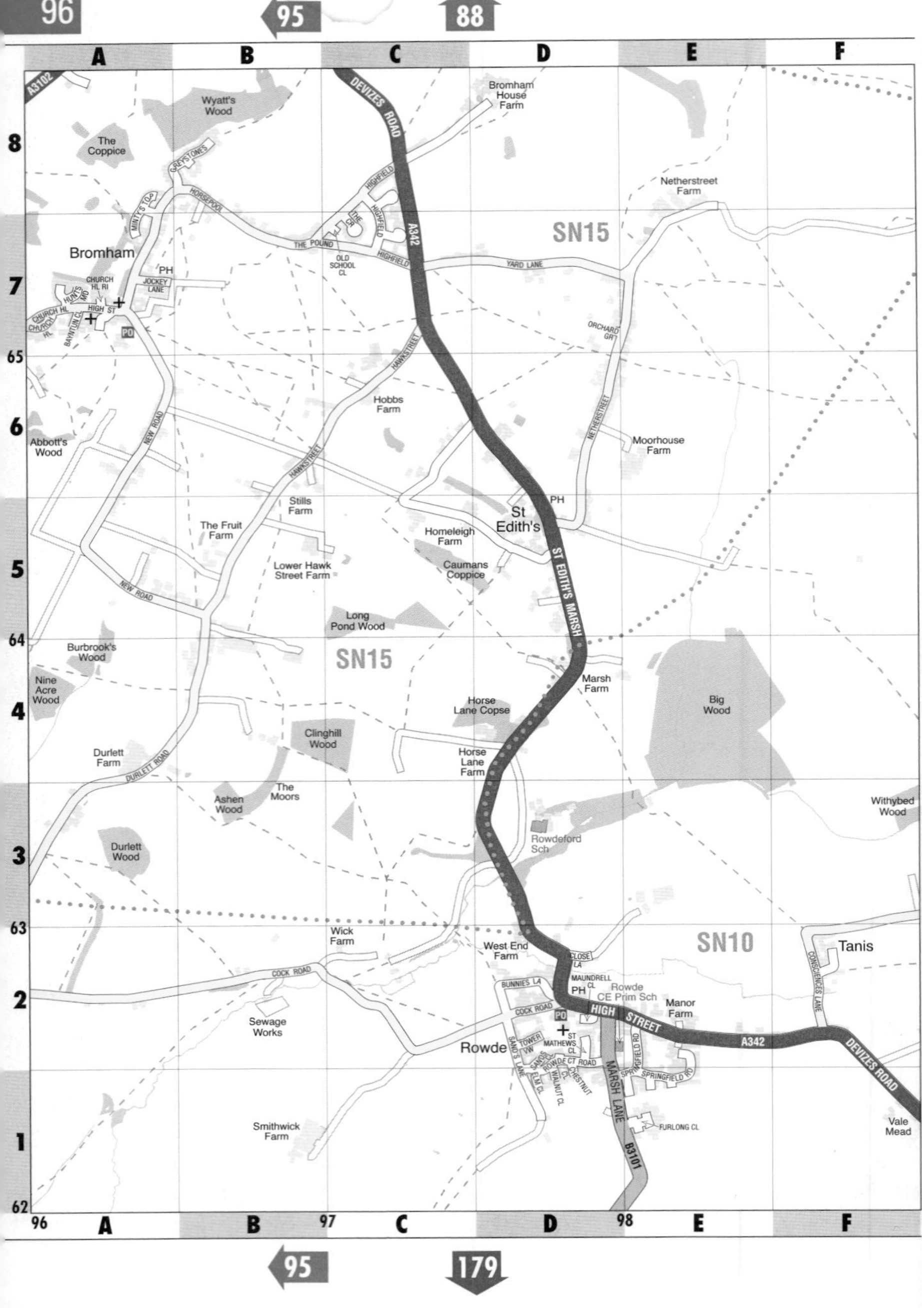
A3102
Wyatt's Wood
The Coppice
Bromham House Farm
DEVIZES ROAD
GREYSTONES
HORSEPOOL
MINTY'S TOP
HIGHFIELD
THE CRS
Netherstreet Farm
SN15
A342
Bromham
THE POUND
OLD SCHOOL CL
YARD LANE
PH
CHURCH HL RI
JOCKEY LANE
HUNTS MD
HIGH ST
CHURCH HL
BAYNTUN CL
PO
ORCHARD GR
HAWKSTREET
Hobbs Farm
NETHERSTREET
NEW ROAD
Abbott's Wood
Moorhouse Farm
Stills Farm
St Edith's
The Fruit Farm
Homeleigh Farm
Lower Hawk Street Farm
Caumans Coppice
ST EDITH'S MARSH
Long Pond Wood
Burbrook's Wood
Marsh Farm
Nine Acre Wood
Horse Lane Copse
Big Wood
Clinghill Wood
Durlett Farm
Horse Lane Farm
DURLETT ROAD
The Moors
Ashen Wood
Withybed Wood
Rowdeford Sch
Durlett Wood
Wick Farm
West End Farm
SN10
CLOSE LA
Tanis
COCK ROAD
BUNNIES LA
MAUNDRELL CL
Rowde CE Prim Sch
Sewage Works
HIGH STREET
Manor Farm
TOWER VW
ST MATHEWS CL
Rowde
SANDS CL
ROWDE CT ROAD
SAND'S LANE
ELM CL
WALNUT CL
CHESTNUT
MARSH LANE
SPRINGFIELD RD
CONSCIENCES LANE
DEVIZES ROAD
Vale Mead
FURLONG CL
Smithwick Farm
B3101
A B C D E F
8 7 65 6 5 64 4 3 63 2 1 62
96 97 98

95
179

89
172

179
214
214

F1
1 BRICKHAM RD
2 LE MARCHANT CL
3 CHARTER CL

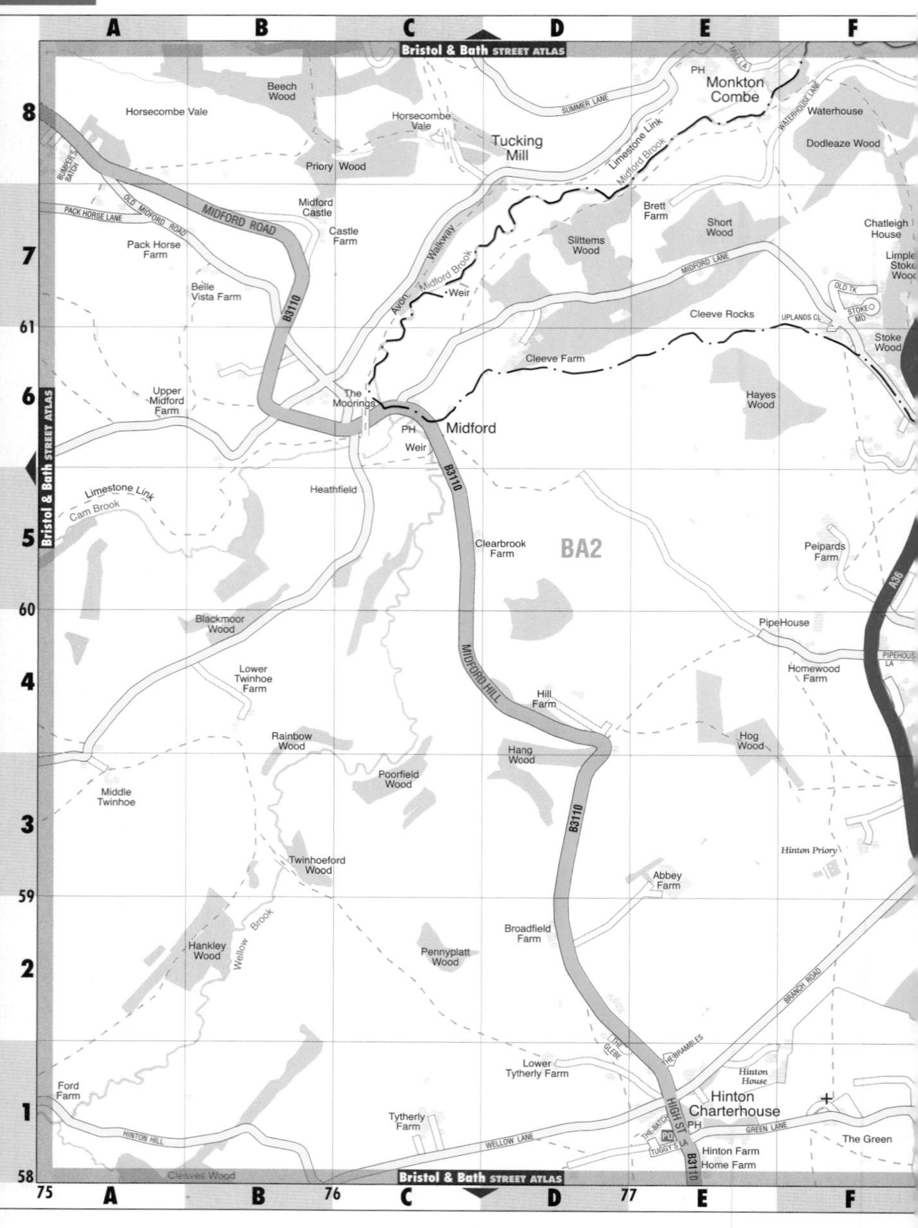
Bristol & Bath STREET ATLAS
Horsecombe Vale
Beech Wood
Horsecombe Vale
Tucking Mill
SUMMER LANE
MILL LA
PH
Monkton Combe
Waterhouse
WATERHOUSE LANE
Dodleaze Wood
Limestone Link
Midford Brook
Priory Wood
BUMPER'S BATCH
PACK HORSE LANE
OLD MIDFORD ROAD
MIDFORD ROAD
Midford Castle
Castle Farm
Pack Horse Farm
Brett Farm
Short Wood
Slittems Wood
Chatleigh House
Limpley Stoke Wood
Avon Walkway
Midford Brook
Weir
MIDFORD LANE
Belle Vista Farm
B3110
OLD TK
STOKE MD
Cleeve Rocks
UPLANDS CL
Stoke Wood
Cleeve Farm
Upper Midford Farm
The Moorings
PH
Midford
Weir
Hayes Wood
Limestone Link
Cam Brook
Heathfield
B3110
Clearbrook Farm
BA2
Peipards Farm
A36
Blackmoor Wood
PipeHouse
PIPEHOUSE LA
Lower Twinhoe Farm
MIDFORD HILL
Homewood Farm
Hill Farm
Rainbow Wood
Hang Wood
Hog Wood
Middle Twinhoe
Poorfield Wood
B3110
Hinton Priory
Twinhoeford Wood
Abbey Farm
Broadfield Farm
Hankley Wood
Wellow Brook
Pennyplatt Wood
BRANCH ROAD
THE GLEBE
THE BRAMBLES
Lower Tytherly Farm
Hinton House
Ford Farm
Hinton Charterhouse
HIGH ST
PH
Tytherly Farm
THE BATCH
PO
TUGGY'S LA
GREEN LANE
The Green
HINTON HILL
WELLOW LANE
B3110
Hinton Farm
Home Farm
Cleaves Wood
Bristol & Bath STREET ATLAS

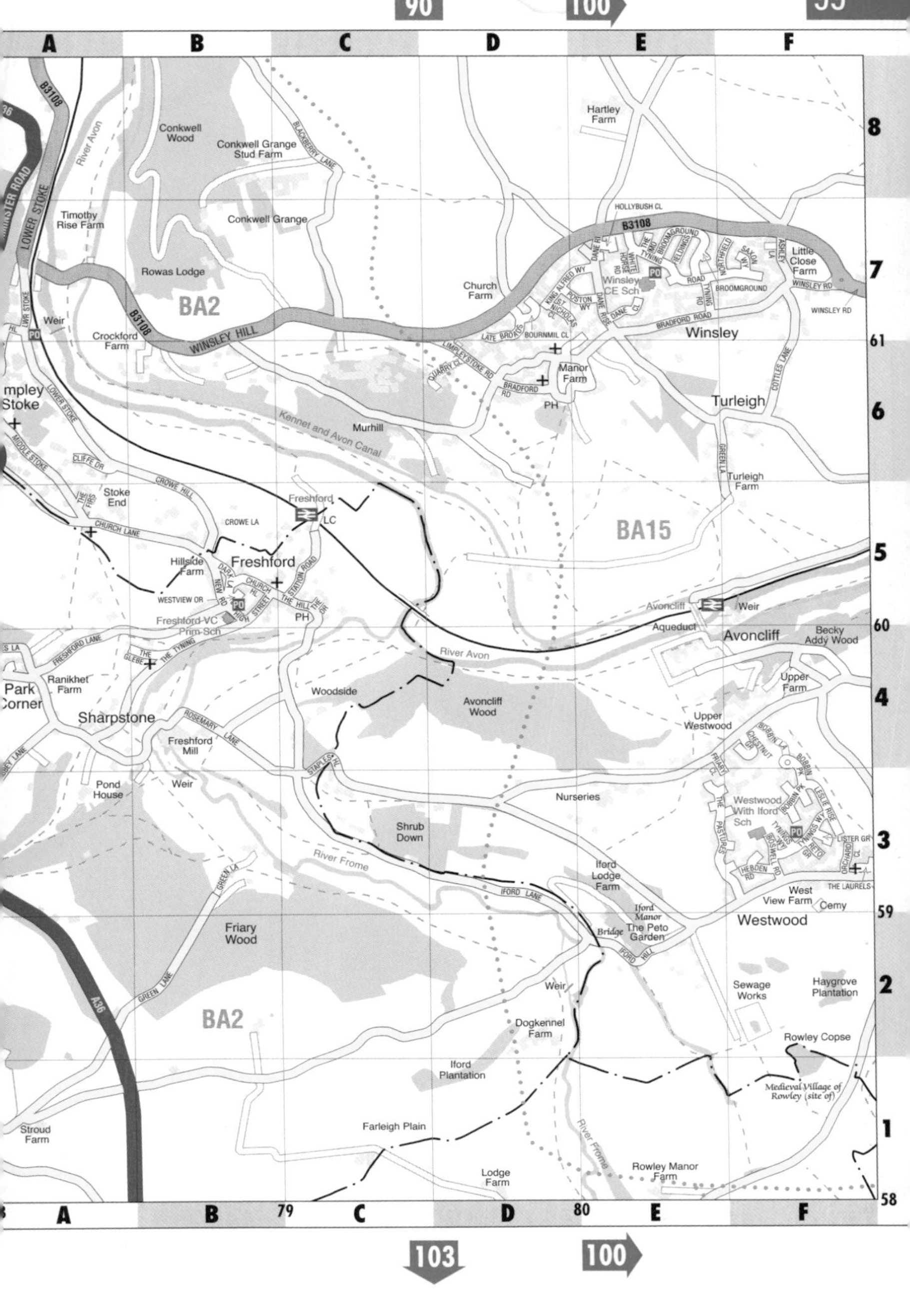
90
100
A B C D E F
8 7 6 5 4 3 2 1
61 60 59 58
79 80
103
100
B3108
LOWER STOKE
Conkwell Wood
Conkwell Grange Stud Farm
BLACKBERRY LANE
Hartley Farm
Timothy Rise Farm
Conkwell Grange
River Avon
HOLLYBUSH CL
Rowas Lodge
BA2
Church Farm
Winsley CE Sch
Little Close Farm
WINSLEY RD
Weir
Crockford Farm
WINSLEY HILL
Winsley
BRADFORD ROAD
BROOMGROUND
Manor Farm
PH
Turleigh
COTTLES LANE
Kennet and Avon Canal
Murhill
Stoke End
CROWE HILL
CHURCH LANE
CLIFFE DR
MIDDLE STOKE
Freshford
LC
BA15
Turleigh Farm
GREEN LA
CROWE LA
Hillside Farm
WESTVIEW DR
STATION ROAD
Freshford VC Prim Sch
HIGH STREET
Avoncliff
Aqueduct
Weir
Becky Addy Wood
River Avon
Ranikhet Farm
Park Corner
Sharpstone
THE TYNING
THE GLEBE
FRESHFORD LANE
Woodside
Avoncliff Wood
Upper Farm
Upper Westwood
ROSEMARY LANE
Freshford Mill
Pond House
STAPLES HL
Nurseries
Westwood With Iford Sch
Shrub Down
River Frome
Iford Lodge Farm
IFORD LANE
LISTER GR
THE LAURELS
West View Farm
Cemy
Westwood
Iford Manor
The Peto Garden
Bridge
IFORD HILL
Friary Wood
GREEN LANE
Weir
Sewage Works
Haygrove Plantation
A36
BA2
Dogkennel Farm
Rowley Copse
Iford Plantation
Medieval Village of Rowley (site of)
Stroud Farm
Farleigh Plain
River Frome
Lodge Farm
Rowley Manor Farm

99
91

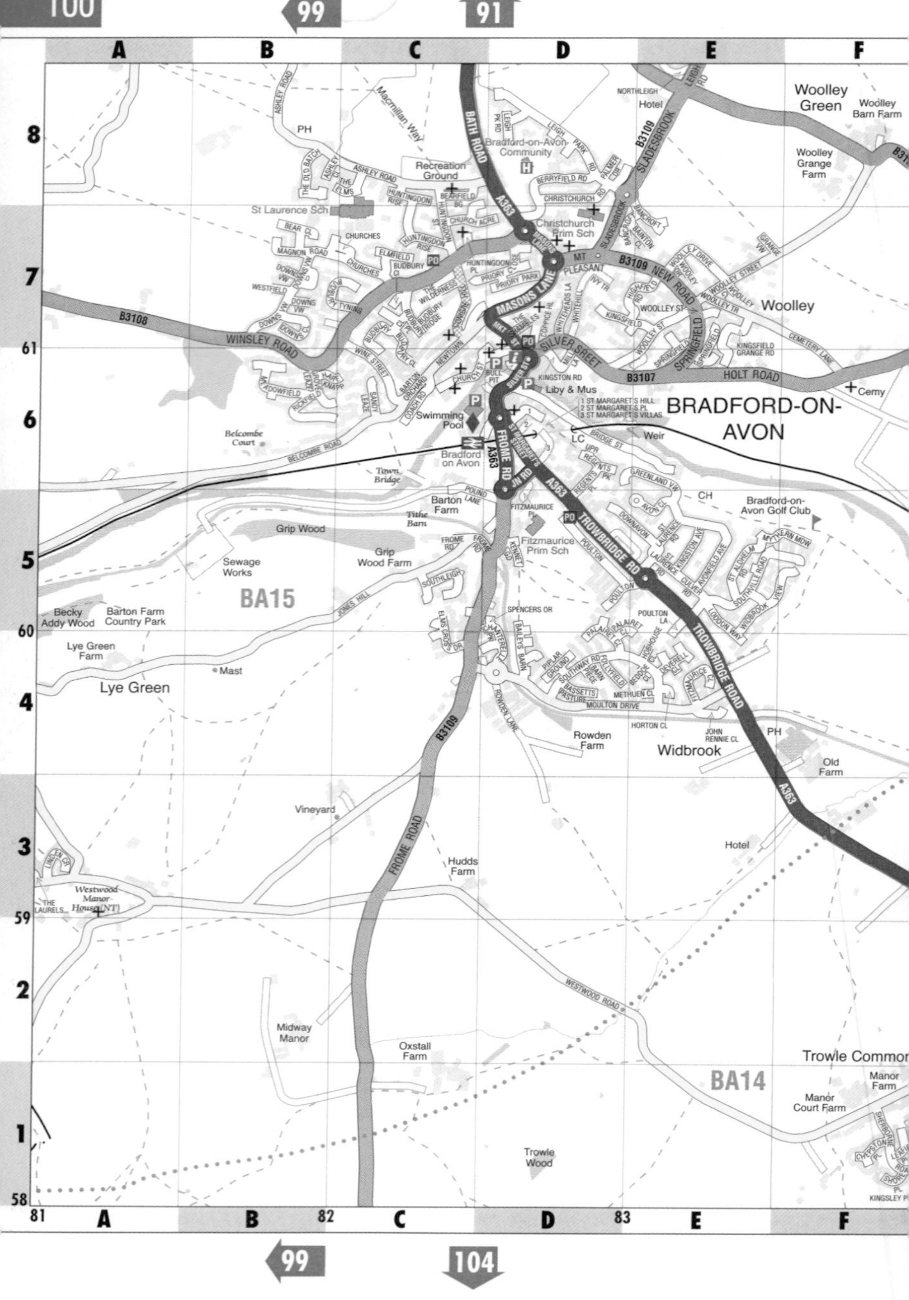
A
B
C
D
E
F
8
7
61
6
5
60
4
3
59
2
1
58
81
82
83
Woolley Green
Woolley Barn Farm
Woolley Grange Farm
Woolley
NORTHLEIGH
Hotel
LEIGH RD
B3109
SLADESBROOK
Macmillan Way
ASHLEY ROAD
PH
BATH ROAD
Bradford-on-Avon Community
Recreation Ground
ASHLEY ROAD
THE OLD BATCH
ASHLEY
THE ELMS
HUNTINGDON RISE
BEARFIELD BG
BERRYFIELD RD
CHRISTCHURCH RD
St Laurence Sch
A363
Christchurch Prim Sch
BEAR CL
CHURCHES
CHURCH ACRE
HUNTINGDON RISE
MAGNON ROAD
ELMFIELD
BUDBURY CL
PO
HUNTINGDON PL
PRIORY CLOSE
PRIORY PARK
MT PLEASANT
B3109
NEW ROAD
WOOLLEY DRIVE
WOOLLEY STREET
WESTFIELD
DOWNS VW
BUDBURY TYNING
THE WILDERNESS
MASONS LANE
IVY TR
HIGHFIELD
WOOLLEY ST
WOOLLEY TR
B3108
WINSLEY ROAD
BUDBURY RIDGE
NEWTOWN
THE SHAMBLES
COPPICE HL
WHITEHEADS LA
WHITEHILL
KINGSFIELD
SPRINGFIELD
KINGSFIELD GRANGE RD
CEMETERY LANE
WINE STREET
SILVER STREET
B3107
HOLT ROAD
MEADOWFIELD
RICKFIELD
BARTON ORCHARD
COACH RD
CHURCH ST
BULL PIT
SILVER ST
KINGSTON RD
Liby & Mus
Cemy
1 ST MARGARET'S HILL
2 ST MARGARET'S PL
3 ST MARGARET'S VILLAS
BRADFORD-ON-AVON
Swimming Pool
Belcombe Court
BELCOMBE ROAD
FROME RD
ST MARGARET'S STREET
BRIDGE ST
LC
Weir
Bradford on Avon
Town Bridge
UPR REGENTS PK
GREENLAND VW
CH
Bradford-on-Avon Golf Club
POUND LANE
Barton Farm
Tithe Barn
FITZMAURICE PL
TROWBRIDGE RD
DOWNAVON
ST LAURENCE RD
KINGSTON AVE
MYRTLE MOW
Grip Wood
Sewage Works
Grip Wood Farm
FROME RD
Fitzmaurice Prim Sch
POULTON
CULVER RD
AVONFIELD AVE
ST ALDHELM RD
SOUTHVILLE ROAD
WIDBROOK VIEW
BA15
SOUTHLEIGH
JONES HILL
Becky Addy Wood
Barton Farm Country Park
SPENCERS OR
POULTON LA
LODDON WAY
Lye Green Farm
Mast
ELMS CROSS DR
BAILEYS BARN
PIPLAR GROUND
SOUTHWAY RD
FOLLYFIELD
BEDDOE CL
DEVERELL CL
FITZMAURICE CL
TROWBRIDGE ROAD
Lye Green
BASSETTS PASTURE
METHUEN CL
MOULTON DRIVE
ROWDEN LANE
HORTON CL
JOHN RENNIE CL
B3109
Rowden Farm
Widbrook
PH
Old Farm
A363
Vineyard
FROME ROAD
Hudds Farm
Hotel
LINDEN CR
THE LAURELS
Westwood Manor House (NT)
WESTWOOD ROAD
Midway Manor
Oxstall Farm
Trowle Common
BA14
Manor Farm
Manor Court Farm
Trowle Wood
KINGSLEY PL

99
104

92
102
A
B
C
D
E
F
8
7
61
6
5
60
4
3
59
2
1
58
84
85
86
Hunt's Hall Farm
Woolley Park Farm
Holt Farm
PH
Ham Green
Kingston Farm
The Street
B3107
Superstore
The Courts Garden (NT)
Holt
Station Rd
Bradley Cl
Station Road
Poplar Farm
Bradford Road
Manor Farm
B3106
Gaston Farm
The Star
Avon View Farm
Forewoods Common
B3105
New Terrace
Weir
Little Bradford Wood
BA15
Staverton
Staverton Farm
Elm Cl
BA14
Earthwork
Great Bradford Wood
Staverton CE Sch
Smallbrook Gd
Marsh Road
PO
School La
Hilperton Marsh Farm
Hammond Way
Marina Drive
Swan Dr
The Slipway
Thestfield Drive
Carisbrooke Cr
Compton Cl
Hill St
Horse Rd
Marshmead
Newleaze
Wyke Rd
Canal Rd
Hilperton Marsh
Kennet and Avon Canal
Aqueduct
Lady Down Farm
Brick Lane
Canal Road
Avon Way
Kennet Way
Hayes Cl
Withy Cl
TROWBRIDGE
Weir
Lady Down Mill
Longscroft Farm
Trowle
Greenway Gd
Victoria Road
Albert Rd
Cemetery Lodge
Cemy
Middle Lane
Parklands
Parochial Junior Sch
Sewage Works
River Biss
Langford Road
Hyde Rd
Avonvale Rd
The Down
Kensington
The Mount
Springfield
Fulford Road
Rodwell Pk
Albany Cl
Hotel
Trowbridge Community
H
Islington
Downhayes Rd
Lower Ct
Prospect
British Row
York Bg
The Mead Com Prim Sch
Victoria Road
Hilperton Road
A361
Cock Hill
A363
Oak Tree Cl
Margaret Stancomb Inf Sch
Upr Broad St 1
Broad St 2
Shails La 3
P
Cross St
Union Street
Church Street
Duke St
St Thomas' Road
Stancomb Av
Larkrise Sch
Paxcroft Prim Sch
Trowle Bridge
Bradford Rd
Linden Pl
Innox Mill Cl
Innox Rd
River Way
Wicker Hill
Back St
Roundstone St
Eastbourne Rd
Eastbourne Gd
Furlong
Quarterway Lane
Cranmore Cl
Broadmead
Chilmark Road
Ancaster Cl
Elliott Pl
Lynwood Rd
City Way
Fore St
Corbin Rd
Kenton Dr
Beeches

101 93 178

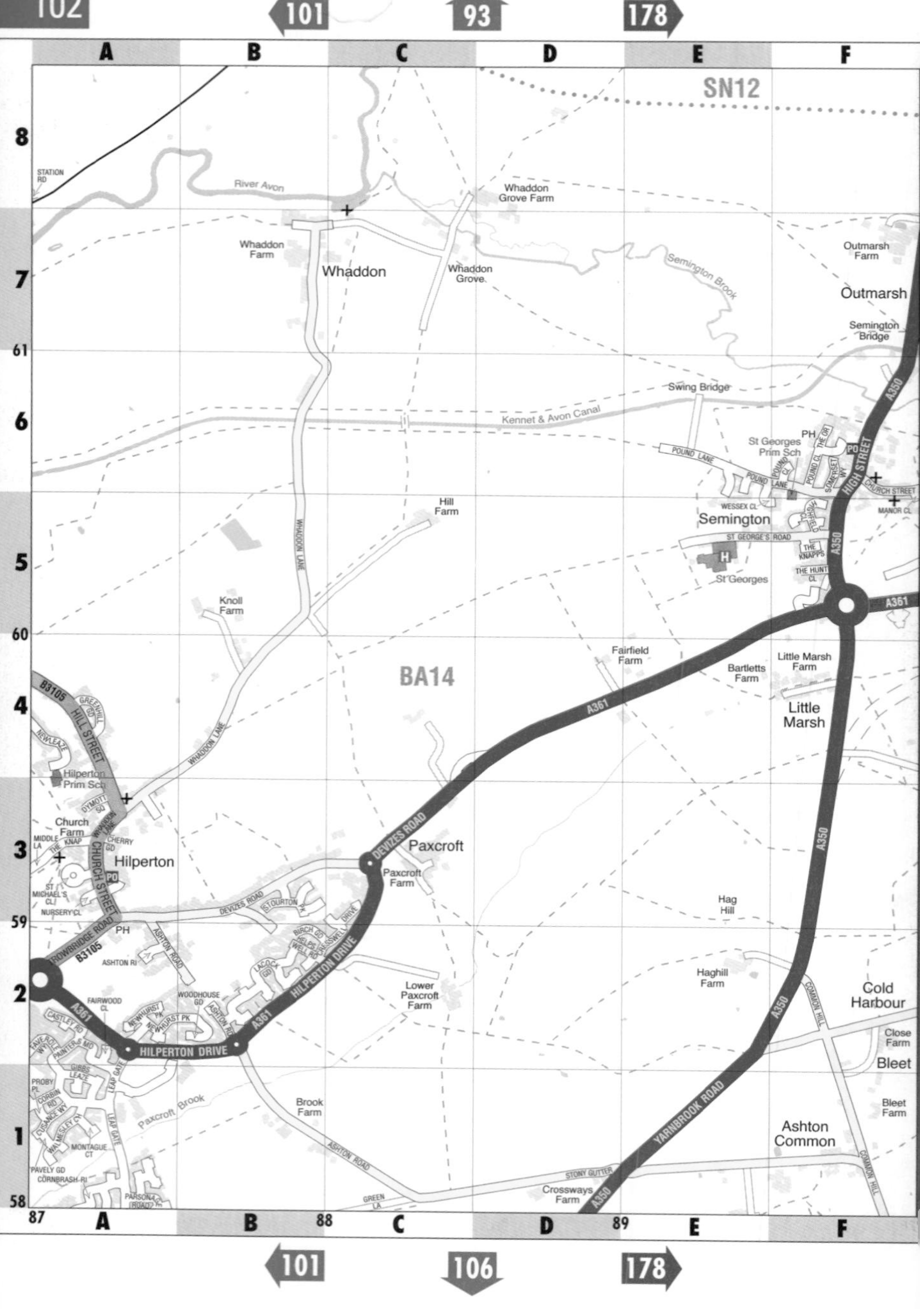
SN12
River Avon
Whaddon Grove Farm
Whaddon Farm
Whaddon
Whaddon Grove
Semington Brook
Outmarsh Farm
Outmarsh
Semington Bridge
Swing Bridge
Kennet & Avon Canal
St Georges Prim Sch
Hill Farm
Semington
St Georges
Knoll Farm
BA14
Fairfield Farm
Bartletts Farm
Little Marsh Farm
Little Marsh
Hilperton Prim Sch
Church Farm
Hilperton
Paxcroft
Paxcroft Farm
Hag Hill
Haghill Farm
Lower Paxcroft Farm
Cold Harbour
Close Farm
Bleet
Bleet Farm
Paxcroft Brook
Brook Farm
Ashton Common
Crossways Farm
WHADDON LANE
HILL STREET
CHURCH STREET
TROWBRIDGE ROAD
DEVIZES ROAD
HILPERTON DRIVE
ASHTON ROAD
YARNBROOK ROAD
HIGH STREET
POUND LANE
ST GEORGE'S ROAD
CHURCH STREET
COMMON HILL
STONY GUTTER
GREEN LA
A361
A350
B3105

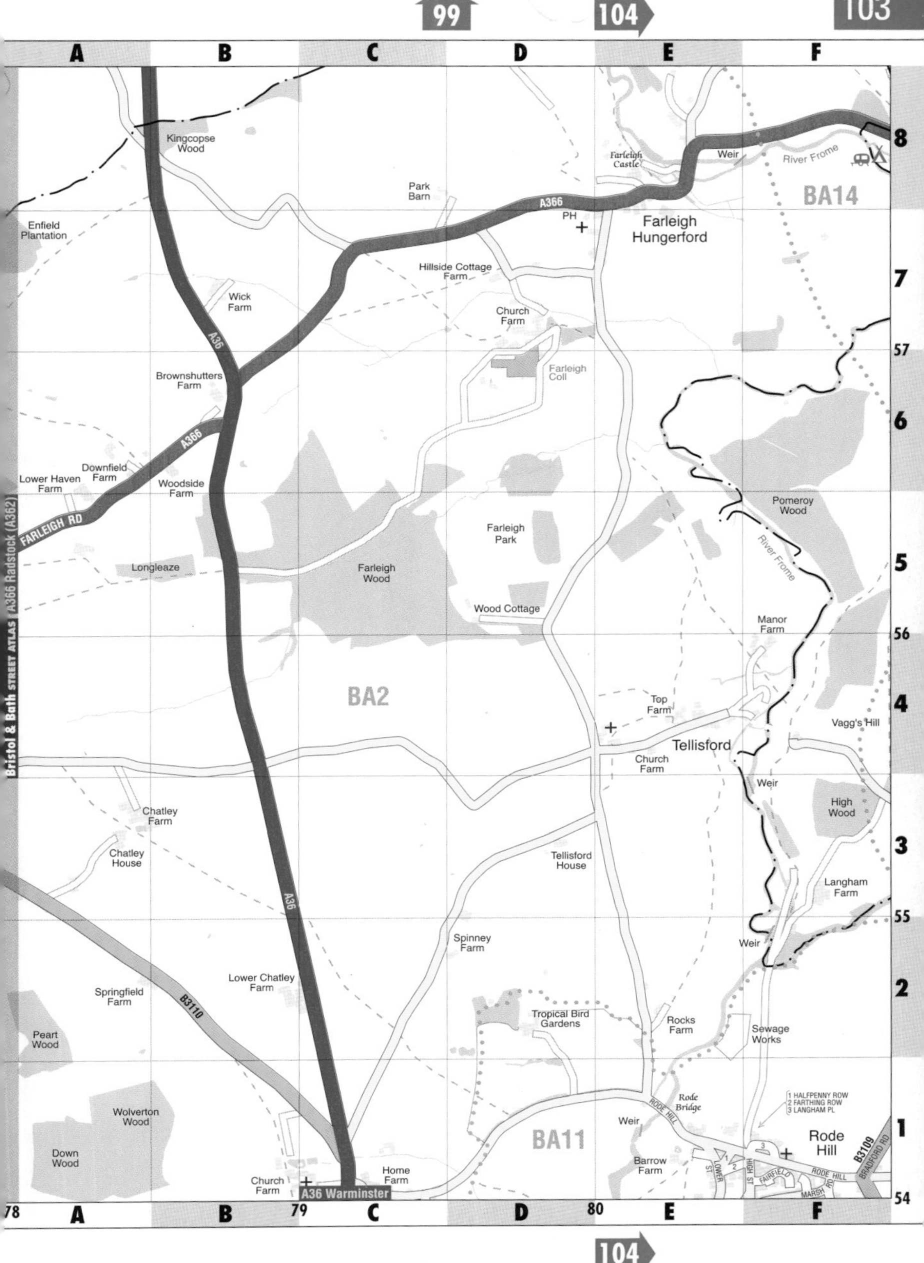
A
B
C
D
E
F
Kingcopse Wood
Farleigh Castle
Weir
River Frome
BA14
Park Barn
A366
PH
Farleigh Hungerford
Enfield Plantation
Hillside Cottage Farm
Wick Farm
Church Farm
A36
Brownshutters Farm
Farleigh Coll
A366
Downfield Farm
Lower Haven Farm
Woodside Farm
Pomeroy Wood
FARLEIGH RD
Farleigh Park
River Frome
Longleaze
Farleigh Wood
Wood Cottage
Manor Farm
BA2
Top Farm
Vagg's Hill
Tellisford
Church Farm
Weir
High Wood
Chatley Farm
Chatley House
Tellisford House
Langham Farm
A36
Spinney Farm
Weir
Lower Chatley Farm
Springfield Farm
B3110
Tropical Bird Gardens
Rocks Farm
Sewage Works
Peart Wood
Rode Bridge
1 HALFPENNY ROW
2 FARTHING ROW
3 LANGHAM PL
Wolverton Wood
Weir
BA11
RODE HILL
Rode Hill
B3109
BRADFORD RD
Down Wood
Barrow Farm
LOWER ST
HIGH ST
FAIRFIELD
MARSH RD
RODE HILL
Church Farm
Home Farm
A36 Warminster
8
7
57
6
5
56
4
3
55
2
1
54
78
79
80
Bristol & Bath STREET ATLAS | A366 Radstock (A362)

103
100

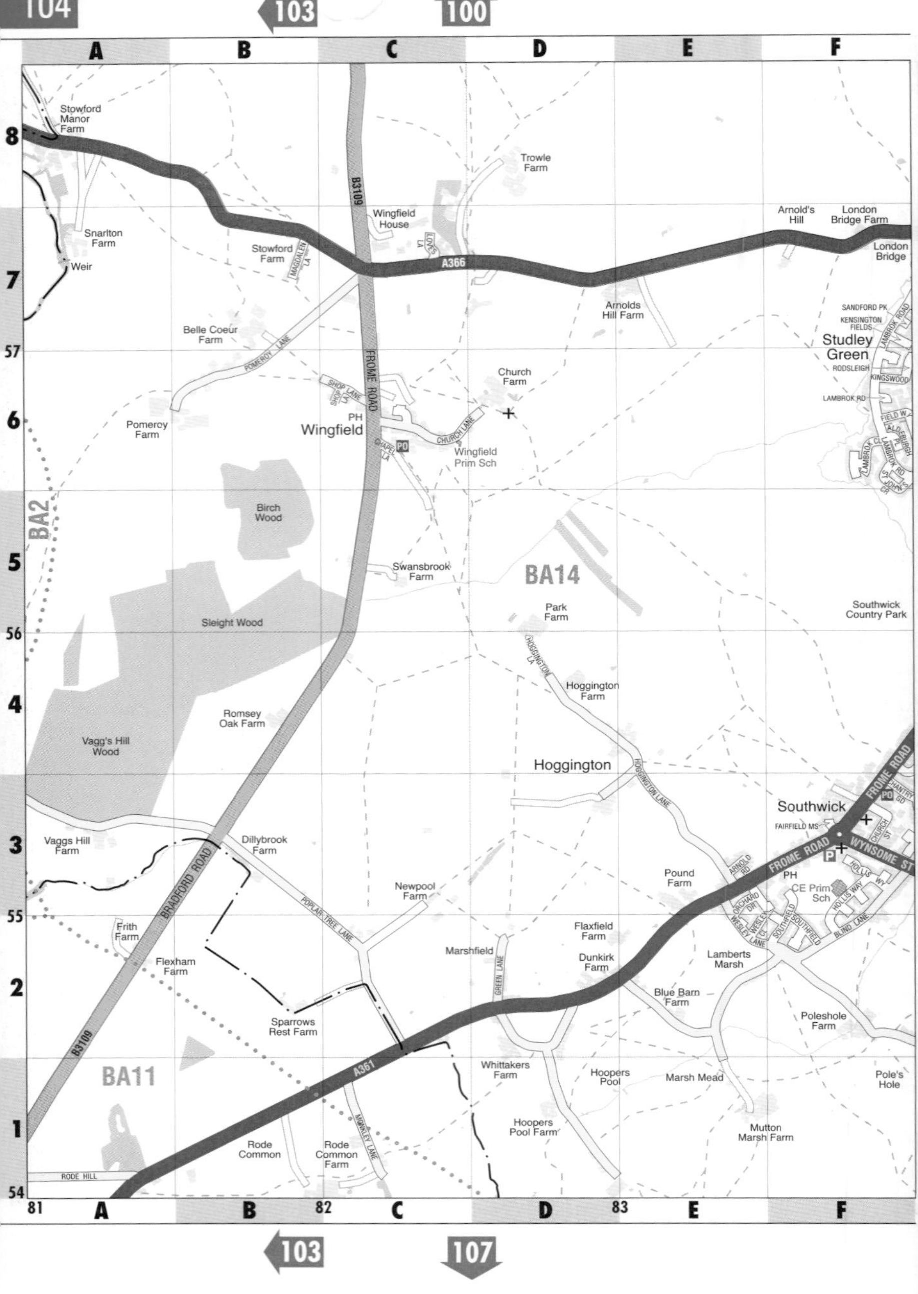

103
107

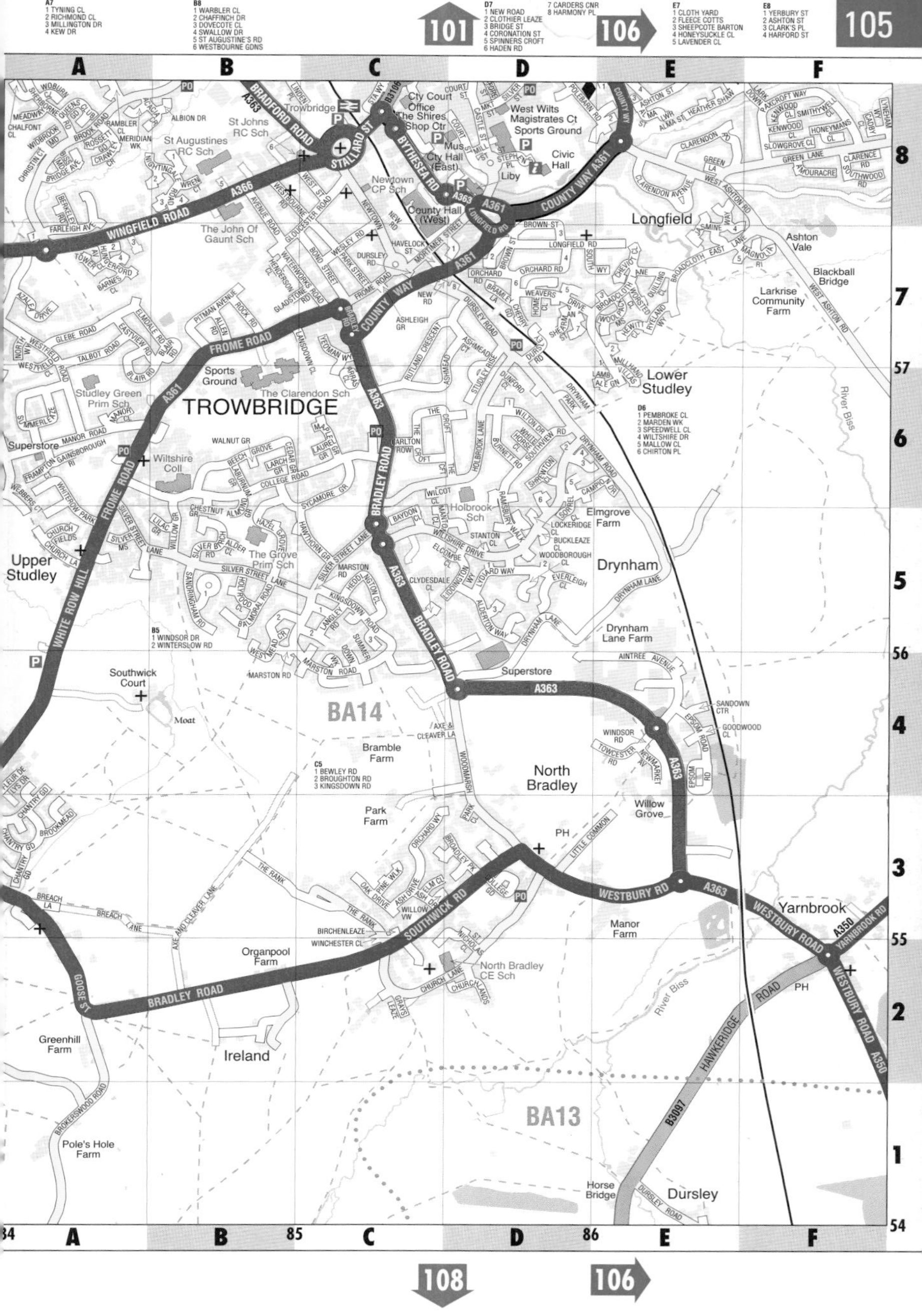
A7
1 TYNING CL
2 RICHMOND CL
3 MILLINGTON DR
4 KEW DR
B8
1 WARBLER CL
2 CHAFFINCH DR
3 DOVECOTE CL
4 SWALLOW DR
5 ST AUGUSTINE'S RD
6 WESTBOURNE GDNS
101
D7
1 NEW ROAD
2 CLOTHIER LEAZE
3 BRIDGE ST
4 CORONATION ST
5 SPINNERS CROFT
6 HADEN RD
7 CARDERS CNR
8 HARMONY PL
106
E7
1 CLOTH YARD
2 FLEECE COTTS
3 SHEEPCOTE BARTON
4 HONEYSUCKLE CL
5 LAVENDER CL
E8
1 YERBURY ST
2 ASHTON ST
3 CLARK'S PL
4 HARFORD ST
A
B
C
D
E
F
8
7
57
6
5
56
4
3
55
2
1
54
84
85
86
Trowbridge
Cty Court Office
The Shires Shop Ctr
St Johns RC Sch
St Augustines RC Sch
West Wilts Magistrates Ct
Sports Ground
Mus
Cty Hall (East)
Civic Hall
Liby
Newtown CP Sch
County Hall (West)
Longfield
Ashton Vale
Blackball Bridge
Larkrise Community Farm
The John Of Gaunt Sch
BRADFORD ROAD
STALLARD ST
BYTHESEA RD
WINGFIELD ROAD
COUNTY WAY
FROME ROAD
BRADLEY ROAD
WHITE ROW HILL
A363
A366
A361
B3106
Sports Ground
The Clarendon Sch
TROWBRIDGE
Studley Green Prim Sch
Superstore
Wiltshire Coll
Holbrook Sch
The Grove Prim Sch
Lower Studley
D6
1 PEMBROKE CL
2 MARDEN WK
3 SPEEDWELL CL
4 WILTSHIRE DR
5 MALLOW CL
6 CHIRTON PL
Elmgrove Farm
Drynham
Drynham Lane Farm
Upper Studley
River Biss
B5
1 WINDSOR DR
2 WINTERSLOW RD
Southwick Court
Moat
BA14
Superstore
Bramble Farm
C5
1 BEWLEY RD
2 BROUGHTON RD
3 KINGSDOWN RD
North Bradley
Willow Grove
Park Farm
PH
WESTBURY RD
SOUTHWICK RD
Yarnbrook
Manor Farm
WESTBURY ROAD
A350
YARNBROOK RD
Organpool Farm
North Bradley CE Sch
BRADLEY ROAD
GOOSE ST
Greenhill Farm
Ireland
HAWKERIDGE ROAD
B3097
River Biss
PH
BA13
Pole's Hole Farm
Horse Bridge
Dursley
DURSLEY ROAD
BROKERSWOOD ROAD
108
106

105 102 178

105 109 178

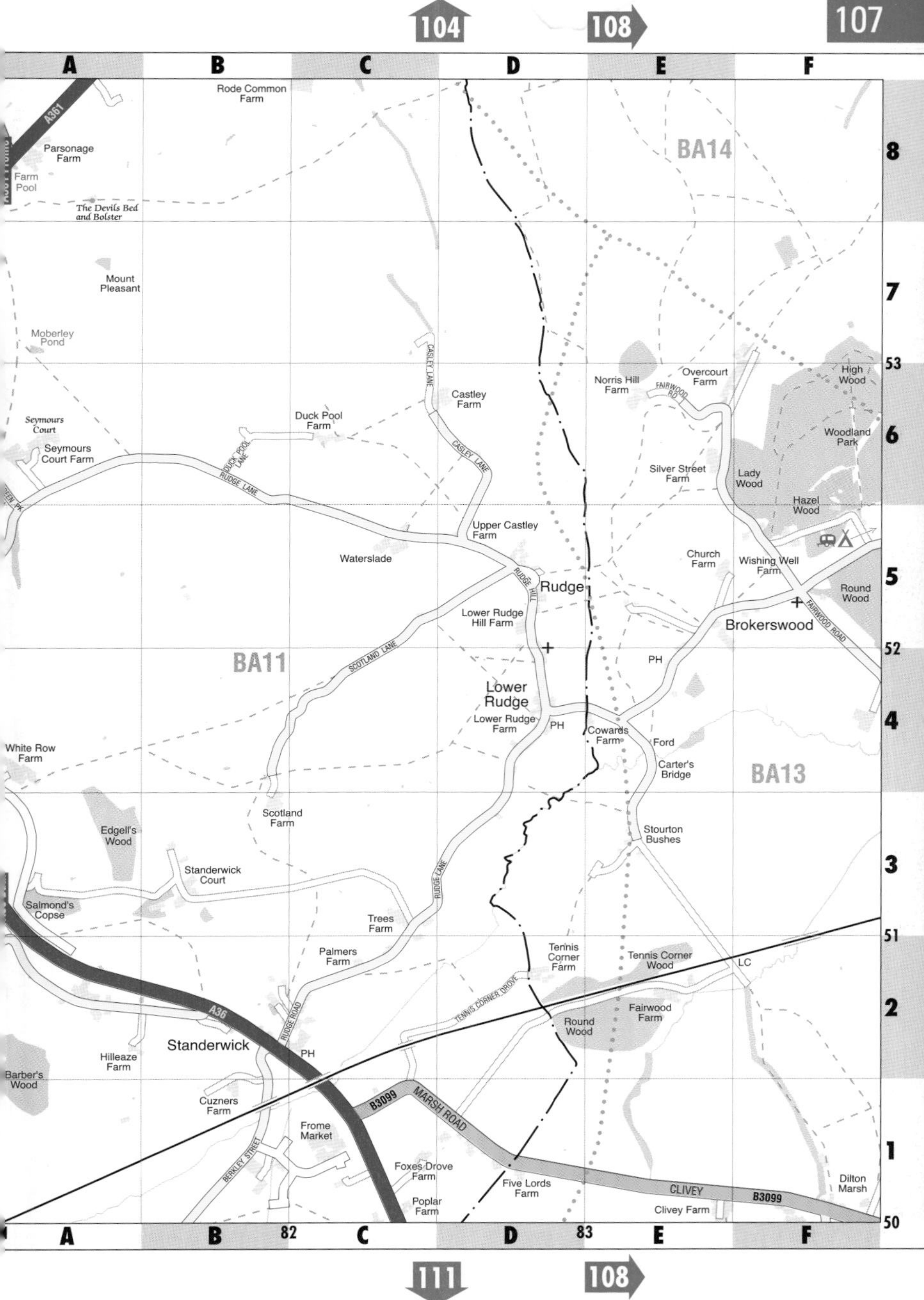
104
108
A
B
C
D
E
F
Rode Common Farm
A361
Parsonage Farm
Farm Pool
The Devils Bed and Bolster
BA14
8
Mount Pleasant
7
Moberley Pond
53
Castley Farm
CASLEY LANE
Norris Hill Farm
FAIRWOOD RD
Overcourt Farm
High Wood
Seymours Court
Duck Pool Farm
Seymours Court Farm
DUCK POOL LANE
RUDGE LANE
Woodland Park
6
Silver Street Farm
Lady Wood
Hazel Wood
Upper Castley Farm
Waterslade
RUDGE HILL
Church Farm
Wishing Well Farm
Rudge
5
Round Wood
Lower Rudge Hill Farm
Brokerswood
FAIRWOOD ROAD
52
BA11
SCOTLAND LANE
PH
Lower Rudge
Lower Rudge Farm
PH
Cowards Farm
Ford
4
White Row Farm
Carter's Bridge
BA13
Scotland Farm
Edgell's Wood
Stourton Bushes
3
Standerwick Court
RUDGE LANE
Salmond's Copse
Trees Farm
51
Palmers Farm
Tennis Corner Farm
Tennis Corner Wood
LC
TENNIS CORNER DROVE
Fairwood Farm
2
A36
Round Wood
RUDGE ROAD
Standerwick
PH
Hilleaze Farm
Barber's Wood
B3099
MARSH ROAD
Cuzners Farm
Frome Market
1
BERKLEY STREET
Foxes Drove Farm
Five Lords Farm
CLIVEY
B3099
Dilton Marsh
Poplar Farm
Clivey Farm
50
A
B
82
C
D
83
E
F
111
108

F1
1 PK VW DR
2 LEIGHTON PK W
3 LAVERTON GN
4 LEIGHTON PK N
5 LEIGHTON PK RD

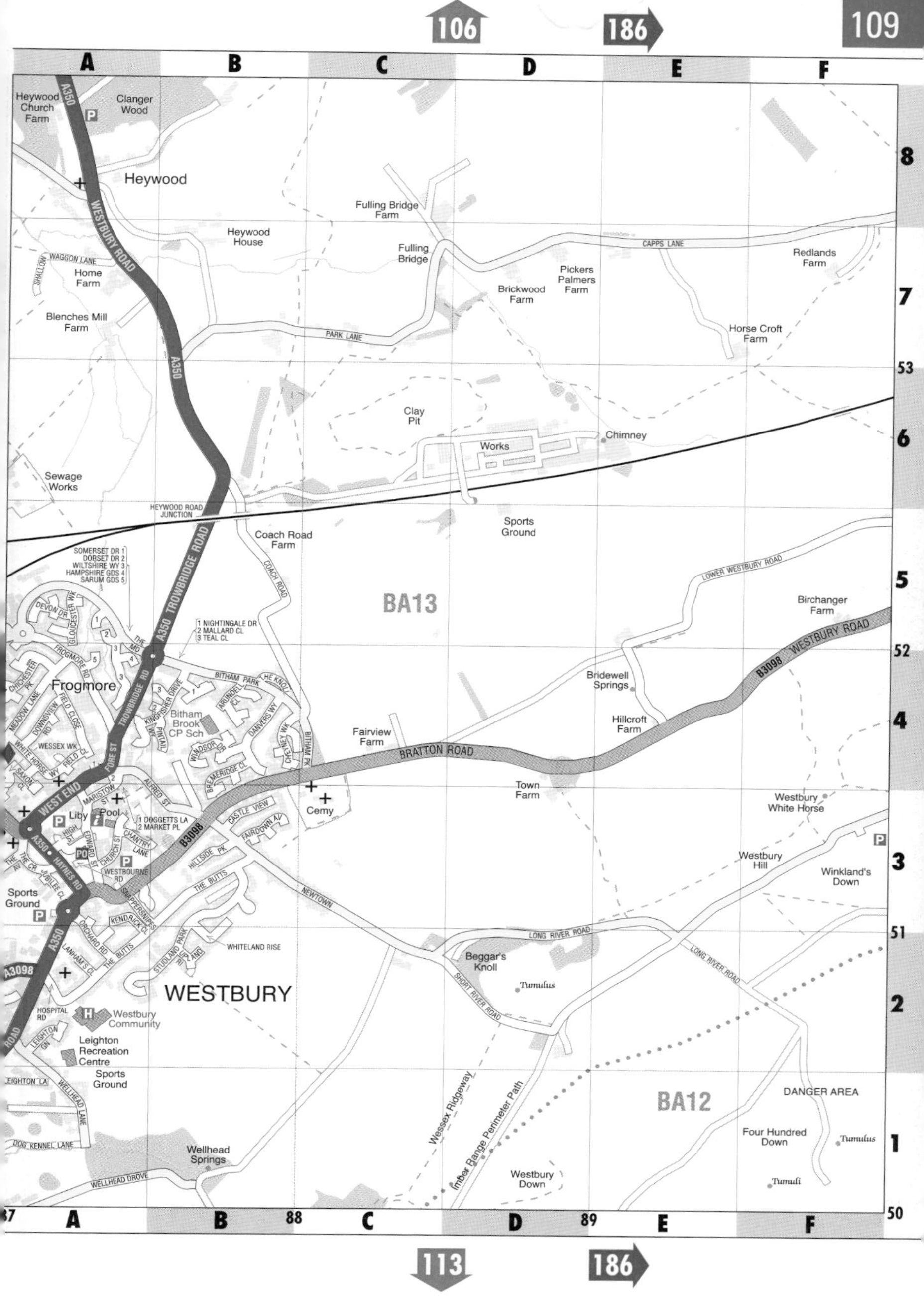
A
B
C
D
E
F
8
7
53
6
5
52
4
3
51
2
1
50
87
88
89
Heywood Church Farm
Clanger Wood
Heywood
WESTBURY ROAD
A350
Fulling Bridge Farm
Heywood House
Fulling Bridge
CAPPS LANE
Redlands Farm
WAGGON LANE
SHALLOW
Home Farm
Pickers Palmers Farm
Brickwood Farm
Blenches Mill Farm
PARK LANE
Horse Croft Farm
Clay Pit
Works
Chimney
Sewage Works
HEYWOOD ROAD JUNCTION
Sports Ground
Coach Road Farm
COACH ROAD
TROWBRIDGE ROAD
SOMERSET DR 1
DORSET DR 2
WILTSHIRE WY 3
HAMPSHIRE GDS 4
SARUM GDS 5
LOWER WESTBURY ROAD
BA13
Birchanger Farm
1 NIGHTINGALE DR
2 MALLARD CL
3 TEAL CL
DEVON DR
GLOUCESTER WK
THE MID
FROGMORE RD
WESTBURY ROAD
B3098
CHICHESTER PK
Frogmore
BITHAM PARK
THE KNOLL
Bridewell Springs
MEADOW LANE
DOWNSVIEW RD
FIELD CLOSE
TROWBRIDGE RD
KINGFISHER DRIVE
ARUNDELL CL
Bitham Brook CP Sch
DANVERS WY
Hillcroft Farm
WESSEX WK
FORE ST
PINTAIL WY
WINDSOR DR
CHEYNEY WK
BITHAM PK
Fairview Farm
BRATTON ROAD
WHITE HORSE WY
FIELD CL
BREMERIDGE CL
SAXON CL
WEST END
MARISTOW ST
ALFRED ST
Town Farm
Westbury White Horse
Pool
Liby
CASTLE VIEW
Cemy
1 DOGGETTS LA
2 MARKET PL
FAIRDOWN AV
HIGH ST
EDWARD ST
CHANTRY LANE
CHURCH ST
B3098
HAYNES RD
THE AV
THE CR
JUBILEE CL
PO
HILLSIDE PK
Westbury Hill
Winkland's Down
WESTBOURNE RD
THE BUTTS
NEWTOWN
Sports Ground
SNAPPERSNIPES
KENDRICK CL
ORCHARD RD
LONG RIVER ROAD
WHITELAND RISE
LANHAM'S CL
THE BUTTS
STUDLAND PARK
UPLAND RI
Beggar's Knoll
LONG RIVER ROAD
A3098
SHORT RIVER ROAD
Tumulus
WESTBURY
HOSPITAL RD
Westbury Community
LEIGHTON GN
Leighton Recreation Centre
ROAD
Sports Ground
LEIGHTON LA
WELLHEAD LANE
Wessex Ridgeway
Imber Range Perimeter Path
BA12
DANGER AREA
Four Hundred Down
Tumulus
DOG KENNEL LANE
Wellhead Springs
Westbury Down
Tumuli
WELLHEAD DROVE

110
A7
1 SELWOOD CR
2 LEVERSEDGE RD
3 MENDIP CL
4 EASTLEIGH CL
5 TANKEY'S CL
6 CHAMPNEY RD
7 NORTHCOTE CR
8 MAPLE CT
9 PRINCESS ANNE RD
218
B7
1 WALNUT WK
2 PINE CT
3 LABURNUM CL
4 BIRCH WK
5 ALDER WK
6 MAYTREE CL
7 FOREST RD
8 SYCAMORE DR
C6
1 HORNBEAM CL
2 PENNEYS PIECE
3 BRAITHWAITE WY
4 GABRIEL CL
5 TREVITHICK CL
6 CLINK FARM CT
7 WIVENHOE CT
8 WHITE HORSE DR
9 WESTCOTT CL
10 LUDLOW CL
11 BARTLETT CL
C7
1 MAGNOLIA CL
2 FOXCOTE GDS
3 SHOSCOMBE GDS
4 CHARTERHOUSE DR
5 WAINWRIGHT DR
6 HAWK'S WORTH CL
7 CYPRESS WY
A361 Trowbridge
OLDFORD HILL
CUCKOO LANE
Hotel
B3090
GIPSY LANE
Frome Community Coll
Leisure Centre
Sports Gnd
GRANGE ROAD
MENDIP DRIVE
Stonebridge
BERKLEY LANE
DARK LANE
POT LANE
Marsh Bridge
Cemy
Berkley Marsh
Fairoak Farm
KEMP'S LANE
Hill Corner
ROOKS LANE
Woodman's Hill
Fishlake Wood
Ridge Copse
BERKLEY CROSS
CLINK ROAD
Tangiers Farm
Lambsgate Farm
LODGE HILL
A3098
A361
BATH ROAD
Fromefield
1 HAWTHORN RD
2 RODDEN RD
3 STONELEIGH RI
4 SPRING RD
BLACKBIRD WY 1
CHAFFINCH AV 2
SWALLOW DR 3
THE COPSE 4
Selwood Middle Sch
Frome Cricket Club
Frome Town FC
BERKLEY ROAD
Hayesdown Fst Sch
Berkley Down
Rodden Lake Stream
FROME
BA11
Wallmarsh Farm
RODDEN ROAD
BEECHWOOD AV
ARMSTRONG RD
ST JOHN'S ROAD
ST MARY'S RD
STYLES HILL
STYLES CL
STYLES AV
WALLBRIDGE
WARMINSTER ROAD
PORTWAY A362
A362 Radstock
GARSTON ROAD
VICTORIA RD
Cemy
Frome
Weir
Rodden Farm
Rodden Manor
Rodden Brook
Rodden Down
Rodden Down Farm
Flintford Farm
Redford Water
FELTHAM DR
MOUNTSFIELD
River Frome
FELTHAM LANE
Feltham Bridge
BIRCHILL LANE
Feltham Farm
FRIGGLE STREET
Grandon Manor
JOLES LANE
Woodcock Farm
78
79
80
A4
1 WALLBRIDGE GDS
2 WALLBRIDGE AV
3 GARSTON LA
4 STATION APP
5 HARCOURT MWS
6 RIVERS REACH
218
114

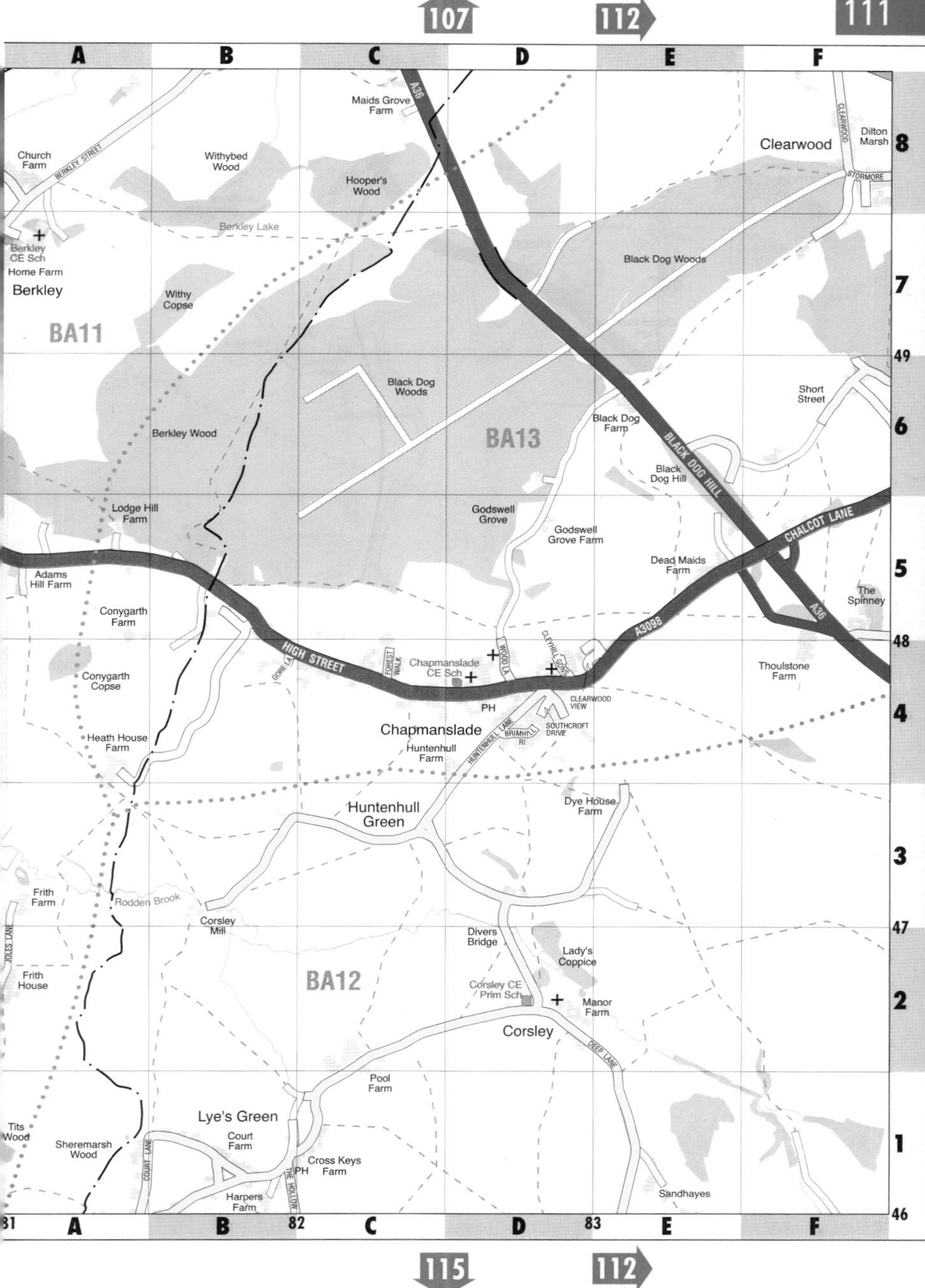
A
B
C
D
E
F
Maids Grove Farm
A36
Church Farm
BERKLEY STREET
Withybed Wood
Hooper's Wood
Clearwood
CLEARWOOD
Dilton Marsh
STORMORE
8
Berkley Lake
Berkley CE Sch
Home Farm
Berkley
Black Dog Woods
Withy Copse
7
BA11
49
Black Dog Woods
Short Street
Berkley Wood
BA13
Black Dog Farm
6
BLACK DOG HILL
Black Dog Hill
Lodge Hill Farm
Godswell Grove
Godswell Grove Farm
CHALCOT LANE
Dead Maids Farm
5
Adams Hill Farm
Conygarth Farm
The Spinney
A3098
A36
48
HIGH STREET
GORE LA
FOREST WALK
Chapmanslade CE Sch
WOOD LA
CLEYHILL GDNS
Thoulstone Farm
Conygarth Copse
PH
CLEARWOOD VIEW
SOUTHCROFT DRIVE
Chapmanslade
HUNTENHULL LANE
BRIMHILL RI
4
Heath House Farm
Huntenhull Farm
Huntenhull Green
Dye House Farm
3
Frith Farm
Rodden Brook
Corsley Mill
47
JOLES LANE
Divers Bridge
Lady's Coppice
Frith House
BA12
Corsley CE Prim Sch
Manor Farm
2
Corsley
DEEP LANE
Pool Farm
Lye's Green
Tits Wood
Sheremarsh Wood
Court Farm
1
COURT LANE
Cross Keys Farm
PH
THE HOLLOW
Harpers Farm
Sandhayes
81
82
83
46

110

A
B
C
D
E
F
8
7
45
6
5
44
4
3
43
2
1
42
78
79
80
BUDGE LANE
A361
A361 Shepton Mallet
Marsh Farm
Bleets Farm
Elliots Green Farm
Lower Grange Farm
Elliots Green
Bollow Hill Farm
FRIGGLE STREET
Redford Water
MILL LANE
Stoneage Farm
Emblems Farm
Elliotts Farm
The Marsh
FELTHAM LANE
EAST WOODLANDS ROAD
Friggle Street Farm
High House Farm
Bollow Farm
Pool Farm
New Farm
SILVER LA
SHEPHERD'S LANE
Ragland Coppice
PH
Timbers Hill
Wraxall Hill
Shepherd's Wood
New Church Farm
Trails End
Cole Hill Farm
East Woodlands
BA11
Hales Castle
THE STALLS
Orchard Farm
Lower Hollies
Roddenbury Hill
Fort
Stalls Farm
Holly Bushes
The Tining
Upper Hollies
Black Coppice
Sand Walk Plantation
Lower Brambles
Lower Woods
Middle Brickhill
BA12
Brambles Farm
Upper Brambles
Longleat House
Trimby's White Marshes Plantation
BUNNS LA
Ashen Copse
Wrangles Wood
B3092
Gully Coppice
High Wood
Cowern Coppice
Gully Copse
Woodhouse Castle (rems of)
Fairbroad Coppice

118

111
116
A
B
C
D
E
F
Chipps Farm
PH
LANES END HILL
Lane End
RODDENBURY VW
GEYS HILL
Corsley Heath
THE HOLLOW
HEATHWAY
Park Farm
DEEP LANE
Cley Hill Farm
Corsley House
HEATH CL
BIRCHWOOD CL
A362
PH
PO
Dertfords
Whitbourne Moor
Popes Farm
Wardens Farm
THE STALLS
Temple Farm
SYDNALLS LANE
Whitbourne Farm
Sturford Mead Farm
Cley Hill Iron Age Hill Fort
Temple
Chapel Barton
STURFORD LANE
National Trust
Dertford's Wood
Temple Coppice
Sturford
Longhedge
Rushpool Farm
Whitbourne Springs
Reeves' Plantation
Winterbourne Screen
Rush Pool
Hares Batch
Green's Coppice
Gattrell's Bottom
King's Bottom
Longleat Safari Park
Hazel Coppice
Wind Hill
Half Mile Pond
BA12
LONGSCOMBE DRIVE
Longleat Park
Redway Bottom
Dod Pool
THE RED WAY
Park Hill
Weir
Centre Parcs Holiday Village
Park Hill Plain
Ford Pond
Weir
Deer Park
Aucombe Bottom
Aucombe
Petit Jean's Island Pond
Weir
Heaven's Gate
Great Island Pond
Nockatt Coppice
Nockatt Plain
Weir
Swancombe Bottom
Little Island Pond
Waterfall
Newbury Wood
8
7
45
6
5
44
4
3
43
2
1
42
82
83
119
116

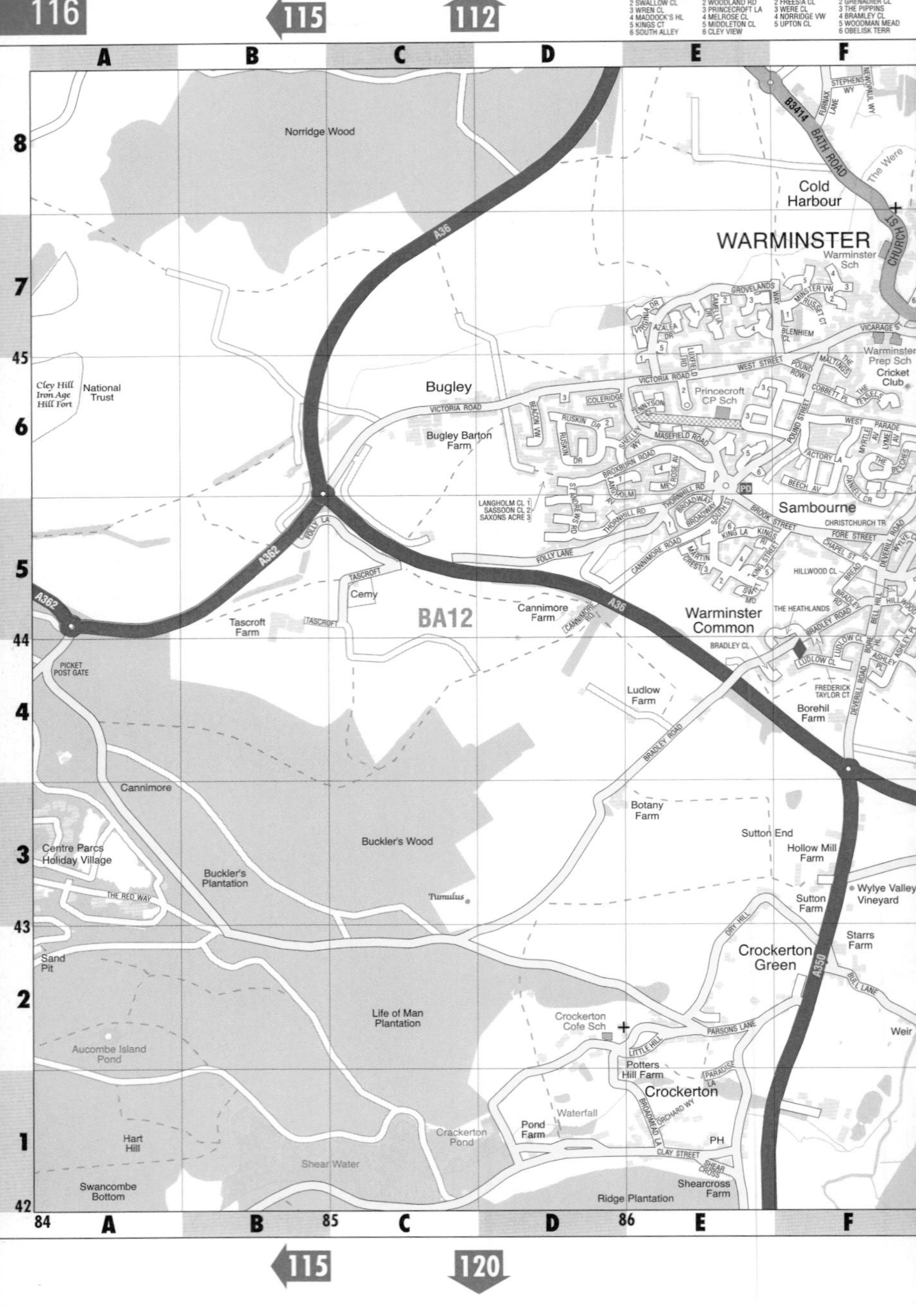
115
112
E5
1 THE HOMELANDS
2 SWALLOW CL
3 WREN CL
4 MADDOCK'S HL
5 KINGS CT
6 SOUTH ALLEY
E6
1 PAMPAS CT
2 WOODLAND RD
3 PRINCECROFT LA
4 MELROSE CL
5 MIDDLETON CL
6 CLEY VIEW
E7
1 PRIMROSE WK
2 FREESIA CL
3 WERE CL
4 NORRIDGE VW
5 UPTON CL
F7
1 CONFERENCE CL
2 GRENADIER CL
3 THE PIPPINS
4 BRAMLEY CL
5 WOODMAN MEAD
6 OBELISK TERR
A
B
C
D
E
F
8
7
45
6
5
44
4
3
43
2
1
42
Norridge Wood
A36
B3414
BATH ROAD
STEPHENS WY
FURNAX LANE
NEWPORT WY
The Were
Cold Harbour
CHURCH ST
WARMINSTER
Warminster Sch
GROVELANDS WAY
MINSTER VW
RUSSET CT
VIRGINIA DR
AZALEA DR
CAMELLIA DR
BLENHEIM CL
VICARAGE ST
Warminster Prep Sch
Cricket Club
POUND ROW
MALTINGS
THE TEASELS
COBBETT PL
LUXFIELD RD
WEST STREET
VICTORIA ROAD
Cley Hill Iron Age Hill Fort
National Trust
Bugley
Princecroft CP Sch
COLERIDGE CL
TENNYSON CL
BEACON VW
RUSKIN DR
MASEFIELD ROAD
SHELLEY WY
POUND STREET
WEST PARADE
MYRTLE AV
LYME AV
THE BEECHES
FACTORY LA
Bugley Barton Farm
BROXBURN ROAD
MELROSE AV
LANGHOLM AV
ST ANDREWS RD
THORNHILL RD
BROADWAY
SOUTH ST
PO
BEECH AV
DANIELL CR
Sambourne
LANGHOLM CL 1
SASSOON CL 2
SAXONS ACRE 3
BROOK STREET
CHRISTCHURCH TR
FORE STREET
KING LA
KINGS RI
KING STREET
CHAPEL ST
DEVERILL ROAD
WYLYE CL
A362
FOLLY LA
FOLLY LANE
CANNIMORE ROAD
MARTIN CREST
SWIFT MD
HILLWOOD CL
BREAD
TASCROFT
Cemy
BA12
Cannimore Farm
CANNIMORE RD
Tascroft Farm
Warminster Common
THE HEATHLANDS
BRADLEY ROAD
BRADLEY CL
LUDLOW CL
BORE HL
BELL HILL
HILLWOOD
ASHLEY PL
PICKET POST GATE
Ludlow Farm
FREDERICK TAYLOR CT
DEVERILL ROAD
Borehil Farm
Cannimore
Botany Farm
Centre Parcs Holiday Village
Buckler's Wood
Buckler's Plantation
Sutton End
Hollow Mill Farm
Wylye Valley Vineyard
THE RED WAY
Tumulus
Sutton Farm
Sand Pit
Starrs Farm
GREY HILL
Crockerton Green
A350
BULL LANE
Life of Man Plantation
Crockerton Cofe Sch
PARSONS LANE
Weir
Aucombe Island Pond
LITTLE HILL
Potters Hill Farm
PARADISE LA
Crockerton
BROADMEAD LA
ORCHARD WY
Waterfall
Pond Farm
Crackerton Pond
Hart Hill
PH
CLAY STREET
Shear Water
SHEAR CROSS
Swancombe Bottom
Shearcross Farm
Ridge Plantation
84
85
86
115
120

A8
1 BROADWOOD CL
2 ARN VW
3 SHERWOOD CL
4 SAVERNAKE CL
5 QUANTOCK CL
6 MENDIP CL
7 MALVERN CL
8 COTSWOLD CL
9 CHILTERN CL
10 BLACKDOWN CL
11 RECTORY CL
113
194
A
B
C
D
E
F
Arn Hill Down
Battlesbury Hill Fort
Battlesbury Hill
Tumulus
Tumuli
Battlesbury Wood
Tech Coll
Warminster
Ind Est Warminster
Avenue Cty Prim Sch
Liby & Dewey Museum
Hall
Depot
Battlesbury Bridge
Woodcock Ind Estate
Battlesbury Barracks
New Close CP Sch
Kingdown Community School
Warminster Town FC
Sports Centre & Swim Pool
St Johns CE Prim Sch
Boating Lake
Woodcock
The Were (Swan River)
St Georges RC Prim Sch
King Barrow
1 HERONSLADE
2 ST GEORGE'S CL
3 CORNER GND
Nature Reserve
Home Farm
Bishopstrow House (Hotel)
Boreham
B3414
BOREHAM ROAD
Knapp Farm
River Wylye
Weir
Henfords Marsh
BA12
Eastleigh Farm
Bishopstrow
Sewage Works
Butler Coombe Farm
Buffage Wood
A36
Woodcroft Wood
Eastleigh Wood
Blasketts Copse
Mast
West Heath
Southleigh Wood
Cooper's Bottom
The Commons Farm
Raxters Farm
Sutton Veny House
Robin Hood's Bower
Camp Farm
PH
Sutton Veny
EAST STREET
HIGH ST
MARKET PL
SILVER ST
GEORGE ST
EMWELL ST
SAMBOURNE GD
SAMBOURNE ROAD
WEYMOUTH STREET
WEYMOUTH ST
UPR MARSH RD
FERRIS MD
WYLYE ROAD
KENNET CL
MARSH STREET
LWR MARSH RD
UPPER MARSH LANE
SMALLBROOK ROAD
SMALLBROOK LANE
HENFORDS MARSH
MOUNT LA
FIVE ASH LANE
WESTBURY ROAD
ORCHARD CL
ELM HILL
IMBER ROAD
HOULDSWORTH AV
GOODWIN CLOSE
FIRBANK CR
PEPPER PLACE
IMBER AVENUE
WILSON SQUARE
WILSON SQ
MORLEY FIELD
THE UPLANDS
COPHEAP LANE
COPHEAP RISE
COPHEAP LA
HILLBOURNE CL
COTTON HOUSE GD
IMBERWOOD CL
WHITFIELD CLOSE
WOODCOCK RD
WOODCOCK ROAD
STATION RD
FAIRFIELD RD
THE RIDGEWAY
PLANTS GN
GIPSY LANE
ROCK LANE
BOREHAM FIELD
PRINCESS GD
QUEENS WY
HERONSLADE
BRADFIELD CLOSE
BARLEY CL
ST JOHN'S ROAD
PRESTBURY DRIVE
WILLOW CRES
SOUTHLEIGH VW
GRANGE LANE
BATTLESBURY ROAD
BISHOPSTROW ROAD
COBBETT RI
WATERY LANE
HIGH STREET
NORTON RD
DEVERILL ROAD
45
44
43
42
8
7
6
5
4
3
2
1
88
89

114

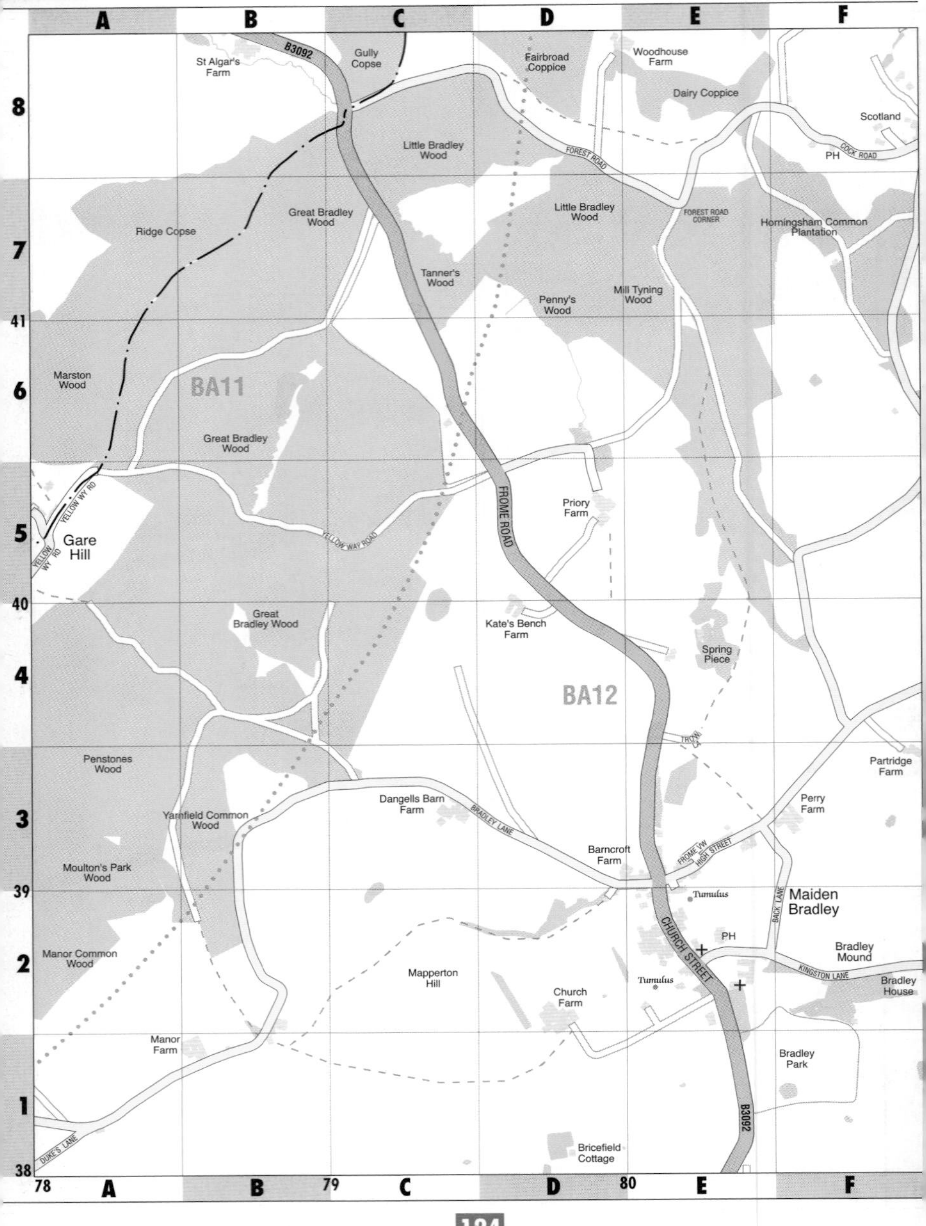
A
B
C
D
E
F
8
7
41
6
5
40
4
3
39
2
1
38
78
79
80
St Algar's Farm
B3092
Gully Copse
Fairbroad Coppice
Woodhouse Farm
Dairy Coppice
Scotland
PH
COCK ROAD
Little Bradley Wood
FOREST ROAD
Ridge Copse
Great Bradley Wood
Little Bradley Wood
FOREST ROAD CORNER
Horningsham Common Plantation
Tanner's Wood
Penny's Wood
Mill Tyning Wood
Marston Wood
BA11
Great Bradley Wood
FROME ROAD
YELLOW WY RD
Gare Hill
YELLOW WY RD
YELLOW WAY ROAD
Priory Farm
Great Bradley Wood
Kate's Bench Farm
Spring Piece
BA12
TROWL LA
Penstones Wood
Partridge Farm
Dangells Barn Farm
BRADLEY LANE
Perry Farm
Yarnfield Common Wood
Barncroft Farm
FROME VW
HIGH STREET
Moulton's Park Wood
Tumulus
BACK LANE
Maiden Bradley
CHURCH STREET
PH
Manor Common Wood
Bradley Mound
KINGSTON LANE
Mapperton Hill
Tumulus
Church Farm
Bradley House
Manor Farm
Bradley Park
B3092
DUKE'S LANE
Bricefield Cottage

124

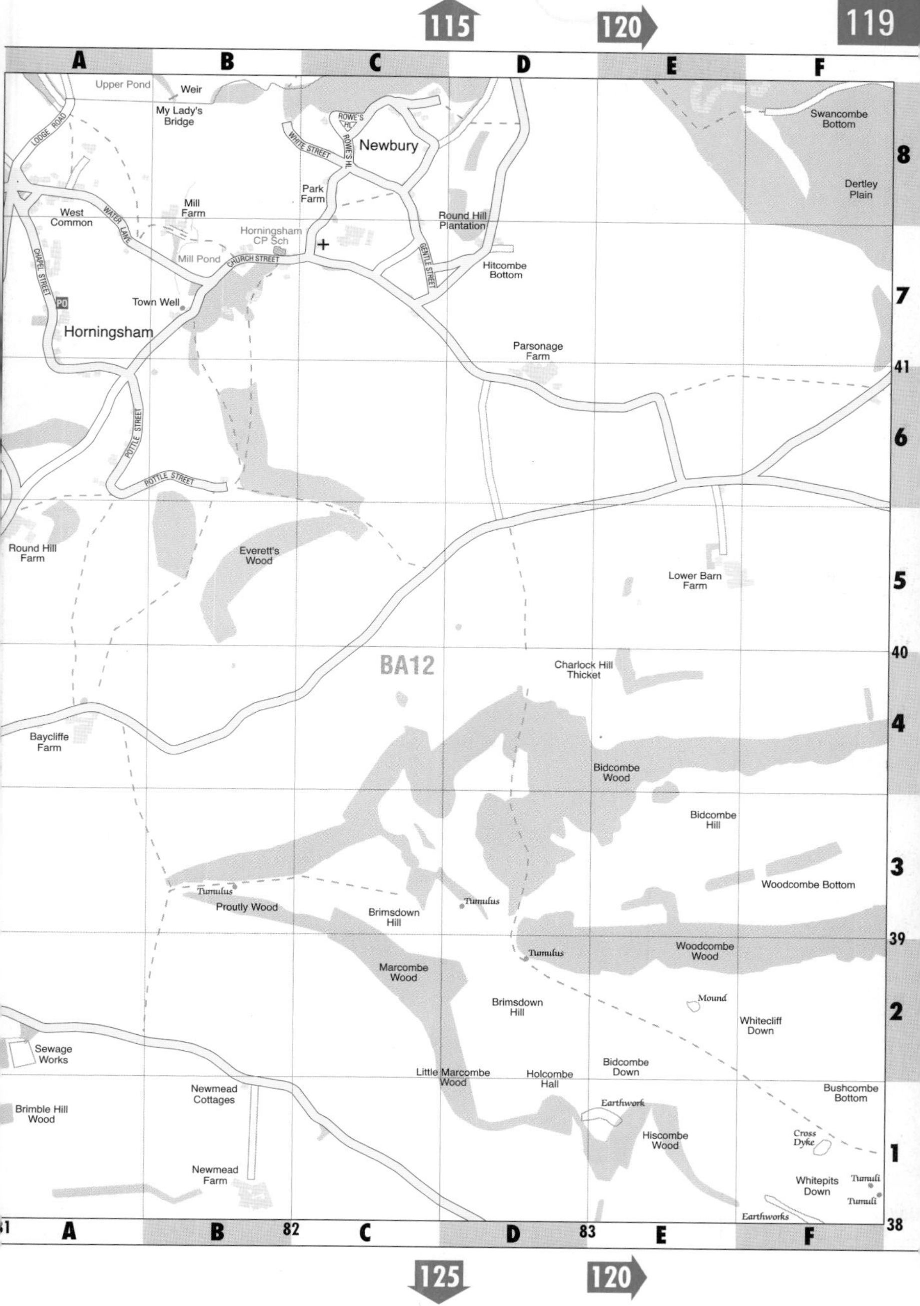
115
120
A
B
C
D
E
F
Upper Pond
Weir
My Lady's Bridge
LODGE ROAD
ROWE'S HL
WHITE STREET
Newbury
Swancombe Bottom
8
Dertley Plain
Park Farm
West Common
WATER LANE
Mill Farm
Round Hill Plantation
Horningsham CP Sch
CHAPEL STREET
Mill Pond
CHURCH STREET
GENTLE STREET
Hitcombe Bottom
PO
Town Well
7
Horningsham
Parsonage Farm
41
POTTLE STREET
6
Round Hill Farm
Everett's Wood
Lower Barn Farm
5
BA12
40
Charlock Hill Thicket
Baycliffe Farm
4
Bidcombe Wood
Bidcombe Hill
3
Tumulus
Proutly Wood
Brimsdown Hill
Woodcombe Bottom
Woodcombe Wood
39
Marcombe Wood
Mound
Brimsdown Hill
2
Whitecliff Down
Sewage Works
Little Marcombe Wood
Holcombe Hall
Bidcombe Down
Bushcombe Bottom
Newmead Cottages
Earthwork
Brimble Hill Wood
Hiscombe Wood
Cross Dyke
1
Newmead Farm
Whitepits Down
Tumuli
Earthworks
38
82
83
125
120

119
116

119
126

A
B
C
D
E
F
Henge
DEVERILL ROAD
The Beeches
Southleigh Wood
WALNUT CL
HIGH ST
DYMOCKS LA
South Leigh Farm
Lynchets
Pickle Farm
8
Sand Pit
Long Ivor Farm
Sandhill Farm
7
FROG LA
SAND ST
Longbridge Hill
41
PH
BA12
6
Sturgess Farm
Cow Down
Settlement
Manor Farm
A350
Whiten Hill
Haycombe Hill Bungalow
Tumulus
5
Haycombe Hill Farm
40
Littlecombe Hill
Tumulus
Field Barn Farm
Sutton Bottom
4
Lord's Hill Farm
3
Parsonage Down
Westcombe
39
SP3
A350
Tumuli
2
Little Down
Parsonage Down Farm
Tumulus
1
Tumuli
Beech Clump
Burnbake
Tumulus
38
7
88
89

A
B
C
D
E
F
8
7
37
6
5
36
4
3
35
2
1
34
72
73
74
Hents Hill Farm
CANNWOOD LANE
Canwood Farm
Hick's Park Wood
Walters Farm
Lipgate Farm
SOCK'S LANE
Forest Gate Farm
Lark Farm
HAMMER STREET
Border Farm
Longfield Farm
Horseshoe Farm
Brewham House
JAMES'S HILL
Jerrards Farm
Green Acres
PH
North Brewham
Treetops Farm
Cooks Farm
TILE HILL
River Brue
Brewham Lodge Farm
Bridge Farm
Mill Farm
PH
Street Farm
CHARCROFT HILL
Earthwork
BA10
STREET LANE
South Brewham
Brook Farm
Haven Farm
STREET LANE
Charcroft Farm
Holland Farm
King's Wood
CHARCROFT HILL
Shave Farm
SHAVE LANE
Jack's Castle Plantation
Tumulus
Macmillan Way
Hookgate Farm
TOWER ROAD
P
Hilcombe Farm
Convent Bottom
Alfred's Tower
Crawley House Farm
KINGSETTLE HILL
Hilcombe Hanging
Brewham Brake Farm
Cards Farm
Berridge
Tower Road Farm
Leland Trail
Brewham Wood
Hardway House
Pillinge Farm
Park Farm
Beaumont's Wood
Hardway
PH
Picketts Farm
Aaron's Hill
Picket's Copse
Moss Cottage
PEN HILL

136

124

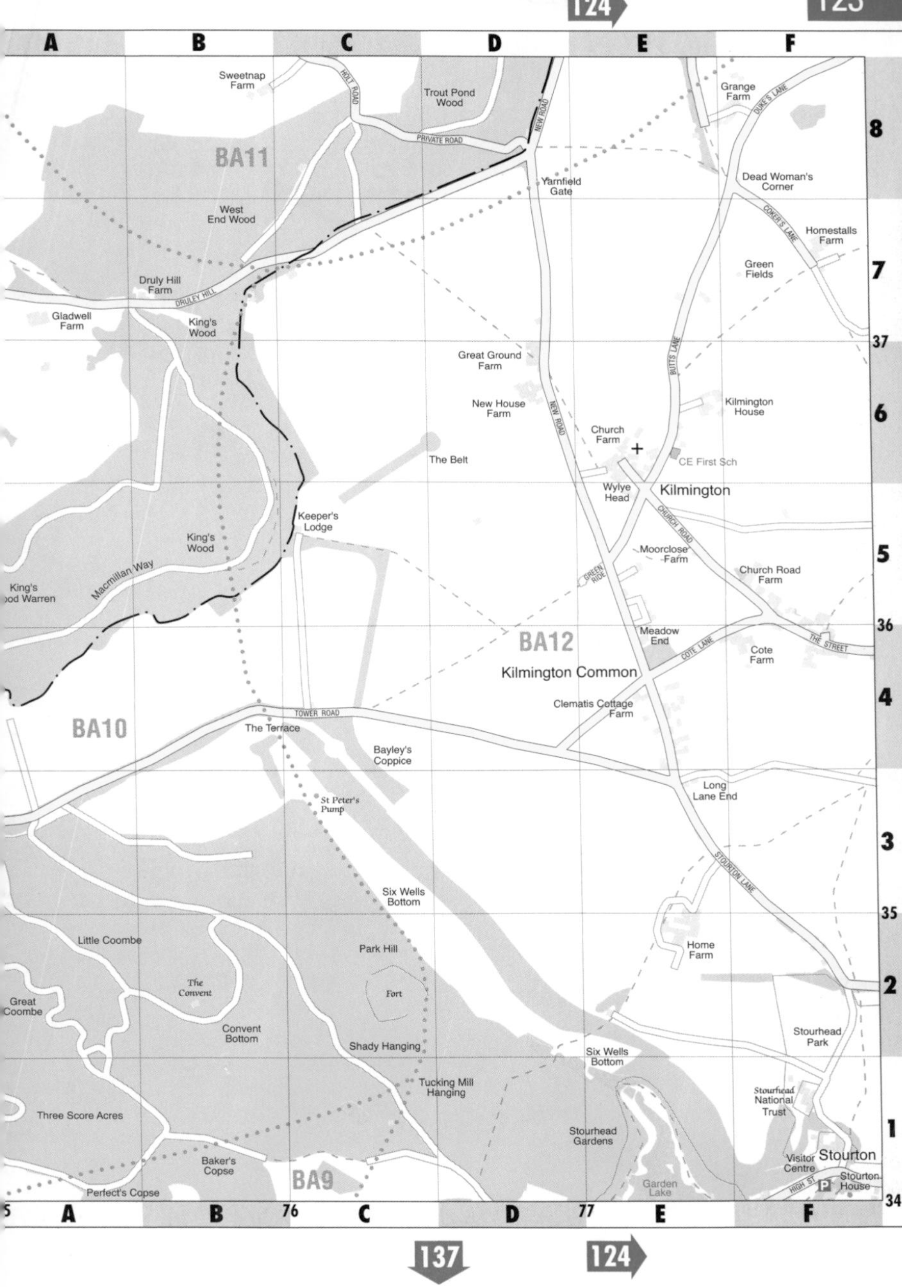
A
B
C
D
E
F
8
7
37
6
5
36
4
3
35
2
1
34
76
77
Sweetnap Farm
Trout Pond Wood
HOLT ROAD
PRIVATE ROAD
NEW ROAD
Grange Farm
DUKE'S LANE
BA11
Yarnfield Gate
Dead Woman's Corner
West End Wood
COKER'S LANE
Homestalls Farm
Green Fields
Druly Hill Farm
DRULEY HILL
Gladwell Farm
King's Wood
Great Ground Farm
BUTTS LANE
New House Farm
Kilmington House
Church Farm
The Belt
CE First Sch
Wylye Head
Kilmington
Keeper's Lodge
CHURCH ROAD
King's Wood
Moorclose Farm
Macmillan Way
King's
ood Warren
GREEN RIDE
Church Road Farm
BA12
Meadow End
THE STREET
COTE LANE
Cote Farm
Kilmington Common
Clematis Cottage Farm
BA10
TOWER ROAD
The Terrace
Bayley's Coppice
Long Lane End
St Peter's Pump
STOURTON LANE
Six Wells Bottom
Park Hill
Home Farm
Little Coombe
The Convent
Fort
Great Coombe
Convent Bottom
Stourhead Park
Shady Hanging
Six Wells Bottom
Tucking Mill Hanging
Stourhead National Trust
Three Score Acres
Stourhead Gardens
Baker's Copse
Visitor Centre
Stourton
BA9
Perfect's Copse
Garden Lake
HIGH ST
P
Stourton House

137
124

123
118

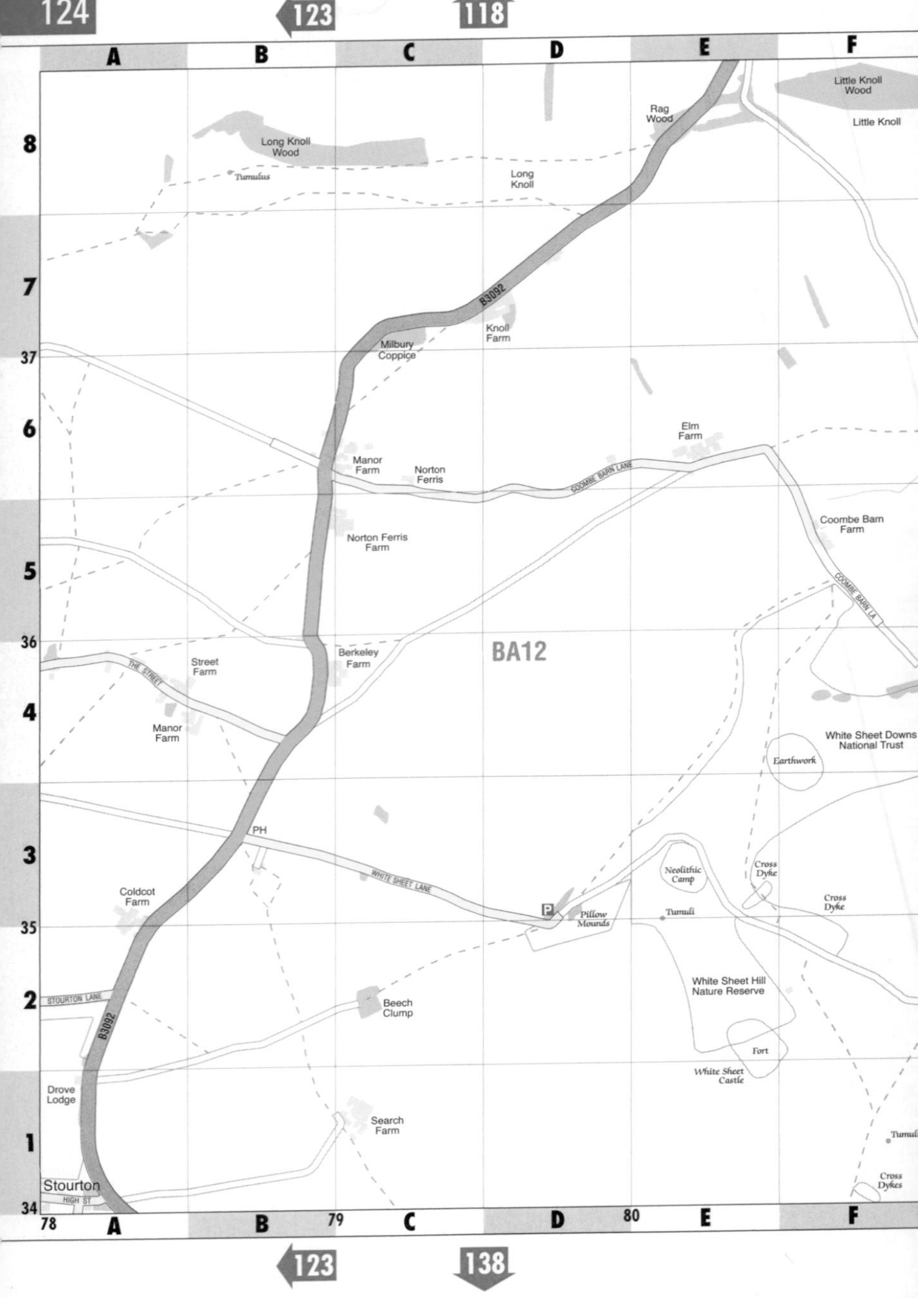

123
138

119
126
A
B
C
D
E
F
Bidcombe Down
Earthworks
Whitepits Down
8
Dairy Farm
Tumulus
Tumulus
River Wylye
7
37
Truncombe Wood
Peter's Penning
Tumulus
Bath Wilts & North Dorset Gliding Club
6
Court Hill
Court Hill Plantation
Rodmead Farm
Tumulus
The Park
Tumulus
5
Rodmead Hill
Danes' Bottom
BA12
36
Tumuli
Earthwork
Tumuli
Rodmead Wood
Cleeve
Danes' Bottom
4
Tumulus
Tumulus
Earthwork
Tumulus
South Down
Cross Dyke
3
The Drusses
Mere Down
Tumulus
35
Tumuli
Pond Bottom
Tumulus
B3095
Mast
2
Mere Down Farm
Cross Dyke
Tumulus
Tumuli
Tumulus
Danger Area
Mere Down
Earthworks
Tumulus
1
Great Bottom
Charnage Down
34
81
82
83
139
126

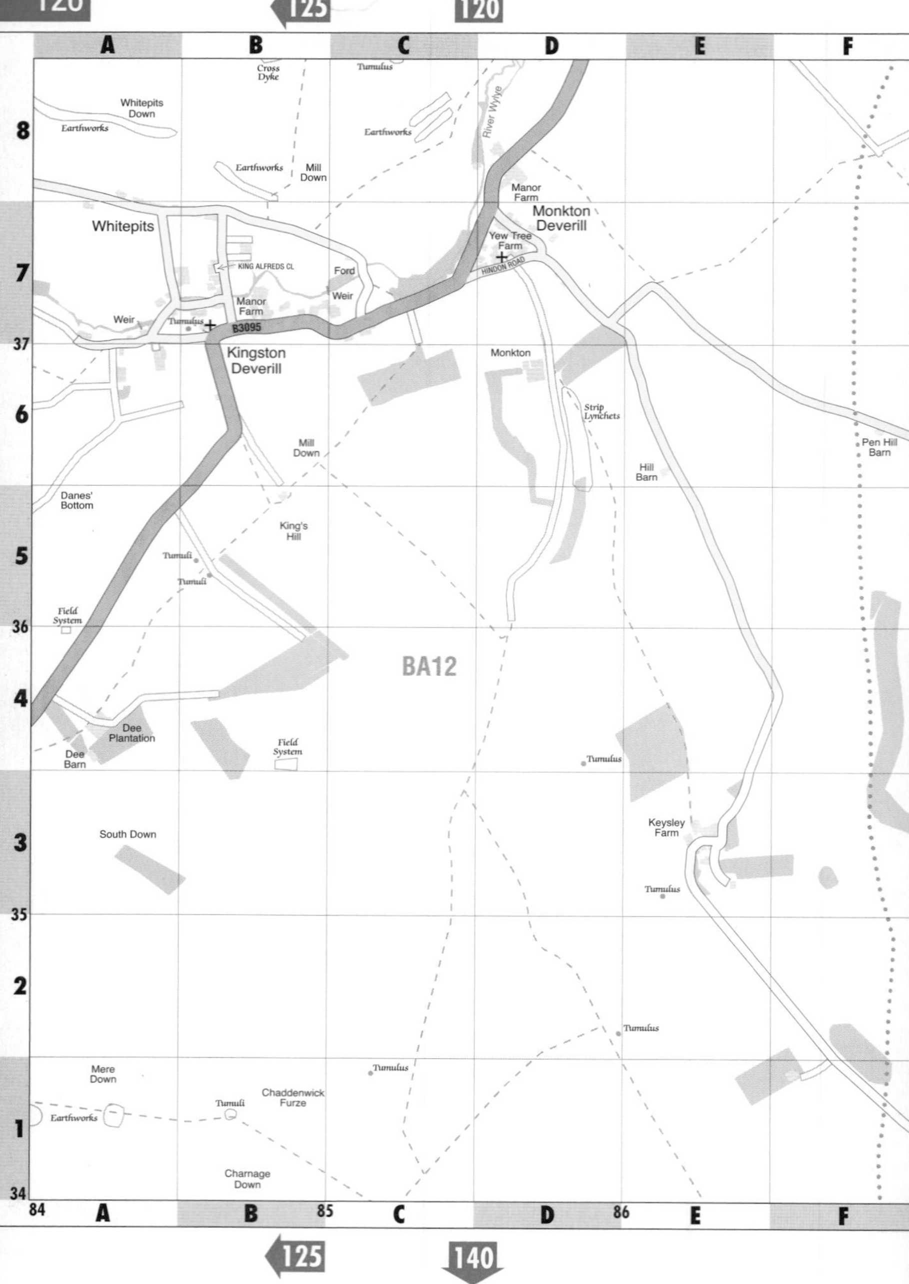
A
B
C
D
E
F
8
7
37
6
5
36
4
3
35
2
1
34
84
85
86
Cross Dyke
Tumulus
Whitepits Down
Earthworks
Earthworks
River Wylye
Earthworks
Mill Down
Manor Farm
Monkton Deverill
Whitepits
Yew Tree Farm
KING ALFREDS CL
Ford
HINDON ROAD
Weir
Manor Farm
Weir
Tumulus
B3095
Kingston Deverill
Monkton
Strip Lynchets
Mill Down
Pen Hill Barn
Hill Barn
Danes' Bottom
King's Hill
Tumuli
Tumuli
Field System
BA12
Dee Plantation
Dee Barn
Field System
Tumulus
South Down
Keysley Farm
Tumulus
Tumulus
Mere Down
Tumulus
Chaddenwick Furze
Tumuli
Earthworks
Charnage Down

A
B
C
D
E
F
Summerslade Down
Field System
Long Barrow
Tumulus
Pertwood Down
Rook Hill
Pertwood Wood
Tumulus
Field System
Tumulus
A350
Tumulus
Botley Oak Brake
Pen Hill Down
Earthwork
Lower Pertwood
SP3
SP3
Pen Hill
St Peter's Church
Pertwood Manor Farm
Higher Pertwood
Tumulus
Upper Pertwood Bushes
Bockerly Hill
Bockerly Coppice
A350
Keysley Down
Field Barn
Tumulus
Knoyle Down Farm
Long Barrow
Tumulus
A350
A303
Tumulus
8
7
37
6
5
36
4
3
35
2
1
34
87
88
89

201
196

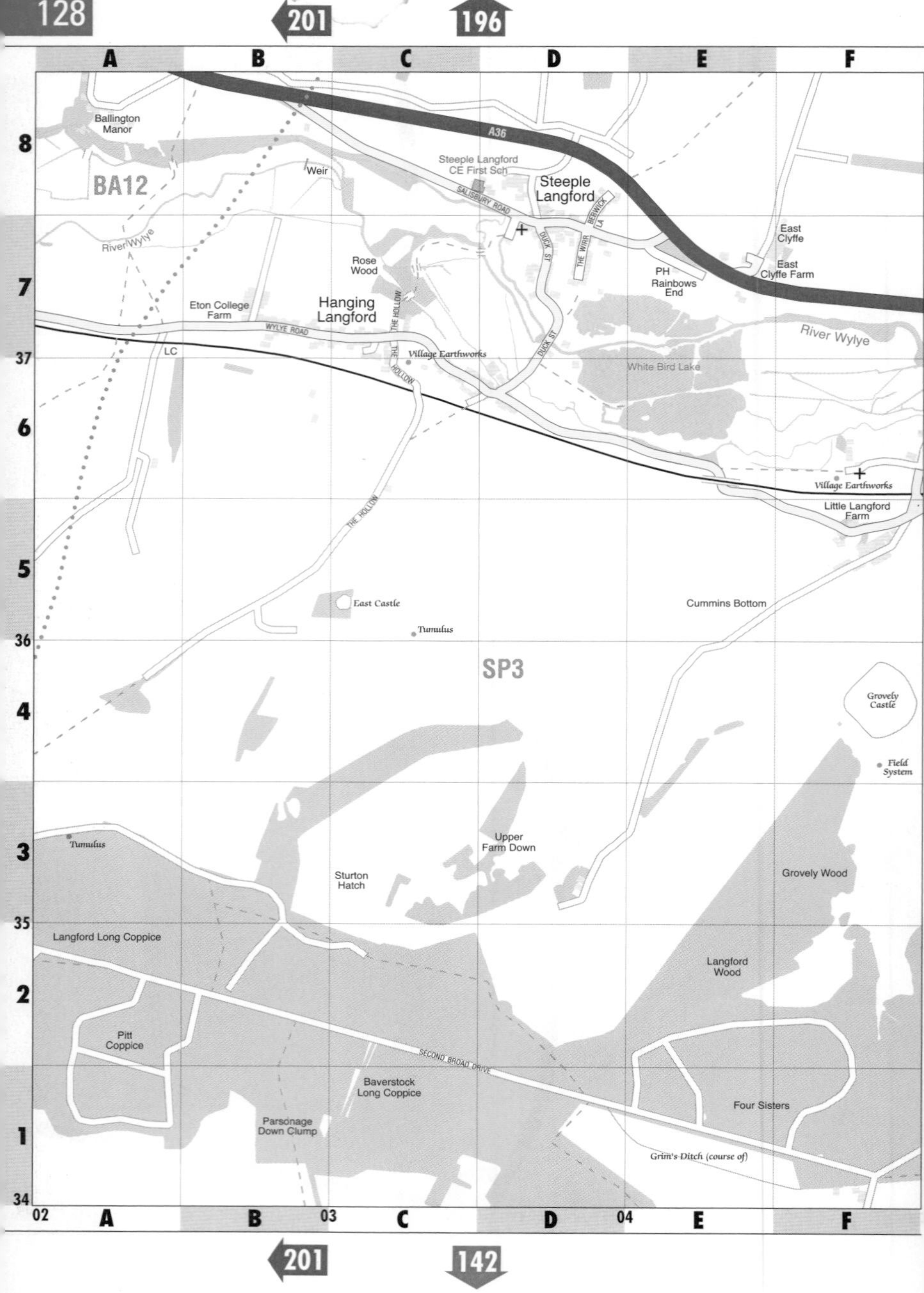

201
142

A
B
C
D
E
F
8
7
37
6
5
36
4
3
35
2
1
34
05
06
07
Stapleford Castle Ring & Bailey
Manor Farm
Bury Bridge
UPPINGTON LANE
RIVERSIDE TR
PO
Brooklet Farm
HILL SIDE
CHURCH FURLONG
B3083
BUTTS HL
Stapleford
BERWICK ROAD
CHAPEL LA
A36
P
Mast
Serrington
CHAIN HILL
CHAIN DROVE
PH
Ford
Little Langford
Hungerford Lodge Farm
Kingsmead Bridge
SP3
Little Wishford
Little Wishford Farm
River Wylye
Strip Lynchets
Manor Farm
PH
LANGFORD RD
FARM LA
MANOR
WEST ST
Ebsbury
Field System
SP2
Ebsbury Hill
Ebsbury Copse
Settlement
Great Wishford
STATION ROAD
Field System
Monarch's Way
Penning Bottom
GROVELY ROAD
Penning Bottom
Hadden Hill
Grovely Wood
Hadden
FIRST BROAD DRIVE
Heath Hill

129
197

129
144

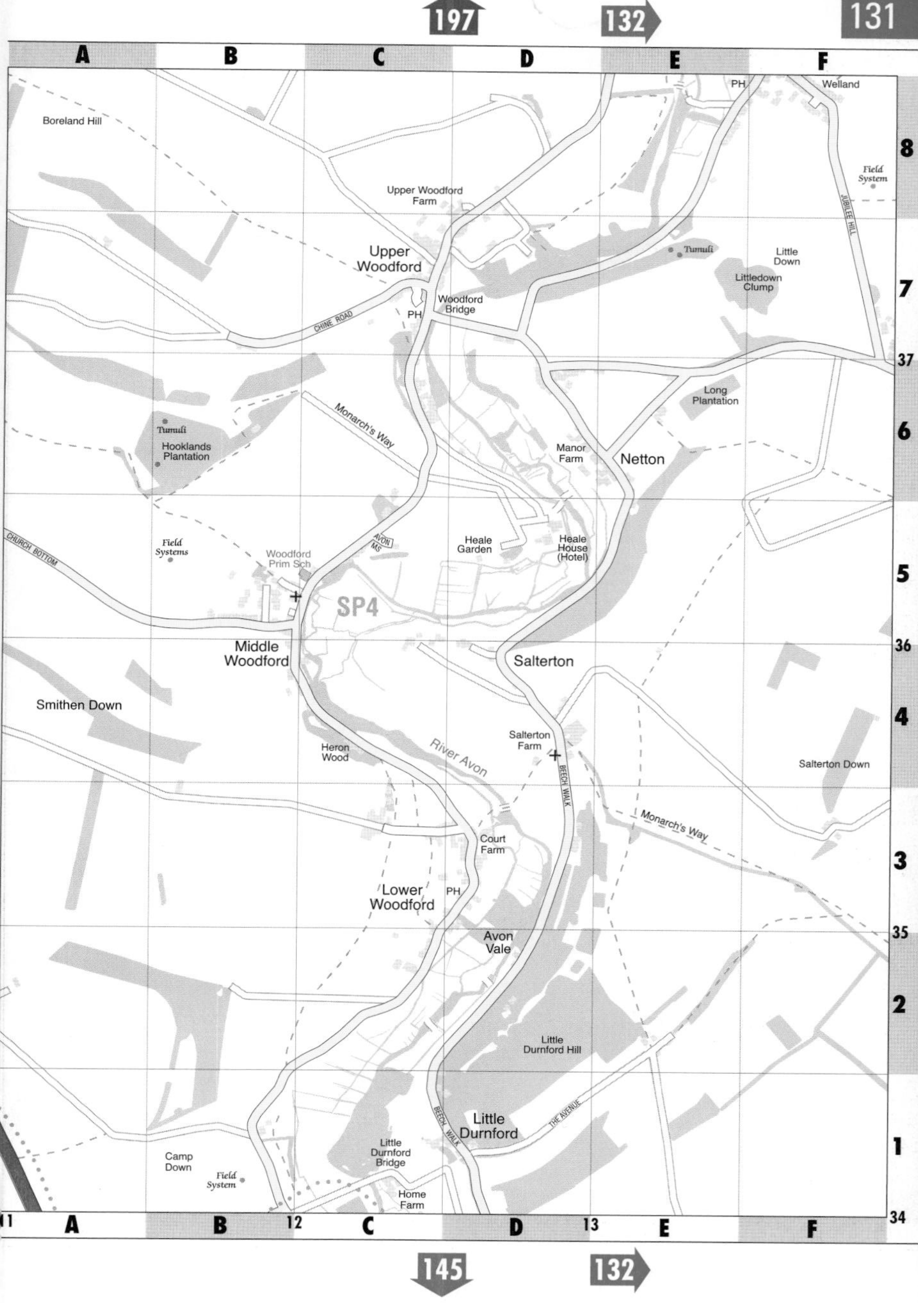
197
132
A
B
C
D
E
F
8
7
37
6
5
36
4
3
35
2
1
34
11
12
13
145
132
Boreland Hill
Upper Woodford Farm
Upper Woodford
Woodford Bridge
PH
CHINE ROAD
Welland
Field System
JUBILEE HILL
Tumuli
Little Down
Littledown Clump
Long Plantation
Monarch's Way
Tumuli
Hooklands Plantation
Manor Farm
Netton
CHURCH BOTTOM
Field Systems
Woodford Prim Sch
AVON MS
Heale Garden
Heale House (Hotel)
SP4
Middle Woodford
Salterton
Smithen Down
Heron Wood
River Avon
Salterton Farm
BEECHE WALK
Salterton Down
Court Farm
Lower Woodford
Avon Vale
Little Durnford Hill
BEECH WALK
THE AVENUE
Little Durnford
Little Durnford Bridge
Camp Down
Field System
Home Farm

131
198

131
146

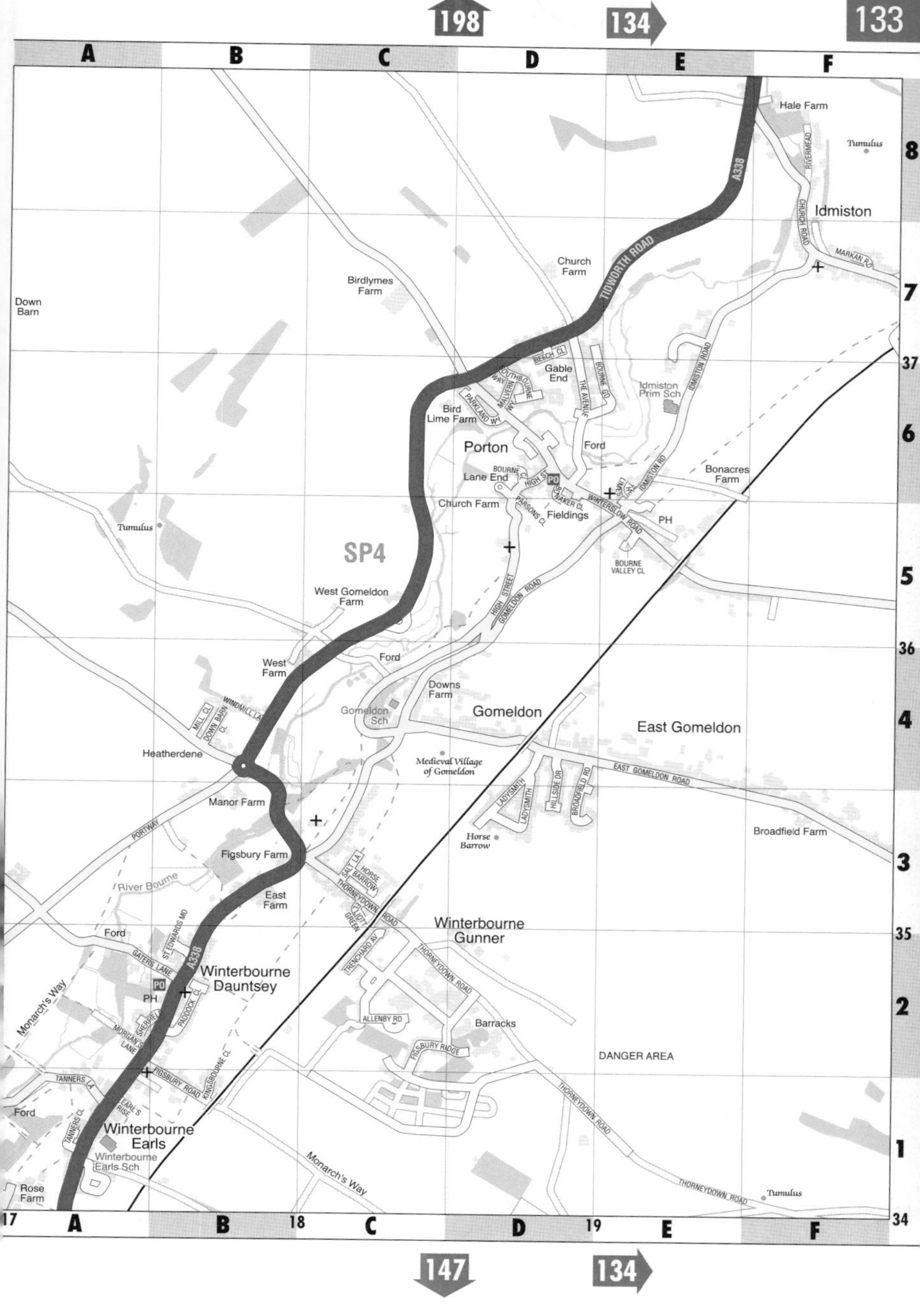
198
134
A
B
C
D
E
F
Hale Farm
Tumulus
RIVERMEAD
A338
Idmiston
CHURCH ROAD
MARKAN RD
Church Farm
TIDWORTH ROAD
Birdlymes Farm
Down Barn
BEECH CL
Gable End
BOURNE GD
THE AVENUE
SOUTHBOURNE WAY
MALVERN WY
PARKLAND WY
Bird Lime Farm
Idmiston Prim Sch
IDMISTON ROAD
Porton
Ford
Bonacres Farm
BOURNE CL
HIGH ST
PO
Lane End
IDMISTON RD
BAKER CL
WINTERSLOW ROAD
Church Farm
PARSONS CL
Fieldings
PH
Tumulus
SP4
BOURNE VALLEY CL
HIGH STREET
GOMELDON ROAD
West Gomeldon Farm
West Farm
Ford
Downs Farm
WINDMILL LA
MILL CL
DOWN BARN CL
Gomeldon Sch
Gomeldon
East Gomeldon
Heatherdene
Medieval Village of Gomeldon
EAST GOMELDON ROAD
LADYSMITH
HILLSIDE DR
BROADFIELD RD
Manor Farm
PORTWAY
Horse Barrow
Broadfield Farm
Figsbury Farm
SALT LA
HORSE BARROW
River Bourne
THORNEYDOWN ROAD
East Farm
FLIGHT GREEN
Winterbourne Gunner
Ford
ST EDWARDS MD
GATERS LANE
A338
Winterbourne Dauntsey
TRENCHARD AV
THORNEYDOWN ROAD
PO
PH
PADDOCK CL
SHERFIELD
Monarch's Way
MORGAN'S LANE
ALLENBY RD
Barracks
FIGSBURY RIDGE
DANGER AREA
KINGSBOURNE CL
TANNERS LA
FIGSBURY ROAD
EARL'S RISE
THORNEYDOWN ROAD
Ford
TANNERS CL
Winterbourne Earls
Winterbourne Earls Sch
Monarch's Way
Rose Farm
THORNEYDOWN ROAD
Tumulus
8
7
37
6
5
36
4
3
35
2
1
34
17
18
19
147
134

133
199

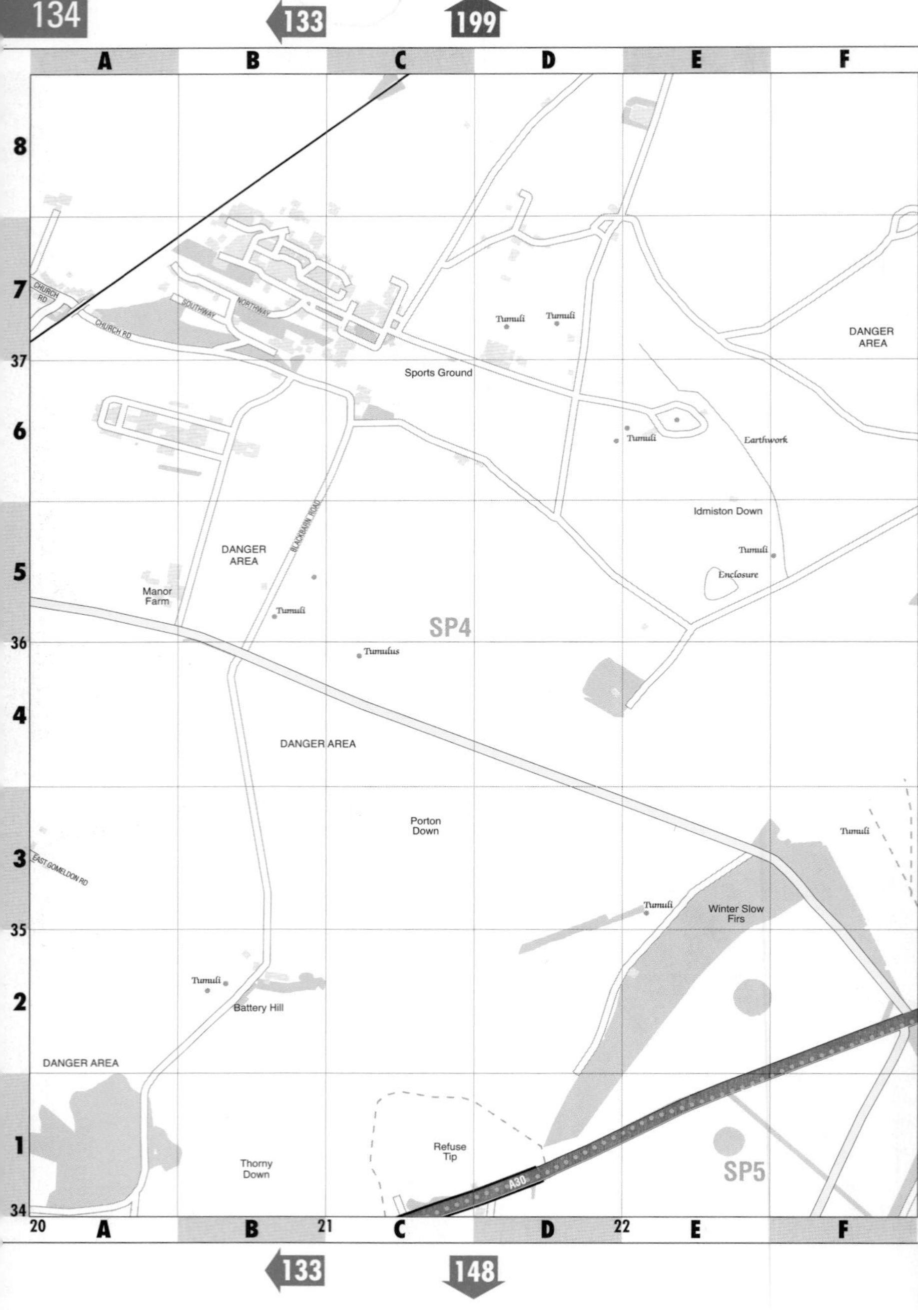

133
148

A B C D E F
8
7
37
6
5
36
4
3
35
2
1
34
North Hampshire STREET ATLAS
A343 Andover
A30 Stockbridge
Earthwork
DANGER AREA
Boscombe Down East
Enclosure
Isle of Wight Hill
Franklin's Well
Tumulus
Forty Acre Plantation
Earthwork
SP4
Earthwork
Blake's Firs
Easton Down
Earthwork
Roche Court Down
A343
Little Firs Farm
Earthwork
LOPCOMBE CORNER
Firs Farm
A30
Lopcombe Corner Farm
Popple Down Farm
Valley Farm
Easton Down Farm
Tumuli
The Pheasant Hotel
A30
Popple Light Copse
SP5
Gutteridge Farm
Ashley's Copse
Howe Copse
Roche Court
Ramshill Copse
3 A B 24 C D 25 E F

122

A
B
C
D
E
F
8
7
33
6
5
32
4
3
31
2
1
30
72
73
74
BA10
Bedlam Green Farm
Coach Road Farm
Leland Trail
Macmillan Way
Blackslough Wood
PEN HILL
Walk Copse
Walk Farm
New Park Farm
Newpark Pond
Newpark Wood
Barrow Lane Farm
Barrow Water Farm
GREY'S CORNER
Horseacres Farm
Cherry Tree Farm
Barrow Corner Farm
Barrow
BARROW WATER LANE
BARROW LANE
Coneygore Wood
Homestead Farm
Stavordale Priory
Motte & Bailey
Somerlea Farm
Canons Farm
Sewage Works
BA9
Cockroad Wood
Common Farm
BARROW LANE
PH
Charlton Musgrove
Brickhouse Farm
Higher Shalford Farm
SHALFORD LANE
Thorney Copse Farm
Monarch's Way
B3081
Pen Forest
Knapp Farm
Rectory Farm
Southmarsh
PARSONAGE LANE
South Marsh Farm
Home Farm
Hillside Farm
RECTORY LANE
Monarch's Way
Greenlands Farm
Bridle Farm
Lower Church Farm
Bitwood Farm
Belmont Farm
Encie Farm

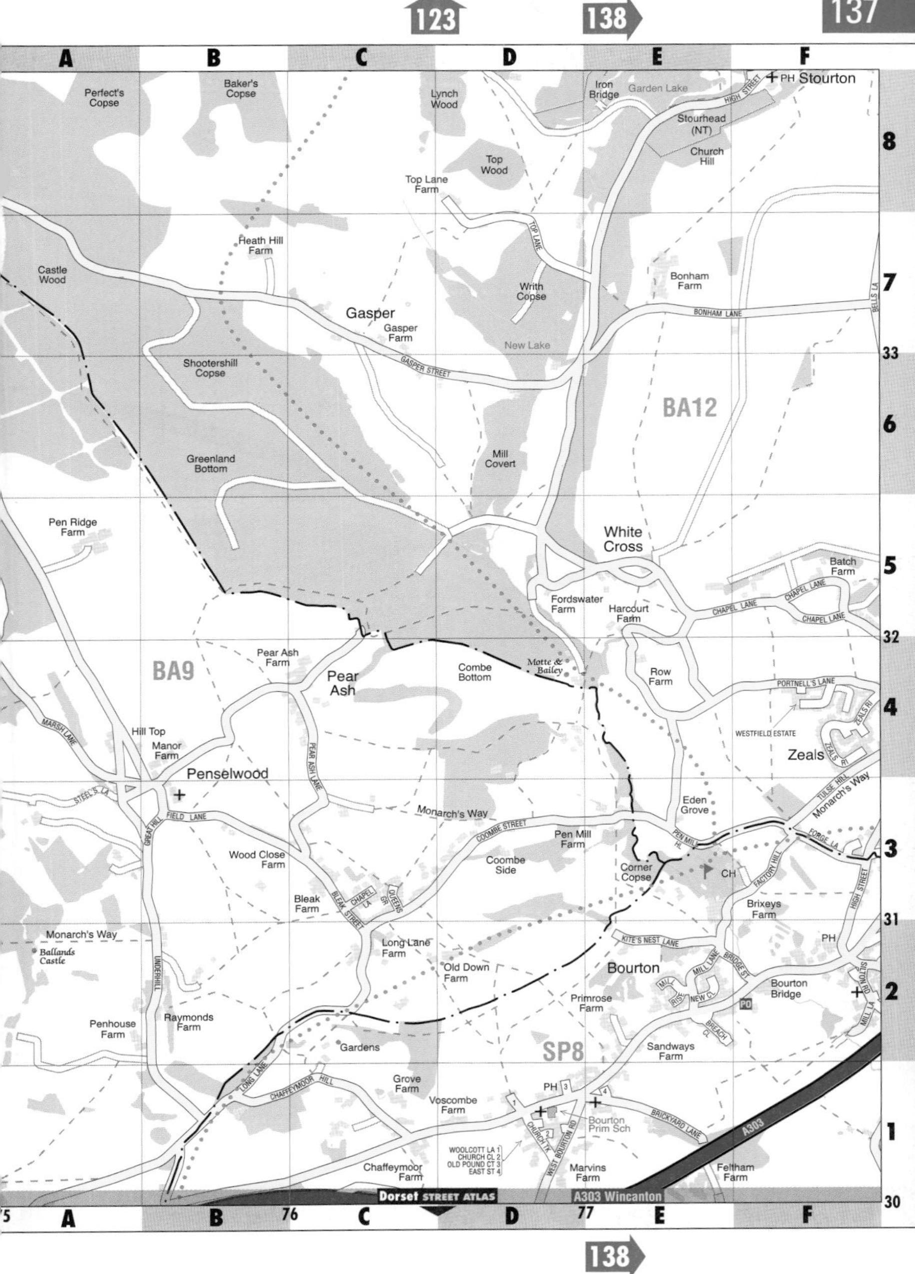
A
B
C
D
E
F
Perfect's Copse
Baker's Copse
Lynch Wood
Iron Bridge
Garden Lake
PH Stourton
HIGH STREET
Stourhead (NT)
Church Hill
Top Wood
Top Lane Farm
TOP LANE
8
Heath Hill Farm
Castle Wood
Writh Copse
Bonham Farm
7
Gasper
Gasper Farm
BONHAM LANE
BELLS LA
New Lake
33
GASPER STREET
Shootershill Copse
BA12
6
Greenland Bottom
Mill Covert
Pen Ridge Farm
White Cross
5
Batch Farm
Fordswater Farm
Harcourt Farm
CHAPEL LANE
32
Pear Ash Farm
BA9
Pear Ash
Combe Bottom
Motte & Bailey
Row Farm
PORTNELL'S LANE
4
MARSH LANE
Hill Top
Manor Farm
PEAR ASH LANE
WESTFIELD ESTATE
ZEALS RI
Zeals
Penselwood
STEEL'S LA
FIELD LANE
Monarch's Way
Eden Grove
TULSE HILL
GREAT HILL
COOMBE STREET
Pen Mill Farm
PEN MILL HL
FORGE LA
3
Wood Close Farm
Coombe Side
Corner Copse
CH
FACTORY HILL
Bleak Farm
CHAPEL LA
QUEENS GR
BLEAK STREET
Brixeys Farm
HIGH STREET
31
Monarch's Way
Ballands Castle
Long Lane Farm
KITE'S NEST LANE
PH
UNDERHILL
Old Down Farm
Bourton
MILL LANE
BRIDGE ST
MILL RISE
NEW CL
OLD STATION
Bourton Bridge
2
Penhouse Farm
Raymonds Farm
Primrose Farm
PO
MILL LA
BREACH CL
Gardens
SP8
Sandways Farm
LONG LANE
CHAFFEYMOOR HILL
Grove Farm
PH
Voscombe Farm
Bourton Prim Sch
BRICKYARD LANE
A303
1
CHURCH TK
WEST BOURTON RD
WOOLCOTT LA 1
CHURCH CL 2
OLD POUND CT 3
EAST ST 4
Chaffeymoor Farm
Marvins Farm
Feltham Farm
A303 Wincanton
30
75
76
77

137
124

A B C D E F
8 7 33 6 5 32 4 3 31 2 1 30
78 79 80
BA12
SP8
Cross Dykes
Wood Farm
Zeals Knoll
Nor Wood
MERE BY-PASS
Mere Castle (site of)
Tumuli
Recn Gd
Long Hill
Quarry Fields Industrial Estate
Quarry Cottages
CADDY LA
UNDERHILL
HOMEFIELD
LONG HL
BRAMLEY HILL
HILLSIDE CL
PROSPECT PL
B3095 CASTLE STREET
TOWNSEND CL
Town End
Greenhouses
B3092
A303
CRAB LANE
BELLS LANE
MANOR ROAD
Long Cross
Lower Zeals
Manor Farm
Zeals House
Castle Ground Farm
St Martin Farm
Zeals First Sch
PO
PH
CHAPEL LANE
PORTNELL'S LA
ZEALS GN DR
TULSE HILL
NEW ROAD
Zeals
Wolverton
Monarch's Way
Zeals Fish Farm
South Lodge
NEW RD
Queen Oak
FANTLEY LANE
TAN LA
Bagmore Wood
Silton Wood
Mapperton Hill Farm
MAPPERTON HILL
Redmoor Farm
CHURCH ROAD
Fitz Farm
DUNN'S LANE
Bagmore Farm
SLODBROOK LANE
Ridge Hill Farm

137

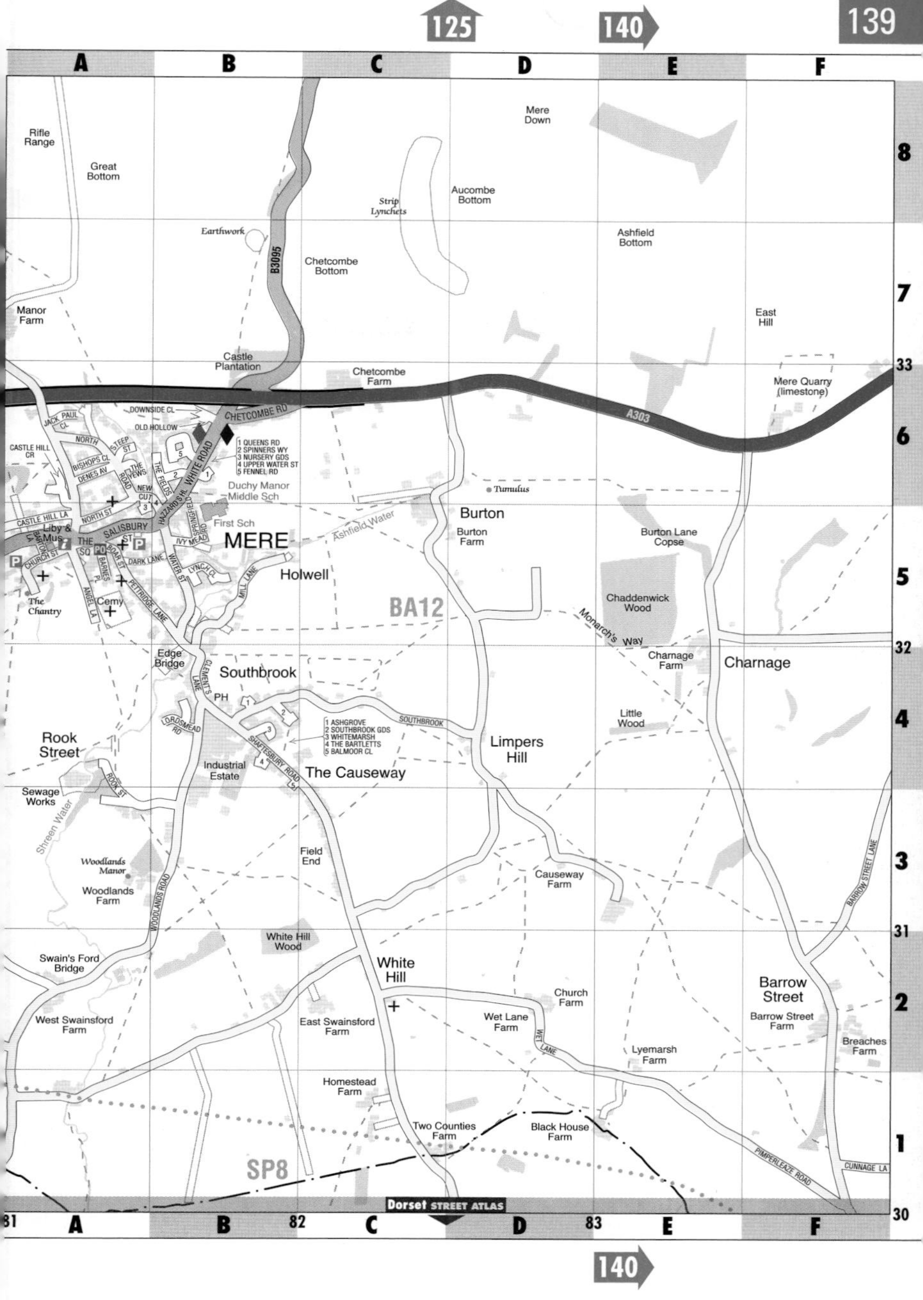
125
140
139
A
B
C
D
E
F
Rifle Range
Great Bottom
Mere Down
Aucombe Bottom
Strip Lynchets
Earthwork
B3095
Chetcombe Bottom
Ashfield Bottom
Manor Farm
East Hill
Castle Plantation
Chetcombe Farm
Mere Quarry (limestone)
A303
JACK PAUL CL
DOWNSIDE CL
OLD HOLLOW
CHETCOMBE RD
CASTLE HILL CR
NORTH ST
STEEP ST
BISHOPS CL
DENES AV
THE MEWS
ROAD
THE FIELDS
WHITE ROAD
NEW CUT
1 QUEENS RD
2 SPINNERS WY
3 NURSERY GDS
4 UPPER WATER ST
5 FENNEL RD
Duchy Manor Middle Sch
Tumulus
CASTLE HILL LA
NORTH ST
HAZZARD'S HL
SPRINGFIELD RD
First Sch
Burton
Liby & Mus
SALISBURY ST
MERE
Ashfield Water
Burton Farm
Burton Lane Copse
BARTON LA
THE SQ
BOAR ST
IVY MEAD
CHURCH ST
DARK LANE
WATER ST
LYNCH CL
BARNES PL
MILL LANE
Holwell
Chaddenwick Wood
The Chantry
Cemy
ANGEL LA
PETTRIDGE LANE
BA12
Monarch's Way
Edge Bridge
Southbrook
CLEMENT'S LANE
Charnage Farm
Charnage
PH
LORDSMEAD RD
1 ASHGROVE
2 SOUTHBROOK GDS
3 WHITEMARSH
4 THE BARTLETTS
5 BALMOOR CL
SOUTHBROOK
Little Wood
Rook Street
Limpers Hill
SHAFTESBURY ROAD
Industrial Estate
The Causeway
ROOK ST
Sewage Works
Shreen Water
Field End
Woodlands Manor
Woodlands Farm
WOODLANDS ROAD
Causeway Farm
BARROW STREET LANE
White Hill Wood
Swain's Ford Bridge
White Hill
Church Farm
Barrow Street
West Swainsford Farm
East Swainsford Farm
Wet Lane Farm
WET LANE
Barrow Street Farm
Lyemarsh Farm
Breaches Farm
Homestead Farm
Two Counties Farm
Black House Farm
PIMPERLEAZE ROAD
CUNNAGE LA
SP8
Dorset STREET ATLAS
8
7
33
6
5
32
4
3
31
2
1
30
81
82
83
140

139
126

139
202

A
B
C
D
E
F
Keysley Down
A303
Two Mile Down
Willoughby Hedge
B3089
Chapel Field Barn
Kemps Barn
B3089
Tumulus
Holden Farm
Monarch's Way
A350
Monarch's Way
Peaked Field Coppice
Upton Bottom Farm
Upton
SUTTON BOTTOM
SP3
WISE LANE
Haddon Hill
Haddon Acre
TOUCHORNE LANE
Sheephouse Farm
Milton
Clouds Farm
Milton Farm
Steeple Close
PH
The Green
Barns Hill
Terrace Wood
NEW ROAD
Warminster Plantation
Mill
Park Farm
WISE LANE
Clouds House
Coombe Bottom
Hindon Plantation
Knoyle Corner
Knoyle Ridge
SANDPIT PL
East Knoyle
HINDON ROAD
PO
Sandpit Coppice
CHURCH RAILS
Summerleaze Pond
Holloway
MILLBROOK LA
A350
Wessex Ridgeway
THE STREET
MILLBROOK LANE
HOLLOWAY LANE
Park Coppice
Great Ground Coppice
Sewage Works
PH
8
7
33
6
5
32
4
3
31
2
1
30
A
B
88
C
D
89
E
F

201
128

201
205

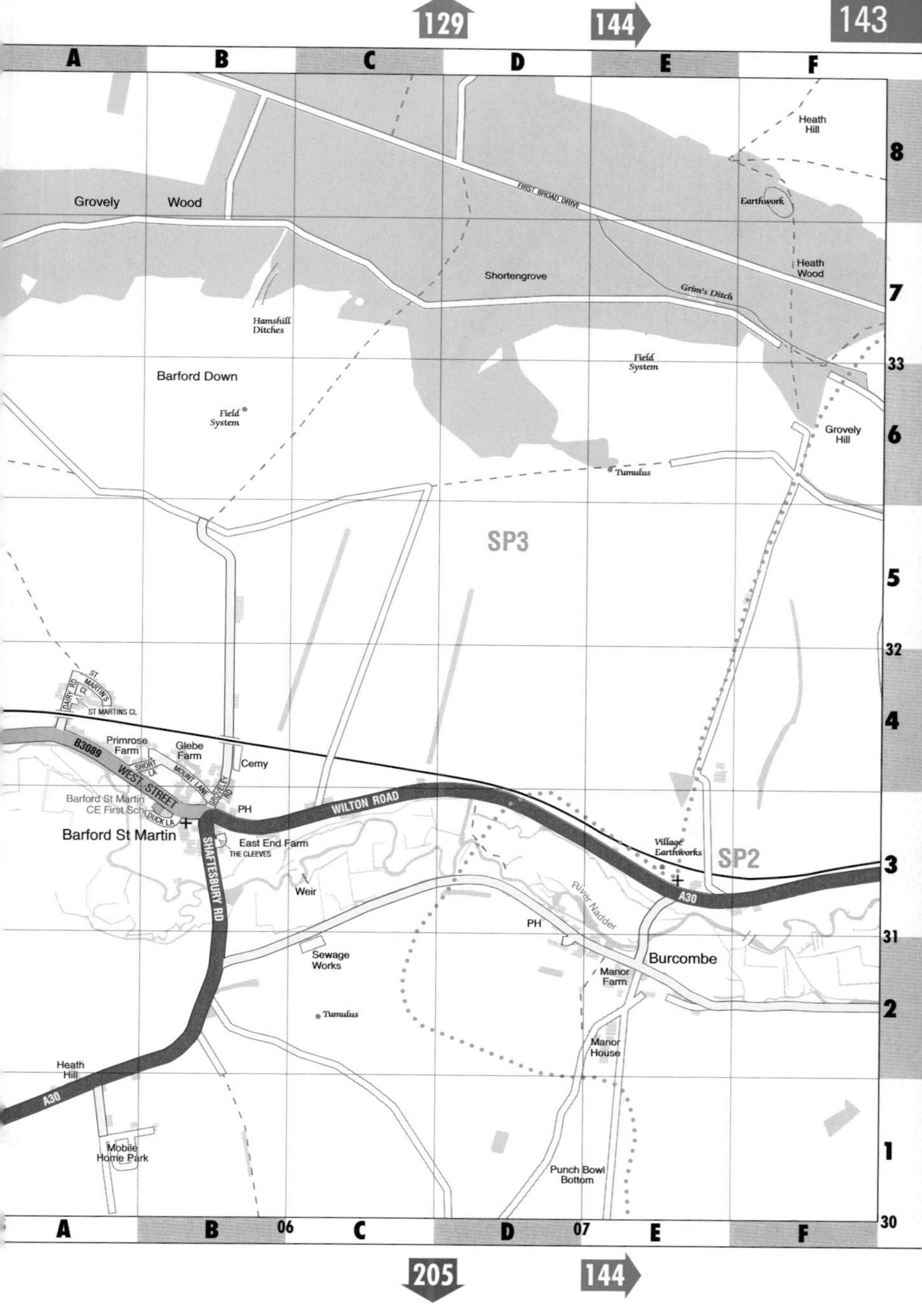
129
144
A
B
C
D
E
F
8
7
6
5
4
3
2
1
33
32
31
30
06
07
Heath Hill
Earthwork
Grovely
Wood
FIRST BROAD DRIVE
Heath Wood
Shortengrove
Grim's Ditch
Hamshill Ditches
Field System
Barford Down
Field System
Grovely Hill
Tumulus
SP3
ST MARTIN'S CL
DAIRY RD
ST MARTINS CL
B3089
Primrose Farm
Glebe Farm
Cemy
SHORT LA
MOUNT LANE
GROVELEY RD
WEST STREET
Barford St Martin CE First Sch
DUCK LA
PH
Barford St Martin
WILTON ROAD
SHAFTESBURY RD
East End Farm
THE CLEEVES
Village Earthworks
SP2
Weir
River Nadder
A30
PH
Burcombe
Sewage Works
Manor Farm
Tumulus
Manor House
Heath Hill
A30
Mobile Home Park
Punch Bowl Bottom
205
144

143
130

143
150

D2
1 CENTURION CL
2 GRAMSHAW RD

E2
1 CHANCERY CL
2 HIGHBURY CL

F1
1 HAWTHORN CL
2 CHARLES ST
3 MEADOW RD
4 STATION TERR
5 MEADOW RD (STH)
6 GEORGE ST (STH)
7 SANDOWN PL
8 SOUTH ST
9 WINDSOR RD
10 WINDSOR ST

F2
1 KENSINGTON RD
2 RICHMOND RD
3 JUBILEE CT

A1
1 CHAPEL PL
2 SUMMERLOCK APP
3 GRIFFINS CT
4 MALTHOUSE LA
5 PRIORY SQ
6 CHEESE MARKET
7 MINSTER ST

B1
1 ROLLESTONE ST
2 ST EDMUNDS CHURCH ST
3 BROWN ST

145

B2
1 SWAYNES CL
2 BELLE VUE RD
3 VENTRY CL
4 THE VENTRY

152

C5
1 NEAL CL
2 GIBBS CL
3 ALDWORTH DRI
4 SHARRAT AVE
5 THE OAKBOURNES
6 THE CRUSADES
7 ST TERESAS CL
8 MANNING CL

D5
1 SAINTES CL
2 FYFIELD CL
3 MONXTON CL
4 ST CHRISTOPHERS CL
5 ST BEDES CL
6 ST MATTHEWS CL
7 MYRRFIELD RD
8 ST LUKES CL
9 ST URSULA'S CL

133
148

153
148

147
134

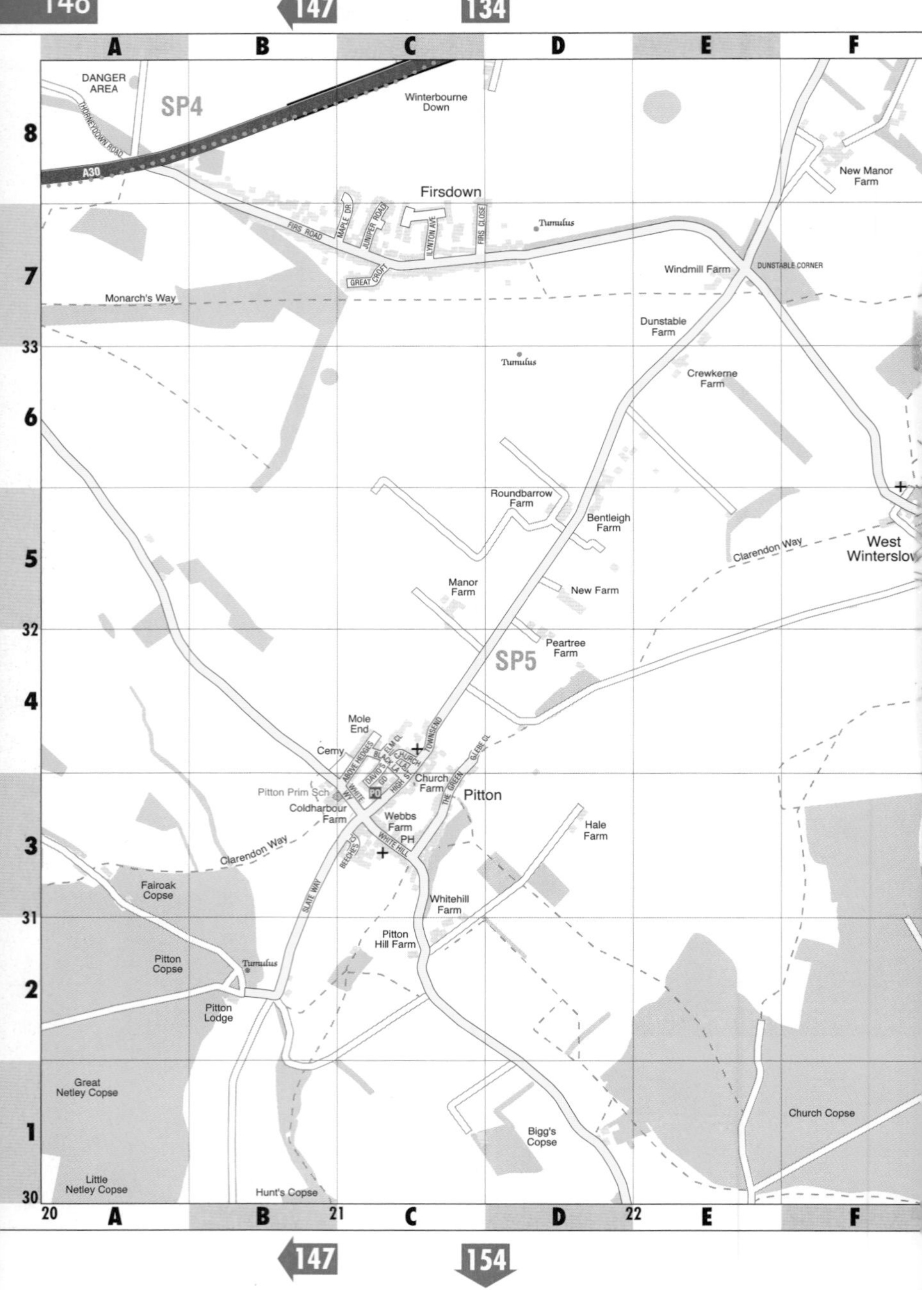

147
154

A B C D E F

East Winterslow
Ramshill Copse
Howe Copse
8
Middle Winterslow
Blackberry Farm
Hill Farm
Clough Lane
Mill Lane
Monarch's Way
Coopers Farm
Noad's Copse
7
The Flood
Middleton
Middleton Rd
The Causeway
Woodland Dr
PH
Tumuli
33
Yew Tree Cl
Highfield Cr
Lansdown Coppice
Saxon Leas
Stone Cl
The Cswy
Hill Top
The Flashett
Glenfield Cl
Mill Lane
Winterslow Prim Sch
Yarmley Lane
Brown's Copse
Middleton Rd
PO
Clarendon Way
Easton Common Hill
6
Youngs Paddock
The Common
PH
Gunville Road
Robin Hill Farm
Gunville Hill
Monarch's Way
The Plantation
Tytherley Road
Bentley Wy
Upper Noad's Copse
The Street
Kings Paddock
Yarmley Farm
Witt Road
Lower Noad's Copse
5
Weston Lane
Weston Hill Farm
Kings Farm
Kingscroft Farm
Hill View Farm
SP5
32
Cotswold Farm
Richwellsted Copse
Hedgemoor Copse
4
Livery Road
Woodgate Farm
Picked Copse
Woodgate Farmhouse
Lower Woodgate Farm
3
Snell Farm
Three Sisters Copse
Smokeway Copse
Old Home Farm
Home Farm
31
Chickard Wood
Bentley Wood
Prior's Copse
Hound Wood
Hooping Oak Copse
2
Livery Hill Farm
Park Lane
1
Beechways Copse
Livery Road
Coalpits Copse
Mapleway Dean Copse
30

North Hampshire STREET ATLAS

23 A B 24 C D 25 E F

205 144 151

205 156

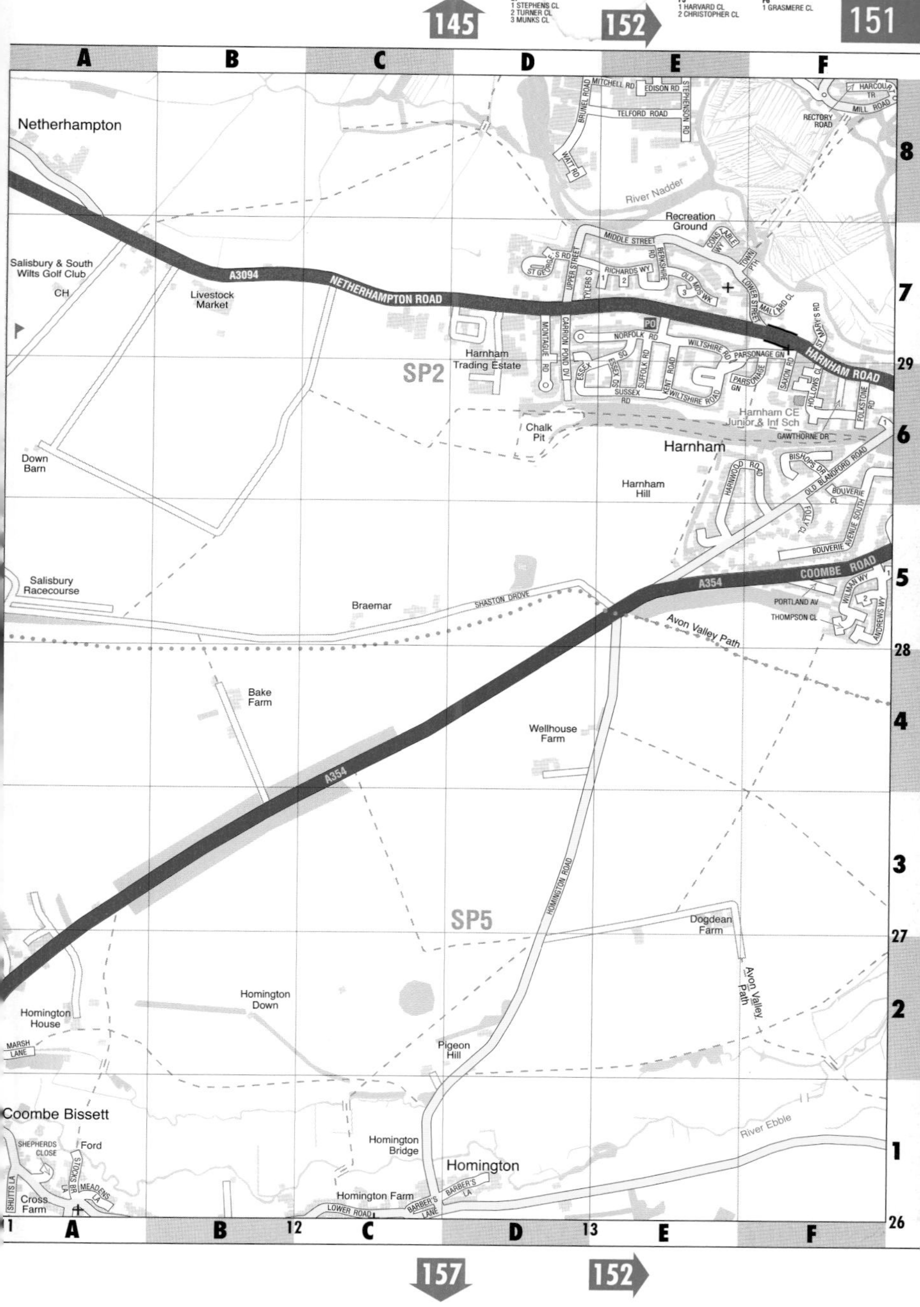
A B C D E F
8 7 29 6 5 28 4 3 27 2 1 26
11 12 13
Netherhampton
Salisbury & South Wilts Golf Club
CH
Livestock Market
A3094
NETHERHAMPTON ROAD
HARNHAM ROAD
Harnham Trading Estate
SP2
SP5
Down Barn
Chalk Pit
Harnham
Harnham Hill
Recreation Ground
River Nadder
MITCHELL RD
EDISON RD
TELFORD ROAD
BRUNEL ROAD
STEPHENSON RD
WATT RD
RECTORY ROAD
MILL ROAD
MIDDLE STREET
UPPER STREET
LOWER STREET
RICHARDS WY
BERKSHIRE RD
OLD MDS WK
CONSTABLE WY
TOWN PTH
MALLARD CL
TYLERS CL
ST GEORGE'S RD
MONTAGUE RD
CARRION POND DV
NORFOLK RD
WILTSHIRE RD
WILTSHIRE ROAD
PARSONAGE GN
ESSEX SQ
SUFFOLK RD
KENT ROAD
SUSSEX RD
SAXON RD
HOLLOWS CL
FOLKSTONE RD
ST MARY'S RD
PO
Harnham CE Junior & Inf Sch
GAWTHORNE DR
BISHOPS DR
HARNWOOD ROAD
OLD BLANDFORD ROAD
BOUVERIE CL
BOUVERIE AVENUE SOUTH
TOLLY CL
A354
COOMBE ROAD
PORTLAND AV
THOMPSON CL
WILMAN WY
ANDREWS WY
Salisbury Racecourse
Braemar
SHASTON DROVE
Avon Valley Path
Bake Farm
Wellhouse Farm
HOMINGTON ROAD
Dogdean Farm
Homington Down
Homington House
MARSH LANE
Pigeon Hill
Coombe Bissett
SHEPHERDS CLOSE
Ford
STOCKS BR
MEADENS LA
SHUTTS LA
Cross Farm
Homington Bridge
Homington
River Ebble
Homington Farm
LOWER ROAD
BARBER'S LANE
BARBER'S LA

A8
1 CHORISTERS SQ
2 ROSEMARY LA
B7
1 WHITEFRIARS RD
151
B8
1 BARNARD ST
2 PAYNE'S HLL
3 GREEN'S CT
4 FRIAR'S ORCHARD
5 ST MARTIN'S CHURCH ST
6 HILL VIEW RD
7 CULVER ST
146
C7
1 POLDEN RD
C8
1 METHUEN DR
2 ST MARGARET'S CL
3 COURTWOOD CL
4 BYWAYS CL
5 THE BEECHES
6 MILFORD HOLLOW
D8
1 BOURNE CL
2 ST JOHN'S CL
A
B
C
D
E
F
8
7
29
6
5
28
4
3
27
2
1
26
14
15
16
Milford
Clarendon Way
Ranger's Lodge Farm
Milford Farm
Mompesson House
Regimental Mus
Medieval Hall
Salisbury Cathedral
Sarum Coll
Bishop Wordsworths Sch
Bishop's Palace
Cath Sch
King's House
Mus
Salisbury Cathedral Sch
St Osmonds Sch
Leaden Hall Sch
YHA
Godolphin Sch
Sch Of English
St Martins CE Jun Sch
St Martins CE Inf Sch
Milford Ind Est
SP1
Dolphin Industrial Estate
Coll Of Tech
SALISBURY
Churchill Gardens
Retail Park
Bourne Retail Park
Petersfinger
Petersfinger Farm
Hatches Bridge
Harnham Bridge
SOUTHAMPTON ROAD
A36
CHURCHILL WAY S
A338
NEW BR RD
A3094
NEW HARNHAM RD
COOMBE ROAD
A354
DOWNTON ROAD
HIGH ROAD
River Avon
Sewage Works
East Harnham Dairy Farm
Harnham
SP5
Long Barn Bridge Farm
The Moat
Britford
Britford Prim Sch
ROWBARROW CLOSE
MILLENNIUM WAY
SP2
FALCONSWAY
LOWER ROAD
CHURCH LANE
ODSTOCK ROAD
Little Woodbury
Manor Farm
PARK LANE
Diens Plantation
Lower Farm
Navigation
Salisbury District
The Grove
Longford Park
Longford Farm
Avon Valley Path
Odstock
Oldstock Bridge
Nunton Bridge
River Ebble
Nunton
Odstock Junior Sch
Bodenham
A5
1 SWALLOWMEAD
2 MARTINS CLOSE
3 MAPLECROFT
4 HAWKSRIDGE
5 SWIFTDOWN
6 LINNETSDENE
7 RAVENSCROFT
8 WRENSCROFT
9 OWLSWOOD
A6
1 BRITFORD LANE WEST
151
B5
1 LONGHILL DRIVE
158

147
154
A
B
C
D
E
F
QUEEN MANOR ROAD
Clarendon Way
King Manor Hill
Little Gilbert's Copse
Great Gilbert's Copse
Crendle Bottom Copse
Grimsditch Copse
Grim's Ditch
8
Ashley Hill
Grimsditch Plantation
Hendon Copse
Long Copse
7
Canon Copse
29
Morley Plantation
Brickkiln Copse
6
Kennel Farm
Claredon Park
A36
Clarendon House
5
SP5
Cupid's Grove
28
CLARENDON ROAD
Hole Farm
Shute End
4
Ivychurch Copse
Ivy Church Farm
End Copse
Lower Bigmans Copse
OLD ROAD
PH
WHITCHERS MD
CLARENDON RD
Common Plantation
River Avon
SHUTE END ROAD
THE GN
Shute End
SILVER WOOD
HIGH ST
OAKWOOD GR
SOUTHAMPTON RD
BRACKEN CL
JUNCTION ROAD
3
Alderbury
FOLLY LA
CHAPEL CL
OLD
Greenways
Alderbury & West Grimstead Sch
SILVER STREET
LIGHT'S LA
WOODLEA GRANGE
27
TUNNEL HILL
SCHOOL HL
Bowden's Copse
OAK DR
FIRS ROAD
FIRS ROAD
WINDMILL CL
PRIORY CL
Alderbury House
SHUTE END ROAD
WALERAN CL
THE COPSE
Hightrees Wood
Firvale
DRIVE
WINDWHISTLE WY
TWINEHAM GD
2
AVON
CANALSIDE
SOUTHAMPTON RD
RECTORY LA
SOUTH WAY
CANAL LA
OAKLEA RD
EYRES DR
Longford Castle
WITHERINGTON ROAD
RECTORY ROAD
PEPPERBOX RI
MATRONS CTS
GRIMSTEAD RD
GRIMSTEAD RD
SHUTE END ROAD
Whaddon
THE SANDRINGHAMS
Spelts Copse
Rectory Farm
KILN CL
PO
CASTLE LANE
SOUTHAMPTON RD
1
Machine Pond Copse
Alderbury Farm
Matrons Coll Farm
PH
17
A
B
18
C
D
19
E
F
26
159
154

153
148

153
160

A
B
C
D
E
F
Livery Farm
The Livery
LIVERY RD
Coalpits Copse
Dean Copse
Farley Farm
PARK LANE
Park Copse
Bentley Wood Nature Reserve
Redridge Copse
Blackmoor Copse
Bentley Wood
Beechwood Copse
LIVERY ROAD
7
Barnridge Copse
Hatchers Farm
Howe Copse East
North Hampshire STREET ATLAS
6
Howe Farm
Barnridge Farm
Dean View Farm
Keepers Cott
Beegarden Copse
LONG DROVE
Hatchers Copse
Heath Copse
Howe Copse West
Hawks Grove
Dean Copse
5
New Berryfield Copse
SP5
Donkey Copse
28
Pilgrims Croft
DEAN ROAD
Upper Highwood Copse
Pegsbrook Copse
Lower Highwood Copse
4
Churchway Copse
Fine Wood
PO
Motte
3
West Dean
RECTORY HL
DEAN ROAD
Dean
HL MOODY'S
LC
Green Acre
27
MOODY'S HILL
Orchard Farm
2
HILLSIDE C
ASHMORE LANE
West Dean Farm
1
Dean Hill
23
A
B
24
C
D
25
E
F
26

205
150

205
209

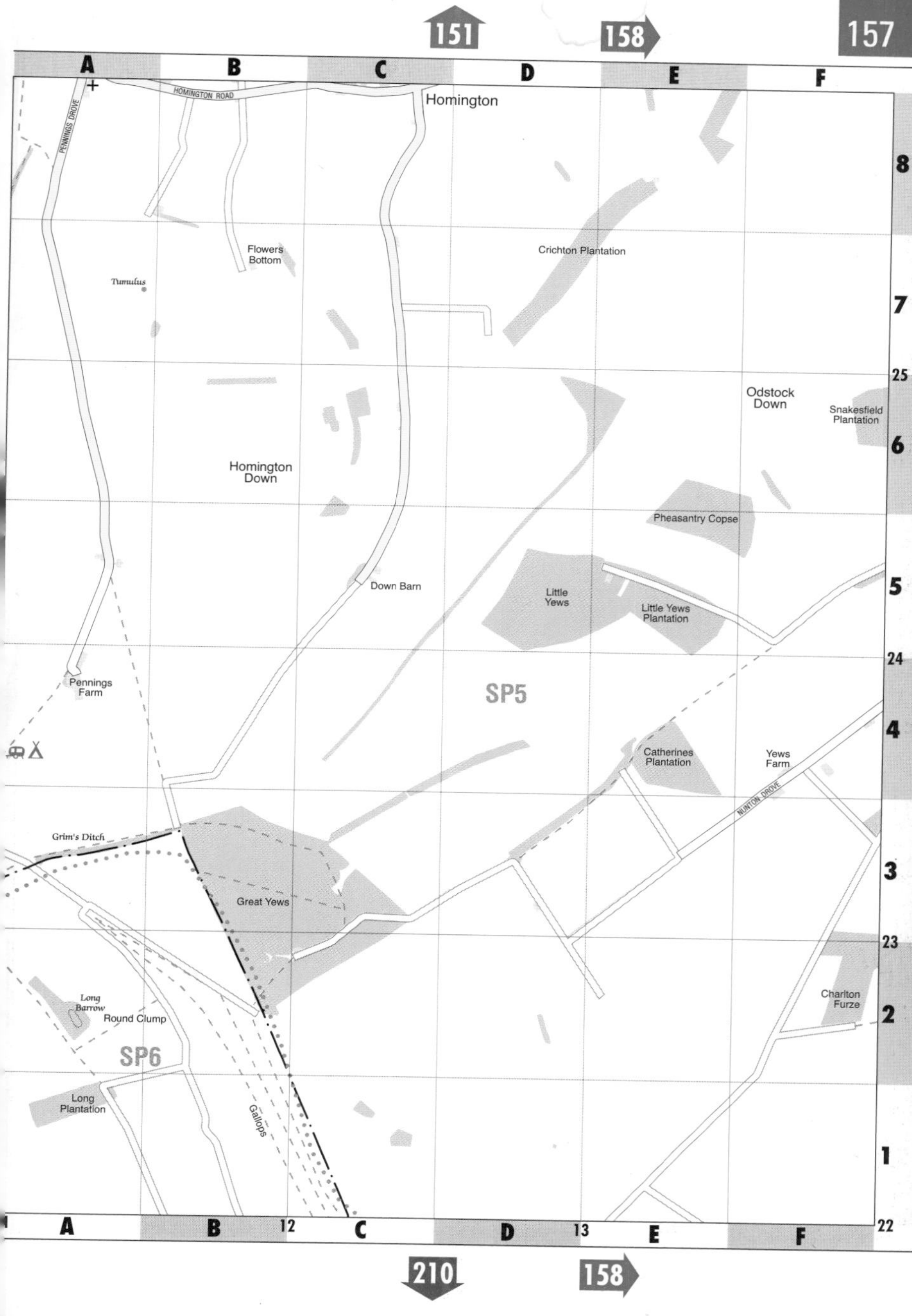
151
158
A
B
C
D
E
F
HOMINGTON ROAD
Homington
PENNINGS DROVE
8
Flowers Bottom
Crichton Plantation
Tumulus
7
25
Odstock Down
Snakesfield Plantation
Homington Down
6
Pheasantry Copse
Down Barn
Little Yews
Little Yews Plantation
5
Pennings Farm
24
SP5
4
Catherines Plantation
Yews Farm
NUNTON DROVE
Grim's Ditch
3
Great Yews
23
Long Barrow
Round Clump
Charlton Furze
2
SP6
Long Plantation
Gallops
1
22
A
B
12
C
D
13
E
F
210
158

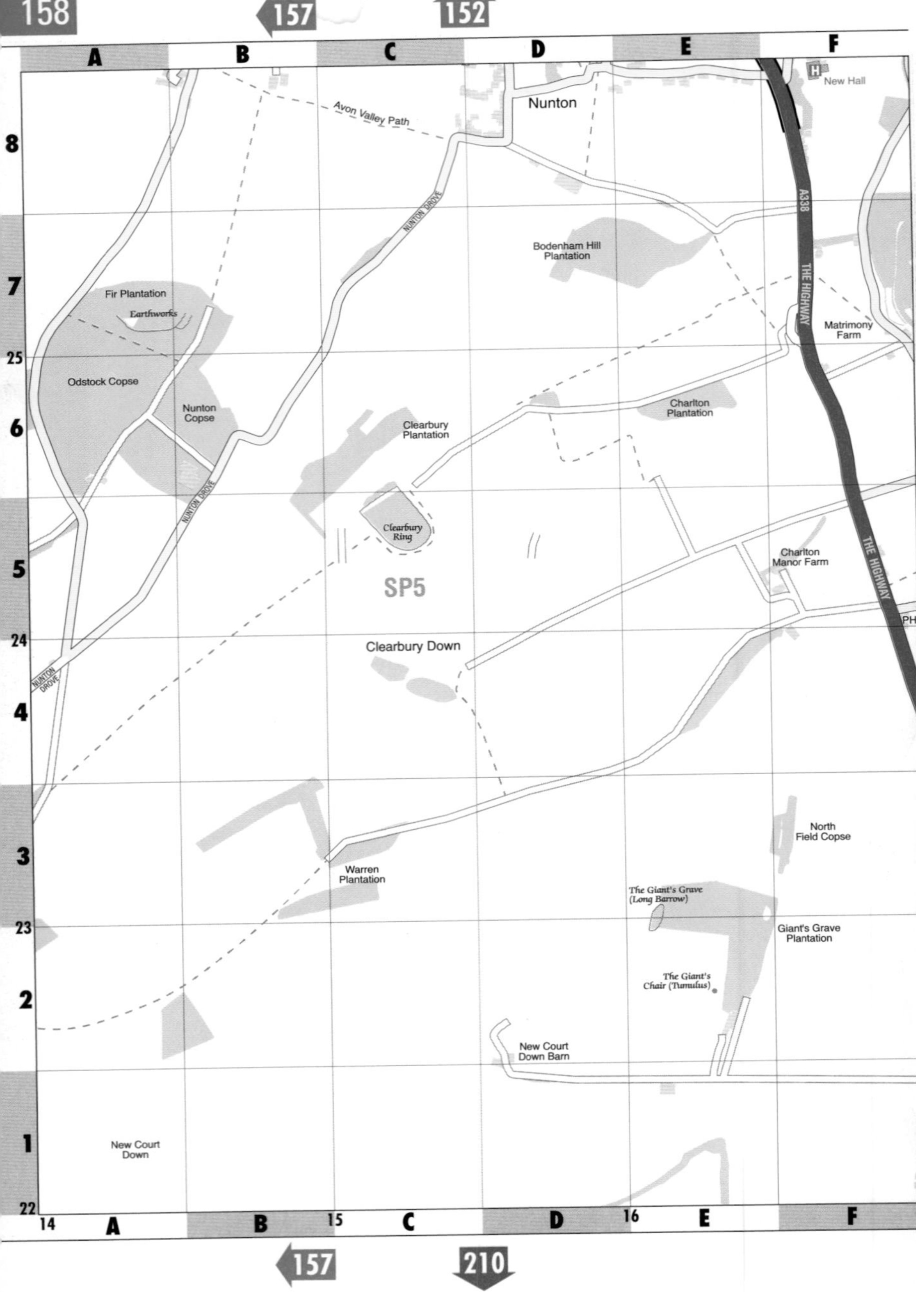
157
152
A
B
C
D
E
F
8
7
25
6
5
24
4
3
23
2
1
22
14
15
16
Nunton
New Hall
Avon Valley Path
NUNTON DROVE
A338
THE HIGHWAY
Bodenham Hill
Plantation
Fir Plantation
Earthworks
Matrimony
Farm
Odstock Copse
Nunton
Copse
Charlton
Plantation
Clearbury
Plantation
Clearbury
Ring
Charlton
Manor Farm
SP5
PH
Clearbury Down
North
Field Copse
Warren
Plantation
The Giant's Grave
(Long Barrow)
Giant's Grave
Plantation
The Giant's
Chair (Tumulus)
New Court
Down Barn
New Court
Down
210

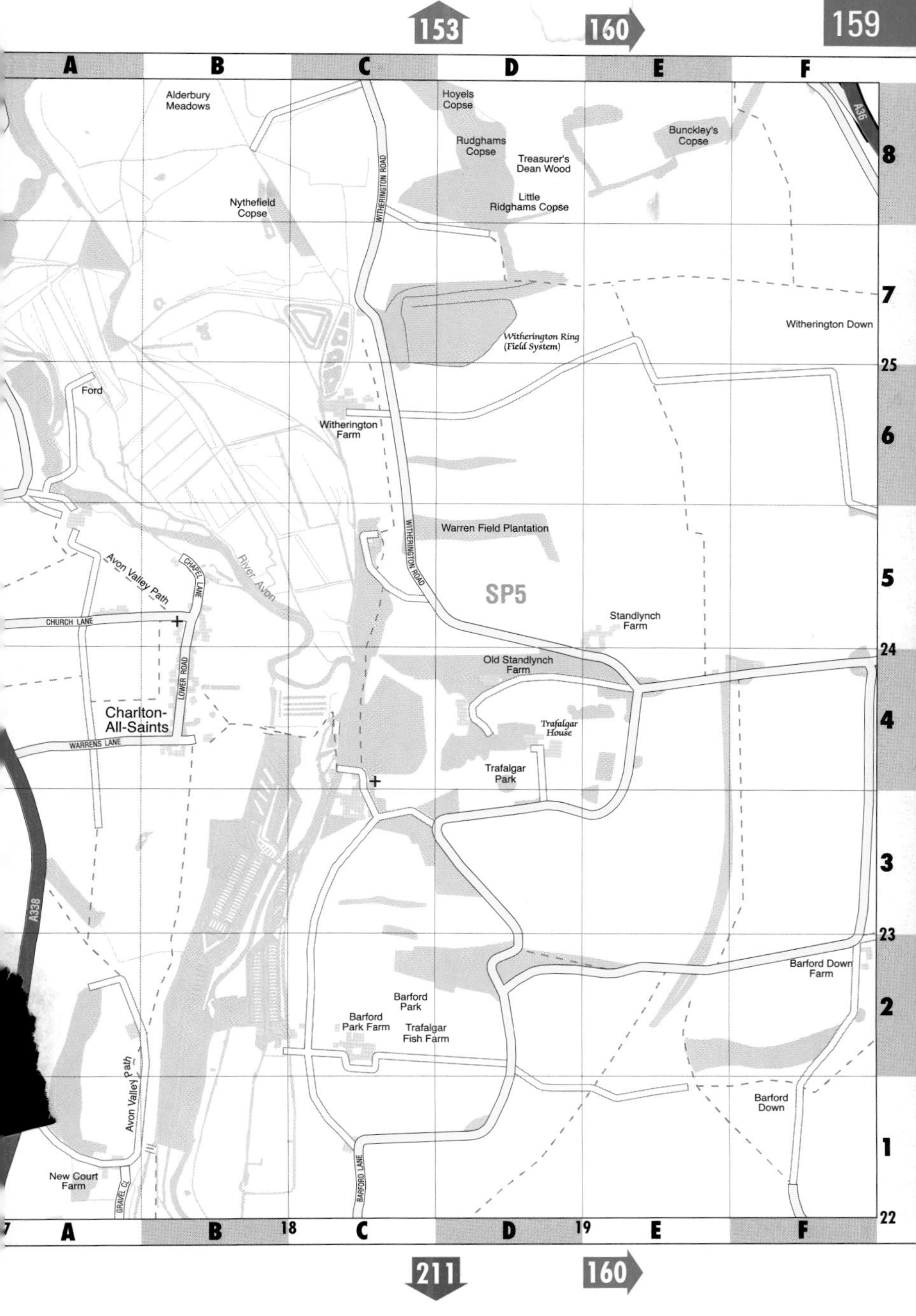
A
B
C
D
E
F
Alderbury Meadows
Hoyels Copse
Rudghams Copse
Treasurer's Dean Wood
Bunckley's Copse
A36
8
Nythefield Copse
Little Ridghams Copse
WITHERINGTON ROAD
7
Witherington Down
Witherington Ring (Field System)
25
Ford
Witherington Farm
6
Warren Field Plantation
WITHERINGTON ROAD
Avon Valley Path
CHAPEL LANE
River Avon
5
SP5
Standlynch Farm
CHURCH LANE
24
Old Standlynch Farm
LOWER ROAD
Charlton-All-Saints
Trafalgar House
4
WARRENS LANE
Trafalgar Park
3
A338
23
Barford Down Farm
Barford Park
2
Barford Park Farm
Trafalgar Fish Farm
Avon Valley Path
Barford Down
1
New Court Farm
GRAVEL CL
BARFORD LANE
22
A
B
18
C
D
19
E
F

159
154

159
211

155
162

212
162

161

A
B
C
D
E
F
North Hampshire STREET ATLAS
Deanhill Barn
8
Biddlesdown Row
COOKS LANE
7
Gatmore Copse
Deanwood Farm
Painshill Farm
25
Well Copse
Dean Copse
6
SP5
Brokes Copse
Bottom Row
Cowesfield House Farm
Worthy Hassock Copse
5
The Plantation
Rowdens Farm
South Hampshire STREET ATLAS
24
Chapel Copse
Lower Cowesfield Farm
Granthams Copse
Testwood Copse
BUNNY LANE
4
Bryce's Farm
Morrisholt Farm
A27
ROMSEY ROAD
Frogmore End
Mill Mound
Great Plantation
SO51
Warren Copse
PARKWATER ROAD
3
Cowesfield Wood
Sandy Close Farm
Yew Tree Farm
CHURCH LANE
Watsons Farm
23
The Heather
Warren Farm
Sole Hill Farm
Church Copse
PARKWATER ROAD
Broxmore Farm
2
A27
THE DRIVE
PO
GRAEMAR LANE
Greenvale Farm
A27 Romsey
Hayter's Wood
Melchet Pond
EASTWOOD
THE DRIVE
THE DRIVE
Fir Copse
St Edwards School
1
MELCHET CL
Sack Hill Farm
GRAEMAR LANE
Broadlands Copse
Sack Copse
22
26
27
28

161
212

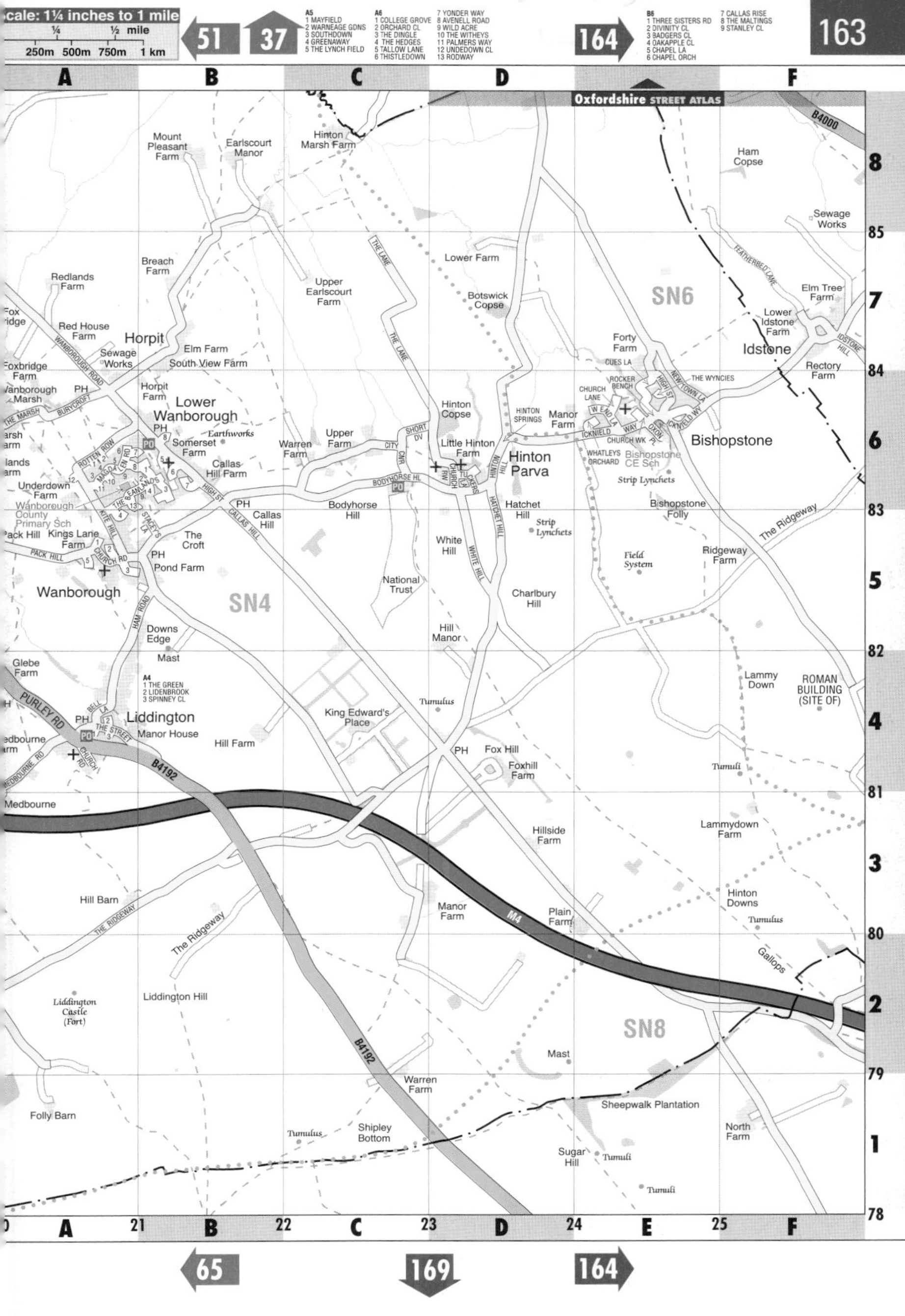
Scale: 1¼ inches to 1 mile
¼
½ mile
250m 500m 750m 1 km
51
37
164
A5
1 MAYFIELD
2 WARNEAGE GDNS
3 SOUTHDOWN
4 GREENAWAY
5 THE LYNCH FIELD
A6
1 COLLEGE GROVE
2 ORCHARD CL
3 THE DINGLE
4 THE HEDGES
5 TALLOW LANE
6 THISTLEDOWN
7 YONDER WAY
8 AVENELL ROAD
9 WILD ACRE
10 THE WITHEYS
11 PALMERS WAY
12 UNDEDOWN CL
13 RODWAY
B6
1 THREE SISTERS RD
2 DIVINITY CL
3 BADGERS CL
4 OAKAPPLE CL
5 CHAPEL LA
6 CHAPEL ORCH
7 CALLAS RISE
8 THE MALTINGS
9 STANLEY CL
Oxfordshire STREET ATLAS
B4000
Mount Pleasant Farm
Earlscourt Manor
Hinton Marsh Farm
Ham Copse
Sewage Works
Breach Farm
Redlands Farm
Upper Earlscourt Farm
THE LANE
Lower Farm
Botswick Copse
SN6
FEATHERBED LANE
Elm Tree Farm
Lower Idstone Farm
Idstone
IDSTONE HILL
Rectory Farm
Red House Farm
Horpit
Sewage Works
Elm Farm
South View Farm
Foxbridge Farm
WANBOROUGH ROAD
Wanborough Marsh
BURYCROFT
THE MARSH
PH
Horpit Farm
Lower Wanborough
Forty Farm
CUES LA
ROCKER BENCH
CHURCH LANE
HIGH ST
NEW TOWN LA
THE WYNCIES
Hinton Copse
HINTON SPRINGS
Manor Farm
W END LA
ICKNIELD WAY
Earthworks
Somerset Farm
ROTTEN ROW
Warren Farm
Upper Farm
SHORT DV
CITY CNR
Little Hinton Farm
CHURCH WK
Bishopstone
WHATLEYS ORCHARD
Bishopstone CE Sch
Hinton Parva
HINTON HILL
Callas Hill Farm
Underdown Farm
THE BEANLANDS
BODYHORSE HL
PO
Strip Lynchets
HIGH ST
Wanborough County Primary Sch
KITE HILL
STACEY'S LA
CALLAS HILL
Callas Hill
Bodyhorse Hill
Hatchet Hill
HATCHET HILL
Bishopstone Folly
The Ridgeway
Pack Hill
Kings Lane Farm
The Croft
White Hill
WHITE HILL
Strip Lynchets
PACK HILL
CHURCH RD
Pond Farm
Field System
Ridgeway Farm
Wanborough
SN4
National Trust
Charlbury Hill
HAM ROAD
Downs Edge
Hill Manor
Mast
Glebe Farm
A4
1 THE GREEN
2 LIDENBROOK
3 SPINNEY CL
Lammy Down
ROMAN BUILDING (SITE OF)
Tumulus
PURLEY RD
BELL LA
Liddington
King Edward's Place
THE STREET
Manor House
Medbourne Farm
Hill Farm
Fox Hill
Foxhill Farm
CHURCH RD
Tumuli
MEDBOURNE RD
B4192
Medbourne
Hillside Farm
Lammydown Farm
Hill Barn
Manor Farm
Hinton Downs
THE RIDGEWAY
M4
Plain Farm
Tumulus
The Ridgeway
Gallops
Liddington Hill
Liddington Castle (Fort)
SN8
B4192
Mast
Warren Farm
Sheepwalk Plantation
Folly Barn
Tumulus
Shipley Bottom
North Farm
Sugar Hill
Tumuli
Tumuli
A B C D E F
8
85
7
84
6
83
5
82
4
81
3
80
2
79
1
78
21 22 23 24 25
65
169
164

163

Scale: 1¼ inches to 1 mile

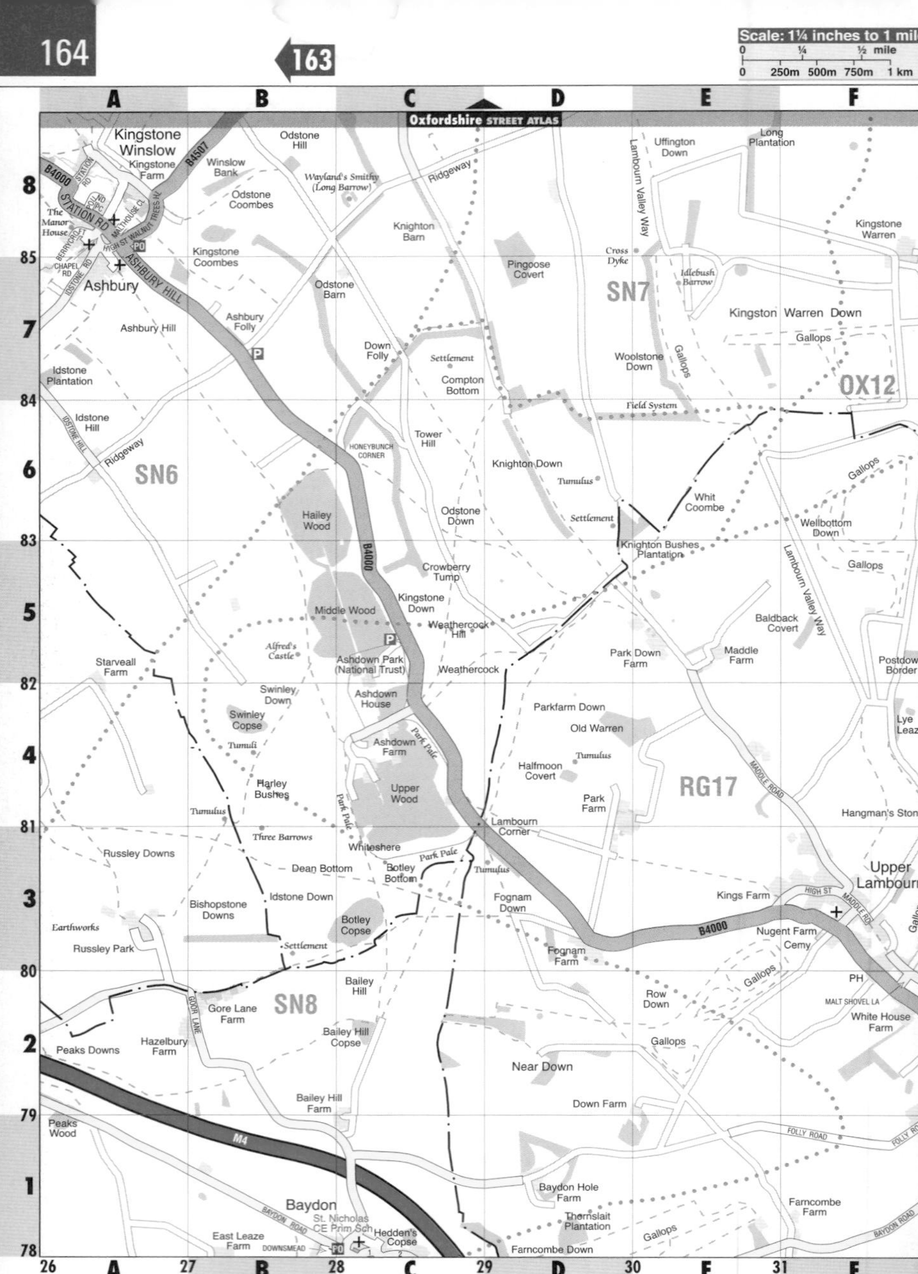

C1
1 ERMIN ST
2 FINCHES LA

163
170

Scale: 1¼ inches to 1 mile
0 ¼ ½ mile
0 250m 500m 750m 1 km

A B C D E F

Oxfordshire STREET ATLAS

Hillbarn Clump
Sincombe Farm
Field Barn
College Farm
Rubblepit Plantation
Ridgeway
Pigtrough Bottom
Hackpen Hill
8
Tumulus
Old Plantation
Hill Barn
Tumulus
Mound
Letcombe Bassett
BASSETT ROAD
Gallop
Down Barn Farm
Sparsholt Firs
Gallops
Tumulus
Devil's Punchbowl
Holburn Hill
HOLBORN HL
KNOLL CL
GRAMP'S HL
RECTORY LA
Rectory Farm
85
Gallops
Mast
Hackpen Hill
Warren Farm East
Church End
Scary Hill
Sparsholt Down
Eastmanton Down Gallops
Childrey Warren
Warren Farm West
Round Hill
Gramp's Hill
Smith's Hill Farm
SMITH'S HILL
7
Moss Hill
Tumulus
Green Down
Ridgeway
Gallop
GRAMP'S HILL
Smiths Hill
Eastmanton Down
B4001
Gallop
Warren Down
Parsonage Hill
Rats Hill
84
Westcot Down
Crog Hill
Greendown Farm
OX12
Parsonagehill Barn
Gallop
Long Barrow
Pit Down
6
Old Warren
Flint Farm
Trabbs Farm
Cockleberry Farm
Nature Reserve
Stancombe Hatts
83
Sevenbarrows House
Gallops
North Plantation
Seven Barrows
Faringdon Road Down
Crow Down
Lang Down
Post Down
Long Covert
Tumuli
Stancombe Farm
5
Postdown Farm
Sheepdrove Farm
Nutwood Down
Poachers Folly
Long Acre Farm
Croker's Hole
Wormhill Bottom
Tumulus
Old Warren Wood
East Ditch
Nut Wood
Hoe Acre Covert
82
Sheepdrove Organic Farm
Cockcrow Bottom
Crow Down
Lambourn Downs
Warren Farm
Mere End Down
Trabbs Farm
Stancombe Down
Bockhampton Down
4
Field System
Lower Valley Farm
Wetherdown Farm
Tumulus
Wether Down
Foxbury Plantation
Pigtrough Bottom
Warren Down
Mile End
81
East Ditch
Littleworth Farm
Newbarn Farm
Foxbury Bottom
Ewe Hill
Hockham Bottom
Warren Down
Old Warren
Lambourn Valley Way
Drive Covert
Foxbury Farm
College Farm
Eastbury Bottom
3
Drain Hill
Warren Plantation
RG17
Washmore Hill
Newbarn Covert
Starlight Farm
Grange Farm
Cranes Copse
SHEEPDROVE ROAD
80
DRAIN HILL
Eastbury Down
Eastbury Grange
Cranes Farm
Sheepdrove
WANTAGE ROAD
SHEEPDROVE ROAD
Lynch Wood
Isbury Farm
Gallops
Tumulus
CHESTNUT LA
Drove Farm
NORTH FARM CL
Pound's Farm
UPR LAMBOURN RD
B4001
Poors' Furze
2
Mill Bottom
North Farm
Fair View
South Cottage Pounds Farm
Lambourn
Oakhedge Copse
OXFORD ST
79
LONG HEDGE
Mill Bottom
MILL LA
ROCKFEL RD
HIGH ST
NEWBURY ST
East Garston Down
DERBY
SOUTHBANK GARDENS
Stables Tour
Sports Club
Eastbury Fields
Upper Bockhampton Farm
Winterdown Bottom
Gallops
Hasham Copse
HILL
HUNGERFORD
BOCKHAMPTON ROAD
NEWBURY ROAD
WOODBURY
1
Lambourn CE Prim Sch
GREENWAYS
LONG HEDGE
B4000
Upshire Farm
Middle Bockhampton Farm
Shepherd's Bottom
Bockhampton Village
Earthwork

Berkshire STREET ATLAS

2 A 33 B 34 C 35 D 36 E 37 F 78

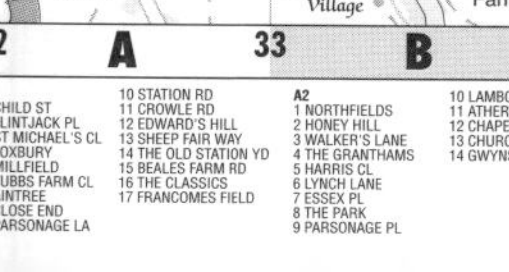
CHILD ST
FLINTJACK PL
ST MICHAEL'S CL
FOXBURY
MILLFIELD
TUBBS FARM CL
AINTREE
CLOSE END
PARSONAGE LA
10 STATION RD
11 CROWLE RD
12 EDWARD'S HILL
13 SHEEP FAIR WAY
14 THE OLD STATION YD
15 BEALES FARM RD
16 THE CLASSICS
17 FRANCOMES FIELD

A2
1 NORTHFIELDS
2 HONEY HILL
3 WALKER'S LANE
4 THE GRANTHAMS
5 HARRIS CL
6 LYNCH LANE
7 ESSEX PL
8 THE PARK
9 PARSONAGE PL
10 LAMBOURN PL
11 ATHERTON PL
12 CHAPEL LANE
13 CHURCH CL
14 GWYNS PIECE

73
60
61

Scale: 1¼ inches to 1 mile

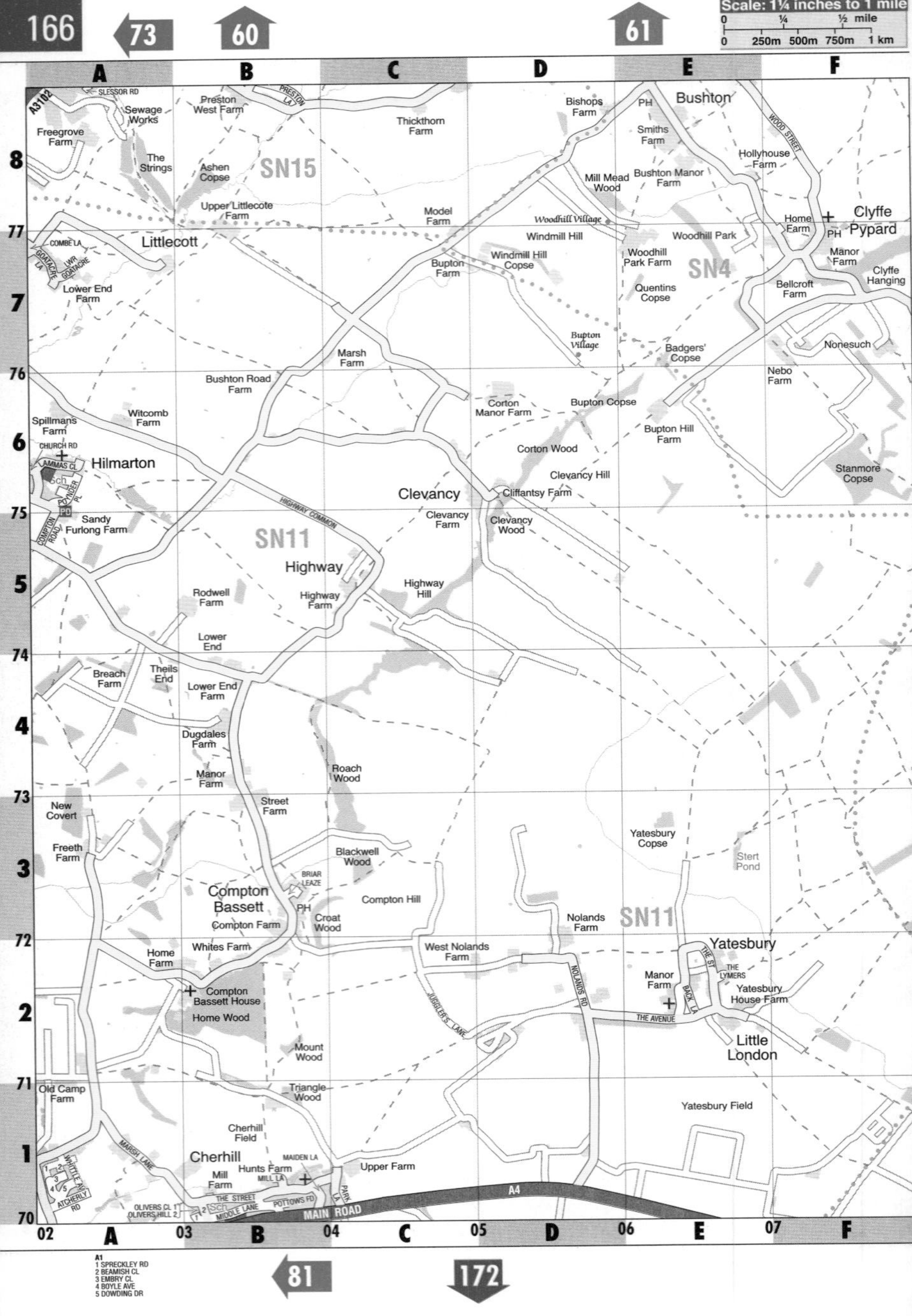

A1
1 SPRECKLEY RD
2 BEAMISH CL
3 EMBRY CL
4 BOYLE AVE
5 DOWDING DR

81
172

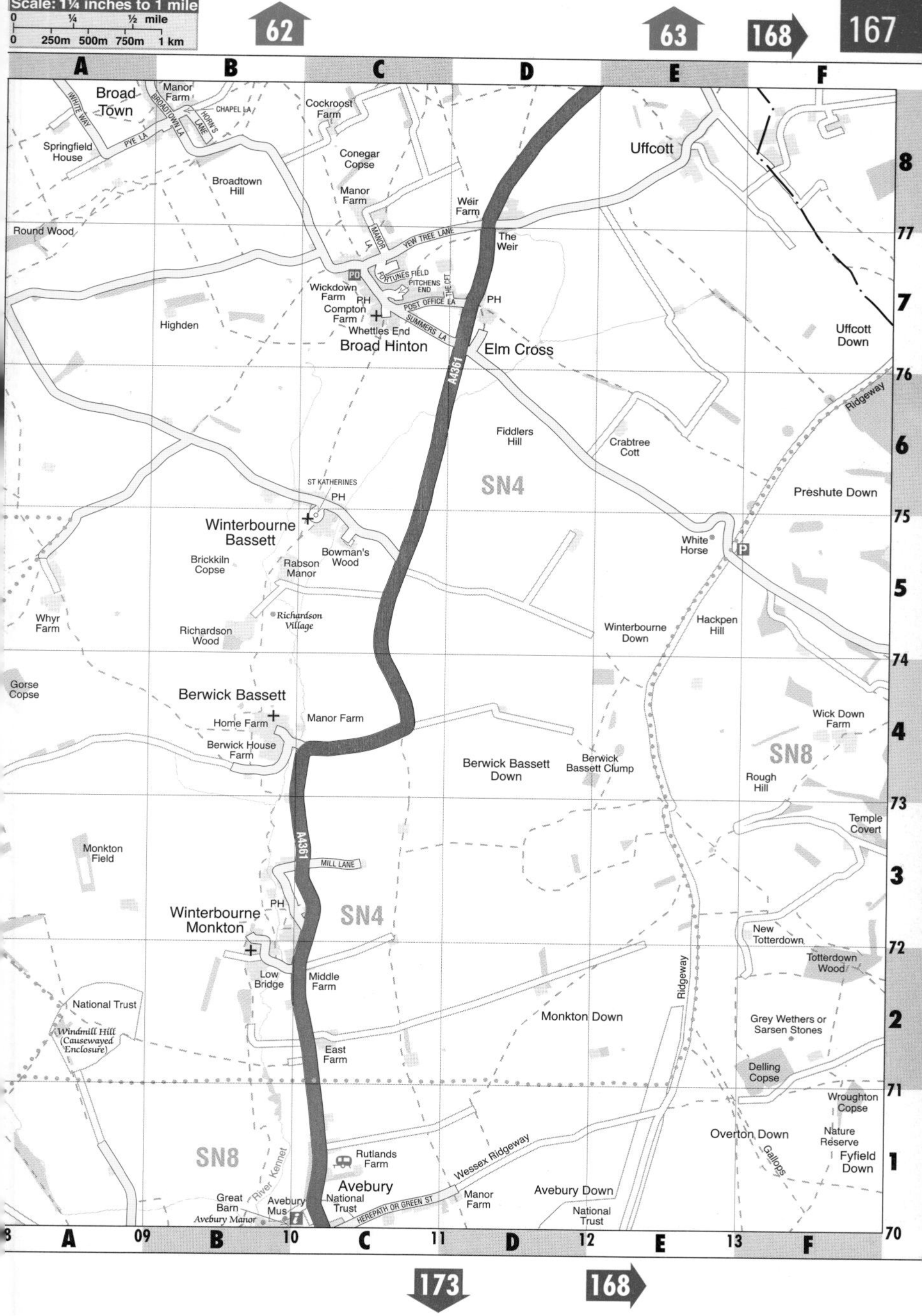

Scale: 1¼ inches to 1 mile
0 ¼ ½ mile
0 250m 500m 750m 1 km
62
63
168
A B C D E F
Broad Town
Manor Farm
WHITE WAY
BROADTOWN LA
CHAPEL LA
HORN'S LANE
PYE LA
Springfield House
Cockroost Farm
Conegar Copse
Broadtown Hill
Manor Farm
Uffcott
Weir Farm
The Weir
Round Wood
MANOR LA
YEW TREE LANE
PO
FORTUNES FIELD
PITCHENS END
THE CFT
Wickdown Farm
PH
Compton Farm
POST OFFICE LA
PH
SUMMERS LA
Whettles End
Broad Hinton
Elm Cross
Highden
Uffcott Down
A4361
Ridgeway
Fiddlers Hill
Crabtree Cott
SN4
ST KATHERINES
PH
Preshute Down
Winterbourne Bassett
Bowman's Wood
White Horse
P
Brickkiln Copse
Rabson Manor
Richardson Village
Whyr Farm
Richardson Wood
Winterbourne Down
Hackpen Hill
Gorse Copse
Berwick Bassett
Home Farm
Manor Farm
Wick Down Farm
Berwick House Farm
Berwick Bassett Down
Berwick Bassett Clump
SN8
Rough Hill
Temple Covert
Monkton Field
A4361
MILL LANE
PH
Winterbourne Monkton
SN4
New Totterdown
Totterdown Wood
Low Bridge
Middle Farm
Ridgeway
National Trust
Windmill Hill (Causewayed Enclosure)
Monkton Down
Grey Wethers or Sarsen Stones
East Farm
Delling Copse
Wroughton Copse
Overton Down
Nature Reserve
Gallops
Fyfield Down
SN8
River Kennet
Rutlands Farm
Wessex Ridgeway
Avebury
Great Barn
Avebury Mus
National Trust
Manor Farm
Avebury Down
National Trust
Avebury Manor
HEREPATH OR GREEN ST
i
8
77
7
76
6
75
5
74
4
73
3
72
2
71
1
70
8 A 09 B 10 C 11 D 12 E 13 F
173
168

167
64
65

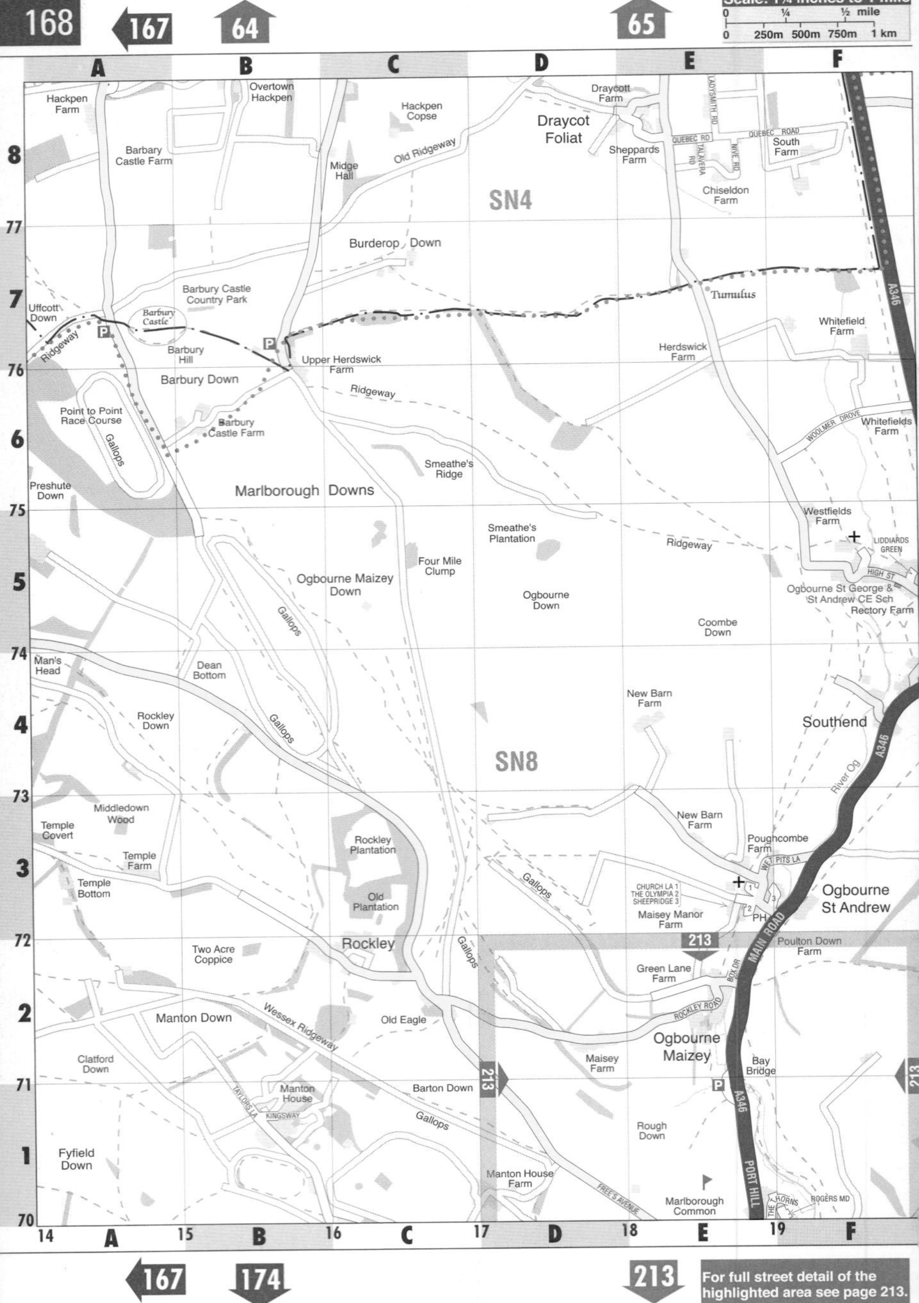

167
174
213
For full street detail of the highlighted area see page 213.

Scale: 1¼ inches to 1 mile
0 ¼ ½ mile
0 250m 500m 750m 1 km
163
170
A B C D E F
Lower Upham Farm
Ridgeway
Upham Village
Upham Copse
Aldbourne Warren Farm
Aldbourne Circular Route
Whitecomb Plantation
Four Barrows
Upper Upham
Upper House Farm
Tumulus
B4192
Snap Village
High Clear Plantation
Aldbourne Circular Route
Tumuli
The Giant's Grave
Whitefield Hill
Woodsend
New Barn
Snap Farm
Woodsend Farm
Lodge Lower Barn
The Dean
Aldbourne Chase
Round Hill Downs
Dudmore Lodge
Briar Farm
High Street Brow
Copse Drove
Chasewood Farm
Ogbourne St George
CH
Little Acre Farm
Jubb's Lane
PH
High St
Bottom Lane
Chase Woods Farm
Chase Woods
Hillwood
St George's Cl
Ewin's Hill
Buckerfield Copse
Laines
Old Chase Rd
Moore's Wood
SN8
Stock Lane
Lewisham Castle
Ewins Hill Farm
Ridgeway
Earthwork
Yielding Copse
Stock Close Farm
Whiteshard Bottom
Pentico Wood
Cottage Copse
Bytham Farm
Hillbarn Copse
Red Lane
Hilldrop Lane
Burney Farm
Warren Farm
Homestead
Smatcham's Copse
Blake's Copse
Mere Farm
Poulton Downs
Red Lane
Leg of Mutton Copse
Cocked Hat Copse
Lopthorn Copse
Woodlands Farm
Lashes Copse
Oldfield Copse
Sound Copse
White's Hill
White's Hill
Minal Woodlands
Sound Bottom
Ramsbury Manor
Upper Thicket Copse
House Farm
Rabley Wood
Ashcroft Cottages
Mildenhall Borders
Axford Farm
Woodlands Road
Greenway Road
Thicket Copse
The Plantation
Thicketts Rd
Axford
Chapel (remains of)
PH
8
77
7
76
6
75
5
74
4
73
3
72
2
71
1
70
20 21 22 23 24 25
175
170

170
A6
1 RECTORY WOOD
2 SOUTHFIELD
3 CLARIDGE CL
4 TURNPIKE
5 MARLBOROUGH RD
6 THE GARLINGS
7 GLEBE CL
8 ST MICHAEL'S CL
9 BACK LA
10 THE PADDOCKS
11 GODDARDS LA
12 THE KNOLL
13 WESTFIELD CH
14 WHITELEY RD
15 HILLWOOD RD
16 HAWKINS RD
169
164
Scale: 1¼ inches to 1 mile
0 ¼ ½ mile
0 250m 500m 750m 1 km
A B C D E F
8
77
7
76
6
75
5
74
4
73
3
72
2
71
1
70
26 27 28 29 30 31
DOWNSMEAD
ERMIN ST
ERMIN CL
FINCHES LA
MANOR LA
WALRONDS CL
Baydon
Sewage Works
Farncombe Down
Windmill Farm
Farn Combe
North Field Barn
Lodge Farm
Lodge Copse
Lodge Down
Coppington Down
B4000
BAYDON ROAD
PLATT LANE
Kingwood House
Great West Wood
Little West Wood
Holly Farm
ALDBOURNE ROAD
Greenhills
Midge Copse
Gore's Copse
A7
1 CHANDLER'S LA
2 LOTTAGE WAY
3 WINDMILL CL
Lottage Farm
ALMA RD
KANDAHAR
CROOKED CR
LOTTAGE RD
OXFORD ST
Green Hill
Woodley's Copse
Coneygre Copse
Common Barn Copse
M4
Hadley Farm
Battens Farm
Baydon Hill Farm
St Michael's C of E Sch
Aldbourne
PH
Liby
WEST ST
PO
B4192
CASTLE ST
STOCK LANE
BUTTS
THE FARM LA
SOUTH ST
SOUTHWARD LANE
THE DOWNS
Pigs' Hill Wood
Baydon Wood
St Johns Wood
Membury Service Area
Hurst Farm
Dixon's Farm
Lyedown Copse
Housedd's Hill
Long Copse
Hillier's Copse
Paxlet Plantation
Membury Castle (site of)
Aerial Farm
Cuckoo Copse
Woodcock Grove
Baydon Manor
Ford Farm
SN8
Marridge Hill
Membury Farm
Lyckweed Farm
Leigh Farm
Moon's Copse
Hoddes Bridge
Anchor Copse
Balak Farm
RG17
Southward Down
Marridge Hill Wood
Witcha Copse
Ballard's Copse
Tumulus
Long Barrow
Preston
Shell's Wood
Ragnal
Crowood Farm
Hunt's Copse
Witcha Farm
Love's Copse
Hails Grove
Raffin Stud
Wiltshire Bottom
Southern Copse
Eastridge House
Pond Wood
Crowood House
Bower Wood
Whittonside Farm
Woodlands Farm
Crooked Soley
Little Wood
Love's Farm
LOVE'S LANE
Whittonditch
Balaam's Wood
Hilldrop Farm
HILLDROP LANE
Boltsridge Copse
Bolstridge Farm
Oaken Coppice
Foxbury Wood
Queen's Coppice
CROWOOD LA
ASHLEY PC
WHITTONDITCH ROAD
HALFWAY LA
Westfield Copse
Ramsbury Sch
Fewley Coppice
Princess Copse
Ramsbury
BACK LA
HIGH ST
OXFORD ST
UNION ST
NEWTOWN ROAD
Manor Farm
New Town
Knighton
Daffy Copse
King's Copse
WHITE'S HILL
MILL LA
Ambrose Farm
Weir
River Kennet
B4192
Chilton Foliat
Spring Hill
Atherton Coppice
Whitehill Coppice
Manor Farm
ROMAN VILLA
The Plantation
Bungalow Bridge Farm
Park Coppice
Littlecote
Hotel
Weir
Bridge Farm
Great Coppice
Darrell's Farm
B2
1 HILLDROP CL
2 KNOWLEDGEHILL
3 LAWRENCE MD
4 BURDETT ST
5 ORCHARD CL
6 ISLES RD
7 SWAN'S BOTTOM
8 CHAPEL LA
9 SWAN'S CL
10 TOWNFIELD
11 WHITEHILL CL
12 ATHERTON CL
13 GREEN ACRES
14 THE PADDOCKS
15 TANKARD LANE
16 SCHOLARD'S LA
169
176

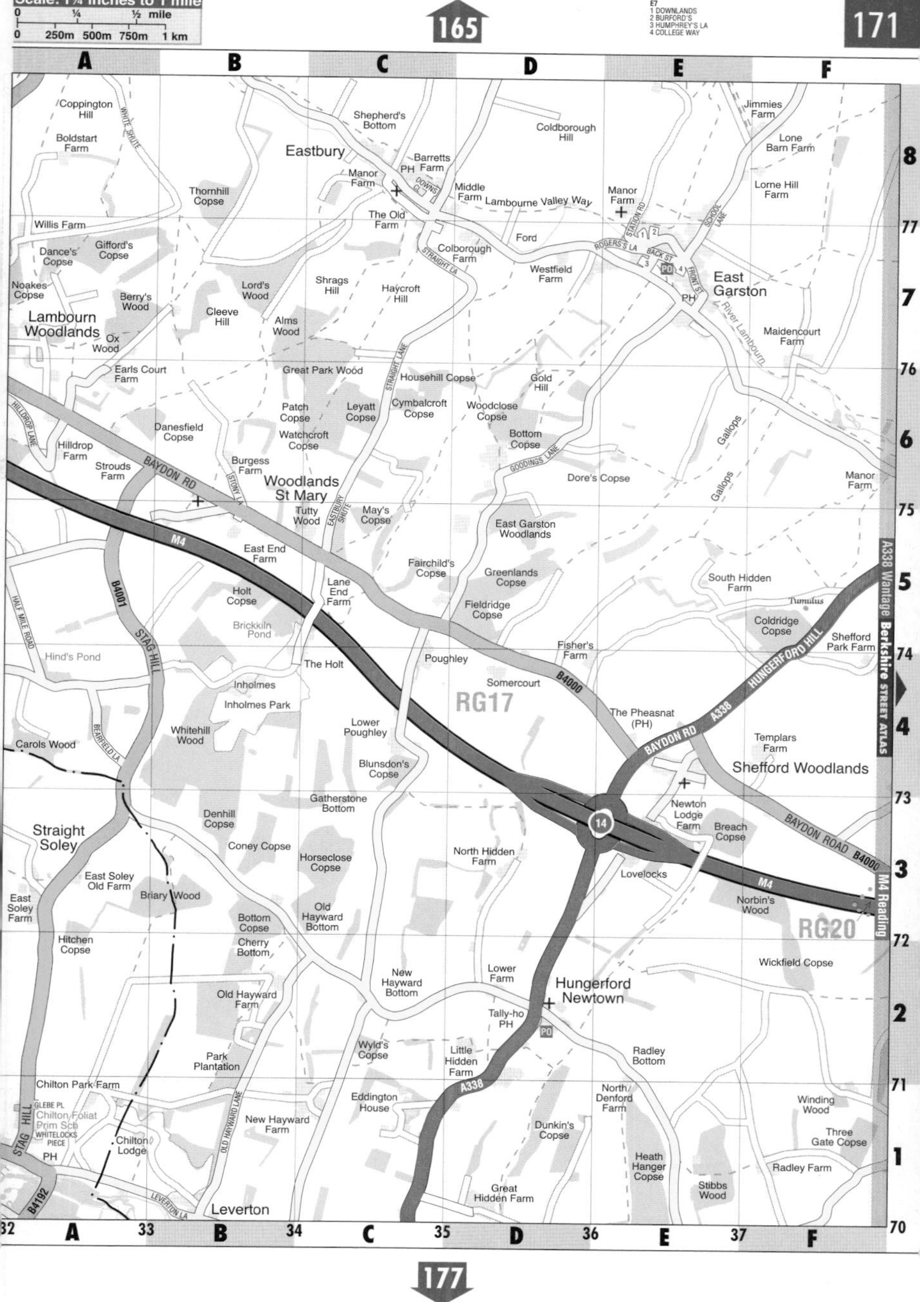

Scale: 1¼ inches to 1 mile
0 ¼ ½ mile
0 250m 500m 750m 1 km
165
E7
1 DOWNLANDS
2 BURFORD'S
3 HUMPHREY'S LA
4 COLLEGE WAY
171
A B C D E F
8 77 7 76 6 75 5 74 4 73 3 72 2 71 1 70
32 33 34 35 36 37
Coppington Hill
WHITE SHUTE
Boldstart Farm
Shepherd's Bottom
Coldborough Hill
Jimmies Farm
Lone Barn Farm
Eastbury
Barretts Farm
PH
Manor Farm
DOWNS CL
Middle Farm
Lambourne Valley Way
Manor Farm
Lorne Hill Farm
Thornhill Copse
The Old Farm
STATION RD
SCHOOL LANE
Willis Farm
Ford
ROGERS'S LA
BACK ST
PO
FRONT ST
Dance's Copse
Gifford's Copse
Colborough Farm
STRAIGHT LA
Westfield Farm
East Garston
Noakes Copse
Lord's Wood
Shrags Hill
Haycroft Hill
PH
Berry's Wood
Cleeve Hill
River Lambourn
Lambourn Woodlands
Alms Wood
Maidencourt Farm
Ox Wood
Earls Court Farm
Great Park Wood
STRAIGHT LANE
Househill Copse
Gold Hill
HILLDROP LANE
Patch Copse
Leyatt Copse
Cymbalcroft Copse
Woodclose Copse
Danesfield Copse
Watchcroft Copse
Bottom Copse
Gallops
Hilldrop Farm
Burgess Farm
GOODINGS LANE
Stroulds Farm
BAYDON RD
STONY LA
Woodlands St Mary
Dore's Copse
Gallops
Manor Farm
Tutty Wood
EASTBURY SHUTE
May's Copse
East Garston Woodlands
M4
East End Farm
A338 Wantage
Berkshire STREET ATLAS
B4001
Fairchild's Copse
Greenlands Copse
South Hidden Farm
Lane End Farm
Holt Copse
Tumulus
HALF MILE ROAD
Fieldridge Copse
Coldridge Copse
Brickkiln Pond
Shefford Park Farm
Fisher's Farm
STAG HILL
Hind's Pond
Poughley
HUNGERFORD HILL
The Holt
Inholmes
Somercourt
B4000
Inholmes Park
RG17
A338
The Pheasnat (PH)
BEARFIELD LA
Whitehill Wood
Lower Poughley
BAYDON RD
Templars Farm
Carols Wood
Blunsdon's Copse
Shefford Woodlands
Gatherstone Bottom
Denhill Copse
14
Newton Lodge Farm
Breach Copse
BAYDON ROAD
Straight Soley
Coney Copse
Horseclose Copse
North Hidden Farm
B4000
East Soley Old Farm
Lovelocks
M4
M4 Reading
Briary Wood
East Soley Farm
Norbin's Wood
Bottom Copse
Old Hayward Bottom
RG20
Hitchen Copse
Cherry Bottom
Wickfield Copse
New Hayward Bottom
Lower Farm
Hungerford Newtown
Old Hayward Farm
Tally-ho PH
PO
Wyld's Copse
Radley Bottom
Park Plantation
Little Hidden Farm
Chilton Park Farm
A338
North Denford Farm
Eddington House
Winding Wood
GLEBE PL
Chilton Foliat Prim Sch
New Hayward Farm
WHITELOCKS PIECE
Dunkin's Copse
STAG HILL
Chilton Lodge
OLD HAYWARD LANE
Three Gate Copse
PH
Heath Hanger Copse
Radley Farm
Stibbs Wood
B4192
LEVERTON LA
Great Hidden Farm
Leverton
177

89
166

Scale: 1¼ inches to 1 mile

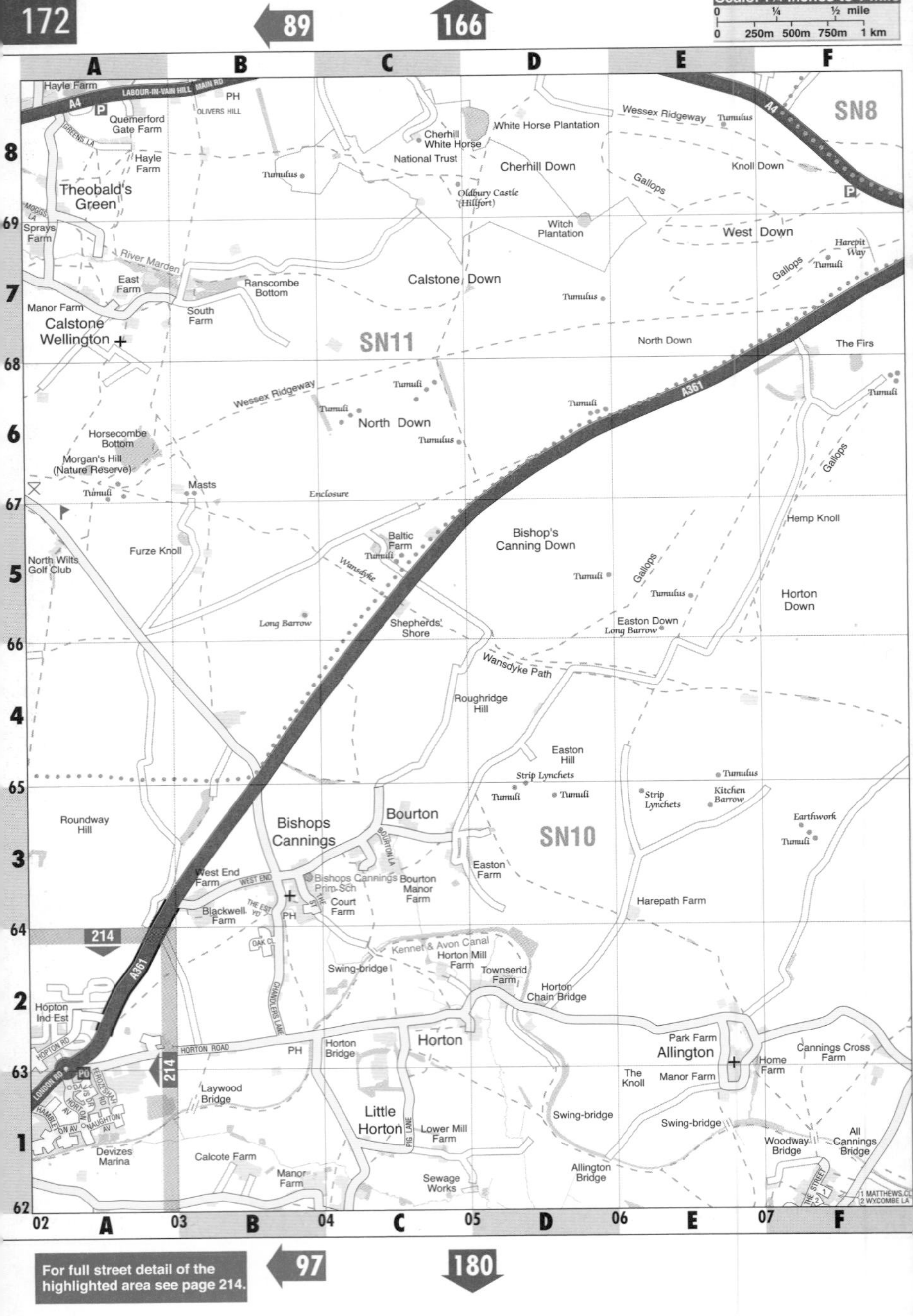

For full street detail of the highlighted area see page 214.
97
180

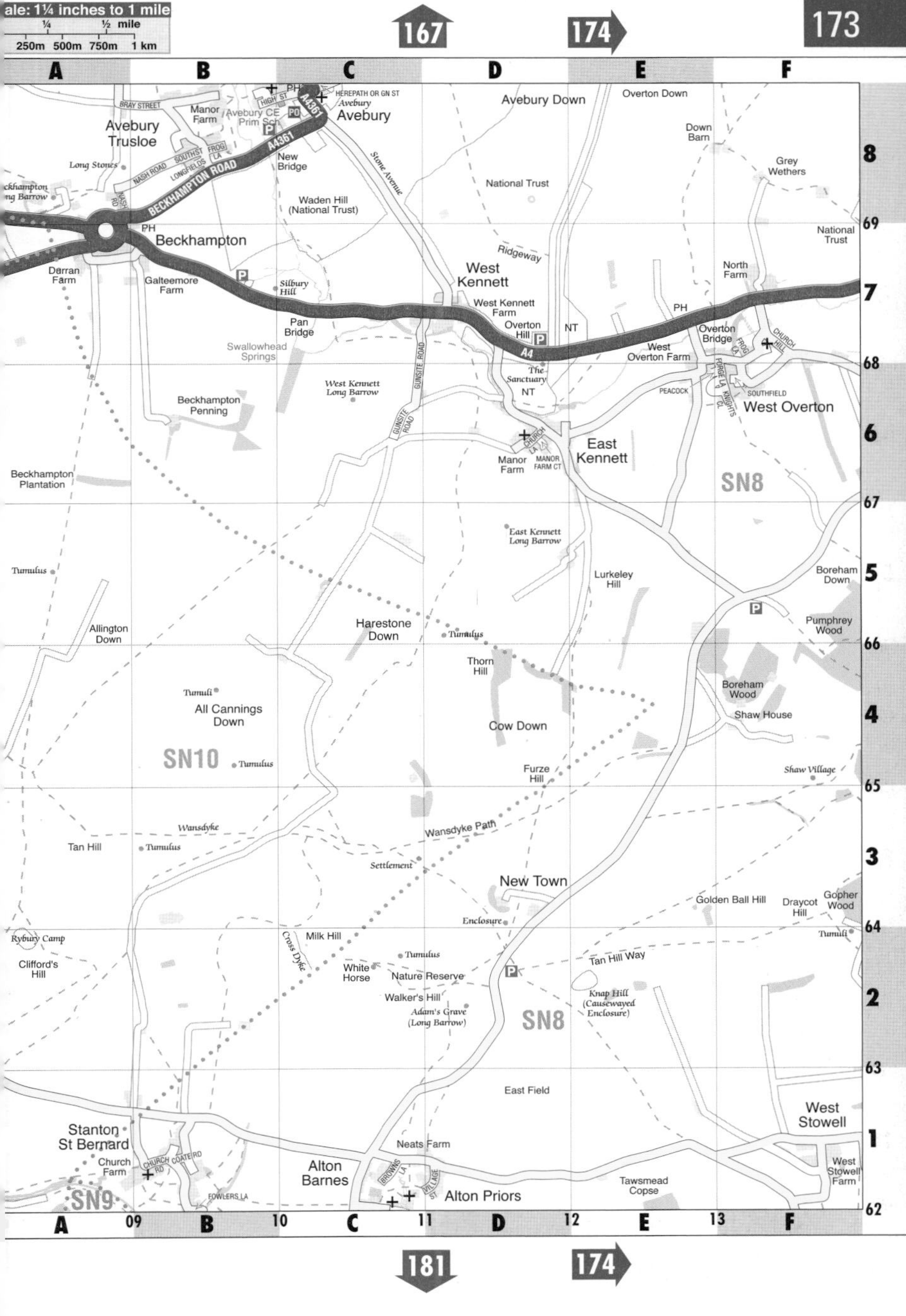

ale: 1¼ inches to 1 mile
¼ ½ mile
250m 500m 750m 1 km
167
174
A B C D E F
Avebury Trusloe
Manor Farm
Avebury CE Prim Sch
Avebury
Avebury Down
Overton Down
Down Barn
Grey Wethers
Long Stones
BECKHAMPTON ROAD
New Bridge
Stone Avenue
National Trust
Waden Hill (National Trust)
Beckhampton
Ridgeway
West Kennett
North Farm
Durran Farm
Galteemore Farm
Silbury Hill
West Kennett Farm
Overton Hill
Pan Bridge
Swallowhead Springs
West Overton Farm
Overton Bridge
The Sanctuary
West Kennett Long Barrow
Beckhampton Penning
West Overton
East Kennett
Manor Farm
Beckhampton Plantation
SN8
East Kennett Long Barrow
Tumulus
Lurkeley Hill
Boreham Down
Allington Down
Harestone Down
Pumphrey Wood
Thorn Hill
Boreham Wood
Shaw House
Tumuli
All Cannings Down
Cow Down
SN10
Furze Hill
Shaw Village
Wansdyke
Wansdyke Path
Tan Hill
Settlement
New Town
Golden Ball Hill
Draycot Hill
Gopher Wood
Enclosure
Rybury Camp
Milk Hill
Cross Dyke
Clifford's Hill
White Horse
Nature Reserve
Tan Hill Way
Knap Hill (Causewayed Enclosure)
Walker's Hill
Adam's Grave (Long Barrow)
East Field
West Stowell
Stanton St Bernard
Neats Farm
Church Farm
Alton Barnes
Alton Priors
Tawsmead Copse
West Stowell Farm
SN9
181
174

173 168 213
For full street detail of the highlighted area see page 213.

Scale: 1¼ inches to 1 mile

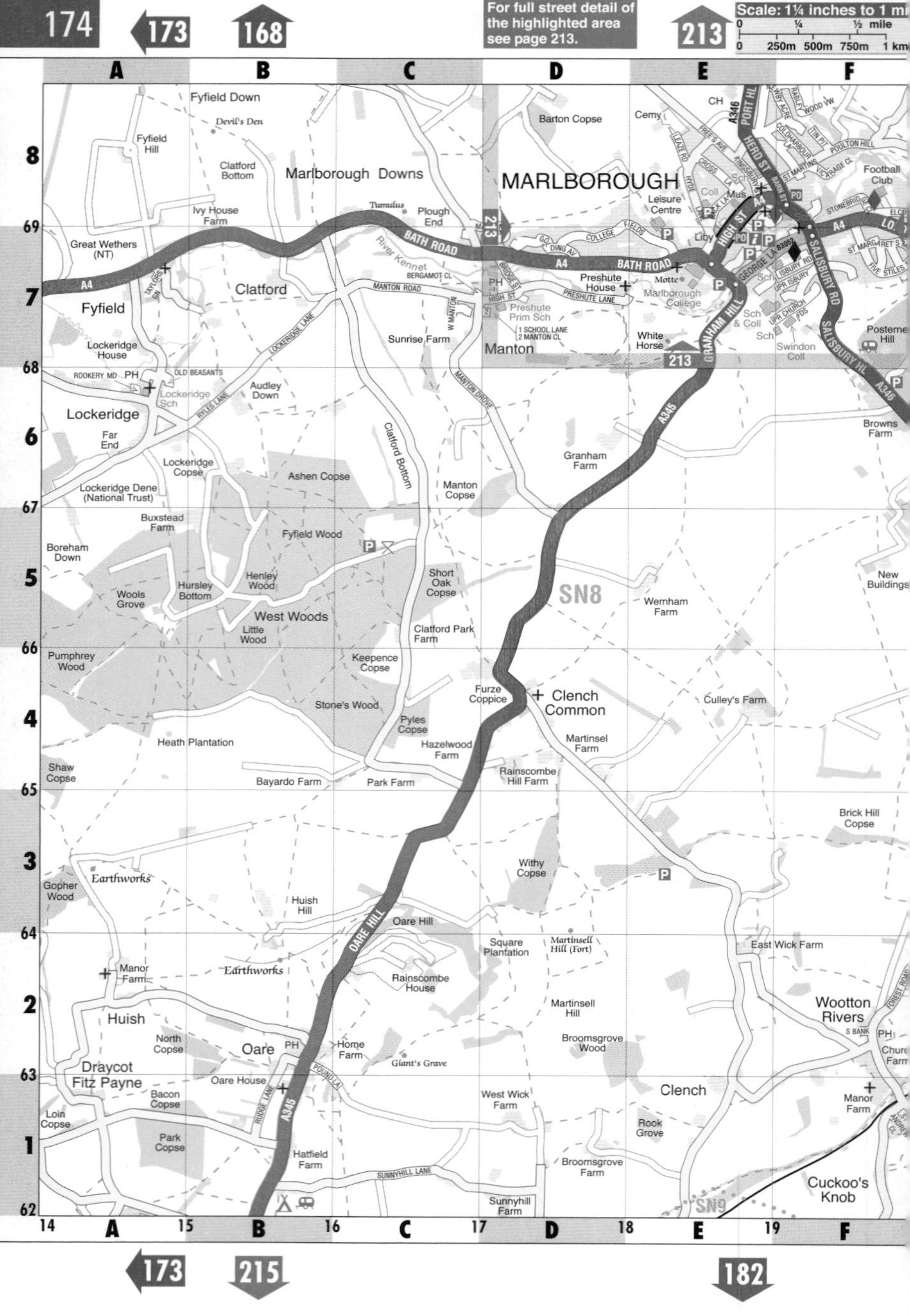

173 215 182

Scale: 1¼ inches to 1 mile
0 ¼ ½ mile
0 250m 500m 750m 1 km

169
176

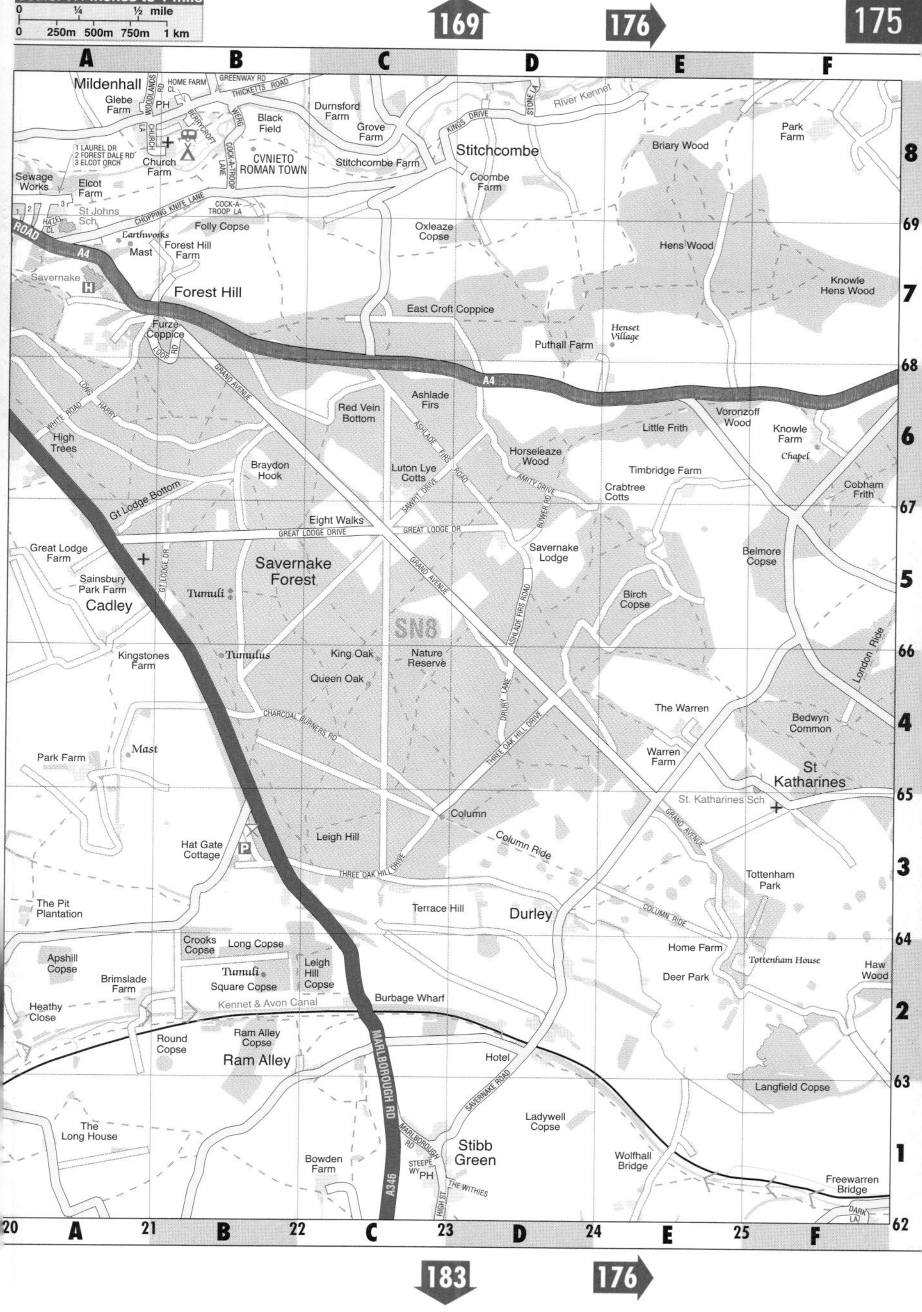

183
176

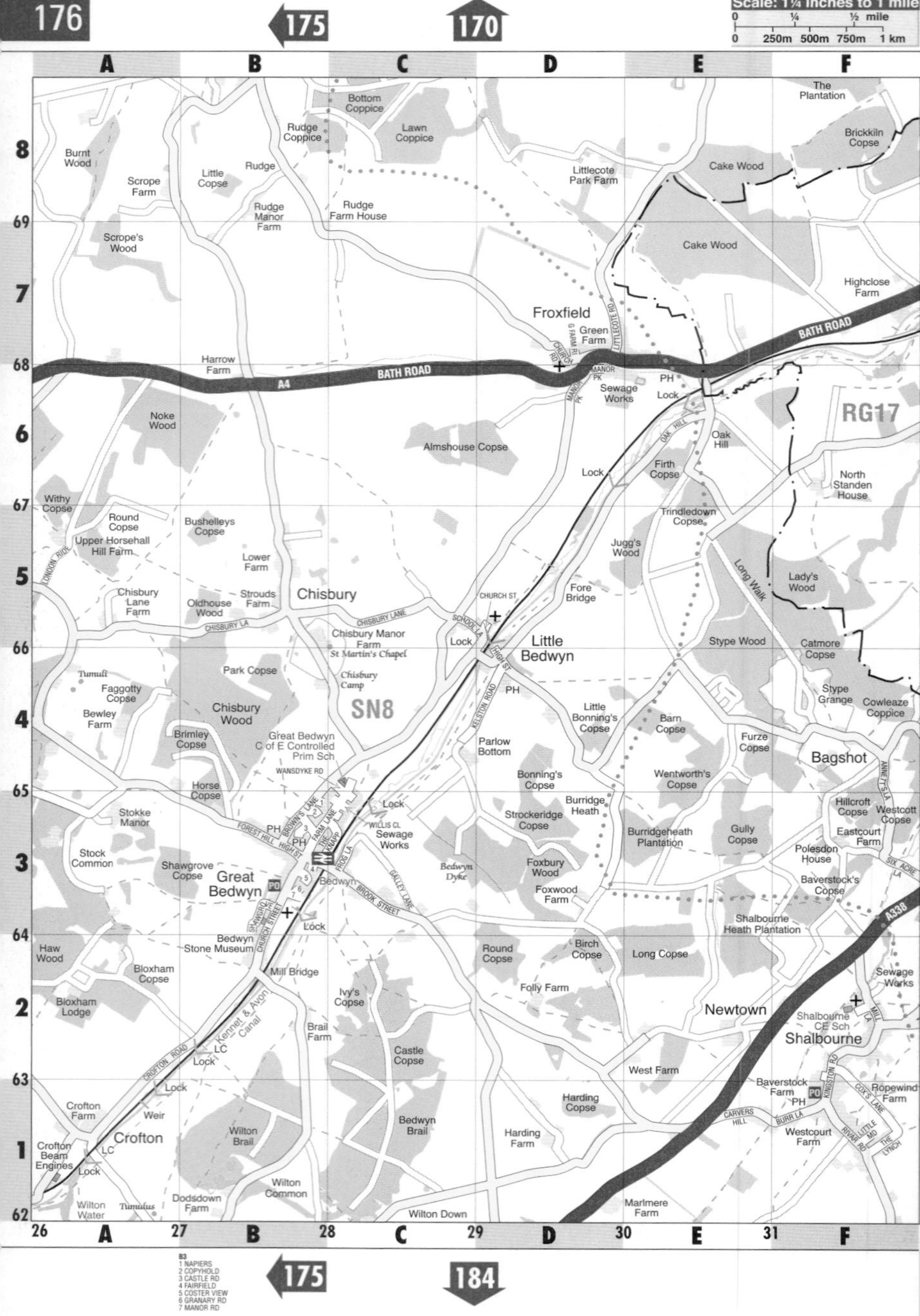
175
170
Scale: 1¼ inches to 1 mile
0 ¼ ½ mile
0 250m 500m 750m 1 km
A B C D E F
8 69 7 68 6 67 5 66 4 65 3 64 2 63 1 62
26 27 28 29 30 31
Bottom Coppice
Lawn Coppice
Rudge Coppice
The Plantation
Brickkiln Copse
Burnt Wood
Scrope Farm
Little Copse
Rudge
Cake Wood
Littlecote Park Farm
Rudge Manor Farm
Rudge Farm House
Scrope's Wood
Cake Wood
Highclose Farm
Froxfield
Green Farm
G FARM RI
CHURCH RD
LITTLECOTE RD
BATH ROAD
Harrow Farm
A4
BATH ROAD
MANOR PK
PH
Sewage Works
Lock
RG17
Noke Wood
Almshouse Copse
OAK HILL
Oak Hill
Lock
Firth Copse
North Standen House
Withy Copse
Round Copse
Bushelleys Copse
Trindledown Copse
Upper Horsehall Hill Farm
Jugg's Wood
Lower Farm
LONDON RIDE
Long Walk
Lady's Wood
Chisbury Lane Farm
Oldhouse Wood
Strouds Farm
Chisbury
Fore Bridge
CHURCH ST
CHISBURY LANE
CHISBURY LA
SCHOOL LA
Chisbury Manor Farm
St Martin's Chapel
Lock
Little Bedwyn
HIGH ST
Stype Wood
Catmore Copse
Tumuli
Park Copse
Chisbury Camp
PH
Faggotty Copse
Stype Grange
Cowleaze Coppice
Bewley Farm
Chisbury Wood
SN8
KELSTON ROAD
Little Bonning's Copse
Barn Copse
Brimley Copse
Great Bedwyn C of E Controlled Prim Sch
Parlow Bottom
Furze Copse
Bagshot
WANSDYKE RD
Bonning's Copse
Wentworth's Copse
ANNETTS LA
Horse Copse
Burridge Heath
Hillcroft Copse
Westcott Copse
Stokke Manor
Lock
Strockeridge Copse
Burridgeheath Plantation
Gully Copse
Eastcourt Farm
FOREST HILL
PH
BROWN'S LANE
FARM LANE
THE KNAPP
WILLIS CL
Sewage Works
HIGH ST
PH
Stock Common
Polesdon House
FROG LA
Foxbury Wood
Bedwyn Dyke
SIX ACRE LA
Shawgrove Copse
Great Bedwyn
PO
Bedwyn
GALLEY LANE
BROOK STREET
Foxwood Farm
Baverstock's Copse
SHAWGROVE
CHURCH STREET
Lock
Shalbourne Heath Plantation
A338
Haw Wood
Bedwyn Stone Museum
Round Copse
Birch Copse
Long Copse
Bloxham Copse
Mill Bridge
Folly Farm
Sewage Works
Bloxham Lodge
Kennet & Avon Canal
Ivy's Copse
Newtown
MILL LA
Shalbourne CE Sch
Brail Farm
Shalbourne
LC
Lock
Castle Copse
CROFTON ROAD
West Farm
Lock
KINGSTON RD
Crofton Farm
Baverstock Farm
PO
PH
Ropewind Farm
COX'S LANE
Harding Copse
Weir
Wilton Brail
Bedwyn Brail
CARVERS HILL
BURR LA
Crofton
Harding Farm
Westcourt Farm
LITTLE MD
RIVAR RD
THE LYNCH
Crofton Beam Engines
LC
Lock
Wilton Common
Wilton Water
Tumulus
Dodsdown Farm
Wilton Down
Marlmere Farm
B3
1 NAPIERS
2 COPYHOLD
3 CASTLE RD
4 FAIRFIELD
5 COSTER VIEW
6 GRANARY RD
7 MANOR RD
175
184

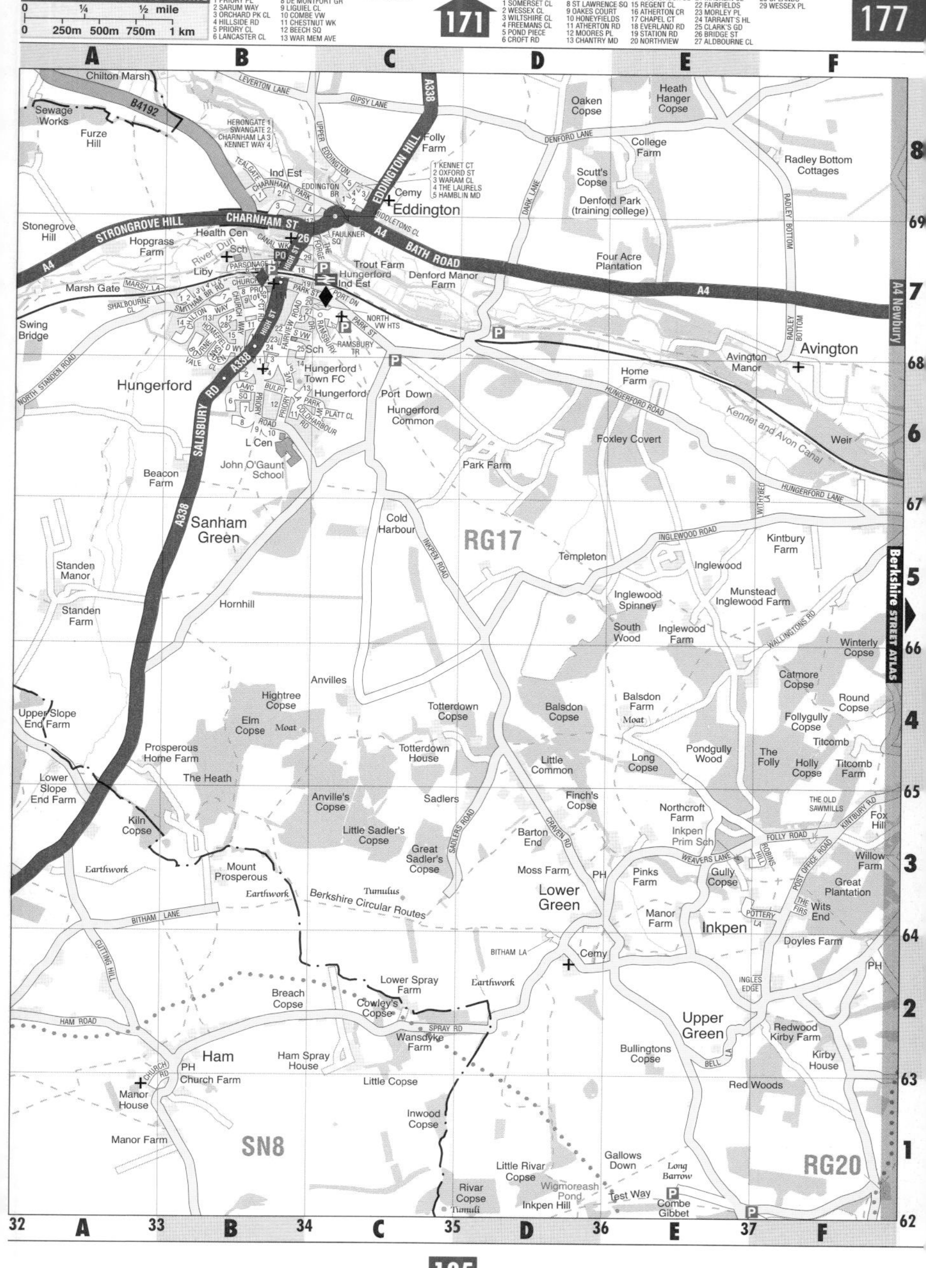
Scale: 1¼ inches to 1 mile
0 ¼ ½ mile
0 250m 500m 750m 1 km
B6
1 PRIORY PL
2 SARUM WAY
3 ORCHARD PK CL
4 HILLSIDE RD
5 PRIORY CL
6 LANCASTER CL
7 YORK RD
8 DE MONTFORT GR
9 LIGUIEL CL
10 COMBE VW
11 CHESTNUT WK
12 BEECH SQ
13 WAR MEM AVE
14 LEWINGTON MS
171
B7
1 SOMERSET CL
2 WESSEX CL
3 WILTSHIRE CL
4 FREEMANS CL
5 POND PIECE
6 CROFT RD
7 CHERRY GR
8 ST LAWRENCE SQ
9 OAKES COURT
10 HONEYFIELDS
11 ATHERTON RD
12 MOORES PL
13 CHANTRY MD
14 WESTBROOK CL
15 REGENT CL
16 ATHERTON CR
17 CHAPEL CT
18 EVERLAND RD
19 STATION RD
20 NORTHVIEW
21 MACKLIN CL
22 FAIRFIELDS
23 MORLEY PL
24 TARRANT'S HL
25 CLARK'S GD
26 BRIDGE ST
27 ALDBOURNE CL
28 UPLANDS
29 WESSEX PL
A B C D E F
Chilton Marsh
B4192
Sewage Works
Furze Hill
LEVERTON LANE
GIPSY LANE
A338
EDDINGTON HILL
UPPER EDDINGTON
HERONGATE 1
SWANGATE 2
CHARNHAM LA 3
KENNET WAY 4
Folly Farm
1 KENNET CT
2 OXFORD ST
3 WARAM CL
4 THE LAURELS
5 HAMBLIN MD
Cemy
Eddington
Ind Est
TEALGATE
CHARNHAM PARK
EDDINGTON BR
MIDDLETONS CL
Oaken Copse
Heath Hanger Copse
DENFORD LANE
College Farm
Scutt's Copse
Denford Park (training college)
DARK LANE
Radley Bottom Cottages
RADLEY BOTTOM
Stonegrove Hill
STRONGROVE HILL
CHARNHAM ST
A4
Health Cen
Hopgrass Farm
River Dun
Sch
Liby
PO
FAULKNER SQ
BATH ROAD
Trout Farm
Hungerford Ind Est
Denford Manor Farm
Four Acre Plantation
Marsh Gate
MARSH LA
CHURCH
PARSONAGE
SHALBOURNE CL
SMITHAM BR RD
CHILTON WAY
CHURCH WAY
HOMEFIELD WY
PARK ST
PORT DN
NORTH VW HTS
RAMSBURY TR
HIGH ST
Swing Bridge
NORTH STANDEN ROAD
BOURNE VALE
Hungerford
SALISBURY RD
Sch
Hungerford Town FC
Hungerford
Port Down
Hungerford Common
BULPIT
PRIORY RD
PRIORY AVE
COLDHARBOUR RD
PLATT CL
L Cen
John O'Gaunt School
Beacon Farm
Park Farm
Home Farm
HUNGERFORD ROAD
Foxley Covert
Avington Manor
Avington
Kennet and Avon Canal
Weir
HUNGERFORD LANE
WITHYBED LA
A4 Newbury
Sanham Green
Cold Harbour
INKPEN ROAD
RG17
Templeton
INGLEWOOD ROAD
Kintbury Farm
Inglewood
Standen Manor
Standen Farm
Hornhill
Inglewood Spinney
Munstead Inglewood Farm
South Wood
Inglewood Farm
WALLINGTONS RD
Winterly Copse
Berkshire STREET ATLAS
Anvilles
Hightree Copse
Totterdown Copse
Balsdon Copse
Balsdon Farm
Catmore Copse
Round Copse
Upper Slope End Farm
Elm Copse
Moat
Moat
Follygully Copse
Titcomb
Prosperous Home Farm
Totterdown House
Little Common
Long Copse
Pondgully Wood
The Folly
Holly Copse
Titcomb Farm
The Heath
Lower Slope End Farm
Anville's Copse
Sadlers
Finch's Copse
Northcroft Farm
THE OLD SAWMILLS
KINTBURY RD
Fox Hill
Kiln Copse
Little Sadler's Copse
SADLERS ROAD
Barton End
CRAVEN RD
Inkpen Prim Sch
FOLLY ROAD
WEAVERS LANE
ROBINS HILL
POST OFFICE ROAD
Willow Farm
Earthwork
Mount Prosperous
Great Sadler's Copse
Moss Farm
PH
Lower Green
Pinks Farm
Gully Copse
Great Plantation
Earthwork
Tumulus
Berkshire Circular Routes
Manor Farm
POTTERY LA
THE FIRS
Wits End
BITHAM LANE
Inkpen
Doyles Farm
CUTTING HILL
BITHAM LA
Cemy
PH
Lower Spray Farm
Earthwork
INGLES EDGE
Breach Copse
Cowley's Copse
HAM ROAD
SPRAY RD
Upper Green
Redwood Kirby Farm
Wansdyke Farm
Ham
Ham Spray House
Bullingtons Copse
BELL LA
Kirby House
CHURCH RD
PH
Church Farm
Little Copse
Red Woods
Manor House
Inwood Copse
Manor Farm
SN8
Gallows Down
Long Barrow
RG20
Little Rivar Copse
Wigmoreash Pond
Test Way
Rivar Copse
Tumuli
Inkpen Hill
Combe Gibbet
8 69 7 68 6 67 5 66 4 65 3 64 2 63 1 62
32 A 33 B 34 C 35 D 36 E 37 F

185

102
94
95

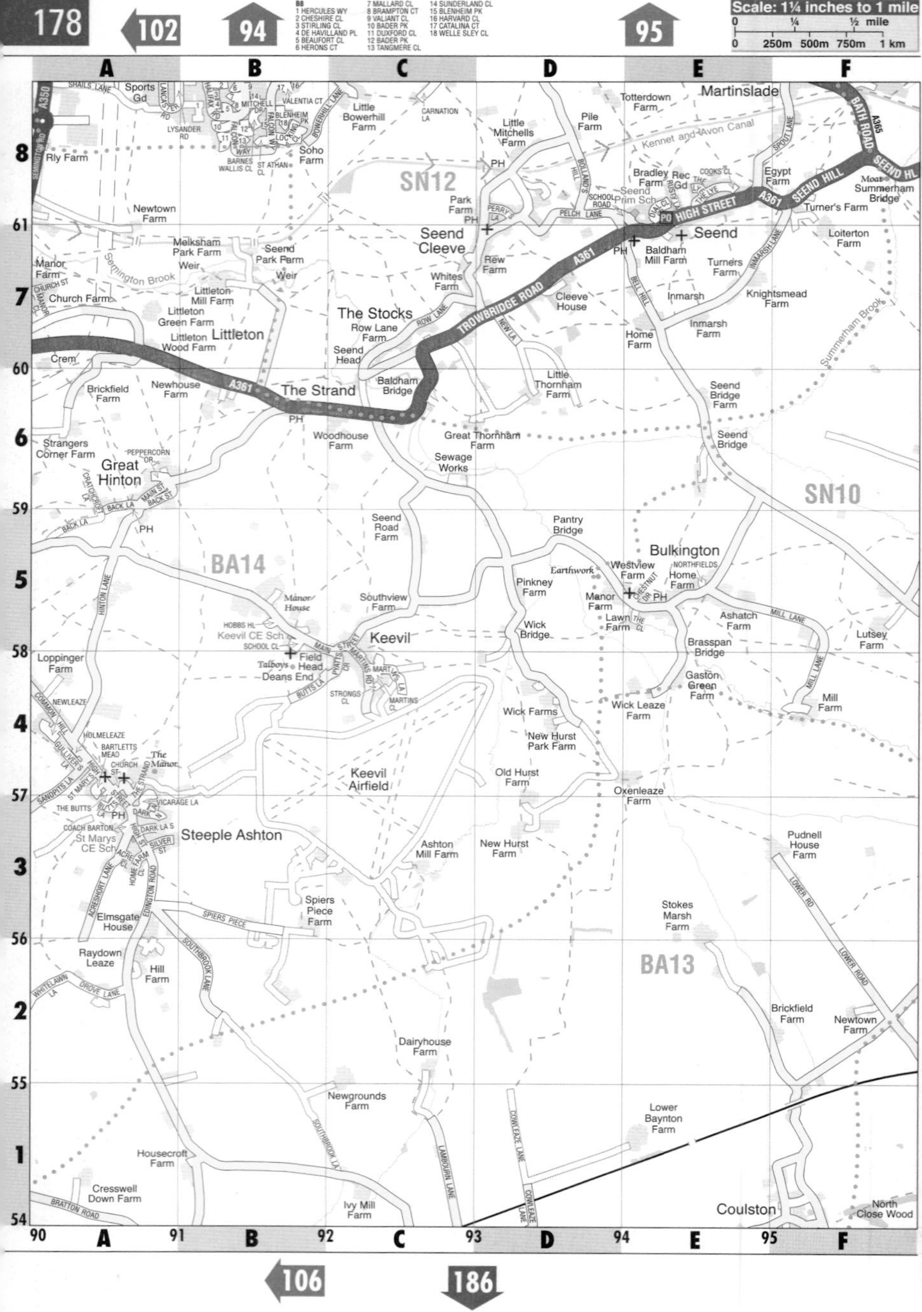

106
186

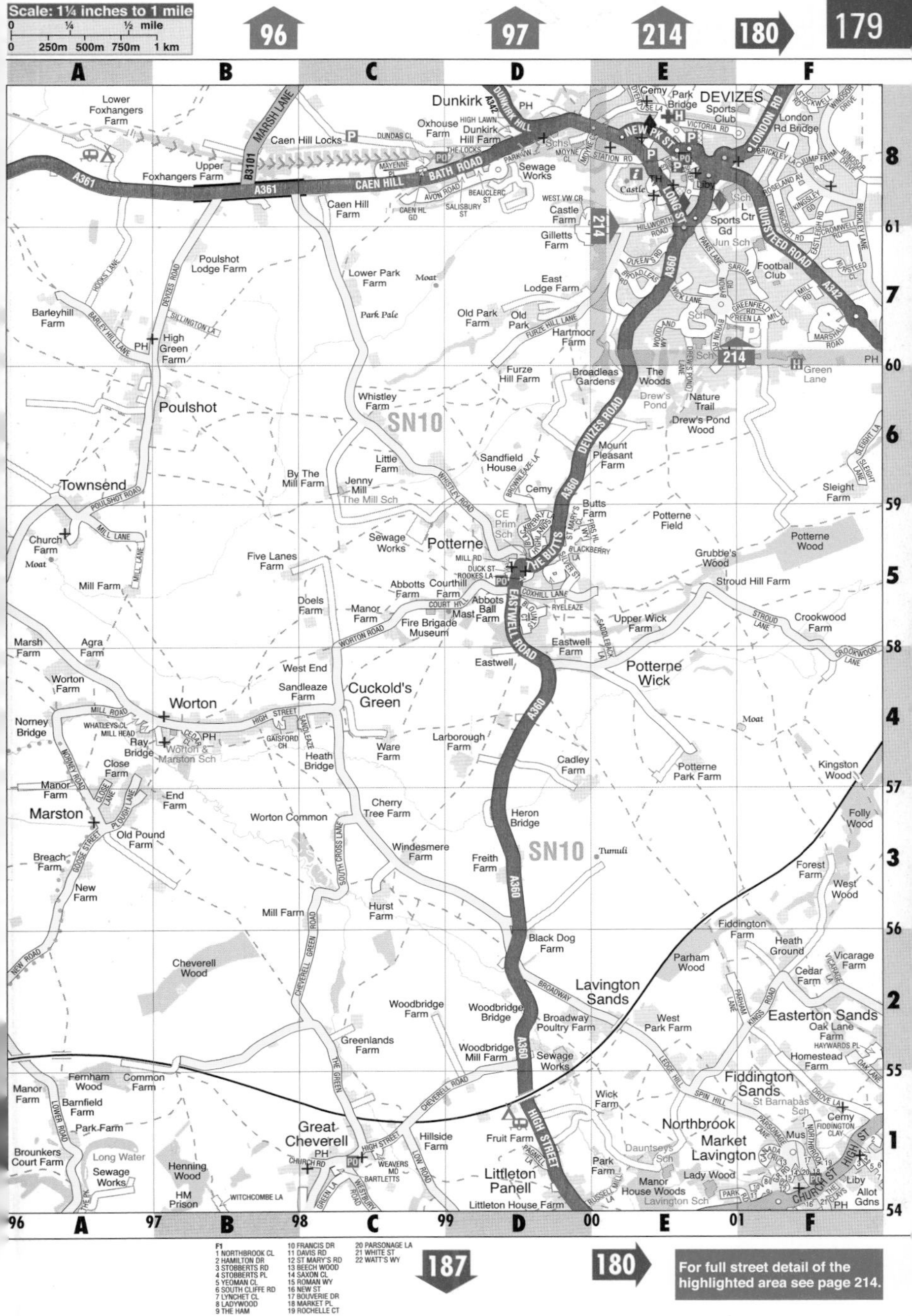

Scale: 1¼ inches to 1 mile
0 ¼ ½ mile
0 250m 500m 750m 1 km
96
97
214
180
179
A B C D E F
Lower Foxhangers Farm
Marsh Lane
B3101
Caen Hill Locks
Dundas Cl
Dunkirk
Dunkirk Hill
A342
PH
Oxhouse Farm
High Lawn
Dunkirk Hill Farm
The Locks
Mayenne Pl
Upper Foxhangers Farm
A361
Caen Hill
Bath Road
Park Vw
Sewage Works
Schs
Avon Road
Beauclerc St
Salisbury St
Caen Hl Gd
Caen Hill Farm
West Vw Cr
Castle Farm
Gilletts Farm
Moyne Cl
Station Rd
New Pk St
Cemy
Park Bridge
DEVIZES
Sports Club
Victoria Rd
London Rd
London Rd Bridge
Stockwell
Windsor Drive
Jump Farm
Brickley La
Castle
TH
Long St
Liby
L Ctr
Sports Gd
Jun Sch
Hillworth Road
Roseland Av
Longcroft Rd
Kingsley Gd
Cromwell Rd
Eastleigh Rd
Nursteed Road
Nursteed Cl
Queen's Rd
Broadleas
A360
Pans Lane
Sarum Dr
Football Club
Mill Rd
A342
Wick Lane
Greenfield Rd
Green La
Mill Cl
Marshall Road
Byron Rd
Woodland
Drew's Pond Lane
Green Lane
PH
61
Poulshot Lodge Farm
Devizes Road
Lower Park Farm
Moat
East Lodge Farm
Hooks Lane
Barleyhill Farm
Barley Hill Lane
Sillington La
High Green Farm
PH
Park Pale
Old Park Farm
Old Park
Furze Hill Lane
Hartmoor Farm
7
60
Furze Hill Farm
Broadleas Gardens
The Woods
Drew's Pond
Nature Trail
Drew's Pond Wood
Poulshot
Whistley Farm
SN10
Devizes Road
6
Mount Pleasant Farm
Sleight Lane
Sleight Farm
Townsend
Poulshot Road
By The Mill Farm
Little Farm
Jenny Mill
The Mill Sch
Whistley Road
Sandfield House
Brownleaze La
Cemy
Butts Farm
59
Potterne Field
Mill Lane
Church Farm
Moat
CE Prim Sch
Sewage Works
Potterne
Highlands
St Mary's Cl
Firs Hl
The Butts
Blackberry La
Grubbe's Wood
Potterne Wood
Five Lanes Farm
Mill Rd
Duck St
Rookes La
PO
Silver St
Mill Farm
Abbotts Farm
Courthill Farm
Abbots Ball Farm
Coxhill Lane
Stroud Hill Farm
5
Doels Farm
Manor Farm
Court Hl
Mast
Blount's Ct
Ryeleaze
Upper Wick Farm
Stroud Lane
Crookwood Farm
Worton Road
Fire Brigade Museum
Eastwell Road
Saddleback La
Marsh Farm
Agra Farm
Eastwell Farm
Crookwood Lane
58
Eastwell
West End
Potterne Wick
Worton Farm
Sandleaze Farm
Cuckold's Green
Worton
Mill Road
High Street
Sandleaze
Norney Bridge
Whatleys Cl
Mill Head
Cedar Cl
PH
Gaisford Ch
Ray Bridge
Worton & Marston Sch
Heath Bridge
Ware Farm
Larborough Farm
A360
Moat
4
Kingston Wood
Cadley Farm
Potterne Park Farm
Close Farm
Norney Road
Close Lane
Plough Lane
Manor Farm
End Farm
Cherry Tree Farm
57
Marston
Worton Common
Heron Bridge
Folly Wood
Old Pound Farm
South Cross Lane
Goose Street
Breach Farm
Windesmere Farm
Freith Farm
SN10
Tumuli
3
Forest Farm
New Farm
West Wood
Hurst Farm
Mill Farm
Cheverell Road
A360
Fiddington Farm
56
Black Dog Farm
Heath Ground
New Road
Cheverell Wood
Parham Wood
Vicarage Farm
Cedar Farm
Vicarage La
Cheverell Green Road
Broadway
Lavington Sands
Parham Lane
Kings Road
2
Woodbridge Farm
Woodbridge Bridge
Broadway Poultry Farm
West Park Farm
Easterton Sands
Oak Lane Farm
Greenlands Farm
Woodbridge Mill Farm
Sewage Works
Haywards Pl
Homestead Farm
Oak Lane
Fernham Wood
Common Farm
Ledge Hill
55
Manor Farm
Lower Road
Barnfield Farm
The Green
Cheverell Road
Wick Farm
Fiddington Sands
Spin Hill
St Barnabas Sch
Drove La
Cemy
Park Farm
High Street
Northbrook
Parsonage Lane
Fiddington Clay
Great Cheverell
Hillside Farm
Fruit Farm
Market Lavington
Mus
Northbrook
High St
1
PH
High Street
Brounkers Court Farm
Long Water
Church Rd
PO
Weavers Md
Bartletts
Low Road
Pagnell La
Dauntseys Sch
Canada Ri
Sewage Works
Henning Wood
Westbury Road
Green La
Littleton Panell
Park Farm
Manor House Woods
Lady Wood
Liby
Allot Gdns
HM Prison
Witchcombe La
Littleton House Farm
Russell Mill La
Lavington Sch
Park
Church St
The Clays
PH
54
96 A 97 B 98 C 99 D 00 E 01 F
F1
1 NORTHBROOK CL
2 HAMILTON DR
3 STOBBERTS RD
4 STOBBERTS PL
5 YEOMAN CL
6 SOUTH CLIFFE RD
7 LYNCHET CL
8 LADYWOOD
9 THE HAM
10 FRANCIS DR
11 DAVIS RD
12 ST MARY'S RD
13 BEECH WOOD
14 SAXON CL
15 ROMAN WY
16 NEW ST
17 BOUVERIE DR
18 MARKET PL
19 ROCHELLE CT
20 PARSONAGE LA
21 WHITE ST
22 WATT'S WY
187
180
For full street detail of the highlighted area see page 214.

For full street detail of the highlighted area see page 214.
214
172

Scale: 1¼ inches to 1 mile

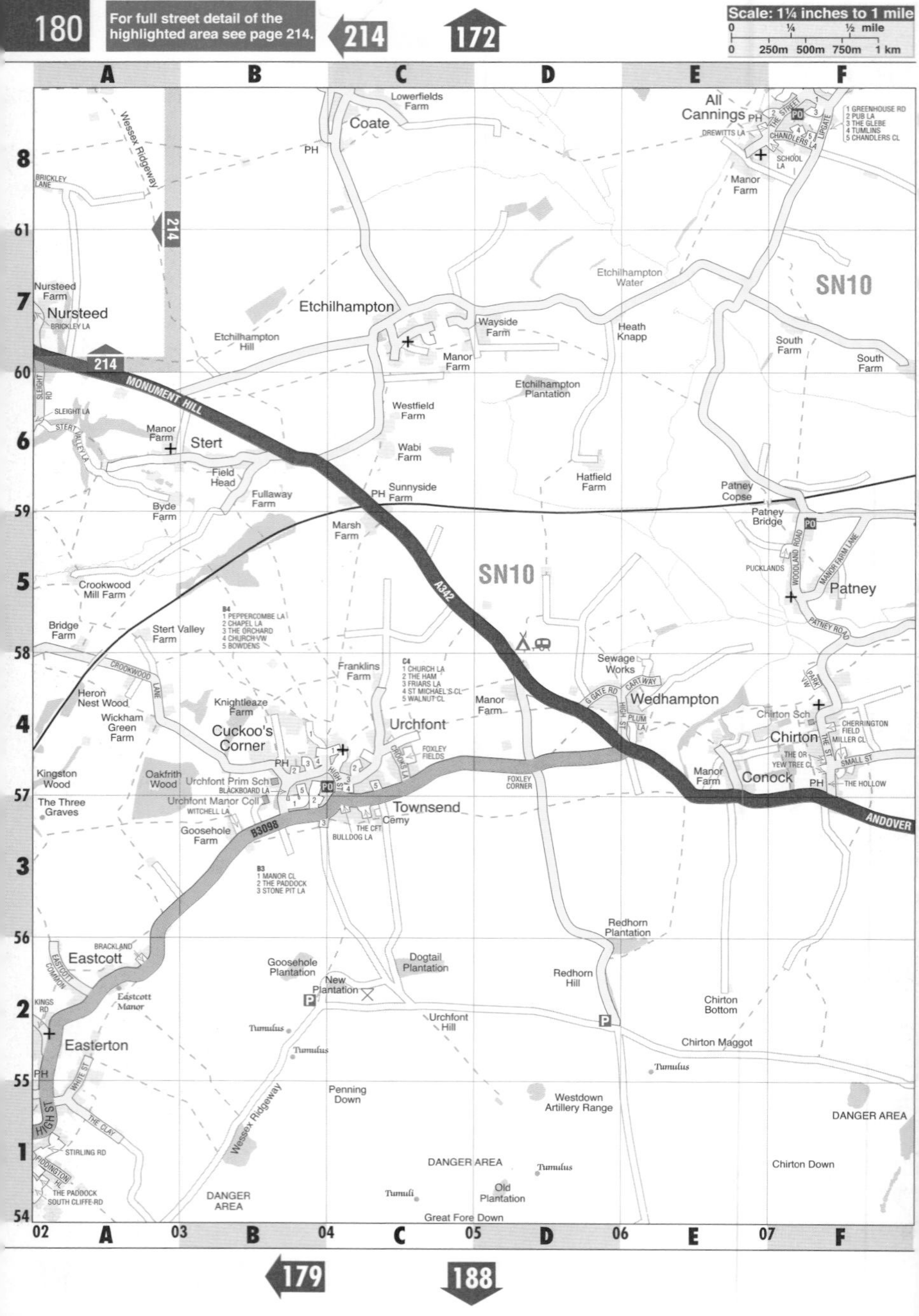

179
188

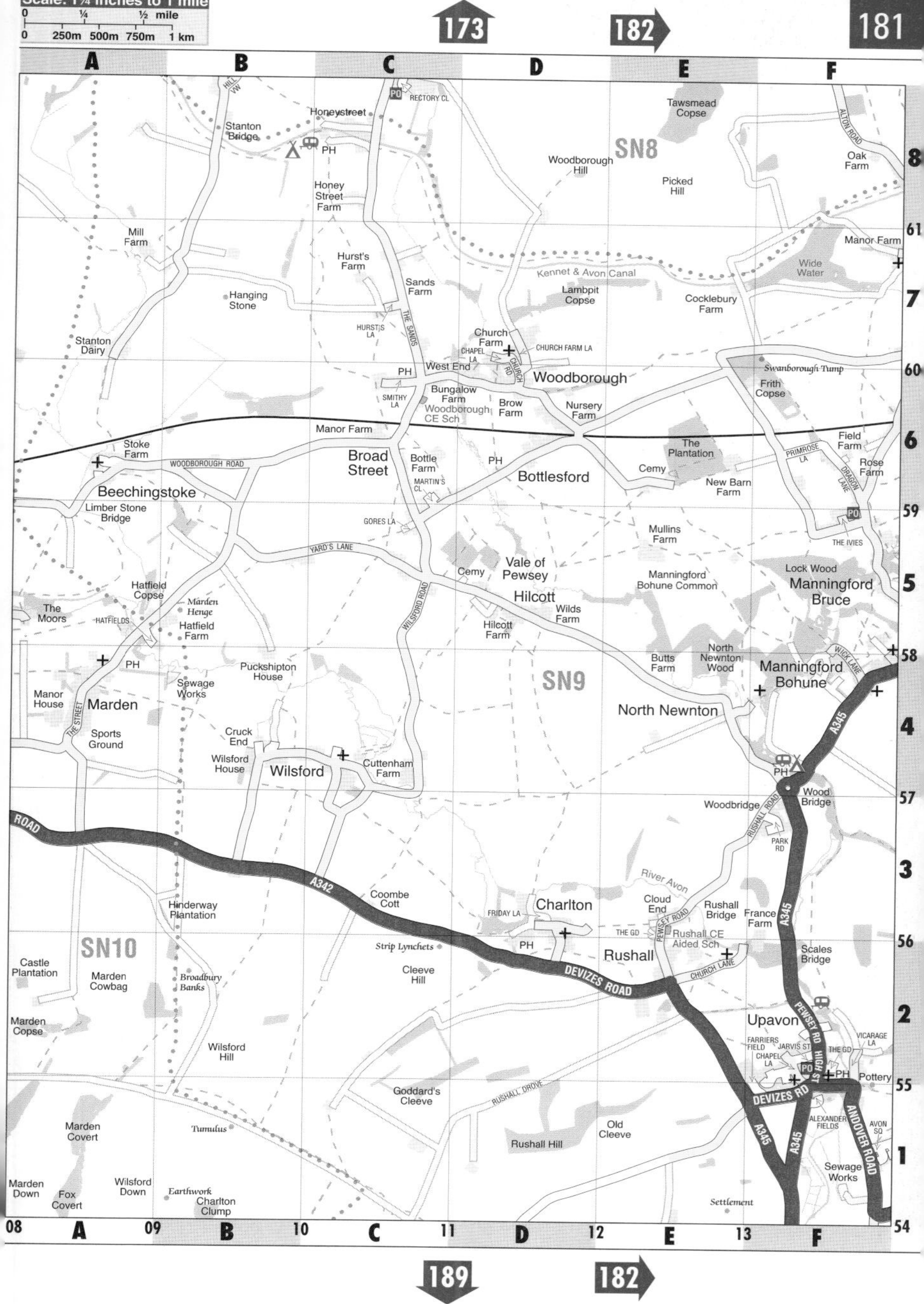
Scale: 1¼ inches to 1 mile
0 ¼ ½ mile
0 250m 500m 750m 1 km
173
182
A B C D E F
Honeystreet
Stanton Bridge
PH
RECTORY CL
Tawsmead Copse
Woodborough Hill
SN8
Picked Hill
Oak Farm
ALTON ROAD
Honey Street Farm
Mill Farm
Hurst's Farm
Sands Farm
Manor Farm
Wide Water
Kennet & Avon Canal
Hanging Stone
Lambpit Copse
Cocklebury Farm
Stanton Dairy
HURST'S LA
THE SANDS
Church Farm
CHAPEL LA
CHURCH RD
CHURCH FARM LA
West End
Woodborough
Swanborough Tump
Frith Copse
SMITHY LA
Bungalow Farm
Woodborough CE Sch
Brow Farm
Nursery Farm
Manor Farm
Stoke Farm
WOODBOROUGH ROAD
Broad Street
Bottle Farm
PH
The Plantation
Field Farm
PRIMROSE LA
Rose Farm
Cemy
Bottlesford
New Barn Farm
DRAGON LANE
Beechingstoke
Limber Stone Bridge
MARTIN'S CL
GORES LA
Mullins Farm
THE IVIES
YARD'S LANE
Cemy
Vale of Pewsey
Lock Wood
Manningford Bohune Common
Manningford Bruce
Hilcott
Hatfield Copse
Marden Henge
The Moors
HATFIELDS
Hatfield Farm
WILSFORD ROAD
Wilds Farm
Hilcott Farm
North Newnton Wood
WICK LANE
PH
Puckshipton House
Sewage Works
Butts Farm
SN9
Manningford Bohune
Manor House
THE STREET
Marden
North Newnton
Sports Ground
Cruck End
Wilsford House
Wilsford
Cuttenham Farm
A345
PH
Wood Bridge
Woodbridge
RUSHALL ROAD
PARK RD
ROAD
A342
River Avon
Hinderway Plantation
Coombe Cott
FRIDAY LA
Charlton
Cloud End
PEWSEY ROAD
Rushall Bridge
France Farm
THE GD
Rushall CE Aided Sch
SN10
Strip Lynchets
PH
Rushall
Scales Bridge
Castle Plantation
Marden Cowbag
Broadbury Banks
Cleeve Hill
DEVIZES ROAD
CHURCH LANE
Marden Copse
Upavon
PEWSEY RD
FARRIERS FIELD
JARVIS ST
HIGH ST
THE GD
VICARAGE LA
Wilsford Hill
CHAPEL LA
PO
PH
Pottery
Goddard's Cleeve
RUSHALL DROVE
DEVIZES RD
Marden Covert
Tumulus
Rushall Hill
Old Cleeve
ALEXANDER FIELDS
AVON SQ
ANDOVER ROAD
Sewage Works
Marden Down
Fox Covert
Wilsford Down
Earthwork
Charlton Clump
Settlement
8 61 7 60 6 59 5 58 4 57 3 56 2 55 1 54
08 09 10 11 12 13

181
For full street detail of the highlighted area see page 215.
174

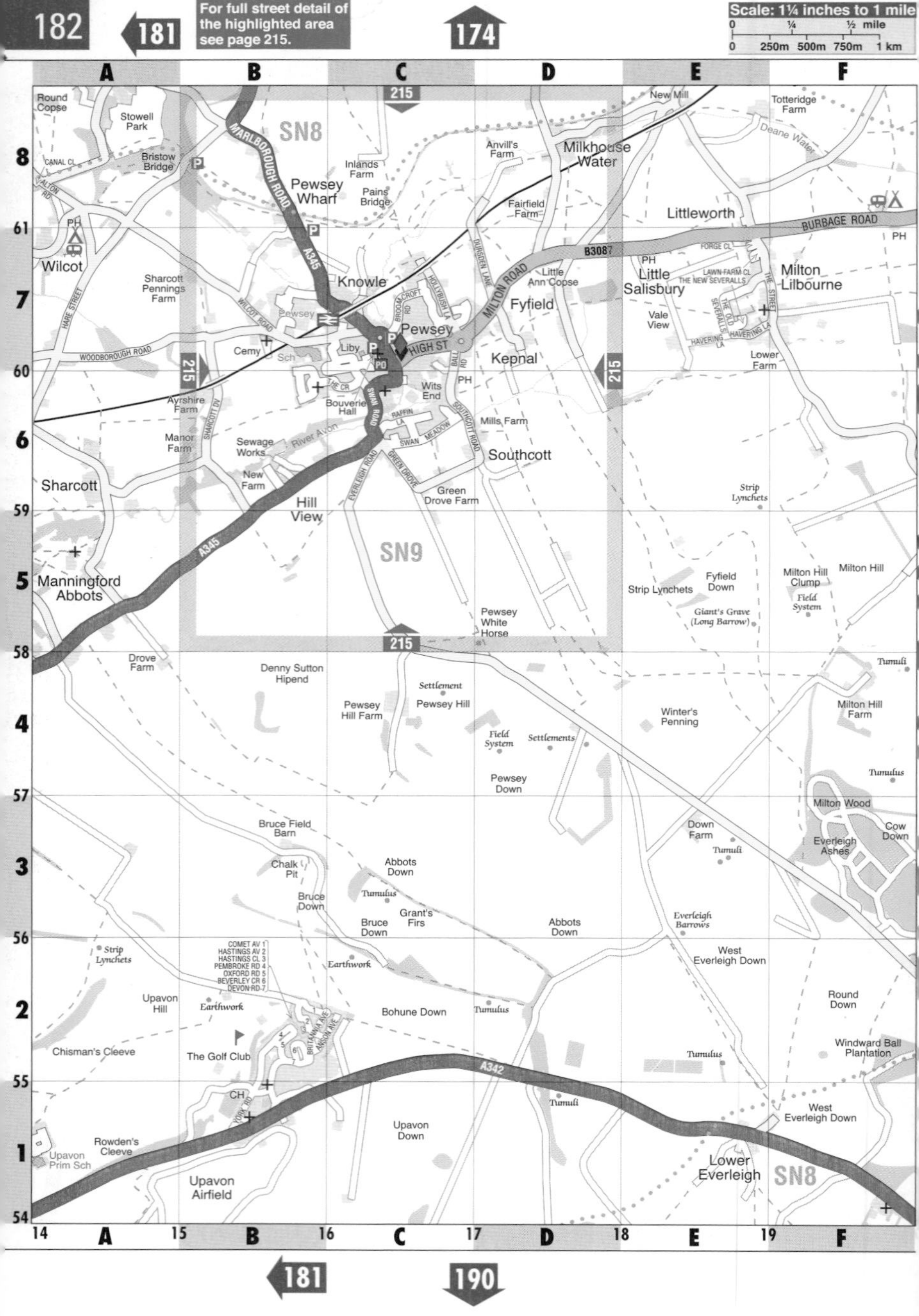

181
190

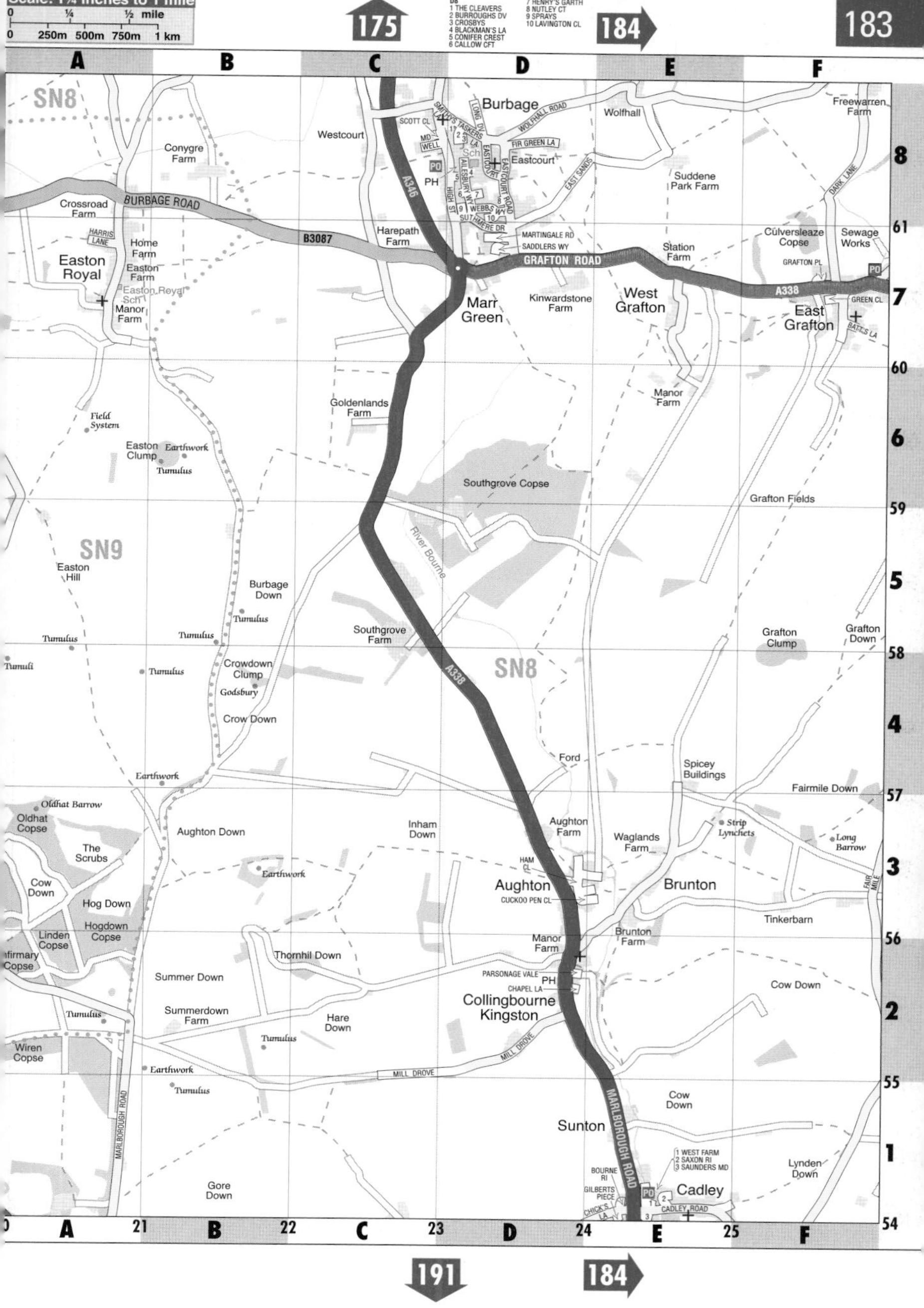
Scale: 1¼ inches to 1 mile
0 ¼ ½ mile
0 250m 500m 750m 1 km
175
184
191
184
D8
1 THE CLEAVERS
2 BURROUGHS DV
3 CROSBYS
4 BLACKMAN'S LA
5 CONIFER CREST
6 CALLOW CFT
7 HENRY'S GARTH
8 NUTLEY CT
9 SPRAYS
10 LAVINGTON CL
Burbage
Westcourt
Wolfhall
Freewarren Farm
Conygre Farm
Eastcourt
Suddene Park Farm
Crossroad Farm
BURBAGE ROAD
B3087
Harepath Farm
GRAFTON ROAD
Station Farm
Culversleaze Copse
Sewage Works
Easton Royal
Home Farm
Easton Farm
Manor Farm
Marr Green
Kinwardstone Farm
West Grafton
East Grafton
A346
A338
Goldenlands Farm
Manor Farm
Field System
Easton Clump
Earthwork
Tumulus
Southgrove Copse
Grafton Fields
SN8
SN9
Easton Hill
River Bourne
Burbage Down
Southgrove Farm
Grafton Clump
Grafton Down
Crowdown Clump
Godsbury
Crow Down
Ford
Spicey Buildings
Fairmile Down
Oldhat Barrow
Oldhat Copse
Aughton Down
Inham Down
Aughton Farm
Waglands Farm
Strip Lynchets
Long Barrow
The Scrubs
Cow Down
Aughton
Brunton
Hog Down
Hogdown Copse
Tinkerbarn
Linden Copse
Thornhil Down
Manor Farm
Brunton Farm
Summer Down
Cow Down
Collingbourne Kingston
Summerdown Farm
Hare Down
Wiren Copse
MILL DROVE
Sunton
MARLBOROUGH ROAD
Cadley
CADLEY ROAD
1 WEST FARM
2 SAXON RI
3 SAUNDERS MD
Gore Down
Lynden Down
A B C D E F
21 22 23 24 25
54 55 56 57 58 59 60 61

183
176

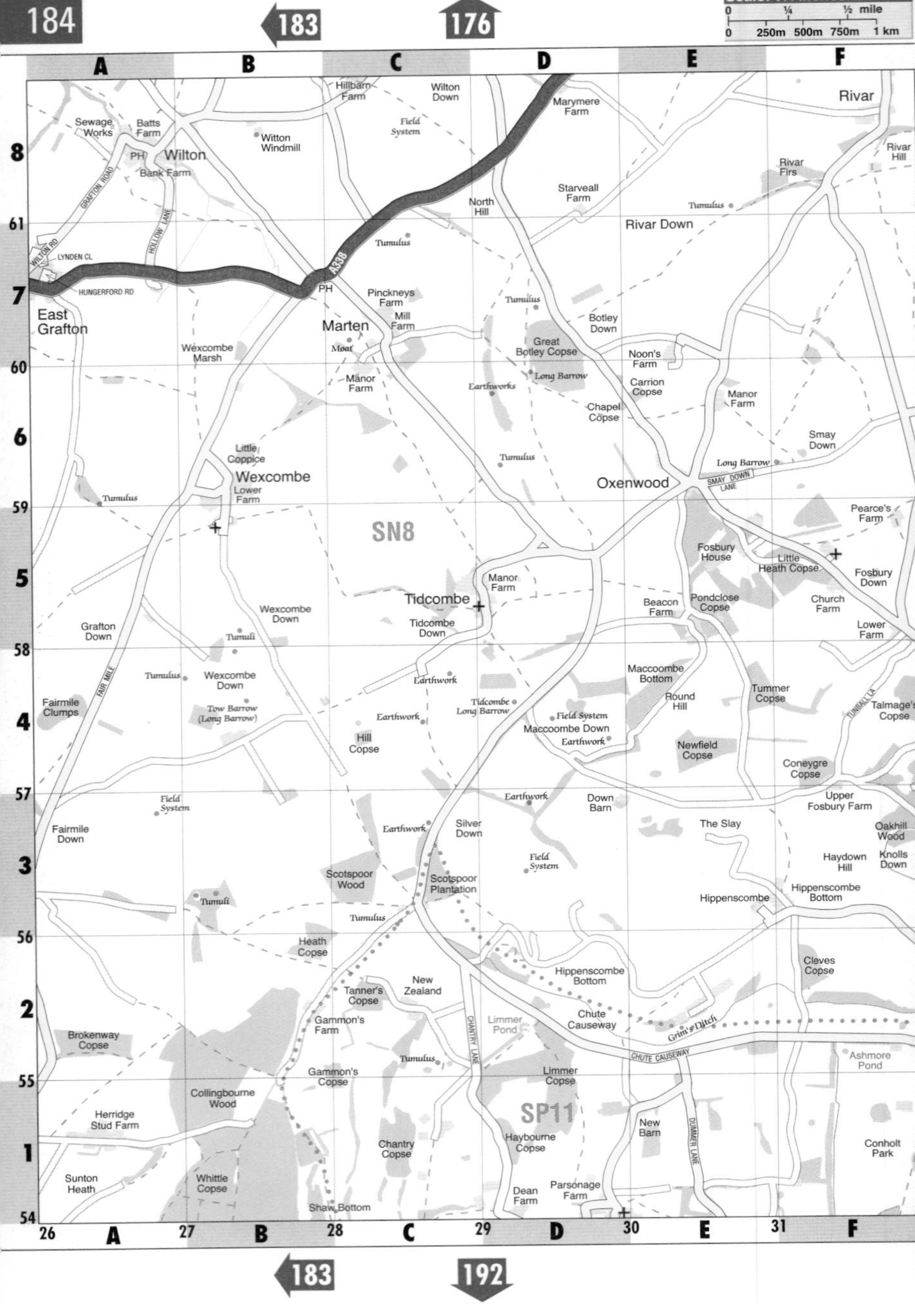

183
192

A B C D E F
Ham Hill
Three Cornered Covert
Wright's Copse
Fort
Walbury Hill
Ashley Down
Earthwork
Town Farm
DOWNS LANE
WOODCOTE ROAD
Buttermere Pond
Pigtrough Copse
Wright's Farm
8
Summer Hill
Inlands Copse
Grange Farm
Buttermere
CHURCH LA
WHITE FARM LA
Belvedere Wood
Combe
Lower Farm
61
Nut Covert
HEATH LANE
Manor Farm
New Buildings
HUNGERFORD ROAD
Buttermere Bottom
SN8
Sheepless Hill
RG17
7
Manor Farm
Wadsmere Down
Test Way
ASHLEY DROVE
Bishop's Barn
Ballyack House
Buttermere Wood
Combe Bottom
Kent's Copse
60
Summerton's Down
Grant's Copse
Rockmoor Down
CHURCH LANE
Moordown Farm
Hogs Hole
Upper Horns Farm
Rockmoor Plantation
Combe Wood
6
Limber Copse
Willis Farm
Henley
Tumulus
Heath Plantation
Birch Copse
Highdown
59
Rockmoor Pond
Test Way
Combe Bottom
Well Wood
ROCKMOOR LANE
Hart Hill Down
Down Copse
Upper Row Farm
Field System
North Hampshire STREET ATLAS
5
Winterside Farm
Cleve Hill
Wissenden Farm
Manor House
Fosbury
Linkenholt
Skites Copse
PO
58
Bulpitt's Copse
Halls Farm
Littledown
Netherton
Earthworks
Netherton House
Vernham Row
Manor Farm
East Down
CHURCH LA
Drove Farm
Box Farm
4
Vernham Street
Oakhill Wood
BOWERS LANE
Harts Bottom
Test Way
57
Bank Copse
SP11
THE DELL
BACK LA
HAYDOWN LEAS
HATCHBURY LA
BULPITS HILL
Sargents Farm
BOWERS LA
SHEPHERDS RI
SCHOOL CL
Netherton Hanging Copse
PO
PH
Vernham Manor
Vernham Bank
Vernham Dean Sch
Sawyers Wood
3
Grim's Ditch
Field System
Vernham Dean
Boats Copse
BOTISDONE CL
Wilster Copse
56
Thornycombe Wood
Farm Copse
Day's Copse
Assam Wood
Upton Manor
Ankers Farm
Conholt Bottom
CONHOLT HILL
CONHOLT LANE
Clinchorn Farm
Test Way
Kiblet Down
2
Parsonage Farm
Upton
PH
Conholt House
Lower Conholt Farm
55
Garden Copse
Little Bourne Farm
Ambley Farm
Forty Acre Wood
Oakdown Copse
Mascombe Copse
Conholt Park
Ambley Wood
HUNGERFORD LA
Well Bottom
Conholt Down
1
Rushmore Farm
Rushmore Down
DUNSTAN'S DROVE
Cow Down
Bevisbury Hill Fort
Enclosure
Lower Down Copse
A 33 B 34 C 35 D 36 E 37 F 54

B7
1 ROSENHEIM RI
2 PEAR TREE OR
3 REDLANDS
4 CARPENTERS LA
5 MANOR FIELDS
6 FLOWERS MD
7 HOLME LA
8 UPR GARSTON LA
9 TYNING LA
10 EMMS
11 ETHENDUN
12 THE PICQUET

109
178

Scale: 1¼ inches to 1 mile

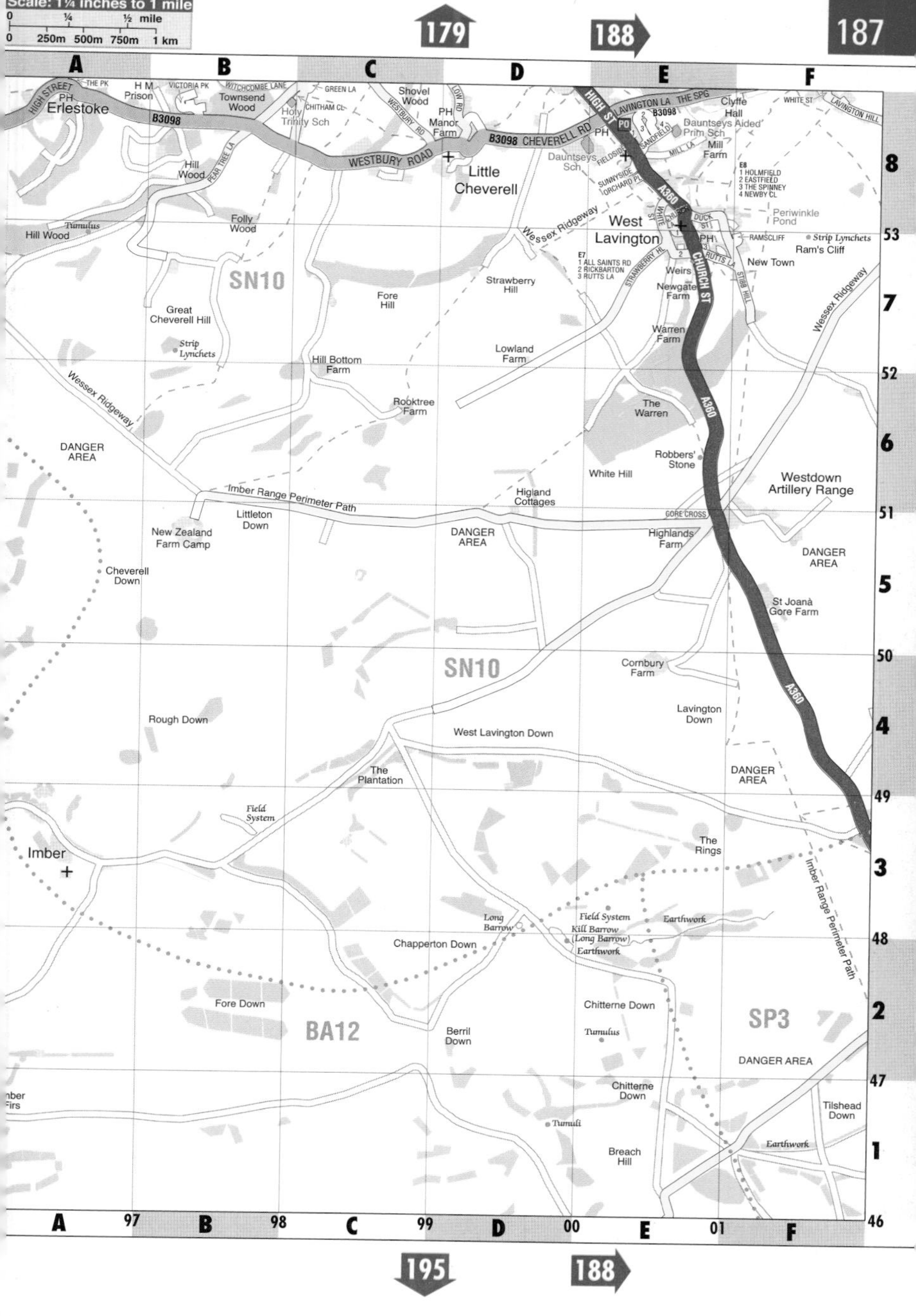
Scale: 1¼ inches to 1 mile
179
188
Erlestoke
H M Prison
Townsend Wood
Holy Trinity Sch
Shovel Wood
Manor Farm
Little Cheverell
B3098
WESTBURY ROAD
CHEVERELL RD
Dauntseys Sch
Clyffe Hall
Dauntseys Aided Prim Sch
Mill Farm
Hill Wood
Folly Wood
Tumulus
West Lavington
Periwinkle Pond
Ram's Cliff
Strip Lynchets
New Town
SN10
Great Cheverell Hill
Fore Hill
Strawberry Hill
Weirs
Newgate Farm
Warren Farm
Lowland Farm
Hill Bottom Farm
Rooktree Farm
The Warren
Wessex Ridgeway
A360
DANGER AREA
Robbers' Stone
White Hill
Westdown Artillery Range
Imber Range Perimeter Path
Higland Cottages
Littleton Down
New Zealand Farm Camp
Highlands Farm
GORE CROSS
Cheverell Down
St Joans Gore Farm
Cornbury Farm
Rough Down
Lavington Down
West Lavington Down
The Plantation
Field System
Imber
The Rings
Long Barrow
Kill Barrow (Long Barrow)
Earthwork
Chapperton Down
Fore Down
BA12
Berril Down
Chitterne Down
Tumulus
SP3
Tilshead Down
Tumuli
Breach Hill
195
188

187
180

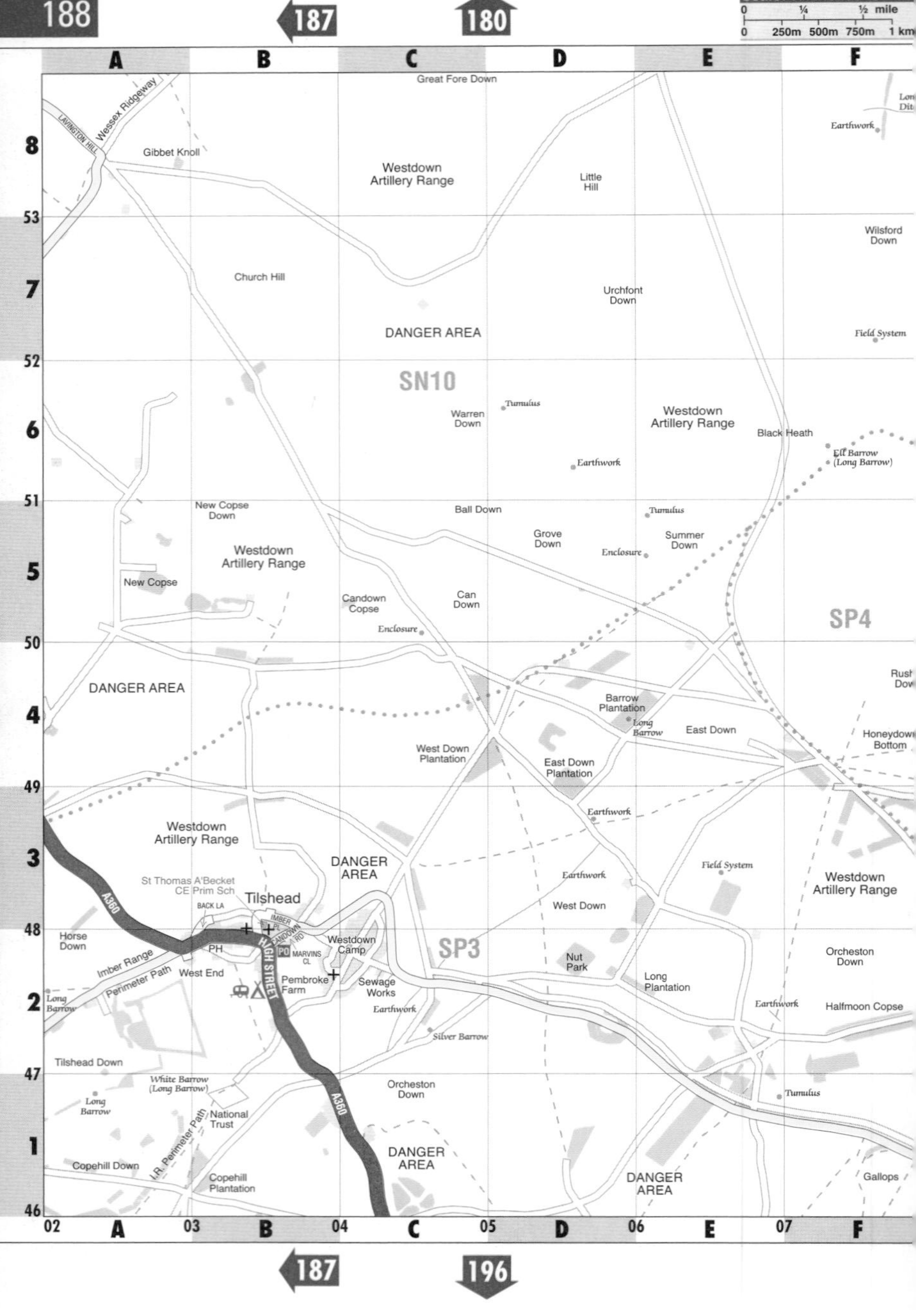

187
196

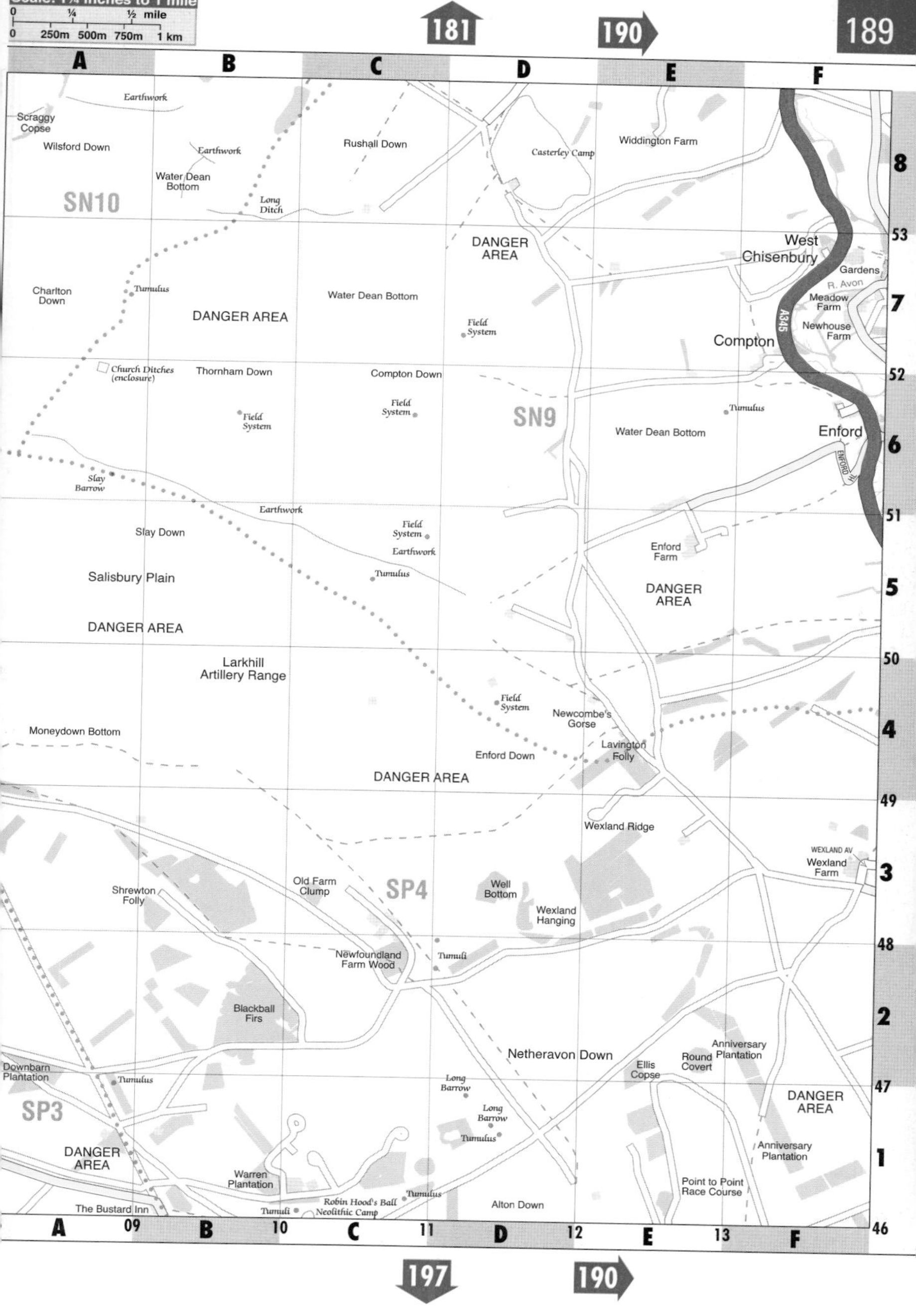
Scale: 1¼ inches to 1 mile
0 ¼ ½ mile
0 250m 500m 750m 1 km
181
190
A B C D E F
Earthwork
Scraggy Copse
Wilsford Down
Earthwork
Water Dean Bottom
Long Ditch
SN10
Rushall Down
Casterley Camp
Widdington Farm
DANGER AREA
West Chisenbury
Gardens
R. Avon
Meadow Farm
Newhouse Farm
Compton
A345
Charlton Down
Tumulus
Water Dean Bottom
DANGER AREA
Field System
Church Ditches (enclosure)
Thornham Down
Compton Down
Field System
Field System
SN9
Water Dean Bottom
Tumulus
Enford
ENFORD HL
Slay Barrow
Earthwork
Slay Down
Field System
Earthwork
Enford Farm
Tumulus
Salisbury Plain
DANGER AREA
DANGER AREA
Larkhill Artillery Range
Field System
Newcombe's Gorse
Moneydown Bottom
Lavington Folly
Enford Down
DANGER AREA
Wexland Ridge
WEXLAND AV
Wexland Farm
Old Farm Clump
SP4
Shrewton Folly
Well Bottom
Wexland Hanging
Newfoundland Farm Wood
Tumuli
Blackball Firs
Anniversary Plantation
Netheravon Down
Round Covert
Ellis Copse
Downbarn Plantation
Tumulus
Long Barrow
DANGER AREA
SP3
Long Barrow
Tumulus
DANGER AREA
Anniversary Plantation
Warren Plantation
Point to Point Race Course
Tumulus
Robin Hood's Ball Neolithic Camp
Tumuli
The Bustard Inn
Alton Down
8
53
7
52
6
51
5
50
4
49
3
48
2
47
1
46
A 09 B 10 C 11 D 12 E 13 F
197
190

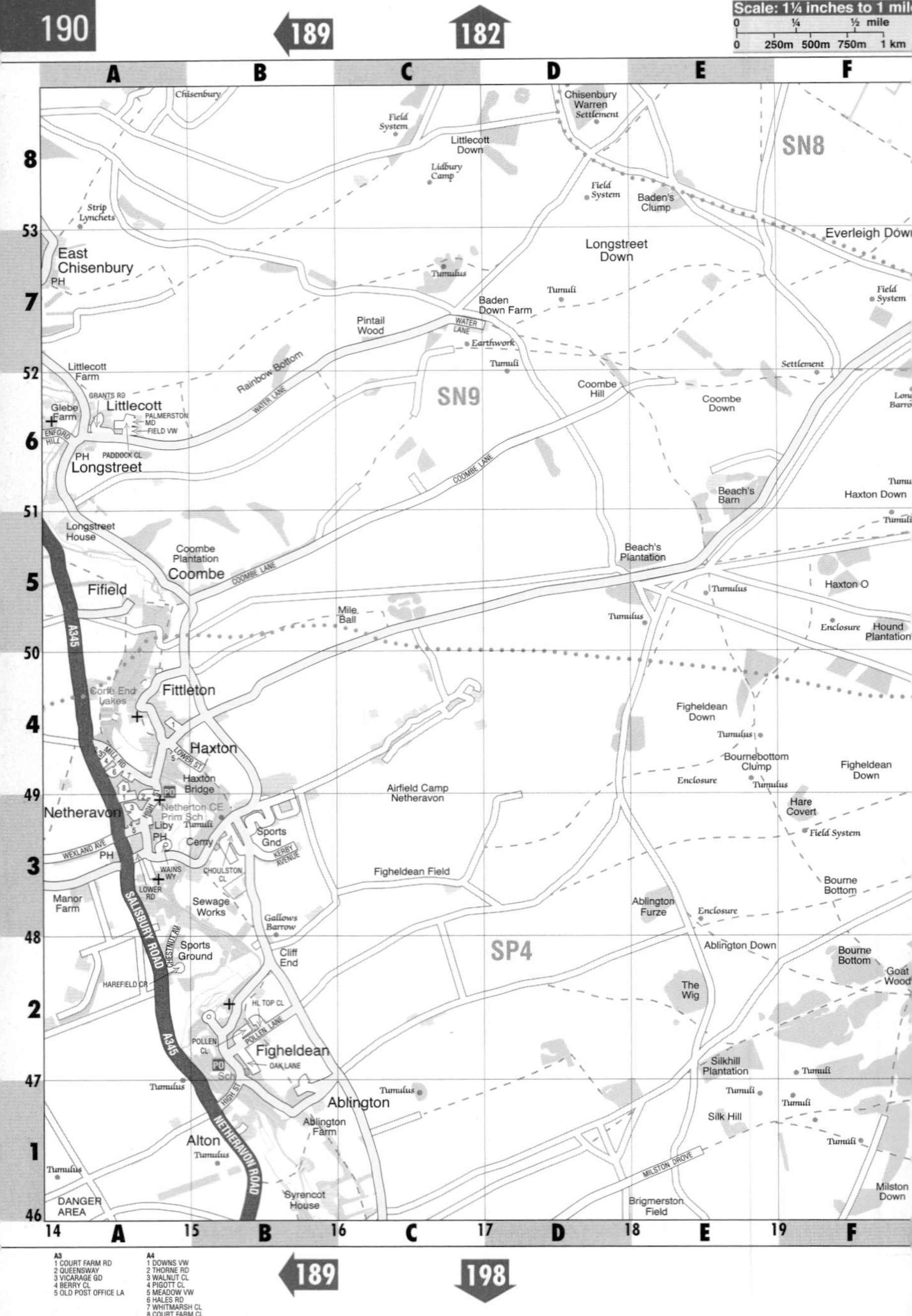
189
182
Scale: 1¼ inches to 1 mile
0 ¼ ½ mile
0 250m 500m 750m 1 km
A
B
C
D
E
F
Chisenbury
Field System
Chisenbury Warren Settlement
Littlecott Down
Lidbury Camp
SN8
Field System
Baden's Clump
Strip Lynchets
Everleigh Down
East Chisenbury
PH
Longstreet Down
Tumulus
Tumuli
Field System
Baden Down Farm
Pintail Wood
WATER LANE
Earthwork
Tumuli
Settlement
Littlecott Farm
Rainbow Bottom
GRANTS RD
Littlecott
SN9
Coombe Hill
Coombe Down
Glebe Farm
PALMERSTON MD
FIELD VW
WATER LANE
ENFORD HILL
PH
PADDOCK CL
Longstreet
COOMBE LANE
Tumuli
Haxton Down
Beach's Barn
Longstreet House
Coombe Plantation
Coombe
COOMBE LANE
Beach's Plantation
Fifield
Mile Ball
Tumulus
Haxton O
Tumulus
Enclosure
Hound Plantation
A345
Corle End Lakes
Fittleton
Figheldean Down
Haxton
MILL RD
LOWER ST
Tumulus
Bournebottom Clump
Figheldean Down
Haxton Bridge
Airfield Camp Netheravon
Enclosure
Tumulus
Netheravon
HIGH
PO
Netherton CE Prim Sch
Hare Covert
Liby
Tumuli
Field System
PH
Sports Gnd
WEXLAND AVE
PH
Cemy
KERBY AVENUE
CHOULSTON CL
Figheldean Field
WAINS WY
Bourne Bottom
Manor Farm
LOWER RD
Sewage Works
Ablington Furze
Enclosure
Gallows Barrow
SALISBURY ROAD
SP4
Ablington Down
Bourne Bottom
Sports Ground
Cliff End
CHESTNUT AV
Goat Wood
HAREFIELD CR
The Wig
HL TOP CL
A345
POLLEN CL
POLLEN LANE
Figheldean
PO
OAK LANE
Silkhill Plantation
Tumuli
Sch
Tumulus
Tumulus
Ablington
Tumuli
HIGH ST
Tumuli
Silk Hill
Ablington Farm
NETHERAVON ROAD
Tumuli
Alton
Tumulus
Tumulus
MILSTON DROVE
Milston Down
DANGER AREA
Syrencot House
Brigmerston Field
8
53
7
52
6
51
5
50
4
49
3
48
2
47
1
46
14
15
16
17
18
19
A3
1 COURT FARM RD
2 QUEENSWAY
3 VICARAGE GD
4 BERRY CL
5 OLD POST OFFICE LA
A4
1 DOWNS VW
2 THORNE RD
3 WALNUT CL
4 PIGOTT CL
5 MEADOW VW
6 HALES RD
7 WHITMARSH CL
8 COURT FARM CL
189
198

For full street detail of the highlighted area see page 216.

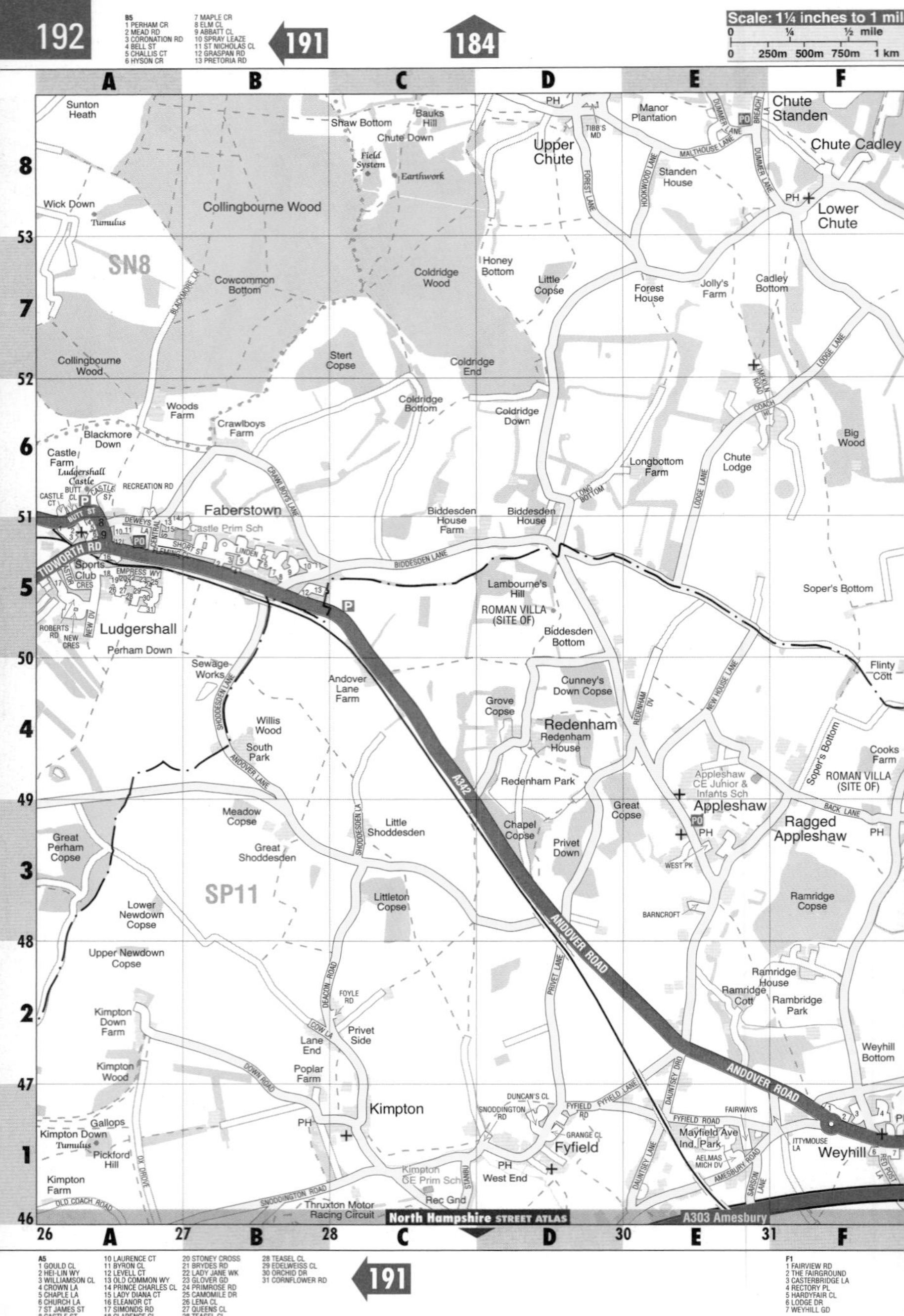
192
B5
1 PERHAM CR
2 MEAD RD
3 CORONATION RD
4 BELL ST
5 CHALLIS CT
6 HYSON CR
7 MAPLE CR
8 ELM CL
9 ABBATT CL
10 SPRAY LEAZE
11 ST NICHOLAS CL
12 GRASPAN RD
13 PRETORIA RD
191
184
Scale: 1¼ inches to 1 mil
0 ¼ ½ mile
0 250m 500m 750m 1 km
A
B
C
D
E
F
Sunton Heath
Shaw Bottom
Bauks Hill
Chute Down
Field System
Earthwork
PH
Upper Chute
TIBB'S MD
FOREST LANE
Manor Plantation
Standen House
HOOKWOOD LANE
MALTHOUSE LANE
DUMMER LANE
BREACH LA
Chute Standen
Chute Cadley
PH
Lower Chute
8
Wick Down
Tumulus
Collingbourne Wood
53
SN8
BLACKMORE LA
Cowcommon Bottom
Coldridge Wood
Honey Bottom
Little Copse
Forest House
Jolly's Farm
Cadley Bottom
7
Collingbourne Wood
Stert Copse
Coldridge End
KILN ROAD
LODGE LANE
52
Woods Farm
Crawlboys Farm
Coldridge Bottom
Coldridge Down
COACH HL
Blackmore Down
Castle Farm
Ludgershall Castle
6
CASTLE CT
BUTT CL
CASTLE ST
RECREATION RD
CRAWLBOYS LANE
Longbottom Farm
LONG BOTTOM
Chute Lodge
LODGE LANE
Big Wood
51
BUTT ST
Faberstown
DEWEYS LA
CENTRAL ST
Castle Prim Sch
SHORT ST
FLEMING CL
LINDEN CL
Biddesden House Farm
Biddesden House
TIDWORTH RD
Sports Club
EMPRESS WY
ASTOR CRES
BIDDESDEN LANE
5
Lambourne's Hill
ROMAN VILLA (SITE OF)
Soper's Bottom
ROBERTS RD
NEW CRES
NEW DV
Ludgershall
Perham Down
Biddesden Bottom
50
Sewage Works
Andover Lane Farm
Cunney's Down Copse
Flinty Cott
REDENHAM DV
NEW HOUSE LANE
SHODDESDEN LANE
Willis Wood
Grove Copse
4
South Park
ANDOVER LANE
Redenham
Redenham House
Soper's Bottom
Cooks Farm
A342
Redenham Park
Appleshaw CE Junior & Infants Sch
ROMAN VILLA (SITE OF)
49
Meadow Copse
SHODDESDEN LA
Little Shoddesden
Great Copse
Appleshaw
BACK LANE
Great Perham Copse
Chapel Copse
Privet Down
PH
Ragged Appleshaw
PH
Great Shoddesden
WEST PK
3
SP11
Littleton Copse
Ramridge Copse
Lower Newdown Copse
ANDOVER ROAD
BARNCROFT
48
Upper Newdown Copse
PRIVET LANE
DEACON ROAD
FOYLE RD
Ramridge House
Ramridge Cott
Rambridge Park
Kimpton Down Farm
2
COW LA
Lane End
Privet Side
Kimpton Wood
DOWN ROAD
Poplar Farm
DAUNTSEY DRO
Weyhill Bottom
ANDOVER ROAD
47
DUNCAN'S CL
FYFIELD LANE
Kimpton
SNODDINGTON RD
FYFIELD RD
FAIRWAYS
PH
Gallops
GRANGE CL
FYFIELD ROAD
Kimpton Down
Tumulus
Pickford Hill
Fyfield
Mayfield Ave Ind. Park
ITTYMOUSE LA
Weyhill
1
PH
West End
AELMAS MICH DV
AMESBURY ROAD
DAUNTSEY LANE
SARSON LANE
RED POST LA
Kimpton Farm
OX DROVE
Kimpton CE Prim Sch
Rec Gnd
OLD COACH ROAD
SNODDINGTON ROAD
Thruxton Motor Racing Circuit
46
North Hampshire STREET ATLAS
A303 Amesbury
26
A
27
B
28
C
D
30
E
31
F
A5
1 GOULD CL
2 HEI-LIN WY
3 WILLIAMSON CL
4 CROWN LA
5 CHAPLE LA
6 CHURCH LA
7 ST JAMES ST
8 CASTLE ST
9 HIGH ST
10 LAURENCE CT
11 BYRON CL
12 LEVELL CT
13 OLD COMMON WY
14 PRINCE CHARLES CL
15 LADY DIANA CT
16 ELEANOR CT
17 SIMONDS RD
18 CLARENCE CL
19 PRINCESS MARY GD
20 STONEY CROSS
21 BRYDES RD
22 LADY JANE WK
23 GLOVER GD
24 PRIMROSE RD
25 CAMOMILE DR
26 LENA CL
27 QUEENS CL
28 TEASEL CL
29 EDELWEISS CL
28 TEASEL CL
29 EDELWEISS CL
30 ORCHID DR
31 CORNFLOWER RD
191
F1
1 FAIRVIEW RD
2 THE FAIRGROUND
3 CASTERBRIDGE LA
4 RECTORY PL
5 HARDYFAIR CL
6 LODGE DR
7 WEYHILL GD

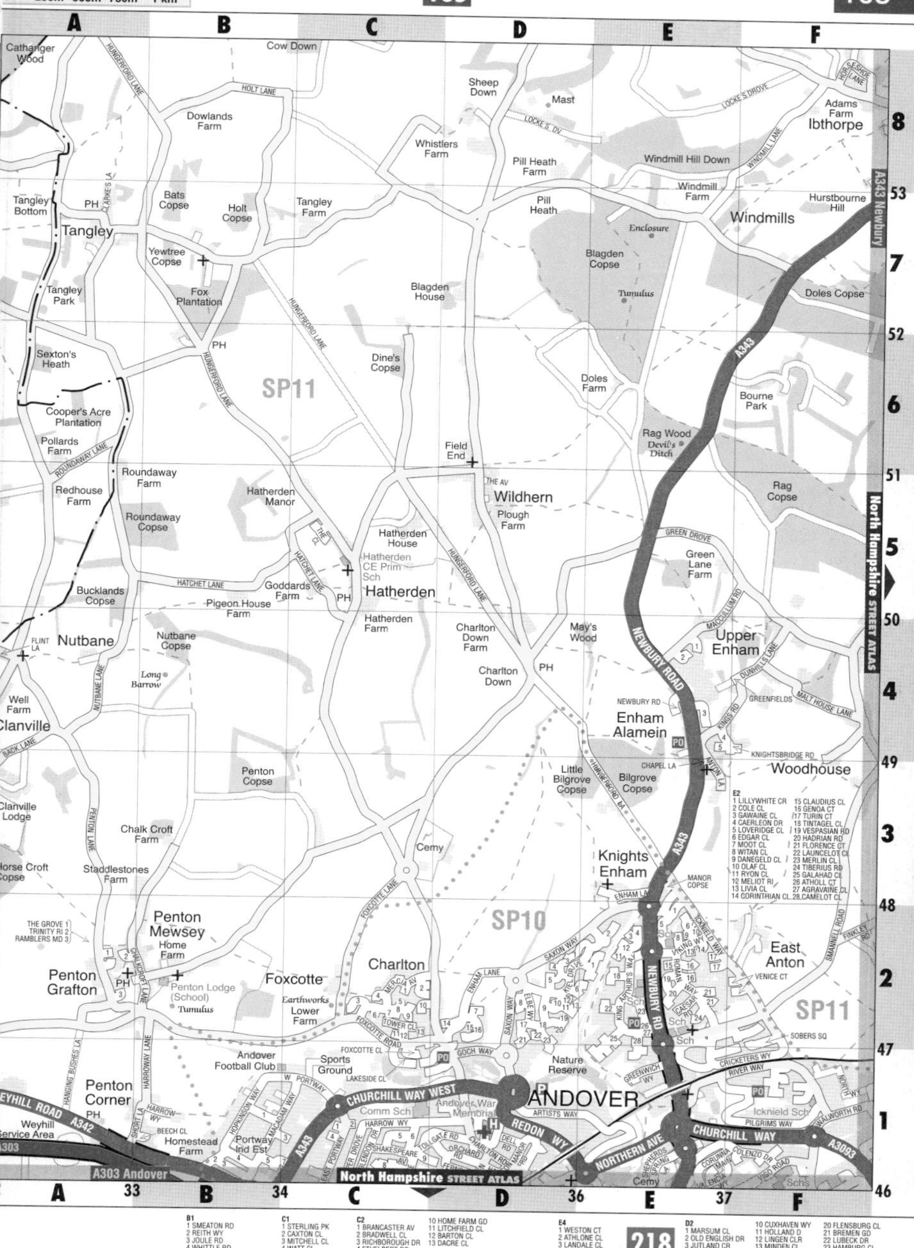

B1
1 SMEATON RD
2 REITH WY
3 JOULE RD
4 WHITTLE RD
5 ROYCE CL

C1
1 STERLING PK
2 CAXTON CL
3 MITCHELL CL
4 WATT CL
5 CHAUCER AV
6 MILTON AV
7 SOPWITH PK
8 BRACKENBURY
9 MAY TREE RD

C2
1 BRANCASTER AV
2 BRADWELL CL
3 RICHBOROUGH DR
4 ETHELBERT DR
5 HENGEST CL
6 RECULVER WY
7 BEDE DR
8 PORCHESTER CL
9 AUGUSTINE WY
10 HOME FARM GD
11 LITCHFIELD CL
12 BARTON CL
13 DACRE CL

E4
1 WESTON CT
2 ATHLONE CL
3 LANDALE CL
4 ALAMEIN RD
5 TOBRUK CL

218

D2
1 MARSUM CL
2 OLD ENGLISH DR
3 JUTLAND CR
4 RUNE DR
5 MONEYER RD
6 ANDEFERAS RD
7 ALDRIN CL
8 BORKUM CL
9 HATTEM PL
10 CUXHAVEN WY
11 HOLLAND D
12 LINGEN CLR
13 MINDEN CL
14 ST THOMAS CL
15 COLLINS CL
16 ARMSTRONG RI
17 ALTONIA GD
18 EMDEN RD
19 VERDEN WY
20 FLENSBURG CL
21 BREMEN GD
22 LUBECK DR
23 HAMBURG CL

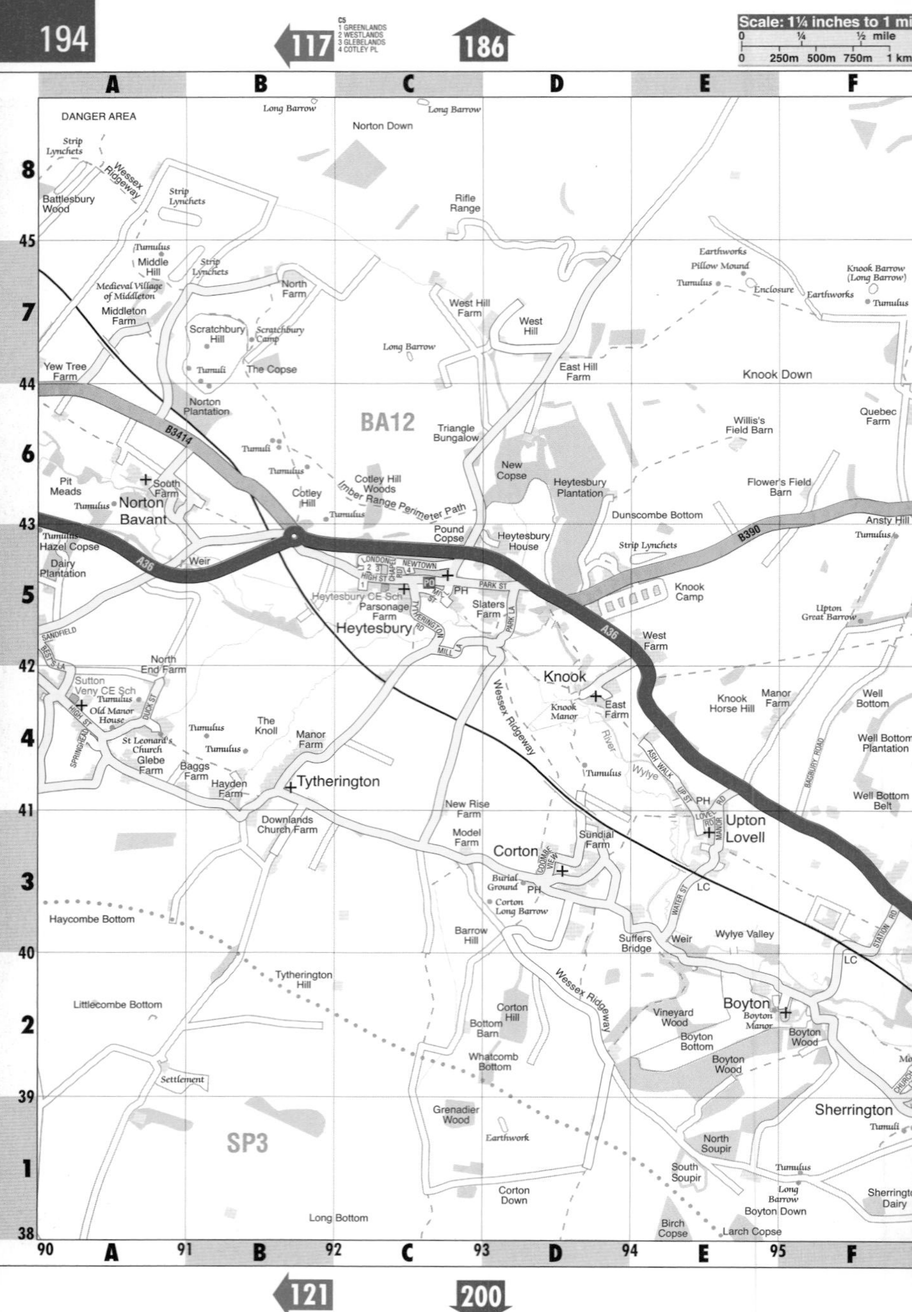
117
CS
1 GREENLANDS
2 WESTLANDS
3 GLEBELANDS
4 COTLEY PL
186
Scale: 1¼ inches to 1 mil
0 ¼ ½ mile
0 250m 500m 750m 1 km
A
B
C
D
E
F
DANGER AREA
Long Barrow
Long Barrow
Norton Down
Strip Lynchets
Wessex Ridgeway
Battlesbury Wood
Strip Lynchets
Rifle Range
Tumulus
Middle Hill
Strip Lynchets
Medieval Village of Middleton
North Farm
West Hill Farm
West Hill
Earthworks
Pillow Mound
Tumulus
Enclosure
Earthworks
Knook Barrow (Long Barrow)
Tumulus
Middleton Farm
Scratchbury Hill
Scratchbury Camp
Long Barrow
Yew Tree Farm
Tumuli
The Copse
East Hill Farm
Knook Down
Norton Plantation
BA12
Triangle Bungalow
Willis's Field Barn
Quebec Farm
B3414
Tumuli
Tumulus
New Copse
Cotley Hill Woods
Imber Range Perimeter Path
Heytesbury Plantation
Flower's Field Barn
Pit Meads
South Farm
Tumulus
Norton Bavant
Cotley Hill
Tumulus
Dunscombe Bottom
Ansty Hill
Pound Copse
Heytesbury House
Tumulus
Tumulus
Hazel Copse
Strip Lynchets
B390
Weir
LONDON
NEWTOWN
HIGH ST
CHAPEL RD
PO
MILL ST
PARK ST
PH
Dairy Plantation
A36
Knook Camp
Heytesbury CE Sch
Parsonage Farm
Slaters Farm
PARK LA
Upton Great Barrow
Heytesbury
TYTHERINGTON RD
MILL LA
SANDFIELD
West Farm
BEST'S LA
North End Farm
Sutton Veny CE Sch
Tumulus
Old Manor House
HIGH ST
DUCK ST
Knook
Knook Manor
East Farm
Wessex Ridgeway
Knook Horse Hill
Manor Farm
Well Bottom
Tumulus
The Knoll
Manor Farm
SPRINGHEAD
St Leonard's Church
Glebe Farm
Tumulus
River Wylye
ASH WALK
Well Bottom Plantation
BAGBURY ROAD
Baggs Farm
Hayden Farm
Tytherington
Tumulus
UP ST
PH
Well Bottom Belt
New Rise Farm
LOVEL RD
MANOR RD
Upton Lovell
Downlands Church Farm
Model Farm
Sundial Farm
Corton
COOMBE VIEW
Burial Ground
PH
Corton Long Barrow
WATER ST
LC
Haycombe Bottom
Barrow Hill
Suffers Bridge
Weir
Wylye Valley
STATION RD
LC
Tytherington Hill
Wessex Ridgeway
Littlecombe Bottom
Corton Hill
Vineyard Wood
Boyton
Boyton Manor
Bottom Barn
Boyton Bottom
Boyton Wood
Whatcomb Bottom
Boyton Wood
CHURCH LA
Settlement
Grenadier Wood
Sherrington
Tumuli
SP3
Earthwork
North Soupir
South Soupir
Tumulus
Long Barrow
Sherrington Dairy
Corton Down
Boyton Down
Long Bottom
Birch Copse
Larch Copse
8
45
7
44
6
43
5
42
4
41
3
40
2
39
1
38
90
91
92
93
94
95

Scale: 1¼ inches to 1 mile

187
196

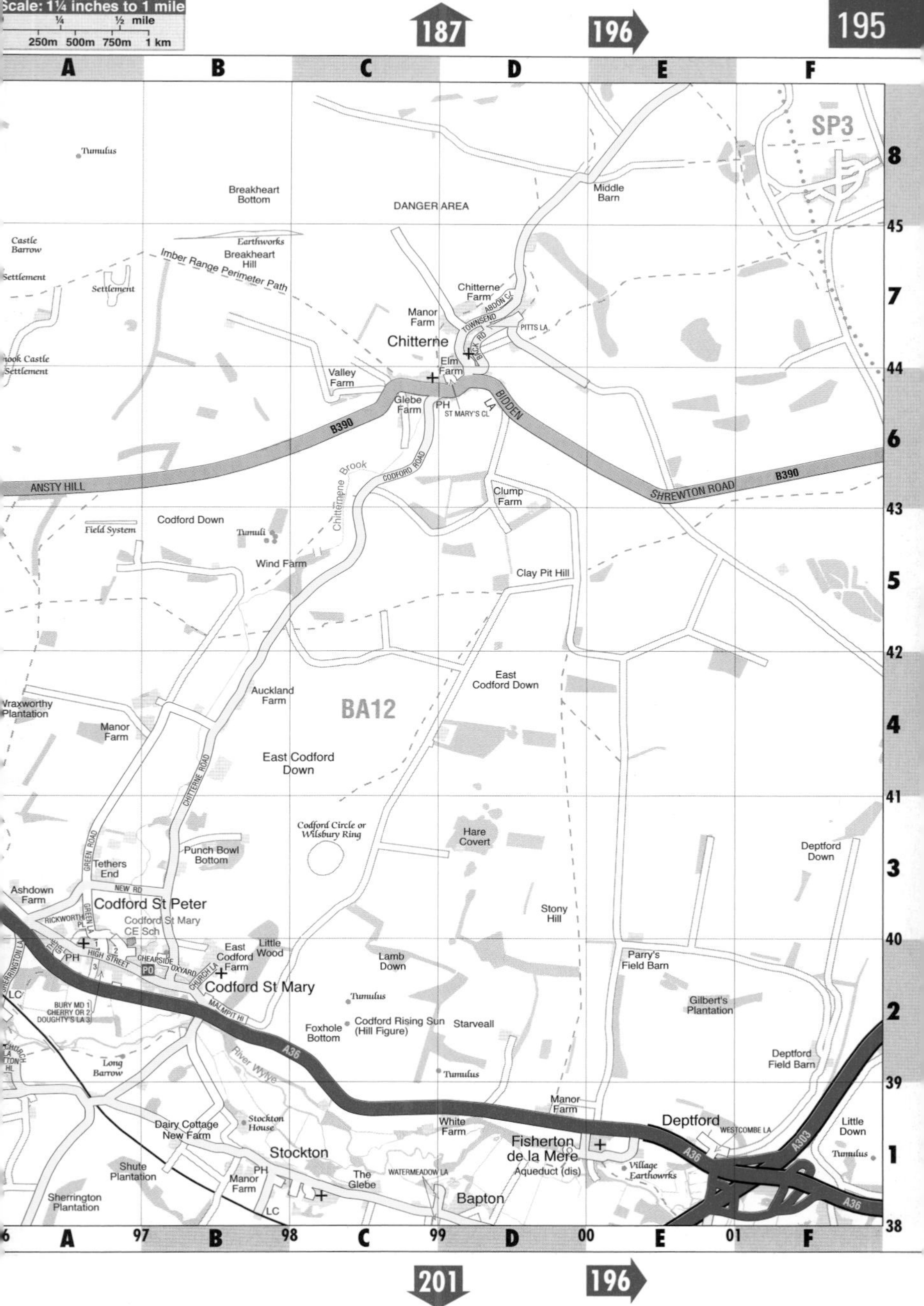

201
196

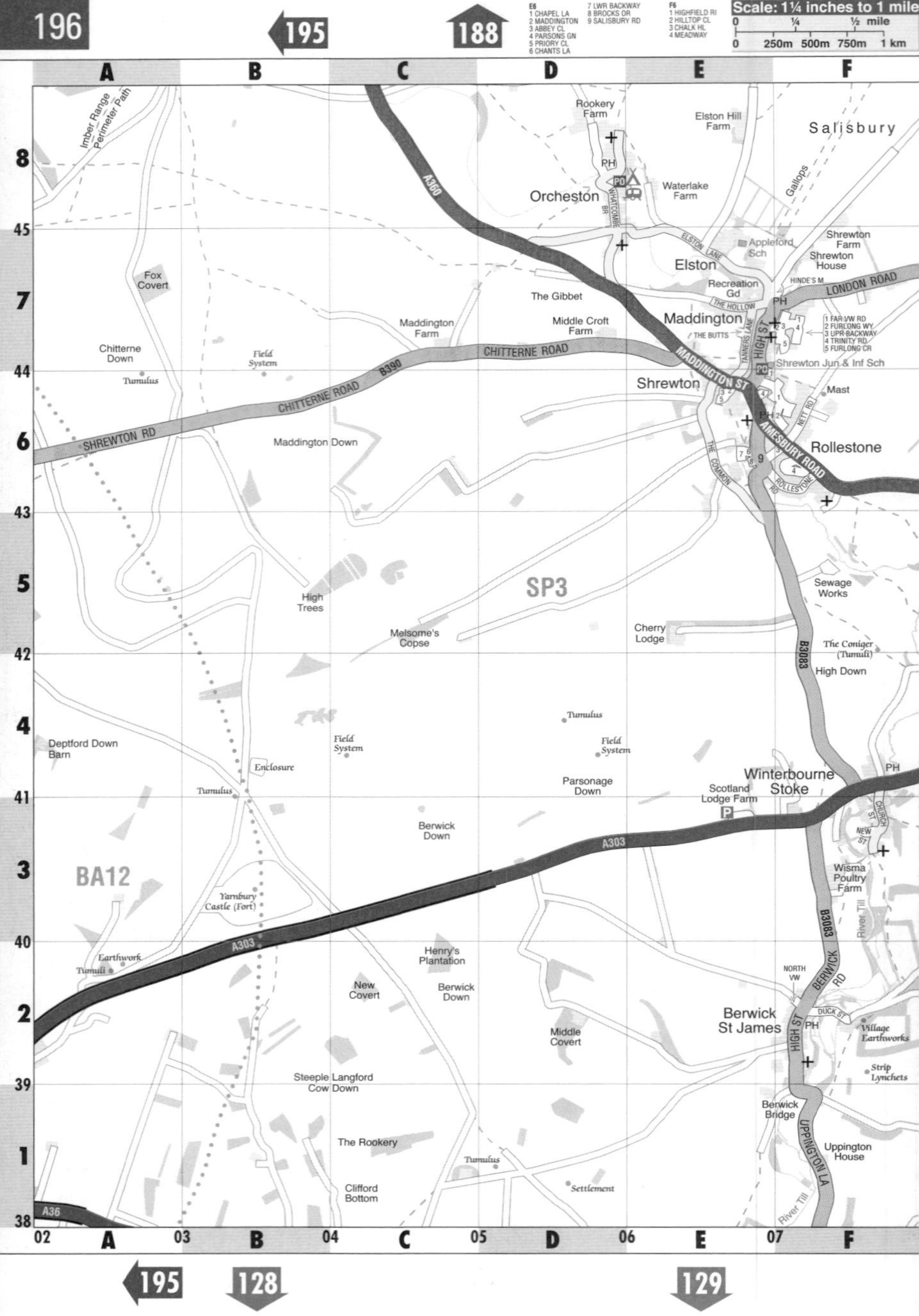
195
188
E6
1 CHAPEL LA
2 MADDINGTON
3 ABBEY CL
4 PARSONS GN
5 PRIORY CL
6 CHANTS LA
7 LWR BACKWAY
8 BROCKS OR
9 SALISBURY RD
F6
1 HIGHFIELD RI
2 HILLTOP CL
3 CHALK HL
4 MEADWAY
Scale: 1¼ inches to 1 mile
0 ¼ ½ mile
0 250m 500m 750m 1 km
Imber Range Perimeter Path
Rookery Farm
Elston Hill Farm
Salisbury
A360
Orcheston
WHATCOMBE BR
Waterlake Farm
Gallops
ELSTON LANE
Appleford Sch
Shrewton Farm
Shrewton House
Elston
Fox Covert
Recreation Gd
HINDE'S M
LONDON ROAD
The Gibbet
THE HOLLOW
Maddington
1 FAR VW RD
2 FURLONG WY
3 UPR BACKWAY
4 TRINITY RD
5 FURLONG CR
Maddington Farm
Middle Croft Farm
THE BUTTS
TANNERS LANE
HIGH ST
Chitterne Down
Field System
CHITTERNE ROAD
B390
MADDINGTON ST
Shrewton Jun & Inf Sch
Tumulus
Shrewton
Mast
CHITTERNE ROAD
NETT RD
SHREWTON RD
Maddington Down
AMESBURY ROAD
Rollestone
THE COMMON
ROLLESTONE RD
SP3
Sewage Works
High Trees
Melsome's Copse
Cherry Lodge
B3083
The Coniger (Tumuli)
High Down
Tumulus
Field System
Field System
Deptford Down Barn
Enclosure
Parsonage Down
Winterbourne Stoke
Scotland Lodge Farm
Tumulus
CHURCH ST
NEW ST
Berwick Down
A303
BA12
Wisma Poultry Farm
Yarnbury Castle (Fort)
River Till
A303
Earthwork
Tumuli
Henry's Plantation
B3083
NORTH VW
BERWICK RD
New Covert
Berwick Down
DUCK ST
Berwick St James
HIGH ST
Village Earthworks
Middle Covert
Strip Lynchets
Steeple Langford Cow Down
Berwick Bridge
The Rookery
UPPINGTON LA
Uppington House
Tumulus
Clifford Bottom
Settlement
River Till
A36
A B C D E F
8 45 7 44 6 43 5 42 4 41 3 40 2 39 1 38
02 03 04 05 06 07
195
128
129

Scale: 1¼ inches to 1 mile
0 ¼ ½ mile
0 250m 500m 750m 1 km
189
198
E6
1 HEATH SQ
2 GARDINER RD
3 MILNE CR
4 ARMITAGE SQ
5 WASON RD
6 DOUGLAS BROWN WK
E7
1 SHRAPNEL RD
2 WHINYATES RD
3 CATOR RD
4 CONGREVE RD
5 COCKS CL
A
B
C
D
E
F
Plain
Tumului
Long Barrow
Alton Down
Crescent Copse
Nelridge Farm
Shrewton Lodge
Alanbrooke's Plantations
Knighton Barrow (Long Barrow)
Sports Ground
DANGER AREA
Rollestone Camp
Tumuli
DANGER AREA
Knighton Down
Royal Sch of Artillery
THE PACKWAY
B3086
Tumuli
THE PACKWAY
Long Barrow
Middle Farm
Tumuli
FARGO ROAD
Durrington Down Plantation
Tumuli
HOWARD-VYSE RD
CP Sch
PH
PO
BRACKENBURY RD
BELL RD
GLOVER RD
BRIND RD
LAWRENCE RD
WATSON RD
ROSS ROAD
POWER RD
BINGHAM RD
WILLOUGHBY RD
WILSON RD
GORE RD
ALANBROOKE RD
LIGHTFOOT ROAD
BINGHAM
NORTHEN TR
Greenland Farm
B3086
FARGO ROAD
Durrington Down
Larkhill
Tumuli
Cursus
Tumuli
Fargo Plantation
Durrington Down Farm
FARGO ROAD
Sewage Works
The Cursus
Long Barrow
A360
Earthwork
AIRMAN'S CORNER
Long Barrow
Tumuli
Tumuli
Tumuli
National Trust
Old King Barrows
Fore Down
Winterbourne Stoke Down
Settlement
Enclosure
A344
The Avenue
P
SP4
Tumuli
Long Barrow
Stonehenge
New King Barrows
Earthwork
Stonehenge Down
National Trust
Tumuli
A303
SP3
Winterbourne Stoke Group (Tumuli)
A360
King Barrow
Long Barrow
Long Barrow
Long Barrow
National Trust
Henge (site of)
Coneybury Hill
Tumulus
LONGBARROW CROSS ROADS
HIGH STREET
A303
Tumuli
Bush Barrow
Tumuli
Tumuli
Winterbourne Stoke Hill
Tumuli
Hill Farm
Wilsford Down
Tumuli
Normanton Down
Oatlands Hill
Earthwork
Earthwork
Tumuli
Horse Down
Long Barrow
Lake Group (Tumuli)
Springbottom Farm
Normanton
Hanging Wood
Wilsford
Wilsford Group (Tumuli)
Lake Down
Asserton Farm
A360
Westfield Farm
Tumuli
Earthwork
Weir
Druid's Lodge
Earthwork
Lake
Tumulus
Lake Down
Field Systems
Lake House
Ham Wood
Druids Head Farm
YORK ROAD
Village Earthwork
Tumulus
Tumulus
Rox Hill Clump
Ham Plantation
Enclosure
Tumuli
Great Durnford
JUBILEE HL
8
45
7
44
6
43
5
42
4
41
3
40
2
39
1
38
08
09
10
11
12
13
130
131
198

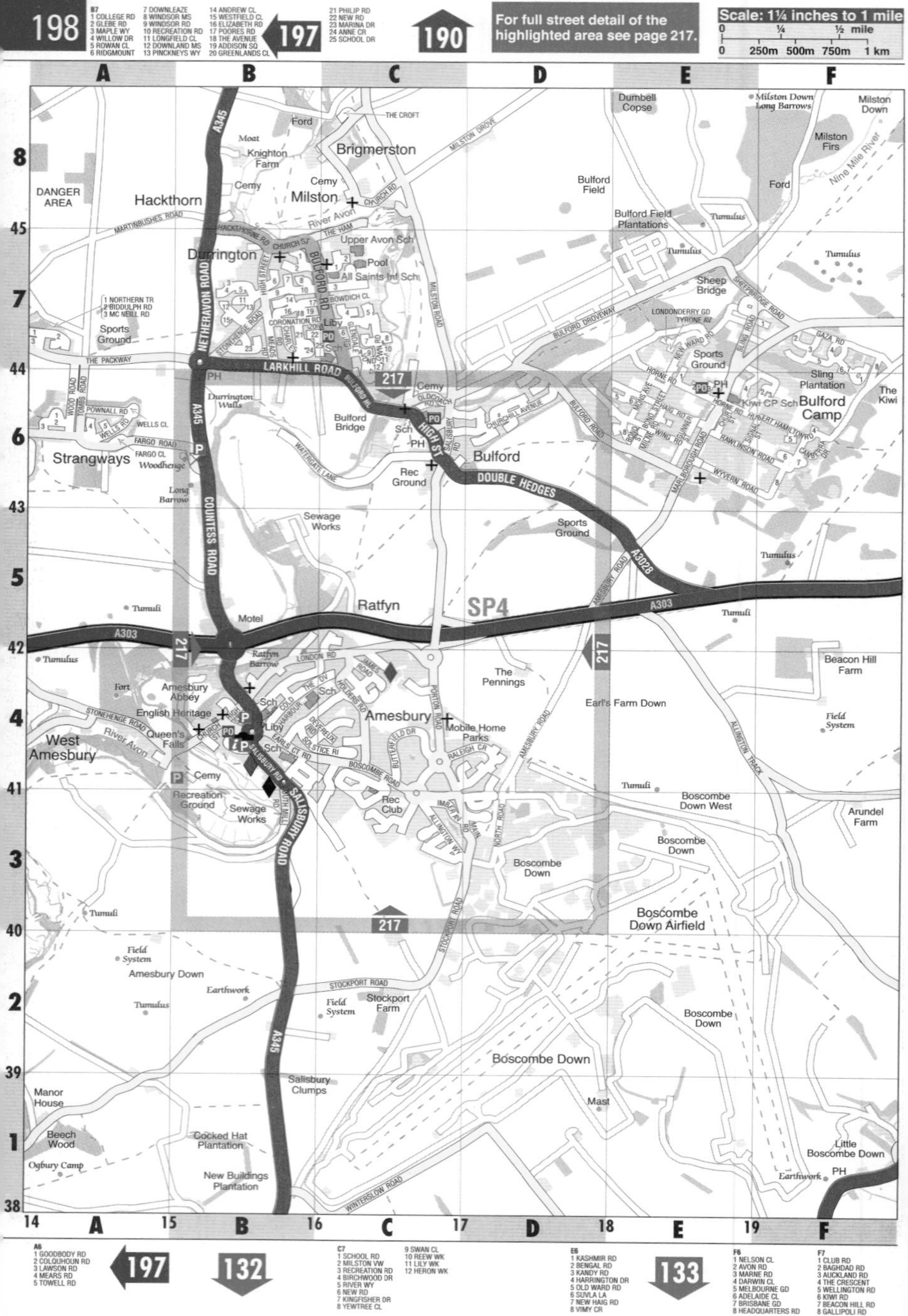
B7
1 COLLEGE RD
2 GLEBE RD
3 MAPLE WY
4 WILLOW DR
5 ROWAN CL
6 RIDGMOUNT
7 DOWNLEAZE
8 WINDSOR MS
9 WINDSOR RD
10 RECREATION RD
11 LONGFIELD CL
12 DOWNLAND MS
13 PINCKNEYS WY
14 ANDREW CL
15 WESTFIELD CL
16 ELIZABETH RD
17 POORES RD
18 THE AVENUE
19 ADDISON SQ
20 GREENLANDS CL
21 PHILIP RD
22 NEW RD
23 MARINA DR
24 ANNE CR
25 SCHOOL DR
197
190
For full street detail of the highlighted area see page 217.
Scale: 1¼ inches to 1 mile
0 ¼ ½ mile
0 250m 500m 750m 1 km
A B C D E F
8
45
7
44
6
43
5
42
4
41
3
40
2
39
1
38
14 15 16 17 18 19
Ford
THE CROFT
Moat
Knighton Farm
Brigmerston
MILSTON DROVE
Dumbell Copse
Milston Down Long Barrows
Milston Down
Milston Firs
Nine Mile River
DANGER AREA
Hackthorn
Cemy
Milston
CHURCH RD
Bulford Field
Ford
A345
MARTINBUSHES ROAD
HACKTHORNE RD
River Avon
THE HAM
Bulford Field Plantations
Tumulus
Durrington
CHURCH ST
BULFORD RD
Upper Avon Sch
Pool
All Saints Inf Sch
Tumulus
Tumulus
1 NORTHERN TR
2 BIDDULPH RD
3 MC NEILL RD
HIGH STREET
BOWDICH CL
MILSTON ROAD
Sheep Bridge
SHEEPBRIDGE ROAD
Sports Ground
STONEHENGE ROAD
CORONATION RD
Liby
PO
GLENDALE
Sch
LONDONDERRY GD
TYRONE AV
BULFORD DROVEWAY
NEW WARD RD
SLING ROAD
GAZA RD
NETHERAVON ROAD
THE PACKWAY
LARKHILL ROAD
BULFORD HL
217
Cemy
Sports Ground
Sling Plantation
The Kiwi
PH
HORNE RD
PH
WOOD ROAD
TOMBS ROAD
Durrington Walls
OLDCOACH RD
Kiwi CP Sch
Bulford Camp
POWNALL RD
WELLS CL
WELLS RD
Bulford Bridge
CHURCHILL AVENUE
BULFORD ROAD
MONS AVE
BOND STREET
SHAIG RD
HUBERT HAMILTON RD
FARGO ROAD
FARGO CL
Strangways
Woodhenge
WATERGATE LANE
Sch
PH
HIGH ST
SALISBURY RD
Bulford
RAWLINSON ROAD
Long Barrow
Rec Ground
DOUBLE HEDGES
MARLBOROUGH ROAD
WYVERN ROAD
COUNTESS ROAD
Sewage Works
Sports Ground
Tumulus
A3028
AMESBURY ROAD
Tumuli
Ratfyn
SP4
A303
Motel
Tumuli
A303
217
Tumulus
Ratfyn Barrow
LONDON RD
The Pennings
Beacon Hill Farm
Fort
Amesbury Abbey
Sch
Earl's Farm Down
English Heritage
STONEHENGE ROAD
Amesbury
PORTON ROAD
Mobile Home Parks
Field System
West Amesbury
River Avon
Queen's Falls
Liby
EARLS CT RD
SOLSTICE RI
RALEIGH CR
AMESBURY ROAD
ALLINGTON TRACK
BOSCOMBE ROAD
BUTTERFIELD DR
Cemy
SALISBURY RD
Tumuli
Boscombe Down West
Recreation Ground
Sewage Works
SALISBURY ROAD
Rec Club
IMBER AV
MAIN RD
NORTH ROAD
ALLINGTON WY
Arundel Farm
Boscombe Down
Boscombe Down
Tumuli
STOCKPORT ROAD
217
Boscombe Down Airfield
Field System
Amesbury Down
STOCKPORT ROAD
Earthwork
Field System
Stockport Farm
Tumulus
A345
Boscombe Down
Boscombe Down
Manor House
Salisbury Clumps
Mast
Beech Wood
Cocked Hat Plantation
Little Boscombe Down
Ogbury Camp
Earthwork
PH
New Buildings Plantation
WINTERSLOW ROAD
A6
1 GOODBODY RD
2 COLQUHOUN RD
3 LAWSON RD
4 MEARS RD
5 TOWELL RD
197
132
C7
1 SCHOOL RD
2 MILSTON VW
3 RECREATION RD
4 BIRCHWOOD DR
5 RIVER WY
6 NEW RD
7 KINGFISHER DR
8 YEWTREE CL
9 SWAN CL
10 REEW WK
11 LILY WK
12 HERON WK
E6
1 KASHMIR RD
2 BENGAL RD
3 KANDY RD
4 HARRINGTON DR
5 OLD WARD RD
6 SUVLA LA
7 NEW HAIG RD
8 VIMY CR
133
F6
1 NELSON CL
2 AVON RD
3 MARNE RD
4 DARWIN CL
5 MELBOURNE GD
6 ADELAIDE CL
7 BRISBANE GD
8 HEADQUARTERS RD
F7
1 CLUB RD
2 BAGHDAD RD
3 AUCKLAND RD
4 THE CRESCENT
5 WELLINGTON RD
6 KIWI RD
7 BEACON HILL RD
8 GALLIPOLI RD

Scale: 1¼ inches to 1 mile

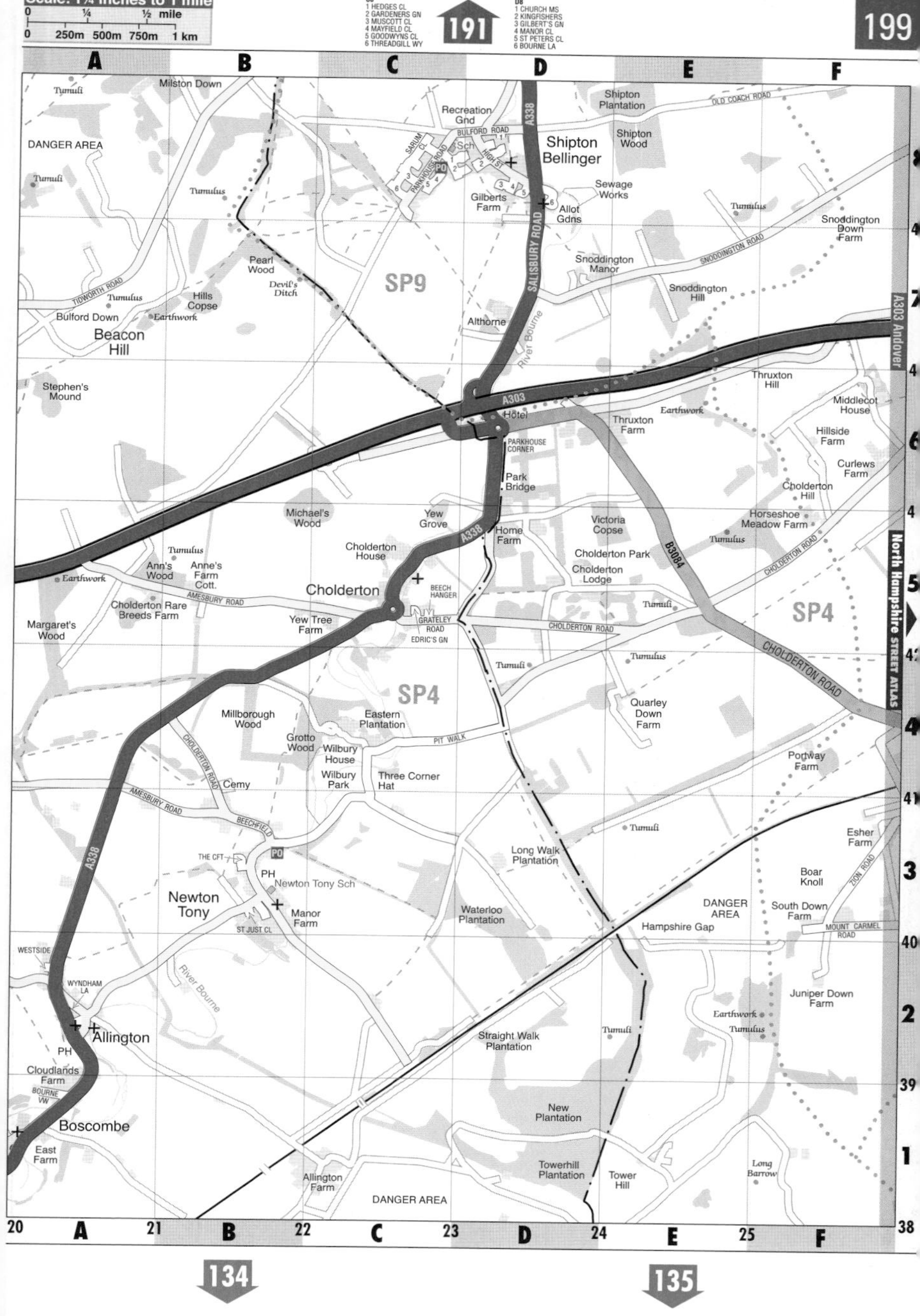

127

194

Scale: 1¼ inches to 1 mile

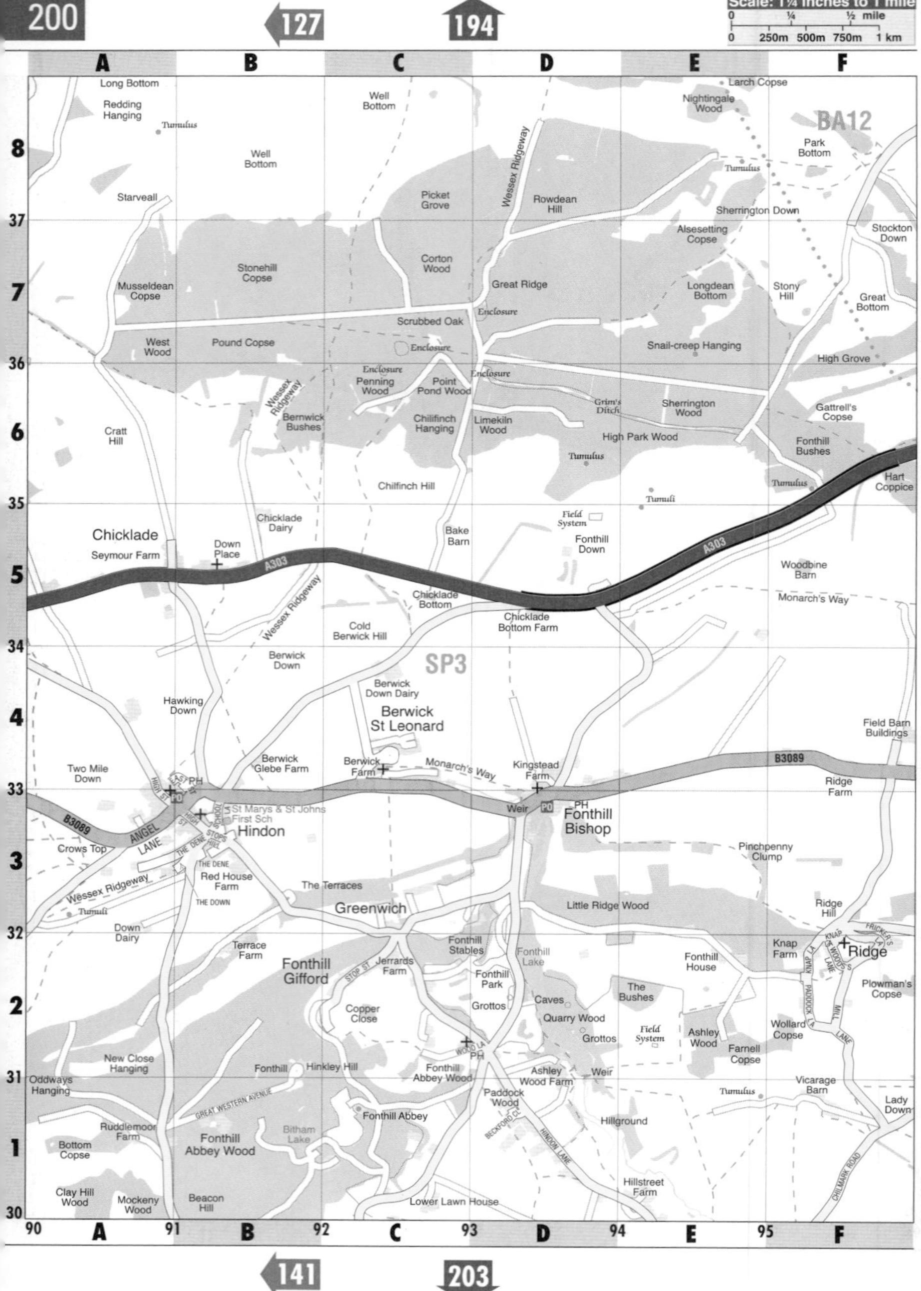

141

203

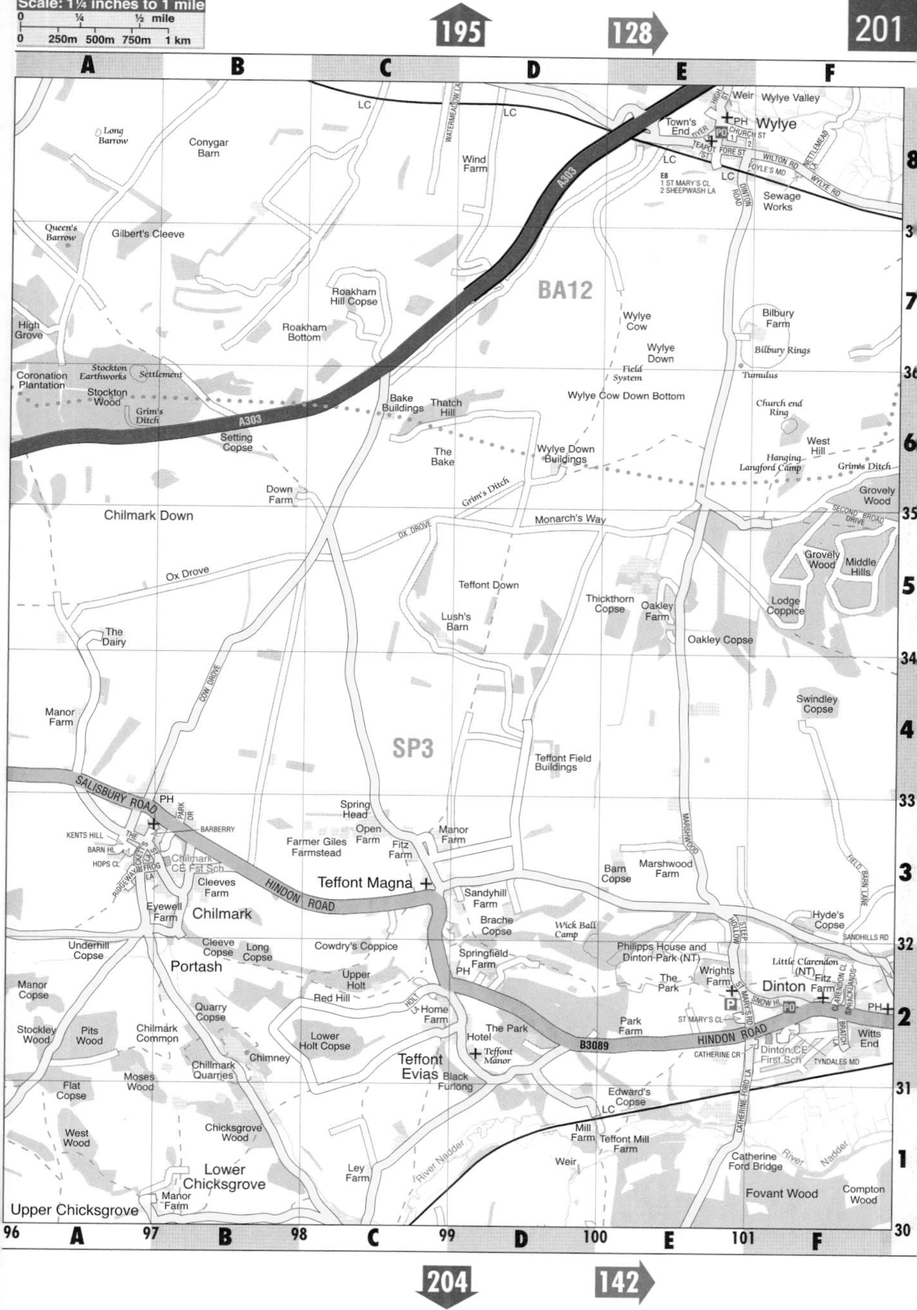
Scale: 1¼ inches to 1 mile
0 ¼ ½ mile
0 250m 500m 750m 1 km
195
128
A
B
C
D
E
F
LC
WATERMEADOW LA
LC
Weir
Wylye Valley
HIGH ST
Town's End
PH
Wylye
DYER LA
CHURCH ST
TEAPOT ST
FORE ST
WILTON RD
NETTLEMEAD LA
FOYLE'S MD
WYLYE RD
LC
LC
E8
1 ST MARY'S CL
2 SHEEPWASH LA
DINTON ROAD
Sewage Works
Long Barrow
Conygar Barn
Wind Farm
A303
Queen's Barrow
Gilbert's Cleeve
BA12
Roakham Hill Copse
Roakham Bottom
High Grove
Wylye Cow
Bilbury Farm
Wylye Down
Bilbury Rings
Field System
Tumulus
Coronation Plantation
Stockton Earthworks
Settlement
Stockton Wood
Grim's Ditch
Bake Buildings
Thatch Hill
Wylye Cow Down Bottom
Church end Ring
A303
Setting Copse
The Bake
Wylye Down Buildings
West Hill
Hanging Langford Camp
Grim's Ditch
Down Farm
Grim's Ditch
Grovely Wood
Chilmark Down
Monarch's Way
SECOND BROAD DRIVE
OX DROVE
Ox Drove
Grovely Wood
Middle Hills
Teffont Down
Thickthorn Copse
Oakley Farm
Lodge Coppice
Lush's Barn
The Dairy
Oakley Copse
COW DROVE
Swindley Copse
Manor Farm
SP3
Teffont Field Buildings
SALISBURY ROAD
PH
PARK DR
BARBERRY
KENTS HILL
BARN HL
HOPS CL
BECKETTS LA
FROG LA
RIDGEWAY
Chilmark CE Fst Sch
Spring Head
Open Farm
Farmer Giles Farmstead
Fitz Farm
Manor Farm
MARSHWOOD
Barn Copse
Marshwood Farm
FIELD BARN LANE
Cleeves Farm
HINDON ROAD
Teffont Magna
Sandyhill Farm
Eyewell Farm
Chilmark
Brache Copse
Wick Ball Camp
Hyde's Copse
SANDHILLS RD
Underhill Copse
Cleeve Copse
Long Copse
Cowdry's Coppice
Springfield Farm
Philipps House and Dinton Park (NT)
HOLLOW
STEEP
Little Clarendon (NT)
Portash
PH
Wrights Farm
The Park
Fitz Farm
CLARENDON CL
SPRACKLANDS
Manor Copse
Upper Holt
Dinton
Red Hill
HOLT LA
Home Farm
SNOW HL
ST MARY'S RD
PH
Quarry Copse
ST MARY'S CL
Stockley Wood
Pits Wood
Chilmark Common
Lower Holt Copse
The Park Hotel
Park Farm
B3089
HINDON ROAD
BRATCH LA
Witts End
Teffont Manor
Chimney
Teffont Evias
Dinton CE First Sch
CATHERINE CR
TYNDALES MD
Chillmark Quarries
Moses Wood
Black Furlong
Flat Copse
Edward's Copse
LC
CATHERINE FORD LA
West Wood
Chicksgrove Wood
Mill Farm
Teffont Mill Farm
River Nadder
River Nadder
Weir
Catherine Ford Bridge
Ley Farm
Lower Chicksgrove
Fovant Wood
Compton Wood
Manor Farm
Upper Chicksgrove
8
37
7
36
6
35
5
34
4
33
3
32
2
31
1
30
96
97
98
99
100
101

204
142

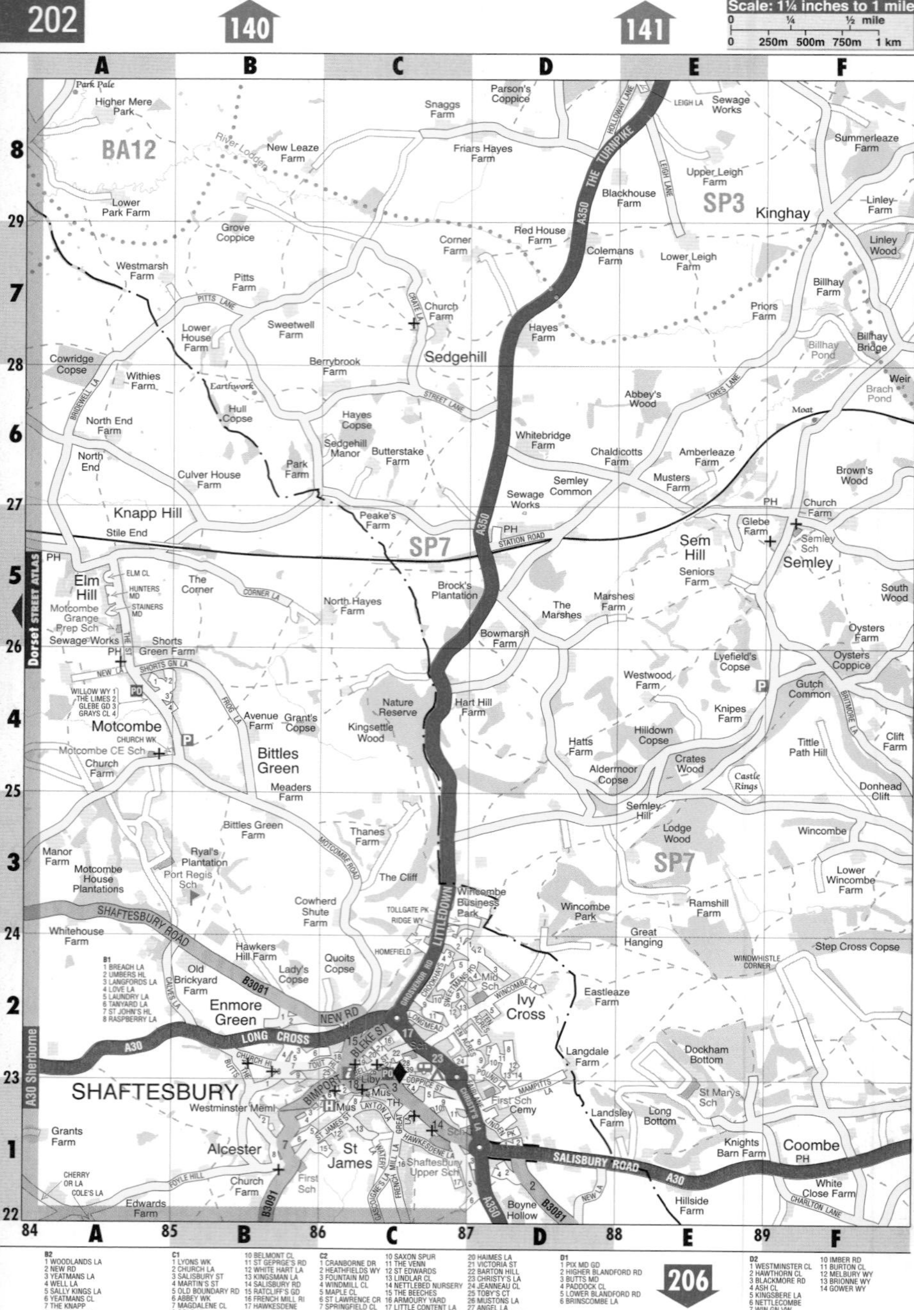

B2
1 WOODLANDS LA
2 NEW RD
3 YEATMANS LA
4 WELL LA
5 SALLY KINGS LA
6 YEATMANS CL
7 THE KNAPP
8 HORSEPONDS
9 CASTLE HL CL

C1
1 LYONS WK
2 CHURCH LA
3 SALISBURY ST
4 MARTIN'S ST
5 OLD BOUNDARY RD
6 ABBEY WK
7 MAGDALENE CL
8 GOLD HL
9 ST RUMBOLD'S RD
10 BELMONT CL
11 ST GEPRGE'S RD
12 WHITE HART LA
13 KINGSMAN LA
14 SALISBURY RD
15 RATCLIFF'S GD
16 FRENCH MILL RI
17 HAWKESDENE
18 HIGH ST

C2
1 CRANBORNE DR
2 HEATHFIELDS WY
3 FOUNTAIN MD
4 WINDMILL CL
5 MAPLE CL
6 ST LAWRENCE CR
7 SPRINGFIELD CL
8 OXENCROFT
9 LANE-SIDE
10 SAXON SPUR
11 THE VENN
12 ST EDWARDS
13 LINDLAR CL
14 NETTLEBED NURSERY
15 THE BEECHES
16 ARMOURY YARD
17 LITTLE CONTENT LA
18 KINGS HILL
19 PARSONS POOL
20 HAIMES LA
21 VICTORIA ST
22 BARTON HILL
23 CHRISTY'S LA
24 JEANNEAU CL
25 TOBY'S CT
26 MUSTONS LA
27 ANGEL LA
28 GRANVILLE GD
29 CHARLES GARRETT CL

D1
1 PIX MD GD
2 HIGHER BLANDFORD RD
3 BUTTS MD
4 PADDOCK CL
5 LOWER BLANDFORD RD
6 BRINSCOMBE LA

206

D2
1 WESTMINSTER CL
2 HAWTHORN CL
3 BLACKMORE RD
4 ASH CL
5 KINGSBERE LA
6 NETTLECOMBE
7 WIN GN VW
8 THOMAS HARDY DR
9 BEAUFOY CL
10 IMBER RD
11 BURTON CL
12 MELBURY WY
13 BRIONNE WY
14 GOWER WY

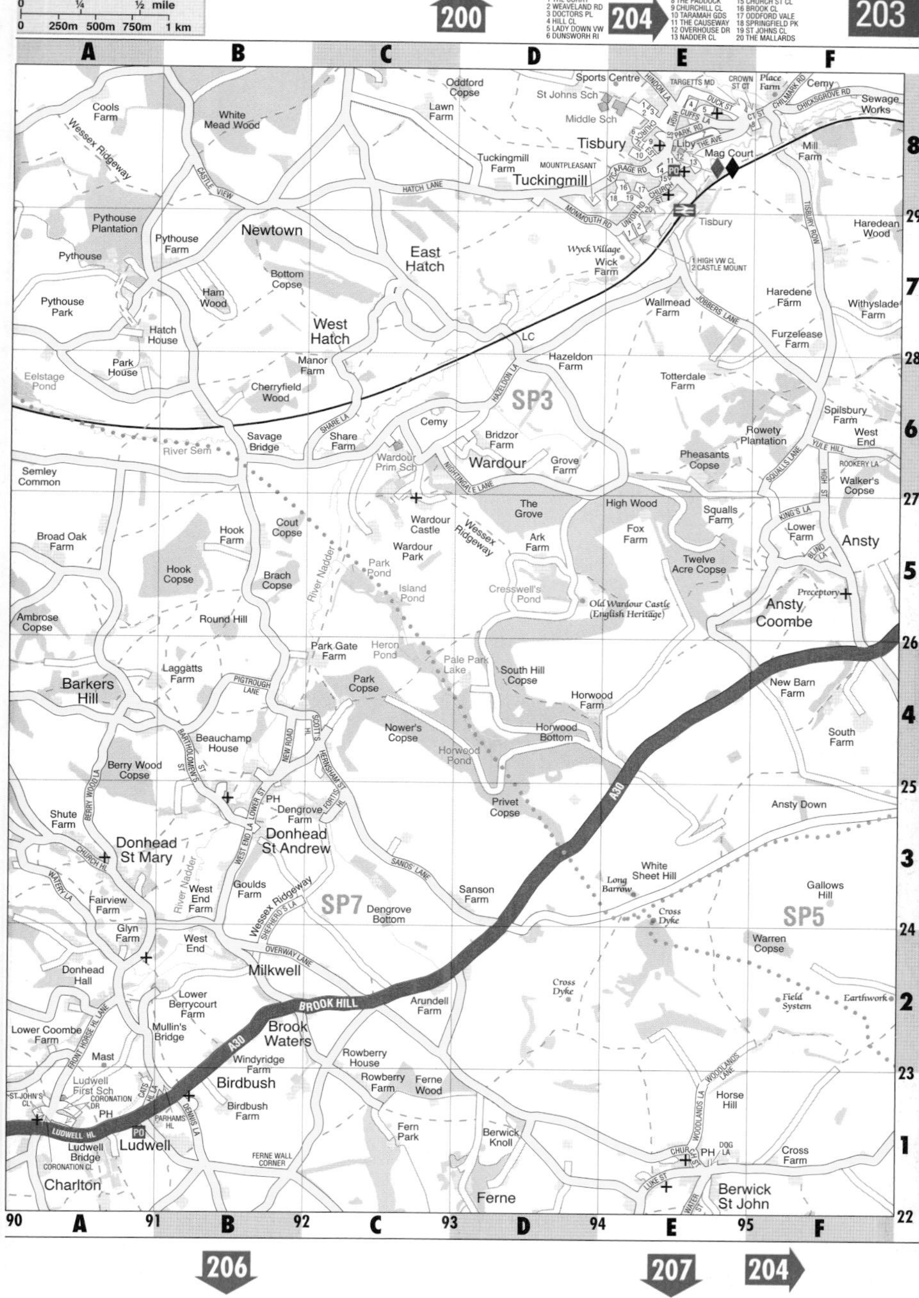
Scale: 1¼ inches to 1 mile
0 ¼ ½ mile
0 250m 500m 750m 1 km
200
E8
1 THE CORRY
2 WEAVELAND RD
3 DOCTORS PL
4 HILL CL
5 LADY DOWN VW
6 DUNSWORH RI
204
7 QUEENS RD
8 THE PADDOCK
9 CHURCHILL CL
10 TARAMAH GDS
11 THE CAUSEWAY
12 OVERHOUSE DR
13 NADDER CL
14 BECKETT ST
15 CHURCH ST CL
16 BROOK CL
17 ODDFORD VALE
18 SPRINGFIELD PK
19 ST JOHNS CL
20 THE MALLARDS
A
B
C
D
E
F
Cools Farm
White Mead Wood
Wessex Ridgeway
Oddford Copse
Lawn Farm
Sports Centre
St Johns Sch
Middle Sch
Tisbury
TARGETTS MD
CROWN ST CT
Place Farm
Cemy
CHILMARK RD
CHICKSGROVE RD
Sewage Works
DUCK ST
CUFFS LA
PARK RD
THE AVE
Mag Court
Mill Farm
Tuckingmill Farm
MOUNTPLEASANT
Tuckingmill
VICARAGE RD
CHURCH ST
HATCH LANE
CASTLE VIEW
MONMOUTH RD
UNION RD
Tisbury
TISBURY ROW
Haredean Wood
Pythouse Plantation
Pythouse Farm
Newtown
Pythouse
East Hatch
Wyck Village
Wick Farm
1 HIGH VW CL
2 CASTLE MOUNT
Bottom Copse
Ham Wood
Pythouse Park
Hatch House
West Hatch
Wallmead Farm
JOBBERS LANE
Haredene Farm
Withyslade Farm
Furzelease Farm
LC
Hazeldon Farm
Park House
Manor Farm
Eelstage Pond
Cherryfield Wood
HAZELDON LA
SP3
Totterdale Farm
Spilsbury Farm
West End
Cemy
Bridzor Farm
Rowety Plantation
YULE HILL
SHARE LA
Share Farm
Savage Bridge
River Sem
Wardour Prim Sch
Wardour
Grove Farm
Pheasants Copse
SQUALLS LANE
ROOKERY LA
HIGH ST
Walker's Copse
Semley Common
NIGHTINGALE LANE
The Grove
High Wood
Squalls Farm
KING'S LA
Lower Farm
Cout Copse
Wardour Castle
Wessex Ridgeway
Fox Farm
Ansty
Broad Oak Farm
Hook Farm
Wardour Park
Ark Farm
Twelve Acre Copse
BLIND LA
Hook Copse
Brach Copse
River Nadder
Park Pond
Island Pond
Cresswell's Pond
Old Wardour Castle (English Heritage)
Preceptory
Ansty Coombe
Ambrose Copse
Round Hill
Park Gate Farm
Heron Pond
Pale Park Lake
South Hill Copse
New Barn Farm
Laggatts Farm
PIGTROUGH LANE
Park Copse
Horwood Farm
Barkers Hill
Beauchamp House
SCOTT'S HL
Nower's Copse
Horwood Bottom
South Farm
BARTHOLOMEW'S ST
NEW ROAD
HERNSHAM ST
Horwood Pond
Berry Wood Copse
BERRY WOOD LA
LOWER ST
FORTIS HL
PH
Dengrove Farm
Privet Copse
A30
Ansty Down
Shute Farm
Donhead St Mary
Donhead St Andrew
CHURCH HL
WEST END LA
SANDS' LANE
White Sheet Hill
Long Barrow
Gallows Hill
WATERY LA
Fairview Farm
River Nadder
West End Farm
Goulds Farm
Wessex Ridgeway
SP7
Dengrove Bottom
Sanson Farm
Cross Dyke
SP5
SHEPHERD'S LA
Glyn Farm
West End
OVERWAY LANE
Warren Copse
Donhead Hall
Milkwell
Cross Dyke
Lower Berrycourt Farm
BROOK HILL
Arundell Farm
Field System
Earthwork
Lower Coombe Farm
FRONT HORSE HL LANE
Mullin's Bridge
Brook Waters
A30
Mast
Windyridge Farm
Rowberry House
WOODLANDS LANE
Ludwell First Sch
CATS HL
Birdbush
Rowberry Farm
Ferne Wood
Horse Hill
ST JOHN'S CL
CORONATION DR
PH
Birdbush Farm
WOODLANDS LA
LUDWELL HL
PO
PARHAMS HL
DENNIS LA
Fern Park
Berwick Knoll
PH
DOG LA
Cross Farm
Ludwell
Ludwell Bridge
FERNE WALL CORNER
CHURCH ST
CORONATION CL
LUKE ST
Charlton
Ferne
WATER ST
Berwick St John
8
29
7
28
6
27
5
26
4
25
3
24
2
23
1
22
90
91
92
93
94
95
206
207
204

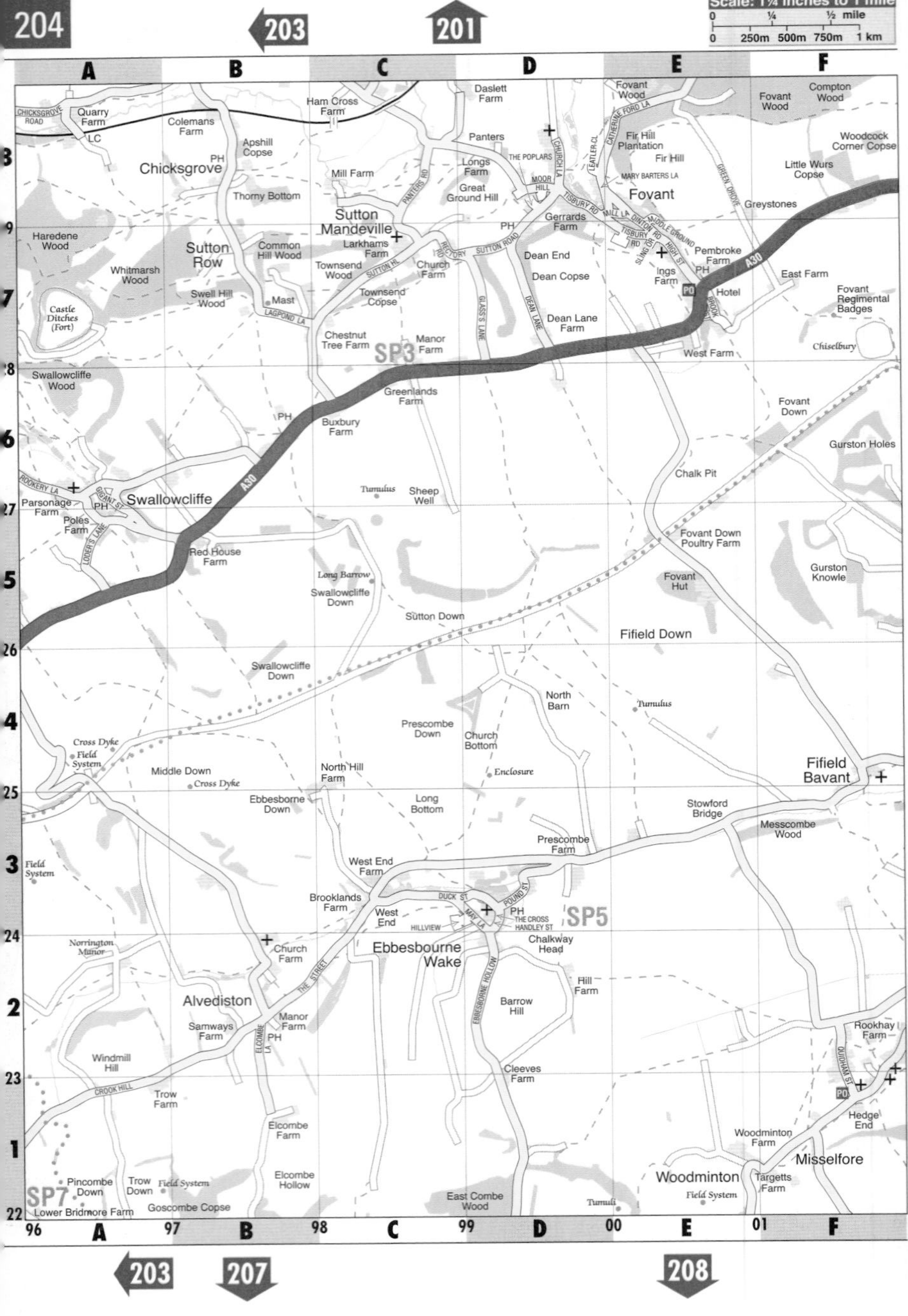
204
203
201
Scale: 1¼ inches to 1 mile
0 ¼ ½ mile
0 250m 500m 750m 1 km
A B C D E F
Chicksgrove Road
Quarry Farm
LC
Colemans Farm
Ham Cross Farm
Daslett Farm
Fovant Wood
Compton Wood
Panters
Apshill Copse
Chicksgrove
PH
Mill Farm
Panters Rd
Longs Farm
The Poplars
Church La
Leatler Cl
Catherine Ford La
Fir Hill Plantation
Fir Hill
Mary Barters La
Woodcock Corner Copse
Little Wurs Copse
Great Ground Hill
Moor Hill
Fovant
Green Drove
Greystones
Thorny Bottom
Sutton Mandeville
Tisbury Rd
Mill La
Dinton Rd
Middle Ground
High St
Gerrards Farm
Sling Or
Haredene Wood
Sutton Row
Common Hill Wood
Larkhams Farm
Rectory Rd
Sutton Road
Dean End
Ings Farm
Pembroke Farm
A30
Whitmarsh Wood
Townsend Wood
Sutton Hl
Church Farm
Dean Copse
East Farm
Castle Ditches (Fort)
Swell Hill Wood
Mast
Townsend Copse
PO
Hotel
Brook
Fovant Regimental Badges
Lagpond La
Glass's Lane
Dean Lane
Dean Lane Farm
Chestnut Tree Farm
Manor Farm
SP3
West Farm
Chiselbury
Swallowcliffe Wood
Greenlands Farm
Fovant Down
Buxbury Farm
Gurston Holes
Chalk Pit
Rookery La
Tumulus
Sheep Well
Swallowcliffe
Parsonage Farm
Gigant St
Poles Farm
Fovant Down Poultry Farm
Loder's Lane
Red House Farm
Gurston Knowle
Fovant Hut
Long Barrow
Swallowcliffe Down
Sutton Down
Fifield Down
Swallowcliffe Down
North Barn
Prescombe Down
Church Bottom
Cross Dyke
Field System
Middle Down
North Hill Farm
Enclosure
Fifield Bavant
Ebbesborne Down
Long Bottom
Stowford Bridge
Messcombe Wood
Prescombe Farm
West End Farm
Duck St
Pound St
Brooklands Farm
West End
May La
The Cross
Handley St
Hillview
SP5
Norrington Manor
Church Farm
Ebbesbourne Wake
Chalkway Head
The Street
Ebbesborne Hollow
Hill Farm
Alvediston
Barrow Hill
Manor Farm
Samways Farm
Elcombe La
Rookhay Farm
Windmill Hill
Cleeves Farm
Quidham St
Crook Hill
Trow Farm
Hedge End
Elcombe Farm
Woodminton Farm
Misselfore
Pincombe Down
Trow Down
Elcombe Hollow
Woodminton
Targetts Farm
SP7
East Combe Wood
Tumuli
Lower Bridmore Farm
Goscombe Copse
8 9 7 6 27 5 26 4 25 3 24 2 23 1 22
96 97 98 99 00 01
203
207
208

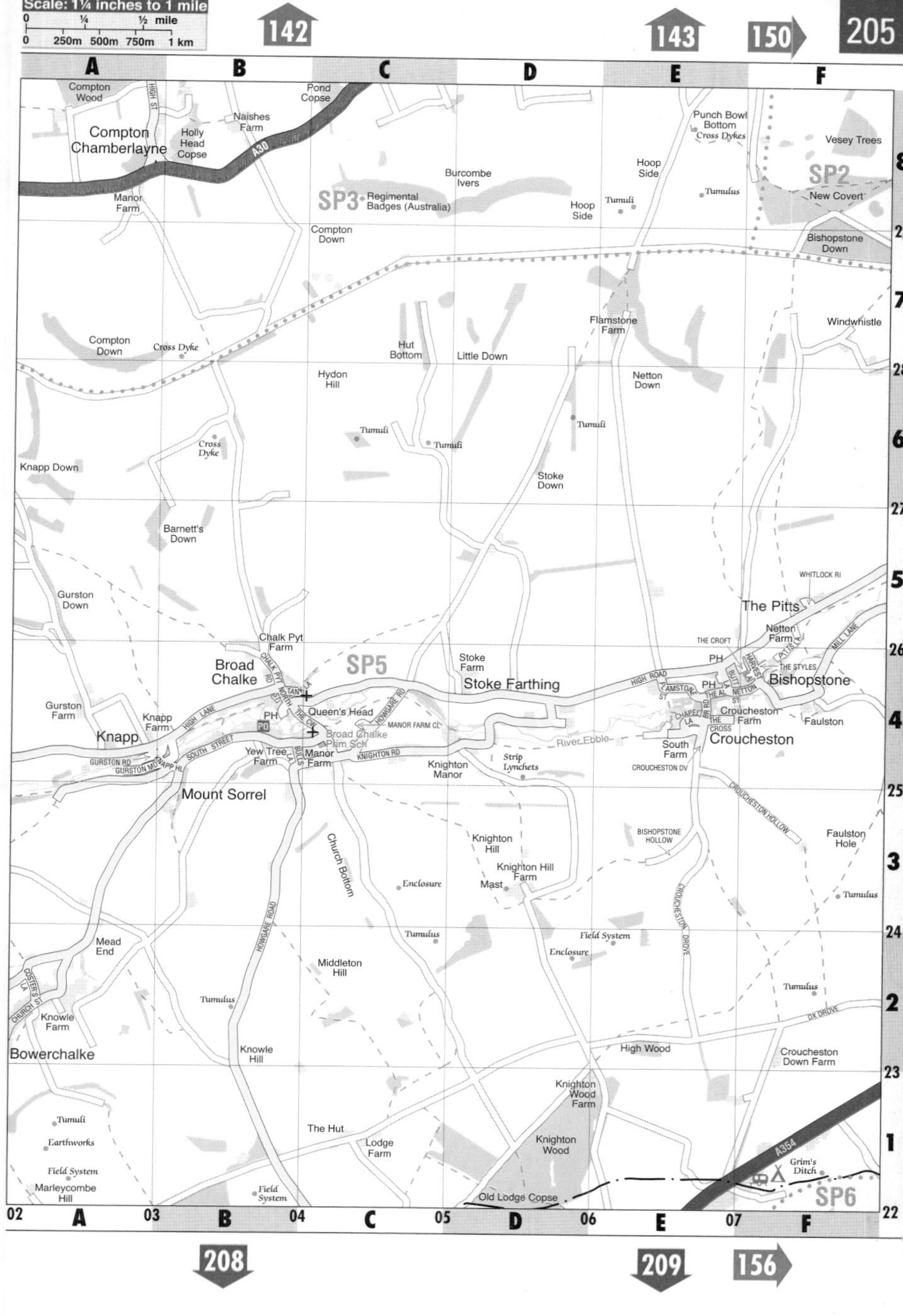
Scale: 1¼ inches to 1 mile
0 ¼ ½ mile
0 250m 500m 750m 1 km
142
143
150
A B C D E F
Compton Wood
Compton Chamberlayne
Holly Head Copse
Naishes Farm
Pond Copse
A30
Manor Farm
SP3
Regimental Badges (Australia)
Burcombe Ivers
Punch Bowl Bottom
Cross Dykes
Vesey Trees
Hoop Side
SP2
New Covert
Tumulus
Tumuli
Compton Down
Bishopstone Down
Flamstone Farm
Windwhistle
Compton Down
Cross Dyke
Hut Bottom
Little Down
Hydon Hill
Netton Down
Tumuli
Cross Dyke
Knapp Down
Stoke Down
Barnett's Down
Whitlock Ri
Gurston Down
The Pitts
Netton Farm
Chalk Pyt Farm
The Croft
Mill Lane
Broad Chalke
SP5
Stoke Farm
PH
High Road
The Styles
Bishopstone
Stoke Farthing
Gurston Farm
Knapp Farm
Queen's Head
Croucheston Farm
Faulston
Knapp
PO
Manor Farm Cl
Broad Chalke Prim Sch
River Ebble
South Farm
Croucheston
Gurston Rd
South Street
Yew Tree Farm
Manor Farm
Knighton Rd
Knighton Manor
Strip Lynchets
Croucheston Dv
Mount Sorrel
Croucheston Hollow
Church Bottom
Knighton Hill
Bishopstone Hollow
Faulston Hole
Knighton Hill Farm
Mast
Enclosure
Croucheston Drove
Howgare Road
Field System
Mead End
Middleton Hill
Coster's St
Church La
Knowle Farm
Tumulus
Ox Drove
Bowerchalke
Knowle Hill
High Wood
Croucheston Down Farm
Knighton Wood Farm
Tumuli
Earthworks
The Hut
Knighton Wood
Lodge Farm
A354
Grim's Ditch
Field System
Marleycombe Hill
Old Lodge Copse
SP6
02 03 04 05 06 07
22 23 24 25 26 27 28
208
209
156

202
203

Scale: 1¼ inches to 1 mile
0 ¼ ½ mile
0 250m 500m 750m 1 km

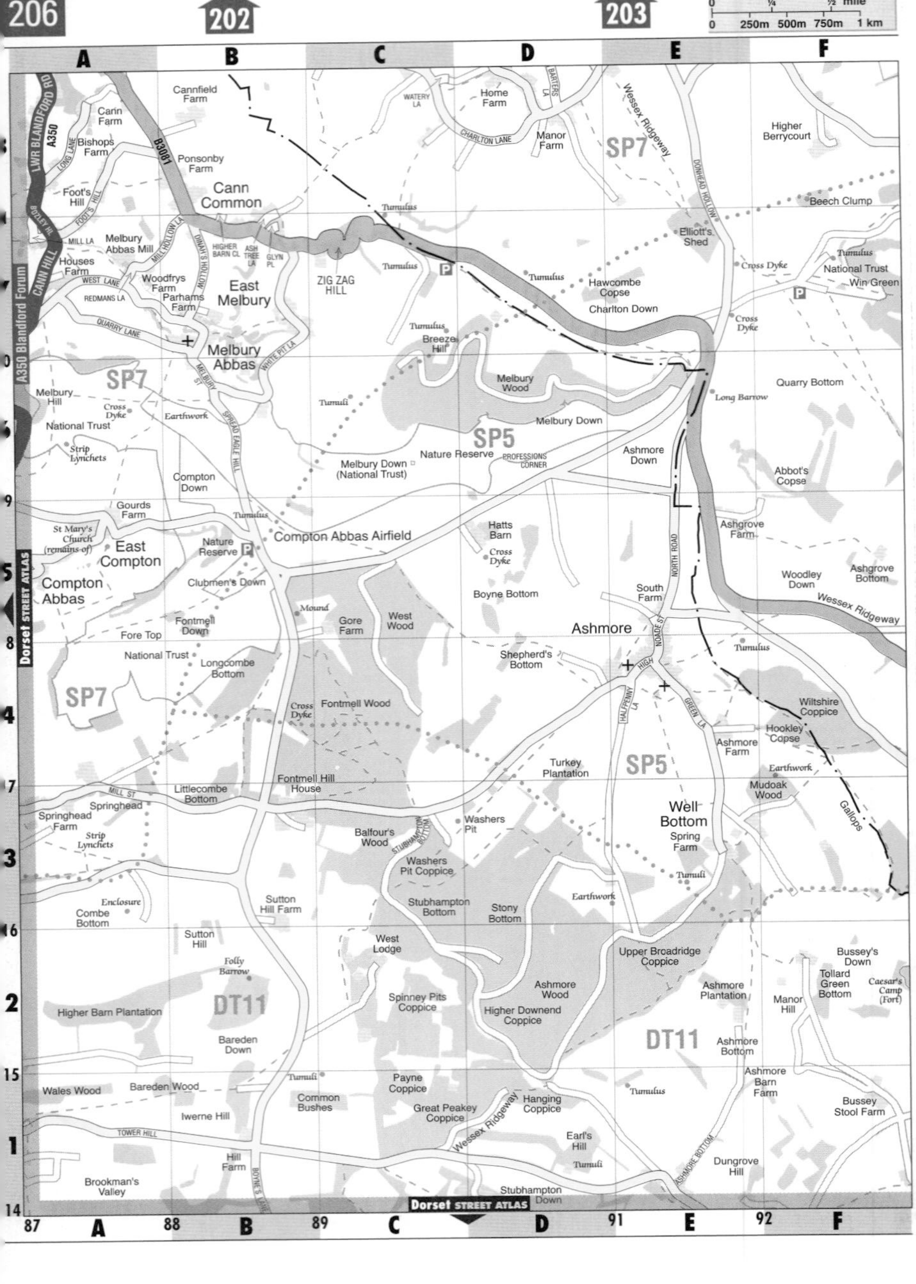

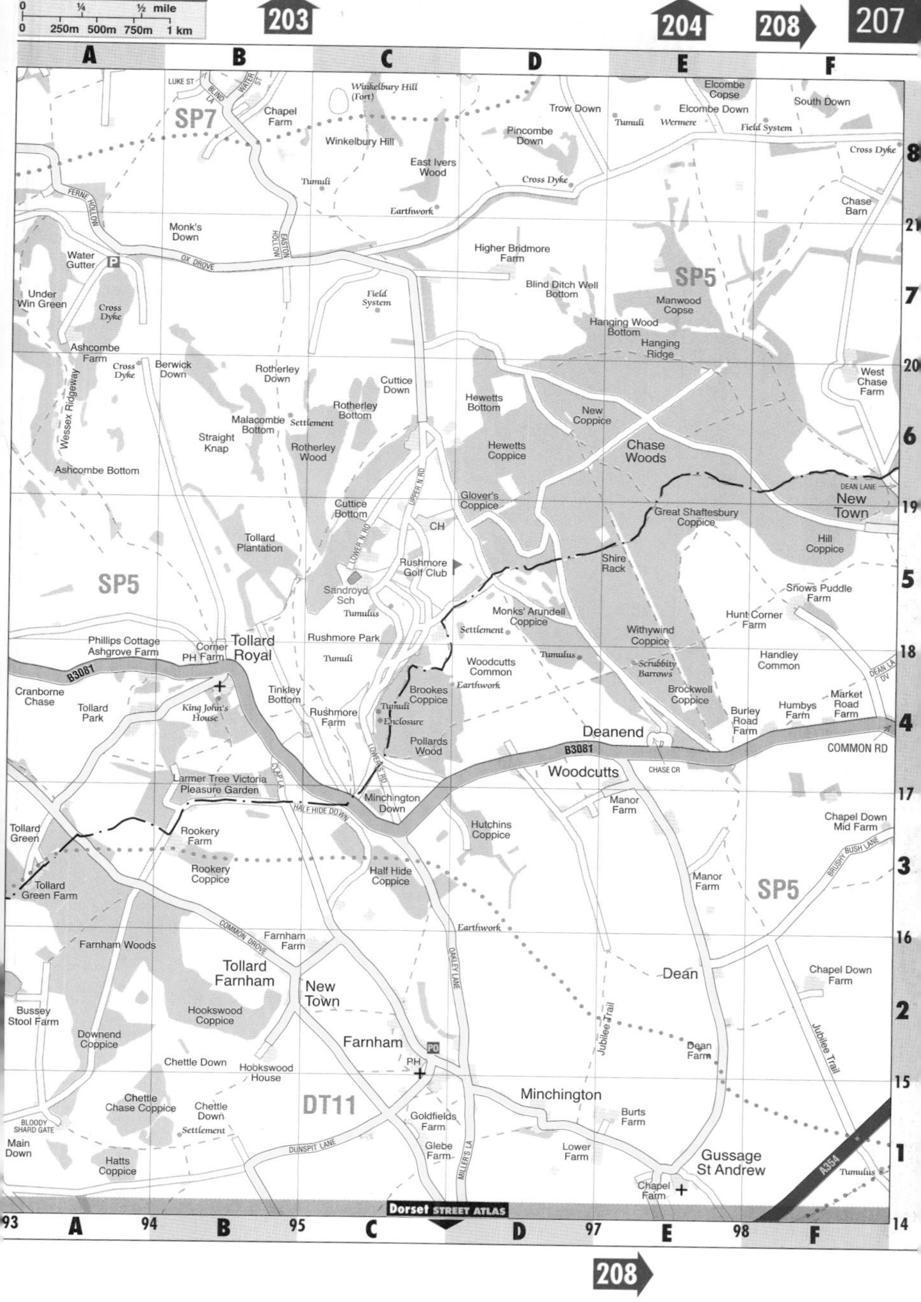
Scale: 1¼ inches to 1 mile
0 ¼ ½ mile
0 250m 500m 750m 1 km
203
204
208
A B C D E F
Luke St
Blind La
Water St
SP7
Chapel Farm
Winkelbury Hill (Fort)
Winkelbury Hill
Trow Down
Pincombe Down
Tumuli
Wermere
Elcombe Copse
Elcombe Down
South Down
Field System
Cross Dyke
East Ivers Wood
Ferne Hollow
Earthwork
Chase Barn
Monk's Down
Easton Hollow
Ox Drove
Water Gutter
Higher Bridmore Farm
Blind Ditch Well Bottom
SP5
Manwood Copse
Under Win Green
Cross Dyke
Field System
Hanging Wood Bottom
Hanging Ridge
Ashcombe Farm
Berwick Down
Rotherley Down
Cuttice Down
West Chase Farm
Wessex Ridgeway
Malacombe Bottom
Settlement
Rotherley Bottom
Hewetts Bottom
New Coppice
Straight Knap
Rotherley Wood
Hewetts Coppice
Chase Woods
Ashcombe Bottom
Upper N Rd
Glover's Coppice
Dean Lane
New Town
Cuttice Bottom
Great Shaftesbury Coppice
Lower N Rd
CH
Tollard Plantation
Hill Coppice
Rushmore Golf Club
Shire Rack
SP5
Sandroyd Sch
Tumulus
Snows Puddle Farm
Monks' Arundell Coppice
Hunt Corner Farm
Phillips Cottage
Ashgrove Farm
Corner PH Farm
Tollard Royal
Rushmore Park
Settlement
Withywind Coppice
Tumuli
Woodcutts Common
Tumulus
Scrubbity Barrows
Handley Common
B3081
Earthwork
Dean La
Cranborne Chase
Tollard Park
King John's House
Tinkley Bottom
Brookes Coppice
Brockwell Coppice
Humbys Farm
Market Road Farm
Rushmore Farm
Tumuli
Enclosure
Burley Road Farm
Deanend
Lower N Rd
Pollards Wood
B3081
Common Rd
Clap La
Woodcutts
Chase Cr
Larmer Tree Victoria Pleasure Garden
Minchington Down
Manor Farm
Half Hide Down
Tollard Green
Rookery Farm
Hutchins Coppice
Chapel Down Mid Farm
Brushy Bush Lane
Rookery Coppice
Half Hide Coppice
Manor Farm
Tollard Green Farm
SP5
Common Drove
Earthwork
Farnham Farm
Farnham Woods
Tollard Farnham
Oakley Lane
Dean
Chapel Down Farm
New Town
Jubilee Trail
Bussey Stool Farm
Hookswood Coppice
Downend Coppice
Farnham
PO
Dean Farm
PH
Chettle Down
Hookswood House
Minchington
Chettle Chase Coppice
DT11
Chettle Down
Goldfields Farm
Burts Farm
Bloody Shard Gate
Settlement
Main Down
Dunspit Lane
Glebe Farm
Miller's La
Lower Farm
Gussage St Andrew
A354
Tumulus
Hatts Copppice
Chapel Farm
Dorset STREET ATLAS
93 94 95 97 98
8 21 7 20 6 19 5 18 4 17 3 16 2 15 1 14
208

Scale: 1¼ inches to 1 mile
0 ¼ ½ mile
0 250m 500m 750m 1 km

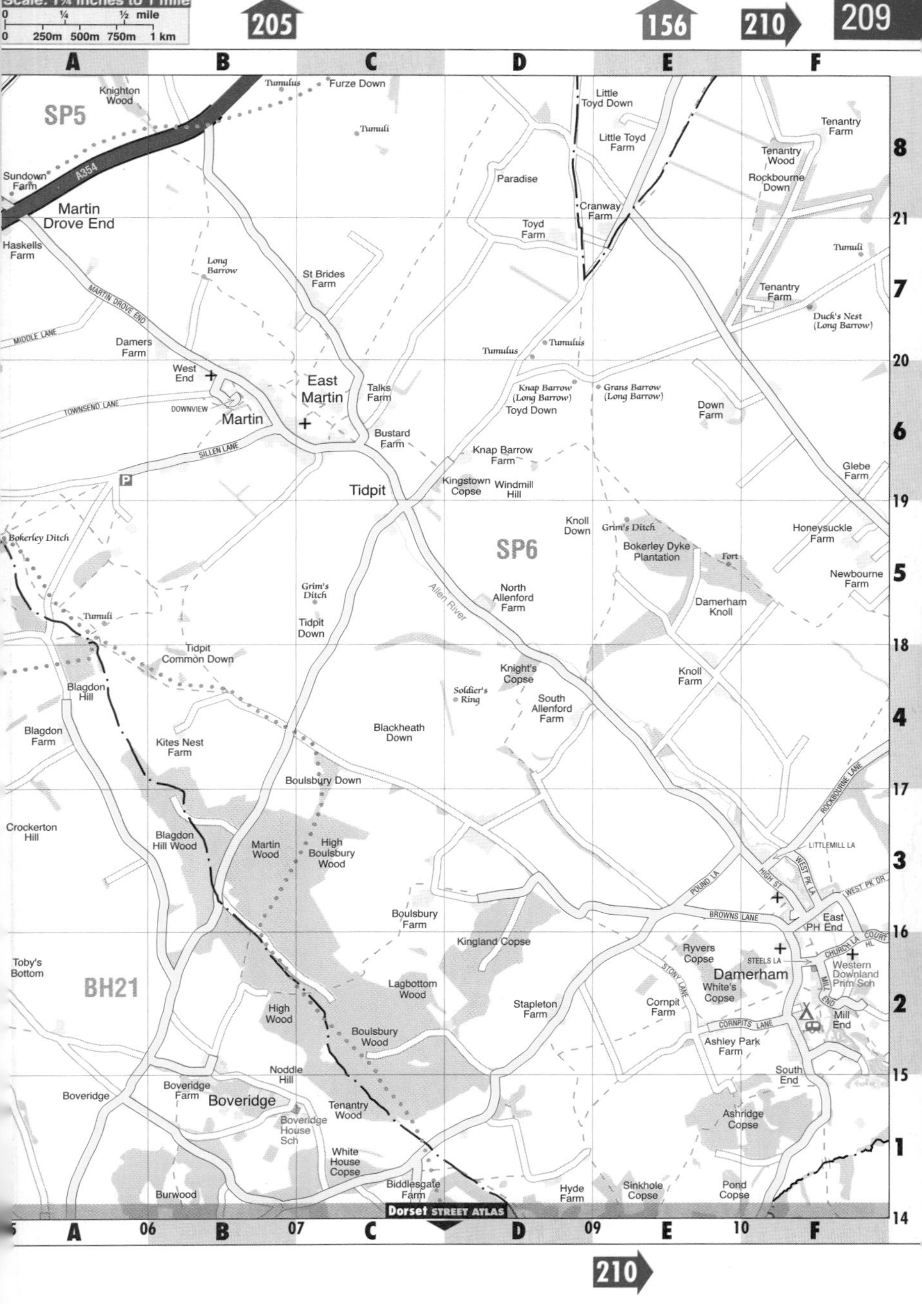
Scale: 1¼ inches to 1 mile
0 ¼ ½ mile
0 250m 500m 750m 1 km
205
156
210
A B C D E F
8
21
7
20
6
19
5
18
4
17
3
16
2
15
1
14
5 A 06 B 07 C D 09 E 10 F
Knighton Wood
SP5
Tumulus
Furze Down
Little Toyd Down
Tenantry Farm
Tumuli
Little Toyd Farm
Tenantry Wood
Sundown Farm
A354
Paradise
Rockbourne Down
Martin Drove End
Cranway Farm
Haskells Farm
Toyd Farm
Tumuli
Long Barrow
St Brides Farm
Tenantry Farm
MARTIN DROVE END
Duck's Nest (Long Barrow)
MIDDLE LANE
Damers Farm
Tumulus
Tumulus
West End
East Martin
Talks Farm
Knap Barrow (Long Barrow)
Grans Barrow (Long Barrow)
Toyd Down
Down Farm
TOWNSEND LANE
DOWNVIEW
Martin
Bustard Farm
Knap Barrow Farm
SILLEN LANE
Glebe Farm
Tidpit
Kingstown Copse
Windmill Hill
Bokerley Ditch
Knoll Down
Grim's Ditch
Honeysuckle Farm
SP6
Bokerley Dyke Plantation
Fort
Newbourne Farm
Grim's Ditch
North Allenford Farm
Allen River
Damerham Knoll
Tumuli
Tidpit Down
Tidpit Common Down
Knight's Copse
Knoll Farm
Blagdon Hill
Soldier's Ring
South Allenford Farm
Blagdon Farm
Blackheath Down
Kites Nest Farm
ROCKBOURNE LANE
Boulsbury Down
Crockerton Hill
Blagdon Hill Wood
Martin Wood
High Boulsbury Wood
LITTLEMILL LA
WEST PK LA
HIGH ST
POUND LA
WEST PK DR
BROWNS LANE
Boulsbury Farm
East End
PH
Kingland Copse
Ryvers Copse
CHURCH LA
COURT HL
STEELS LA
Toby's Bottom
STONY LANE
Damerham
Western Downland Prim Sch
BH21
Lagbottom Wood
White's Copse
MILL END
Stapleton Farm
Cornpit Farm
High Wood
Mill End
Boulsbury Wood
CORNPITS LANE
Ashley Park Farm
Noddle Hill
South End
Boveridge Farm
Boveridge
Boveridge
Tenantry Wood
Ashridge Copse
Boveridge House Sch
White House Copse
Biddlesgate Farm
Hyde Farm
Sinkhole Copse
Pond Copse
Burwood
Dorset STREET ATLAS
210

210
209
157
158
F8
1 WEEKE CL
2 GREENACRES
3 ELIZABETH CL
4 JOANNA CL
5 MARIE AVE
Scale: 1¼ inches to 1 mil
0 ¼ ½ mile
0 250m 500m 750m 1 km
A B C D E F
Long Barrow
Whitsbury Down
Gallops
Wick Down
Gallows Hill
WICK LANE
Wick Farm
SP5
Botleys Farm
Sports Gd
Middle Wick Farm
Well Bottom
Tumuli
Grim's Ditch
NORTH CHARFORD DROVE
Northayes Farm
Breamore Down
Grim's Ditch (course of)
Scotland Cottage
Mizmaze
Tumulus
Giant's Grave (Long Barrow)
North Charford Down Farm
South Charford Down Buildings
Earthwork
Manor Farm
Manor House
Castle Ditches (Fort)
SOUTH CHARFORD DROVE
A338
Down Farm
Breamore Wood
Whitsbury Wood
Provost Farm
Dunberry Hill
Round Copse
Majors Farm
WELL HO CL
PO
Lower Farm
Whitsbury
PH
LONG STEEPLE LANE
Breamore House
Breamore Park
North Street
South Charford Farm
Lime Kiln Farm
Breamore Countryside Museum
Upper Street
LOWER GR
Rockbourne
NEW RD
Manor House
Gravelhill Copse
ROOKERY LA
North Street Farm
SALISBURY ROAD
RECTORY LA
Western Downland Sch
Long Copse
Roundhill Farm
Whitsbury Common
Topps Farm
Breamore
Marsh Farm
Hursts Coppice
Outwick
Breamore CE Prim Sch
Weir
Rockstead Copse
Rockstead Farm
Greenlane Wood
Kiln Wood
MARSH LANE
Arch Farm
ROCKBOURNE LANE
Marsh Farm
SP6
THE SHALLOWS
The Shallows
Whip's Hill Copse
Radnall Wood
Floodstreet Copse
Flood Street
Shallows Farm
ROCKBOURNE ROMAN VILLA
Rockbourne Mus
CLACK LA
Sagles Spring
Brookheath
Peas Ash Copse
Peasash Farm
West Park
GREEN LANE
Upper Burgate
Palmer's Copse
WEST PK DR
Fryern Court Farm
Mist Farm
FRYERN COURT ROAD
Ct Farm
COURT HILL
Allen's Farm
Fryern Court
Folds Farm
West Park Farm
Fiddlesticks Farm
Sweatfords Water
Lower Burgate
Courtvale Farm
Lower Breach Copse
Sandle Dairy Farm
Avon Valley Path
Burgate Manor Farm
FB
Wilkins's Coomb
Fordingbridge Jun & Inf Sch
River Avon
Hurley Farm
The Burgate Sch
Frankenbury
Brickhops Copse
Courtwood Farm
PUDDLESLOSH LA
BEACON CT
SHARPLEY CL
WHITSBURY RD
DUDLEY
BURGATE FIELDS
Sandle Home Farm
ALLEN WATER DR
WAVERLEY RD
LANGLEY GD
Sandleheath
TANNERS LA
PEMBRIDGE RD
WOODFERN
WOODLING CR
LARCH ROW
Lower Court Wood
Thorps Farm
ELMS CL
OLD BRICKYARD ROAD
Sandle Manor
MARL LANE
Sandle Manor Sch
LYSTER RD
Sandle Manor Farm
FORDINGBRIDGE
Sandy Balls
ALEXANDRA RD
PARK RD
BRUYN RD
Hawkhill Farm
ALDERHOLT RD
Reeve's Copse
STATION ROAD
JUBILEE ROAD
Ashford
Criddlestyle
Weir
Mews Hill Copse
SANDLE COPSE
VICTORIA RD
Fordingbridge
Andrew's Copse
MARL LA
ASHFORD RD
Hotel
Liby
SOUTHAMPTON ROAD
B3078
Ashford Water
STUCKTON RD
Avonside Farm
SANDLEHEATH RD
Avon Farm
TH
BLISSFORD ROAD
South Hampshire STREET ATLAS
A338 Ringwood
8 21 7 20 6 19 5 18 4 17 3 16 2 15 1 14
11 12 13 15 16
209
C1
1 MANOR FARM RD
2 MAYFIELD RD
3 JUBILEE CL
4 MARBREAN CL
5 BRYMPTON CL
6 ELMWOOD AV
7 DOWNWOOD CL
8 FALCONWOOD CL
9 ROOKWOOD GD
10 THE OLD VINERIES
11 ASHFORD CL
12 THE PANTILES
13 BEECHWOOD
14 VICTORIA GD
D1
1 AVON MEADE
2 GARENDON CT
3 PARSONAGE PK DR
4 MAYFLY CL
5 WILLOW AV
6 PEALSHAM GD
7 STEPHEN MARTIN GD
8 MEADOW CL
9 RIVERDALE CL
10 MEADOW AV
11 MEADOW CT
12 OAKLANDS CL
13 COTTAGE MS
14 NORMANDY WY
15 FLAXFIELDS END
16 VIMOUTIERS CT
17 WESTGROVE
18 MILL CT
19 SHAFTESBURY ST
20 BARTONS RD
21 MOXHAMS
22 WEST ST
23 PROVOST ST
24 HIGH ST
25 ROUND HILL
26 SALISBURY ST
27 RINGWOOD RD
28 MANOR CL
29 THE BARTONS
30 LWR BARTONS
31 PARSONAGE CL
32 QUEENS GD
33 ALBIONRD
34 ORCHARD CL
35 ST GEORGES RD
D2
1 HERTFORD CL
2 BEDFORD CL
3 PENNY'S CL
4 PENNY'S CR
5 BURNHAM RD
6 MERTON CL
7 WAVERLEY CL
8 PLAYER CT
9 CHARNWOOD DR

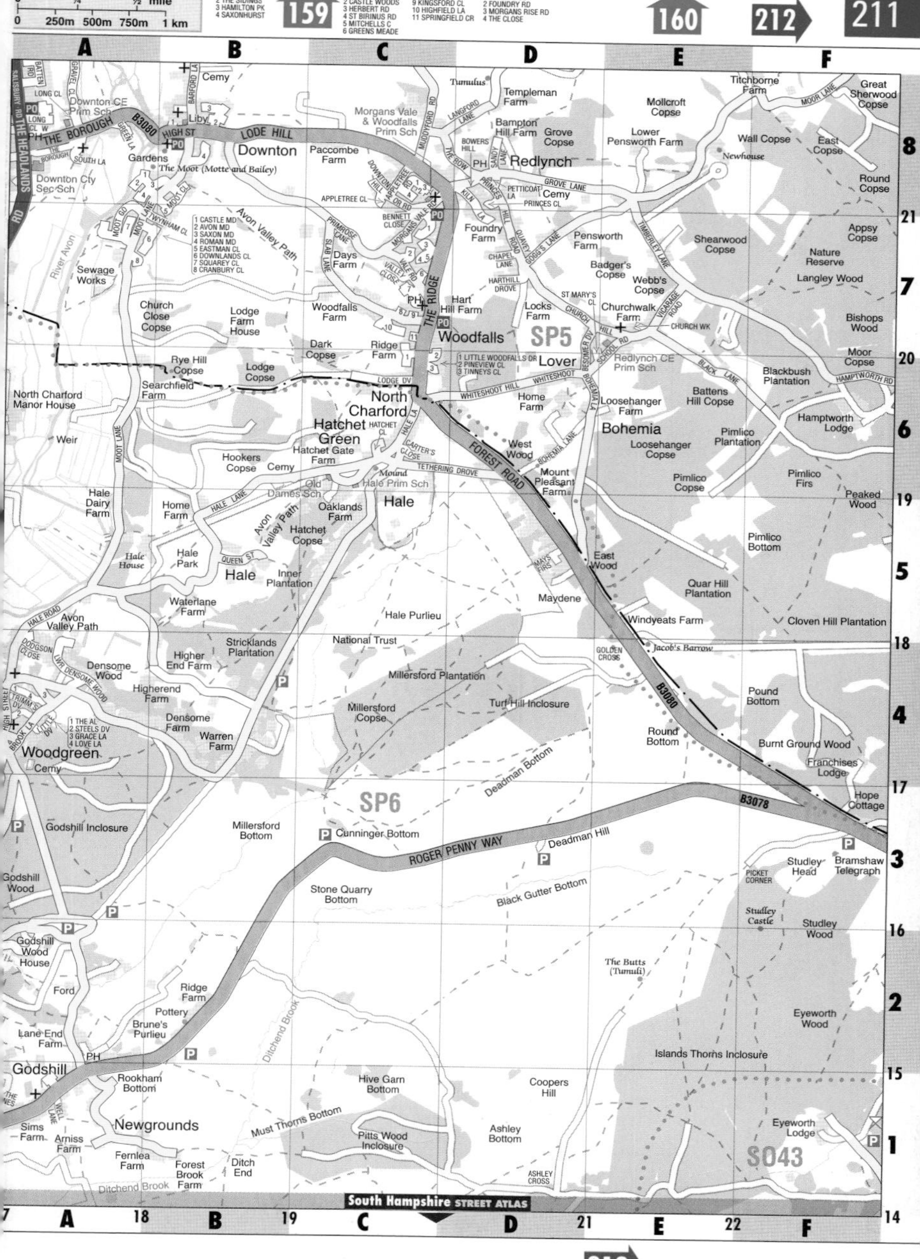
Scale: 1¼ inches to 1 mile
0 ¼ ½ mile
0 250m 500m 750m 1 km
B8
1 CHURCH HATCH
2 THE SIDINGS
3 HAMILTON PK
4 SAXONHURST
159
C7
1 VICARAGE PK
2 CASTLE WOODS
3 HERBERT RD
4 ST BIRINUS RD
5 MITCHELLS C
6 GREENS MEADE
7 ELMFIELD CL
8 DAIRY CL
9 KINGSFORD CL
10 HIGHFIELD LA
11 SPRINGFIELD CR
C8
1 CHALK'S CL
2 FOUNDRY RD
3 MORGANS RISE RD
4 THE CLOSE
160
212
A
B
C
D
E
F
Cemy
Downton CE Prim Sch
Morgans Vale & Woodfalls Prim Sch
Tumulus
Templeman Farm
Mollcroft Copse
Titchborne Farm
Great Sherwood Copse
THE BOROUGH
B3080
HIGH ST
LODE HILL
Liby
Downton
Paccombe Farm
Bampton Hill Farm
Grove Copse
Lower Pensworth Farm
Wall Copse
East Copse
Newhouse
8
Gardens
The Moot (Motte and Bailey)
Downton Cty Sec Sch
Redlynch
GROVE LANE
PETTICOAT LA
PRINCES CL
APPLETREE CL
Round Copse
21
1 CASTLE MD
2 AVON MD
3 SAXON MD
4 ROMAN MD
5 EASTMAN CL
6 DOWNLANDS CL
7 SQUAREY CL
8 CRANBURY CL
Avon Valley Path
Foundry Farm
Pensworth Farm
Shearwood Copse
Appsy Copse
Sewage Works
Days Farm
Badger's Copse
Webb's Copse
Nature Reserve
Langley Wood
7
Church Close Copse
Lodge Farm House
Woodfalls Farm
THE RIDGE
Hart Hill Farm
Locks Farm
Churchwalk Farm
CHURCH WK
Bishops Wood
Woodfalls
SP5
Dark Copse
Ridge Farm
1 LITTLE WOODFALLS DR
2 PINEVIEW CL
3 TINNEYS CL
Lover
Redlynch CE Prim Sch
Moor Copse
20
Rye Hill Copse
Lodge Copse
Searchfield Farm
LODGE DV
WHITESHOOT HILL
Home Farm
Blackbush Plantation
Battens Hill Copse
HAMPTWORTH RD
North Charford Manor House
North Charford
Hatchet Green
Loosehanger Farm
Bohemia
Hamptworth Lodge
Weir
MOOT LANE
Hookers Copse
Hatchet Gate Farm
Cemy
West Wood
Loosehanger Copse
Pimlico Plantation
6
FOREST ROAD
TETHERING DROVE
Mount Pleasant Farm
Mound
Hale Prim Sch
Old Dames Sch
Hale
Pimlico Copse
Pimlico Firs
Hale Dairy Farm
Home Farm
HALE LANE
Oaklands Farm
Peaked Wood
19
Hatchet Copse
Pimlico Bottom
Hale House
Hale Park
QUEEN ST
Hale
Inner Plantation
East Wood
Quar Hill Plantation
5
Waterlane Farm
Maydene
HALE ROAD
Avon Valley Path
Hale Purlieu
Windyeats Farm
Cloven Hill Plantation
Stricklands Plantation
National Trust
Jacob's Barrow
18
Densome Wood
Higher End Farm
GOLDEN CROSS
Millersford Plantation
Higherend Farm
Turf Hill Inclosure
Pound Bottom
1 THE AL
2 STEELS DV
3 GRACE LA
4 LOVE LA
Densome Farm
Warren Farm
Millersford Copse
Round Bottom
Burnt Ground Wood
4
Woodgreen
Cemy
Deadman Bottom
Franchises Lodge
17
SP6
B3078
Hope Cottage
Godshill Inclosure
Millersford Bottom
Cunninger Bottom
ROGER PENNY WAY
Deadman Hill
Godshill Wood
Studley Head
Bramshaw Telegraph
3
PICKET CORNER
Stone Quarry Bottom
Black Gutter Bottom
Studley Castle
Studley Wood
16
Godshill Wood House
The Butts (Tumuli)
Ridge Farm
Ford
Pottery
Brune's Purlieu
Ditchend Brook
Eyeworth Wood
2
Lane End Farm
PH
Islands Thorns Inclosure
Godshill
Rookham Bottom
Hive Garn Bottom
Coopers Hill
15
Newgrounds
Must Thorns Bottom
Pitts Wood Inclosure
Ashley Bottom
Eyeworth Lodge
Sims Farm
Arniss Farm
1
Fernlea Farm
Forest Brook Farm
Ditch End
ASHLEY CROSS
SO43
Ditchend Brook
South Hampshire STREET ATLAS
A
18
B
19
C
D
21
E
22
F
14

212

Scale: 1¼ inches to 1 mile
0 ¼ ½ mile
0 250m 500m 750m 1 km

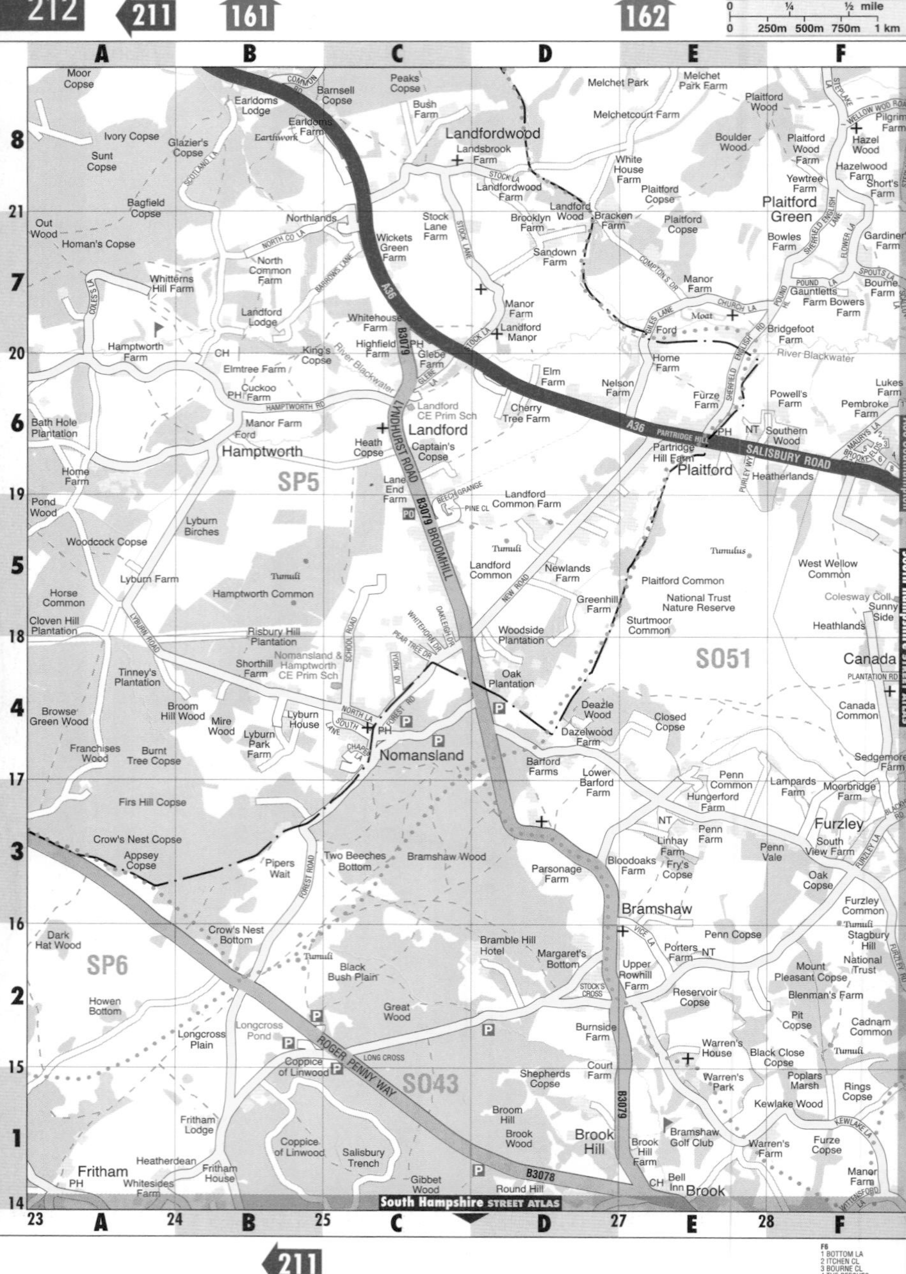

8
21
7
20
6
19
5
18
4
17
3
16
2
15
1
14

23 A 24 B 25 C D 27 E 28 F

F6
1 BOTTOM LA
2 ITCHEN CL
3 BOURNE CL
4 THE BEECHES
5 STOUR CL
6 ARUN WY
7 PEARTREE CL
8 NIGHTINGALE CL

168 168 169

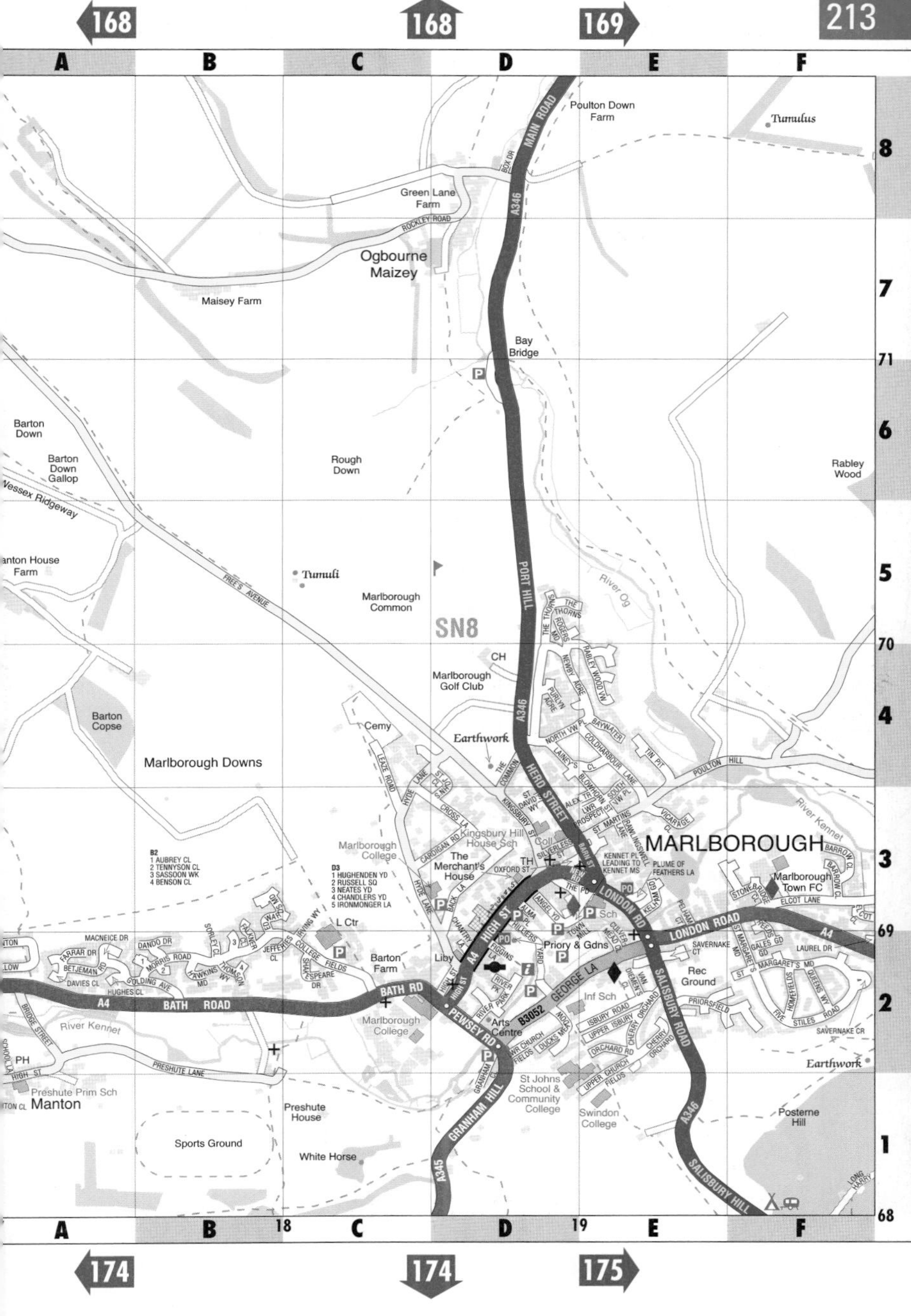

174 174 175

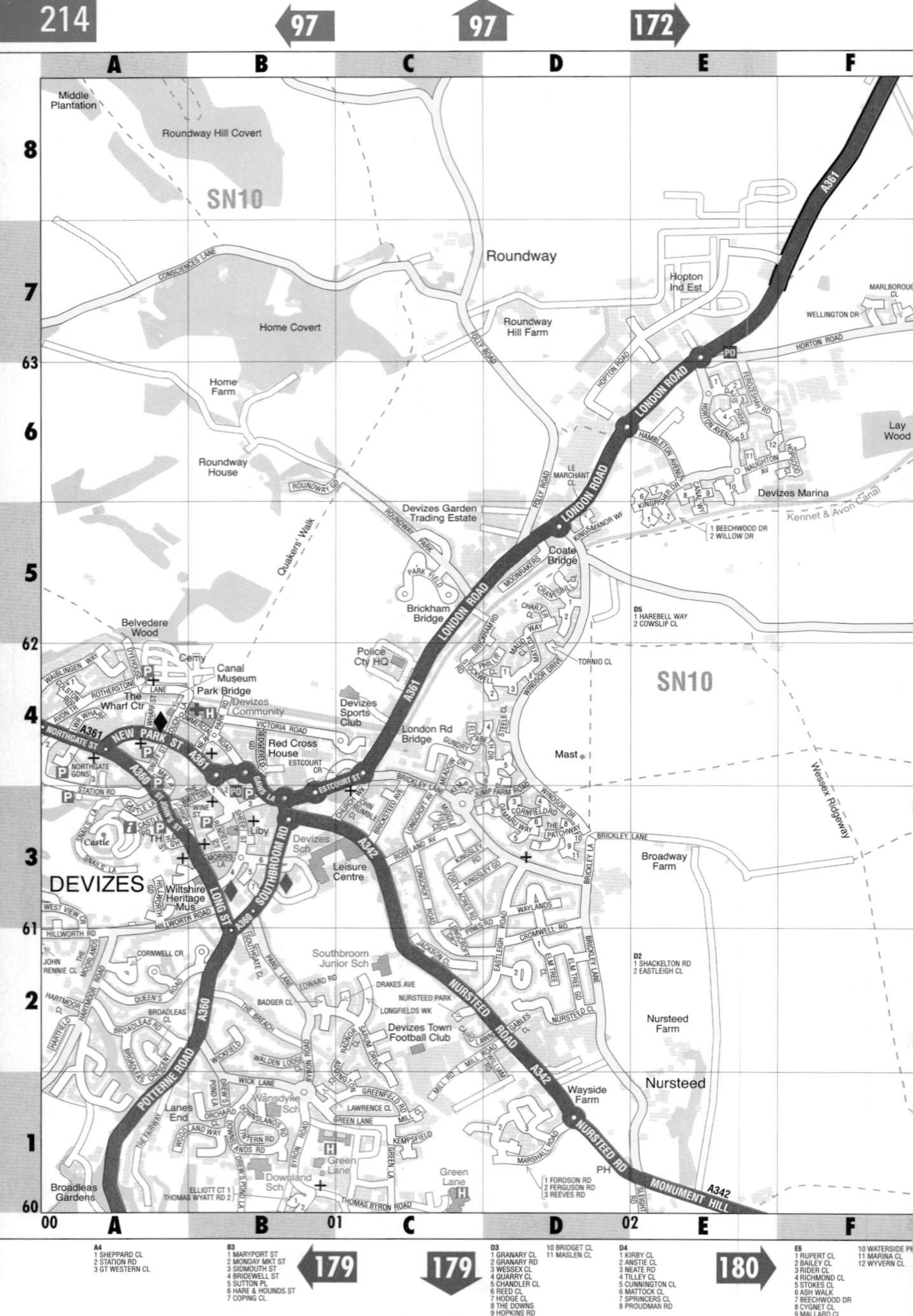

214
97
97
172
A
B
C
D
E
F
8
7
63
6
5
62
4
3
61
2
1
60
00
01
02
Middle Plantation
Roundway Hill Covert
SN10
Roundway
Hopton Ind Est
A361
MARLBOROUGH CL
WELLINGTON DR
CONSCIENCES LANE
Home Covert
Roundway Hill Farm
FOLLY ROAD
HORTON ROAD
PO
Home Farm
HOPTON ROAD
LONDON ROAD
DAVIS DRIVE
FEROZESHAH RD
HORTON AVENUE
Lay Wood
HAMBLETON AVENUE
NAUGHTON AV
HOPGOOD CL
Roundway House
ROUNDWAY GD
LE MARCHANT CL
KINGFISHER DR
CANAL WY
Devizes Marina
Devizes Garden Trading Estate
KINGSMANOR WF
Kennet & Avon Canal
1 BEECHWOOD DR
2 WILLOW DR
ROUNDWAY PARK
Coate Bridge
Quakers' Walk
PARK FIELD
MOONRAKERS
CRANESBILL CL
Brickham Bridge
CHARTER CL
D5
1 HAREBELL WAY
2 COWSLIP CL
Belvedere Wood
BRICKHAM RD
MAUD CL
MATILDA WAY
PHILLIP CL
Police Cty HQ
TORNIO CL
WAIBLINGEN WAY
DYEHOUSE
Cemy
Canal Museum
STOCKWELL RD
WINDSOR DRIVE
SN10
COLSTON RD
ROTHERSTONE
LANE
Park Bridge
Devizes Sports Club
The Wharf Ctr
Devizes Community
AVON TR
LWR WHARF
WHARF ST
COMMERCIAL RD
VICTORIA ROAD
London Rd Bridge
GUNDRY CL
STEELE CL
A361
NORTHGATE ST
NEW PARK ST
SEDGEFIELD GD
Red Cross House
ELIZABETH DR
Mast
A361
ESTCOURT CR
NORTHGATE GDNS
ESTCOURT ST
BRICKLEY LANE
MEADOW DR
JUMP FARM ROAD
STATION RD
MKT PL
WINDSOR DR
THE BRITTOX
JOHN RUMBLE CL
BRICKSTEAD AVE
LONGCROFT AV
CORNFIELD RD
SNAILS LA
CASTLE LA
WINE ST
SHEEP ST
CHURCH WK
OAMARU WAY
THE PATCHWAY
BRICKLEY LANE
Castle
TH
Liby
SOUTHBROOM RD
Devizes Sch
ROSELAND AV
KINGSLEY RD
Broadway Farm
SNAILS LA
MORRIS LA
Leisure Centre
A342
KINGSLEY GD
Wessex Ridgeway
DEVIZES
Wiltshire Heritage Mus
LONG ST
FORTY ACRES RD
BRICKLEY LA
WEST VIEW CR
HILLWORTH ROAD
A360
WAYLANDS
LONGCROFT ROAD
PINES RD
HILLWORTH RD
CROMWELL RD
JACKSON CL
EASTLEIGH ROAD
ELM TREE CL
SOUTHGATE CL
PANS LANE
CORNWELL CR
Southbroom Junior Sch
D2
1 SHACKELTON RD
2 EASTLEIGH CL
JOHN RENNIE CL
THE MOORLANDS
HARTMOOR ROAD
QUEEN'S ROAD
EDWARD RD
DRAKES AVE
ELM TREE GD
BRICKLEY LANE
HARTMOOR CL
BADGER CL
NURSTEED PARK
BROADLEAS CL
THE BREACH
LONGFIELDS WK
NURSTEED CL
HARTFIELD
BROADLEAS RD
RADNOR CL
SARUM DRIVE
Devizes Town Football Club
GABLES CL
Nursteed Farm
A360
CAIRD LAWNS
NURSTEED ROAD
BROADLEAS CRESCENT
WICKFIELD
WALDEN LODGE CL
BYRON ROAD
MILL ROAD
WILLIAM CL
A342
POTTERNE ROAD
WICK LANE
ADDINGTON CL
GREENFIELD RD
MILL RD
Nursteed
DREW'S
POND LA
LAWRENCE CL
Wayside Farm
Lanes End
ORCHARD
DOWNSLANDS RD
Wansdyke Sch
MILL CL
GREEN LANE
WOODLAND WAY
TERN RD
NURSTEED RD
KEMPSFIELD
MARSHALL ROAD
THE FAIRWAY
DOWNSLANDS RD
BYRON ROAD
Green Lane
GREEN LA
PH
DREW'S POND LA
Green Lane
1 FORDSON RD
2 FERGUSON RD
3 REEVES RD
Downland Sch
SLEIGHT RD
MONUMENT HILL
A342
Broadleas Gardens
ELLIOTT CT 1
THOMAS WYATT RD 2
THOMAS BYRON ROAD
A4
1 SHEPPARD CL
2 STATION RD
3 GT WESTERN CL
B3
1 MARYPORT ST
2 MONDAY MKT ST
3 SIDMOUTH ST
4 BRIDEWELL ST
5 SUTTON PL
6 HARE & HOUNDS ST
7 COPING CL
179
179
D3
1 GRANARY CL
2 GRANARY RD
3 WESSEX CL
4 QUARRY CL
5 CHANDLER CL
6 REED CL
7 HODGE CL
8 THE DOWNS
9 HOPKINS RD
10 BRIDGET CL
11 MASLEN CL
D4
1 KIRBY CL
2 ANSTIE CL
3 NEATE RD
4 TILLEY CL
5 CUNNINGTON CL
6 MATTOCK CL
7 SPRINCERS CL
8 PROUDMAN RD
180
E6
1 RUPERT CL
2 BAILEY CL
3 RIDER CL
4 RICHMOND CL
5 STOKES CL
6 ASH WALK
7 BEECHWOOD DR
8 CYGNET CL
9 MALLARD CL
10 WATERSIDE PK
11 MARINA CL
12 WYVERN CL

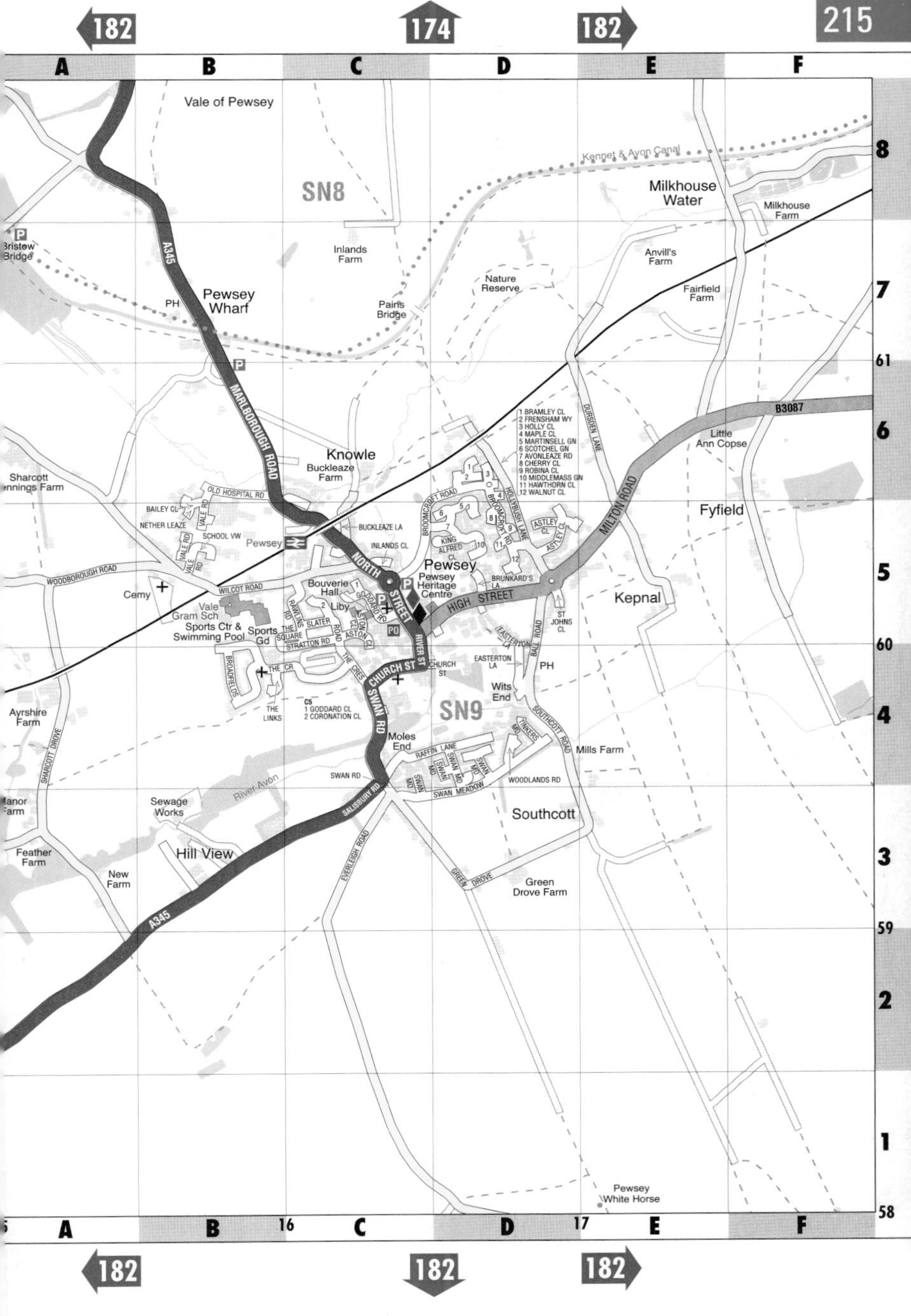

182
174
182
A
B
C
D
E
F
Vale of Pewsey
SN8
Kennet & Avon Canal
Milkhouse Water
Milkhouse Farm
Bristow Bridge
A345
Inlands Farm
Anvill's Farm
Nature Reserve
Fairfield Farm
PH
Pewsey Wharf
Pains Bridge
MARLBOROUGH ROAD
1 BRAMLEY CL
2 FRENSHAM WY
3 HOLLY CL
4 MAPLE CL
5 MARTINSELL GN
6 SCOTCHEL GN
7 AVONLEAZE RD
8 CHERRY CL
9 ROBINA CL
10 MIDDLEMASS GN
11 HAWTHORN CL
12 WALNUT CL
DURSDEN LANE
B3087
Little Ann Copse
Knowle
Buckleaze Farm
Sharcott
Jennings Farm
OLD HOSPITAL RD
BROOMCROFT ROAD
HOLLYBUSH LANE
MILTON ROAD
Fyfield
BAILEY CL
VALE RD
NETHER LEAZE
SCHOOL VW
BUCKLEAZE LA
INLANDS CL
ASTLEY CL
Pewsey
KING ALFRED CL
WOODBOROUGH ROAD
NORTH STREET
Pewsey Heritage Centre
BRUNKARD'S LA
Cemy
WILCOT ROAD
Bouverie Hall
Liby
GODDARD RD
HIGH STREET
Kepnal
Vale Gram Sch
Sports Ctr & Swimming Pool
Sports Gd
RAWLINS RD
SLATER ROAD
ASTON CL
THE SQUARE
STRATTON RD
PO
RIVER ST
EASTERTON LA
BALL ROAD
ST JOHNS CL
PH
BROADFIELDS
THE CR
THE CRES
CHURCH ST
Wits End
THE LINKS
C5
1 GODDARD CL
2 CORONATION CL
SWAN RD
SN9
Ayrshire Farm
SHARCOTT DROVE
TINKERS MD
SOUTHCOTT ROAD
Mills Farm
Moles End
RAFFIN LANE
SWAN MD
SWAN RD
WOODLANDS RD
SWAN MEADOW
Manor Farm
Sewage Works
River Avon
SALISBURY RD
Southcott
Feather Farm
Hill View
EVERLEIGH ROAD
New Farm
GREEN DROVE
Green Drove Farm
Pewsey White Horse
8
7
61
6
5
60
4
3
59
2
1
58
16
17

191
191

191
199

198
198
198
A
B
C
D
E
F
PH
ROBIN HL LA
BULFORD HILL
CYGNET DR
CHURCH LA
LEDGER HL CL 1
CHURCHILL AV 2
Cemy
MILSTON ROAD
BULFORD DROVEWAY
DORSET CL
WILTSHIRE CL
HAIG RD
HAMPSHIRE CLOSE
Manor Farm
OLD COACH ROAD
WATER ST
CAMILLA CL
Bulford Bridge
Avondale Sch
HIGH STREET
PO
ST LEONARD'S CL
MEADOW RD
MEADOW
JOHN FRENCH WY
CHURCHILL AVENUE
BULFORD ROAD
Bulford Camp
1 CLAYTON RD
2 THE LEAZE
3 DUKE'S WY
4 SWATTONS CL
NEWMANS WY
Bulford
SALISBURY ROAD
CRESCENT RD
Durrington Walls
A345
FARGO ROAD
River Avon
WATERGATE LANE
Recreation Ground
A3028
DOUBLE HEDGES
Woodhenge
Long Barrow
Totterdown Clump
COUNTESS ROAD
Long Barrow
Tumuli
Sports Ground
Sewage Works
Mast
Tumuli
Countess
Ratfyn
Tumuli
AMESBURY ROAD
TOLLGATE CL
Folly Bottom
Motel
A303
A303
BEACON CL
Home Farm
RATFYN ROAD
Ratfyn Barrow
BEACON HILL
OAK PL
LONDON ROAD
PORTON ROAD
COOPERS CL
ALANBROOK CL
ARAGON CL
JAMES ROAD
ANNETTS CL
LORDS CFT
DARRELL RD
QUEENSBERRY
Amesbury Abbey
HILLVIEW CL
RD
THE DROVE
Sports Ground
The Pennings
Tumuli
Tumuli
MILLS WY
SP4
COUNTESS RD
KITCHENER
CARLETON PL
The Stonehenge Sch
HUDSON RD
LANE'S CL
Earl's Farm Down
THE CENTRE
Amesbury Jun School
GAUNTLET RD
ANTROBUS ROAD
ST ANNES CL
FAIRFAX CL
HARBOUR
Amesbury
English Heritage
HIGH STREET
Mkt
COLD
Amesbury Cty Inf Sch
LANFEAR CL
Queen's Falls
SALISBURY ST
Liby
COLTSFOOT CL
HOLDERS ROAD
Tumuli
Mobile Home Park
EDWARDS RD
EARLS COURT ROAD
ANTROBUS RD
DEVEREUX ROAD
BUTTERFIELD DRIVE
CHURCH STREET
CHURCH LA
ORCHARD WY
SIMMANCE WAY
RALEIGH CRES
FLOWER LA
Christ The King Sch
SOLSTICE RISE
BRAMLEY WY
BUTTERFIELD DR
River Avon
COACH HOUSE MS
BOSCOMBE ROAD
JAGGARD VIEW
TANNERS FIELD
HAMILTON CL
RALEIGH CRES
OLD GRANARY LA
PARSONAGE RD
HIGHFIELD RD
PILOTS VW
VWY
PORTON ROAD
LYNCHETS RD
LYNDHURST ROAD
Cemy
SOUTH MILL RD
SALISBURY ROAD
Rec Club
BEAUMONT
Recreation Gd
MILLGREEN RD
Lark Side
BOSCOMBE ROAD
MILTON RD
NORTH ROAD
41
ABBESS CL 1
AVONSTOKE CL 2
SOUTH MILL CL 3
BEAULIEU RD
IMBER AVE
CADNAM CR
Mast
Sewage Works
SOUTH MILL ROAD
ASHLEY WK
EARLS CL
ROBBINS RIDGE
BLACKCROSS RD
UNDERWOOD DR
KICKDOM CL
Boscombe Down
Strip Lynchets
EVERGREEN WAY
CHAMBERS AVE
ROMSEY RD
ALLINGTON WAY
MAIN ROAD
WINCHESTER CL
WILCOT CL
ORFORD RD
MARTLESHAM RD
STOCKPORT ROAD
Southmill Hill Plantation
SOUTHMILL HILL
A345
STOCKPORT ROAD
Boscombe Down Airfield
8
7
43
6
5
42
4
3
41
2
1
40
15
A
B
16
C
D
17
E
F
B3
1 SCHOOL LA
2 SMITHFIELD ST
3 CHAPLINS PL
4 NURSERY CL
5 JOHN GAY RD
6 HAYWAIN
7 LYNCHFIELD RD
198
C2
1 MILLGREEN RD
2 BEAULIEU RD
3 PAINS WY
4 FLIT CROFT
5 HARVARD WY
6 TUCKER CL
7 WITTENHAM VW
8 DIDDLEDOWN RD
C3
1 FINNIS RD
2 CHERRY TREE WY
3 GENEVILLE RI
4 LAWRENCE CL
5 RINGWOOD AV
198
D2
1 LIGHTNING RD
2 HAVARD WY
3 MCKIE RD
4 LEONARD CHESHIRE CL
5 BEYER RD
6 BAWDSEY RD
D3
1 BEAUCHAMP DR
2 CARLTON CL
3 WESTLAND CL
4 FOSTERS BUSHES
5 HURLEY CL
6 JAVELIN CL
7 MOYNE GD
8 LUMLEY WK
9 TEMPEST RD
10 CANTERBURY CL
198
E3
1 VIRGINIA CL
2 VERNON CL
3 CHESTERFIELD CL
4 PURVIS CL
5 CONISTON CL
6 NICOLSON CL
7 BURWOOD CL
8 HEYFORD CL
9 BARNES WALLIS CL
10 THURLOW CL

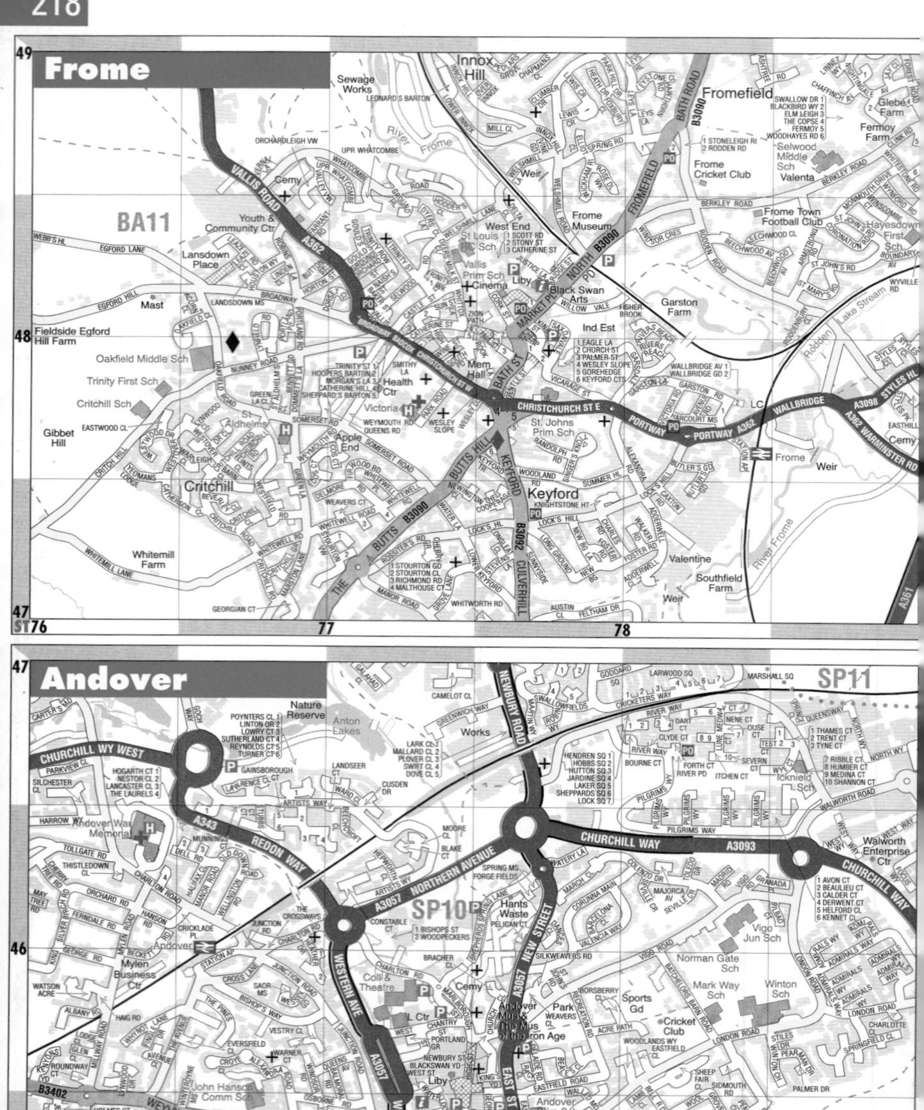
Frome
Innox Hill
Sewage Works
River Frome
Fromefield
BA11
Cemy
Youth & Community Ctr
Lansdown Place
Weir
West End
Frome Museum
Frome Cricket Club
Selwood Middle Sch
Valenta
Frome Town Football Club
Hayesdown First Sch
Glebe Farm
Fermoy Farm
St Louis RC Sch
Valls Prim Sch
Cinema
Liby
Black Swan Arts
Garston Farm
Mast
Fieldside Egford Hill Farm
Oakfield Middle Sch
Trinity First Sch
Critchill Sch
Gibbet Hill
Health Ctr
Victoria
Mem Hall
Ind Est
St. Johns Prim Sch
Apple End
Critchill
Keyford
Frome
Weir
Whitemill Farm
Valentine
Southfield Farm
VALLIS ROAD
A362
BATH ROAD
B3090
FROMEFIELD
CHRISTCHURCH ST E
PORTWAY
WALLBRIDGE
A3098
A362 WARMINSTER RD
BUTTS HILL
KEYFORD
B3092
CULVERHILL
THE BUTTS
A361
ST76
77
78
49
48
47
Andover
Nature Reserve
Anton Lakes
Works
CHURCHILL WY WEST
NEWBURY ROAD
SP11
Icknield Sch
Andover War Memorial
A343
REDON WAY
CHURCHILL WAY
A3093
Walworth Enterprise Ctr
A3057 NORTHERN AVENUE
SP10
Hants Waste
Andover
Mylen Business Ctr
WESTERN AVE
Coll & Theatre
Cemy
L Ctr
Andover Mus & The Mus of the Iron Age
Park
Sports Gd
Cricket Club
Vigo Jun Sch
Norman Gate Sch
Mark Way Sch
Winton Sch
Liby
John Hanson Comm Sch
Rookwood Sch
B3402
WEYHILL ROAD
WESTERN RD
Andover Prim Sch
Wolverdene School
NEW STREET
EAST ST
SU35
36
37
47
46
45

Scale: 5 inches to 1 mile
0 110 yards 220 yards
0 125 m 250 m

One-way streets

House numbers
1 59
HIGH ST

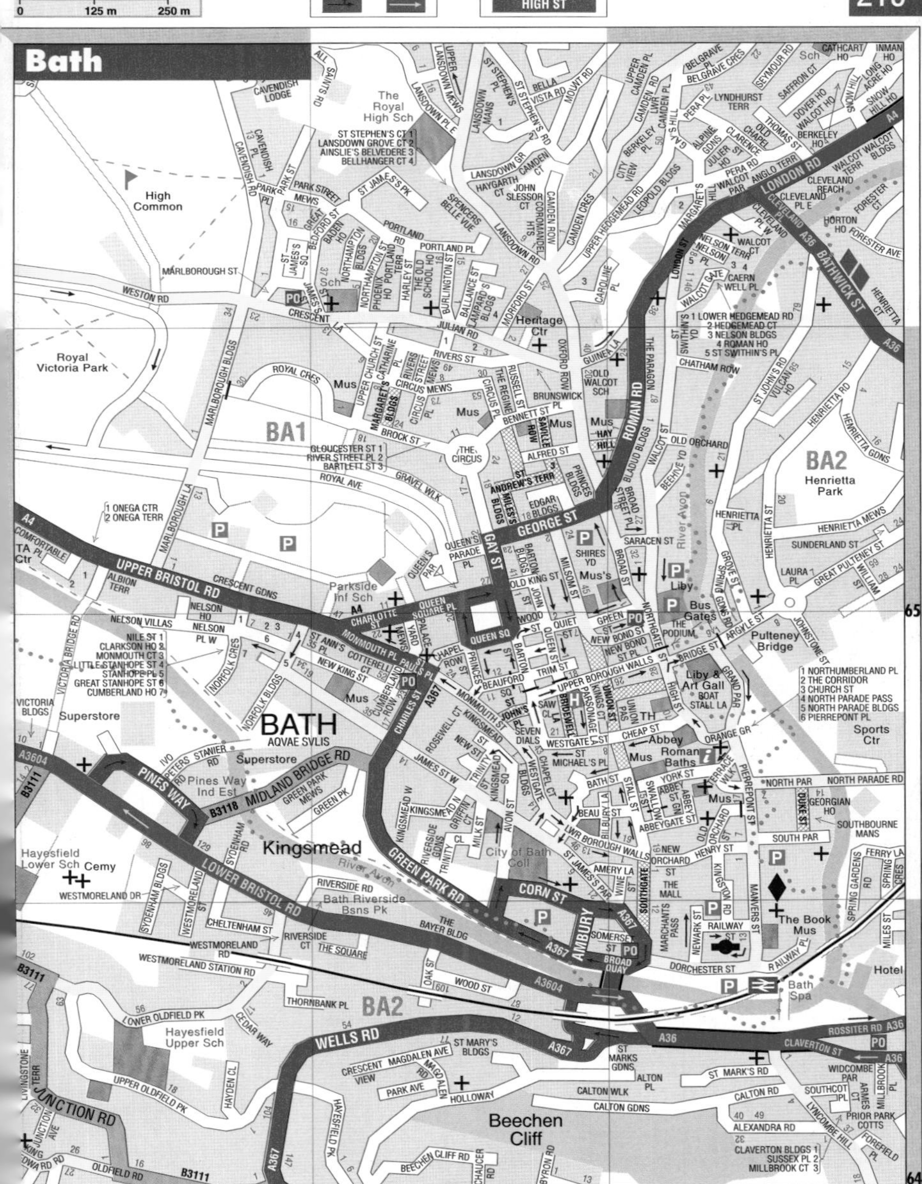

Index

Church Rd **6** Beckenham BR2..........**53** C6

Place name	Location number	Locality, town or village	Postcode district	Page and grid square
May be abbreviated on the map	Present when a number indicates the place's position in a crowded area of mapping	Shown when more than one place has the same name	District for the indexed place	Page number and grid reference for the standard mapping

Public and commercial buildings are highlighted in magenta. Places of interest are highlighted in blue with a star★

Abbreviations used in the index

Acad	**Academy**	Comm	**Common**	Gd	**Ground**	L	**Leisure**	Prom	**Promenade**
App	**Approach**	Cott	**Cottage**	Gdn	**Garden**	La	**Lane**	Rd	**Road**
Arc	**Arcade**	Cres	**Crescent**	Gn	**Green**	Liby	**Library**	Recn	**Recreation**
Ave	**Avenue**	Cswy	**Causeway**	Gr	**Grove**	Mdw	**Meadow**	Ret	**Retail**
Bglw	**Bungalow**	Ct	**Court**	H	**Hall**	Meml	**Memorial**	Sh	**Shopping**
Bldg	**Building**	Ctr	**Centre**	Ho	**House**	Mkt	**Market**	Sq	**Square**
Bsns, Bus	**Business**	Ctry	**Country**	Hospl	**Hospital**	Mus	**Museum**	St	**Street**
Bvd	**Boulevard**	Cty	**County**	HQ	**Headquarters**	Orch	**Orchard**	Sta	**Station**
Cath	**Cathedral**	Dr	**Drive**	Hts	**Heights**	Pal	**Palace**	Terr	**Terrace**
Cir	**Circus**	Dro	**Drove**	Ind	**Industrial**	Par	**Parade**	TH	**Town Hall**
Cl	**Close**	Ed	**Education**	Inst	**Institute**	Pas	**Passage**	Univ	**University**
Cnr	**Corner**	Emb	**Embankment**	Int	**International**	Pk	**Park**	Wk, Wlk	**Walk**
Coll	**College**	Est	**Estate**	Intc	**Interchange**	Pl	**Place**	Wr	**Water**
Com	**Community**	Ex	**Exhibition**	Junc	**Junction**	Prec	**Precinct**	Yd	**Yard**

Index of localities, towns and villages

A

Ablington 190 B1
Acton Turville 52 F6
Alcester 202 B1
Alcombe 82 F8
Aldbourne 170 A6
Alderbury 153 C3
Alderton 39 F2
All Cannings 180 E8
Allington 69 E3
Allington 172 E2
Allington 199 A2
Allington Bar 69 F2
Alton 190 B1
Alton Barnes 173 C1
Alton Priors 173 D1
Alvediston 204 B2
Amesbury 217 C4
Ansty 203 F5
Ansty Coombe 203 F5
Appleshaw 192 E3
Ashbury 164 A7
Ashford 210 C1
Ashley 3 A2
Ashley 83 A6
Ashmore 206 D5
Ashton Common 102 F1
Ashton Keynes 6 F1
Atworth 92 F8
Aughton 183 D3
Avebury 173 C8
Avebury Trusloe 173 B8
Avington 177 F7
Avon 71 F6
Avoncliff 99 F4
Axford 169 D1

B

Badbury 65 F5
Badbury Wick 65 D8
Badminton 38 F2
Bagshot 176 F4
Ballard's Ash 47 D5
Bapton 195 D1
Barford St Martin 143 A3
Barkers Hill 203 A4
Barrow 136 C5
Barrow Street 139 F2
Batheaston 82 A3
Bathford 82 B2
Baverstock 142 B4
Baydon 170 C8
Beanacre 94 A8
Beckhampton 173 B7
Beechingstoke 181 A6
Bemerton 145 C2
Bemerton Heath 145 C4
Berkley 111 A7
Berkley Down 110 C5
Berryfield 93 F1
Berwick Bassett 167 B4
Berwick St James 196 E2
Berwick St John 203 E1
Berwick St Leonard 200 C4
Bewley Common 86 E5
Biddestone 76 F8
Birdbush 203 B1
Bishopdown 146 C4
Bishops Cannings 172 B3
Bishopstone 163 E6
Bishopstone 205 F4
Bishopstrow 117 E4
Bittles Green 202 B4
Blackland 89 F6
Bleet 102 F2
Blue Vein 83 D3
Blunsdon St Andrew 34 E8
Bodenham 152 F1
Bohemia 211 E6
Boreham 117 C5
Boscombe 199 A1
Bottlesford 181 D6
Bourton 137 E2
Bourton 172 C3
Boveridge 209 B1
Bowden Hill 87 B4
Bowerchalke 205 A2
Bowerhill 94 D1
Bowldown 70 E8
Box 83 D6
Box Hill 83 F7
Boyton 194 E2
Bradenstoke 59 C3
Bradford Leigh 91 F1
Bradford-on-Avon 100 E6
Bramshaw 212 E3
Bratton 186 B7
Breamore 210 F5
Bremhill 80 E7
Brigmerston 198 C8
Brinkworth 45 E5
Britford 152 E5
Brixton Deverill 120 E2
Broad Blunsdon 21 C2
Broad Chalke 205 B4
Broad Hinton 167 C7
Broad Street 181 C6
Broad Town 167 A8
Broad's Green 88 F3
Broadbush 21 D1
Brokenborough 27 D7
Brokerswood 107 F5
Bromham 96 A7
Brook 212 E1
Brook Hill 212 D1
Brook Waters 203 B2
Broomfield 55 A1
Broughton Gifford 93 C4
Brunton 183 E3
Bugley 116 C6
Bulbridge 144 B1
Bulford 217 E8
Bulford Camp 198 F6
Bulkington 178 E5
Bullenhill 106 E8
Bullock's Horn 15 E1
Burbage 183 D8
Burcombe 143 E2
Burton 53 B4
Burton 139 D5
Buscot Wick 12 D8
Bushton 166 E8
Buttermere 185 B8

C

Cadley 175 A5
Calcutt 20 A7
Callow Hill 46 D6
Calne 81 B2
Calne Marsh 81 C4
Calstone Wellington 172 A7
Canada 212 F4
Cann Common 206 B8
Castle Combe 68 A7
Castle Eaton 10 B4
Catcomb 73 D6
Cerney Wick 7 F5
Chalford 113 A8
Chapel Barton 115 D6
Chapel Knapp 85 D5
Chapel Plaister 84 A5
Chapmanslade 111 C4
Charlcutt 72 F4
Charlton 29 A6
Charlton 181 D3
Charlton 193 C2
Charlton 203 A1
Charlton Heath 29 D6
Charlton Musgrove 136 B4
Charlton-All-Saints 159 A4
Charnage 139 E4
Chedglow 14 C7
Chelworth 4 C1
Chelworth Lower Green 19 A5
Chelworth Upper Green 19 A6
Cherhill 166 B1
Chicklade 200 A5
Chicksgrove 204 B8
Chilmark 201 B3
Chilton Foliat 170 F1
Chippenham 78 E7
Chirton 180 F4
Chisbury 176 B5
Chiseldon 65 D3
Chitterne 195 C7
Chittoe 87 E2
Cholderton 199 C5
Christian Malford 58 B2
Churchfields 145 D1
Chute Cadley 192 F8
Chute Standen 192 F8
Clanville 56 E4
Clanville 193 A4
Clatford 174 B7
Claverton 90 B5
Clearwood 111 F8
Clench 174 E1
Clench Common 174 D4
Clevancy 166 C6
Cleverton 44 D8
Cloatley 15 E2
Cloatley End 16 B1
Clyffe Pypard 166 F8
Coate 51 C2
Coate 180 C8
Cobley 208 D7
Codford St Mary 195 B2
Codford St Peter 195 A3
Cold Harbour 102 F2
Cold Harbour 116 F8
Colerne 75 B3
Collingbourne Ducis 191 E8
Collingbourne Kingston 183 D2
Combe 185 F8
Common Platt 33 F2
Compton 189 F7
Compton Abbas 206 A5
Compton Bassett 166 B3
Compton Chamberlayne 205 A8
Conkwell 90 D1
Conock 180 E4
Coombe 190 B5
Coombe 202 F1
Coombe Bissett 150 F1
Coped Hall 47 F4
Corsham 85 A8
Corsley 111 D2
Corsley Heath 115 B8
Corston 42 E5

Corton 194 D3
Cotmarsh 62 B4
Cotswold Community 6 D4
Coulston 178 E1
Covingham 51 D7
Cowesfield Green 161 F4
Cricklade 19 E7
Criddlestyle 210 E1
Crockerton 116 E1
Crockerton Green 116 F2
Crofton 176 A1
Crooked Soley 170 F3
Cross Keys 77 A3
Croucheston 205 F4
Crudwell 14 E6
Cuckold's Green 179 C4
Cuckoo's Corner 180 B4
Cuckoo's Knob 174 F1
Culkerton 3 A5
Culverslade 66 A2

D

Damerham 209 F2
Dauntsey 45 B1
Dauntsey Lock 59 B5
Dean 207 E2
Deanend 207 E4
Deanland 208 A5
Deptford 195 E1
Derry Fields 17 F8
Derry Hill 79 F2
Dertfords 115 B7
Devizes 214 A3
Didmarton 24 C3
Dilton Marsh 112 B8
Dinton 201 F2
Ditchampton 144 C4
Ditteridge 83 B8
Dogridge 32 F3
Donhead St Andrew 203 B3
Donhead St Mary 203 A3
Dorcan 51 D5
Down Ampney 8 D7
Downton 211 B8
Draycot Cerne 56 F1
Draycot Fitz Payne 174 A2
Draycot Foliat 168 D8
Drynham 105 E5
Dunfield 10 A8
Dunge 106 E1
Dunkirk 179 D8
Durley 175 D3
Durrington 198 B7
Dursley 105 E1

E

East Anton 193 F2
East Chisenbury 190 A7
East Compton 206 A5
East Everleigh 191 A8
East Garston 171 E7
East Gomeldon 133 E4
East Grafton 183 F7
East Grimstead 154 F4
East Hatch 203 C7
East Kennett 173 E6
East Knoyle 141 C2
East Martin 209 C6
East Melbury 206 B7
East Town 106 E4
East Tytherton 72 B2
East Winterslow 149 C8
East Woodlands 114 B5
Eastbury 171 C8
Eastcott 180 A2
Eastcourt 15 D6
Easterton 180 A2
Easterton Sands 179 F2
Eastleaze 49 B6
Easton 77 D2
Easton Grey 26 C3
Easton Royal 183 A7
Easton Town 25 D1
Eastrip 75 D4
Ebbesbourne Wake 204 C2
Eddington 177 C8
Eden Vale 108 E3
Edington 186 C8
Elcombe 63 E5
Eldene 51 C5
Elliots Green 114 D8
Elm Cross 167 D7
Elm Hill 202 A5
Elston 196 E7
Enford 189 F6
Enham Alamein 193 E4
Enmore Green 202 B2
Erlestoke 187 A8
Etchilhampton 180 C7
Even Swindon 49 E6
Everleigh 191 A8
Ewen 5 C8

F

Faberstown 192 B6
Fairford 1 E7
Fairwood 108 B4
Farleigh Hungerford 103 E7
Farleigh Wick 90 F5
Farley 154 D8
Farnham 207 C2
Ferne 203 D1
Fiddington Sands 179 F1
Fifield 190 A5
Fifield Bavant 204 F4
Figheldean 190 B2
Filands 28 A6
Firsdown 148 C8
Fisherton de la Mere 195 D1
Fittleton 190 A4
Flaxlands 47 D6
Flood Street 210 E4
Fonthill Bishop 200 D3
Fonthill Gifford 200 B2
Ford 68 A2
Ford 146 D7
Fordingbridge 210 E1
Forest Hill 175 B7
Forewoods Common 101 C7
Fosbury 185 A5
Foscote 54 E3
Fovant 204 E8
Foxcotte 193 C2
Foxham 72 D7
Foxley 41 F8
Fresh Brook 49 A4
Freshford 99 B5
Fritham 212 A1
Frogmore 109 A4
Frome 110 A5
Fromefield 110 A6
Froxfield 176 D7
Fugglestone St Peter 144 F4
Furzley 212 F3
Fyfield 192 D1
Fyfield 215 E5

G

Gare Hill 118 A5
Garsdon 29 B4
Gasper 137 C7
Gastard 85 D6
Giddeahall 68 D2
Goatacre 73 F7
Godshill 211 A1
Gomeldon 133 D4
Gorse Hill 35 D1
Grange Park 48 F5
Great Ashley 91 A1
Great Bedwyn 176 B3
Great Chalfield 92 E3
Great Cheverell 179 C1
Great Durnford 197 F1
Great Hinton 178 A6
Great Somerford 44 B2
Great Wishford 129 F3
Greatfield 47 F8
Green Hill 32 D1
Greenmeadow 35 B4
Greenwich 200 C3
Grittenham 46 C2
Grittleton 54 D5
Gussage St Andrew 207 E1

H

Hackthorn 198 A8
Hailstone Hill 8 A1
Halcombe 27 E3
Hale 211 C5
Half Way Firs 76 C1
Halfway 113 A4
Ham 177 B2
Ham Green 101 C8
Hampshire Gate 185 A1
Hampton 22 D5
Hampton Hill 22 E5
Hamptworth 212 B6
Hanging Langford 128 C7
Hankerton 15 C2
Hannington 22 B7
Hannington Wick 11 A4
Hardway 122 A1
Haresfield 23 B8
Harnham 151 E6
Hatchet Green 211 C6
Hatherden 193 C5
Hawkeridge 108 E8
Haxton 190 B4
Haydon Wick 34 E5
Hayes Knoll 19 E2
Heddington 89 B1
Heddington Wick 88 E2
Henley 83 C4
Henley 185 A6
Heytesbury 194 C5
Heywood 109 A8
Higher Pertwood 127 E4
Highway 166 B5
Highworth 23 B5
Hilcott 181 D5
Hill Corner 110 E7
Hill Deverill 120 F5
Hill View 215 B3
Hilmarton 166 A6
Hilperton 102 A3
Hilperton Marsh 101 F4
Hindon 200 B3
Hinton Charterhouse 98 E1
Hinton Parva 163 D6
Hisomley 112 C7
Hodson 65 A5
Hoggington 104 D4
Holloway 141 A1
Holt 92 E1
Holwell 139 B5
Homington 151 D1
Hook 47 F6
Hook Street 48 B6
Horningsham 119 A7
Horpit 163 B7
Horton 172 C2
Hudswell 84 C8
Huish 174 A2
Hullavington 41 E1
Hungerford 177 A6
Hungerford Newtown 171 D2
Huntenhull Green 111 C3
Hurdcott 146 F8
Hyde 35 D7

I

Ibthorpe 193 F8
Idmiston 133 F8
Idstone 163 F7
Imber 187 A3
Inglesham 2 B1
Inkpen 177 E3
Ireland 105 B2
Ivy Cross 202 D2

K

Keevil 178 C5
Kellaways 71 E4
Kemble 4 E7
Kemble Wick 4 E4
Kempsford 10 E6
Kepnal 215 E5
Kilmington 123 E5
Kilmington Common 123 D4
Kimpton 192 C1
Kinghay 202 F8
Kingsdown 35 F5
Kingsdown 82 F3
Kingshill 50 B5
Kingston Deverill 126 B6
Kingstone Winslow 164 A8
Kington Langley 70 E7
Kington St Michael 70 A8
Knapp 205 A4
Knapp Hill 202 A5
Knighton 170 D2
Knights Enham 193 E3
Knockdown 24 F5
Knook 194 D4
Knowle 215 C6

L

Lacock 86 D5
Lake 197 F2
Lambourn 165 B2
Lambourn Woodlands 171 A7
Landford 212 C6
Landfordwood 212 D8
Lane End 115 A8
Langley Burrell 71 A3
Larkhill 197 F6
Latton 8 C4
Laverstock 146 E2
Lavington Sands 179 E2
Lawn 50 F3
Lea 28 F1
Leafield 84 E7
Lechlade-on-Thames 2 D4
Leigh 18 C5
Leigh Delamere 55 C3
Letcombe Bassett 165 F8
Leverton 171 B1
Liddington 163 B4
Liden 51 D3
Limpers Hill 139 D4
Limpley Stoke 99 A6
Linkenholt 185 E5
Little Ashley 91 A2
Little Badminton 38 E5
Little Bedwyn 176 D5
Little Chalfield 92 C3
Little Cheverell 187 D8
Little Durnford 131 D1
Little Faringdon 2 F8
Little Horton 172 C1
Little Langford 129 A6
Little London 166 E2
Little Marsh 102 F4
Little Salisbury 182 E7
Little Somerford 44 B5
Littlecott 166 A7
Littlecott 190 A6
Littledown 185 D4
Littleton 178 B7
Littleton Drew 53 E5
Littleton Panell 179 D1
Littleworth 182 E8
Lockeridge 174 A6
Long Cross 138 B5
Long Dean 68 C4
Long Newnton 13 C5
Longbridge Deverill 120 F6
Longfield 105 E8
Longhedge 115 D5
Longstreet 190 A6
Lover 211 D6
Lower Blunsdon 21 B3
Lower Burgate 210 D2
Lower Chicksgrove 201 B1
Lower Chute 192 F8
Lower Everleigh 182 E1
Lower Green 177 D3
Lower Moor 17 A4
Lower Rudge 107 D4
Lower Seagry 57 F7
Lower Stanton St Quintin 56 D6
Lower Stratton 36 B2
Lower Studley 105 E6
Lower Wanborough 163 B6
Lower Woodford 131 C3
Lower Wraxall 91 E5
Lower Zeals 138 D5
Luckington 39 E4
Ludgershall 192 A5
Ludwell 203 A1
Lydiard Green 48 B8
Lydiard Millicent 33 D1
Lydiard Plain 32 B1
Lydiard Tregoze 48 E6
Lye Green 100 A4
Lye's Green 111 B1
Lyneham 60 B2

M

Maddington 196 E7
Maiden Bradley 118 F2
Malmesbury 28 B3
Manningford Abbots 182 A5
Manningford Bohune 181 F4
Manningford Bruce 181 F5
Manton 213 A1
Marden 181 A4
Market Lavington 179 E1
Marlborough 213 F3
Marr Green 183 D7
Marshfield 74 A8
Marston 179 A3
Marston Hill 1 C4
Marston Meysey 9 D7
Marten 184 C7
Martin 209 B6
Martin Drove End 209 A8
Martinslade 178 E8
Melbury Abbas 206 B7
Melksham 94 A5
Melksham Forest 94 D6
Mere 139 B5
Meysey Hampton 1 A5
Middle Winterslow 149 B7
Middle Woodford 131 B4
Middlehill 83 A6
Middlewick 76 D3
Midford 98 C6
Milbourne 28 D4
Mildenhall 175 A8
Mile Elm 89 A7
Mile End 165 A3
Milford 152 E8
Milkhouse Water 215 E8
Milkwell 203 B2
Milston 198 B8
Milton 141 B3
Milton Lilbourne 182 F7
Minchington 207 D1
Minety 17 B2
Minety Common 31 C8
Misselfore 204 F1
Monk's Park 85 A6
Monkton Combe 98 E8
Monkton Deverill 126 D7
Monkton Farleigh 90 F7
Moor Green 84 D6
Moredon 34 E3
Motcombe 202 A4
Mount Sorrel 205 B3
Mountain Bower 66 F4
Murcott 14 F4

N

Neston 84 E6
Netheravon 190 A3
Netherhampton 151 A8
Netherton 185 F4
Nettleton 53 C1
Nettleton Green 53 B1
Nettleton Shrub 67 C7
Netton 131 E6
New Town 50 D6
New Town 170 C2
New Town 173 D3
New Town 207 C2
New Town 207 F6
Newbury 119 C8
Newgrounds 211 B1
Newton 161 B2
Newton Tony 199 B3
Newtown 176 E2
Newtown 203 B7
Nine Elms 49 A8
Nomansland 212 C4
Norleaze 108 F8
Normanton 197 F3
Norrington Common 93 C6
North Bradley 105 D4
North Brewham 122 A6
North Charford 211 C6
North End 6 E2
North Newnton 181 E4
North Street 210 E5
North Tidworth 216 D8
North Wraxall 67 B3
North Wroughton 64 A8
Northbrook 179 E1
Northend 82 A5
Norton 41 D5
Norton Bavant 194 A6
Notton 86 B8
Nunton 152 D1
Nursteed 214 E1
Nutbane 193 A4
Nythe 51 C7

O

Oaksey 15 F7
Oare 174 B2
Odstock 152 A1
Ogbourne Maizey 213 C7
Ogbourne St Andrew 168 F3
Ogbourne St George 169 A5
Okus 50 A4
Old Town 50 D3
Oldbury on the Hill 24 B5
Orcheston 196 D8
Outmarsh 102 F7
Outwick 210 D4
Overtown 64 D4
Oxenwood 184 E6

P

Park 51 A5
Park Corner 99 A4
Patney 180 F5
Paxcroft 102 C3
Pear Ash 137 C4
Peckingell 71 B2
Penhill 35 C5
Penknap 112 E8
Penleigh 108 D2
Penselwood 137 B4
Penton Corner 193 A1
Penton Grafton 193 A2
Penton Mewsey 193 B2
Pentridge 208 E4
Perham Down 191 F4
Perry Green 29 B7
Petersfinger 152 E7
Petty France 38 B8
Pewsey 215 D5
Pewsey Wharf 215 B7
Pickwick 76 E2

Pinckney Green .90 E5
Pinehurst .35 D3
Pinkney .25 E2
Pitton .148 C3
Plaitford .212 E6
Plaitford Green .212 F8
Poole Keynes .5 C4
Portash .201 B2
Porton .133 D6
Potterne .179 D5
Potterne Wick .179 E4
Poulshot .179 B6
Preston .60 D1
Preston .170 B4
Purlpit .93 A8
Purton .33 B4
Purton Common .33 A5
Purton Stoke .19 C1

Q

Queen Oak .138 A3
Queen Street .31 B3
Quemerford .89 D8
Quidhampton .145 A2

R

Ragged Appleshaw .192 F3
Ram Alley .175 B2
Ramsbury .170 A2
Ratford .80 E5
Ratfyn .217 C5
Redenham .192 D4
Redlands .22 F3
Redlynch .211 D8
Redstocks .95 A2
Restrop .33 A2
Reybridge .86 D7
Ridge .200 F2
Rivar .184 F8
Rockbourne .210 A5
Rockley .168 C2
Rodbourne .35 A1
Rodbourne .43 A3
Rodbourne Bottom .43 A2
Rodbourne Cheney .35 B2
Rode Hill .103 F1
Rodmarton .3 C8
Rollestone .196 F6
Rollestone Camp .197 B7
Rood Ashton .106 D4
Rook Street .139 A4
Roughmoor .34 B1
Roundway .214 D7
Rowde .96 D2
Rudge .107 D5
Rudloe .76 B1
Rushall .181 E2

S

St Edith's .96 D5
St James .202 C1
St Katharines .175 F4
Salisbury .152 C7
Salterton .131 D4
Sambourne .116 F5
Sandleheath .210 B2
Sandy Lane .88 B4
Sanham Green .177 B5
Sawyers Hill .17 A2
Sedgehill .202 C7
Seend .178 E7
Seend Cleeve .178 C7
Sells Green .95 E1
Sem Hill .202 E5
Semington .102 E5
Semley .202 F5
Serrington .129 D7
Sevenhampton .23 B2
Sevington .55 A2
Shaftesbury .202 A1
Shalbourne .176 F2
Sharcott .182 A6
Sharpstone .99 A4
Shaw .49 B7
Shaw .93 D7
Sheepdrove .165 B2
Shefford Woodlands .171 F4
Sherrington .194 F1
Sherston .25 C1
Shipton Bellinger .199 D8
Shipton Moyne .26 E8
Shorncote .6 A6
Shrewton .196 E6
Sixpenny Handley .208 A3
Slaughterford .76 A8
Sodom .59 C7
Somerford Keynes .5 F3
Sopworth .24 D1
South Brewham .122 A4
South Cerney .7 A6
South Marston .36 F5
South Marston Park .36 D7
South Newton .130 B2
South Tidworth .216 D4
South Wraxall .91 D6
Southbrook .139 B4
Southcott .215 D3
Southend .168 F4
Southwick .104 F3
Spirthill .73 B4
Standerwick .107 B2
Stanley .80 A6
Stanton Fitzwarren .22 B1
Stanton St Bernard .173 A1
Stanton St Quintin .56 B4
Stapleford .129 E7
Startley .43 D1
Staverton .101 C6
Steeple Ashton .178 B3
Steeple Langford .128 D8
Stert .180 B6
Stibb Green .175 D1
Stitchcombe .175 D8
Stockley .89 C4
Stockton .195 B1
Stoford .130 A3
Stoke Farthing .205 D4
Stonebridge .110 C7
Stormore .112 A8
Stourton .123 F1
Straight Soley .171 A3
Strangways .198 A6
Stratford sub Castle .145 F5
Stratford Tony .150 C2
Stratton St Margaret .36 A3
Studley .80 B3
Studley Green .104 F7
Sturford .115 E6
Sunton .183 E1
Sutton Benger .57 C2
Sutton Mandeville .204 C8
Sutton Row .204 B7
Sutton Veny .117 F1
Swallett Gate .59 A6
Swallowcliffe .204 A6
Swanborough .22 C4
Swindon .50 E4

T

Tangley .193 A7
Tanis .96 F2
Teffont Evias .201 C2
Teffont Magna .201 C3
Tellisford .103 E4
Temple .115 C6
The Causeway .139 C4
The Common .46 B7
The Common .93 B5
The Common .149 C6
The Fox .33 F3
The Gibb .53 F3
The Green .141 A3
The Ham .108 E5
The Linleys .85 B6
The Pitts .205 F5
The Ridge .85 B5
The Shoe .66 F1
The Spa .94 C2
The Stocks .178 C7
The Strand .178 B6
Theobald's Green .172 A8
Thickwood .75 D6
Thingley .77 F1
Thornend .58 C1
Thornhill .61 F1
Tidcombe .184 C5
Tidpit .209 C6
Tidworth .216 E7
Tilshead .188 B3
Tisbury .203 D8
Tockenham .60 E3
Tockenham Wick .60 D7
Tollard Farnham .207 B2
Tollard Royal .207 B4
Toothill .49 C4
Townsend .179 A6
Townsend .180 C3
Trowbridge .101 E3
Trowle Common .100 F2
Tucking Mill .98 D8
Tuckingmill .203 D8
Turleigh .99 F6
Tytherington .194 B4
Tytherton Lucas .71 D1

U

Uffcott .167 E8
Ugford .144 A3
Underhill .140 F2
Upavon .181 F2
Upper Burgate .210 E3
Upper Castle Combe .68 B8
Upper Chicksgrove .201 A1
Upper Chute .192 D8
Upper Enham .193 F4
Upper Green .177 E2
Upper Inglesham .12 B5
Upper Lambourn .164 F3
Upper Minety .16 D3
Upper Pickwick .76 C3
Upper Seagry .57 D6
Upper Stratton .35 E4
Upper Street .210 D5
Upper Studley .105 A5
Upper Town .58 D4
Upper Up .6 E6
Upper Upham .169 C8
Upper Woodford .131 C7
Upper Wraxall .66 E2
Upton .141 A5
Upton .185 D2
Upton Lovell .194 E3
Upton Scudamore .112 E5
Urchfont .180 C4

V

Vastern .60 F8
Vernham Bank .185 B3
Vernham Dean .185 C3
Vernham Row .185 B4
Vernham Street .185 D4

W

Wadswick .84 B4
Walcot East .50 F6
Walcot West .50 E5
Wanborough .163 A5
Wardour .203 D6
Warleigh .90 D5
Warminster .116 E7
Warminster Common .116 E5
Waterhay .18 C7
Wedhampton .180 E4
Well Bottom .206 E3
West Amesbury .198 A4
West Ashton .106 B3
West Chisenbury .189 F7
West Crudwell .14 D7
West Dean .155 F3
West Grafton .183 E7
West Grimstead .154 C2
West Hatch .203 C7
West Kennett .173 D7
West Kington .66 F7
West Kington Wick .67 B6
West Knoyle .140 E6
West Lavington .187 E8
West Overton .173 F6
West Stowell .173 F1
West Winterslow .148 F5
West Yatton .68 D3
Westbrook .95 E8
Westbury .109 B2
Westbury Leigh .108 E1
Westlea .49 D5
Westonbirt .25 D8
Westrop .77 C1
Westwells .84 C6
Westwood .99 F2
Westwood .145 B5
Wexcombe .184 B6
Weyhill .192 F1
Whaddon .102 C7
Whaddon .153 E1
Whitbourne Springs .115 E5
White Cross .137 E5
White Hill .139 C2
Whiteparish .161 D4
Whitepits .126 A7
Whitley .85 C1
Whitsbury .210 B5
Whittonditch .170 D3
Wick .210 F8
Widbrook .100 E4
Widham .33 C5
Wilcot .182 A7
Wildhern .193 D5
Willesley .25 C6
Wilsford .181 B4
Wilsford .197 F2
Wilton .144 C3
Wilton .184 A8
Windmills .193 F7
Wingfield .104 C6
Winsley .99 E7
Winterbourne Bassett .167 B5
Winterbourne Dauntsey .133 B2
Winterbourne Earls .133 A1
Winterbourne Gunner .133 D3
Winterbourne Monkton .167 B3
Winterbourne Stoke .196 F4
Wolverton .138 B4
Woodborough .181 D6
Woodcock .117 C6
Woodcutts .207 D4
Woodfalls .211 D7
Woodgreen .211 A4
Woodhouse .193 F3
Woodlands St Mary .171 B6
Woodminton .204 E1
Woodsend .169 C7
Woodshaw .48 A2
Woodyates .208 D6
Woolley .100 E7
Woolley Green .100 F8
Wootton Bassett .47 C2
Wootton Rivers .174 F2
Worton .179 B4
Wroughton .64 A5
Wylye .201 F8

Y

Yarnbrook .105 F3
Yatesbury .166 E2
Yatton Keynell .68 E6

Z

Zeals .137 F4

A

Abberd La SN11 .81 D3
Abberd Way SN11 .81 C3
Abbess Cl SP4 .217 B2
Abbey CE Fst Sch The SP7 .202 B1
Abbey Cl
Chippenham SN15 .79 B5
3 Shrewton SP3 .196 E6
Abbey La BA2 .99 A3
Abbey Rw SN16 .28 A3
Abbey View Rd SN25 .34 E3
Abbey Wlk 6 SP7 .202 C1
Abbeyfield Sch SN14 .70 C2
Abbeymeads Com Prim Sch SN2 .35 A7
Abbot Rd SP1 .146 C4
Abbots Wlk GL7 .2 D4
Abbotsbury Way SN25 .35 A8
Abbotts Cl SP9 .216 C7
Abbotts Gdn SN16 .28 A3
Abbotts Rd SP9 .216 C7
Abdon Cl BA12 .195 D7
Abingdon Ct La SN6 .19 E8
Abington Way SN2 .35 D5
Abney Moor SN3 .51 E2
Abotts Cl BA13 .108 F3
Above Hedges SP5 .148 C3
Acacia Cl SN14 .70 A1
Acacia Cres BA14 .105 A8
Acacia Dr BA11 .110 C7
Acacia Gr SN2 .35 C2
Academy Dr SN13 .76 E2
Acorn Cl SN3 .51 C5
Acre Cl BA14 .178 A3
Acres Rd SN10 .214 C3
Acreshort La BA14 .178 A3
Activity Zone Leisure Ctr SN16 .27 F3
Adam's Grave (Long Barrow)* SN8 .173 D2
Adampur Rd SP9 .216 A4
Adcroft Dr BA14 .101 D1
Adcroft St BA14 .101 C1
Adderwell BA11 .110 A3
Adderwell Cl BA11 .110 A3
Addington Cl SN10 .214 C2
Addison Cres SN2 .35 F3
Addison Rd SN12 .93 F6
Addison Sq 19 SP4 .198 B7
Adelaide Cl 6 SP4 .198 F6
Adwalton Cl SN5 .49 B4
Aelmas Mich Dro SP11 .192 E1
Affleck Cl SN5 .49 C5
Agra Rd SP9 .216 A4
Agravaine Cl 27 SP10 .193 E2
Ailesbury Cl SN15 .79 A4
Ailesbury Way SN8 .183 D8
Ainsworth Rd SN3 .51 A4
Aintree 7 RG17 .165 A1
Aintree Ave BA14 .105 E4
Aintree Dr SN14 .77 F6
Airman's Cnr SP3 .197 B5
Aisne Rd SN4 .65 D1
Akenfield Cl SN25 .34 F5
Akers Ct SN26 .21 C2
Akers Way SN2 .34 E2
Alamein Rd 4 SP11 .193 E4
Alan Powell La BA13 .112 B8
Alanbrook Cl SP4 .217 B4
Alanbrooke Cres SN2 .35 A2
Alanbrooke Rd SP4 .197 E6
Alba Cl 11 SN5 .48 F8
Albany Cl BA14 .101 F2
Albany Rd SP1 .146 B1
Albert Rd BA14 .101 F3
Albert St SN1 .50 D4
Albion Dr BA14 .105 B8
Albion Rd 33 SP6 .210 D1
Albion St SN1 .50 A5
Aldborough Cl 2 SN5 .49 C6
Aldbourne Cl
Blunsdon St Andrew SN2 .35 C6
27 Hungerford RG17 .177 B7
Aldbourne Four Barrows* SN8 .169 E8
Aldbourne Rd SN8 .170 B7
Aldeburgh Pl BA14 .104 F6
Alder Cl Swindon SN2 .34 D4
Trowbridge BA14 .105 B5
Alder Way SN12 .94 A4
Alder Wlk 5 BA11 .110 B7
Alderbury & W Grimstead Sch SP5 .153 E3
Alderholt Rd SP6 .210 B1
Alderney Cl 6 SN4 .48 A2
Alderton Rd
Grittleton SN14 .54 D5
Luckington SN14 .53 D6
Alderton Way BA14 .105 D5
Aldrin Cl 7 SP10 .193 D2
Aldworth Dr 3 SP1 .146 C5
Alexander Fields SN9 .181 F1
Alexander Rd SN16 .27 F4
Alexander Terr SN13 .77 A1
Alexandra Cl SP2 .145 C3
Alexandra Rd
Fordingbridge SP6 .210 D1
Frome BA11 .110 A4
1 Swindon SN1 .50 C7
Alexandra Terr SN8 .213 D3
Alfred St Swindon SN1 .50 C7
Westbury BA13 .109 A4
Alfred's Castle* RG17 .164 B5
Alfred's Twr* BA10 .122 F3
All Saints CE Prim Sch SP5 .161 D3
All Saints Rd 1 SN10 .187 E7
Allen Rd Corsham SN13 .84 C8
Trowbridge BA14 .105 B7
Allen Wr Dr SP6 .210 D2
Allenby Rd SP4 .133 C2
Allengrove La SN14 .39 C3
Alley The
Bishopstone SP5 .205 E4
Woodgreen SP6 .211 A4
Allington Rd SN2 .35 B5
Allington Tk SP4 .198 E4
Allington Way
Amesbury SP4 .217 D2
2 Chippenham SN14 .70 A1
Alma Pl SN8 .213 D3
Alma Rd SN8 .170 A7
Alma St BA14 .105 E8
Alma Terr SN11 .81 B3
Almond Gr BA14 .105 B5
Alnwick SN5 .49 B4
Aloeric GM Prim Sch SN12 .94 A3
Alpine Cl 6 SN5 .49 A7
Alton Barnes White Horse* SN8 .173 C2
Alton Cl SN2 .35 C5
Alton Rd SN8 .181 F8
Altona Gdns 17 SP10 .193 D2
Alvescot Rd SN3 .50 D5
Alveston Cl SN5 .49 D6
Amber Ct SN1 .50 D7
Amberley Cl SN25 .35 C4
Ambrose House Con & Management Ctr SN1 .50 B6
Ambrose Rd SN1 .50 C2
American Mus In Britain* BA2 .90 A5
Amersham Rd SN3 .51 B3
Amesbury Cl 4 SN2 .35 C6
Amesbury Cty Inf Sch SP4 .217 B4
Amesbury Jun Sch SP4 .217 B4
Amesbury Rd
Amesbury SP4 .217 F4
Amport SP11 .192 E1
Newton Tony SP4 .199 A3
Shrewton SP3 .196 E6
Amity Dr SN8 .175 D6
Amouracre BA14 .105 F8
Ancaster Cl BA14 .101 A1
Anchor Rd SN11 .81 C2
Ancona Cl 12 SN5 .49 A7
Andeferas Rd 6 SP10 .193 D2
Anderson Cl SN3 .51 D3
Anderson Rd SP1 .146 C4
Andover La SP11 .192 B4
Andover Rd
Amport SP11 .192 E2
Chirton SN10 .180 F3
Fyfield SP11 .192 D3
Upavon SN9 .181 F1
Andover St 4 SN1 .50 A5
Andrew Cl 14 SP4 .198 B7
Andrews Cl SN14 .78 B7
Andrews Way SP2 .151 F5
Angel La Hindon SP3 .200 A3
Mere BA12 .139 A5
27 Shaftesbury SP7 .202 C2
Angel Yd SN8 .213 D3
Angelica Cl 6 SN2 .34 D4
Angler Rd
Salisbury SP2 .145 C5
Swindon SN5 .49 B7
Anglesey Cl 5 SN5 .49 C6
Anglesey Mead SN15 .79 A4
Angrove Cotts SN16 .43 D4
Angus Cl SN5 .49 B7
Anise Cl 4 SN2 .34 C4
Ann Edwards Sch GL7 .6 E6
Anne Cres 24 SP4 .198 B7
Annett's La RG17 .176 F4
Annetts Cl SP4 .217 C4
Anson Ave SN9 .182 B2
Anson Gr SN12 .94 C1
Anson Pl SN14 .56 C7
Anstey Pl SN15 .79 A4
Ansty Hill BA12 .195 A6
Anthony Cl SN16 .25 C1
Anthony Rd SN4 .64 A7
Anton La SP11 .193 E4
Antrobus Rd SP4 .217 B3
Apollo Rd SN15 .59 E3
Apostle Way SP1 .146 C5
Appleford Sch SP3 .196 E7
Appleshaw CE Jun & Infants Sch SP11 .192 E4
Appleshaw Way
Perham Down SP11 .191 F3
Salisbury SP1 .146 D5
Appletree Cl SP5 .211 C8
Appletree Rd SP5 .211 C8
Applewood Cl SN14 .78 B8
Applewood Ct SN5 .49 D5
Aragon Cl SP4 .217 C4
Archer Cl SN2 .35 F5
Arches La SN16 .27 F2
Arcot Rd SP9 .216 B3
Arden Cl SN12 .94 C5
Argosy Rd SN15 .60 B1
Argyle Dr SN14 .70 C3
Argyle St SN2 .35 D1
Arkwright Rd SN25 .35 D6
Arley Cl SN25 .35 A5
Arlington Cl SN3 .51 B7
Armitage Sq 4 SP4 .197 E6
Armoury Yd 16 SP7 .202 C2
Armstrong Rd BA11 .110 B5
Armstrong Rise 16 SP10 .193 D2
Armstrong St 2 SN1 .50 C7
Arn View 2 BA12 .117 A8
Arney Cl SN13 .84 E8
Arnfield Moor SN3 .51 E2
Arnhem Cross SN15 .60 B2
Arnold Rd BA14 .104 E3
Arnolds Mead SN13 .76 F2
Arran Cl 5 SN4 .48 A2
Arran Way SN6 .22 F7
Arras Cl BA14 .105 C6
Artis Ave SN4 .64 B7
Arun Rd SN25 .34 F3
Arun Way 6 SO51 .212 F6
Arundel Cl
Chippenham SN14 .78 A7
Swindon SN3 .50 F3
Arundell Cl BA13 .109 B4
Ascham Rd SN5 .49 A5
Ascot Cl SN14 .78 A5
Ash Cl Lyneham SN15 .60 B2
4 Shaftesbury SP7 .202 D2
Swindon SN5 .34 A2
Tidworth SP9 .216 E7
Ash Cres SP1 .146 C5
Ash Dr BA14 .105 C3
Ash Gdns SN3 .36 E4
Ash Gr 1 Melksham SN12 .94 A2
Swindon SN2 .35 C2
Ash Rd SN14 .75 A5
Ash Tree La SP7 .206 B7
Ash Wlk
Upton Lovell BA12 .194 E4
Warminster BA12 .117 A7
Ashburnham Cl 7 SN5 .49 A4
Ashbury Ave SN3 .51 B7
Ashbury Hill SN6 .164 A7
Ashcroft Cotts SN8 .169 B1
Ashdown Dr SN12 .94 D6
Ashdown Pk* RG17 .164 C5
Ashdown Terr SP9 .216 D5
Ashdown Way SN2 .34 C4
Ashe Cres SN15 .70 D1
Ashen Copse Rd SN4 .63 F7
Ashes La Freshford BA2 .99 A4
Kington Langley SN15 .70 E7
Ashfield Rd
Chippenham SN15 .70 D1
Salisbury SP2 .145 E1
Ashford Cl 11 SP6 .210 C1
Ashford Rd
Fordingbridge SP6 .210 C1
Swindon SN1 .50 B4
Ashford Trad Est SP2 .145 E1
Ashgrove BA12 .139 B4
Ashie Cl SN5 .34 B2
Ashkirk Cl SN3 .50 E6
Ashlade Firs Rd SN8 .175 C6
Ashlands SP4 .146 D6
Ashleigh Cl SP2 .130 B2
Ashleigh Gr BA14 .105 C7
Ashley Cl
Atworth/Whitley SN12 .85 D1
Bradford-on-Avon BA15 .100 B8
Swindon SN3 .50 F6
Ashley Coombe BA12 .117 A4
Ashley Dro SN8 .185 A7
Ashley La BA15 .99 F7
Ashley Piece SN8 .170 C2
Ashley Pl BA12 .116 F4
Ashley Rd Bath BA1 .82 C2
Bradford-on-Avon BA15 .91 B1
Salisbury SP2 .145 F2
Ashley Wlk SP4 .217 D2
Ashleycross SP6 .211 D1
Ashmead BA14 .105 D6
Ashmead Ct BA14 .105 D7
Ashmore Bottom DT11 .206 E1
Ashmore Cl
Swindon SN3 .51 C6
Whiteparish SP5 .161 D4
Ashmore La
West Dean SP5 .155 E2
Whiteparish SP5 .161 D6
Ashton Keynes CE Sch SN6 .17 F8
Ashton Rd
Ashton Keynes SN16 .17 E7
Siddington GL7 .6 D8
Trowbridge BA14 .102 A2
Ashton Rise BA14 .102 A2
Ashton St 2 BA14 .105 E8
Ashtree Rd BA11 .110 A7
Ashwell Cl SN3 .50 F5
Ashwicke Rd SN14 .74 B3
Ashwood Rd SN13 .76 A1
Ashworth Rd SN5 .49 E6
Askerton Cl 5 SN5 .48 F8
Askew Cl 3 SN5 .48 F5
Aspen Cl Colerne SN14 .74 F6
Frome BA11 .110 B7
Wootton Bassett SN4 .47 E3
Assisi Rd SP1 .146 A4
Astley Cl SN9 .215 D5
Aston Cl SN9 .215 C5
Aston Mead SP1 .146 C3
Astor Cres SP11 .192 A5
Atbara Cl SN25 .35 A3
Atcherly Rd SN11 .166 A1
Athelstan Mus* SN16 .28 A3
Athelstan Rd SN16 .27 F4
Athena Ave SN2 .35 E1
Atherton Cl 12 SN8 .170 B2
Atherton Cres 16 RG17 .177 B7
Atherton Pl 11 RG17 .165 A2
Atherton Rd 11 RG17 .177 B7
Athlone Cl 2 SP11 .193 E4
Atholl Ct 26 SP10 .193 E2
Attlee Cres SN2 .35 E3
Attwood Rd SP1 .146 A3
Atwell-Wilson Motor Mus* SN11 .89 D7
Atworth Cl SN2 .35 B6
Atworth CP Sch SN12 .92 E8
Atworth La SN13 .84 E4
Atyec Cl BA13 .112 B8
Atyeo Cl BA13 .112 B8
Aubrey Rise 6 SN16 .28 A5
Auckland Cl SP9 .216 E6
Auckland Rd 3 SP4 .198 F7
Auden Cl SN25 .34 F5
Audley Cl 2 SN5 .48 F4
Audley Gate BA13 .108 E2
Audley Rd SN14 .78 C8
Augustine Way 9 SP10 .193 C2
Austen Cres SN3 .51 D4
Australian Ave SP2 .145 D2
Ave Cty Prim Sch The BA12 .117 B7
Avebury CE Prim Sch SN8 .173 C8
Avebury Cl Calne SN11 .81 A3
Westbury BA13 .108 F4
Avebury Manor* SN8 .167 B1
Avebury Mus* SN8 .167 B1
Avebury Rd
Chippenham SN14 .78 A6
Swindon SN2 .35 B5
Avebury Stone Circle & Henge* SN8 .173 C8
Avenell Rd 8 SN4 .163 A6
Avening St SN2 .35 D1
Avens Cl SN2 .34 D4
Avenue La Fleche SN15 .78 D6
Avenue Rd Frome BA11 .110 A4
Swindon SN1 .50 C4
Trowbridge BA14 .105 B8
Avenue The*
Amesbury SP4 .197 E5
Cherhill SN11 .166 E2
Claverton BA2 .90 A4
Durnford SP4 .131 D1
18 Durrington/Bulford SP4 .198 B7
Porton SP4 .133 D6
Salisbury SP1 .146 C1
South Tedworth SP9 .216 C4
Stanton Fitzwarren SN6 .22 B1
Tangley SP11 .193 D5
Tisbury SP3 .203 E8
Warminster BA12 .117 A7
Westbury BA13 .109 A3
Westbury BA13 .112 B8
Wilton SP2 .144 F5
Woodford SP2 .145 A8
Avil's La SN14 .56 F6
Avocet Cl SN3 .51 E6
Avon App SP2 .146 A1
Avon Cl BA15 .100 E5
Avon Ct BA1 .82 A4
Avon Dr SP5 .153 E2
Avon Mdw SP5 .211 A8
Avon Mdws SP4 .131 C5
Avon Mead SN15 .78 F8
Avon Meade 1 SP6 .210 D1
Avon Mid Sch SP2 .145 D4
Avon Mills SN16 .28 B2
Avon Rd Devizes SN10 .179 C8
2 Durrington/Bulford SP4 .198 F6
Malmesbury SN16 .27 F4
Melksham SN12 .94 A6
Tidworth SP9 .216 C5
Warminster BA12 .117 A5
Avon Reach SN15 .78 D7
Avon Rise SN14 .39 E4
Avon Sq SN9 .181 F1
Avon Terr
Devizes SN10 .214 A4
Salisbury SP2 .145 F2
Avon View SP6 .210 F1
Avon Way BA14 .101 D3
Avoncliff Sta BA15 .99 E5
Avondale Sch SP4 .217 C8
Avondown Rd SP4 .198 C7
Avonfield BA14 .101 F8
Avonfield Ave BA15 .100 E5
Avonleaze Rd SN9 .215 D5
Avonmead SN25 .34 F4
Avonstoke Cl SP4 .217 B2
Avonvale Rd BA14 .101 D2
Avonweir La SN15 .57 F3
Avro Way SN12 .94 C1
Awdry Ave SN12 .94 C6
Awdry Cl
Chippenham SN14 .77 F7
Heddington SN11 .89 A2
Axbridge Cl SN3 .51 A5
Axe & Cleaver La BA14 .105 C4
Aylesbury St SN1 .50 C7
Ayleswade Rd SP2 .152 A6
Aymer Pl SN3 .51 C5
Ayr Cl SN14 .77 F5
Ayrshire Cl
Salisbury SP2 .145 B5
Swindon SN5 .49 B7
Azalea Cl SN11 .81 C1
Azalea Dr
Trowbridge BA14 .105 A7
Warminster BA12 .116 E7
Azelin Ct SN3 .36 B3

B

Babington Pk 9 SN5 .48 F5
Back La
9 Aldbourne SN8 .170 A6
Blunsdon St Andrew SN26 .21 B3
Calne Without SN15 .88 B4
Cherhill SN11 .166 E2
Great Hinton BA14 .178 A5
Maiden Bradley with Yarnfield BA12 .118 F2
Marlborough SN8 .213 D3
Penton Grafton SP11 .193 A3
Ramsbury SN8 .170 B2
Sixpenny Handley SP5 .208 A4
Tilshead SP3 .188 B3
Vernhams Dean SP11 .185 C3
Back Rd Calne SN11 .81 B2
Chitterne BA12 .195 D7
Back St
Ashton Keynes SN6 .6 F1
East Garston RG17 .171 E7
Great Hinton BA14 .178 A6
Trowbridge BA14 .101 C1
Bader Pk 10 SN12 .178 B8
Badger Cl
Devizes SN10 .214 B2
2 Wootton Bassett SN4 .47 F2
Badgers Cl 3 SN4 .163 B6
Badminton House* GL9 .38 F2
Badminton Pk* GL9 .38 F3
Bagbury Rd BA12 .194 F4
Baghdad Rd 2 SP4 .198 F7
Bailey Cl SN9 .215 B5
Bailey's Mead SN4 .48 A2
Baileys Barn BA15 .100 D5
Baileys Way SN4 .64 B7
Bailiffe Piece SN6 .8 D1
Bainbridge Cl 2 SN5 .49 A5
Bainton Cl BA15 .100 D7
Baird Cl SN5 .49 B8
Bakers Field SN15 .60 A3
Bakers Rd SN4 .64 B5
Balden Cl SN4 .63 F6
Baldwin Cl SN4 .65 D4
Bale Cl 6 SN5 .48 F5
Ball Rd SN9 .215 D4
Ballands Castle* BA9 .137 A2
Balmoor Cl BA12 .139 B3
Balmoral Cl SN3 .51 A3
Balmoral Rd
Salisbury SP1 .146 B4
Trowbridge BA14 .105 B5
Bampton Gr SN3 .50 E6
Banbury Cl SN3 .50 F3
Bancroft BA15 .100 D7
Bancroft Cl SN5 .48 F6
Bank Street SN12 .94 A4
Bank The SN14 .75 C3
Bankfoot Cl 3 SN5 .49 B7
Bankside SN1 .49 F4
Bannerdown Cl BA1 .82 B4
Bannerdown Dr BA1 .82 A4
Bannerdown Rd BA1 .82 C5
Banwell Ave SN3 .51 A5
Barbara's Rd SN13 .84 D8
Barber's La SP5 .151 C1
Barberry SP3 .201 B3
Barbury Castle* SN4 .168 A7
Barbury Castle Ctry Pk* SN4 .168 B7
Barcelona Cres SN4 .64 A7
Bardsey Cl 5 SN4 .47 F2
Barford La SP5 .159 C1
Barford St Martin CE Fst Sch SP3 .143 B3
Bargates SN13 .83 D6
Barken Rd
4 Chippenham SN14 .70 A1
Chippenham SN14 .78 A8
Barkstead Cl 3 SN5 .49 B4
Barley Cl
Malmesbury SN16 .28 A2
Warminster BA12 .117 C5
Barley Hill La SN10 .179 A7
Barlow Cl SN25 .35 A8
Barn Cl
Chippenham SN14 .78 A8
Corsham SN13 .76 E1
Barn End SN14 .74 A8
Barn Glebe BA14 .101 E1
Barn Hill SP3 .201 A3
Barn Moor Cl SN3 .51 E3
Barn Owl Rd SN14 .70 B2
Barn Piece Box SN13 .83 D6
Bradford-on-Avon BA15 .100 D4
Barn St SN8 .213 D3
Barnack Cl BA14 .101 A1
Barnard Cl SN3 .51 B7
Barnard St 1 SP1 .152 B8
Barnards Hill Dr SP2 .145 C4
Barncroft SP11 .192 E3
Barnes Cl BA14 .105 A7
Barnes Gn SN15 .45 F6
Barnes Pl BA12 .139 A5
Barnes Wallis Cl
9 Amesbury SP4 .217 E3
Melksham Without BA14 .178 B8
Barnetts Hill SN13 .83 F7
Barnfield Cl SN2 .49 F7
Barnfield Rd SN2 .49 E7

Barnfield Way BA1 ....82 B4
Barnstaple Cl SN3 ....51 B5
Barnum Ct SN2 ....50 A7
Baroda Rd SP9 ....216 A4
Baron Cl Lyneham SN15 ....59 C4
4 Swindon SN3 ....36 B3
Barons Mead SN14 ....78 A8
Barra Cl SN6 ....22 E6
Barracks SN14 ....74 F4
Barrett La SN15 ....57 D2
Barrett Way SN4 ....64 B6
Barrington Cl SN3 ....51 D3
Barrington Rd SP1 ....146 C3
Barrow Cl SN8 ....213 F3
Barrow Gn SN15 ....70 E2
Barrow La BA9 ....136 B5
Barrow St La
Mere BA12 ....139 F3
West Knoyle BA12 ....140 A4
Barrow Water La BA9 ....136 A5
Barrowby Gate SN3 ....36 A4
Barrows La SP5 ....212 B7
Barry Glen Cl SN2 ....35 E1
Barry Pl SN11 ....79 F2
Barters La SP7 ....206 D8
Bartlett Cl 11 BA11 ....110 C6
Bartlett Rd SP1 ....146 B4
Bartletts SN10 ....179 C1
Bartletts Mead BA14 ....178 A4
Bartletts The BA12 ....139 B4
Barton Cl 12 SP10 ....193 C2
Barton Farm Ctry Pk* BA15 ....100 A5
Barton Heritage Collection* SP2 ....145 F1
Barton Hill 22 SP7 ....202 C2
Barton Hill House Sch SP7 ....202 C2
Barton La BA12 ....139 A5
Barton Orch BA15 ....100 C6
Barton Rd SN25 ....34 E3
Barton Way SN16 ....42 E4
Bartons Rd 20 SP6 ....210 D1
Bartons The 29 SP6 ....210 D1
Basil Cl SN2 ....34 D4
Basil Hill Rd SN13 ....84 C7
Basingstoke Cl 5 SN5 ....49 A4
Baskerville Rd SN3 ....51 E7
Bassett Rd OX12 ....165 F8
Bassetts Pasture BA15 ....100 D4
Bassetts The SN13 ....83 D6
Batch The BA2 ....98 E1
Bath Acad of Art SN13 ....77 A2
Bath Rd Atworth SN12 ....84 D2
Atworth/Whitley SN12 ....93 A8
Box SN13 ....83 A6
Bradford-on-Avon BA15 ....91 C1
Chippenham Without SN14 ....77 F5
Colerne SN14 ....74 F3
Corsham SN13 ....77 B4
Cricklade SN6 ....19 D8
Devizes SN10 ....179 C8
Frome BA11 ....110 A6
Hungerford RG17 ....176 F7
Marlborough SN8 ....213 B2
Melksham SN12 ....94 A5
Melksham Without SN12 ....93 E7
Preshute SN8 ....174 C7
Seend SN12 ....95 C1
Swindon SN1 ....50 C4
Upton Scudamore BA12 ....112 D2
Warminster BA12 ....112 E1
Westonbirt with Lasborough GL8 ....25 D8
Wootton Bassett SN4 ....47 C1
Bath Rd Ind Est SN14 ....78 B6
Bathampton St SN1 ....50 A6
Bathford CE Prim Sch BA1 ....82 C2
Bathford Hill BA1 ....82 B2
Bathurst Rd SN1 ....50 D6
Batt's La SN8 ....183 F7
Batten Rd SP5 ....211 A8
Battens The 3 SN14 ....70 A1
Battlesbury Barracks BA12 ....117 E6
Battlesbury Hill Fort* BA12 ....117 F8
Battlesbury Rd BA12 ....117 E7
Battlewell SN5 ....33 A3
Baverstock La SP3 ....142 B5
Bawdsey Rd 6 SP4 ....217 D2
Baxter Cl SN25 ....35 A7
Bay Cl SN11 ....89 C8
Baydon Cl BA14 ....105 C5
Baydon Gr SN11 ....81 B4
Baydon Rd
Aldbourne SN8 ....164 B1
Great Shefford RG17 ....171 E4
Lambourn RG17 ....171 A6
Baydons La SN15 ....78 E6
Bayleaf Ave SN2 ....34 D4
Bayliffes Cl SN15 ....79 A7
Baynton Way BA13 ....186 D8
Bayntun Cl SN15 ....96 A7
Baywater SN8 ....213 E4
Bazaar Rd SP9 ....216 B5
Beacon Cl
Amesbury SP4 ....217 C4
8 Swindon SN1 ....49 F4
Beacon Ct SP6 ....210 D2
Beacon Hill Rd 7 SP4 ....198 F7
Beacon View BA12 ....116 D6
Beaconsfield Way BA11 ....110 B7
Beale Ct SN14 ....78 A7
Beale's Barton BA14 ....101 F8
Beales Cl SN1 ....50 B7
Beales Farm Rd 15 RG17 ....165 A1
Beamish Cl 2 SN11 ....166 A1
Beanacre Manor* SN12 ....94 A8
Beanacre Rd
Melksham SN12 ....94 A7
Melksham Without SN12 ....86 A1
Beanlands The SN4 ....163 A6
Bear Cl BA15 ....100 B7
Bearfield Bldgs BA15 ....100 C8
Bearfield La RG17 ....171 A4
Beatrice Rd SP1 ....146 A4
Beatrice St SN2 ....50 C8
Beauchamp Dr 1 SP4 ....217 D3
Beauclerc St SN10 ....179 D8
Beaufort Cl 5 SN12 ....178 B8
Beaufort Gn SN3 ....51 B5
Beaufort Rd SN4 ....64 A7
Beaufoy Cl 9 SP7 ....202 D2
Beaulieu Cl SN5 ....49 C4
Beaulieu Rd 2 SP4 ....217 C2
Beaumaris Rd SN5 ....49 B5
Beaumont Rd SN3 ....50 E6
Beaumont Way SP4 ....217 D2
Beaven Cl SN15 ....78 F4
Becket Way SP1 ....146 D1
Beckett St 14 SP3 ....203 E8
Beckett's La SP3 ....201 A3
Beckford Cl
Tisbury SP3 ....200 D1
Warminster BA12 ....117 B6
Beckhampton (Long Barrow)* SN8 ....173 A8
Beckhampton Rd SN8 ....173 B8
Beckhampton St SN1 ....50 C6
Beddington Ct SN2 ....36 A5
Beddoe Cl BA15 ....100 E4
Bede Dr 7 SP10 ....193 C2
Bedford Cl 2 SP6 ....210 D2
Bedford Rd
Salisbury SP2 ....145 E2
6 Swindon SN3 ....50 F6
Bedwin St SP1 ....146 B1
Bedwyn Cl SN2 ....35 C3
Bedwyn Dyke* SN8 ....176 C3
Bedwyn Sta SN8 ....176 B3
Bedwyn Stone Mus* SN8 ....176 B2
Beech Ave
Melksham SN12 ....94 A3
Swindon SN2 ....35 A2
Warminster BA12 ....116 F6
Beech Cl Andover SP11 ....193 B1
Porton SP4 ....133 D6
Beech Ct BA11 ....110 B7
Beech Dr SN5 ....34 A2
Beech Gr Highworth SN6 ....22 F5
Trowbridge BA14 ....105 B6
Beech Grange SP5 ....212 C5
Beech Hanger SP4 ....199 C5
Beech Hill Rd SP9 ....216 E7
Beech Lea
Broad Blunsdon SN26 ....21 C1
Meysey Hampton GL7 ....1 A4
Beech Rd Colerne SN14 ....75 A5
Corsham SN13 ....83 E7
Beech Sq 12 RG17 ....177 B6
Beech Wlk SP4 ....131 C1
Beech Wood 13 SN10 ....179 F1
Beechcroft Inf Sch SN2 ....35 D4
Beechcroft Rd
Salisbury SP1 ....146 D1
Swindon SN2 ....35 E4
Beeches Cl SP5 ....148 C3
Beeches La SN15 ....59 A5
Beeches The
Bradford-on-Avon BA15 ....101 A7
Coombe Bissett SP5 ....156 F7
Lydiard Millicent SN5 ....33 B1
Melksham Without SN12 ....93 C7
5 Salisbury SP1 ....152 C8
15 Shaftesbury SP7 ....202 C2
Trowbridge BA14 ....101 F2
Warminster BA12 ....116 F6
4 West Wellow SO51 ....212 F6
Beechfield SP4 ....199 B3
Beechfield Dr SN10 ....214 E5
Beechfield Rd SN13 ....76 E1
Beechgrove BA12 ....117 B8
Beechwood 13 SP6 ....210 C1
Beechwood Ave BA11 ....110 A5
Beechwood Cl BA11 ....110 A5
Beechwood Rd SN14 ....78 B8
Beehive Cl 1 SN5 ....49 A8
Belcombe Ct* BA15 ....100 B6
Belcombe Rd BA15 ....100 B6
Belfast Mead SN15 ....60 C2
Belfry Dr SN14 ....41 E1
Belgrave St SN1 ....50 C5
Bell Gdns SN3 ....36 E4
Bell Hill Seend SN12 ....178 E7
Warminster BA12 ....116 F5
Bell La Inkpen RG17 ....177 E2
Lechlade GL7 ....2 C3
Liddington SN4 ....163 A4
Sutton Benger SN15 ....57 D2
Bell Piece SN15 ....57 D2
Bell Rd SP4 ....197 F7
Bell St
4 Ludgershall SP11 ....192 B5
Shaftesbury SP7 ....202 C2
Bellamy La SP1 ....152 B8
Belle Vue Rd
Salisbury SP1 ....146 A1
Swindon SN1 ....50 D4
Bellefield Cres BA14 ....101 D1
Bellinger Cl SN15 ....70 C3
Bellingham La SN6 ....23 A2
Bellot Dr
3 Corsham SN13 ....76 E1
Corsham SN13 ....84 E8
Bells La BA12 ....137 F7
Bellver SN5 ....49 B5
Belmont Cl
10 Shaftesbury SP7 ....202 C1
Swindon SN3 ....36 A4
Belmont Cres SN1 ....50 A3
Belsay SN5 ....49 C4
Belvedere Rd SN3 ....51 A3
Bembridge Cl SN3 ....51 B4
Bemerton Prim Sch SP2 ....145 C1
Ben La SP5 ....154 F7
Bences La SN13 ....77 A2
Bendy Bow SN16 ....15 F7
Benin Rd SP11 ....191 F3
Bennett Cl SP5 ....211 C7
Bennett Hill Cl 3 SN4 ....47 F2
Bentham Cl SN5 ....49 D6
Bentham La SN5 ....33 A8
Bentley Cl SN3 ....51 A6
Bentley Gr SN11 ....81 C2
Bentley Way SP5 ....149 D5
Benwell Cl SN5 ....49 C6
Beranburh Field SN4 ....64 E2
Berenger Cl SN1 ....50 D3
Beresford Cl 1 SN3 ....51 C4
Bergamot Cl SN8 ....174 C7
Bergman Cl SN2 ....35 B6
Berhills La SN10 ....95 F2
Bericot La SN4 ....65 E6
Berkeley Cl
Melksham SN12 ....94 A2
South Cerney GL7 ....6 F6
Berkeley Lawns SN3 ....50 F3
Berkeley Rd
Trowbridge BA14 ....105 A8
Wroughton SN4 ....64 B7
Berkely Cl 2 SN14 ....78 A7
Berkley CE Sch BA11 ....111 A7
Berkley Cross BA11 ....110 F6
Berkley La BA11 ....110 D8
Berkley Rd BA11 ....110 A5
Berkley St BA11 ....107 B1
Berkshire Dr SN5 ....49 A7
Berkshire Rd SP2 ....151 E7
Berrington Rd SN3 ....51 A3
Berry Cl 4 SP4 ....190 A3
Berry Rd BA13 ....186 D8
Berry Wood La SP7 ....203 A3
Berrycroft
Ashbury SN6 ....164 A7
Mildenhall SN8 ....175 B8
Berryfield Cl SN12 ....93 F1
Berryfield La SN12 ....93 F1
Berryfield Pk SN12 ....93 F1
Berryfield Rd BA15 ....100 D8
Bertha's Field GL9 ....24 B4
Berton Cl SN26 ....21 C2
Berwick La SP3 ....128 D7
Berwick Rd
Berwick St James SP3 ....196 F2
Stapleford SP3 ....129 E7
Besomer Dro SP5 ....211 D6
Bess Rd SN5 ....48 F4
Bessemer Cl SN2 ....35 A1
Bessemer Rd E SN2 ....35 A1
Bessemer Rd W SN2 ....34 F1
Best's La BA12 ....194 A5
Bethel Rd SN13 ....76 E1
Betjeman Ave SN4 ....47 E3
Betjeman Rd SN8 ....213 A2
Betony Cl SN25 ....34 E5
Bettertons Cl GL7 ....1 F7
Bevan Cl SN2 ....35 F3
Beverley SN5 ....49 C4
Beverley Cl SN12 ....94 C1
Beverley Cres SN9 ....182 B2
Beverley Way SN14 ....77 F5
Beversbrook Rd SN11 ....81 B5
Beverstone Gr SN3 ....50 F4
Bevil SN5 ....49 A3
Bevisbury Hill Fort* SP11 ....185 A1
Bevisland SN3 ....51 C3
Bewley Ct* SN15 ....86 F6
Bewley La SN15 ....86 F5
Bewley Rd 1 BA14 ....105 C5
Beyer Rd 5 SP4 ....217 D2
Bibury Rd SN3 ....50 E5
Bicton Rd SN25 ....34 F6
Biddel Springs SN6 ....23 B6
Bidden La BA12 ....195 D6
Biddesden La SP11 ....192 C5
Biddestone La SN14 ....68 E3
Biddestone Manor* SN14 ....76 F7
Biddulph Rd SP4 ....198 A7
Bideford Cl SN3 ....51 A5
Big La RG17 ....165 A2
Bilbury Rings* BA12 ....201 F7
Bimport SP7 ....202 B1
Bincknoll Castle* SN4 ....62 F3
Bindon Cl SN5 ....49 A5
Bingham Rd
Durrington SP4 ....197 E7
Salisbury SP1 ....146 C4
Birch Gdns BA14 ....102 B2
Birch Glade SN6 ....17 F8
Birch Gr Bower Hill SN12 ....94 C1
Chippenham SN15 ....70 E1
Birch St SN1 ....49 F5
Birch Wlk 4 BA11 ....110 B7
Birchenleaze BA14 ....105 C3
Birches The SN3 ....51 B2
Birchill La BA11 ....110 A1
Birchwood Cl BA12 ....115 C7
Birchwood Dr 4 SP4 ....198 C7
Birchwood Rd SN3 ....36 B2
Birdbrook Rd SN2 ....35 E5
Birdcombe Rd 1 SN5 ....49 C5
Birds Marsh View SN15 ....70 E2
Bishop Rd SN11 ....81 B4
Bishop Wordsworths Sch SP1 ....152 A8
Bishop's Pal* SP1 ....152 A7
Bishop's Wlk SP1 ....152 A8
Bishopdale Cl 2 SN5 ....34 A1
Bishopdown Rd SP1 ....146 B3
Bishops Cannings Prim Sch SN10 ....172 B3
Bishops Cl
Chippenham SN15 ....78 F4
Mere BA12 ....139 A6
Tidworth SP9 ....216 D4
Bishops Dr SP2 ....151 F6
Bishops Mead SP1 ....146 E4
Bishopsfield 6 SN6 ....19 D8
Bishopstone CE Sch SN6 ....163 E6
Bishopstone Hollow SP5 ....205 E3
Bishopstrow Rd BA12 ....117 E4
Bisley SN16 ....29 A6
Bisley Cl SN3 ....51 A5
Biss Cl BA12 ....112 F4
Biss Mdw BA14 ....105 A8
Bitham Brook CP Sch BA13 ....109 B4
Bitham La RG17 ....177 A3
Bitham Pk BA13 ....109 B4
Bittern Rd SN3 ....51 E6
Black Bridge Rd SN15 ....78 F8
Black Dog Hill
Calne Without SN11 ....80 D2
Chapmanslade BA13 ....111 E6
Black Horse La
Westbury BA13 ....108 D1
Winterbourne SP4 ....146 F8
Black La
Pitton & Farley SP5 ....148 C4
Redlynch SP5 ....211 E6
Blackbarn Rd SP4 ....134 B5
Blackberry Cl SN14 ....70 A2
Blackberry La
Potterne SN10 ....179 D5
Winsley BA15 ....90 C1
Blackbird Way BA11 ....110 B6
Blackboard La SN10 ....180 B4
Blackcross SN15 ....78 F6
Blackcross Rd SP4 ....217 C2
Blackdown Cl 10 BA12 ....117 A8
Blackford La SN6 ....10 C4
Blackfriars Way SP1 ....152 B8
Blackhill Rd SO51 ....212 F3
Blackland Pk* SN11 ....89 E7
Blacklands Crossroads SN11 ....89 E6
Blackman's La 4 SN8 ....183 D8
Blackmore Cl 1 SN3 ....51 E7
Blackmore La SN8 ....192 A7
Blackmore Rd
Melksham SN12 ....94 C4
3 Shaftesbury SP7 ....202 D2
Blackstone Ave SN3 ....51 C4
Blackthorn Cl SN4 ....47 E4
Blackthorn Mews SN15 ....78 F5
Blackworth SN6 ....22 F8
Blagdon Wlk BA11 ....110 C7
Blair Rd BA14 ....105 B7
Blake Cres SN3 ....36 C2
Blakeney Ave SN3 ....51 B7
Blakesley Cl 3 SN3 ....50 F4
Blakey Rd SP1 ....152 C8
Blandford Alley SN6 ....23 A5
Blandford Rd SP5 ....150 F1
Bleak St BA9 ....137 C3
Bleke St SP7 ....202 C2
Blendon Dr SP10 ....193 C1
Blenheim Gdns SN14 ....56 C6
Blenheim Pk 15 SN12 ....178 B8
Blenheim Rd SN4 ....64 A7
Blenhiem Cl BA12 ....116 F7
Bletchley Cl 5 SN3 ....51 C4
Blick's Hill SN16 ....28 B4
Blicks Cl SN14 ....41 F1
Blicks Hill SN16 ....28 B3
Blind La Ansty SP3 ....203 F5
Berwick St John SP7 ....207 B8
Southwick BA14 ....104 F2
Blissford Rd SP6 ....210 F1
Bloody Shard Gate DT11 ....207 A1
Bloomsbury Cl 2 SN5 ....49 B4
Blounts Ct SN10 ....179 D5
Blowhorn St SN8 ....213 D4
Blue Boar Row SP1 ....146 A1
Bluebell Dr SN14 ....70 B3
Bluebell Gr SN11 ....81 B5
Blunsdon Rd SN25 ....34 F4
Blyth Way SP1 ....146 D4
Boar St BA12 ....139 A5
Bobbin La BA15 ....99 F4
Bobbin Pk BA15 ....99 F3
Bockhampton Rd RG17 ....165 A1
Bockhampton Village* RG17 ....165 B1
Bodiam Dr SN5 ....49 D4
Bodiam Dr N 4 SN5 ....49 D5
Bodiam Dr S 3 SN5 ....49 D4
Bodman Cl SN15 ....78 F4
Bodmin Cl SN3 ....51 A6
Bodyhorse Hill SN4 ....163 C6
Bohemia La SP5 ....211 D6
Bokerley Ditch* SP6 ....209 A5
Bokerley Junc SP5 ....208 E6
Boldrewood SN3 ....51 D3
Bolehyde Manor* SN14 ....69 E4
Boleyn Cl SN5 ....49 A6
Bolingbroke Cl SN5 ....47 F6
Bolingbroke Rd SN2 ....34 F2
Bolland's Hill SN12 ....178 D8
Bonaker Cl SP4 ....133 D6
Bond St
Durrington/Bulford SP4 ....198 E6
Trowbridge BA14 ....105 C7
Boness Rd SN4 ....64 A7
Bonham La BA12 ....137 E7
Bonner Cl 10 SN5 ....48 F5
Bonners Cl SN16 ....28 A5
Boothmead SN14 ....78 B8
Borage Cl SN2 ....34 D5
Border Cl SN25 ....34 C5
Bore Hill BA12 ....116 F4
Boreham Cl BA12 ....117 C6
Boreham Field BA12 ....117 D6
Boreham Rd BA12 ....117 E5
Borkum Cl 8 SP10 ....193 D2
Borough Fields SN4 ....47 D2
Borough The SP5 ....211 A8
Boscombe Down Airfield SP4 ....198 E3
Boscombe Rd
Amesbury SP4 ....217 C3
Swindon SN25 ....34 E4
Bosham Cl 6 SN5 ....49 B4
Boswell Rd BA15 ....99 F3
Bosworth Rd SN5 ....49 A5
Botany SN6 ....22 E5
Bothwell Rd SN3 ....50 F7
Botisdone Cl SP11 ....185 C3
Botley Copse SN5 ....34 A2
Bottlebush La BH21 ....208 E1
Bottom La
Ogbourne St George SN8 ....169 A5
1 West Wellow SO51 ....212 F6
Bouchers Way SP2 ....152 A5
Boulton Cl BA13 ....108 E1
Boundary Ave BA11 ....110 B5
Boundary Cl
Lyneham SN15 ....59 C3
Swindon SN2 ....35 F6
Boundary Rd
Chippenham SN15 ....78 F8
Salisbury SP1 ....146 E2
Bourbon Cl BA12 ....117 B5
Bourne Ave SP1 ....146 C2
Bourne Cl Porton SP4 ....133 D6
1 Salisbury SP1 ....152 D8
Warminster BA12 ....117 A5
3 West Wellow SO51 ....212 F6
Bourne Gdns SP4 ....133 D6
Bourne Hill SP1 ....146 B1
Bourne La 6 SP9 ....199 D8
Bourne Lake Pk SN6 ....18 E6
Bourne Pk* SP11 ....193 F6
Bourne Rd Swindon SN2 ....34 F2
Tidworth SP9 ....216 D6
Bourne Ret Pk SP1 ....152 D7
Bourne Rise SN8 ....183 E1
Bourne Vale RG17 ....177 B7
Bourne Valley Cl SP4 ....133 E5
Bourne View SP4 ....199 A1
Bourne Way SP1 ....152 D7
Bournmil Cl BA15 ....99 D7
Bourton Ave SN3 ....36 B2
Bourton La SN10 ....172 C3
Bourton Prim Sch SP8 ....137 E1
Bouverie Ave
Salisbury SP2 ....152 A6
Swindon SN3 ....50 D3
Bouverie Ave S SP2 ....151 F5
Bouverie Cl SP2 ....151 F6
Bouverie Dr 17 SN10 ....179 F1
Bouverie Pk SN14 ....56 B5
Boveridge House Sch BH21 ....209 B1
Bow Wow GL7 ....7 A7
Bowd's La SN15 ....60 A6
Bowden Cres SN12 ....94 C6
Bowden Pk* SN15 ....87 B5
Bowdich Cl SP4 ....198 C7
Bower Gdns SP1 ....152 C8
Bower Hill Rd SP1 ....146 C2
Bower Rd SN8 ....175 D5
Bowerhill CP Sch SN12 ....94 C1
Bowerhill La SN12 ....94 E1
Bowers Hill SP5 ....211 D8
Bowers La SP11 ....185 B4
Bowes Lyon Ct SP2 ....145 D3
Bowldown Rd GL8 ....25 F8
Bowles Rd SN25 ....35 A5
Bowleymead SN3 ....51 D5
Bowling Gn La
Pentridge SP5 ....208 D5
Swindon SN1 ....50 C3
Bowls Barrow (Long Barrow)* BA12 ....186 E1
Bowman Cl 5 SN3 ....36 B3
Bowood Cl SN11 ....79 F3

Bowood Golf & Ctry Club SN11 88 A8
Bowood House* SN11 88 C8
Bowood Rd SN1 50 B4
Box CE Sch SN13 83 D6
Box Dr SN8 213 D8
Box Highlands Sch SN13 84 B8
Box Hill Box SN13 76 A1
Corsham SN13 83 E7
Box Rd BA1 82 C3
Box View SN14 75 B2
Boxbush Rd GL7 7 A7
Boxfields Rd SN13 83 F7
Boydell Cl SN5 49 B8
Boyle Ave 4 SN11 166 A1
Boyne's La DT11 206 B1
Boyton Manor* BA12 194 E2
Bozley Hill SP7 206 A8
Bracken Cl SP5 153 D3
Brackenbury 8 SP10 193 C1
Brackenbury Rd SP4 197 E7
Brackland SN10 180 A2
Bradbury Cl SN15 79 A5
Bradene Cl 3 SN4 47 E2
Bradenham Rd SN5 49 A5
Bradenstoke Abbey* SN15 59 B3
Bradfield Cl BA12 117 D5
Bradford Rd
Atworth SN12 92 E7
Bathford BA1 82 B2
Box SN13 83 F3
Broughton Gifford SN12 93 F4
Corsham SN13 76 C1
Holt BA14 101 D8
Melksham SN12 94 A5
Rode BA11 103 F1
Swindon SN1 50 C4
Trowbridge BA14 101 B1
Winsley BA15 99 D6
Bradford-on-Avon Com Hospl BA15 100 D8
Bradford-on-Avon Golf Club BA15 100 E5
Bradford-on-Avon Swimming Pool BA15 100 C6
Bradley Cl Holt BA14 101 F8
Warminster BA12 116 E4
Bradley La Holt BA14 92 F1
Maiden Bradley with Yarnfield BA12 118 C3
Bradley Mound* BA12 118 F2
Bradley Pk* BA12 118 F1
Bradley Rd
Southwick BA14 105 B2
Swindon SN2 35 D4
Trowbridge BA14 105 C5
Warminster BA12 116 E4
Bradon Forest Comp Sch SN5 33 C3
Bradwell Cl 2 SP10 193 C2
Bradwell Moor SN3 51 D2
Braemar Cl SN3 50 F3
Braemar Rise SP1 146 B4
Braemor Rd SN11 81 A4
Braemore CE Prim Sch SP6 210 E4
Braithwaite Way 3 BA11 110 C6
Brake Mead SN15 78 F7
Brakspear Dr SN13 76 E1
Bramble Cl SN2 35 E1
Bramble Dr SN15 79 A4
Bramble Rd SN2 35 E1
Brambles The
Hinton Charterhouse BA2 98 E1
Salisbury SP1 146 C2
Bramdean Cl SN25 34 F5
Bramley Cl
Pewsey SN9 215 D6
4 Warminster BA12 116 F7
Bramley Dr BA11 110 C6
Bramley Hill BA12 138 F5
Bramley La BA14 105 D7
Bramley Way SP4 217 C3
Bramleys The SP5 161 D3
Brampton Ct 8 SN12 178 B8
Bramptons The SN5 49 B7
Bramshaw Golf Club SO43 212 E1
Bramshaw Telegraph* SP6 211 F3
Bramwell Cl SN2 35 E6
Brancaster Ave 1 SP10 193 C2
Branch Rd BA2 98 F2
Branders 4 SN6 19 D8
Brandon Cl SN5 49 A5
Branksome Rd SN25 34 E3
Branscombe Dr SN4 47 E1
Bransdown Hill
Easton Grey SN16 26 A3
Sherston SN16 25 F2
Brassknocker Hill BA2 90 A1
Bratch La SP3 201 F2
Bratton Camp* BA13 186 A6
Bratton Cl SN2 35 B5
Bratton CP Sch BA13 186 B7
Bratton Rd
West Ashton BA14 106 B4
Westbury BA13 109 C4
Bray St SN8 173 A8
Braybrooke Cl 2 SN5 48 F8
Braydon La SN6 18 F4
Breach Cl SP8 137 E2
Breach La Chute SP11 192 E8
Breach La *continued*
1 Shaftesbury SP7 202 B1
Southwick BA14 105 A3
Wootton Bassett SN4 61 B5
Breach The SN10 214 B2
Bread St BA12 116 F5
Bream Cl SN12 94 D6
Breamore Countryside Mus* SP6 210 E5
Breamore House* SP6 210 E6
Breamore Rd SP5 210 F7
Brecon Cl
Melksham SN12 94 D4
Swindon SN3 50 E2
Bremen Gdns 21 SP10 193 D2
Bremeridge Cl BA13 109 B3
Bremhill Cl SN2 35 C4
Bremhill View SN11 81 A4
Bremilham Rd SN16 27 F4
Bremilham Rise SN16 27 E3
Breton Rd BA13 108 F2
Brettingham Gate SN3 64 F8
Brewer Mead SN15 78 F4
Brewers La SN11 81 C1
Brewery St SN6 23 A5
Briar Cl Frome BA11 110 B7
Westbury BA13 108 F4
Briar Fields SN1 50 E7
Briar Leaze SN11 166 B3
Briars Cl SN4 47 E3
Briary Rd GL7 2 C6
Brick Hill SN15 95 D6
Brick La Salisbury SP2 145 C2
Trowbridge BA14 101 D3
Brickham Rd 1 SN10 214 D5
Brickley La SN10 214 D2
Bricksteed Ave SN10 214 C3
Brickworth La SP5 160 E4
Brickyard La SP8 137 E1
Bridewell La SP7 202 A6
Bridge Ave BA14 105 A8
Bridge End Rd SN3 35 F1
Bridge Rd SP5 205 E4
Bridge St Bourton SP8 137 E2
Bradford-on-Avon BA15 100 D6
Fordingbridge SP6 210 D1
26 Hungerford RG17 177 B7
Marlborough SN8 213 A2
Salisbury SP2 152 A8
Swindon SN1 50 B6
3 Trowbridge BA14 105 D7
Bridge The SN15 78 D7
Bridgeman Cl SN3 36 B2
Bridgemead Cl SN5 49 D7
Bridgewater Cl SN2 50 A7
Bridport Rd SN3 51 B4
Briery Cl SN3 36 A4
Bright Cl 3 SN15 78 F5
Bright St SN2 50 D8
Brighton Way SN14 77 F6
Brimble Hill SN4 64 D5
Brimble Hill Specl Sch SN3 51 B5
Brimhill Rise BA13 111 D4
Brind Cl SN3 51 E6
Brind Rd SP4 197 F7
Brindley Cl SN2 34 E1
Brington Rd SN3 51 B8
Brinkworth Cl SN14 77 F7
Brinkworth Earl Danbys Sch SN15 45 E5
Brinkworth Golf Club SN15 45 C8
Brinkworth Rd SN15 45 C3
Brinscombe La 6 SP7 202 D1
Brionne Way 18 SP7 202 D2
Brisbane Gdns 7 SP4 198 F6
Bristol Rd
Chippenham SN14 78 C8
Chippenham Without SN14 69 E2
Luckington SN14 39 D3
Bristol St
3 Malmesbury SN16 28 A3
Swindon SN1 50 A6
Britannia Ave SN9 182 B2
Britannia Cres SN15 60 B2
Britannia Pl SN1 50 D4
Britford La SP2 152 B6
Britford La W 1 SP2 152 A6
Britford Prim Sch SP5 152 D5
British Row BA14 101 C1
Britmore La SP7 202 F4
Brittain Cl SN14 77 F7
Brittox The SN10 214 B3
Brixham Ave SN3 50 E5
Broad Chalke Prim Sch SP5 205 C4
Broad Hinton (Hackpen) White Horse* SN4 167 E5
Broad St Swindon SN1 50 C7
Trowbridge BA14 101 C1
Broad Stones BA15 90 E7
Broad Town CE Prim Sch SN4 62 B1
Broadacres SN4 62 B2
Broadbury Banks* SN9 181 B2
Broadcloth E La BA14 105 E7
Broadcloth La BA14 105 E7
Broadfield Rd SP4 133 D3
Broadfields SN9 215 B4
Broadlands Cl SP1 146 B4
Broadleas Cl SN10 214 A2
Broadleas Cres SN10 214 A2
Broadleas Gdns* SN10 214 A1
Broadleas Rd SN10 214 A2
Broadleaze
Down Ampney GL7 8 E8
Seagry SN15 57 D6
Broadley Pk BA14 105 D3
Broadmead
Corsham SN13 85 B7
Trowbridge BA14 101 A1
Broadmead La BA12 116 E1
Broadmoor Rd SN3 36 D7
Broadtown La
Broad Town SN4 62 B3
Wootton Bassett SN4 61 F5
Broadway
Market Lavington SN10 179 D2
Warminster BA12 116 E5
Broadway Cl GL7 10 D7
Broadway E BA13 108 D6
Broadway La GL7 7 A5
Broadway The SN25 35 A3
Broadwood Ave SN13 84 B8
Broadwood Cl 1 BA12 117 A8
Brockley Rise SN2 36 A5
Brocks Orch 8 SP3 196 E6
Broken Cross
Calne SN11 81 B3
Laverstock SP4 146 F6
Brokerswood Rd BA14 105 A1
Bromley Cl 2 SN3 50 E6
Bronte Cl 2 SN3 51 D4
Brook Cl 16 SP3 203 E8
Brook Dr SN13 85 B7
Brook Dro BA13 108 C4
Brook Hill
Donhead St Andrew SP7 203 B2
Sherston SN16 40 C8
Brook La
Westbury BA13 108 D4
Woodgreen SP6 211 A4
Brook Rd BA14 101 B1
Brook St
Chippenham SN14 78 B8
Fovant SP3 204 E7
Great Bedwyn SN8 176 C3
Warminster BA12 116 E5
Brook Way SN11 81 C3
Brookdene SN25 34 E4
Brookfield SN6 22 F7
Brookfield Prim Sch SN5 49 A8
Brookfield Rise SN12 85 D1
Brookfields SO51 212 F6
Brooklands SN15 45 E5
Brooklands Ave SN2 34 F1
Brookleaze SN13 84 E5
Brooklime Cl 1 SN2 34 D4
Brookmead BA14 105 A3
Brooks Cl SN2 35 E5
Brooksby Way SN3 51 B8
Brookside
Crudwell SN16 14 E6
Hullavington SN14 41 F2
Brookwell Cl SN14 70 C2
Broomcroft Rd SN9 215 C5
Broome Manor La SN3 50 F2
Broomfield SN15 70 D2
Broomground BA15 99 E7
Broomhill SP5 212 C5
Brotherton Cl SN15 78 F5
Broughton Gifford Sch SN12 93 B3
Broughton Grange 6 SN3 50 F4
Broughton Rd 2 BA14 105 C5
Brouncker's Well* BA12 186 F5
Brow The SN25 34 E4
Brown St
3 Salisbury SP1 146 B1
Salisbury SP1 152 B8
Trowbridge BA14 105 D7
Brown's Folly* BA1 82 C1
Brown's La SN8 176 B3
Browning Cl 1 SN3 36 B3
Brownings The SN13 83 D5
Brownleaze La SN10 179 D6
Browns La Alton SN8 173 C1
Damerham SP6 209 E3
Broxburn Rd BA12 116 D6
Bruce St SN2 49 F7
Bruddel Gr SN3 50 E2
Bruges Cl SN15 78 F7
Brunel Ct SN15 78 B6
Brunel Rd SP2 145 D1
Brunel Way Box SN13 83 D6
Frome BA11 110 C7
Brunkard's La SN9 215 D5
Brunswick St SN1 50 C4
Brushy Bush La SP5 207 F3
Bruyn Rd SP6 210 E1
Bryans Cl Rd SN11 81 B3
Bryanston Way SN3 51 C6
Bryant Rd SN25 34 C5
Brydes Rd 21 SP11 192 A5
Brympton Cl 5 SP6 210 C1
Brynards Hill SN4 47 E1
Bryony Way SN2 34 D4
Bryworth La GL7 2 A6
Buckhurst Cres SN3 51 A6
Buckingham Rd
Chippenham SN15 79 A5
Swindon SN3 51 A3
Buckland Cl SN3 51 A6
Buckleaze Cl BA14 105 D5
Buckleaze La SN9 215 C5
Bucklebury Cl SN3 36 A1
Buckthorn Dr SN2 34 D4
Budbury Circ BA15 100 C7
Budbury Cl BA15 100 C7
Budbury Pl BA15 100 C7
Budbury Ridge BA15 100 C7
Budbury Tyning BA15 100 C7
Budge La BA11 114 A8
Buettell Way SN16 27 F5
Buie Cl SN5 34 B2
Bulbridge Rd SP2 144 B1
Bulford Droveway SP4 198 D7
Bulford Hill SP4 217 C8
Bulford Rd Bulford SP4 217 F8
Durrington/Bulford SP4 198 B7
Shipton Bellinger SP9 199 C8
South Tedworth SP9 216 A4
Bull La BA12 116 F2
Bull Pit BA15 100 D6
Bulldog La SN10 180 C3
Buller St SN2 35 D1
Bullfinch Cl SN3 51 D6
Bullock's Horn La
Charlton SN16 29 D7
Hankerton SN16 15 D1
Bulls La Box SN13 83 D6
Broad Chalke SP5 205 B4
Bulpit La RG17 177 B6
Bulpits Hill SP11 185 C3
Bumper's Batch BA2 98 A8
Bumpers Way SN14 70 A1
Bunce Rd SN3 36 A2
Bunnies La SN10 96 D2
Bunns La BA11 114 A2
Bunny La SP5 162 C4
Buntings The SN3 51 D7
Bupton Village* SN11 166 D7
Burbage CP Sch SN8 183 D8
Burbage Rd
Easton SN9 183 A8
Milton Lilbourne SN9 182 F7
Swindon SN2 35 C6
Burbage Wharf* SN8 175 C2
Burcombe La SP2 144 B2
Burden Cl SN3 36 C1
Burderop Cl
1 Trowbridge BA14 105 D5
Wroughton SN4 64 B8
Burderop Pk* SN4 64 F5
Burdett St 4 SN8 170 B2
Burford Ave
Salisbury SP2 152 B6
Swindon SN3 50 E5
Burford Rd SP2 152 B6
Burford St GL7 2 C4
Burford's 2 RG17 171 E7
Burgate Fields SP6 210 D2
Burgate Sch The SP6 210 E2
Burgess Cl SN3 36 A1
Burgess Gn SP1 146 C4
Burghley Cl SN3 51 A6
Burlands Rd SN15 78 E6
Burleaze SN15 78 C5
Burn Rd SN13 76 E1
Burnet Cl
Melksham SN12 94 B2
Swindon SN2 34 D5
Burnet Way SP1 146 D4
Burnett Rd BA14 105 D6
Burnham Rd
5 Fordingbridge SP6 210 D2
4 Malmesbury SN16 28 A4
Swindon SN3 51 B6
Burnhams Cl 1 SP10 193 E2
Burnivale SN16 28 A3
Burns Way SN2 35 E4
Burnston Cl SN12 94 D5
Burr La SN8 176 F1
Burroughs Dro 2 SN8 183 D8
Burton Cl 11 SP7 202 D2
Burton Farm Cl SN14 53 B3
Burton Hill Sch SN16 28 A1
Burton Rd GL9 52 F6
Burtons La SN13 83 C5
Burwood Cl 7 SP4 217 E3
Bury Camp (Hill Fort)* SN14 67 B1
Bury Fields SN5 33 D1
Bury Hill (Settlement)* SN6 18 B1
Bury La BA13 186 B7
Bury Mead BA12 195 A2
Burycroft SN4 163 A6
Burytown La SN26 21 C2
Buscote Old Parsonage (National Trust)* SN7 2 E1
Bush Barrow* SP4 197 D4
Bush Farm Bison Ctr* BA12 140 B3
Bustlers Hill SN16 40 D8
Bute Cl SN6 22 F7
Butler Cl SP2 152 B6
Butler's Field GL7 2 C5
Butler's Gdns BA11 110 A4
Butlers Cl SN16 25 C1
Butt Cl SP11 192 A6
Butt La SP5 205 E4
Butt St SP11 192 A5
Butt's La BA15 90 F7
Butter Furlong Rd SP5 154 C3
Buttercup Cl SN14 70 B3
Butterfield Dr SP4 217 D3
Buttermere SN3 51 E3
Butterworth St SN1 50 A5
Buttons Yd BA12 117 B7
Butts (Tumuli) The* SP6 211 E2
Butts Cl SN14 76 E7
Butts Hill SP3 129 E7
Butts La
Kilmington BA12 123 E6
Steeple Ashton BA14 178 A3
Butts Mead 3 SP7 202 D1
Butts Rd Chiseldown SN4 65 D5
Salisbury SP1 146 A2
Butts Terr SP2 146 A2
Butts The
Aldbourne SN8 170 A6
Biddestone SN14 76 D7
Bratton BA13 186 B7
Chippenham SN15 78 E6
Crudwell SN16 14 E6
Lydiard Millicent SN5 48 C8
Potterne SN10 179 D5
Shaftesbury SP7 202 B2
Shrewton SP3 196 E7
Steeple Ashton BA14 178 A3
Westbury BA13 109 A2
Bydemill Gdns SN6 22 E5
Byfield Way SN3 51 B8
Byrd Cl 13 SN5 48 F5
Byron Ave SN4 47 F2
Byron Cl 11 SP11 192 A5
Byron Ct SN3 36 E5
Byron Rd SN10 214 B1
Byron St 3 SN1 50 C5
Bythebrook SN14 70 B1
Bythesea Rd BA14 105 C8
Byways Cl 4 SP1 152 C8

C

Cabot Dr SN5 48 F6
Cabul Rd SP9 216 B5
Cadby Cl BA14 105 F8
Caddy La BA12 138 F5
Cadley Cl SN2 35 D2
Cadley Rd SN8 183 E1
Cadnam Cres SP4 217 E2
Caen Hill SN10 179 C8
Caen Hill Gdns SN10 179 C8
Caen Hill Locks* SN10 179 C8
Caen View SN1 49 E4
Caerleon Dr 4 SP10 193 E2
Caesar Rd SP10 193 E2
Caesar's Camp (Fort)* DT11 206 F2
Cagney Dr SN25 35 A5
Caird Lawns SN10 214 C2
Cairndow Way SN2 35 E5
Calcutt St SN6 19 E8
Calder Cl SN25 34 F5
Callaghan Cl 2 SN3 36 B2
Callas Hill SN4 163 B5
Callas Rise 7 SN4 163 B6
Callenders SN5 49 E5
Callow Croft 6 SN8 183 D8
Callows Cross SN15 46 C6
Calne Coll SN11 81 B2
Calne Dunstan CE Jun Sch SN11 81 C4
Calne Rd SN15 60 A1
Calvert Rd SN3 50 E6
Calves La SP7 202 A2
Cambrai Rd SN4 65 D1
Cambria Bridge Rd SN1 50 A5
Cambria Pl SN1 50 A5
Cambridge Cl SN3 50 F4
Cambridge Rd SP1 146 B3
Camden Cl SN5 49 A5
Camellia Dr BA12 116 E7
Camelot Cl 28 SP10 193 E2
Cameron Cl SN3 36 A1
Camilla Cl SP4 217 D8
Camomile Dr 25 SP11 192 A5
Campbell Rd SP1 146 B2
Campden Rd SN3 50 E5
Campion Cl SN11 81 B5
Campion Dr
Melksham SN12 94 C2
Trowbridge BA14 105 D6
Campion Gate SN5 48 F5
Camton Rd SN5 48 F7
Canada Rd SO51 212 F5
Canada Rise SN10 179 F1
Canadian Ave SP2 145 D2
Canal Cl Calne SN11 81 A2
Wilcot SN8 182 A8
Canal La SP5 153 E2
Canal Mus* SN10 214 B4
Canal Rd
Chippenham SN15 78 F5
Trowbridge BA14 101 E4
Canal Way SN10 214 E6
Canal Wlk
Hungerford RG17 177 B7
Swindon SN1 50 B6
Canalside SP5 153 E2
Canberra Dr SP4 198 F6
Candown Rd SP3 188 B2
Canford Cl SN3 51 C6
Cann Hill SP7 206 A7
Canney Cl SN4 65 D4
Cannimore Rd BA12 116 D5
Cannon Sq SN12 94 A4
Cannon St SN1 50 C5
Cannwood La BA10 122 D8

Canons Cl
Tidworth SP9 216 D4
Warminster BA12 117 C5
Cantax Hill SN15 86 C6
Canterbury Cl
10 Amesbury SP4 217 D3
Swindon SN3 50 F3
Canterbury St SN14 78 C8
Cantors Way SN16 17 C2
Capesthorne Dr SN25 34 E6
Capitol Cl SN3 36 D1
Capps La BA13 109 E7
Caprice Cl 1 SN5 49 A7
Capulet Rd SP1 145 F4
Caraway Dr SN2 34 C4
Carders Cnr 7 BA14 105 D7
Cardigan Cl SN3 50 E4
Cardigan Rd SN8 213 C3
Cardwell Cl 1 SN3 51 B7
Carey Cl SN5 49 A5
Carfax Cl 1 SN1 50 C6
Carfax St SN1 50 C6
Carisbrook Rd SN12 94 B2
Carisbrook Terr SN4 65 C3
Carisbrooke Cres BA14 101 E5
Carleton Pl SP4 217 A4
Carlisle Ave SN3 50 D3
Carlton Cl 2 SP4 217 D3
Carlton Gate SN3 50 F1
Carlton Row BA14 105 C6
Carman Cl SN3 36 B3
Carmelite Way SP1 152 B7
Carnarvon Cl SN14 78 A7
Carnation La SN12 178 C8
Carpenter Cl 5 SN15 78 F5
Carpenter's Cl SN11 80 F4
Carpenters Cl SN16 25 D1
Carpenters La
4 Bratton BA13 186 B7
Swindon SN2 50 D8
Carr St SN1 50 B6
Carrick Cl SN15 79 A8
Carrion Pond Dro SP2 151 D7
Carroll Cl SN3 51 D4
Carronbridge Rd SN5 49 B6
Carshalton Rd SN3 51 B3
Carstairs Ave SN3 51 A3
Carter's Cl SP6 211 C6
Cartway SN10 180 E4
Cartwright Dr SN5 49 B8
Carvers Hill SN8 176 E1
Cary Glen SN15 79 A4
Casley La BA11 107 C7
Casson Rd SN3 36 A2
Casterbridge La 3 SP11 192 F1
Casterley Camp* SN9 189 D8
Castle Barrow* BA12 195 A7
Castle Combe Golf Club SN14 68 A8
Castle Combe Motor Racing Circuit* SN14 68 C6
Castle Combe Motte & Baileys* SN14 67 F8
Castle Ct SP11 192 A6
Castle Ditches Hill Fort* SP3 204 A7
Castle Dore SN5 49 A5
Castle Hill (Fort)* SN26 21 D3
Castle Hill Cl 9 SP7 202 B2
Castle Hill Cres BA12 139 A6
Castle Hill La BA12 139 A5
Castle Keep
Salisbury SP1 145 E4
4 Wilton SP2 144 D3
Castle La Alderbury SP5 153 E1
Devizes SN10 214 A3
Wilton SP2 144 D3
Castle Mdw SP5 211 A8
Castle Prim Sch SP11 192 B5
Castle Rd Bratton BA13 186 A6
Devizes SN10 214 A3
3 Great Bedwyn SN8 176 B3
Salisbury SP1 146 A3
Castle St
Aldbourne SN8 170 A6
Calne SN11 81 B2
8 Ludgershall SP11 192 A5
Mere BA12 138 F5
Salisbury SP2 146 A2
Trowbridge BA14 105 D8
Castle View
West Tisbury SP3 203 B8
Westbury BA13 109 B3
Castle View Cl SN4 65 E4
Castle View Rd
Chiseldown SN4 65 E4
Swindon SN3 36 C1
Castle Woods 2 SP5 211 C7
Castledown Comp Sch SP11 191 F5
Castlefield Cl 3 SN5 49 C6
Castlefields SN11 81 A3
Castlehaven Cl SN15 79 A5
Castleton Rd SN5 49 A7
Castley Rd BA14 102 A2
Catalina Ct 17 SN12 178 B8
Cathedral Sch SP1 152 A7
Catherine Cres
Dinton SP3 201 E2
Downton SP5 210 F8
Catherine Ford La
Dinton SP3 201 E1
Fovant SP3 204 E8
Catherine St
Salisbury SP1 152 B8
5 Swindon SN1 50 B6
Catherine Waite Prim Sch SN25 34 F6
Catherine Way BA1 82 A5
Catherine Wayte Cl SN25 34 F4
Catmint Cl SN2 34 D4
Cator Rd 3 SP4 197 E7
Cats Hill La SP7 203 A1
Catterick Cl 7 SN14 77 F6
Caulfield Rd SN2 50 D8
Causeway The SN15 45 D6
Caversham Cl SN3 50 F5
Cavie Cl SN5 49 A8
Caxton Cl
2 Andover SP10 193 C1
2 Swindon SN3 50 F4
Caxton Rd BA11 110 A3
Cayenne Pk SN2 34 C4
Cecil Ave SP2 152 A5
Cecil Rd SN3 51 A6
Cecil Terr SP2 145 D1
Cedar Cl Melksham SN12 94 A3
Salisbury SP2 145 B4
Worton SN10 179 B4
Cedar Gr
Chippenham SN15 70 E1
Trowbridge BA14 105 B6
Cedars Cl SN2 35 A2
Celandine Way SN14 70 B2
Cemetery La BA15 100 F7
Central St SP11 192 A5
Centre The SP4 217 A4
Centurion Cl
Chippenham SN15 79 A5
1 Salisbury SP2 145 D2
Centurion Way SN3 51 C8
Cerney Wick La GL7 7 D5
Chaddenwick Hill BA12 140 B7
Chaffeymoor Hill SP8 137 B1
Chaffinch Ave BA11 110 B6
Chaffinch Dr 2 BA14 105 B8
Chafyn Gr Sch SP1 146 C2
Chain Dro
South Newton SP3 130 B6
Stapleford SP3 129 F7
Chain Hill SP3 129 E7
Chain La BA12 117 C6
Chalcot La
Chapmanslade BA13 111 F5
Upton Scudamore BA13 112 A6
Chalet Specl Sch The SN1 50 E6
Chalfield Cres SN12 94 C5
Chalfont Cl BA14 105 A8
Chalford Ave SN3 51 B7
Chalk Hill 3 SP3 196 F6
Chalk Pyt Rd SP5 205 B4
Chalk's Cl 1 SP5 211 C8
Chalkcroft La SP11 193 A2
Challis Ct 5 SP11 192 B5
Chamberlain Rd
Chippenham Without SN14 77 F7
Swindon SN3 36 A2
Chambers Ave SP4 217 C2
Chambon Cl SN16 17 A2
Champney Rd 6 BA11 110 A7
Chancel Way GL7 2 C4
Chancellor Cl SN5 48 F6
Chancery Cl 1 SP2 145 E2
Chancery La BA12 117 C6
Chandler Cl SN3 50 D5
Chandler Way 3 SN15 78 F4
Chandler's La 1 SN8 170 A7
Chandlers Cl SN10 180 F8
Chandlers La
All Cannings SN10 180 F8
Bishops Cannings SN10 172 B2
Chandos Cl SN5 49 A6
Chanterelle Pk BA15 100 D5
Chantry Gdns BA14 104 F3
Chantry La Chute SP11 184 C2
Marlborough SN8 213 D2
Westbury BA13 109 A3
Chantry Mead 13 RG17 177 B7
Chantry Rd Swindon SN2 34 F2
Wilton SP2 144 C1
Chantry The* BA12 139 A5
Chants La 6 SP3 196 E6
Chapel Cl GL7 10 D6
Chapel Cnr SN14 41 F1
Chapel Ct 17 RG17 177 B7
Chapel Hill
Broad Blunsdon SN26 21 B2
Grimstead SP5 154 B2
Lacock SN15 86 C6
Chapel La
Acton Turville GL9 53 A6
Andover SP11 193 E3
Bishopstone SP5 205 E4
Box SN13 83 D5
Broad Town SN4 167 B8
Chippenham SN15 78 E7
Collingbourne Kingston SN8 183 D2
Corsham SN13 84 E4
Downton SP5 159 B5
Hankerton SN16 15 C2
12 Lambourn RG17 165 A2
5 Ludgershall SP11 192 A5
Melksham Without SN12 86 A1
Chapel La *continued*
Minety SN16 17 A2
Nomansland SP5 212 C4
Oaksey SN16 15 E8
Pen Selwood BA9 137 C3
8 Ramsbury SN8 170 B2
Redlynch SP5 211 D7
1 Shrewton SP3 196 E6
South Marston SN3 36 E5
Stapleford SP3 129 E7
Upavon SN9 181 F2
5 Wanborough SN4 163 B6
Wingfield BA14 104 C6
Woodborough SN9 181 D7
Zennor BA12 137 E5
Chapel Orch 6 SN4 163 B6
Chapel Path SN14 75 B3
Chapel Pl 1 SP2 146 A1
Chapel Rd
Ashbury SN6 164 A7
Heytesbury BA12 194 C5
Kempsford GL7 10 D7
Chapel Rise SN12 92 E8
Chapel St
Horningsham BA12 119 A7
Swindon SN2 50 D8
Warminster BA12 116 F5
Chapel Wlk GL9 24 B3
Chaplins Pl 3 SP4 217 B3
Chapmanslade CE Sch BA13 111 C4
Charcoal Burners Rd SN8 175 B4
Charcroft Hill BA10 122 A5
Charfield Cl SN3 51 A4
Charlbury Cl SN25 34 E3
Charles Garrett Cl 39 SP7 202 C2
Charles Rd SP4 198 B7
Charles St
Corsham SN13 76 F2
2 Salisbury SP2 145 F1
Trowbridge BA14 101 C1
Charlham La GL7 8 D7
Charlieu Ave SN11 89 C8
Charlotte Mews SN3 50 D4
Charlotte St BA14 101 D1
Charlton Cl SN2 35 D5
Charlton Hill BA13 186 D8
Charlton La SP7 202 F1
Charlton Pk* SN16 28 E7
Charlton Rd SN16 28 E5
Charlwood Rd SN13 84 F8
Charminster Cl SN3 51 C6
Charnham La RG17 177 B8
Charnham Pk RG17 177 B8
Charnwood Dr 9 SP6 210 D2
Charnwood Rd
Salisbury SP2 145 E1
Trowbridge BA14 101 A1
Charter Cl 3 SN10 214 D5
Charter CP Sch SN15 78 E6
Charter Rd SN15 78 D7
Charterhouse Dr 4 BA11 110 C7
Chartley Gn 1 SN5 49 A5
Chase Cres SP5 207 E4
Chase Wood SN5 34 A2
Chatham Cl SP1 145 F4
Chatsworth Rd SN25 34 F5
Chaucer Ave 5 SP10 193 C1
Chaucer Cl SN4 47 E3
Chaveywell Ct SN11 81 B2
Cheapside BA12 195 A2
Cheddar Cl BA11 110 C7
Cheddar Rd SN25 34 E3
Chedworth Gate SN3 50 F1
Cheese Mkt 6 SP1 146 A1
Chelmsford Rd SN5 49 C7
Cheltenham Dr SN14 78 A5
Cheltenham St SN1 50 B7
Chelwood Cl SN14 78 B6
Chelworth House SN16 4 B1
Chelworth Rd SN6 19 B6
Chemical Rd BA13 108 C6
Cheney Manor Ind Est SN2 34 E1
Cheney Manor Rd SN2 34 F2
Chepston Pl BA14 100 F1
Chepstow Cl
4 Chippenham SN14 78 A5
Swindon SN5 49 C3
Cheraton Cl SN3 51 B7
Cherhill Prim Sch SN11 166 B1
Cherhill White Horse* SN11 172 C8
Cherrington Field SN10 180 F4
Cherry Cl Pewsey SN9 215 D5
Salisbury SP2 145 D1
Cherry Gdns BA14 102 A3
Cherry Gr 7 RG17 177 B7
Cherry Orch
Codford St Peter BA12 195 A2
Highworth SN6 23 A5
Marlborough SN8 213 E2
Cherry Orch La
Cann SP7 202 A1
Luckington SN14 39 C5
Salisbury SP2 145 D1
Cherry Rd SN14 75 A5
Cherry Tree Ave SP9 216 E7
Cherry Tree Ct SN11 81 B4
Cherry Tree Gr SN2 35 C2
Cherry Tree Rd SN6 19 D8
Cherry Tree Way 2 SP4 217 C3
Chervil Cl 3 SN2 34 C4
Chesford Cl SN3 51 A3
Cheshire Cl
2 Bower Hill SN12 178 B8
Salisbury SP2 145 C4
Chester St SN1 50 B6
Chester Way SN14 78 A5
Chesterfield Cl
3 Amesbury SP4 217 E3
4 Swindon SN5 49 C6
Chesters The SN5 49 C6
Chestnut Ave
Netheravon SP4 190 A2
Swindon SN2 35 C3
Tidworth SP9 216 D7
Chestnut Cl
Down Ampney GL7 8 D7
Frome BA11 110 B7
Rowde SN10 96 D2
Salisbury SP1 146 D3
Chestnut Dr SN10 178 E5
Chestnut Gr
Trowbridge BA14 105 B5
Westwood BA15 99 F4
Chestnut Grange SN13 76 D1
Chestnut La RG17 165 C2
Chestnut Mews SN12 94 A3
Chestnut Rd
Chippenham SN14 78 B8
Sutton Benger SN15 57 D2
Chestnut Springs SN5 33 D1
Chestnut Wlk 11 RG17 177 B6
Chetcombe Rd BA12 139 B6
Chevalier Cl 13 SN5 48 F8
Cheverell Ave SP1 146 C3
Cheverell Gn Rd SN10 179 C2
Cheverell Rd
Cheverell Parva SN10 179 C1
West Lavington SN10 187 D8
Cheviot Cl Swindon SN5 49 A6
Trowbridge BA14 105 E7
Chevral Cl SN14 70 B2
Cheyney Wlk BA13 109 B4
Chichester Cl SP2 152 B6
Chichester Pk BA13 109 A4
Chick's La SN8 183 E1
Chickerell Rd SN3 51 A6
Chicksgrove Rd SP3 203 F8
Chicory Cl SN2 34 C3
Child St 1 RG17 165 A1
Chilmark CE Fst Sch SP3 201 B3
Chilmark Rd
Tisbury SP3 200 F1
Trowbridge BA14 101 A1
Chiltern Cl
Melksham SN12 94 C4
9 Warminster BA12 117 A8
Chilton Foliat Prim Sch RG17 171 A1
Chilton Way RG17 177 B7
Chilvester Hill SN11 80 E2
Chine Rd SP4 131 C7
Chippenham Coll SN15 78 E8
Chippenham Com Hospl SN15 78 C6
Chippenham Golf Club SN14 70 B4
Chippenham Hardenhuish Sch SN14 70 B2
Chippenham La SN14 77 B7
Chippenham Mus* SN15 78 E7
Chippenham Rd
Lyneham & Bradenstoke SN15 59 E3
Marshfield SN14 74 A8
Chippenham Sta SN15 78 E8
Chipper La SP1 146 A1
Chirton Pl 6 BA14 105 D6
Chirton Sch SN10 180 F4
Chisbury Camp* SN8 176 C4
Chisbury La SN8 176 C5
Chiselbury Gr SP2 152 A6
Chiseldon Ct SN4 65 D4
Chiseldon Prim Sch SN4 65 E4
Chitham Cl SN10 187 C8
Chitterne Rd
Codford BA12 195 B3
Shrewton SP3 196 B6
Chittoe Heath SN15 88 A2
Chivers Rd SN15 78 E5
Chives Way SN2 34 D4
Chobham Cl SN2 36 A5
Cholderton Rare Breeds Farm* SP4 199 A5
Cholderton Rd
Amport SP4 199 D5
Quarley SP4 199 F5
Chopping Knife La SN8 175 A7
Choristers Sq 1 SP1 152 A8
Choulston Cl SP4 190 B3
Christ the King Sch SP4 217 B3
Christchurch Prim Sch BA15 100 D7
Christchurch Rd BA15 100 D8
Christchurch Terr BA12 116 F5
Christian Malford CE Prim Sch SN15 58 A2
Christie Cl SN3 51 D4
Christie Miller Rd SP2 145 E2
Christie Miller Sports Ctr SN12 94 B1
Christin Ct BA14 105 A8
Christopher Cl 2 SP2 151 F5
Christopher Dr SN15 79 A4
Christy's La 23 SP7 202 C2
Chubb Cl SN16 28 A5
Chudleigh SN5 49 B4
Chur St SP4 198 E6
Church Acre
Bradford-on-Avon BA15 100 C7
Seagry SN15 57 F6
Church Bottom SP4 131 A5
Church Cl Bath BA1 82 B2
Bourton SP8 137 D1
13 Lambourn RG17 165 A2
Church Farm La
South Marston SN3 36 E4
Woodborough SN9 181 D7
Church Fields BA14 105 A5
Church Furlong SP3 129 E7
Church Hatch 1 SP5 211 B8
Church Hill
Bromham SN15 95 F7
Donhead St Mary SP7 203 A3
Limpley Stoke BA2 99 B5
Nettleton SN14 53 B3
Redlynch SP5 211 D7
Shaftesbury SP7 202 B2
West Overton SN8 173 F7
Wroughton SN4 63 F5
Church Hill Rise SN15 96 A7
Church La
Amesbury SP4 217 A3
Bishopstone SP5 150 A1
Bishopstone SN6 163 E6
Box SN13 83 C5
Bratton BA13 186 B7
Britford SP5 152 E5
Brokenborough SN16 27 D7
Buttermere SN8 185 C7
Codford St Peter BA12 195 B2
5 Cricklade SN6 19 D8
Damerham SP6 209 F2
Dauntsey SN15 44 E1
Downton SP5 159 A5
Durrington/Bulford SP4 217 D8
East Kennet SN8 173 D6
Fovant SP3 204 D8
Hankerton SN16 15 C2
Hawkesbury GL9 38 E5
Kington Langley SN15 70 E6
Limpley Stoke BA2 99 A5
6 Ludgershall SP11 192 A5
Lyneham SN15 60 A2
Marshfield SN14 74 A8
Melchet Park & Plaitford SO51 212 E7
Melksham SN12 94 C6
Mildenhall SN8 175 A8
Norton SN16 41 D5
Ogbourne St Andrew SN8 168 E3
Pitton & Farley SP5 148 C4
Rushall SN9 181 E2
Salisbury SP2 145 C2
2 Shaftesbury SP7 202 C1
Sherfield English SO51 162 F3
Sherrington BA12 194 F2
Sopworth SN14 24 D1
South Cerney GL7 6 F7
Stanton St Quintin SN14 56 B5
Tidworth SP9 216 D4
Trowbridge BA14 105 A5
Vernhams Dean SP11 185 B4
West Lavington SN10 187 E8
Westbury BA13 108 E1
Wingfield BA14 104 C6
Church Piece SN15 57 D2
Church Pl
Lydiard Millicent SN5 33 C1
Swindon SN1 50 A6
Church Rails SP3 141 B1
Church Rd
Biddestone SN14 76 E7
Bratton BA13 186 B6
Calne Without SN11 80 A2
Cheverell Magna SN10 179 B1
Christian Malford SN15 58 A2
Derry Hill/Studley SN11 79 F2
Froxfield SN8 176 D7
Ham SN8 177 A1
Hilmarton SN11 73 F3
Idmiston SP4 133 F8
Kemble GL7 4 F7
Kilmington BA12 123 E5
Kington Langley SN15 70 E6
Liddington SN4 163 A4
Luckington SN14 39 E4
Milston SP4 198 C8
Pitton & Farley SP5 154 E7
St Paul Malmesbury Without SN16 43 A3
Salisbury SP1 146 E3
Sherston GL8 25 B5
Silton SP8 138 A1
Stanton St Bernard SN8 173 B1
Swindon SN1 50 D4
Wanborough SN4 163 A5
Woodborough SN9 181 D7
Church Rise SN13 84 E5
Church Row SN4 163 D6
Church St
Amesbury SP4 217 A3
Atworth SN12 92 D8
Bath BA1 82 B2
Berwick St John SP7 203 E1
Bower Chalke SP5 205 A2
Bradford-on-Avon BA15 100 C6
Calne SN11 81 B2
Chiseldown SN4 65 D4

Church St continued
Collingbourne Ducis SN8 ...191 E8
Corsham SN13 ...77 A2
Durrington/Bulford SP4 ...198 B7
Great Bedwyn SN8 ...176 B2
Grimstead SP5 ...154 C2
Horningsham BA12 ...119 B7
Hungerford RG17 ...177 B7
Keevil BA14 ...178 A4
Lacock SN15 ...86 D6
Little Bedwyn SN8 ...176 D5
Longbridge Deverill BA12 ...120 F7
Maiden Bradley with Yarnfield BA12 ...118 E2
Market Lavington SN10 ...179 F1
Melksham SN12 ...94 A4
Mere BA12 ...139 A5
Pewsey SN9 ...215 D4
Purton SN5 ...33 C4
Semington BA14 ...102 F6
Sherston SN16 ...25 C1
Southwick BA14 ...104 F3
Swindon SN3 ...36 B3
Tisbury SP3 ...203 E8
Trowbridge BA14 ...101 D1
Trowbridge BA14 ...102 A3
Warminster BA12 ...116 F7
West Lavington SN10 ...187 E7
Westbury BA13 ...109 A3
Winterbourne Stoke SP3 ...196 F3
Wootton Bassett SN4 ...47 C2
Wylye BA12 ...201 E8
Church St Cl 15 SP3 ...203 E8
Church Tk SP8 ...137 D1
Church View
Castle Eaton SN6 ...10 B4
Chippenham SN14 ...70 C2
Church Way
Hungerford RG17 ...177 B7
7 Swindon SN3 ...36 B3
Church Wlk
Ashton Keynes SN6 ...6 E1
Bishopstone SN6 ...163 E6
Devizes SN10 ...214 C3
Melksham SN12 ...94 A4
Motcombe SP7 ...202 A4
Redlynch SP5 ...211 E7
Swindon SN2 ...35 E3
Church Wlk N SN25 ...34 F3
Church Wlk S SN2 ...34 F3
Churches BA15 ...100 C7
Churchfield SN25 ...34 F4
Churchfield Upper Sch SN3 ...50 F5
Churchfields Ind Est SP2 ...145 E1
Churchfields Lower Sch SN3 ...50 F4
Churchfields Rd SP2 ...145 E1
Churchill Ave
Broad Blunsdon SN26 ...21 C2
Durrington/Bulford SP4 ...217 D8
Melksham SN12 ...94 D5
Churchill Cl Calne SN11 ...81 C1
North Tidworth SP9 ...216 B8
9 Tisbury SP3 ...203 E8
3 Wootton Bassett SN4 ...47 F3
Churchill Ct SP2 ...144 D3
Churchill Est SP3 ...203 E8
Churchill Way E SP1 ...146 B1
Churchill Way N SP1 ...146 A2
Churchill Way S SP1 ...152 B7
Churchill Way W
Charlton SP10 ...193 C1
Salisbury SP2 ...146 A1
Churchlands BA14 ...105 D2
Churchward Ave SN2 ...35 A1
Churchward Dr BA11 ...110 C7
Churchway SN26 ...21 C2
Churn Cl GL7 ...6 F7
Chute Cswy SP11 ...184 E2
Circle The SN2 ...35 C2
Cirencester Rd
Fairford GL7 ...1 F6
Latton GL7 ...7 E8
Cirencester Way SN2 ...50 D8
City Cnr SN4 ...163 C6
City The SN12 ...94 A5
Clack La SP6 ...210 B3
Clanfield Rd SN3 ...51 B5
Clap La SP5 ...207 B4
Clardon La SN5 ...33 C6
Clare Wlk SN5 ...49 B4
Clarence Cl 18 SP11 ...192 A5
Clarence Rd
Chippenham SN14 ...77 F7
Trowbridge BA14 ...105 F8
Clarence St SN1 ...50 C6
Clarendon Ave BA14 ...105 E8
Clarendon Cl SP3 ...201 F2
Clarendon Cty Jun & Inf Sch SP9 ...216 D6
Clarendon Dr SN4 ...47 E1
Clarendon La 1 SN1 ...50 A5
Clarendon Pal* SP5 ...147 C1
Clarendon Rd
Alderbury SP5 ...153 D3
Clarendon Park SP5 ...152 F6
Grimstead SP5 ...154 A4
Salisbury SP1 ...146 C1
Trowbridge BA14 ...105 E8
Clarendon Sch The BA14 ...105 C6
Claridge Cl 3 SN8 ...170 A6
Clark Ave SN11 ...81 C5
Clark's Gdns 25 RG17 ...177 B7
Clark's Pl 3 BA14 ...105 E8
Clarke Dr SN5 ...49 B8
Clarke's La SP11 ...193 A7
Clarkes Leaze SN14 ...68 F6
Clary Rd SN2 ...34 D5
Classics The 16 RG17 ...165 A1
Claudius Cl 15 SP10 ...193 E2
Claverton Pumping Sta* BA1 ...90 C5
Clay Cl BA13 ...112 C8
Clay St
Little Somerford SN15 ...44 C6
Longbridge Deverill BA12 ...116 E1
Whiteparish SP5 ...161 C3
Clay The SN10 ...180 A1
Clayfurlong Gr GL7 ...4 F8
Clayhill Copse SN5 ...34 A2
Clays Cl SN2 ...35 E3
Clays The SN10 ...179 F1
Clayton Rd SP4 ...217 E8
Clearbury Ring* SP5 ...158 C5
Clearwood BA13 ...111 F8
Clearwood View BA13 ...111 D4
Cleasby Cl SN5 ...49 D6
Cleavers The 1 SN8 ...183 D8
Cleaves Ave SN14 ...75 A3
Cleeve Lawns SN3 ...50 F3
Cleeve The BA12 ...140 A6
Cleevedale Rd SN13 ...85 A8
Cleeves Cl SN5 ...49 A6
Cleeves The SP3 ...143 B3
Clement's La BA12 ...139 B4
Clevedon Cl SN3 ...51 A6
Cleveland Gdns BA14 ...101 E2
Cleveland Way BA13 ...108 E2
Cley Hill (Hill Fort)* BA12 ...116 A6
Cley View 6 BA12 ...116 E6
Cleyhill Gdns BA13 ...111 D5
Cliff Rd SN16 ...40 C8
Cliffe Dr BA2 ...99 A6
Cliffords SN6 ...19 C8
Clift Ave SN15 ...70 E1
Clift Cl SN13 ...84 A8
Clifton Cl SN14 ...78 B8
Clifton Rd SP2 ...145 F2
Clifton St SN1 ...50 B5
Clink Farm Ct 6 BA11 ...110 C6
Clink Rd BA11 ...110 E6
Clinton Cl SN5 ...48 F4
Clipsham Rise BA14 ...101 A1
Clivey BA13 ...107 E1
Cloatley Manor* SN16 ...15 D2
Cloatley Rd SN16 ...15 C2
Cloche Way SN2 ...35 E3
Cloford Cl BA14 ...101 A1
Close End 8 RG17 ...165 A1
Close La Marston SN10 ...179 A3
Rowde SN10 ...96 D2
Close The
Bulkington SN10 ...178 E5
Corsham SN13 ...85 C6
Kington St Michael SN14 ...70 A8
Laverstock SP4 ...146 D8
Lechlade GL7 ...2 C5
Lydiard Millicent SN5 ...48 D8
Melksham SN12 ...94 B3
4 Redlynch SP5 ...211 C8
Tangley SP11 ...193 C5
Warminster BA12 ...117 A7
Cloth Yd 1 BA14 ...105 E7
Clothier Leaze 2 BA14 ...105 D7
Cloudberry Rd SN25 ...34 E5
Clough La SP5 ...149 B7
Clover Cl SN12 ...94 C3
Clover Dean SN14 ...78 A6
Clover Gdns 23 SP11 ...192 A5
Clover Pk SN2 ...34 D4
Cloverlands SN25 ...34 D4
Club La SP9 ...216 C4
Club Rd 1 SP4 ...198 F7
Clydesdale Cl
5 Swindon SN5 ...49 A7
Trowbridge BA14 ...105 C5
Clydesdale Rd SN13 ...83 D5
Coach Barton BA14 ...178 A3
Coach Hill SP11 ...192 E6
Coach Ho Mews SP4 ...217 B3
Coach Rd
Bradford-on-Avon BA15 ...100 C6
Westbury BA13 ...109 B5
Coalpit Rd BA1 ...82 A4
Coate Agricultural Mus* SN3 ...51 B2
Coate Rd SN8 ...173 B1
Coate Water Ctry Pk* SN3 ...51 A1
Cobbett Cl SN2 ...35 A7
Cobbett Pl BA12 ...116 F6
Cobbett Rise BA12 ...117 E4
Cobden Rd SN2 ...50 A8
Cobley Cl SP5 ...208 D6
Cock Hill BA14 ...101 A1
Cock Rd
Horningsham BA12 ...118 F8
Rowde SN10 ...95 F2
Cock-a-troop La SN8 ...175 B8
Cocklebury La SN15 ...70 F1
Cocklebury Rd SN15 ...78 E8
Cocks Cl 5 SP4 ...197 E7
Codford Circ or Wilsbury Ring* BA12 ...195 C3
Codford Rd BA12 ...195 C6
Codford Rising Sun (Hill Figure)* BA12 ...195 C2
Codford St Mary CE Sch BA12 ...195 A3
Coker's La BA12 ...123 F7
Colbert Pk SN25 ...34 F6
Colborne Cl SN15 ...79 B5
Colbourne St SN1 ...50 D7
Colchester Cl SN5 ...49 D4
Cold Harbour SP4 ...217 B3
Coldharbour La
Marlborough SN8 ...213 E4
Salisbury SP2 ...145 F2
Coldharbour Rd RG17 ...177 B6
Cole Cl 2 Andover SP10 ...193 E2
Swindon SN3 ...51 D6
Cole's La SP7 ...202 A1
Colebrook Rd SN3 ...36 B1
Coleridge Cl
Warminster BA12 ...116 D6
Wootton Bassett SN4 ...47 E3
Coleridge Rd SN25 ...34 F6
Colerne Airfield SN14 ...74 E3
Colerne CE Prim Sch SN14 ...75 B3
Colerne Pk* SN14 ...75 F6
Coles's La SP5 ...212 A7
Colesway Coll SO51 ...212 F5
College Cl SN15 ...78 F8
College Fields SN8 ...213 C2
College Gdns BA14 ...105 D3
College Gr 1 SN4 ...163 A6
College Rd
1 Durrington/Bulford SP4 ...198 B7
Purton SN5 ...33 C4
Trowbridge BA14 ...105 B6
College St
Salisbury SP1 ...146 B1
Swindon SN1 ...50 C6
College Way 4 RG17 ...171 E7
Collen Cl 1 SN14 ...78 A7
Collett Ave SN2 ...35 A1
Collett Way BA11 ...110 C7
Collingbourne CE Prim Sch SN8 ...191 E8
Collingbourne Cl 2 BA14 ...105 D5
Collingsmead SN3 ...51 C5
Collins Cl 15 SP10 ...193 D2
Collins Ct SP9 ...216 C8
Collins La SN5 ...33 E5
Coln Cres SN25 ...35 A4
Coln Ho Specl Sch GL7 ...1 F6
Colquhoun Rd 2 SP4 ...198 A6
Colston Cl SN3 ...51 A4
Colston Rd SN10 ...214 A4
Coltsfoot Cl SP4 ...217 C3
Column Ride SN8 ...175 E3
Combe La
Bratton BA13 ...186 B7
Hilmarton SN11 ...73 F6
Combe View
10 Hungerford RG17 ...177 B6
Yatton Keynell SN14 ...68 F5
Comet Ave SN9 ...182 B2
Comet Cl SN15 ...60 B2
Comfrey Cl SN2 ...34 D4
Commercial Rd
Devizes SN10 ...214 A4
Swindon SN1 ...50 B5
Common Dro DT11 ...207 B3
Common Hill
Cricklade SN6 ...19 B7
Great Hinton BA14 ...102 F2
Steeple Ashton BA14 ...106 F8
Common Rd
St Paul Malmesbury Without SN16 ...27 D1
Sixpenny Handley SP5 ...207 F4
Whiteparish SP5 ...161 E1
Common Slip SN15 ...78 E7
Common The
Bromham SN15 ...95 E6
Holt BA14 ...92 F1
Kington Langley SN15 ...70 E6
Marlborough SN8 ...213 D4
Minety SN16 ...17 C1
Shrewton SP3 ...196 E6
The Common SP5 ...149 D6
Commonweal Rd SN1 ...50 B3
Commonweal Sch SN1 ...50 B3
Commonwood La SN16 ...40 D5
Compton Abbas Airfield SP5 ...206 C5
Compton Cl
4 Swindon SN3 ...51 C4
Trowbridge BA14 ...101 E4
Compton Gdns BA11 ...110 C7
Compton Pk* SP3 ...142 C1
Compton Rd SN11 ...73 F3
Compton's Dr SO51 ...212 E7
Conan Doyle Wlk SN3 ...51 D4
Conference Cl 1 BA12 ...116 F7
Congreve Rd 4 SP4 ...197 E7
Conholt Hill SP11 ...185 A2
Conholt La SP11 ...185 B2
Conholt Pk* SP11 ...184 F1
Conifer Crest 5 SN8 ...183 D8
Coniger The (Tumuli)* SP3 ...196 F5
Conigre Cl SN12 ...94 A3
Conigre Hill BA15 ...100 C7
Conisborough SN5 ...49 C5
Coniston Cl 5 SP4 ...217 E3
Coniston Rd
Chippenham SN14 ...77 F6
Trowbridge BA14 ...101 E2
Conrad Cl SN3 ...51 D4
Consciences La SN10 ...214 A7
Constable Rd SN2 ...35 E2
Constable Way SP2 ...151 E7
Convent The* BA10 ...123 B2
Conway Cres SN12 ...94 B2
Conway Rd
Chippenham SN14 ...78 A7
Swindon SN3 ...51 C3
Conyers Cl 5 SN5 ...48 F4
Cooks Cl
Hullavington SN14 ...56 D6
Salisbury SP2 ...145 B5
Seend SN12 ...178 E8
Cooks La SO51 ...162 F7
Coombe Barn La BA12 ...124 D5
Coombe Bissett Sch SP5 ...150 F1
Coombe Cl SN4 ...64 C5
Coombe La
Atworth SN12 ...92 C7
Enford SN9 ...190 C6
Coombe Rd
Salisbury SP2 ...151 F5
Swindon SN25 ...34 F3
Coombe St BA9 ...137 D3
Coombe View BA12 ...194 D3
Cooper Fields SN25 ...35 A5
Coopers Cl
Amesbury SP4 ...217 B4
2 Malmesbury SN16 ...28 A5
Cop Croft SN11 ...81 B3
Copheap La BA12 ...117 B7
Copheap Rise BA12 ...117 B8
Copper Beeches SN6 ...22 F5
Coppice Cl SN2 ...34 D3
Coppice Hill BA15 ...100 D7
Coppice St SP7 ...202 C1
Copse Ave SN1 ...50 E8
Copse Dro SN8 ...169 B5
Copse The
Alderbury SP5 ...153 D2
Frome BA11 ...110 B6
Copyhold 2 SN8 ...176 B3
Corbin Rd BA14 ...101 F1
Corby Ave SN3 ...50 E3
Corfe Cl SN25 ...35 A4
Corfe Cres SN11 ...81 A4
Corfe Rd Melksham SN12 ...94 B3
Swindon SN5 ...49 B4
Coriander Way SN2 ...34 D5
Corinthian Cl 14 SP10 ...193 E2
Corn Gastons SN16 ...27 E3
Cornbrash Rise BA14 ...102 A1
Corner Gd BA12 ...117 E5
Corner La SP7 ...202 B5
Cornfield Rd SN10 ...214 D3
Cornflower Cl SN11 ...81 C5
Cornflower Rd SN25 ...34 D5
Cornflower Way
31 Ludgershall SP11 ...192 A5
Melksham SN12 ...94 B3
Cornmarsh Way SN3 ...51 E7
Cornpits La SP6 ...209 E2
Cornwall Ave SN2 ...35 A1
Cornwall Cres SN12 ...94 C4
Cornwall Rd SP1 ...146 A3
Cornwell Cres SN10 ...214 A2
Coronation Cl
Christian Malford SN15 ...58 A1
Donhead St Mary SP7 ...203 A1
2 Pewsey SN9 ...215 C5
Sutton Benger SN15 ...57 F1
Coronation Dr SP7 ...203 A1
Coronation Rd
Atworth/Whitley SN12 ...92 E8
Durrington/Bulford SP4 ...198 B7
Frome BA11 ...110 B5
3 Ludgershall SP11 ...192 B5
Melksham SN12 ...94 B3
Salisbury SP2 ...145 D3
Tidworth SP9 ...216 C8
Wroughton SN4 ...64 A6
Coronation St
Fairford GL7 ...1 F7
4 Trowbridge BA14 ...105 D7
Corporation St SN2 ...50 C7
Corral Cl SN5 ...34 A1
Corry The 1 SP3 ...203 E8
Corsham CP Sch SN13 ...77 A1
Corsham Ct* SN13 ...77 A2
Corsham Pk* SN13 ...77 B2
Corsham Rd
Atworth/Whitley SN12 ...85 D1
Lacock SN13 ...85 F8
Swindon SN2 ...35 C5
Corsham Regis Sch SN13 ...76 F2
Corsham Sch The SN13 ...76 F1
Corsham Sports & Cricket Club SN13 ...77 A1
Corsley CE Prim Sch BA12 ...111 D2
Corton (Long Barrow)* BA12 ...194 D3
Corton Cres SN5 ...49 B6
Coster View 5 SN8 ...176 B3
Coster's La SP5 ...205 A2
Cote La BA12 ...123 E4
Cotley Pl 4 BA12 ...194 C5
Cotswold Cl Calne SN11 ...81 D2
Melksham SN12 ...94 C4
8 Warminster BA12 ...117 A8
Cotswold Wr Pk* SN6 ...6 F4
Cottage Mews 13 SP6 ...210 D1
Cottars Cl 3 SN3 ...36 B3
Cottington Cl SN5 ...49 A4
Cottle Mead SN13 ...84 E8
Cottles La BA15 ...99 F6
Cotton House Gdns BA12 ...117 B7
Couch La SN10 ...214 A4
Coulston Hollow BA13 ...186 F8
Coulston Rd SN13 ...77 A3
Council Houses The SN15 ...44 A4
Countess Rd SP4 ...217 A4
County Rd SN1 ...50 D7
County Way BA14 ...101 E1
Court Farm Cl 8 SP4 ...190 A4
Court Farm Rd 1 SP4 ...190 A3
Court Gdns Bath BA1 ...82 A3
Stanton St Quintin SN14 ...56 B4
Court Hill
Damerham SP6 ...209 F2
Potterne SN10 ...179 C5
Court La Bathford BA1 ...82 B1
Bratton BA13 ...186 B7
Corsley BA12 ...111 B1
Edington BA13 ...186 D8
Court St Sherston SN16 ...25 C1
Tisbury SP3 ...203 E8
Trowbridge BA14 ...105 D8
Court St Cl SP3 ...203 E8
Courtenay Rd SN3 ...51 A6
Courts Gdns (National Trust) The* BA14 ...101 E8
Courtsknap Ct 7 SN1 ...50 A5
Courtwood Cl 3 SP1 ...152 C8
Coventry Cl SN4 ...64 B7
Covingham Dr SN3 ...51 C8
Covingham Pk Cty Jun & Inf Sch SN3 ...51 D7
Cow Dro SP3 ...201 B4
Cow La Kimpton SP11 ...192 B2
Laverstock SP1 ...146 C1
Cow St SN5 ...19 B1
Cowbridge Cres SN16 ...28 C1
Cowdrey Cl SN5 ...49 B4
Cowleaze Cres SN4 ...63 F6
Cowleaze La BA13 ...186 D8
Cowley Way SN15 ...57 D1
Cowslip Gr SN11 ...81 B5
Cowslip Way SN14 ...70 B3
Cox's Hill
Ashton Keynes SN6 ...6 E2
Calne SN11 ...81 B2
Cox's La SN8 ...176 F1
Coxhill La SN10 ...179 D5
Coxstalls SN4 ...47 D2
Crab La Zennor BA12 ...138 A7
Zennor BA12 ...138 B6
Crab Mill La SN16 ...28 E1
Crabtree Copse SN5 ...34 A2
Crampton Rd SN3 ...51 A7
Cranborne Chase SN2 ...34 C4
Cranborne Dr 1 SP7 ...202 C2
Cranbury Cl SP5 ...211 A7
Crandon Lea BA14 ...92 F1
Crane Furlong SN6 ...23 A7
Cranebridge Rd SP2 ...152 A8
Cranesbill Cl SN10 ...214 D5
Cranfield Univ SN1 ...50 C6
Cranmore Ave SN3 ...51 A3
Cranmore Cl BA14 ...101 A1
Cratchcroft La BA14 ...178 A6
Crate La SP7 ...202 C7
Craven Rd RG17 ...177 D3
Crawford Cl SN5 ...49 A4
Crawlboys La SP11 ...192 B6
Crawley Ave SN3 ...36 B1
Crawley Cres BA14 ...105 A8
Craybourne Rd SN12 ...94 C6
Crays The SN12 ...94 C5
Crescent Rd
Durrington/Bulford SP4 ...217 D7
Melksham SN12 ...94 C6
Crescent The
Bromham SN15 ...96 C7
Calne SN11 ...89 F8
Chiseldown SN4 ...65 C3
4 Durrington/Bulford SP4 ...198 F7
Pewsey SN9 ...215 B4
Swindon SN5 ...33 F2
Westbury BA13 ...109 A3
Wilton SP2 ...144 B2
Cresswell Dr BA14 ...102 B2
Cresswell La SN15 ...44 B8
Crestmount Dr SP2 ...145 C3
Creswells SN13 ...84 F8
Cricketts La SN15 ...78 F5
Cricklade Leisure Ctr SN6 ...19 C8
Cricklade Mus* SN6 ...19 E8
Cricklade Rd
Highworth SN6 ...22 F5
Purton SN5 ...19 C2
Swindon SN2 ...35 D1
Cricklade St SN1 ...50 D5
Crieff Cl SN3 ...51 B6
Crispin Cl 6 SN3 ...36 B3
Crockerton Cofe Sch BA12 ...116 D2
Crockford Rd SP5 ...154 B2
Croft Hts SP5 ...161 D3
Croft La SN6 ...8 C4
Croft Rd
6 Hungerford RG17 ...177 B7
Swindon SN1 ...50 C1
Wroughton SN1 ...50 B1
Croft Sports Hall SN1 ...50 D3
Croft The
Bishopstone SP5 ...205 E5
Broad Hinton SN4 ...167 D7
Milston SP4 ...198 C8
Newton Tony SP4 ...199 B3

Croft The *continued*
Trowbridge BA14 105 C6
Urchfont SN10 180 C3
Crofton Beam Engines*
SN8 176 A1
Crofton Rd SN8 176 A1
Crombey St SN1 50 B5
Cromhall La SN14 69 A7
Crompton Rd SN25 35 D6
Cromwell SN5 49 B3
Cromwell Rd SN10 214 D2
Crook Hill SP5 204 A1
Crooked Cnr SN8 170 A6
Crookhays SP7 202 C2
Crooks La SN10 180 C4
Crookwood La SN10 179 F4
Crosbys 3 SN8 183 D8
Croscombe Gdns
BA11 110 D6
Cross Hayes La SN16 28 A3
Cross Keys Rd SN13 77 A3
Cross La SN8 213 D3
Cross St Swindon SN1 50 C5
Trowbridge BA14 101 D1
Cross The
Bishopstone SP5 205 E4
Ebbesborne Wake SP5 204 D3
Crossing La SN15 71 B3
Crossways SN4 46 D6
Crossways Ave SN25 35 C3
Crosswood Rd SN3 51 A3
Croucheston Dro SP5 205 E3
Croucheston Hollow
SP5 205 E4
Crowdys Hill Sch SN2 35 D2
Crowe Hill BA2 99 B6
Crowe La BA2 99 B5
Crowle Rd 11 RG17 165 A1
Crown Cl
Chippenham SN15 79 A5
Salisbury SP2 145 D3
Crown La 4 SP11 192 A5
Crowood La SN8 170 B2
Crudwell La
Crudwell SN16 14 B6
Long Newnton GL8 13 D6
Crusades The 6 SP1 146 C5
Cruse Cl SN14 77 F8
Cswy The
Broad Chalke SP5 205 B4
Chippenham SN15 78 E7
The Common SP5 149 C7
11 Tisbury SP3 203 E8
Cuckoo La BA11 110 A8
Cuckoo Pen Cl SN8 183 D3
Cues La SN6 163 E7
Cuffs La SP3 203 E8
Cullerne Rd SN3 36 C1
Cullerns The SN6 23 A6
Culver Rd BA15 100 E5
Culver St 7 SP1 152 B8
Culvermead Cl SN8 213 E3
Culverwell Rd SN14 78 A7
Cumberland Rd SN3 50 E6
Cumberwell Pk Golf Club
BA15 91 B3
Cunetio Rd SN3 51 C8
Cunnage La BA12 139 F1
Cunningham Rd SN2 35 A2
Curlcroft Rd SN13 84 D7
Curlew Dr SN14 70 A2
Curnicks The SN4 65 C4
Cursus The*
Amesbury SP4 197 D6
Lechlade GL7 2 C5
Curtis Orch SN12 93 B4
Curtis St SN1 50 B5
Curzon Cl SN11 81 A3
Curzon St SN11 81 A3
Cusance Way BA14 102 A1
Cuthwine Pl GL7 2 C5
Cutting Hill RG17 177 A2
Cuttle La SN14 76 E8
Cutts Cl SN15 46 A7
Cuxhaven Way 10 SP10 193 D2
Cvnieto Roman Town*
SN8 175 B8
Cygnet Dr SP4 217 C8
Cyppa Ct SN15 78 E6
Cypress Gr SN2 35 A3
Cypress Way 7 BA11 110 C7
Cypress Wlk SN14 74 F6

D

Dacre Cl 18 SP10 193 C2
Dacre Rd SN3 51 A6
Dairy Cl 8 SP5 211 C7
Dairy Mdw La SP1 152 D7
Dairy Rd
Barford St Martin SP3 143 A4
Chiseldon SN4 64 F4
Daisy Cl Melksham SN12 94 C3
Swindon SN2 34 C3
Dales Cl SN25 35 A7
Dales Rd BA13 108 E2
Dalewood Rise SP1 146 E2
Dallas Ave SN3 51 B7
Dallas Rd SN14 78 C8
Dalton Cl SN3 50 F7
Dalwood Cl SN3 51 B3
Damask Way BA12 117 A5
Dammas La SN3 50 D4
Damy Gn SN13 84 E5
Dando Dr SN8 213 B2
Dane Cl BA15 99 E7
Dane Rise BA15 99 E7
Danegeld Cl 9 SP10 193 E2
Danes Cl SN15 78 F5
Danestone Cl SN5 48 F7
Daniel Cl 9 SN1 49 F4
Daniel's Well* SN16 28 A3
Daniell Crest BA12 116 F6
Danvers Mead SN15 79 A4
Danvers Rd SN13 76 E1
Danvers Way BA13 109 B4
Darby Cl SN2 34 E1
Darcey Cl SN5 48 F6
Darcy Cl SN15 78 F8
Darius Way SN25 35 A6
Dark La Berkley BA11 110 E8
Castle Combe SN14 68 B7
Grafton SN8 175 F1
Kintbury RG17 177 D8
Limpley Stoke BA2 99 B5
Malmesbury SN16 27 F3
Mere BA12 139 A5
Dark La N BA14 178 A3
Dark La S BA14 178 A3
Darnley Cl SN3 50 F6
Darrell Rd SP4 217 C4
Dart Ave SN25 35 A3
Dartmoor Cl 7 SN1 49 F4
Darwin Cl
4 Durrington/Bulford
SP4 198 F6
Swindon SN3 51 B7
Dasna Rd SP9 216 B5
Daunch Cl SP9 216 B7
Dauntsey Dro SP11 192 E1
Dauntsey La SP11 192 E1
Dauntsey Pk* SN15 44 E2
Dauntsey Rd SN15 44 C2
Dauntseys Prim Sch
SN10 187 E8
Dauntseys Sch
Market Lavington SN10 179 E1
West Lavington SN10 187 D8
Davenham Cl SN3 51 A3
Davenwood SN2 35 F4
David's Gdn SP5 148 C3
Davies Cl SN8 213 A2
Davis Dr SN10 214 E6
Davis Pl SN1 50 B6
Davis Rd 11 SN10 179 F1
Dawlish Rd SN3 51 B5
Dawneys The SN16 14 E6
Day Ho La SN3 51 C2
Day's Cl SN3 36 A1
Day's La SN15 56 D2
Days Ct SN16 14 E6
De Havilland Pl 4 SN12 178 B8
De Montfort Gr 8 RG17 177 B6
De Vaux Pl SP1 152 A7
Deacon Rd SP11 192 B2
Deacon St SN1 50 B5
Dean Cl Frome BA11 110 C6
Melksham SN12 94 C6
Dean La Fovant SP3 204 D7
Sixpenny Handley SP5 207 F6
Whiteparish SP5 161 D4
Dean La Dro SP5 207 F4
Dean Rd SP5 155 B3
Dean St SN1 49 F5
Dean Sta SP5 155 F3
Deans Cl SP9 216 D4
Deansfield SN6 19 D7
Deansway SN15 70 D2
Deben Cres SN25 34 F5
Deburgh St SN2 49 F6
Deep La BA12 111 D2
Deer Pk* SN8 175 E2
Deerhurst Way 1 SN5 49 D4
Delamere Dr SN3 36 A4
Delamere Rd BA14 101 D2
Dell The SP11 185 B3
Denbeck Wood SN5 49 B6
Denbigh Cl SN3 50 E3
Dene The SP3 200 B3
Denes Ave BA12 139 A6
Denford La RG17 177 D8
Denholme Rd SN3 51 A3
Denison Rise SP1 146 C3
Dennis La SP7 203 B1
Derby Cl
Chippenham SN15 78 F5
Lambourn RG17 165 A1
Derriads La 3 SN14 77 F6
Derry Hill CE Sch SN11 80 A2
Derry Pk SN16 17 C2
Derry The SN6 17 F8
Derwent Dr SN2 35 F4
Desborough SN5 49 A3
Deva Cl SN3 51 D8
Deverell Cl BA15 100 E4
Devereux Cl 8 SN5 48 F5
Devereux Rd SP4 217 B3
Deverill Rd
Sutton Veny BA12 117 E1
Warminster BA12 116 F4
Devils Bed & Bolster The*
BA11 107 A8
Devizes Castle* SN10 214 A3
Devizes Com Hospl
SN10 214 B4
Devizes Gdn Trading Est
SN10 214 C5
Devizes Leisure Ctr
SN10 214 B3
Devizes Rd Box SN13 83 E4
Bromham SN15 88 B4
Calne Without SN11 87 F7
Devizes Rd *continued*
Charlton SN9 181 D2
Derry Hill/Studley SN11 79 F1
Hilperton BA14 102 C3
Potterne SN10 179 D6
Poulshot SN10 179 B7
Rowde SN10 96 F2
Salisbury SP2 145 E2
Swindon SN1 50 D4
Trowbridge BA14 102 B3
Wroughton SN4 64 B6
Devizes Sch SN10 214 B3
Devizes Sports Club
SN10 214 C4
Devon Cl 5 SN14 77 F6
Devon Dr BA13 109 A5
Devon Rd Swindon SN2 35 B1
Upavon Down SN9 182 B2
Devonshire Pl SN12 94 C5
Devonshire Rd SP1 146 A3
Dew Cl SN13 85 A8
Dew's Rd SP2 145 F1
Dewell Mews SN1 50 D3
Dewey Cl SN4 65 D4
Deweys La SP11 192 A5
Dexter Cl SN5 49 B7
Dial Cl SN12 178 E8
Dianmer Cl SN4 47 F5
Dickens Ave SN13 76 F2
Dickens Cl SN3 51 D3
Dickenson Rd SN25 34 C5
Dicketts Rd SN13 85 A7
Dickson Rd SN15 60 A1
Dickson Way 2 SN15 78 F5
Diddledown Rd 8 SP4 217 C2
Dilton Ct BA13 112 B6
Dilton Marsh CE Cont Prim
Sch BA13 112 B8
Dilton Marsh Sta
BA13 108 C1
Dinah's Hollow SP7 206 B7
Dingle The 3 SN4 163 A6
Dinmore Rd SN25 34 F6
Dinton CE Fst Sch
SP3 201 F2
Dinton Rd Fovant SP3 204 E8
Wylye BA12 201 E8
Discover Salisbury (Medieval
Hall)* SP1 152 A8
Divinity Cl 2 SN4 163 B6
Dixon St SN1 50 B5
Dixon Way SN11 81 B4
Dobbin Cl SN3 51 E7
Dobson Cl SN25 35 A8
Dockle Way SN2 35 F4
Doctors Hill SN13 83 B5
Doctors Pl 3 SP3 203 E8
Dodford La SN15 58 D6
Dodgson Cl SP6 211 A4
Dog Kennel La BA13 109 A1
Dog La SP7 203 E1
Dog Trap La SN16 16 E1
Doggetts La BA13 109 A4
Dogridge SN5 33 A3
Dolphin Ind Est SP1 152 D7
Dolphin St SP1 152 B8
Don Cl SN25 35 A4
Donaldson Rd SP1 146 A2
Doncombe Hill SN14 74 E7
Doncombe La SN14 75 A6
Donhead Hollow SP7 206 E8
Donnington Gr SN3 50 F4
Dorcan Tech Coll SN3 51 D6
Dorcan Way SN3 51 A8
Dorchester Rd SN3 50 F3
Dores Ct SN2 35 E3
Dores Rd SN2 35 D3
Dormers The SN6 23 A6
Dorney Cl BA13 108 F1
Dorset Cl SP4 217 E8
Dorset Cres SN12 94 C3
Dorset Dr BA13 109 A5
Dorset Rd SP1 146 B3
Double Hedges SP4 217 E7
Doubledays SN6 19 D8
Doughty's La BA12 195 A2
Douglas Brown's Wlk 6
SP4 197 E6
Douglas Haig Rd SP1 146 A3
Douglas Rd 5 SN3 50 F6
Dovecote Cl 3 BA14 105 B8
Dovecote Dr SN13 76 F2
Dover St
Chippenham SN14 78 C7
Swindon SN1 50 C5
Dovers La BA1 82 C2
Dovers Pk BA1 82 C2
Doves La SP5 161 C3
Dovetrees SN3 51 D7
Doveys Terr SN15 70 E7
Dowding Ave SN13 84 B8
Dowding Dr 5 SN11 166 A1
Dowding Way SN12 94 C1
Dowling St SN1 50 C5
Down Ampney CE Prim Sch
GL7 8 E7
Down Ampney House*
GL7 8 D6
Down Ampney Rd GL7 8 B6
Down Barn Cl SP4 133 B4
Down Barn Rd SP4 132 F6
Down Rd Kimpton SP11 192 B2
Marshfield SN14 66 C2
Down The Hindon SP3 200 B3
Trowbridge BA14 101 D2
Down View Rd SP1 146 E2
Downavon BA15 100 D5
Downham Mead SN15 78 F8
Downhayes Rd BA14 101 D2
Downing St SN14 78 C8
Downland Rd
Calne SN11 81 A2
Swindon SN2 34 D4
Downland Sch SN10 214 B1
Downland Way 12 SP4 198 B7
Downlands 1 RG17 171 E7
Downlands Cl SP5 211 A7
Downlands The BA12 117 B7
Downleaze 7 SP4 198 B7
Downs Cl
Bradford-on-Avon BA15 100 B7
Lambourn RG17 171 C8
Downs La SN8 185 B8
Downs Rd SN4 65 E4
Downs The SN8 170 A5
Downs View
Bradford-on-Avon BA15 100 B7
Highworth SN6 23 A6
1 Netheravon SP4 190 A4
Warminster BA12 117 C6
Wootton Bassett SN4 47 D1
Downs View Rd SN3 50 F2
Downside Cl BA12 139 A6
Downside Pk BA14 101 E2
Downslands Rd SN10 214 B1
Downsmead SN8 164 B1
Downsview BA13 186 C7
Downsview Rd BA13 109 A4
Downsview Way SP11 191 F3
Downsway SP1 146 B4
Downton CE Prim Sch
SP5 211 A8
Downton Cty Sec Sch
SP5 211 A8
Downton Hill SP5 211 C8
Downton Meml Gdns*
SP5 211 A8
Downton Rd
Salisbury SP2 152 B5
Swindon SN2 35 B5
Downview Rd SP6 209 B6
Downwood Cl 7 SP6 210 C1
Doyle Cl SN25 34 C5
Dragon La SN9 181 F6
Drain Hill RG17 165 A2
Drake Cres SN14 77 F6
Drake's Way
Swindon SN3 50 E6
Swindon SN3 51 A8
Drakes Ave SN10 214 C2
Draycot Rd SN4 65 C3
Draycott Cl SN3 51 A5
Drew St SN2 49 E7
Drew's Pond La SN10 214 B1
Drewitts La SN10 180 E8
Drifton Hill SN14 66 E7
Drive The
Melchet Park & Plaitford
SO51 162 C1
Swindon SN3 51 B7
Drove Cl SP5 150 F2
Drove Infs Sch The
SN1 50 D6
Drove Jun Sch The
SN3 50 D6
Drove La
Coombe Bissett SP5 150 F3
Market Lavington SN10 179 F1
Steeple Ashton BA14 178 A2
Drove Rd SN1 50 D5
Drove The
Amesbury SP4 217 B4
Andover SP10 193 C1
Druley Hill BA10 123 B7
Drury Cl SN5 47 F6
Drury La SN8 175 D4
Dry Hill BA12 116 E2
Dryden Cl SP2 152 B5
Dryden St SN1 50 B5
Drynham La BA14 105 D5
Drynham Pk BA14 105 D6
Drynham Rd BA14 105 D6
Duchess Way SN2 35 D5
Duchy Manor Mid Sch
BA12 139 B6
Duck La
Barford St Martin SP3 143 B3
Laverstock SP1 152 E8
Salisbury SP1 146 D2
Duck Pool La BA11 107 B6
Duck St
Berwick St James SP3 196 F2
Ebbesborne Wake SP5 204 C3
Potterne SN10 179 D5
Steeple Langford SP3 128 D7
Sutton Veny BA12 194 A4
Tisbury SP3 203 E8
West Lavington SN10 187 E8
Duck's Nest (Long Barrow)*
SP6 209 F7
Ducks Mdw SN8 213 D2
Dudley Ave SP6 210 D2
Dudley Rd SN3 50 F6
Dudmore Rd SN3 50 D6
Duke St BA14 101 D1
Duke's La BA12 118 A1
Duke's Way SP4 217 E8
Dukes Cl SN2 35 E5
Dulverton Ave SN3 51 A5
Dumbarton Terr 2 SN1 50 C5
Dummer La SP11 184 E1
Dummer Way SN15 79 A5
Dunbar Rd SN4 64 A7
Dunbeath Ct SN2 35 E1
Dunbeath Rd SN2 35 E1
Duncan St SN11 81 B5
Duncan's Cl SP11 192 D1
Dunch La SN12 93 F7
Dundas Aqueduct*
BA2 90 B2
Dundas Cl SN10 179 C8
Dunedin Cl SP9 216 E6
Dunford Cl BA14 105 D6
Dunhills La SP11 193 F4
Dunkirk Hill
Devizes SN10 179 D8
Rowde SN10 97 A1
Dunley Way SP1 146 C5
Dunn's La SP8 138 A1
Dunnet Cl SN11 81 B4
Dunnington Rd SN4 61 D8
Dunns La SN14 68 B8
Dunraven Cl SN3 50 F4
Dunsford Cl SN1 49 F4
Dunspit La DT11 207 B1
Dunstable Cnr SP5 148 E7
Dunstan's Dro SP11 185 E1
Dunster Cl SN3 50 E3
Dunwich Dr SN5 49 D4
Dunworth Rise 6 SP3 203 E8
Durham St SN1 50 C5
Durlett Rd SN10 95 F2
Durley Pk SN13 84 D6
Durnford Rd SN2 35 C5
Durrington All Saints Inf Sch
SP4 198 C7
Durrington Jun Sch
SP4 198 C7
Durrington Swimming Pool
SP4 198 C7
Durrington Walls*
SP4 217 A8
Dursden La SN9 215 E6
Dursley Rd
Heywood BA13 108 F8
North Bradley BA13 105 E1
Dutts BA13 108 B1
Duxford Cl 11 SN12 178 B8
Dyehouse La SN10 214 A4
Dyer La BA12 201 E8
Dyer's Cl SN15 79 A6
Dyke Mews SN4 65 D4
Dymocks La BA12 121 F8
Dymott Sq BA14 102 A3

E

Eagle Cl SN3 51 E7
Eagle Field SP2 145 D4
Earl Cl SN5 48 F7
Earl's Rise SP4 133 A1
Earls Cl SP4 217 E2
Earls Cnr SN16 15 E8
Earls Ct Rd SP4 217 B3
Earthpits La SP5 208 E4
East Dunley Cotts SN14 40 E1
East End BA12 117 B6
East End Ave BA12 117 B6
East End La SN15 44 D5
East Gomeldon Rd
SP4 133 E4
East Kennett (Long
Barrow)* SN8 173 D5
East La SN12 93 B3
East Portway SP10 193 C1
East Sands SN8 183 D8
East St Bourton SP8 137 E1
Hindon SP3 200 A4
Lacock SN15 86 D6
Salisbury SP2 145 F1
Swindon SN1 50 B6
Warminster BA12 117 B6
East Town Rd BA14 106 D3
East Woodlands Rd
BA11 114 A7
East Yewstock Cres
SN15 70 C1
Eastbourne Gdns
BA14 101 E1
Eastbourne Rd BA14 101 E1
Eastbury Shute RG17 171 C5
Eastcott Comm SN10 180 A2
Eastcott Hill 5 SN1 50 C5
Eastcott Rd SN1 50 C5
Eastcourt SN8 183 D8
Eastcourt Rd SN8 183 D8
Eastern Ave
Chippenham SN15 78 F8
Swindon SN3 50 E6
Easterton La SN9 215 D4
Eastfield
Ashton Keynes SN6 6 F1
2 Littleton Panell SN10 187 E8
Easthill BA11 110 B4
Eastleaze Rd SN5 49 C6
Eastleigh Cl 4 BA11 110 A7
Eastleigh Rd SN10 214 D2
Eastman Cl SP5 211 B7
Eastmere SN3 51 E3
Easton Comm Hill
SP5 149 E6
Easton Hollow SP5 207 B7
Easton La SN14 77 F3
Easton Royal Sch SN9 183 A7
Easton Sq SN16 25 D1
Easton Town SN16 25 C1
Eastrip La SN14 75 C3
Eastrop SN6 23 B5
Eastrop Cty Inf Sch
SN6 23 A5
Eastview Rd BA14 105 A7
Eastville Rd SN25 35 C3
Eastwell Rd SN10 179 D5

Eastwood SO51 162 E1
Eastwood Ave SN4 47 E1
Eaton Cl 1 SN3 51 A4
Ebbesborne Hollow
SP5 204 D2
Ebble Cl SP9 216 D7
Ebble Cres BA12 117 A5
Ebor Cl SN25 34 F7
Ebor Gdns SN11 89 C8
Ebor Paddock SN11 89 C8
Eccleston Cl SN3 51 B3
Ecklington SN3 51 C5
Edale Moor SN3 51 E3
Eddington Hill RG17 177 C8
Edelweiss Cl 29 SP11 192 A5
Eden Gr SN12 85 D1
Eden Pk Cl BA1 82 A4
Eden Pk Dr BA1 82 A4
Eden Vale Rd BA13 108 F3
Edencroft SN6 23 B8
Edgam Pl SP2 144 F3
Edgar Cl 6 SP10 193 E2
Edgar Row Cl 1 SN4 64 A6
Edgecorner La SN14 53 A3
Edgehill SN5 49 B3
Edgeware Rd SN1 50 C6
Edgeworth Cl 4 SN5 49 B7
Edinburgh Rd SN11 81 F1
Edinburgh St SN2 35 D1
Edinburgh Way SN13 84 E7
Edington Cl SN5 49 B5
Edington Priory*
BA13 186 C8
Edington Rd BA14 178 A3
Edison Rd
Salisbury SP2 151 E8
Swindon SN3 51 D5
Edmund St SN1 50 C5
Edric's Gn SP4 199 C5
Edridge Cl SN15 78 F8
Edridge Pl 1 SN13 76 E1
Edward Rd SN10 214 B2
Edward St BA13 109 A3
Edwards Hill 12 RG17 165 A1
Edwards Mdw SN8 213 B3
Edwards Rd SP4 217 B3
Egerton Cl SN3 51 B7
Eider Ave SN15 60 A1
Elbe Way SP10 193 D2
Elborough Rd SN2 34 D3
Elcombe Ave 3 SN4 64 A6
Elcombe Cl BA14 105 C5
Elcombe La SP5 204 B2
Elcot Cl SN8 213 F3
Elcot La SN8 213 F3
Elcot Orch SN8 175 A8
Elden Rd SP9 191 D5
Eldene Dr SN3 51 C4
Eldene Jun & Inf Sch
SN3 51 C5
Elder Cl SN2 34 C3
Eleanor Ct 16 SP11 192 A5
Elgin Dr SN2 35 E1
Eliot Cl SN3 51 D3
Elizabeth Cl
3 Downton SP5 210 F8
Melksham Without SN12 93 F1
Elizabeth Dr SN10 214 C4
Elizabeth Gdns GL7 1 A5
Elizabeth Pl SN15 79 A4
Elizabeth Rd
16 Durrington/Bulford
SP4 198 B7
Wilton SP2 144 B5
Elley Gn SN13 84 E6
Ellingdon Rd SN4 63 F7
Elliott Ct SN10 214 B1
Elliott Gn SP4 133 C3
Elliott Pl BA14 101 A1
Elm Cl Bower Hill SN12 94 C1
Calne SN11 89 C8
8 Ludgershall SP11 192 B5
Lyneham SN15 60 B2
Motcombe SP7 202 A5
Pitton & Farley SP5 148 C4
Rowde SN10 96 D1
Salisbury SP1 146 D3
Staverton BA14 101 D6
Trowbridge BA14 105 C3
Wootton Bassett SN4 47 E4
Elm Gr Corsham SN13 76 E1
Salisbury SP1 146 C1
Swindon SN5 49 A8
Elm Gr Rd SP1 146 B1
Elm Hayes SN13 85 A7
Elm Hill BA12 113 C1
Elm Leigh BA11 110 C6
Elm Pk SN4 47 D1
Elm Rd Colerne SN14 75 A5
Swindon SN2 35 A2
Elm Tree Cl SN10 214 D2
Elm Tree Gdns SN10 214 D2
Elm View GL7 5 F4
Elmdale Rd BA14 105 A7
Elmer Cl SN16 28 A5
Elmfield BA15 100 C7
Elmfield Cl 7 SP5 211 C7
Elmina Rd SN1 50 C7
Elmore SN3 51 C5
Elms Cl SP6 210 B1
Elms Cross Dr BA15 100 C5
Elms The
Bradford-on-Avon BA15 100 B8
Highworth SN6 22 F5
Holt BA14 92 E1
Swindon SN5 48 F8
Elmswood Cl SN2 35 E5
Elmwood SN15 70 E2
Elmwood Ave 6 SP6 210 C1
Elsham Way SN25 35 A5
Elston La SP3 196 E7
Elstree Way
Haydon Wick SN25 34 F6
Swindon SN25 34 F6
Ely Cl SN5 49 C4
Embankment SN1 50 D3
Embry Cl 3 SN11 166 A1
Emden Rd 18 SP10 193 D2
Emerson Cl SN2 35 A6
Emery La SN15 78 E7
Emlyn Sq SN1 50 B6
Emmanuel Cl SN25 35 A4
Emms La 10 BA13 186 B7
Empire Rd SP2 145 C2
Empress Way SP11 192 A5
Emwell St BA12 117 A7
Endless St SP1 146 A1
Enford Ave SN2 35 C6
Enford Hill SN9 189 F6
Engineer Rd BA13 108 C6
Englefield SN4 47 E1
Enham La SP10 193 E3
Eningen View SN11 81 B1
Ensor Cl SN25 35 A8
Epping Cl BA12 117 A8
Epping Dr SN12 94 C6
Epsom Cl SN14 77 F6
Epsom Rd BA14 105 E4
Erin Ct 2 SN1 50 A5
Erleigh Dr SN15 78 C7
Erlestoke Sands Golf Club
SN10 186 F8
Ermin Cl SN8 170 C8
Ermin St 1 Baydon SN8 164 C1
Baydon SN8 170 C8
Blunsdon St Andrew SN26 20 F2
Swindon SN2 35 F4
Erneston Cres SN13 76 F1
Ernle Rd SN11 81 C4
Erskine Barracks SP2 144 F4
Escott Cl 4 SN15 78 F4
Esmead SN15 78 F8
Essex Pl 7 RG17 165 A2
Essex Sq SP2 151 D6
Estate Yard The SN10 172 B3
Estcourt Cres SN10 214 B4
Estcourt Rd SP1 146 B1
Estcourt St SN10 214 B3
Eston Medieval Village of*
SN14 69 D8
Ethelbert Dr 4 SP10 193 C2
Ethelred Pl SN13 76 E1
Ethendun 11 BA13 186 B7
Euclid St SN1 50 C6
Evans Cl SN15 70 E1
Eveleigh Rd SN4 47 E2
Evelyn St SN1 50 D3
Even Swindon Sch SN2 49 E7
Eveque Ct SP2 144 F3
Evergreen Way SP4 217 C2
Evergreens Cl SN3 36 C1
Everland Rd 18 RG17 177 B7
Everleigh Barrows*
SN9 182 E3
Everleigh Cl BA14 105 D5
Everleigh Rd
Collingbourne Ducis
SN8 191 D8
Pewsey SN9 215 C3
Swindon SN2 35 C5
Eworth Cl SN5 48 F5
Exbury Cl 2 SN25 35 A6
Exe Cl SN25 35 A4
Exeter Cl SN14 77 F5
Exeter House Specl Sch
SP1 146 B3
Exeter St Salisbury SP1 152 B7
Swindon SN1 50 A6
Exmoor Cl 1 SN2 34 C4
Eyres Dr SP5 153 E2
Eyres Way SP1 152 B8

F

Factory Hill SP8 137 F3
Factory La BA12 116 F6
Fair Mile
Collingbourne Kingston
SN8 183 F3
Grafton SN8 184 A4
Fair View Rd SP2 144 E4
Fairdown Ave BA13 109 B3
Fairfax Cl
Amesbury SP4 217 A4
Swindon SN3 50 F7
Fairfield 1 Cricklade SN6 19 D8
4 Great Bedwyn SN8 176 B3
Rode BA11 103 F1
Wootton Bassett SN4 47 E3
Fairfield Cl SN14 74 A8
Fairfield Mdws BA14 104 F3
Fairfield Rd
Salisbury SP1 146 A4
Warminster BA12 117 B7
Fairfields 22 RG17 177 B7
Fairfoot Cl SN14 78 A7
Fairford Airfield GL7 1 E1
Fairford Cres SN25 35 C3
Fairground The 2 SP11 192 F1
Fairhaven BA13 108 D1
Fairholm Way SN2 35 F4
Fairlane SP7 202 C1
Fairlawn SN3 51 D3
Fairleigh Rise SN15 70 F7
Fairview Colerne SN14 75 C6
Fairview *continued*
Swindon SN1 50 B5
Fairview Rd
1 Andover SP11 192 F1
Hungerford RG17 177 B7
Salisbury SP1 146 C1
Fairway Calne SN11 89 C8
Melksham SN12 94 C5
Fairway The SN10 214 A1
Fairways Amport SP11 192 E1
Dilton Marsh BA13 108 D1
Fairwood Cl BA14 102 A2
Fairwood Rd
Dilton Marsh BA13 108 C3
North Bradley BA13 107 F5
Falcon Cl SP9 216 D7
Falcon Rd SN11 81 D3
Falcon Way SN12 94 D1
Falconscroft SN3 51 C8
Falconsway SP2 152 A5
Falconwood Cl 8 SP6 210 C1
Falkirk Rd SN4 64 A7
Falkner Cl SN8 213 B3
Fallow Field Cl SN14 70 B2
Falmouth Gr SN3 50 E4
Fanshaw Way BA12 117 A5
Fanstones Rd SN3 51 C4
Fantley La SP8 138 B1
Far View Rd SP3 196 F7
Faraday Rd
Salisbury SP2 145 E1
Swindon SN3 51 E5
Fareham Cl SN3 51 B5
Farfield La SN6 19 E4
Fargo Cl SP4 198 A6
Fargo Rd SP4 217 A7
Faringdon Rd 2 SN1 50 B6
Farleigh Ave
Melksham SN12 94 B3
Trowbridge BA14 105 A7
Farleigh Castle* BA2 103 E8
Farleigh Cl
1 Chippenham SN14 77 F6
Westbury BA13 108 F4
Farleigh Coll BA2 103 D6
Farleigh Cres SN3 50 E3
Farleigh Pk* BA2 103 D5
Farleigh Rd BA2 103 A5
Farleigh Rise BA1 82 D1
Farley Cl BA11 110 C6
Farley Rd SP1 152 C7
Farleys All Saints Prim Sch
SP5 154 E8
Farm La Aldbourne SN8 170 A6
Great Bedwyn SN8 176 B3
Salisbury SP2 145 E1
Farman Cl SN3 51 C4
Farmer Cl SN15 70 E1
Farmhouse Cl SN15 78 F4
Farnborough Rd SN3 51 B3
Farne Way SN4 48 A2
Farnsby St SN1 50 B6
Farrar Dr SN8 213 A2
Farrells Field SN14 68 F4
Farrfield SN2 35 E4
Farriers Cl SN1 50 E8
Farriers Field SN9 181 F2
Farthing Row BA11 103 E1
Faulkner Sq RG17 177 C7
Faverole Way BA14 102 A2
Feather Wood SN5 49 D5
Featherbed La SN6 163 F7
Fell Rd BA13 108 E2
Feltham Dr BA11 110 A3
Feltham La BA11 110 A2
Fenland Cl
8 Swindon SN5 48 F8
5 Swindon SN5 49 A8
Fennel Cl SN2 34 D4
Fennel Rd BA12 139 B6
Ferguson Rd SN10 214 D1
Fermoy BA11 110 B6
Ferndale Rd SN2 49 F8
Ferne Hollow SP5 207 A8
Ferne Wall Cnr SP7 203 B1
Fernham Rd SN25 34 E3
Ferozeshah Rd SN10 214 E6
Ferrers Dr SN5 48 F4
Ferris Gr SN12 94 C4
Ferris Mead BA12 117 A6
Festival Ave SP2 145 C3
Feversham Rd SP1 146 B3
Fiddington Clay SN10 179 F1
Fiddington Hill SN10 180 A1
Fiddle The SN6 19 C7
Field Barn La SP3 201 F3
Field Cl South Cerney GL7 7 A7
Westbury BA13 109 A4
Field La BA9 137 B3
Field Rise SN1 50 A3
Field View
Chippenham SN15 78 D7
Enford SN9 190 A6
Field Way BA14 104 F6
Fieldfare SN3 51 D7
Fieldings BA15 99 E7
Fields The BA12 139 B6
Fieldside SN10 187 E8
Figgins La SN8 213 D2
Figsbury Rd SP4 133 B1
Figsbury Ridge SP4 133 C2
Figsbury Ring* SP4 147 D8
Finchdale SN3 51 D8
Finches La
2 Baydon SN8 164 C1
Baydon SN8 170 C8
Finchley Rd SP2 145 E2
Finkley Rd SP11 193 F2
Finnis Rd 1 SP4 217 C3
Fir Gn La SN8 183 D8
Fir Gr SN11 89 D8
Fir Rd SN14 74 F6
Fir Tree Cl SN2 35 A2
Firbank Cres BA12 117 D8
Fire Brigade Mus*
SN10 179 C5
Firecrest View 3 SN3 51 E6
Firs Cl SP5 148 C7
Firs Hill Way SN10 179 E5
Firs Rd Alderbury SP5 153 E2
Firsdown SP5 148 B7
Firs The Inkpen RG17 177 F3
Limpley Stoke BA2 99 A5
First Broad Dr
Barford St Martin SP3 129 A1
Wilton SP2 144 A7
First La SN12 85 C1
Firth Cl SN25 35 A3
Fisherton Island SP2 145 F1
Fisherton Manor Mid Sch
SP2 145 E2
Fisherton St SP2 145 F1
Fitzmaurice Cl
Bradford-on-Avon BA15 100 E4
Calne Without SN11 79 F2
Swindon SN3 51 D7
Fitzmaurice Pl BA15 100 D5
Fitzmaurice Prim Sch
BA15 100 D5
Fitzroy Rd SN1 50 C2
Fitzwarren Cl SN15 79 A4
Five Ash La BA12 117 C2
Five Stiles Rd SN8 213 F2
Five Thorn La SN15 57 D6
Flamstone St SP5 205 E4
Flashett The SP5 149 D6
Flaxfields End 15 SP6 210 D1
Fleece Cotts 2 BA14 105 E7
Fleet Rd SN15 78 D8
Fleet St SN1 50 B6
Fleetwood Cl SN13 84 E6
Fleetwood Rise SN12 93 A8
Fleming Cl SP11 192 A5
Fleming Way SN1 50 C6
Flensburg Cl 20 SP10 193 D2
Fleur De Lys Dr BA14 105 A4
Flint Hill SN5 49 C4
Flint La SP11 193 A4
Flintjack Pl 2 RG17 165 A1
Flisteridge Rd SN16 16 C3
Flit Croft 4 SP4 217 C2
Flood The SP5 149 B7
Florence Ct 21 SP10 193 E2
Florence St SN2 50 C8
Flower La
Amesbury SP4 217 A3
Melchet Park & Plaitford
SO51 212 F7
Flowers Mead 6 BA13 186 B7
Foghamshire SN15 78 D7
Folkestone Cl SN14 78 A6
Folkestone Rd SN1 50 B4
Folkstone Rd SP2 151 F6
Folly Barrow* DT11 206 B2
Folly Cl Highworth SN6 23 A7
Salisbury SP2 151 F5
Folly Cres SN6 23 A7
Folly Dr SN6 23 A7
Folly La Alderbury SP5 153 C3
Melksham Without SN12 93 B8
Salisbury SP2 145 D3
Warminster BA12 116 B5
Folly La E SN15 86 C5
Folly La W SN15 86 B5
Folly Rd Inkpen RG17 177 F3
Lambourn SN8 164 F1
Roundway SN10 214 C7
Folly The SN15 44 A2
Folly View SP2 145 C5
Folly Way SN6 23 A7
Follyfield
Bradford-on-Avon BA15 100 D4
Hankerton SN16 15 B2
Foot's Hill Cann SP7 206 A7
Salisbury SP2 145 A3
Ford St SN1 50 A5
Fordingbridge Hospl
SP6 210 D1
Fordingbridge Jun & Inf Sch
SP6 210 D2
Fordson Rd SN10 214 D1
Fore St Ashton Keynes SN6 6 F1
Trowbridge BA14 101 D1
Warminster BA12 116 F5
Westbury BA13 109 A4
Wylye BA12 201 E8
Forest Dale Rd SN8 175 A8
Forest Dr SP9 216 E7
Forest Hill SN8 176 B3
Forest La
Chippenham SN15 78 E3
Chute SP11 192 D8
Melksham Without SN12 86 F2
Forest Rd
Bramshaw SP5 212 B3
7 Frome BA11 110 B7
Horningsham BA12 118 D8
Melksham SN12 94 B5
Redlynch SP6 211 D6
Wooton Rivers SN8 174 F2
Forest Rd Cnr BA12 118 E7
Forest Wlk BA13 111 C4
Forester Cl 6 SN3 51 D4
Foresters Pk Rd SN12 94 C4
Forge Cl
Milton Lilbourne SN9 182 E7
Forge Cl *continued*
South Newton SP2 130 B1
Forge Fields SN5 48 D8
Forge La
West Overton SN8 173 F7
Zennor BA12 137 F3
Forge The RG17 177 C7
Forman St SN11 81 C3
Forrester Gn SN14 75 B3
Forsey Cl 4 SN3 51 E7
Fortis Hill SP7 203 C3
Fortune Way SN15 78 F5
Fortunes Field SN4 167 C7
Forty Acres Rd SN10 214 C3
Forty The SN6 19 D7
Forum Cl SN3 51 C8
Fosbury Hill Fort*
SN8 185 A3
Fosse Cl SN2 49 F6
Fosse Cotts SN16 27 A6
Fosse La BA1 82 A4
Fosseway Cl SN14 75 B3
Foster Rd BA11 110 A3
Fosters Bushes 4 SP4 217 D3
Fotherby Cres SP1 146 C4
Foundry La SN15 70 E1
Foundry Rd
3 Malmesbury SN16 28 A4
2 Redlynch SP5 211 C8
Fountain Mead 3 SP7 202 C2
Four Acre Cl SN6 18 A8
Fourmile Hill SP4 132 B3
Fovant Cl SN5 34 A1
Fovant Regimental Badges*
SP3 204 F7
Fowey SN5 49 A3
Fowler's Hill SP1 152 C8
Fowler's Rd SP1 152 B8
Fowlers La SN8 173 B1
Fox Brook SN4 47 F2
Fox Cl SN14 70 B1
Fox Croft Wlk SN15 78 F4
Fox Talbot Mus* SN15 86 D5
Fox Wood SN5 49 D5
Foxbridge SN3 51 D7
Foxbury 4 RG17 165 A1
Foxcote Gdns 2 BA11 110 C7
Foxcott SN6 8 C4
Foxcotte Cl SP10 193 C1
Foxcotte La SP11 193 C2
Foxcotte Rd SP10 193 C2
Foxglove Cl SN12 94 C3
Foxglove Dr BA14 101 E4
Foxglove Rd SN25 34 D5
Foxglove Way SN11 81 B5
Foxgrove SN14 70 A2
Foxleaze SN6 8 D1
Foxley Cl SN2 35 E4
Foxley Cnr SN10 180 D4
Foxley Fields SN10 180 C4
Foxley Rd Norton SN16 41 E8
St Paul Malmesbury Without
SN16 27 D2
Foyle Hill SP7 202 B1
Foyle Rd SP11 192 C2
Foyle's Mead BA12 201 E8
Frampton Cl SN5 49 B6
Frampton Ct BA14 105 A6
Francis Rd 10 SN10 179 F1
Francis St BA14 101 C1
Francis Way SP2 152 A5
Francomes SN25 34 E4
Francomes Field 17
RG17 165 A1
Frank Warman Ct 8 SN3 36 B3
Frankenbury* SP6 210 F2
Frankland Rd SN1 48 E3
Frankton Gdns 2 SN3 36 B2
Fraser Cl SN3 51 B7
Frederick Taylor Ct
BA12 116 F4
Free's Ave SN8 213 B5
Freegrove Rd SN15 73 F8
Freemans Cl 4 RG17 177 B7
Freesia Cl 2 BA12 116 E7
Fremantle Rd SP11 191 F4
French Mill La SP7 202 C1
French Mill Rise 16 SP7 202 C1
Frensham Way SN9 215 D6
Fresden Village* SN6 23 E4
Freshbrook Prim Sch
SN5 49 A3
Freshbrook Way SN5 49 B4
Freshford La BA2 99 A4
Freshford Sta BA2 99 C5
Freshford VC Prim Sch
BA2 99 B5
Friar's Orch 4 SP1 152 B8
Friars Cl BA13 112 C8
Friars The SN12 94 C6
Friary Cl BA15 99 E4
Friary La SP1 152 B7
Friary The SP1 152 B8
Fricker's La SP3 200 F3
Friday La SN9 181 D3
Friday St SN15 58 C3
Fridays Ham La SN6 7 B3
Friesian Cl SN5 49 A7
Friesland Cl SN5 49 A7
Friggle St BA11 110 D1
Frilford Dr SN3 36 A1
Frith Copse SN5 34 A2
Frobisher Dr SN3 50 F6
Frog La Avebury SN8 173 B8
Chilmark SP3 201 A3

Frog La *continued*
Great Bedwyn SN8 176 C3
Great Somerford SN15 44 B3
Hullavington SN14 41 F1
Longbridge Deverill BA12 121 A6
Motcombe SP7 202 B4
West Overton SN8 173 F7
Frogmore Rd BA13 108 F5
Frogwell
Chippenham SN14 77 F8
Chippenham Without SN14 77 E8
Frogwell Pk SN14 78 A8
Frogwell Prim Sch SN14 78 A7
Frome Com Coll BA11 110 A7
Frome Leisure Ctr BA11 110 A7
Frome Mkt BA11 107 C1
Frome Rd
Bradford-on-Avon BA15 100 C5
Maiden Bradley with Yarnfield BA12 118 D5
Southwick BA14 104 F3
Swindon SN25 34 F4
Trowbridge BA14 105 C7
Westwood BA15 100 C3
Wingfield BA14 104 C6
Frome Sta BA11 110 B4
Frome View BA12 118 E3
Front Horse Hill La SP7 203 A1
Front La SN26 21 A4
Front St RG17 171 E7
Fry Cl 2 SN1 49 F4
Fryern Ct Rd SP6 210 D3
Fugglestone SP2 144 F3
Fulford Rd BA14 101 E2
Fuller Ave SN13 84 E8
Fuller Cl SN2 35 F5
Fuller's Cl SN12 94 B5
Fullers Ave SN6 19 D8
Fullerton Wlk 6 SN1 49 F4
Fulmar Cl SN12 94 D1
Fulney Cl BA14 101 F2
Furlong BA12 117 B6
Furlong Cl Rowde SN10 96 E1
Swindon SN25 34 E5
Furlong Cres SP3 196 F7
Furlong Gdns BA14 101 E1
Furlong Way SP3 196 F7
Furnax La BA12 112 F1
Furse Hill Rd SP9 216 D5
Furze Cl SN5 34 A2
Furze Dr SP11 191 F3
Furze Hill La SN10 179 D7
Furzehill SN13 84 F8
Furzley La SO51 212 F3
Furzley Rd SO51 212 F2
Fussells Lodge (Long Barrow)* SP5 147 D5
Fyfield Ave SN2 35 C5
Fyfield Cl 2 SP1 146 D5
Fyfield La SP11 192 D1
Fyfield Rd SP11 192 E1
Fyfield Way SP11 191 F3
Fyne Cl 3 SN5 34 B2

G

Gable Cl SN2 35 B6
Gables Cl SN10 214 D2
Gabriel Cl 4 BA11 110 C6
Gains La SN10 214 B4
Gainsborough Ave SN4 47 F3
Gainsborough Cl SP2 145 C3
Gainsborough Rise BA14 105 A6
Gainsborough Way SN5 49 A3
Gairlock Cl SN5 34 B2
Gaisford Chase SN10 179 B4
Galahad Cl 25 SP10 193 E2
Gales Cl SN15 78 F8
Gales Gd SN8 213 F2
Galley La SN8 176 C3
Gallipoli Rd 8 SP4 198 F7
Galloway Cl 13 SN5 49 A7
Galloway Dr SN2 34 C5
Gallows Barrow* SP4 190 B3
Galsworthy Cl SN3 51 D4
Galton Way SN2 49 F8
Gambia St SN1 50 D6
Gamekeepers Cl SN25 34 F7
Gantlettdene SN3 51 E6
Ganton Way SN2 35 E1
Gardeners Gn 2 SP9 199 C8
Gardiner Rd 2 SP4 197 E6
Gardners Dr SN14 55 E8
Garendon Ct 2 SP6 210 D1
Garfield Cl SN3 51 C3
Garlings The 6 SN8 170 A6
Garrard Way SN3 51 A8
Garraways 6 SN4 47 F2
Garsdon Mill SN16 28 F5
Garston La 3 BA11 110 A4
Garston Rd BA11 110 A4
Garstons The BA1 82 D2
Garth Cl SN14 70 B3
Gartons Rd SN5 48 F7
Gas La Cricklade SN6 19 D8
Salisbury SP2 145 F1
Gascelyn Cl SN14 78 A7
Gascoigne's La SP7 202 C1
Gason Hill Rd SP9 216 C8
Gasper St BA12 137 C6
Gassons Rd GL7 2 C5
Gassons Way GL7 2 C4
Gaston La SN16 40 C8
Gaston's Rd SN14 78 C8
Gastons Rd SN16 27 F3
Gaters La SP4 133 A2
Gauntlet Rd SP4 217 B4
Gawaine Cl 3 SP10 193 E2
Gawthorne Dr SP2 151 F6
Gay's Pl SN2 35 F4
Gaynor Cl SN25 35 A6
Gaza Rd SP4 198 F7
Gdn The SN2 35 E5
Gdns The SN9 181 E3
Geneville Rise 3 SP4 217 C3
Genoa Ct 16 SP10 193 E2
Gentle St BA12 119 C7
George Cl SN11 81 C3
George Gay Gdns 7 SN3 50 F4
George La SN8 213 D2
George St (South) 6 SP2 145 F1
George St
Salisbury SP2 145 F1
Swindon SN1 50 A6
Trowbridge BA14 101 D1
Warminster BA12 117 A7
George VI Rd SP9 216 C8
George Ward Comp Sch SN12 93 F6
Gerard Wlk SN5 49 A6
Germain's La SN14 76 A8
Geys Hill BA12 115 A7
Giant's Cave (Long Barrow)* SN14 39 C2
Giant's Chair The (Tumulus)* SP5 158 E2
Giant's Grave*
Breamore SP6 210 C7
Aldbourne SN8 169 E7
Downton SP5 158 E3
Milton Lilbourne SN9 182 E5
Wilcot SN8 174 C2
Gibbs Cl 2 Salisbury SP1 146 C5
Swindon SN3 51 E7
Gibbs La SN14 55 F8
Gibbs Leaze BA14 102 A1
Gibson Cl SN12 94 C1
Gifford Rd SN3 36 B3
Gigant St Salisbury SP1 152 B8
Swallowcliffe SP3 204 A6
Gilbert Way SP1 146 C4
Gilbert's Gn 3 SP9 199 D8
Gilberts Hill Sch SN1 50 C5
Gilberts Piece SN8 183 E1
Giles Ave 1 SN6 19 D7
Giles La SO51 212 E7
Gilling Way SN3 51 D6
Gilman Cl SN25 35 A8
Gipsy La
Chippenham SN15 78 D6
Frome BA11 110 B7
Holt BA14 92 F2
Hungerford RG17 177 C8
Swindon SN2 50 E8
Warminster BA12 117 B5
Gisbourne Cl SP9 216 E6
Gladstone Rd
Chippenham SN15 78 D7
Trowbridge BA14 105 B7
Gladstone St SN1 50 C7
Glass's La SP3 204 D7
Glebe Cl
7 Aldbourne SN8 170 A6
Pitton & Farley SP5 148 C4
Glebe Field BA12 117 A6
Glebe Gdns SP7 202 A4
Glebe La Kemble GL7 4 F7
Landford SP5 212 C6
Glebe Pl RG17 171 A1
Glebe Rd
2 Durrington/Bulford SP4 198 B7
Trowbridge BA14 105 A7
Wootton Bassett SN4 47 D1
Glebe The
All Cannings SN10 180 F8
Calne SN11 81 C3
Freshford BA2 99 B4
Hinton Charterhouse BA2 98 D2
Glebe Way SN13 76 E1
Glebelands 3 BA12 194 C5
Glendale Cres SP1 152 D8
Glendale Rd SP4 198 C7
Gleneagles Cl SN15 78 F7
Glenfield Cl SP5 149 D6
Glenmore Rd
Haydon Wick SN25 34 C5
Salisbury SP1 146 C3
Glenside SN12 94 C6
Glenville Cl SN4 61 E8
Glenwood Cl SN1 50 C2
Glevum Cl SN5 33 C5
Glevum Rd SN3 36 C1
Globe St SN1 50 C4
Gloucester Cl 3 SN14 78 A6
Gloucester Rd
Calne Without SN11 81 F1
Malmesbury SN16 28 A4
Trowbridge BA14 105 B7
Gloucester Sq SN12 94 C4
Gloucester St SN1 50 B7
Gloucester Wlk BA13 109 A4
Glover Rd SP4 197 F7
Glyn Pl SP7 206 B7
Glyndebourne Cl SP2 145 C3
Goatacre La SN11 73 F7
Goddard Ave SN1 50 B4
Goddard Cl 1 SN9 215 C5
Goddard Pk Prim Sch SN3 51 A4
Goddard Rd SN9 215 C5
Goddards La 11 SN8 170 A6
Godley Rd SP2 152 A6
Godolphin Cl SN5 49 A3
Godolphin Prep Sch SP1 146 C1
Godolphin Sch SP1 152 C8
Godolphin Sch Douglas House SP1 146 C1
Godwin Rd SN3 36 B3
Godwins Cl SN12 84 E1
Gogg's La SP5 211 D7
Gold Hill 8 SP7 202 C1
Gold View SN1 49 F4
Golden Cross SP6 211 E4
Golding Ave SN8 213 A2
Goldney Ave SN14 78 C7
Goldsborough Cl SN5 49 B6
Gomeldon Medieval Village of* SP4 133 C4
Gomeldon Rd SP4 133 D5
Gomeldon Sch SP4 133 C4
Gooch Cl BA11 110 D6
Gooch St SN1 50 C7
Goodbody Rd 1 SP4 198 A6
Goodes Hill
Corsham SN13 85 D3
Melksham Without SN12 85 D2
Goodings La RG17 171 D6
Goodwin Cl BA12 117 E8
Goodwood Cl BA14 105 E4
Goodwood Way 3 SN14 77 F5
Goodwyns Cl 5 SP9 199 C8
Goor La SN8 164 B2
Goose Gn RG17 165 A2
Goose St Marston SN10 179 A3
Southwick BA14 105 A2
Gooselands
Crudwell SN16 14 D5
Westbury BA13 108 F2
Gordon Gdns 4 SN1 50 C6
Gordon Rd 5 SN1 50 C6
Gore Cross SN10 187 E5
Gore La BA13 111 B4
Gore Rd SP4 197 E7
Gores La SN9 181 C5
Gorringe Rd SP2 145 D1
Gorse Hill Jun Sch SN2 35 D1
Gosditch
Ashton Keynes SN6 17 E8
Latton SN6 8 C4
Goughs Way SN4 47 E2
Gould Cl 1 SP11 192 A5
Goulding Cl 3 SN3 36 B2
Gower Cl Swindon SN2 35 F2
1 Swindon SN5 48 F5
Gower Rd 14 SP7 202 D2
Grace Cl SP2 145 B5
Grace La SP6 211 A4
Graemar La SO51 162 E1
Grafton Pl SN8 183 F7
Grafton Rd
Burbage SN8 183 D7
Swindon SN2 35 C5
Graham St SN1 50 D7
Grailey Cl SN3 51 C4
Gramp's Hill OX12 165 F7
Gramshaw Rd 2 SP2 145 D2
Granary Cl 4 SN5 48 F8
Granary Rd 6 SN8 176 B3
Grand Ave SN8 175 E3
Grand Trunk Rd SP9 216 B4
Grandison Cl SN5 49 A6
Grange Cl
Atworth/Whitley SN12 85 D1
Fyfield SP11 192 D1
Highworth SN6 23 A5
Grange Dr SN3 36 B1
Grange Gdns SP1 146 C2
Grange Inf Sch SN3 36 B3
Grange Jun Sch SN3 36 B2
Grange La
St Paul Malmesbury Without SN16 43 B5
Warminster BA12 117 E5
Grange Pk Way SN5 48 F5
Grange Rd BA11 110 A7
Grange View BA15 100 E7
Granger Cl SN15 78 F4
Granham Cl SN8 213 D1
Granham Hill SN8 213 D1
Grans Barrow (Long Barrow)* SP6 209 E6
Grantham Cl SN5 49 B3
Granthams The 4 RG17 165 A2
Grantley Cl SN3 51 A3
Grants Rd SN9 190 A6
Granville Gdns 28 SP7 202 C2
Granville Rd SN12 94 A6
Granville St SN1 50 C6
Grasmere
Bower Hill SN12 94 D1
Swindon SN3 51 E3
Trowbridge BA14 101 E2
Grasmere Cl 1 SP2 151 F6
Graspan Rd 12 SP11 192 B5
Grateley Rd SP4 199 C5
Gravel Cl SP5 211 A8
Gravel The BA14 92 E1
Grays Cl SP7 202 A4
Grays Leaze BA14 105 C2
Graythwaite Cl 3 SN25 34 F6
Great Barn* SN8 167 B1
Great Bedwyn C of E Controlled Prim Sch SN8 176 C4
Great Chalfield Manor (National Trust)* BA14 92 D3
Great Croft SP5 148 C7
Great Dro SP4 132 F1
Great Hill BA9 137 B3
Great La SP7 202 C1
Great Lodge Dr SN8 175 B5
Great Parks BA14 92 F1
Great Roc Rd BA13 108 E3
Great Western Ave SP3 200 B1
Great Western Way SN5 48 F3
Great Wethers (National Trust)* SN8 174 A7
Greater La BA13 186 C8
Greatwoods BA13 186 C8
Green Acres 13 SN8 170 B2
Green Beeches SN12 93 D8
Green Cl
East Grafton SN8 183 F7
Holt BA14 101 F8
Whiteparish SP5 161 D4
Green Dro Fovant SP3 204 E8
Grimstead SP5 154 B4
Pewsey SN9 215 D3
Smannell SP11 193 E5
Green Farm Rise SN8 176 D7
Green Gate Rd SN10 180 D4
Green La Ashmore SP5 206 E4
Cheverell Magna SN10 179 C1
Codford BA12 195 A3
Colerne SN14 75 A3
Devizes SN10 214 B1
Downton SP5 211 A8
Fordingbridge SP6 210 D1
Hinton Charterhouse BA2 98 E1
Laverstock SP4 146 D8
Rockbourne SP6 210 C3
Salisbury SP1 146 D6
Sherston SN16 25 C1
Southwick BA14 104 D2
Steeple Ashton BA14 102 C1
Trowbridge BA14 105 E8
Westbury BA13 108 F2
Winsley BA15 99 E6
Green La Hospl SN10 214 B1
Green Mdw Ave SN25 34 F4
Green Pk La BA11 107 A6
Green Rd Codford BA12 195 A3
Corsham SN13 85 B4
Swindon SN2 35 E3
Green Ride BA12 123 E5
Green St SN8 167 C1
Green The
Alderbury SP5 153 C3
Biddestone SN14 76 E8
Brokenborough SN16 27 D7
Calne SN11 81 B2
Cheverell Magna SN10 179 C2
Dauntsey SN15 59 A8
Fairford GL7 1 F7
Highworth SN6 22 F5
1 Liddington SN4 163 A4
Lyneham & Bradenstoke SN15 60 A4
Oaksey SN16 15 F7
Pitton & Farley SP5 148 C3
Salisbury SP1 146 D2
Whiteparish SP5 161 D4
Green Valley Ave SN25 34 F4
Green's Ct 3 SP1 152 B8
Green's La SN4 64 B5
Greenacres
Dilton Marsh BA13 112 A8
2 Downton SP5 210 F8
Greenacres Way SN11 80 F4
Greenaway 4 SN4 163 A5
Greenbridge Ind Est SN3 51 A7
Greenbridge Rd SN3 51 A7
Greenbridge Ret Pk SN3 51 A8
Greencroft St SP1 146 B1
Greenfield Rd SN10 214 C1
Greenfields
Grimstead SP5 154 C2
Smannell SP11 193 F4
South Marston SN3 36 E5
Greenhill Gdns BA14 102 A4
Greenhill Rd SN2 34 E2
Greenhills BA13 186 C8
Greenhouse Rd SN10 180 F8
Greenland Cl SN12 92 E8
Greenland View BA15 100 D6
Greenlands 1 BA12 194 C5
Greenlands Cl 20 SP4 198 B7
Greenlands Rd SN2 35 E3
Greenlane Cl SP4 146 D6
Greenmeadow Prim Sch SN25 35 A4
Greens Cl SN14 41 F1
Greens La SN11 172 A8
Greens Meade 6 SP5 211 C7
Greensand Cl SN25 34 F7
Greenway SN4 60 F2
Greenway Ave SN15 70 D1
Greenway Cl SN3 51 B7
Greenway Dr SN15 73 F8
Greenway Gdns
Chippenham SN15 70 D1
Greenway Gdns *continued*
Trowbridge BA14 101 E3
Greenway La SN15 70 D2
Greenway Pk SN15 70 D1
Greenway Rd SN8 169 B1
Greenways RG17 165 A1
Greenwich Cl SN25 35 A5
Greenwood Ave SP1 146 D1
Greenwood Rd SN12 94 A3
Gregory Cl SN15 57 C1
Grenadier Cl 2 BA12 116 F7
Gresham Cl SN3 50 F6
Grey Wethers or Sarsen Stones* SN8 167 F2
Grey's Cnr BA9 136 A5
Greyfriars Cl SP1 152 B7
Greyhound La 1 SP2 144 D3
Greystones SN15 96 B8
Greywethers Ave SN3 50 E3
Grierson Cl SN11 81 B3
Griffin Alley 6 SN16 28 A3
Griffins Ct 3 SP2 146 A1
Griffiths Cl SN3 36 B1
Grimstead Beeches (National Trust)* SP5 160 D7
Grimstead Rd SP5 153 F1
Grindal Dr SN5 48 F5
Grittleton House Sch SN14 54 E4
Grocyn Cl SN14 75 B3
Grosmont Dr SN5 49 B5
Grosvenor Rd
Shaftesbury SP7 202 C2
Swindon SN1 50 A4
Ground Cnr BA14 101 D8
Groundwell Rd SN1 50 D5
Grove Hill SN6 23 A7
Grove La
Kington St Michael SN14 69 F8
Redlynch SP5 211 D8
Yatton Keynell SN14 69 A6
Grove Leaze BA15 100 B6
Grove Orch SN6 22 F7
Grove Prim Sch The BA14 105 B5
Grove Rd Corsham SN13 77 A1
Market Lavington SN10 179 F1
Sherston SN16 40 C8
Grove The
Codford St Peter BA12 195 A2
Crudwell SN16 4 C1
Penton Mewsey SP11 193 A2
Warminster BA12 117 A7
Grovelands Ave SN1 50 C3
Grovelands Way BA12 116 E7
Groveley Rd SP3 143 B3
Grovely Castle* SP3 128 F4
Grovely Rd SP3 129 E2
Grovely View SP2 144 B1
Groves St SN2 49 F6
Grundys SN3 51 D3
Gryphon Cl BA13 108 E3
Guilder La SP1 152 B8
Guildford Ave SN3 50 F3
Gullet The SN13 83 F7
Gulliver's La BA14 178 A4
Gundry Cl
Chippenham SN15 78 F5
Devizes SN10 214 C4
Gunner St SP4 198 E6
Gunsite Rd SN8 173 C6
Gunville Hill SP5 149 E6
Gunville Rd SP5 149 D6
Guppy St SN2 49 F7
Gurston Mdw SP5 205 A4
Gurston Rd SP5 205 A4
Guthrie CE Inf Sch SN11 81 C4
Guthrie Cl SN11 81 C4
Guyers La SN13 76 D2
Gwyns Piece 14 RG17 165 A2

H

Ha'penny Bridge* GL7 2 C3
Habrel's Cl SN15 78 F6
Hackett Cl SN2 35 E4
Hackleton Rise SN3 51 B8
Hackpen Cl SN4 64 B7
Hackthorne Rd SP4 198 B7
Haddon Cl 14 SN5 48 F5
Haddons Cl SN16 27 E2
Haden Rd 6 BA14 105 D7
Hadleigh Cl SN5 49 C6
Hadleigh Rise SN2 36 A5
Hadrian Rd 20 SP10 193 E2
Hadrians Cl
Salisbury SP2 145 C1
Swindon SN3 51 C8
Haig Cl SN2 35 E4
Haig Rd SP4 217 F8
Haimes La 20 SP7 202 C2
Hale House* SP6 211 A5
Hale La SP6 211 B5
Hale Prim Sch SP6 211 C6
Hale Rd SP6 211 A5
Hales Castle* BA11 114 D5
Hales Rd 6 SP4 190 A4
Half Hide Down SP5 207 B3
Half Mile Rd RG17 171 A5
Halfpenny La SP5 206 E4
Halfpenny Row BA11 103 E1
Halfway Cl BA14 101 F2
Halfway La SN8 170 C2
Halifax Cl SN4 64 A7
Halifax Rd SN12 94 C1
Hall Cl SN4 64 A6

Hallam Moor SN3 ....51 E2
Hallsfield SN6 ....8 D1
Hallum Cl SP1 ....146 D4
Halton Rd SP11 ....191 F4
Halve The BA14 ....101 D1
Ham Cl SN8 ....183 D3
Ham La Biddestone SN14 ....76 C8
Kempsford GL7 ....10 E6
South Cerney GL7 ....6 F6
Ham Rd Ham RG17 ....177 A2
Liddington SN4 ....163 A5
Ham The
Durrington/Bulford SP4 ....198 C7
Kington St Michael SN14 ....70 A8
9 Market Lavington SN10 ....179 F1
Westbury BA13 ....108 E5
Hambidge La GL7 ....2 C5
Hamble Rd SN25 ....34 F4
Hambleton Ave SN10 ....214 E6
Hamblin Mdw RG17 ....177 C8
Hamilton Cl
Amesbury SP4 ....217 E3
Swindon SN3 ....50 F7
Hamilton Dr
Chippenham SN14 ....77 F5
2 Market Lavington SN10 ....179 F1
Hamilton Pk 3 SP5 ....211 B8
Hamilton Rd SP1 ....146 A2
Hamlet Ct SN15 ....70 D1
Hamlet The SN15 ....70 E1
Hammer St BA10 ....122 C7
Hammond Way BA14 ....101 D4
Hammonds SN6 ....19 E8
Hampshire Cl
Durrington/Bulford SP4 ....217 E8
7 Swindon SN5 ....49 A7
Hampshire Gdns
BA13 ....109 A4
Hampshire Pl SN12 ....94 B5
Hampstead Way SN25 ....34 F7
Hampton Cl SN12 ....94 C1
Hampton Ct SP2 ....144 F2
Hampton Dr SN5 ....48 F5
Hamptworth Rd SP5 ....211 F6
Hamshill Ditches*
SP3 ....143 B7
Hamworthy Rd SN3 ....51 C6
Hanbury Rd SN3 ....51 A4
Hancock Cl SN15 ....79 A5
Handel St SN2 ....50 C8
Handley St SP5 ....204 D3
Hanging Bushes La
SP11 ....193 A1
Hanging Langford Camp*
BA12 ....201 F6
Hanging Stone* SN9 ....181 B7
Hangman's Stone*
RG17 ....164 F4
Hankerton Priory SN16 ....15 B4
Hankerton Rd SN16 ....16 C2
Hanks Cl SN16 ....28 A5
Hannington Cl SN2 ....35 B6
Hanover Cl BA14 ....101 E4
Harbour Cl SN25 ....34 F3
Harcourt Mews 5 BA11 ....110 A4
Harcourt Rd SN2 ....50 A8
Harcourt Terr SP2 ....151 F8
Hardenhuish Ave SN15 ....70 C1
Hardenhuish La SN14 ....70 B1
Hardenhuish Pk*
SN14 ....70 C1
Hardens Cl SN15 ....79 A5
Hardens Mead SN15 ....79 A6
Hardhams Rise SN13 ....84 F8
Hardie Cl SN3 ....36 A1
Harding St 6 SN1 ....50 B6
Hardwick Cl SN25 ....35 A5
Hardyfair Cl 5 SP11 ....192 F1
Hare Cl SN2 ....35 F5
Hare Knapp BA15 ....100 B6
Hare St Bremhill SN15 ....72 C5
Pewsey SN9 ....182 A7
Hare Warren Cl SP2 ....144 C1
Harebell Cl SN25 ....34 D5
Harefield Cres SP4 ....190 A2
Harepit Way* SN11 ....172 F7
Hares Patch SN14 ....70 B2
Haresdown Hill GL7 ....3 F7
Harford Cl 4 SN15 ....78 F5
Harford St 4 BA14 ....105 E8
Hargreaves Rd SN25 ....35 D6
Harlech Cl SN5 ....49 B4
Harlestone Rd SN3 ....51 B8
Harmony Pl 8 BA14 ....105 D7
Harnham CE Jun & Inf Sch
SP2 ....151 F6
Harnham Rd SP2 ....151 F7
Harnham Trad Est
SP2 ....151 D7
Harnish Way SN14 ....70 B2
Harnwood Rd SP2 ....151 E6
Harper Rd SP2 ....145 D2
Harper's La SN16 ....27 F3
Harptree Cl SN5 ....49 A8
Harriers The SN3 ....51 C7
Harrington Dr 4 SP4 ....198 E6
Harris Cl 5 RG17 ....165 A2
Harris La SN9 ....183 A7
Harris Rd
Ashton Keynes SN6 ....7 A1
Calne SN11 ....81 C5
Swindon SN2 ....35 A2
Harrow Cl SN3 ....36 A1
Harrow Gr SN15 ....60 B2
Harrow Way SP11 ....193 B1
Harrow Way Com Sch
SP10 ....193 C1
Harroway La SP11 ....193 B1
Hartfield SN10 ....214 A2
Hartham La SN13 ....76 E5
Harthill Dro SP5 ....211 D7
Hartington Rd SP2 ....145 E2
Hartland Cl SN3 ....51 A5
Hartley Way SP1 ....146 D5
Hartmoor Cl SN10 ....214 A2
Hartmoor Rd SN10 ....214 A2
Harts La SN14 ....76 E8
Harvard Cl
16 Bower Hill SN12 ....178 B8
1 Salisbury SP2 ....151 F5
Harvest La SP5 ....205 F4
Harvester Cl 7 SN5 ....48 F8
Harvey Gr SN2 ....34 F2
Hastings Ave SN9 ....182 B2
Hastings Cl SN9 ....182 B2
Hastings Dr SN15 ....60 B2
Hastings Rd SN13 ....85 A8
Hatch La SP3 ....203 C8
Hatchbury La SP11 ....185 C3
Hatcher's Cres SN26 ....21 B2
Hatches La SP1 ....152 D7
Hatchet Cl SP6 ....211 C6
Hatchet Hill SN4 ....163 D6
Hatchet La SP11 ....193 B5
Hatfield Cl SN25 ....34 E6
Hatfields SN10 ....181 A5
Hathaway Cl SP1 ....145 F4
Hathaway Rd SN2 ....35 E5
Hathaway Ret Pk SN15 ....78 E8
Hatherden CE Prim Sch
SP11 ....193 C5
Hatherell Rd SN15 ....78 F4
Hatherhall Cl SN3 ....36 C2
Hatherley Rd SN3 ....51 B7
Hathersage Moor SN3 ....51 E2
Hattem Pl 23 SP10 ....193 D2
Hatton Gr SN3 ....50 F6
Hatton Way SN13 ....76 E1
Havard Way 2 SP4 ....217 D2
Havelock St
Swindon SN1 ....50 B5
Trowbridge BA14 ....105 C7
Haven Cl SN3 ....51 B8
Havering La SN9 ....182 E7
Hawcroft BA14 ....92 E1
Hawfinch Cl SN3 ....51 E5
Hawk's Worth Cl 6
BA11 ....110 C7
Hawker Rd SN3 ....51 C4
Hawkeridge Pk BA13 ....108 E5
Hawkeridge Rd BA14 ....105 E2
Hawkesdene 17 SP7 ....202 C1
Hawkesdene La SP7 ....202 C1
Hawkins Cl SN15 ....78 F5
Hawkins Mdw SN8 ....213 B2
Hawkins Rd 16 SN8 ....170 A6
Hawkins St SN2 ....50 A7
Hawksridge 4 SP2 ....152 A5
Hawkstreet SN15 ....96 B6
Hawkswood SN3 ....51 D8
Hawksworth Way SN2 ....50 A7
Hawthorn Ave SN2 ....35 C2
Hawthorn Cl
Pewsey SN9 ....215 D5
1 Salisbury SP2 ....145 F1
2 Shaftesbury SP7 ....202 D2
Hawthorn Gr BA14 ....105 C5
Hawthorn Rd
Chippenham SN15 ....70 E1
Frome BA11 ....110 A6
Tidworth SP9 ....216 D7
Hay La Swindon SN5 ....48 F6
Wroughton SN4 ....48 F1
Hay St SN14 ....74 A8
Haydock Cl 4 SN14 ....77 F5
Haydon Ct SN25 ....34 E5
Haydon Ct Dr SN25 ....34 E5
Haydon End La SN25 ....34 D6
Haydon St SN1 ....50 C7
Haydon View Rd SN25 ....35 C3
Haydonleigh Dr SN25 ....34 E4
Haydonleigh Sch SN25 ....34 E5
Haydown Leas SP11 ....185 C3
Haye's La GL9 ....38 E2
Hayes Cl BA14 ....101 E3
Hayesdown Fst Sch
BA11 ....110 B5
Hayfield SN14 ....74 A8
Haynes Cl SN3 ....51 C4
Haynes Rd BA13 ....109 A3
Haywain 6 SP4 ....217 B3
Hayward Cl
Chippenham SN15 ....78 F5
Swindon SN25 ....35 A6
Hayward Pl BA13 ....108 F5
Haywards Pl SN10 ....179 F2
Hazel Cl
Marlborough SN8 ....175 A7
Salisbury SP2 ....145 B3
Hazel Copse 2 SN14 ....77 F6
Hazel End SN4 ....47 E1
Hazel Gr Calne SN11 ....81 B1
Swindon SN2 ....35 C3
Trowbridge BA14 ....105 B5
Hazel Way SN14 ....75 A5
Hazelbury Cres SN3 ....51 C7
Hazelbury Hill SN13 ....83 D6
Hazeldon La SP3 ....203 D6
Hazelwood Rd SN12 ....94 A3
Hazlemere Cl SN3 ....51 B4
Hazzard's Hill BA12 ....139 B5
Headlands Comp Sch
SN2 ....35 D3
Headlands Gr SN2 ....35 E3
Headquarters Rd
8 Durrington/Bulford
SP4 ....198 F6
Westbury BA13 ....108 C6
Heale Gdn* SP4 ....131 D5
Heath Cl BA12 ....115 B8
Heath La
Buttermere SN8 ....185 C7
Great Somerford SN15 ....43 D2
Heath Rd SP2 ....145 D4
Heath Sq 1 SP4 ....197 E6
Heath Way SN3 ....51 B8
Heathcote Rd SN12 ....94 C5
Heather Ave SN12 ....94 C4
Heather Cl BA13 ....108 F4
Heather Shaw BA14 ....105 E8
Heather Way SN11 ....81 C1
Heathfield SN15 ....70 E2
Heathfields Way 2 SP7 ....202 C2
Heathlands The BA12 ....116 F5
Heathway BA12 ....115 C8
Heaton Cl SN25 ....35 A6
Heaven's Gate* BA12 ....115 C1
Hebden Rd BA15 ....99 F3
Heddington CE Prim Sch
SN11 ....89 B1
Heddington Cl
Swindon SN2 ....35 B5
Trowbridge BA14 ....105 C5
Hedge Row SN15 ....79 A4
Hedgeditch La GL8 ....26 D7
Hedges Cl
1 Shipton Bellinger SP9 ....199 C8
Swindon SN3 ....36 B3
Hedges The 4 SN4 ....163 A6
Hedgesparrow La SN13 ....83 F8
Hei-lin Way 2 SP11 ....192 A5
Helena Terr SP1 ....146 B1
Helmdon Rd BA14 ....101 A1
Helmsdale SN25 ....34 F4
Helps Well Rd BA14 ....102 B2
Helston Rd SN3 ....51 A5
Henderson Cl BA14 ....105 B7
Henfords Marsh BA12 ....117 B4
Hengest Cl 5 SP10 ....193 C2
Henley Dr SN6 ....23 A7
Henley La SN13 ....83 C4
Henley Rd 2 SN3 ....51 A4
Henman Cl SN25 ....35 A5
Henn La SN15 ....57 C6
Henry St 1 SN1 ....50 B6
Henry's Garth 7 SN8 ....183 D8
Henset Village* SN8 ....175 E7
Hepworth Rd 5 SN25 ....34 F6
Herbert Rd
3 Redlynch SP5 ....211 C7
Salisbury SP2 ....145 C3
Hercules Way 1 SN12 ....178 B8
Herd St SN8 ....213 D4
Hereford Cl SN14 ....78 A5
Hereford Lawns SN3 ....50 F3
Herepath SN8 ....167 C1
Herman Miller Ind Est
SN14 ....78 B5
Hermitage La SN2 ....35 E3
Hernsham St SP7 ....203 C4
Herod Prim Sch SN2 ....34 E3
Heron Cl SN11 ....81 D3
Heron Way SN14 ....77 F6
Heron Wlk 12 SP4 ....198 C7
Heronbridge Cl 2 SN5 ....49 C5
Herongate RG17 ....177 B8
Herons Ct 6 SN12 ....178 B8
Heronscroft SN3 ....51 D7
Heronslade BA12 ....117 D5
Heronswood SP2 ....152 A5
Hertford Cl
1 Fordingbridge SP6 ....210 D2
4 Swindon SN3 ....50 F6
Hesketh Cres SN1 ....50 D3
Hewitt Cl Swindon SN3 ....51 C4
Trowbridge BA14 ....105 E7
Hewlett Cl SN15 ....79 A5
Hexham Cl
4 Chippenham SN14 ....77 F6
Swindon SN5 ....49 B5
Heyford Cl 8 SP4 ....217 E3
Heytesbury CE Sch
BA12 ....194 C5
Heytsbury Gdns 4 SN5 ....48 F4
Heywood Cl SN2 ....35 B5
Heywood Prep Sch The
SN13 ....77 A2
Hicks Cl SN4 ....64 A6
High Bannerdown BA1 ....82 B4
High La SP5 ....205 B4
High Lawn SN10 ....179 D8
High Mead SN4 ....47 F2
High Post Golf Club
SP4 ....132 C5
High Rd
Ashton Keynes SN6 ....6 F1
Bishopstone SP5 ....205 E4
Britford SP5 ....152 D4
High St Alderbury SP5 ....153 C3
Amesbury SP4 ....217 A3
Ansty SP3 ....203 F6
Ashbury SN6 ....164 A8
Ashmore SP5 ....206 E4
Avebury SN8 ....173 B8
Badminton GL9 ....38 E2
Bath BA1 ....82 D2
Berwick St James SP3 ....196 F2
Bishopstone SN6 ....163 E6
Box SN13 ....83 C5
Broad Blunsdon SN26 ....21 B1
Bromham SN15 ....96 A7
Bulford SP4 ....217 D8
High St *continued*
Burbage SN8 ....175 C1
Calne SN11 ....81 B3
Chapmanslade BA13 ....111 B4
Cheverell Magna SN10 ....179 C1
Chippenham SN15 ....78 D7
Chiseldown SN4 ....65 D4
Codford BA12 ....195 A2
Colerne SN14 ....75 B3
Collingbourne Ducis SN8 ....191 E8
Compton Chamberlayne
SP3 ....205 A8
Corsham SN13 ....77 A1
Cricklade SN6 ....19 E8
Damerham SP6 ....209 F3
Devizes SN10 ....214 A3
Downton SP5 ....211 B8
Durrington/Bulford SP4 ....198 B7
Erlestoke SN10 ....187 A8
Figheldean SP4 ....190 B1
24 Fordingbridge SP6 ....210 D1
Fovant SP3 ....204 E7
Great Bedwyn SN8 ....176 B3
Heytesbury BA12 ....194 C5
Highworth SN6 ....23 A5
Hindon SP3 ....200 A4
Hinton Charterhouse BA2 ....98 E1
Hungerford RG17 ....177 B7
Idmiston SP4 ....133 D5
Kempsford GL7 ....10 C7
Lacock SN15 ....86 D5
Lambourn RG17 ....164 F3
Lechlade GL7 ....2 C4
Limpley Stoke BA2 ....99 B5
Little Bedwyn SN8 ....176 D4
Littleton Panell SN10 ....187 D8
9 Ludgershall SP11 ....192 A5
Maiden Bradley with Yarnfield
BA12 ....118 E3
Malmesbury SN16 ....28 A3
Market Lavington SN10 ....179 F1
Marlborough SN8 ....213 A1
Melksham SN12 ....94 A4
Meysey Hampton GL7 ....1 A5
Netheravon SP4 ....190 A3
Ogbourne St George
SN8 ....168 F5
Pewsey SN9 ....215 D5
Pitton & Farley SP5 ....148 C3
Porton SP4 ....133 D6
Purton SN5 ....33 B4
Ramsbury SN8 ....170 B2
Rode BA11 ....103 F1
Rowde SN10 ....96 D2
Salisbury SP1 ....152 A8
Seend SN12 ....178 E8
Semington BA14 ....102 F6
18 Shaftesbury SP7 ....202 C1
Sherston SN16 ....40 C8
Sherston SN16 ....40 C8
Shipton Bellinger SP9 ....199 D8
Shrewton SP3 ....196 E7
Sixpenny Handley SP5 ....208 A4
South Cerney GL7 ....6 F6
Steeple Ashton BA14 ....178 A3
Stourton with Gasper
BA12 ....123 F1
Sutton Benger SN15 ....57 C2
Sutton Veny BA12 ....117 F1
Swindon SN25 ....34 E4
Swindon SN3 ....50 D4
Tilshead SP3 ....188 B2
Tisbury SP3 ....203 E8
Upavon SN9 ....181 F2
Urchfont SN10 ....180 C4
Wanborough SN4 ....163 B6
Warminster BA12 ....117 A7
West Lavington SN10 ....179 D1
Westbury BA13 ....109 A3
Westbury BA13 ....112 C8
Winterbourne Stoke SP3 ....197 A4
Woodgreen SP6 ....211 A4
Wootton Bassett SN4 ....47 D1
Worton SN10 ....179 B4
Wroughton SN4 ....64 A5
Wylye BA12 ....201 E8
Zeale SP8 ....137 F3
High St Brow SN8 ....169 A6
High View Cl SP3 ....203 E7
Highbury Ave SP2 ....145 E2
Highbury Cl 2 SP2 ....145 E2
Highbury Fst Sch SP2 ....145 E2
Highbury Pk BA12 ....117 C6
Highclere Ave SN3 ....50 F4
Highdown Way SN25 ....35 A7
Higher Barn Cl SP7 ....206 B7
Higher Blandford Rd 2
SP7 ....202 D1
Higher Mere Pk*
BA12 ....202 A8
Highfield SN15 ....96 C7
Highfield Cl BA14 ....102 F5
Highfield Cres SP5 ....149 B6
Highfield La 10 SP5 ....211 C7
Highfield Rd
Amesbury SP4 ....217 B3
Bradford-on-Avon BA15 ....100 D7
Salisbury SP2 ....145 E2
Highfield Rise 1 SP3 ....196 F6
Highfold SN4 ....47 F1
Highgate Cottage SN4 ....46 F5
Highgrove Cl SN11 ....81 D2
Highland Cl 8 SN5 ....49 A7
Highland View SP2 ....130 A2
Highlands SN10 ....179 D5
Highlands Cl SN13 ....84 A8
Highlands Rd SP2 ....152 A6
Highlands Way SP5 ....161 D4
Highmoor Copse SN5 ....34 A1
Highnam Cl SN3 ....36 A1
Highridge Cl SN5 ....33 A3
Highway Comm SN11 ....166 B6
Highway The SP5 ....158 F5
Highwood Cl 4 SN2 ....34 D4
Highworth Golf Club
SN6 ....22 F4
Highworth Rd
Highworth SN6 ....22 D1
Shrivenham SN6 ....23 E1
South Marston SN3 ....36 E6
Swindon SN3 ....36 A4
Highworth Recn Ctr
SN6 ....22 F5
Highworth Warneford Comp
Sch SN6 ....23 A5
Hill Beech Rd SP9 ....216 E7
Hill Cl 4 SP3 ....203 E8
Hill Cnr Rd SN15 ....70 E2
Hill Deverill Manor*
BA12 ....120 F5
Hill Deverill Medieval Village
of* BA12 ....120 F5
Hill Hayes La SN14 ....41 E1
Hill Moody's SP5 ....155 E3
Hill Rd SP1 ....146 E2
Hill Rise SN15 ....70 E2
Hill Side SP3 ....129 E8
Hill St BA14 ....101 C1
Hill The
Limpley Stoke BA2 ....99 C5
Little Somerford SN15 ....44 B6
Hill Top Ave SP9 ....216 C8
Hill Top Cl SP4 ....190 B2
Hill View SN8 ....181 B8
Hill View Rd
6 Salisbury SP1 ....152 B8
Swindon SN3 ....36 C1
Hillary Cl SN25 ....35 C4
Hillbourne Cl BA12 ....117 B7
Hillcrest Colerne SN14 ....75 C6
Malmesbury SN16 ....28 B2
Hilldrop Cl 1 SN8 ....170 B2
Hilldrop La
Lambourn RG17 ....171 A6
Ramsbury SN8 ....169 F3
Hilliers Yd SN8 ....213 D3
Hillingdon Rd SN3 ....51 B4
Hillmead Dr SN5 ....34 B1
Hillocks The SN4 ....60 B5
Hillside Leigh SN6 ....18 C5
Nettleton SN14 ....53 A4
Hillside Ave SN1 ....50 A4
Hillside Cl
Heddington SN11 ....89 B1
Mere BA12 ....138 E5
West Tytherley SP5 ....155 F2
Hillside Ct SN1 ....50 A4
Hillside Dr SP4 ....133 D3
Hillside Pk BA13 ....109 B3
Hillside Rd
4 Hungerford RG17 ....177 B6
South Newton SP2 ....130 B2
Hillside Way SN26 ....21 A1
Hilltop Cl 2 SP3 ....196 F6
Hilltop Way SP1 ....146 A5
Hillview SP5 ....204 C3
Hillview Cl SP4 ....217 B4
Hillwell SN16 ....15 B2
Hillwood Cl BA12 ....116 F5
Hillwood La BA12 ....116 F5
Hillwood Rd 15 SN8 ....170 A6
Hillworth Gdns SN10 ....214 A3
Hillworth Rd SN10 ....214 A2
Hillyard Cl 3 SN5 ....48 F4
Hilmarton Ave 1 SN2 ....35 C5
Hilmarton CP Sch
SN11 ....166 A6
Hilperton Dr BA14 ....102 A2
Hilperton Prim Sch
BA14 ....102 A4
Hilperton Rd BA14 ....101 E1
Hinde's Mdw SP3 ....196 F7
Hindon La SP3 ....200 D1
Hindon Rd
Chilmark SP3 ....201 B3
East Knoyle SP3 ....141 C2
Kingston Deverill BA12 ....126 D7
Hinton Hill
Bishopstone SN4 ....163 D6
Hinton Charterhouse BA2 ....98 A1
Hinton Ho* BA2 ....98 E1
Hinton La BA14 ....178 A5
Hinton Priory* BA2 ....98 F3
Hinton Springs SN6 ....163 D6
Hinton St SN2 ....50 D8
Hitchings Skilling SN14 ....75 B3
Hither Cl SN14 ....78 A8
Hither Spring SN13 ....84 F8
Hither Way SN15 ....86 D5
Hoadley Gn SP1 ....146 D4
Hobbes Cl SN16 ....27 F4
Hobbs Hill BA14 ....178 B5
Hobhouse Cl BA15 ....100 E4
Hobley Drive SN3 ....36 A3
Hocketts Cl SN15 ....60 A3
Hodds Hill SN5 ....34 B2
Hodge La SN16 ....27 F4
Hodges Barn Gdns*
GL8 ....26 F8
Hodson Rd SN4 ....65 C4
Hoggington La BA14 ....104 D4
Hoggs La SN5 ....33 A4
Holborn Hill OX12 ....165 E8

Holbrook La BA14 105 D6
Holbrook Sch BA14 105 D5
Holbrook Vale SN12 93 F1
Holbrook Way SN1 50 B6
Holcombe La BA2 82 A1
Holdcroft Cl SN26 21 C2
Holden Garson Rd SN2 35 B6
Holders Rd SP4 217 C4
Holford Cres GL7 10 E6
Holinshed Mews 3 SN5 49 A5
Holland Cl SN15 79 A4
Holland Dr 11 SP10 193 D2
Holliday Cl SN25 35 A6
Hollies La BA1 82 A6
Hollins Moor SN3 51 D2
Hollis Gdns SN14 39 E4
Hollis Way BA14 104 F3
Hollow La SN8 184 A7
Hollow St SN15 43 F2
Hollow The
Bratton BA13 186 A7
Chirton SN10 180 F4
Corsley BA12 111 B1
Dilton Marsh BA13 112 C8
Shrewton SP3 196 E7
Sixpenny Handley SP5 208 A4
Steeple Langford SP3 128 C5
Hollow Way SN15 59 D3
Holloway SN16 28 A3
Holloway Hill SN14 66 E8
Holloway La SP3 141 B1
Hollows Cl SP2 151 F6
Hollows The SP2 144 B4
Holly Cl Calne SN11 81 C1
Pewsey SN9 215 D6
Swindon SN2 35 A2
Holly Ct BA11 110 B7
Holly Dr SN14 74 F6
Hollybush Cl
Acton Turville GL9 53 A6
Chippenham Without SN14 70 A2
Winsley BA15 99 E7
Hollybush La SN9 215 D6
Hollybush Rd BA12 117 A8
Holmbury Cl BA11 110 C6
Holme La 7 BA13 186 B7
Holmeleaze BA14 178 A4
Holmes Cl SN15 78 F4
Holmfield 1 SN10 187 E8
Holmleigh SN25 34 E4
Holmoak Ct SN3 50 D4
Holt La Tangley SP11 193 B8
Teffont SP3 201 C2
Holt Prim Sch BA14 92 F1
Holt Rd
Bradford-on-Avon BA15 100 E6
Witham Friary BA11 123 C8
Holy Family RC Jun & Inf Sch SN3 51 B6
Holy Rd Church* SN3 50 E4
Holy Rood Inf Sch SN1 50 D5
Holy Trinity Sch
Calne SN11 81 C1
Cheverell Magna SN10 187 B8
Holyrood Cl BA14 105 B5
Holyrood RC Jun Sch SN3 50 D5
Home Cl Chiseldown SN4 65 C4
Trowbridge BA14 105 D7
Home Farm Cl
Mildenhall SN8 175 B8
Steeple Ashton BA14 178 A3
Home Farm Gdns 10 SP10 193 C2
Home Farm Rd SP2 144 C1
Home Fields SN14 68 F5
Home Gd Cricklade SN6 19 C8
Wootton Bassett SN4 48 A2
Homefarm SN6 22 F6
Homefield Mere BA12 138 F5
Motcombe SP7 202 C2
Wootton Bassett SN4 47 E2
Homefield Way RG17 177 B7
Homefields
Longbridge Deverill BA12 120 F6
Marlborough SN8 213 F2
Homelands The 1 BA12 116 E5
Homington Rd
Britford SP5 151 D3
Coombe Bissett SP5 157 B8
Honey Garston SN11 81 C3
Honey Hill 2 RG17 165 A2
Honey Knob Hill SN14 55 F1
Honey La Norton SN16 41 E6
Westbury BA13 112 D8
Honeybrook Cl SN14 78 B8
Honeybunch Cnr SN8 164 C6
Honeyfields 10 RG17 177 B7
Honeylight View 3 SN25 35 A6
Honeymans Cl BA14 105 F8
Honeymead SN11 81 C3
Honeysuckle Cl
Calne Without SN11 80 F4
Chippenham Without SN14 70 B3
Swindon SN25 34 D5
4 Trowbridge BA14 105 E7
Honiton Rd SN3 51 B5
Hook Cl SN5 34 A1
Hook St SN5 48 F4
Hooks Hill SN5 33 C4
Hooks La SN10 179 A7
Hookwood La SP11 192 E8
Hoopers Pl SN1 50 D4
Hopgood Cl SN10 214 F6
Hopkinson Way SP10 193 B1
Hops Cl SP3 201 A3
Hopton Cl SN5 49 B3
Hopton Ind Est SN10 214 E7
Hopton Rd SN10 214 D6
Horace St SN2 49 F7
Horcott Rd GL7 1 F6
Horham Cres SN3 51 A4
Horn's La SN4 167 B8
Hornbeam Cl 1 BA11 110 C6
Hornbeam Cres SN12 94 A3
Hornbury Cl SN16 17 A2
Hornbury Hill SN16 17 A2
Horne Rd SP4 198 E6
Horningsham CP Sch BA12 119 B7
Hornsey Gdns SN2 36 A5
Horse Barrow* SP4 133 D3
Horse Fair La SN6 19 E8
Horse Rd BA14 101 F4
Horse Shoe La SP3 142 C3
Horsebrook Pk SN11 81 B2
Horsebrook The SN11 81 C2
Horsefair La SN15 59 C3
Horsell Cl 2 SN4 47 E2
Horseponds 8 SP7 202 B2
Horsepool SN15 96 B8
Horseshoe Cres SN5 34 A1
Horseshoe La SP11 193 F8
Horton Ave SN10 214 E6
Horton Cl BA15 100 E4
Horton Rd
Bishops Cannings SN10 172 B2
Devizes SN10 214 F7
Swindon SN2 35 E6
Hospital Rd BA13 109 A2
Hossil La SN6 22 B1
Houldsworth Ave BA12 117 D8
Howard Cl SN3 50 F6
Howard-Vyse Rd SP4 197 F7
Howgare Rd SP5 205 B2
Hubert Hamilton Rd SP4 198 E6
Huddleston Cl SN2 50 D8
Hudson Rd
Amesbury SP4 217 C4
Malmesbury SN16 27 F4
Salisbury SP1 145 F3
Hudson Way SN25 35 A5
Hudswell La SN13 84 C8
Hughes Cl SN8 213 A2
Hughes St SN2 49 F7
Hugo Dr SN25 35 A6
Hulbert Cl SN13 76 E1
Hullavington Airfield SN14 56 A7
Hullavington Sch SN14 41 F1
Hulse Rd SP1 146 A2
Humber La SP9 216 B4
Humphrey's La 3 RG17 171 E7
Hungerdown La SN14 78 A6
Hungerford Ave BA14 105 A7
Hungerford CP Sch RG17 177 B7
Hungerford Hill
Great Shefford RG17 171 F4
Lambourn RG17 165 A1
Hungerford La
Andover SP10 193 E3
Chute SP11 185 A1
Kintbury RG17 177 F6
Tangley SP11 193 A8
Hungerford Leisure Ctr RG17 177 B6
Hungerford Rd
Buttermere SN8 185 B7
Calne SN11 81 B4
Chippenham SN15 70 D1
Grafton SN8 184 A7
Hungerford RG17 177 D6
Hungerford Sta RG17 177 C7
Hunsdon Cl SN3 51 A6
Hunt Cl The BA14 102 F5
Hunt St SN1 50 C5
Huntenhull La BA13 111 D4
Hunter's Gr SN2 35 B1
Hunters Mdw SN14 68 F5
Hunters Mead SP7 202 A5
Huntingdon Pl BA15 100 C7
Huntingdon Rise BA15 100 C7
Huntingdon St BA15 100 C8
Huntingdon Way SN14 78 A6
Huntley Cl SN3 50 F7
Hunts Hill SN26 21 B2
Hunts Mead SN15 96 A7
Hunts Mill Rd SN4 61 A8
Hunts Rise SN3 36 C7
Huntsland SN4 47 F2
Hurdcott La SP4 146 F8
Hurley Cl 5 SP4 217 D3
Hurricane Rd SN12 94 C1
Hurst Cres SN2 35 C3
Hurst's La SN9 181 C7
Huxley Ct GL7 7 A7
Hyam Cotts SN16 27 C4
Hyde La
Marlborough SN8 213 C3
Purton SN5 33 C4
Hyde Rd Swindon SN25 35 D6
Trowbridge BA14 101 C2
Hyde The SN5 33 D4
Hylder Cl SN2 34 D4
Hyson Cres 6 SP11 192 B5
Hysopp Cl SN2 34 C4
Hythe Rd SN1 50 B5

I

Icknield Way
Andover SP10 193 E2
Bishopstone SN6 163 E6
Icomb Cl SN5 49 C4
Idlebush Barrow* SN7 164 E7
Idmiston Prim Sch SP4 133 E6
Idmiston Rd SP4 133 E6
Idovers Dr SN5 49 C4
Idstone Hill SN6 163 F7
Idstone Rd SN6 164 A7
Iffley Rd SN2 49 F8
Iford Hill BA15 99 E2
Iford La BA15 99 D3
Iford Manor* BA15 99 E3
Iles Ct SN11 73 F7
Ilynton Ave SP5 148 C7
Imber Ave
Amesbury SP4 217 D2
Warminster BA12 117 C7
Imber Pl SP3 188 B3
Imber Rd Bratton BA12 186 C6
10 Shaftesbury SP7 202 D2
Warminster BA12 117 D8
Imberwood Cl BA12 117 C7
Imby Cl BA12 117 F1
India Ave SP2 145 E2
Indigo Gdns BA13 108 F3
Indigo La BA13 108 F3
Ingles Edge RG17 177 E2
Inglesham Cl 3 BA14 105 D5
Inglesham Rd SN2 35 C4
Inglesham Village* SN6 2 B1
Inglewood Rd RG17 177 E5
Ingram Pl BA13 108 F4
Ingram Rd SN12 94 D5
Ingram St SN16 28 A3
Inkpen Prim Sch RG17 177 E3
Inkpen Rd RG17 177 C5
Inlands Cl SN9 215 C5
Inmarsh La SN12 178 E7
Inmead BA13 186 C8
Innox Mill Cl BA14 101 B1
Innox Rd BA14 101 B1
Inverary Rd SN4 64 A7
Ipswich St SN2 50 C8
Irston Way 4 SN5 49 B4
Irving Way SN8 213 C2
Isbury Rd SN8 213 E2
Isis Cl SN25 35 A3
Islandsmead SN3 51 C6
Islay Cres SN6 22 F6
Isles Rd 6 SN8 170 B2
Islington BA14 101 D1
Islington St SN1 50 C6
Itchen Cl 2 SO51 212 F6
Ivies The SN9 181 F5
Ivy Field SN13 77 A2
Ivy La
Broad Blunsdon SN26 21 B2
South Wraxall BA15 91 E5
Ivy La Prim Sch SN15 78 D7
Ivy Lane SN15 78 D7
Ivy Mead BA12 139 B5
Ivy Rd SN15 78 D7
Ivy St SP1 152 B8
Ivy Terr BA15 100 D7
Ixworth Cl 10 SN5 49 A7

J

Jack Paul Cl BA12 139 A6
Jack Thorne Cl SN5 34 A2
Jack's Hedge Cnr BH21 208 F2
Jackaments Barn GL7 4 B6
Jacksom's La SN15 70 D5
Jackson Cl SN10 214 C2
Jacob's Barrow* SP5 211 E4
Jacobs Wlk SN3 51 D4
Jagdalik Rd SP9 216 C4
Jaggard View SP4 217 C3
Jaggards La SN13 84 D5
James Cl SN15 79 A4
James Rd SP4 217 C4
James St Salisbury SP2 145 F1
Trowbridge BA14 101 D2
James Watt Cl SN2 50 A7
James's Hill BA10 122 A7
Jamrud Rd SP9 216 B5
Jarvis St SN9 181 F2
Jasmine Cl Calne SN11 81 B1
Chippenham SN14 70 A1
Swindon SN2 34 D4
Jasmine Way BA14 105 E7
Javelin Cl 6 SP4 217 D3
Jay Cl BA11 110 B6
Jeanneau Cl 24 SP7 202 C2
Jefferies Ave SN2 35 D2
Jefferies Cl SN8 213 B2
Jenkins St BA14 101 C1
Jennings St SN2 49 F6
Jersey Pk SN5 49 B8
Jewel Cl 2 SN5 48 F5
Jewell Cl SP1 146 D4
Joanna Cl 4 SP5 210 F8
Jobbers La SP3 203 E7
Jockey La SN15 96 A7
John Aubrey Cl SN14 68 F6
John Bentley Sch The SN11 81 B1
John Betjeman Cl 1 SN16 28 A5
John French Way SP4 217 E8
John Gay Rd 5 SP4 217 B3
John Herring Cres SN3 36 A1
John O'Gaunt Sch RG17 177 B6
John of Gaunt Rd GL7 10 D6
John of Gaunt Sch The BA14 105 B7
John Rennie Cl
Bradford-on-Avon BA15 100 E4
Devizes SN10 214 A2
John Rumble Cl SN10 214 C3
John St SN1 50 B6
Jole Cl SN2 35 E5
Joles La BA11 110 F1
Jolliffe St 8 SN1 50 A5
Jones Hill BA15 100 C5
Jordan Cl SN15 78 F5
Joseph St 5 SN1 50 A5
Joule Rd 3 SP10 193 B1
Joyce Cl SN2 35 A6
Jubb's La SN8 169 A5
Jubilee Cl
3 Sandleheath SP6 210 C1
Westbury BA13 109 A3
Jubilee Ct 3 SP2 145 F2
Jubilee Gdns GL7 6 F7
Jubilee Hill SP4 197 F1
Jubilee Rd
Sandleheath SP6 210 C1
Swindon SN2 34 D3
Juggler's La SN11 166 C2
Juliana Cl 2 SN5 49 A7
Jump Farm Rd SN10 214 C3
Junction Rd
Alderbury SP5 153 E3
Bradford-on-Avon BA15 100 D6
Juniper Cl SN3 51 B8
Juniper Dr SP1 146 A5
Juniper Rd SP5 148 C7
Juno Way SN1 49 F4
Jutland Cres 3 SP10 193 D2

K

Kandahar SN8 170 A7
Kandy Rd 3 SP4 198 E6
Karachi Cl SP9 216 C7
Karslake Cl 6 SN3 51 C4
Kashmir Rd 1 SP4 198 E6
Katherine's Wlk GL7 2 D4
Katifer La SN16 28 A3
Keates Cl BA14 101 D1
Keats Cl SN4 47 F3
Keble Cl Lechlade GL7 2 D5
Swindon SN3 51 C7
Keels SN6 8 C1
Keevil Airfield BA14 178 C4
Keevil Ave SN11 81 A3
Keevil CE Sch BA14 178 B5
Kelham Cl 8 SN3 50 F4
Kelham Gdns SN8 213 E3
Kellsborough Rd SN4 63 F7
Kelly Gdns SN25 34 F6
Kelmscot Rd SN25 35 C3
Kelsey Rd SP1 146 B1
Kelso Ct 3 SN14 78 A5
Kelston Rd SN8 176 C4
Kelvin Rd SN3 51 A7
Kemble CP Sch GL7 4 F7
Kemble Dr SN2 50 A7
Kemble Sta GL7 4 F8
Kembles Cl SN16 28 C2
Kembrey Bsns Pk SN2 35 E2
Kembrey St SN2 35 D2
Kemmel Rd SP11 191 F4
Kemp Cl SN10 214 C3
Kemp's La BA11 110 F7
Kempsfield SN10 214 C1
Kempton Pk Ct 10 SN14 77 F6
Kendal SN5 49 B4
Kendrick Cl BA13 109 A3
Kenilworth Gdns SN12 94 B3
Kenilworth Lawns SN3 50 F3
Kennedy Ave SN12 85 D1
Kennedy Dr SN3 51 D4
Kennel Dr GL9 38 E2
Kennet Ave SN25 35 B3
Kennet Cl
Melksham SN12 94 A6
Warminster BA12 117 A5
Kennet Ct RG17 177 C8
Kennet Gdns BA15 100 D5
Kennet Mews SN8 213 E3
Kennet Pl SN8 213 E3
Kennet Rd
South Tedworth SP9 216 E6
Wroughton SN4 64 A7
Kennet Way
Hungerford RG17 177 B8
Trowbridge BA14 101 D3
Kensington Cl BA14 101 D2
Kensington Fields BA14 104 F7
Kensington Rd 1 SP2 145 F2
Kensington Way SN14 77 F7
Kent Cl SN14 78 A6
Kent End SN6 7 A1
Kent Rd Salisbury SP2 151 E6
Swindon SN1 50 B4
Kenton Cl SN3 51 B6
Kenton Dr BA14 101 F1
Kents Hill SP3 201 A3
Kenwin Cl SN3 36 B2
Kenwood Cl BA14 105 F8
Kerby Ave SP4 190 B3
Kerrs Way SN4 64 A6
Kerry Cl
Derry Hill/Studley SN11 79 F2
Swindon SN5 49 A7
Kershaw Rd SN3 51 C4
Kestrel Cl SP9 216 E7
Kestrel Dr SN3 51 E6
Keswick Rd SN3 51 B3
Kettle La BA14 106 A2
Ketton Cl BA14 101 A1
Kew Dr 4 BA14 105 A7
Kewlake La SO51 212 F1
Keynes Ctry Pk* GL7 6 B5
Keyneston Rd SN3 50 F5
Kibblewhite Cl SN5 33 B3
Kickdom Cl SP4 217 D2
Kidston Way SN13 84 A8
Kiel Dr SP10 193 D2
Kilben Cl SN5 48 F7
Kilda Rd SN6 22 E7
Kill Barrow (Long Barrow)* BA12 187 D3
Kilmington CE Fst Sch BA12 123 E6
Kiln Cl SP5 153 F1
Kiln La Redlynch SP5 211 D8
Swindon SN2 34 F1
Kilns The SN11 81 C4
Kilsby Dr SN3 51 B8
Kilsyth Cl SN5 49 B5
Kilverts Cl SN14 78 A6
Kimberley Rd SN3 51 A4
Kimbolton Cl 6 SN5 49 A4
Kimmeridge Cl SN3 51 C6
Kimpton CE Prim Sch SP11 192 C1
King Alfred Cl SN9 215 D5
King Alfred St SN15 78 C8
King Alfred Way BA15 99 D7
King Alfred's Mid Sch SP7 202 D2
King Alfreds Cl BA12 126 B7
King Arthur's Way SP10 193 E2
King Barrow*
Bishopstrow BA12 117 F5
Winterbourne Stoke SP4 197 C4
King Charles Rd SN5 49 B4
King Henry Dr
Chippenham SN15 79 A4
Swindon SN5 48 F4
King John St SN1 50 D4
King John's Ho* SP5 207 B4
King La BA12 116 E5
King Oak* SN8 175 C4
King St Melksham SN12 94 A3
3 Swindon SN1 50 B6
Warminster BA12 116 E5
Wilton SP2 144 D4
King William St SN1 50 C4
King William St CE Prim Sch SN1 50 C4
King's House* SP1 152 A7
King's La SP3 203 F5
King's Rd SP1 146 A2
King's Wall SN16 28 A3
Kingdown Comp Sch BA12 117 D6
Kingfisher Cl SP2 152 A5
Kingfisher Dr
Bower Hill SN12 94 D1
Devizes SN10 214 E5
7 Durrington/Bulford SP4 198 C7
Swindon SN3 51 D7
Westbury BA13 109 A4
Kingfishers 2 SP9 199 D8
Kingham Cl SN14 78 C7
Kings Ave
Chippenham Without SN14 77 F6
Corsham SN13 76 F2
Highworth SN6 23 A5
Kings Ct 5 BA12 116 E5
Kings Dr SN8 175 C8
Kings Gate SP2 144 E4
Kings Gdns BA14 101 E5
Kings Hill 18 SP7 202 C2
Kings Lodge Sch SN15 79 A5
Kings Mdw SN16 14 D5
Kings Paddock SP5 149 A5
Kings Rd
Easterton SN10 180 A2
Enham Alamein SP11 193 E4
Market Lavington SN10 179 F2
Kings Rise BA12 116 E5
Kingsbere La 5 SP7 202 D2
Kingsbourne Cl SP4 133 B1
Kingsbury Cl SN12 94 B3
Kingsbury Hill House Sch SN8 213 D3
Kingsbury Sq 3 SP2 144 D3
Kingsbury St
Calne SN11 81 B2
Marlborough SN8 213 D3
Kingscote Cl 1 SN5 48 F8
Kingsdown Golf Club SN13 83 A3
Kingsdown Gr BA1 82 F2
Kingsdown La SN2 35 D8
Kingsdown Rd
Stratton St Margaret SN2 36 A6
Swindon SN2 35 F5
3 Trowbridge BA14 105 C5

Kingsdown Sch SN2 .....35 F5
Kingsettle Hill BA10 ....122 C2
Kingsfield BA15 ....100 D7
Kingsfield Grange Rd
BA15 ....100 E7
Kingsford Cl 9 SP5 .....211 C7
Kingshill Rd SN1 ....50 A4
Kingsland Rd SP2 ....145 F2
Kingsley Ave SN4 ....47 E3
Kingsley Gdns SN10 .....214 C3
Kingsley Pl BA14 ....100 F1
Kingsley Rd
Chippenham SN14 ....78 B6
Devizes SN10 ....214 C3
Kingsley Way SN2 ....35 D5
Kingsman La 13 SP7 ....202 C1
Kingsmanor Wharf
SN10 ....214 D5
Kingsmead GL7 ....2 C5
Kingsmead House
SN15 ....44 A5
Kingsmead Mill* SN15 ...43 F6
Kingston SN16 ....43 F8
Kingston Ave BA15 ......100 E5
Kingston La BA12 ....118 F2
Kingston Rd
Bradford-on-Avon BA15 ...100 D6
Shalbourne SN8 ....176 F1
Swindon SN3 ....51 A4
Kingsway Preshute SN8 ..168 B1
Wilton SP2 ....144 E5
Kingsway Cl 1 SN3 ....50 F4
Kingswood BA14 ....104 F6
Kingswood Ave SN3 ....51 A5
Kington La SN14 ....56 B4
Kington St Michael CE Prim
Sch SN14 ....70 A8
Kingway View SN16 ....42 E4
Kintbury Rd RG17 ....177 F3
Kipling Gdns SN2 ....35 E4
Kirby Cl SN3 ....50 F4
Kirby Rd SN13 ....76 E1
Kirkee Rd SP9 ....216 C5
Kirkstall Cl SN5 ....49 C4
Kirktonhill Rd SN5 ....49 D6
Kishorn Cl 5 SN5 ....34 B2
Kitchen Barrow*
SN10 ....172 E3
Kitchener Rd SP4 ....217 B4
Kitchener St SN2 ....50 C8
Kite Hill SN4 ....163 A5
Kite's Nest La SP8 ......137 E2
Kitefield 2 SN6 ....19 D8
Kivel Ct SP2 ....146 A2
Kiwi CP Sch SP4 ....198 E6
Kiwi Rd 6 SP4 ....198 F7
Kiwi The* SP4 ....198 F6
Knap Barrow (Long
Barrow)* SP6 ....209 D6
Knap Hill (Causewayed
Enclosure)* SN8 ......173 E2
Knap La SP3 ....200 F2
Knap The BA14 ....102 A3
Knapp Cl SN2 ....35 A2
Knapp Hill SP5 ....205 A4
Knapp The Calne SN11 ....81 C3
Great Bedwyn SN8 ....176 B3
7 Shaftesbury SP7 ......202 B2
Knapps The BA14 ....102 F5
Knighton Barrow (Long
Barrow)* SP4 ....197 E8
Knighton Rd SP5 ....205 C4
Knights Cl
1 Chippenham SN15 ......78 F4
West Overton SN8 ....173 F6
Knights Enham Inf Sch
SP10 ....193 E2
Knightsbridge Rd
SP11 ....193 F4
Knockdown Rd SN16 ....25 C1
Knoll Cl OX12 ....165 F8
Knoll The
12 Aldbourne SN8 ....170 A6
Kempsford GL7 ....10 D7
Westbury BA13 ....109 B4
Knook Barrow (Long
Barrow)* BA12 ....194 F7
Knook Castle* BA12 ....195 A7
Knook Manor* BA12 .....194 D4
Knowlands SN6 ....23 A7
Knowle The SN13 ....84 F8
Knowledge Hill 2 SN8 ...170 B2
Knowsley Rd SN3 ....51 A4
Kohat Cl SP9 ....216 B7
Komat Rd SP9 ....216 C5
Kyneton Way SN14 ....70 A8

L

La Retraite Sch SP1 .....146 B2
Labour-in-Vain Hill
SN11 ....172 A8
Laburnam Dr SN4 ....47 E3
Laburnum Cl 3 BA11 ....110 B7
Laburnum Dr SN12 ....94 A3
Laburnum Gr BA14 ....105 B6
Laburnum Rd SN2 ....35 C3
Lacemakers Rd SN16 ......28 A5
Lackham Cir SN14 ....78 B6
Lackham Coll SN15 ....78 E1
Lacock Abbey* SN15 .....86 D5
Lacock Gdns BA14 ....102 B2
Lacock Prim Sch SN15 ....86 D5
Lacock Rd
Corsham SN13 ....85 D8
Swindon SN2 ....35 C4
Ladbrook La SN13 ....77 C1
Ladds La SN15 ....78 E7
Lady Coventry Rd SN15 ...78 F7
Lady Diana Ct 15 SP11 ..192 A5
Lady Down View 5 SP3 ..203 E8
Lady Godley Cl SP9 .....216 C5
Lady Jane Wlk 22 SP11 ..192 A5
Lady La SN25 ....21 B1
Lady Mead SN6 ....19 D8
Ladyfield Rd SN14 ....78 B7
Ladysmith SP4 ....133 D3
Ladysmith Rd
Chiseldon SN4 ....65 D1
Salisbury SP2 ....145 D3
Ladywood 8 SN10 ....179 F1
Laggar The SN13 ....77 A2
Lagos St 3 SN1 ....50 C7
Lagpond La SP3 ....204 B7
Lahore Cl SP9 ....216 C7
Lahore Rd SP9 ....216 C5
Laines Head SN14 ....70 C2
Lainey's Cl SN8 ....213 D4
Lainsmead Jun & Inf Sch
SN3 ....50 E5
Lake Group (Tumuli)*
SP4 ....197 D3
Lake House* SP4 ....197 F1
Lakeside Fairford GL7 .....1 F6
South Cerney GL7 ....7 B7
Swindon SN3 ....50 E3
Lakeside Cl SP10 ....193 C1
Lamb Ale Gn BA14 ....105 D6
Lambdown App SP11 .....191 F3
Lambdown Terr
North Tidworth SP11 ....216 F6
Perham Down SP11 ....191 F4
Lambert Cl SN5 ....49 B3
Lamberts SN14 ....78 A8
Lambourn Ave SN3 ....50 E3
Lambourn CE Prim Sch
RG17 ....165 A1
Lambourn La BA13 ....186 C8
Lambourn Pl 10 RG17 ....165 A2
Lambourne Cres SN12 .....94 B4
Lambrok Cl BA14 ....104 F6
Lambrok Rd BA14 ....104 F6
Lammas Cl SN11 ....166 A6
Lamora Cl 12 SN5 ....48 F8
Lanac Rd SN3 ....36 A1
Lancaster Cl 6 RG17 ....177 B6
Lancaster Mews SN3 ......36 C6
Lancaster Pl SN3 ....36 C6
Lancaster Rd
Bower Hill SN12 ....94 B1
Kempsford GL7 ....10 E6
Wroughton SN4 ....64 A6
Lancaster Sq
Hungerford RG17 ....177 B6
Lyneham SN15 ....60 A2
Landale Cl 3 SP11 ......193 E4
Landford CE Prim Sch
SP5 ....212 C6
Landor Rd SN25 ....34 F8
Lane The SN4 ....163 C7
Lane's Cl SP4 ....217 C4
Lane-side 9 SP7 ....202 C2
Lanes End SN13 ....85 D5
Lanes End Hill BA12 ....115 A8
Lanfear Cl SP4 ....217 C4
Langdale Dr SN5 ....49 B3
Langet GL7 ....6 E6
Langford Gr SN3 ....50 E6
Langford La SP5 ....160 A3
Langford Rd
Great Wishford SP2 .....129 F4
Trowbridge BA14 ....101 C2
Langfords La 3 SP7 ....202 B1
Langham Pl BA11 ....103 F1
Langholm Ave BA12 .....116 D6
Langholm Cl BA12 ......116 D6
Langley Fitzurе CE Sch
SN15 ....70 E6
Langley Gdn SP6 ....210 E2
Langley Rd
Chippenham SN15 ....70 E1
Swindon SN5 ....34 B1
Trowbridge BA14 ....105 C5
Langport Cl 1 SN5 ....49 B4
Langstone Way SN5 ....49 C6
Lanham's Cl BA13 ......109 A2
Lanhill (Long Barrow)*
SN14 ....69 B2
Lanhill View SN14 ....70 B2
Lanhydrock Cl 9 SN5 ....49 A4
Lansbury Dr SN2 ....35 F4
Lansdown Cl
Melksham SN12 ....94 D6
Trowbridge BA14 ....105 B7
Lansdown Gr SN15 ....70 D1
Lansdown Rd SN1 ....50 B4
Lansdowne Cl SN11 ....81 A4
Lansdowne Cres SN11 .....79 F2
Lapwing Cl 1 SN3 ....51 E6
Lapwing Cres SN14 ....70 B2
Larch Cl SN12 ....94 A3
Larch Gr BA14 ....105 B6
Larch Rd SN14 ....74 F6
Larch Row SP6 ....210 F1
Larchfield Cl BA11 .....110 B7
Larchmore Cl SN25 ....35 A3
Lark Cl SP9 ....216 D7
Lark Down BA14 ....101 E1
Larkham Rise SN15 ....78 F6
Larkhill CP Sch SP4 ....197 E7
Larkhill Rd SP4 ....198 B7
Larkrise Sch BA14 ......101 F1
Larksfield SN3 ....51 C8
Larmer Tree Victorian
Pleasure Garden*
SP5 ....207 B3
Late Broads BA15 ....99 D7
Latimer Gdns SN14 ....41 E1
Latton Cl SN2 ....35 B6
Laughton Way SN25 ....35 A6
Launcelot Cl 22 SP10 ...193 E2
Laundry La 5 SP7 ....202 B1
Laurel Cl BA11 ....110 B7
Laurel Dr Colerne SN14 ...74 F6
Marlborough SN8 ....213 F2
Laurel Gr BA14 ....105 C6
Laurels The
Hungerford RG17 ....177 C8
Melksham Without SN12 ...86 A1
Westwood BA15 ....99 F3
Laurence Ct 10 SP11 ....192 A5
Lavender Cl
Melksham SN12 ....94 C3
5 Trowbridge BA14 .....105 E7
Lavender Ct BA11 ....110 B7
Lavender Dr SN11 ....81 B1
Laverstock Pk SP1 ......146 D1
Laverstock Pk W SP1 ...146 D2
Laverstock Rd SP1 ......146 C1
Laverton Gn 3 BA13 ....108 F1
Laverton Rd BA13 ....108 F1
Lavington Cl 10 SN8 ...183 D8
Lavington Hill SN10 ....187 F8
Lavington La SN10 ......187 E8
Lavington Sch SN10 .....179 E1
Lawn Farm Cl SN9 ....182 E7
Lawn Jun & Inf Sch
SN3 ....50 F2
Lawns The SN4 ....47 D2
Lawrence Cl
4 Amesbury SP4 ....217 C3
Devizes SN10 ....214 C1
Swindon SN3 ....51 C4
Lawrence Mead 3 SN8 ...170 B2
Lawrence Rd SP4 ....197 F7
Lawson Rd 3 SP4 ....198 A6
Lawton Cl SN3 ....51 A3
Layton La SP7 ....202 C1
Le Marchant Cl 2 SN10 .214 D5
Lea Cl SN25 ....35 A7
Lea House SN16 ....28 D1
Leaden Hall Sch SP2 ....152 A7
Leafield Ind Est SN13 ...84 E6
Leafield Pl BA14 ....100 F1
Leafield Rd SN13 ....84 E6
Leafield Way SN13 ....84 E6
Leafy La SN13 ....76 A1
Leamington Gr SN3 ....50 F2
Leap Gate
Hilperton BA14 ....102 A1
Trowbridge BA14 ....106 A8
Leatler Cl SP3 ....204 D8
Leaze Rd
Marlborough SN8 ....213 C4
Melksham SN12 ....94 C6
Leaze The
Ashton Keynes SN6 ....6 F1
Durrington/Bulford SP4 ..217 E8
South Cerney GL7 ....6 F6
Lechlade Rd Buscot SN7 ....2 E2
Highworth SN6 ....23 A7
Inglesham SN6 ....12 A6
Ledge Hill SN10 ....179 E2
Ledger Hill Cl SP4 .....217 D8
Lee Cres SN15 ....57 C1
Legate Cl SN15 ....79 B5
Leicester St SN1 ....50 D6
Leigh CE Sch SN6 ....18 C5
Leigh Cl BA13 ....108 E1
Leigh La SP3 ....202 E8
Leigh Pk Rd BA15 ....100 D8
Leigh Rd
Bradford-on-Avon BA15 ....91 E1
Holt BA14 ....92 C1
Swindon SN2 ....35 C4
Westbury BA13 ....108 F2
Leighton Ave SN3 ....50 F4
Leighton Gn BA13 ....109 A2
Leighton La BA13 ....109 A1
Leighton Pk N 4 BA13 ..108 F1
Leighton Pk Rd 5 BA13 .108 F1
Leighton Pk W 2 BA13 ..108 F1
Leighton Recn Ctr
BA13 ....109 A2
Leland Cl 5 SN16 ....28 A5
Lena Cl 26 SP11 ....192 A5
Lennards The GL7 ....7 A7
Lennox Dr SN3 ....50 E6
Lenton Cl SN14 ....77 F7
Leonard Cheshire Cl 4
SP4 ....217 D2
Leslie Cl SN5 ....49 A4
Leslie Rise BA15 ....99 F3
Lethbridge Prim Sch
SN1 ....50 C3
Lethbridge Rd SN1 ....50 C3
Letterage Rd SN5 ....34 A2
Levell Ct 12 SP11 ......192 A5
Leven SN5 ....49 A3
Leversedge Rd 2 BA11 ..110 A7
Leverton Gate SN3 ....50 F1
Leverton La RG17 ......171 B1
Lewington Mews 14
RG17 ....177 B6
Lewisham Castle*
SN8 ....169 E4
Lewisham Cl SN25 ....34 F3
Ley The SN13 ....83 D5
Leylands Rd SN13 ....76 B1
Leys Hill BA11 ....110 A6
Leys La BA11 ....110 A6
Leystone Cl BA11 ......110 A6
Lichen Cl 3 SN2 ....34 D4
Lickhill Rd SN11 ....81 A4
Lidbury Camp* SN9 .....190 C8
Liddiards Gn SN8 ....168 F5
Liddington Castle (Fort)*
SN4 ....163 A2
Liddington St SN2 ....35 C3
Liddington Way BA14 ...105 D5
Liden Dr Swindon SN3 ....51 D4
Swindon SN3 ....51 E4
Liden Infs Sch SN3 ......51 D3
Liden Jun Sch SN3 ....51 D3
Lidenbrook 2 SN4 ....163 A4
Light Cl SN13 ....77 A2
Light's La SP5 ....153 C2
Lightfoot Rd SP4 ....197 F7
Lightning Rd 1 SP4 ....217 D2
Liguiel Cl 9 RG17 .....177 B6
Lilac Gr BA14 ....105 B5
Lilac Way SN11 ....81 B1
Lillywhite Cres 1 SP10 .193 E2
Lily Wlk 11 SP4 ....198 C7
Lime Ave Badminton GL9 ...38 C1
Melksham SN12 ....94 A3
Lime Cl Colerne SN14 ....75 A5
Frome BA11 ....110 B7
Lyneham & Bradenstoke
SN15 ....60 C2
Lime Kiln SN4 ....47 D3
Lime Kiln Sports Ctr
SN4 ....47 D3
Lime Kiln Way SP2 .....152 A5
Lime Tree Cl SN11 ....81 A3
Lime Trees SN15 ....58 A2
Limekiln Rd SP11 ....192 E6
Limes Ave SN2 ....35 B3
Limes Pl SN6 ....8 C4
Limes Rd GL7 ....4 F7
Limes The
Badminton GL9 ....38 E2
Motcombe SP7 ....202 A4
Porton SP4 ....133 E6
Limpley Stoke Rd BA15 ...99 D6
Lincoln Gn SN12 ....94 C7
Lincoln Gr SN12 ....94 C1
Lincoln St SN1 ....50 C6
Linden Ave SN2 ....35 C3
Linden Cl Calne SN11 ....81 B2
Colerne SN14 ....74 F6
Ludgershall SP11 ....192 B5
Salisbury SP1 ....146 D1
Wootton Bassett SN4 .....47 E3
Linden Cres BA15 ....100 A3
Linden Gr 2 SN12 ....94 A2
Linden Pk SP7 ....202 D1
Linden Pl BA14 ....101 B1
Linden Way SN5 ....34 A2
Lindford Rd SP1 ....146 D5
Lindisfarne 1 SN4 ....48 A2
Lindlar Cl 18 SP7 ......202 C2
Lineacre Cl SN5 ....48 F4
Lingen Cl 12 SP10 ......193 D2
Lingfield Cl 6 SN14 .....77 F5
Link Ave SN5 ....49 B5
Link La BA15 ....83 A1
Link Leisure Ctr SN5 ....49 B5
Link Rd BA13 ....108 E7
Link Way SP1 ....146 C3
Links The Corsham SN13 ...84 B7
Pewsey SN9 ....215 B4
Linley Cl SN1 ....50 C2
Linley Rd SN26 ....21 C2
Linnet Way BA11 ....110 B6
Linnetsdene
6 Salisbury SP2 ....152 A5
Swindon SN3 ....51 C8
Linslade SN2 ....50 A7
Linslade St SN2 ....49 F6
Linsvale Cl BA11 ....110 C5
Linsvale Dr BA11 ....110 C5
Lipgate SN10 ....180 F8
Liskeard Way SN5 ....49 B4
Lisle Cl SN5 ....49 A5
Lismore Rd SN6 ....22 E6
Lister Gr BA15 ....99 F3
Lister Rd SN4 ....64 B7
Litchfield Cl 11 SP10 ..193 C2
Little Ave SN2 ....35 A1
Little Badminton La
SN16 ....28 F2
Little Challows SN14 ....76 D7
Little Clarendon (National
Trust)* SP3 ....201 F2
Little Comm BA14 ....105 D3
Little Content La 17
SP7 ....202 C2
Little Ct La BA13 ......186 D8
Little Down SN14 ....78 B7
Little Dro SP6 ....211 A4
Little Hill BA12 ....116 E2
Little London
Heytesbury BA12 ....194 C5
Swindon SN1 ....50 D4
Little Mead SN8 ....176 F1
Little Parks BA14 ....92 F1
Little Pk Cl SN15 ....59 F1
Little Rose La SN26 .....20 F5
Little Sands SN14 ....68 F5
Little Woodbury*
SP5 ....152 B4
Little Woodfalls Dr
SP5 ....211 C6
Littlecote Cl 3 SN5 .....49 D5
Littlecote Rd
Chippenham SN14 ....78 A6
Froxfield SN8 ....176 D7
Littlecote Roman Villa*
RG17 ....170 D1
Littledown SP7 ....202 C2
Littlefield La SP5 .....208 A4
Littlejohn Ave SN12 .....94 C6
Littlemead SN13 ....83 B5
Littlemill La SP6 ......209 F3
Littleworth La SN12 .....85 C2
Livery Rd
West Dean SP5 ....155 B7
Winterslow SP5 ....149 B4
Livia Cl 13 SP10 ....193 E2
Lock's Hill BA11 ....110 A3
Lock's La SP2 ....145 A3
Locke's Dro SP11 ....193 E8
Lockeridge Cl BA14 ....105 D5
Lockeridge La SN8 .....174 B7
Lockeridge Sch SN8 ....174 A6
Locking Cl SN12 ....178 B8
Locks La SN5 ....33 B5
Locks The SN10 ....179 D8
Locksgreen Cres 1 SN2 ...34 E3
Lockside 1 SN15 ....78 F5
Lockswell Cl SN15 ....79 A4
Loddon Way BA15 ....100 E5
Lode Hill SP5 ....211 B8
Loder's La SP3 ....204 A5
Lodersfield GL7 ....2 C4
Lodge Cl SN11 ....81 A3
Lodge Dr 6 SP11 ....192 F1
Lodge Dro SP5 ....211 C6
Lodge Hill BA11 ....110 F5
Lodge La SP11 ....192 E6
Lodge Rd
Chippenham SN15 ....79 A5
Horningsham BA12 ......119 A8
Lodowicks SN11 ....80 D7
Logan Cl 1 SN3 ....50 E6
Lomond Cl SN5 ....34 B2
London La SN5 ....17 C1
London Rd
Amesbury SP4 ....217 B4
Bishops Cannings SN10 ..214 E6
Box SN13 ....83 D7
Calne SN11 ....81 B2
Chippenham SN15 ....78 F6
Marlborough SN8 ....213 E2
Salisbury SP1 ....146 C3
Shrewton SP3 ....196 F7
London Rd E BA1 ....82 A3
London Ride SN8 ....176 A5
London St SN1 ....50 B6
Londonderry Gdns
SP4 ....198 E7
Long Acre SN5 ....33 B4
Long Barrow Rd SN11 ....81 A3
Long Bottom SP11 ......192 D6
Long Cl
Chippenham SN15 ....78 F6
Downton SP5 ....211 A8
Long Cl Ave SN13 ....76 B1
Long Cl W SP5 ....211 A8
Long Cross
Bramshaw SO43 ....212 C2
Shaftesbury SP7 ....202 B2
Long Dro Burbage SN8 ..183 D8
Grimstead SP5 ....154 B4
Long Harry SN8 ....213 F1
Long Hedge RG17 ....165 B1
Long Hill BA12 ....138 F5
Long Hollow BA13 ......186 D7
Long La Bourton SP8 ...137 B1
Cann SP7 ....206 A8
Long Leaze La SN12 .....94 C3
Long Ridings SN14 ......70 C2
Long River Rd BA13 ....109 D2
Long Row SN6 ....10 B4
Long St SN10 ....214 B3
Long Steeple La SP6 ...210 C6
Long Stones* SN8 .....173 A8
Longbarrow Cross Roads
SP4 ....197 C4
Longcombe Dr BA12 ....115 E3
Longcroft Ave SN10 ....214 C3
Longcroft Cres SN10 ...214 C3
Longcroft Rd SN10 .....214 C3
Longfellow Cl SN25 .....35 A8
Longfellow Cres SN4 ....47 F3
Longfield Cl 11 SP4 ...198 B7
Longfield Rd BA14 .....105 D7
Longfields SN8 ....173 B8
Longfields Wlk SN10 ..214 C2
Longford Castle*
SP5 ....153 A2
Longford Pk* SP5 .....152 E2
Longford Rd SN12 ....94 A2
Longhill Dr 1 SP2 .....152 B5
Longland SP2 ....145 E1
Longlands Cl BA13 ....186 C7
Longleat House*
BA12 ....114 F3
Longleat Safari Pk*
BA12 ....115 B4
Longleaze SN4 ....47 E3
Longleaze CP Sch SN4 ...47 E3
Longmead SP7 ....202 C2
Longsplatt SN13 ....83 D3
Longstock Ct SN5 ....49 B6
Longstone Rd 1 SN14 ....70 A1
Longthorpe Cl SN5 ......49 D4
Lonsdale Cl SN26 ....21 C2
Loop Rd SN8 ....175 A7
Lopcombe Cnr SP4 .....135 D3
Lopes Way BA13 ....108 F4
Lord's La SN15 ....78 E7

Lord's Mead SN14 78 A8
Lords Croft SP4 217 B4
Lordsmead Rd BA12 139 B4
Lorne St SN1 50 A5
Lottage Rd SN8 170 A7
Lottage Way 2 SN8 170 A7
Lotts The SN6 17 F8
Loughborough Cl 1 SN5 48 F4
Louviers Way SN1 50 C2
Love La Box SN13 83 F7
Salisbury SP1 152 B8
4 Shaftesbury SP7 202 B1
Woodgreen SP6 211 A4
Love's La SN8 170 B3
Loveage Cl 5 SN2 34 D4
Lovel Rd BA12 194 E3
Lovell Cl SN3 51 D7
Lover's La SN16 28 A4
Loveridge Cl
5 Andover SP10 193 E2
Swindon SN2 35 E6
Loves La BA14 104 C7
Lovett Gn SP1 146 C4
Low La SN11 81 D2
Low Rd SN10 179 C1
Lowa Cl SP9 216 C6
Lowa Rd SP9 216 B6
Lowbourne SN12 94 B4
Lowbourne Sch SN12 94 B5
Lowden SN15 78 C7
Lowden Ave SN14 78 C8
Lowden Hill SN15 78 C7
Lower Alma St BA14 105 E8
Lower Backway 7 SP3 196 E6
Lower Bartons 30 SP6 210 D1
Lower Blandford Rd
Cann SP7 206 A8
5 Shaftesbury SP7 202 D1
Lower Church Fields
SN8 213 D2
Lower Ct BA14 101 D1
Lower Densome Wood
SP6 211 A4
Lower Folly SP2 144 B1
Lower Goatacre SN11 166 A7
Lower Gr SP6 210 B5
Lower Ho SN16 15 B8
Lower Kingsdown Rd
SN13 83 A4
Lower Marsh Rd BA12 117 A5
Lower N Rd SP5 207 C5
Lower Prospect SN8 213 E3
Lower Rd Bratton BA13 186 B7
Britford SP5 152 C5
Coombe Bissett SP5 151 C1
Downton SP5 159 B4
Edington BA13 186 C8
Erlestoke BA13 178 F2
Netheravon SP4 190 A3
Odstock SP5 152 D4
Salisbury SP2 144 F2
Lower S Rd SP5 207 C4
Lower St
Donhead St Andrew SP7 203 B3
Netheravon SP4 190 A4
Rode BA11 103 E1
Salisbury SP2 151 E7
Lower Stoke
Limpley Stoke BA2 99 A6
Monkton Combe BA2 90 A1
Lower Westbury Rd
BA13 109 E5
Lower Wharf SN10 214 A4
Lower Woodrow SN12 86 F1
Lowes Cl 2 SN5 34 B2
Lowmead BA14 101 E1
Loxley Cl SN12 94 B6
Loyalty St SN14 78 C7
Lubeck Dr 22 SP10 193 D2
Lucerne Cl
10 Swindon SN5 48 F8
Wootton Bassett SN4 47 D4
Lucewood La SP5 154 C7
Luckett Way SN11 81 C4
Luckington CP Sch
SN14 39 E5
Luckington Ct* SN14 39 F5
Lucknam Pk* SN14 75 B6
Luddesdown Rd SN5 49 C4
Ludgershall Castle*
SP11 192 A6
Ludgershall Rd
Collingbourne Ducis SN8 191 E8
4 Swindon SN1 49 F4
Tidworth SP9 216 D7
Ludgershall Sports Club
SP11 192 A5
Ludlow Cl
Chippenham SN15 79 A5
10 Frome BA11 110 C6
Swindon SN3 50 F4
Warminster BA12 116 F4
Westbury BA13 108 F4
Ludmead Rd SN13 85 A8
Ludwell Fst Sch SP7 203 A1
Ludwell Hill SP7 203 A1
Lugbury (Long Barrow)*
SN14 53 E2
Luke St SP7 203 E1
Lulworth Rd SN25 34 E3
Lumley Cl 2 SN5 49 A4
Lumley Wlk 8 SP4 217 D3
Luxfield Rd BA12 116 E7
Lyall Cl SN25 34 F8
Lyburn Rd SP5 212 A5
Lydford Cl 4 SN5 49 A8
Lydiard Ctry Pk* SN5 48 E6
Lydiard Rd SN14 78 A6
Lydiard Way BA14 105 D5
Lye The SN12 178 E8
Lyes Gr BA13 112 B8
Lyme Ave BA12 116 F6
Lyme Way SN25 35 A5
Lymers The SN11 166 E2
Lynch Cl BA12 139 B5
Lynch Field The 5 SN4 163 A5
Lynch La 6 RG17 165 A2
Lynch The SN8 176 F1
Lynchet Cl 7 SN10 179 F1
Lynchets Rd SP4 217 B3
Lynchfield Rd 7 SP4 217 B3
Lynden Cl SN8 184 A7
Lyndhurst Cres SN3 51 A6
Lyndhurst Rd
Amesbury SP4 217 C3
Landford SP5 212 C6
Lyneham Cl SN2 35 B6
Lyneham Jun & Inf Sch
SN15 60 B2
Lyneham Way BA14 105 F8
Lynt Rd SN6 12 A5
Lynton Rd SN2 34 E1
Lynwood Gr SN2 34 D3
Lynwood Rd BA14 101 A1
Lyons Wlk 1 SP7 202 C1
Lypiatt SN13 84 F6
Lypiatt Mead SN13 85 A8
Lypiatt Rd SN13 85 A7
Lysander Rd
Bower Hill SN12 94 B1
Laverstock SP4 146 C8
Melksham Without SN12 178 B8
Lysley Cl SN15 79 A5
Lyster Rd SP6 210 E1
Lytchett Way SN3 51 C6
Lytham Cl SN15 78 F7

M

Macadam Way SP10 193 B1
Maccullum Rd SP11 193 E4
Mackenzie Cl 1 SN3 51 D4
Macklin Cl 21 RG17 177 B7
Macklin Rd SP2 145 E2
Macneice Dr SN8 213 A2
Maddington 2 SP3 196 E6
Maddington St SP3 196 E7
Maddle Rd RG17 164 E4
Maddock's Hill 4 BA12 116 E5
Magdalen La BA14 104 B7
Magdalen Rd SN4 163 A6
Magdalene La 7 SP7 202 C1
Magister Rd SN12 94 D1
Magnolia Cl 1 BA11 110 C7
Magnolia Rise
Calne SN11 81 B1
Trowbridge BA14 105 E7
Magnon Rd BA15 100 B7
Magpie La SN3 51 E6
Maiden La SN11 166 B1
Maidstone Rd SN1 50 B4
Main Rd Amesbury SP4 217 D2
Ogbourne St Andrew
SN8 213 D8
Cherhill SN11 166 B1
St Paul Malmesbury Without
SN16 42 E4
Christian Malford SN15 58 E5
Sutton Benger SN15 57 F2
Main St
Great Hinton BA14 178 A6
Westbury BA13 108 C6
Maitland Cl SN15 79 A4
Maitland Rd SN3 51 A7
Majestic Cl 4 SN5 49 A7
Maldwyn Cl 9 SN5 48 F8
Mall The
South Tedworth SP9 216 A4
Swindon SN1 50 B3
Mallard Ave SN15 60 B1
Mallard Cl
7 Bower Hill SN12 178 B8
Calne SN11 81 D2
Salisbury SP2 151 F7
Swindon SN3 51 E6
Westbury BA13 109 B4
Mallards The 20 SP3 203 E8
Mallow Cl 2 Swindon SN2 34 D4
5 Trowbridge BA14 105 D6
Malmesbury Abbey*
SN16 28 A3
Malmesbury C of E Prim Sch
SN16 27 F6
Malmesbury Com Hospl
SN16 28 B1
Malmesbury Rd
Chippenham SN15 70 C1
Leigh SN5 17 E3
Malmesbury Sch SN16 27 E3
Malmesbury Swimming Pool
SN16 27 E4
Malmpit Hill BA12 195 B2
Malt House La SP11 193 F4
Malt Shovel La RG17 164 F2
Malthouse Cl
Ashbury SN6 164 A8
Broad Blunsdon SN26 21 C2
Malthouse La
Chute SP11 192 E8
4 Salisbury SP2 146 A1
Maltings The
Malmesbury SN16 28 A3
Maltings The *continued*
Salisbury SP2 146 A1
8 Wanborough SN4 163 B6
Warminster BA12 116 F6
Wootton Bassett SN4 47 D1
Yatton Keynell SN14 68 F6
Malvern Cl
Melksham SN12 94 D4
7 Warminster BA12 117 A8
Malvern Rd SN2 35 C1
Malvern Way SP4 133 D6
Mampitts La SP7 202 D1
Manchester Rd SN1 50 C7
Mand Wood BA14 101 F8
Manning Cl 8 SP1 146 C5
Mannington La SN5 49 D5
Mannington Pk SN2 49 F7
Mannington Ret Pk
SN1 49 E4
Manor Bridge Ct SP9 216 D7
Manor Cl
Broad Blunsdon SN26 21 C2
28 Fordingbridge SP6 210 D1
Semington BA14 102 F5
Sherston SN16 25 C1
4 Shipton Bellinger SP9 199 D8
Trowbridge BA14 105 A6
Wroughton SN4 64 B5
Manor Copse SP11 193 E3
Manor Cotts SN14 24 D1
Manor Cres SN2 34 C2
Manor Dr BA1 82 B2
Manor Farm Cl SP5 205 C4
Manor Farm Cl SN8 173 D6
Manor Farm Dr SN15 57 C2
Manor Farm La
Great Wishford SP2 129 F4
Patney SN10 180 F5
Manor Farm Rd
Salisbury SP1 146 C1
1 Sandleheath SP6 210 C1
Manor Fields 5 BA13 186 B7
Manor Gdns
Swindon SN2 34 F1
Warminster BA12 117 A7
Manor Ho SN14 68 E5
Manor La Baydon SN8 170 C8
Broad Hinton SN4 167 C7
Manor Orch SN6 19 E8
Manor Pk
Froxfield SN8 176 D6
Great Somerford SN15 44 A2
South Marston SN3 36 E4
Manor Rd
Chippenham SN14 78 A8
Corsham SN13 76 F2
7 Great Bedwyn SN8 176 B3
Mere BA12 138 F7
Salisbury SP1 146 C1
Swindon SN1 49 F5
Trowbridge BA14 105 A6
Upton Lovell BA12 194 E3
Manor The*
Keevil BA14 178 A4
Longbridge Deverill
BA12 120 F5
Manor View SN16 28 F2
Manton Cl
Marlborough SN8 213 A1
Trowbridge BA14 105 C6
Manton Dro SN8 174 C6
Manton Hollow SN8 213 A2
Manton Rd SN8 174 C7
Manton St SN2 49 F7
Maple Cl Calne SN11 81 B1
Melksham SN12 94 D5
Pewsey SN9 215 D6
5 Shaftesbury SP7 202 C2
Maple Cres
7 Ludgershall SP11 192 B5
Wilton SP2 144 F3
Maple Ct 8 BA11 110 A7
Maple Dr Firsdown SP5 148 C7
Wootton Bassett SN4 47 E4
Maple Gr Swindon SN2 35 C2
Trowbridge BA14 105 C6
Maple Way
Chippenham SN15 70 D2
3 Durrington/Bulford
SP4 198 B7
Maplecroft 3 SP2 152 A5
Mapperton Hill SP8 138 E1
Marbrean Cl 4 SP6 210 C1
March Cl SN25 35 A6
Marden Henge* SN9 181 B5
Marden Way SN11 81 A2
Marden Wlk 2 BA14 105 D6
Margaret Stancomb Inf Sch
BA14 101 C1
Margha Rd SP9 216 C6
Marie Ave 5 SP5 210 F8
Marigold Cl
Melksham SN12 94 C3
Swindon SN2 34 D4
Marina Dr BA14 101 D4
Marina Rd
23 Durrington/Bulford
SP4 198 B7
Salisbury SP1 152 C7
Marine Cl SN4 64 B7
Maristow St BA13 109 A3
Marjoram Cl SN2 34 D5
Markan Rd SP4 133 F7
Markenfield 2 SN5 49 D4
Market Hill SN11 81 B3
Market Lavington Mus*
SN10 179 F1
Market Pl Box SN13 83 D6
Market Pl *continued*
Chippenham SN15 78 E7
Colerne SN14 75 B3
Lechlade GL7 2 C4
18 Market Lavington SN10 179 F1
Marshfield SN14 74 A8
Warminster BA12 117 A7
Westbury BA13 109 A4
Market Place The
SN10 214 A4
Market Sq SN3 50 D4
Market St
Bradford-on-Avon BA15 100 D7
4 Malmesbury SN16 28 A3
Swindon SN1 50 B6
Trowbridge BA14 105 D8
Markham Cl SN3 50 F7
Markham Rd SN4 64 A5
Marl La SP6 210 D1
Marlborough Cl SN10 214 F7
Marlborough Coll
SN8 213 C2
Marlborough Ct SN14 78 C7
Marlborough Golf Club
SN8 213 D4
Marlborough La SN1 50 D3
Marlborough Leisure Ctr
SN8 213 C3
Marlborough Rd
5 Aldbourne SN8 170 A6
Bulford SP4 198 E6
Burbage SN8 175 C1
Chiseldon SN3 51 C2
Chiseldon SN4 65 E7
Chiseldown SN4 65 E4
Collingbourne Ducis SN8 183 E1
Everleigh SN8 183 A1
Liddington SN4 51 E1
Pewsey SN9 215 B6
Salisbury SP1 146 A2
Swindon SN3 50 D3
Wootton Bassett SN4 61 E7
Wroughton SN4 64 B6
Marlborough St 6 SN1 50 A5
Marlborough White Horse*
SN8 213 C1
Marlowe Ave SN3 50 F7
Marlowe Way SN4 47 F3
Marne Rd 3 SP4 198 F6
Marney Rd SN5 49 A5
Marsh La
Breamore SP6 210 E4
Cherhill SN11 166 A1
Coombe Bissett SP5 150 F2
Hungerford RG17 177 A7
Nettleton SN14 53 C4
Pen Selwood BA9 137 A4
Rowde SN10 96 D2
Salisbury SP2 145 F2
Marsh Rd Berkley BA11 107 C1
Rode BA11 103 F1
Trowbridge BA14 101 E5
Marsh St BA12 117 A5
Marsh The SN4 51 F3
Marshall Rd
Roundway SN10 214 D1
Swindon SN5 49 B8
Marshall St SN14 78 C7
Marshfield Prim Sch
SN14 74 A8
Marshfield Rd SN15 78 C8
Marshfield Way SN3 36 A2
Marshgate SN1 50 F8
Marshmead BA14 101 F4
Marshmead Cl SP5 152 F6
Marshwood SP3 201 E3
Marsland Rd SN2 35 D2
Marston Ave SN2 35 D4
Marston Rd BA14 105 B4
Marsum Cl 1 SP10 193 D2
Martha's La SP3 140 F4
Marti Cl SN12 94 C4
Martigny Rd SN12 94 B3
Martin Cl SP9 216 E6
Martin Crest BA12 116 E5
Martin Dro End SP6 209 A7
Martin Way SN11 81 D3
Martin's Cl SN9 181 C6
Martin's St 4 SP7 202 C1
Martinbushes Rd SP4 198 A7
Martinfield SN3 51 D7
Martingale Rd SN8 183 D7
Martins Cl
Chippenham SN15 79 A8
2 Salisbury SP2 152 A5
Steeple Ashton BA14 178 C4
Martins Croft SN14 75 B3
Martins La BA14 178 C4
Martins Rd BA14 178 C5
Martins Rise SP5 161 C4
Martinsell Gn SN9 215 D5
Martinsell Hill (Fort)*
SN8 174 D2
Martlesham Rd SP4 217 D2
Martlet Cl SN12 94 D1
Martor Ind Est SN14 66 A2
Marvins Cl SP3 188 B2
Mary Barters La SP3 204 E8
Maryland Cl SP2 145 B5
Masefield SN4 47 F3
Masefield Ave SN2 35 E3
Masefield Rd BA12 116 E6
Maskeleyne Way SN4 63 F6
Masons La BA15 100 D7
Masons The SN5 33 A3
Masons Way SN13 76 D1
Matford Hill SN15 79 A8
Matilda Way SN10 214 D4
Matley Moor SN3 51 E2
Matravers Cl BA13 108 F3
Matravers Sch BA13 108 F2
Matrons Cotts SP5 153 F1
Matthews Cl SN10 172 F1
Maud Cl SN10 214 D4
Maud Heath Prim Sch
SN15 72 A2
Maud Heath's Cswy
Chippenham SN15 70 E1
Langley Burrell Without
SN15 71 B3
Maud Heath's Mon*
SN11 80 C8
Maud Heath's Stone*
SN11 80 C8
Maulton Cl BA14 101 D8
Maundrell Cl SN10 96 D2
Maundrell Rd SN11 81 C5
Maunsell Way SN4 63 F7
Maur Cl SN15 78 C7
Maurys La SO51 212 F6
Maxey Cl SN5 49 B8
Maxwell St SN1 50 A6
May Cl SN2 35 C1
May La SP5 204 D3
May Tree Rd 9 SP10 193 C1
May's La SN4 65 D4
Mayenne Pl SN10 179 C8
Mayfair Rd SP1 146 D1
Mayfield 1 SN4 163 A5
Mayfield Ave Ind. Pk
SP11 192 E1
Mayfield Cl
4 Shipton Bellinger SP9 199 C8
Swindon SN3 51 B7
Mayfield Rd 2 SP6 210 C1
Mayfly Cl 4 SP6 210 D1
Mayo Cl SN13 76 E2
Mays Firs SP6 211 D5
Maytree Cl 6 BA11 110 B7
Mc Neill Rd SP4 198 A7
Mckie Rd 3 SP4 217 D2
Mead Com Prim Sch The
BA14 101 F2
Mead Pk SN12 84 F1
Mead The
Ashton Keynes SN6 17 F8
Warminster BA12 117 A7
Westbury BA13 109 A5
Winsley BA15 99 E7
Mead Way Swindon SN5 34 B2
Swindon SN5 49 D6
Meade Rd 2 SP11 192 B5
Meadens La SP5 151 A1
Meadland SN13 76 E1
Meadow Ave 10 SP6 210 D1
Meadow Cl
Chippenham SN14 78 A7
8 Fordingbridge SP6 210 D1
Yatton Keynell SN14 68 F6
Meadow Ct
11 Fordingbridge SP6 210 D1
Whiteparish SP5 161 E4
Meadow Dr SN10 214 C3
Meadow La
Little Somerford SN15 44 A5
Westbury BA13 109 A4
Meadow Pk BA1 82 B3
Meadow Rd (South) 5
SP2 145 F1
Meadow Rd
Durrington/Bulford SP4 217 E8
Melksham SN12 94 C7
3 Salisbury SP2 145 F1
Swindon SN2 49 E7
Meadow Springs SN5 48 E8
Meadow View 5 SP4 190 A4
Meadow Way
Chiseldon SN4 65 E7
South Cerney GL7 6 F7
Meadow Well SN8 183 C8
Meadowcroft SN2 35 F3
Meadowfield BA15 100 B6
Meadows The
Lydiard Tregoze SN5 47 F5
Salisbury SP1 152 D8
Meadowsweet Cl 2
SN25 34 E5
Meadowsweet Dr SN11 80 F3
Meads Rd SP4 198 B7
Meads The SN14 53 B3
Meadway
4 Shrewton SP3 196 F6
Wingfield BA14 105 A8
Meares Dr SN5 49 B8
Mears Rd 4 SP4 198 A6
Medbourne SN4 163 A3
Medbourne Rd SN4 163 A4
Medgbury Pl SN1 50 D6
Medgbury Rd SN1 50 C6
Medina Way SN2 35 F4
Medway Rd SN25 34 F4
Meerut Rd SP9 216 C6
Melbourne Cl SN3 50 F3
Melbourne Gdns 5 SP4 198 F6
Melbourne St BA13 186 B7
Melbury Abbas Mill*
SP7 206 A7
Melbury Down (National
Trust)* SP5 206 C6
Melbury St SP7 206 B6
Melbury Way 12 SP7 202 D2
Melchet Cl SO51 162 D1
Melfort Cl SN5 34 B2
Meliot Rise 12 SP10 193 E2
Melksham Cl SN2 35 B6

Melksham Com Hospl SN12 . . . 94 B3
Melksham La SN12 . . . 93 C4
Melksham Rd Holt SN12 . . . 93 A2
Lacock SN15 . . . 86 D5
Melksham Sta SN12 . . . 94 A6
Mellow Gd SN25 . . . 34 E5
Melrose Ave BA12 . . . 116 E6
Melrose Cl
1 Swindon SN5 . . . 49 C6
4 Warminster BA12 . . . 116 E6
Melsome Rd SN15 . . . 59 F1
Melton Rd BA14 . . . 101 C2
Melville Cl 8 SN3 . . . 50 F6
Melvin Cl SP1 . . . 146 D1
Mendip Cl
3 Frome BA11 . . . 110 A7
Melksham SN12 . . . 94 C4
Swindon SN25 . . . 35 C3
6 Warminster BA12 . . . 117 A8
Mendip Dr BA11 . . . 110 A7
Menham Cl SN2 . . . 35 D2
Merchants House The* SN8 . . . 213 D3
Mercia Ave SP10 . . . 193 C2
Mere Ave SN14 . . . 41 F1
Mere Castle* BA12 . . . 138 F6
Mere Fst Sch BA12 . . . 139 B5
Meridian Wlk BA14 . . . 105 A8
Merlin Cl 23 SP10 . . . 193 E2
Merlin Way
Bower Hill SN12 . . . 94 B1
Stratton St Margaret SN3 . . . 51 D8
Swindon SN3 . . . 36 D1
Merrifield Rd SP4 . . . 146 C6
Merrivale Gr SN3 . . . 50 E5
Merton Ave SN2 . . . 35 D4
Merton Cl 6 SP6 . . . 210 D2
Merton St 2 SN1 . . . 50 C6
Mervyn Webb Pl SN2 . . . 50 D8
Mesh Pond SP5 . . . 210 F8
Methuen Ave SN12 . . . 94 B6
Methuen Cl BA15 . . . 100 E4
Methuen Dr 1 SP1 . . . 152 C8
Methuen Pk 5 SN14 . . . 77 F5
Mews The
Highworth SN6 . . . 23 A6
Lydiard Millicent SN5 . . . 48 D8
Warminster BA12 . . . 117 A7
Meyrick Ave SP2 . . . 152 A5
Meysey Cl GL7 . . . 1 A5
Michael Pym's Rd 3 SN16 . . . 28 A5
Middle Field Cl SN10 . . . 214 C3
Middle Gd Cricklade SN6 . . . 19 C8
Fovant SP3 . . . 204 E7
Wootton Bassett SN4 . . . 48 A2
Middle La
Atworth/Whitley SN12 . . . 85 D1
Cherhill SN11 . . . 166 B1
Martin SP6 . . . 209 A7
Trowbridge BA14 . . . 101 F2
Middle St SP2 . . . 151 E7
Middle Stoke BA2 . . . 99 A6
Middleleaze Dr SN5 . . . 48 F8
Middlemass Gn SN9 . . . 215 D5
Middleton SP5 . . . 149 B7
Middleton Cl
Swindon SN3 . . . 50 F6
5 Warminster BA12 . . . 116 E6
Middleton Medieval Village of* BA12 . . . 194 A7
Middleton Rd
Salisbury SP2 . . . 145 F2
The Common SP5 . . . 149 B7
Middletons Cl RG17 . . . 177 C8
Middlewick La SN13 . . . 76 D3
Midford Hill BA2 . . . 98 C4
Midford La BA2 . . . 98 E7
Midford Rd BA2 . . . 98 B7
Midhurst Ave SN3 . . . 51 B5
Midlands Ind Est The BA14 . . . 92 E1
Midlands The BA14 . . . 92 E1
Midwinter Cl SN5 . . . 34 B2
Milbourne La SN16 . . . 28 C4
Milbourne Pk SN16 . . . 28 C4
Mildmay Cl 12 SN5 . . . 48 F5
Mile Dr SN15 . . . 44 E1
Miles's La SP5 . . . 161 E5
Milestone Way SN15 . . . 70 C2
Milford Hill SP1 . . . 152 B8
Milford Hollow 6 SP1 . . . 152 C8
Milford Ind Est SP1 . . . 152 C8
Milford Manor Gdns SP1 . . . 152 D8
Milford Mill Rd SP1 . . . 152 D8
Milford Pk SP1 . . . 152 D8
Milford St
Salisbury SP1 . . . 152 B8
Swindon SN1 . . . 50 C6
Milford Way SN15 . . . 78 F4
Mill Cl Devizes SN10 . . . 214 C1
Longbridge Deverill BA12 . . . 120 F6
South Cerney GL7 . . . 7 A7
Winterbourne SP4 . . . 133 B4
Wroughton SN4 . . . 64 B6
Mill Ct 18 SP6 . . . 210 D1
Mill Dro SN8 . . . 183 C1
Mill End SP6 . . . 209 F2
Mill Head SN10 . . . 179 A4
Mill Hill Ave SP9 . . . 216 C8
Mill Hollow La SP7 . . . 206 A7
Mill La Bishopstone SP5 . . . 150 A1
Bourton SP8 . . . 137 E2
Box SN13 . . . 83 C7
Bradford-on-Avon BA15 . . . 100 D6
Mill La *continued*
Broughton Gifford SN12 . . . 93 C3
Bulkington SN10 . . . 178 E5
Cherhill SN11 . . . 166 B1
Chilmark SP3 . . . 200 F2
Fairford GL7 . . . 1 F7
Fovant SP3 . . . 204 D8
Heytesbury BA12 . . . 194 C5
Lambourn RG17 . . . 165 B1
Lechlade GL7 . . . 2 F4
Little Somerford SN15 . . . 43 F5
Malmesbury SN16 . . . 28 A3
Melbury Abbas SP7 . . . 206 A7
Mere BA12 . . . 139 B5
Monkton Combe BA2 . . . 98 E8
Poulshot SN10 . . . 179 A5
Ramsbury SN8 . . . 170 B2
St Paul Malmesbury Without SN16 . . . 42 E5
Salisbury SP1 . . . 145 E5
Selwood BA11 . . . 114 F8
Shalbourne SN8 . . . 176 F2
Stanton Fitzwarren SN6 . . . 22 A2
Swindon SN1 . . . 50 A3
The Common SP5 . . . 149 E6
West Lavington SN10 . . . 187 E8
Westbury BA13 . . . 112 D8
Winterbourne Monkton SN4 . . . 167 C3
Winterslow SP5 . . . 149 D7
Zeale SP8 . . . 137 F2
Mill Rd Devizes SN10 . . . 214 C1
Netheravon SP4 . . . 190 A4
Potterne SN10 . . . 179 D5
Salisbury SP2 . . . 145 F1
Worton SN10 . . . 179 A4
Mill Rise SP8 . . . 137 E2
Mill Sch The SN10 . . . 179 C6
Mill St Calne SN11 . . . 81 B2
Fontmell Magna SP7 . . . 206 A3
Heytesbury BA12 . . . 194 C5
Trowbridge BA14 . . . 105 D8
Mill Stream App SP2 . . . 146 A1
Milland Cl SN25 . . . 35 B6
Millard Cl 2 SN15 . . . 78 F4
Millbrook 2 SP1 . . . 146 B2
Millbrook La SP3 . . . 141 C1
Millbuck Cl SN2 . . . 35 E1
Millennium Pk Ctr* GL7 . . . 6 B3
Millennium Way SP2 . . . 152 B5
Miller Cl Chirton SN10 . . . 180 F4
Salisbury SP1 . . . 145 E5
Swindon SN5 . . . 48 F8
Miller's La DT11 . . . 207 D1
Millfield 5 RG17 . . . 165 A1
Millgreen Rd 1 SP4 . . . 217 C2
Millhand Villas BA14 . . . 105 E7
Millington Dr 3 BA14 . . . 105 A7
Mills Rd SN12 . . . 94 C4
Mills Way SP4 . . . 217 D4
Milne Cres 3 SP4 . . . 197 E6
Milne Rd SP4 . . . 198 E6
Milston Ave SN2 . . . 35 C5
Milston Down (Long Barrows)* SP4 . . . 198 E8
Milston Dro SP4 . . . 190 E1
Milston Rd Bulford SP4 . . . 198 C7
Durrington/Bulford SP4 . . . 217 D8
Milston View 2 SP4 . . . 198 C7
Milton Ave
6 Andover SP10 . . . 193 C1
Melksham SN12 . . . 94 B4
Milton Pl GL7 . . . 1 F6
Milton Rd
Amesbury SP4 . . . 217 E2
Pewsey SN9 . . . 215 E5
Salisbury SP2 . . . 152 B6
Swindon SN1 . . . 50 B6
Milton St GL7 . . . 1 F6
Milton's Way SN4 . . . 47 C1
Minden Cl 13 SP10 . . . 193 D2
Minety CE Sch SN16 . . . 17 B2
Minety La SN16 . . . 16 A7
Minety Rd SN2 . . . 35 B5
Minster Cl SN25 . . . 34 F7
Minster St
7 Salisbury SP1 . . . 146 A1
Wilton SP2 . . . 144 D3
Minster View BA12 . . . 116 F7
Minster Way SN14 . . . 78 A5
Mint Cl SN2 . . . 34 D4
Minty's Top SN15 . . . 96 A7
Mitchell Cl 3 SP10 . . . 193 C1
Mitchell Dr SN12 . . . 178 B8
Mitchell Rd SP2 . . . 151 D8
Mitchells Cl 5 SP5 . . . 211 C7
Mizmaze* SP6 . . . 210 D7
Moat Rd BA13 . . . 108 D6
Moberly Rd SP1 . . . 146 B3
Moffat Rise SN16 . . . 28 A5
Moggs La SN11 . . . 172 A8
Mompesson Ho* SP2 . . . 152 A8
Monastery Rd BA13 . . . 186 C8
Monet Cl SN25 . . . 34 F6
Moneyer Rd 5 SP10 . . . 193 D2
Monk's La SN13 . . . 85 B6
Monkley La BA14 . . . 104 C1
Monks Cl SP9 . . . 216 C7
Monks Pk SN16 . . . 28 D4
Monks Pk Gdns SN13 . . . 85 B5
Monks Way SN15 . . . 79 A4
Monkton Cl SN3 . . . 51 B4
Monkton Dro BH21 . . . 208 D1
Monkton Farleigh Prim Sch BA15 . . . 90 E7
Monkton Hill SN15 . . . 78 D7
Monkton House* SN12 . . . 93 C1
Monkton Pk Prim Sch SN15 . . . 78 E7
Monmouth Cl 4 SN3 . . . 50 F4
Monmouth Dr BA11 . . . 110 B5
Monmouth Rd SP3 . . . 203 D8
Mons Ave SP4 . . . 198 E6
Mons La SN15 . . . 86 D8
Montagu St SN2 . . . 49 F7
Montague Cl SN15 . . . 79 A7
Montague Ct BA14 . . . 102 A1
Montague Pl SN12 . . . 94 C5
Montague Rd SP2 . . . 151 D7
Monteagle Cl SN5 . . . 49 A4
Montessori Sch SP2 . . . 144 D3
Montgomery Ave SN2 . . . 35 B2
Montgomery Gdns SP2 . . . 145 E2
Montrose Cl SN2 . . . 34 E2
Monument Hill SN10 . . . 214 E1
Monxton Cl 3 SP1 . . . 146 D5
Moody's Hill SP5 . . . 155 E2
Moon Cl SN14 . . . 75 B3
Moonrakers SN10 . . . 214 D5
Moor Barton SN13 . . . 84 D6
Moor Hill SP3 . . . 204 D8
Moor La SP5 . . . 161 A1
Moor Pk SN13 . . . 84 C6
Moore Cl SN4 . . . 64 C8
Moore's Pl 12 RG17 . . . 177 B7
Moorgate GL7 . . . 2 B4
Moorhen Cl SN3 . . . 51 E5
Moorlands SN15 . . . 70 E2
Moorlands The SN10 . . . 214 A2
Moormead Rd SN4 . . . 64 B6
Moors Cl SN15 . . . 70 C5
Moot (Motte & Bailey) The* SP5 . . . 211 B8
Moot Cl 7 Andover SP10 . . . 193 E2
Downton SP5 . . . 211 B7
Moot Gdns SP5 . . . 211 A7
Moot La SP5 . . . 211 A7
Mopes La SN5 . . . 33 C7
Moray Rd SN2 . . . 35 E1
Moredon Jun Sch SN2 . . . 34 E2
Moredon Pk SN2 . . . 34 D3
Moredon Rd SN25 . . . 34 F3
Moresby Cl SN5 . . . 49 C6
Morgan Wlk BA13 . . . 108 E2
Morgan's La
Pentridge SP5 . . . 208 E5
Winterbourne SP4 . . . 133 A2
Morgans Rise Rd 3 SP5 . . . 211 C8
Morgans Vale & Woodfalls Prim Sch SP5 . . . 211 C8
Morgans Vale Rd SP5 . . . 211 C7
Morie Cl SN5 . . . 34 B1
Morley Field BA12 . . . 117 C7
Morley Pl 23 RG17 . . . 177 B7
Morley St SN1 . . . 50 C5
Morris La Bath BA1 . . . 82 B3
Devizes SN10 . . . 214 B3
Morris Rd SN8 . . . 213 B2
Morris St SN2 . . . 49 E6
Morrison St SN2 . . . 49 F7
Morse Cl SN15 . . . 78 E4
Morse St SN1 . . . 50 B5
Morstone Rd SN4 . . . 61 D8
Mortimer Cl 5 SN5 . . . 49 B7
Mortimer St BA14 . . . 105 C7
Moss Mead SN14 . . . 77 F8
Motcombe CE Sch SP7 . . . 202 A4
Motcombe Grange Prep Sch SP7 . . . 202 A5
Motcombe Rd SP7 . . . 202 B3
Moulton Dr BA15 . . . 100 D4
Mount Carmel Rd SP11 . . . 199 F3
Mount La
Barford St Martin SP3 . . . 143 B4
Warminster BA12 . . . 117 A5
Mount Pleasant
Atworth SN12 . . . 85 A1
Atworth/Whitley SN12 . . . 93 A8
Bradford-on-Avon BA15 . . . 100 D7
Lechlade GL7 . . . 2 C4
South Newton SP2 . . . 130 A4
Mount The BA14 . . . 101 D2
Mountain Wood BA1 . . . 82 B2
Mountford Manor Jun & Inf Sch SN3 . . . 50 F6
Mountings The SN4 . . . 64 B8
Mountpleasant SP3 . . . 203 D8
Mountsfield BA11 . . . 110 A2
Moxhams 21 SP6 . . . 210 D1
Moyne Cl SN10 . . . 179 D8
Moyne Gdns 7 SP4 . . . 217 D3
Mud La SN5 . . . 32 F2
Muddyford Rd SP5 . . . 211 C8
Mulberry Cl SN14 . . . 70 B1
Mulberry Ct
Frome BA11 . . . 110 B7
Sixpenny Handley SP5 . . . 208 B4
Mulberry Gr SN2 . . . 35 A2
Mulcaster Ave SN5 . . . 48 F5
Mulling Cl SN14 . . . 75 A3
Mundy Ave SN3 . . . 51 C4
Munks Cl 3 SP2 . . . 151 E7
Munro Cl SN3 . . . 50 E6
Murdock Rd SN3 . . . 51 E6
Murray Rd BA14 . . . 101 D2
Murray Wlk SN12 . . . 94 B5
Murrayfield SN15 . . . 70 E1
Muscott Cl 3 SP9 . . . 199 C8
Muscovey Cl SN15 . . . 60 A2
Mustons La 26 SP7 . . . 202 C2
Myrrfield Rd 7 SP1 . . . 146 D5
Myrtle Ave BA12 . . . 116 F6
Myrtle Gdns SN2 . . . 35 C2
Mythern Mdw BA15 . . . 100 E5

N

Nadder CE Mid Sch SP3 . . . 203 E8
Nadder Cl 13 SP3 . . . 203 E8
Nadder La SP2 . . . 144 F2
Nadder Rd SP9 . . . 216 D6
Nadder Terr SP2 . . . 144 C2
Naini Tal Rd SP9 . . . 216 C6
Nantwich SN5 . . . 49 A3
Napier Cl Swindon SN2 . . . 50 A7
Tidworth SP9 . . . 216 E6
Napier Cres SP1 . . . 146 D1
Napiers 1 SN8 . . . 176 B3
Nash Cl SN25 . . . 35 A8
Nash Rd SN8 . . . 173 A8
Naughton Ave SN10 . . . 214 E6
Naunton Rd SN3 . . . 51 A6
Navigator Cl BA14 . . . 101 E4
Neal Cl 1 SP1 . . . 146 C5
Neale's Barrow* SP2 . . . 150 A6
Neeld Cl SN14 . . . 68 F6
Neeld Cres SN14 . . . 78 B8
Neigh Bridge Ctry Pk* GL7 . . . 5 F2
Nell Hill SN6 . . . 22 A7
Nelson Cl 1 SP4 . . . 198 F6
Nelson Rd SP2 . . . 146 A2
Nelson St SN1 . . . 49 F5
Nepaul Rd SP9 . . . 216 C7
Ness Cl 1 SN5 . . . 34 B2
Neston Cres SN13 . . . 84 E6
Neston Pk* SN13 . . . 84 E3
Neston Prim Sch SN13 . . . 84 E5
Nether Leaze SN9 . . . 215 B5
Netheravon Rd
Durrington SP4 . . . 198 B7
Figheldean SP4 . . . 190 B1
Salisbury SP1 . . . 146 B2
Nethercote Hill SN15 . . . 86 D6
Netherhampton Rd
Netherhampton SP2 . . . 150 F8
Quidhampton SP2 . . . 144 F1
Netherstreet SN15 . . . 96 D6
Netherton CE Prim Sch SP4 . . . 190 A3
Netherton Cl SN3 . . . 51 B4
Netherton House* SP11 . . . 185 F4
Nett Rd SP3 . . . 196 F6
Nettlebed Nursery 14 SP7 . . . 202 C2
Nettlecombe 6 SP7 . . . 202 D2
Nettlemead La BA12 . . . 201 F8
Nettleton & Burton CE Prim Sch SN14 . . . 53 B3
Nettleton Rd SN14 . . . 53 B3
Netton St SP5 . . . 205 E4
Neville Cl SP1 . . . 146 C4
Neville Terr SN15 . . . 57 D1
Nevis Cl SN5 . . . 34 B2
New Bottom Rd SP4 . . . 145 E7
New Bridge Cl 4 SN1 . . . 50 C7
New Bridge Rd SP1 . . . 152 A7
New Broughton Rd SN12 . . . 94 A5
New Canal SP1 . . . 152 A8
New Cl Bourton SP8 . . . 137 E2
West Knoyle BA12 . . . 140 E7
New Cl CP Sch BA12 . . . 117 B6
New Coll SN3 . . . 50 F5
New Cres SP11 . . . 192 A5
New Cut BA12 . . . 139 A6
New Dro SP11 . . . 192 A5
New Haig Rd 7 SP4 . . . 198 E6
New Hall Hospl SP5 . . . 158 F8
New Harnham Rd SP2 . . . 152 A6
New House La SP11 . . . 192 E4
New King Barrows* SP4 . . . 197 F5
New La Cann SP7 . . . 202 D1
Seend SN12 . . . 178 D7
New Lawns SN12 . . . 94 B4
New Pk Rd SN10 . . . 214 B4
New Pk St SN10 . . . 214 A4
New Rd Bath BA1 . . . 82 C2
Bradford-on-Avon BA15 . . . 100 E7
Bromham SN15 . . . 96 A5
Calne SN11 . . . 81 B2
Calne Without SN11 . . . 79 F3
Chippenham SN15 . . . 78 D7
Chiseldon SN4 . . . 65 D3
Codford BA12 . . . 195 A3
Donhead St Andrew SP7 . . . 203 B4
22 Durrington/Bulford SP4 . . . 198 B7
East Knoyle SP3 . . . 141 B3
Erlestoke BA13 . . . 179 A2
Kilmington BA12 . . . 123 D6
Landford SP5 . . . 212 D5
Limpley Stoke BA2 . . . 99 B5
Maiden Bradley with Yarnfield BA11 . . . 123 D8
Marlborough SN8 . . . 213 D3
Melksham Without SN12 . . . 94 E7
Purton SN5 . . . 33 C5
Rockbourne SP6 . . . 210 A5
2 Shaftesbury SP7 . . . 202 B2
1 Trowbridge BA14 . . . 105 D7
Wootton Bassett SN4 . . . 47 D1
Zeale SP8 . . . 138 A3
New Severalls The SN9 . . . 182 E7
New St
16 Market Lavington SN10 . . . 179 F1
Salisbury SP1 . . . 152 A8
Winterbourne Stoke SP3 . . . 196 F3
New Terrace BA14 . . . 101 C7
New Town La SN6 . . . 163 E6
New Ward Rd SP4 . . . 198 E7
New Zealand Ave SP2 . . . 145 D2
Newall Tuck Rd SN15 . . . 78 F7
Newark Cl SN5 . . . 49 B3
Newbourne Gdns SN14 . . . 56 D6
Newburgh Pl SN6 . . . 22 F6
Newburn Cres SN1 . . . 49 F5
Newbury Dr
Chippenham SN14 . . . 77 F5
Swindon SN5 . . . 49 B3
Newbury Rd
Enham Alamein SP11 . . . 193 E4
Lambourn RG17 . . . 165 B1
Newbury Road SP10 . . . 193 E2
Newbury St RG17 . . . 165 A1
Newby Acre SN8 . . . 213 D4
Newby Cl 4 SN10 . . . 187 E8
Newcastle St SN1 . . . 50 D6
Newcombe Dr SN2 . . . 50 A7
Newcroft Cl SN11 . . . 81 B4
Newcroft Rd SN11 . . . 81 B4
Newhall St SN1 . . . 50 B5
Newhurst Pk BA14 . . . 102 A2
Newland Rd SN25 . . . 35 A3
Newlands Cl SN15 . . . 70 E7
Newlands Rd SN13 . . . 77 A1
Newleaze
Steeple Ashton BA14 . . . 178 A4
Trowbridge BA14 . . . 101 F4
Newleaze Pk SN12 . . . 93 B4
Newmans Way SP4 . . . 217 E7
Newmarket Ave BA14 . . . 105 E4
Newmarket Cl 9 SN14 . . . 77 F6
Newmeadow Copse SN5 . . . 34 A1
Newopaul Way BA12 . . . 116 F8
Newport BA12 . . . 117 A7
Newport St SN1 . . . 50 D3
Newstead Cl 1 SN25 . . . 34 F6
Newth's La SN5 . . . 19 D2
Newton Abbot Cl 6 SN14 . . . 77 F6
Newton Barrow* SP2 . . . 130 E3
Newton Cl SP5 . . . 161 C3
Newton La SP5 . . . 161 B3
Newton Rd SP2 . . . 145 D1
Newton Toney Sch SP4 . . . 199 B3
Newton Way SN2 . . . 35 C4
Newtown
Bradford-on-Avon BA15 . . . 100 C6
Heytesbury BA12 . . . 194 C5
Hullavington SN14 . . . 41 F1
Trowbridge BA14 . . . 105 C8
Westbury BA13 . . . 109 C3
Newtown CP Sch BA14 . . . 105 C8
Newtown Rd SN8 . . . 170 C2
Nicolson Cl 6 SP4 . . . 217 E3
Niebull Cl SN16 . . . 28 A5
Nightingale Ave BA11 . . . 110 B6
Nightingale Cl 8 SO51 . . . 212 F6
Nightingale Dr BA13 . . . 109 B4
Nightingale La
South Marston SN3 . . . 36 F4
Tisbury SP3 . . . 203 C6
Nightingale Rd BA14 . . . 105 A8
Nightwood Copse 3 SN5 . . . 34 A1
Nindum Rd SN3 . . . 36 C1
Nive Rd SN4 . . . 168 E8
Noade St SP5 . . . 206 E4
Noble St SN16 . . . 40 C8
Nolan Cl SN25 . . . 34 F8
Nolands Rd SN11 . . . 166 D2
Nomansland & Hamptworth CE Prim Sch SP5 . . . 212 B4
Norcliffe Rd SN3 . . . 51 B4
Nore Marsh Rd SN4 . . . 47 E1
Noredown Way SN4 . . . 47 E1
Noremarsh Jun Sch SN4 . . . 47 E1
Norfolk Cl 1 SN3 . . . 50 F6
Norfolk Rd SP2 . . . 151 E7
Norley La SN11 . . . 80 C3
Norman Cl SN15 . . . 79 A4
Norman Rd SN2 . . . 35 C1
Normandy Way 14 SP6 . . . 210 D1
Norney Rd BA13 . . . 179 A4
Norridge View 4 BA12 . . . 116 E7
Norrington La SN12 . . . 93 C6
Norrington Manor* SP5 . . . 204 A2
Norris Cl SN4 . . . 65 C3
North Bank Rise SN4 . . . 47 F2
North Bradley CE Sch BA14 . . . 105 D2
North Charford Crossing SP6 . . . 210 F6
North Charford Dro SP6 . . . 210 C8
North Comm La SP5 . . . 212 B7
North Cote SN11 . . . 81 A4
North End SN11 . . . 81 A4
North End Gdns SN16 . . . 25 C1
North Farm Cl RG17 . . . 165 B2
North La SP5 . . . 212 C4
North Leaze Cl SN2 . . . 34 F3
North Mdw Rd SN6 . . . 8 C1

North Rd
Amesbury SP4 217 E2
Ashmore SP5 206 E5
Mere BA12 139 A6
North Row BA12 117 A7
North St
Broad Chalke SP5 205 B4
Calne SN11 81 B4
Mere BA12 139 A5
Pewsey SN9 215 C5
Salisbury SP2 145 F1
Swindon SN1 50 C5
Wilton SP2 144 D3
North Standen Rd
RG17 177 A6
North Star Ave SN2 50 B8
North View
Berwick St James SP3 196 F2
Highworth SN6 22 F5
North View Hts RG17 177 C7
North View Pl SN8 213 D4
North Wall SN6 19 D8
North Way Calne SN11 81 A4
Trowbridge BA14 105 A7
North Wilts Golf Club
SN11 172 A5
North Wlk SP1 152 A8
Northampton St SN1 50 D6
Northbourne Rd SN25 35 A7
Northbrook SN10 179 F1
Northbrook Cl 1 SN10 179 F1
Northbrook Rd SN12 93 F7
Northcote Cres 7 BA11 110 A7
Northcroft Rd 2 SN13 76 B1
Northen Cl GL7 10 E6
Northen Terr
Durrington SP4 197 F7
Larkhill SP4 198 A7
Northern Rd SN2 35 A1
Northfield BA15 99 F7
Northfield La SN14 66 A2
Northfield Way SN3 51 B7
Northfields
Bulkington SN10 178 E5
Calne SN11 81 A4
1 Lambourn RG17 165 A2
Northgate Gdns SN10 214 A4
Northgate St SN10 214 A4
Northlands Ind Est
BA12 117 B7
Northleigh BA15 91 E1
Northmoor La GL7 6 F8
Northside SP4 146 D8
Northview 20 RG17 177 B7
Northview Prim Sch
SN6 23 A7
Northway SP4 134 B7
Northwood SN15 70 E2
Norton Dr SP4 146 D6
Norton Gr SN3 50 D5
Norton Rd BA12 117 F1
Norwood Castle (site of)*
SN16 4 F2
Norwood Cl 3 SN3 51 D4
Noyes Cl
Chippenham SN14 77 F8
Haydon Wick SN2 34 C5
Nuffield Cl SN5 49 B8
Nunns Pk SP5 161 D4
Nunton Dro SP5 152 D1
Nurseries The
Christian Malford SN15 58 A2
Swindon SN1 50 A5
Nursery Cl
4 Amesbury SP4 217 B3
Atworth/Whitley SN12 92 E8
Trowbridge BA14 102 A3
Nursery Gdns
Corsham SN13 85 A8
Mere BA12 139 A5
Nursery Rd
Colerne SN14 75 A3
Salisbury SP2 145 E1
Nursery The SN16 27 F6
Nursteed Cl SN10 214 D2
Nursteed Pk SN10 214 C2
Nursteed Rd SN10 214 C2
Nutbane La SP11 193 A4
Nuthatch Cl 4 SN3 51 E6
Nutley Ct 8 SN8 183 D8
Nutmeg Cl 7 SN2 34 D4
Nyland Rd SN3 51 C7
Nythe Prim Sch SN3 51 C7
Nythe Rd SN3 36 B1

O

O'Donnell Cl SN15 70 E1
Oak Ash Gn SP2 144 C2
Oak Cl
Bishops Cannings SN10 172 B2
Pitton & Farley SP5 154 E7
South Newton SP2 130 B2
Tidworth SP9 216 E7
Oak Dr Alderbury SP5 153 D2
Highworth SN6 22 F5
Trowbridge BA14 105 C3
Oak Gdns SN3 36 A4
Oak Hill SN8 176 E6
Oak La Easterton SN10 179 F2
Figheldean SP4 190 B2
Oak Lodge Cl SN14 78 C8
Oak Pl SP4 217 C4
Oak Rd
Chippenham Without
SN14 77 F6
Colerne SN14 74 F5
Down Ampney GL7 8 E6
Oak St GL7 2 C4
Oak Tree Ave SN2 35 D3
Oak Tree Cl BA14 101 B1
Oak Way GL7 6 F6
Oakapple Cl 4 SN4 163 B6
Oakbournes The 5 SP1 146 C5
Oakes Ct 9 RG17 177 B7
Oakes La GL9 52 B5
Oakford La SN14 74 B2
Oakham Cl SN5 49 C5
Oakie Cl SN25 35 A5
Oaklands SN15 70 D2
Oaklands Cl 12 SP6 210 D1
Oaklea La SP5 153 E2
Oakleaze SN16 17 B2
Oakleigh Dr SP5 212 C5
Oakley Flats GL7 10 D6
Oakley La DT11 207 D2
Oaks The
Chippenham SN15 70 D2
Kemble GL7 4 F7
Warminster BA12 117 A8
Oaksey Prim Sch SN16 15 F8
Oaksey Rd Minety SN16 16 C4
Swindon SN2 35 C4
Oakwood Dr SN12 94 B4
Oakwood Gr SP5 153 D3
Oakwood Rd SN5 49 C7
Oamaru Way SN10 214 D3
Oare Hill SN8 174 C2
Oasis Leisure Ctr SN2 50 B7
Oasthouse Cl 3 SN5 49 A8
Oate Hill SN15 78 F6
Oathill La GL7 3 B8
Oathills SN13 84 F8
Obelisk Terr 6 BA12 116 F7
Oberon Way SN25 35 A5
Ocotal Way SN1 50 D8
Odcroft Cl SN15 79 A7
Oddford Vale 17 SP3 203 E8
Odstock Jun Sch SP5 152 B1
Odstock Rd
Britford SP2 152 B4
Swindon SN2 35 C6
Ogbourne SN14 75 B3
Ogbourne St George & St.
Andrew CE Sch SN8 168 F5
Ogbury Camp* SP4 198 A1
Ogilvie Sq SN11 81 C3
Okebourne Pk SN3 51 C3
Okeford Cl SN3 51 C7
Okus Gr SN2 35 D4
Okus Rd SN1 49 F3
Olaf Cl 10 SP10 193 E2
Old Alexander Rd SN16 27 F4
Old Bakery Cl SN16 28 F2
Old Barn GL8 3 C5
Old Batch The BA15 100 B8
Old Beasants SN8 174 A6
Old Blandford Rd SP2 151 F6
Old Boundary Rd 5
SP7 202 C1
Old Brickyard Rd SP6 210 B1
Old Broughton Rd
SN12 94 A5
Old Cann Sch SP7 202 C1
Old Castle Rd SP1 146 A5
Old Chapel Cl SP5 153 D3
Old Chase Rd SN8 169 A4
Old Coach Rd
Durrington/Bulford SP4 217 D8
North Wraxall SN14 67 D2
Shipton Bellinger SP11 191 F1
Old Comm Way 13 SP11 192 A5
Old Ct SN4 47 D1
Old Dames Sch SP6 211 C6
Old Derry Hill
Calne Without SN15 79 D2
Calne Without SN11 79 E2
Old Dilton Rd BA13 112 E7
Old Down Rd GL9 52 C8
Old English Dr 2 SP10 193 D2
Old Granary La SP4 217 B3
Old Hardenhuish La
SN14 70 B1
Old Hayward La RG17 171 B1
Old Hollow BA12 139 B6
Old Hospl Rd SN9 215 B6
Old King Barrows*
SP4 197 F5
Old Malmesbury Rd
SN4 47 E4
Old Malthouse La SP4 147 B7
Old Manor Hospl SP2 145 E1
Old Manor House*
BA12 194 A4
Old Mdws Wlk SP2 151 E7
Old Midford Rd BA2 98 A7
Old Mill La SN3 50 D3
Old Orch The SN16 28 A6
Old Post Office La 5
SP4 190 A3
Old Pound Ct SP8 137 D1
Old Rd Alderbury SP5 153 C4
Chippenham SN15 78 D8
Derry Hill/Studley SN11 80 B2
Old Rly Cl 1 SN16 28 A4
Old Sarum* SP1 145 F6
Old Sarum Barracks
SP4 146 C8
Old Sarum Pk SP4 146 D8
Old Sawmills The
RG17 177 F3
Old Sch Cl SN15 96 C7
Old Severalls The SN9 182 E7
Old Shaft Rd SN13 84 C7
Old Shaftesbury Dro
SP2 150 A6
Old Shaw La SN5 48 F8
Old Sodom La SN15 59 B8
Old St SP2 152 A6
Old Sta Yd The 14 RG17 165 A1
Old Tk BA2 98 F7
Old Vicarage La GL7 4 F7
Old Vineries The 10
SP6 210 C1
Old Ward Rd 5 SP4 198 E6
Old Wardour Castle*
SP3 203 D5
Oldbury Castle (Hill Fort)*
SN11 172 C8
Oldbury Prior SN11 81 C1
Oldbury Way SN11 81 A3
Oldfield Pk BA13 108 E3
Oldfield Rd
Salisbury SP1 146 C5
Westbury BA13 108 E4
Oldford Hill BA11 110 A8
Oldhat Barrow* SN9 183 A3
Olive Gr SN2 35 B3
Olivemead La SN15 45 C1
Oliver Ave SN13 76 F2
Oliver Cl SN5 48 F6
Oliver's Castle (Fort)*
SN10 97 C6
Oliver's La 5 SN16 28 A3
Olivers Cl SN11 166 B1
Olivers Hill SN11 166 B1
Olivier Cl SP2 145 C5
Olivier Rd Swindon SN2 35 B6
Wilton SP2 144 B5
Olympia The SN8 168 E3
Olympiad L Ctr* SN15 78 E8
Omdurman St SN2 35 B1
Orange Cl SN6 23 A6
Orchard Cl Calne SN11 81 C2
Devizes SN10 214 B1
34 Fordingbridge SP6 210 D1
Lechlade GL7 2 B4
5 Ramsbury SN8 170 B2
2 Wanborough SN4 163 A6
Warminster BA12 117 B8
West Ashton BA14 106 B4
Westbury BA13 112 C8
Westwood BA15 99 F3
Orchard Cres SN14 78 B7
Orchard Ct
Bratton BA13 186 A7
St Paul Malmesbury Without
SN16 28 A2
Orchard Dr BA14 104 E2
Orchard End SP4 217 D8
Orchard Gdns
Melksham SN12 94 A3
Purton SN5 33 A3
Orchard Gr
Bromham SN15 96 D7
Swindon SN2 35 D3
Orchard Mead 3 SN4 48 A2
Orchard Pk Cl 3 RG17 177 B6
Orchard Pl SN10 187 E8
Orchard Rd
Chippenham SN14 78 B7
Corsham SN13 77 A2
Marlborough SN8 213 E2
Redlynch SP5 211 C8
Salisbury SP2 145 D2
Trowbridge BA14 105 D7
Westbury BA13 109 A3
Orchard The
Chirton SN10 180 F4
Kington St Michael SN14 70 A8
Limpley Stoke BA2 99 C5
Semington BA14 102 F6
Sixpenny Handley SP5 208 B4
Upton Scudamore BA12 112 F4
Orchard Way
Amesbury SP4 217 C3
Longbridge Deverill
BA12 116 E1
Trowbridge BA14 105 C3
Orchid Dr 30 SP11 192 A5
Ordnance Rd SP9 216 D6
Orford Rd SP4 217 D2
Orkney Cl SN5 49 B7
Orlando Cl 4 SN5 48 F5
Orrin Cl SN5 34 B1
Orwell Cl
Malmesbury SN16 28 A5
Swindon SN25 35 A5
Osborne Rd BA14 101 E3
Osborne St SN2 50 B8
Oslings La BA1 82 B2
Osprey Cl
Bower Hill SN12 94 D1
Swindon SN3 51 E6
Osterley Rd SN25 34 E6
Otter Way SN4 47 F2
Overbrook SN3 51 C3
Overhouse Dr 12 SP3 203 E8
Overton Gdns SN3 36 B2
Overtown Hill SN4 64 C5
Overway La SP7 203 B2
Owl Cl SN3 51 E6
Owlswood 9 SP2 152 A5
Ox Dro
Berwick St John SP5 207 B7
Bishopstone SP5 205 F2
Bower Chalke SP5 208 A8
Kimpton SP11 192 A1
Teffont SP3 201 C5
Oxencroft 8 SP7 202 C2
Oxford Rd Calne SN11 81 B3
Swindon SN3 36 A1
Upavon Down SN9 182 B2
Oxford St
Aldbourne SN8 170 A6
Hungerford RG17 177 C8
Lambourn RG17 165 A1
Malmesbury SN16 28 A3
Marlborough SN8 213 D3
Ramsbury SN8 170 B2
Swindon SN1 50 B6
Oxon Pl SN6 163 E6
Oxyard BA12 195 B2

P

Pack Hill SN4 51 F2
Pack Horse La BA2 98 A7
Packhorse Bridge*
SN15 86 E5
Packhorse La SN5 33 E8
Packington Cl SN5 49 B7
Packway The
Durrington SP4 197 D7
Shrewton SP3 197 A7
Paddington Dr SN5 49 E5
Paddock Cl Enford SN9 190 A6
Great Somerford SN15 44 A2
4 Shaftesbury SP7 202 D1
Sixpenny Handley SP5 208 A3
Swindon SN25 34 E5
Winterbourne SP4 133 B2
Paddock End SN14 70 A7
Paddock La
Chilmark SP3 200 F2
Corsham SN13 84 D8
Paddock The
Highworth SN6 23 A5
Market Lavington SN10 180 A1
8 Tisbury SP3 203 E8
Paddock Way SP1 146 E2
Paddocks The
10 Aldbourne SN8 170 A6
Chippenham SN15 78 E6
14 Ramsbury SN8 170 B2
5 Swindon SN3 36 A2
Padfield Gdns SN12 93 F1
Page Cl Calne SN11 81 C3
Chippenham SN14 78 A7
Paget Cl SP9 216 B8
Pagnell La SN10 179 D1
Pains Way 3 SP4 217 C2
Painters Mead BA14 102 A2
Pakenham Rd SN3 51 B4
Palairet Cl BA15 100 D4
Palm Rd SN14 75 A5
Palmer Dr BA15 100 D8
Palmer Rd
Salisbury SP2 145 E2
Trowbridge BA14 101 D2
Palmer St SN14 78 C7
Palmers Way 11 SN4 163 A6
Palmerston Mdw SN9 190 A6
Pampas Ct 1 BA12 116 E6
Pans La SN10 214 B2
Panters Rd SP3 204 C8
Pantiles The 12 SP6 210 C1
Parade The
Marlborough SN8 213 D3
Swindon SN1 50 C6
Paradise La BA12 116 E1
Parham La SN10 179 E2
Parham Wlk 7 SN5 48 F5
Parhams Ct SN4 47 E1
Parhams Hill SP7 203 B1
Park Ave
Chippenham SN14 78 B8
Corsham SN13 84 A8
Highworth SN6 23 A5
Park Cl Calne SN11 81 C2
Salisbury SP1 146 A4
Trowbridge BA14 105 D3
Park Dr SP3 201 B3
Park End SN6 17 F8
Park Field SN10 214 C5
Park Fields SN15 78 C8
Park La
Castle Combe SN14 68 A7
Cherhill SN11 166 C1
Chippenham SN15 78 D8
Corsham SN13 76 D1
Great Somerford SN15 44 A2
Heytesbury BA12 194 D5
Heywood BA13 109 C7
Lea & Cleverton SN16 29 D3
Lydiard Millicent SN5 48 D7
Malmesbury SN16 27 E5
North Wraxall SN14 68 A2
Odstock SP5 152 D4
Salisbury SP1 146 A3
Sutton Benger SN15 57 D2
Swindon SN1 50 A6
West Dean SP5 149 F1
Park Mead SN16 27 F4
Park Pl SN6 6 F1
Park Rd
Fordingbridge SP6 210 D1
Malmesbury SN16 27 F4
Market Lavington SN10 179 E1
Rushall SN9 181 F3
Salisbury SP1 146 D2
Tidworth SP9 216 D5
Tisbury SP3 203 E8
Westbury BA13 112 B8
Park Springs SN5 49 C5
Park St Charlton SN16 29 A6
Park St *continued*
Heytesbury BA12 194 C5
Hungerford RG17 177 B7
Salisbury SP1 146 B2
Swindon SN3 36 C2
Trowbridge BA14 105 C7
Park The
Erlestoke SN10 179 A1
8 Lambourn RG17 165 A2
Park View
Chirton SN10 180 F4
Devizes SN10 179 D8
Park View Dr
Lydiard Millicent SN5 48 D8
1 Westbury BA13 108 F1
Park Way RG17 177 B6
Parkers La SN15 70 D6
Parkhouse Cnr SP4 199 D6
Parkhouse Rd SP9 199 C8
Parkland Way SP4 133 D6
Parklands
Malmesbury SN16 27 E4
Trowbridge BA14 101 D2
Parklands Cl SN16 27 E4
Parklands Rd SN3 50 D5
Parklands The SN14 55 E8
Parkside
Chippenham SN15 78 D8
Swindon SN3 36 A3
Parkwater Rd SP5 161 E1
Parliament St SN14 78 B7
Parr Cl SN5 49 A6
Parsley Cl SN2 34 D5
Parsonage Cl
31 Fordingbridge SP6 210 D1
Salisbury SP1 145 E5
Parsonage Gn SP2 151 E6
Parsonage Hill SP5 154 D7
Parsonage La
Charlton Musgrove BA9 136 C2
Hungerford RG17 177 B7
9 Lambourn RG17 165 A1
20 Market Lavington SN10 179 F1
Parsonage Pk Dr 3
SP6 210 D1
Parsonage Pl 9 RG17 165 A2
Parsonage Rd
Amesbury SP4 217 B3
Swindon SN3 36 A3
Trowbridge BA14 102 A1
Parsonage The SP5 208 B4
Parsonage Vale SN8 183 D2
Parsonage Way SN15 70 F1
Parsons Cl SP4 133 D5
Parsons Gn 4 SP3 196 E6
Parsons La BA12 116 E2
Parsons Pool 19 SP7 202 C2
Parsons Way SN4 47 E1
Partridge Cl
Chippenham SN14 70 B2
Corsham SN13 76 E1
Swindon SN3 51 E6
Partridge Hill SP5 212 E6
Partridge Way SP4 146 C8
Passmore Cl SN3 51 E7
Pasture Cl SN2 49 E7
Pastures The BA15 99 E3
Pat-Yat GL7 4 B5
Patchway SN14 78 B8
Patchway The SN10 214 D3
Patney Rd SN10 180 F5
Paul St SN13 76 F1
Paul's Dene Cres SP1 146 A5
Paul's Dene Rd SP1 146 A5
Paulet Cl 3 SN5 49 A4
Pauls Croft SN6 19 D7
Pavely Cl SN15 78 C6
Pavely Gdns BA14 102 A1
Paven Cl SN5 33 A4
Pavenhill SN5 33 A4
Paxcroft Prim Sch
BA14 101 F1
Paxcroft Way BA14 105 F8
Payne Cl SN15 78 E4
Payne's Hill 2 SP1 152 B8
Peacock SN8 173 E6
Peak The SN5 33 B3
Peaks Down SN5 34 B2
Pealsham Gdns 6 SP6 210 D1
Pear Ash La BA9 137 C4
Pear Tree Dr SP5 212 C5
Pear Tree La SN10 187 B8
Pear Tree Orch 2 BA13 186 B7
Pearce Cl SN2 35 E6
Pearce Way SP1 146 D5
Pearl Rd SN5 49 A7
Peartree Cl
Atworth/Whitley SN12 85 C1
Purton SN5 33 C5
7 West Wellow SO51 212 F6
Peatmoor Way SN5 34 A1
Peel Cir SN13 84 D8
Pegasus Way SN12 94 C1
Pelch La SN12 178 D8
Pelham Ct SN8 213 E3
Pembridge Rd SP6 210 E1
Pembroke Cl 1 BA14 105 D6
Pembroke Gdns SN25 34 E3
Pembroke Gn SN16 28 F1
Pembroke Pk Cty Fst Sch
SP2 145 C3
Pembroke Rd
Chippenham SN15 79 A4
Melksham SN12 94 B4
Salisbury SP2 145 C2
Upavon Down SN9 182 B2
Pembroke St SN1 50 B4
Pen Cl SN25 35 A4

Pen Hill BA10 122 F1
Pen Mill Hill BA9 137 E3
Pendennis Rd SN5 49 A3
Penfold Gdns SN1 50 C4
Penhill Dr SN2 35 C4
Penhill Jun Sch SN2 35 C5
Penleigh Cl SN13 84 F8
Penleigh Rd BA13 108 D2
Penn Hill Rd SN11 81 C3
Penneys Piece 2 BA11 110 C6
Pennine Cl SN12 94 D4
Pennine Way SN25 34 F7
Penning Rd SP2 145 B4
Pennings Dro SP5 157 A8
Pennings Rd
North Tidworth SP9 191 D5
Tidworth SP9 216 C8
Penny Hill SN8 191 E8
Penny La
Chippenham SN15 78 F4
Swindon SN3 50 F7
Penny Royal Cl SN11 80 F3
Penny's Cl 3 SP6 210 D2
Penny's Cres 4 SP6 210 D2
Penny's La
Pitton & Farley SP5 154 E7
2 Wilton SP2 144 D3
Pennycress Cl SN25 34 E4
Pennycress Dr SN12 94 C3
Pennyfarthing St SP1 146 B1
Pennys La SP6 210 D2
Penruddock Cl SP2 145 C3
Pensford Way BA11 110 D6
Penton La SP11 193 A3
Penton Lodge School SP11 193 B2
Pentridge Cl SN3 51 C7
Pentylands Cl SN6 22 F7
Penzance Dr SN5 49 F5
Pepper Pl BA12 117 D7
Pepperacre La BA14 101 F1
Pepperbox Hill SN5 34 B2
Pepperbox Rise SP5 153 E2
Pepperbox The* SP5 160 C6
Peppercorn Orch BA14 178 A6
Percheron Cl 11 SN5 49 A7
Percy St SN2 49 F7
Peregrine Cl SN3 51 D8
Perham Cres 1 SP11 192 B5
Periwinkle Cl SN2 34 C3
Perrinsfield GL7 2 D6
Perry's La Seend SN12 178 D8
Wroughton SN4 64 A6
Peters Finger Rd SP5 152 E7
Petersfield Rd SN3 51 B4
Peto Gdn The* BA15 99 E2
Petter Cl SN4 64 B7
Petticoat La
Redlynch SP5 211 D8
Westbury BA13 112 C8
Pettridge La BA12 139 A5
Petty La SN11 79 F3
Pevensey Way SN5 49 C5
Pewsey Rd
Marlborough SN8 213 D2
Rushall SN9 181 E2
Upavon SN9 181 F2
Pewsey Sports Ctr & Swimming Pool SN9 215 B5
Pewsey Sta SN9 215 B5
Pewsey Vale Gram Sch SN9 215 B5
Pewsham Lock SN15 78 E5
Pewsham Rd SN2 35 D5
Pewsham Way SN15 78 E4
Pheasant Bsns Pk SN14 78 B5
Pheasant Cl
8 Chippenham Without SN14 77 F6
Swindon SN3 51 E5
Tidworth SP9 216 D6
Pheasantry The GL7 8 E7
Philip Cl SN12 94 C6
Philip Rd
21 Durrington/Bulford SP4 198 B7
Wilton SP2 144 B5
Philipps House & Dinton Pk* SP3 201 E2
Phillip Cl SN10 214 C4
Phillips Cl SN14 77 F7
Phillips La
Salisbury SP4 145 E6
Swindon SN1 50 D4
Phipps Cl BA13 108 F4
Phoenix Rise BA13 108 E3
Picket Cl SP6 210 D1
Picket Cnr SP6 211 F3
Picket Post Gate BA12 116 A4
Picketleaze SN14 78 A7
Pickford Way SN25 35 B6
Pickwick Cl SN2 35 E5
Pickwick Rd SN13 76 F2
Picquet The 12 BA13 186 B7
Picton Rd SN5 49 A7
Pictor Cl SN13 76 D1
Pig La
Bishops Cannings SN10 172 C1
Hullavington SN16 41 A3
Pigeon House La SN3 36 A3
Pigott Cl 4 SP4 190 A4
Pigtrough La SP7 203 B4
Pike Cnr SN16 17 D7
Pike House Cl SN6 19 C8
Pikefield Cres SN16 29 A6
Pilgrim Cl SN5 49 A7
Pilgrims Mead SP1 146 C5
Pill Hill SP5 161 C4
Pilots View SP4 217 D3
Pilton Cl SN5 49 A8
Pimperleaze Rd BA12 139 F1
Pinckneys Way 13 SP4 198 B7
Pine Cl Corsham SN13 76 A1
Landford SP5 212 C5
Melksham SN12 94 A3
Pine Ct 2 BA11 110 B7
Pine Wlk BA14 105 C3
Pinehurst Infs Sch SN2 35 B2
Pinehurst Jun Sch SN2 35 B2
Pinehurst Rd SN2 35 C2
Pinehurst Youth & Sports Ctr SN2 35 B3
Pines Rd SN10 214 C2
Pines The SP6 211 A1
Pinetree Rise SN2 35 B3
Pineview Cl SP5 211 C6
Pinewood Way
Colerne SN14 74 F7
Salisbury SP2 145 B4
Pinewoods Cl SP2 145 B4
Pinfield La SN15 78 F4
Pinhills SN11 81 A2
Pink La SN16 29 E5
Pinkney Pk* SN16 25 F1
Pinnegar Way SN3 51 E6
Pinnocks Pl SN2 35 F4
Pintail Ct SN15 60 B1
Pintail Way BA13 109 B4
Pioneer Cl 3 SN5 49 A7
Pipehouse La BA2 98 F4
Pipers Cl SN4 61 D8
Pipers Way SN1 50 C1
Pipitdene SN3 51 D7
Piplar Gd BA15 100 D4
Pippin The SN11 81 B3
Pippins The 3 BA12 116 F7
Pipsmore Rd
5 Chippenham SN14 70 A1
Chippenham SN14 78 A8
Pit Wlk SP4 199 C4
Pitchens End SN4 167 C7
Pitchens The SN4 64 B5
Pitman Ave BA14 105 B7
Pitton Prim Sch SP5 148 B3
Pitton Rd SP5 154 D8
Pitts Croft SN13 84 E5
Pitts La
Bishopstone SP5 205 F4
Chitterne BA12 195 D7
Sedgehill & Semley SP7 202 B7
Pittsfield SN6 19 D7
Pix Mead Gdns 1 SP7 202 D1
Place Rd SN12 94 A4
Plane Tree Cl SN12 85 C1
Planks The SN3 50 D4
Plantation Rd
Chippenham SN14 78 C8
Tidworth SP9 216 D5
Wellow SO51 212 F4
Plantation The SP5 149 A5
Plants Gn BA12 117 B6
Plassey Rd SP9 216 C7
Platford St SN11 81 B2
Platt Cl RG17 177 C6
Platt La RG17 170 E7
Plattes Cl SN5 49 B8
Play Cl SN5 33 C4
Player Ct 8 SP6 210 D2
Pleydell Rd SN1 50 C2
Pleydells 3 SN6 19 D8
Plough La
Kington Langley SN15 70 C5
Marston SN10 179 A3
Plum La SN10 180 E4
Plume of Feathers La SN8 213 E3
Plummer Cl SN4 64 A6
Plumpton Cl SN14 77 F6
Plymouth St SN1 50 D6
Pockeredge Dr SN13 84 C7
Pockeridge Rd SN13 84 E7
Polden Rd 1 SP1 152 C7
Polebarn Rd BA14 105 D8
Pollen Cl SP4 190 B2
Pollen La SP4 190 B2
Poltondale SN3 51 D7
Pomeroy La BA14 104 B6
Pond La SN5 19 B1
Pond St SN25 34 F5
Ponting St SN1 50 C7
Ponting's Cl SN26 21 C2
Pool Gastons Rd SN16 27 F3
Pool Gn SN13 84 E6
Poole Keynes House GL7 5 B4
Poole Rd SN25 34 E3
Poores Rd 17 SP4 198 B7
Pope Cl SN25 34 F5
Popham Ct SN15 78 E6
Poplar Ave SN2 35 C2
Poplar Tree La BA14 104 B3
Poplar Way
Colerne SN14 75 A5
Salisbury SP1 146 C5
Poplars The
Chippenham SN14 70 A1
Fovant SP3 204 D8
Popplechurch Dr 5 SN3 51 E7
Poppy Cl SN11 80 F4
Porchester Cl 8 SP10 193 C2
Port Down RG17 177 C7
Port Hill SN8 213 D5
Port Regis Sch SP7 202 B3
Port Way BA13 186 A6
Portal Ave SN13 84 B8
Portal Pl SN15 60 A1
Portal Rd SN2 35 A2
Porte Marsh Ind Est SN11 81 C5
Porte Marsh Rd SN11 81 C5
Portfield Rd SP5 150 A4
Portland Ave
Britford SP2 151 F5
Swindon SN1 50 A4
Portland Way SN11 81 C2
Portman Rd SN12 94 A6
Portmore Cl SN5 34 C2
Portnell's La BA12 137 F4
Porton Rd SP4 217 D3
Portsmouth St SN1 50 D6
Portway
Chippenham SN14 78 B6
Frome BA11 110 A4
Laverstock SP4 146 B7
Warminster BA12 117 A7
Winterbourne SP4 133 A3
Portway Ind Est SP10 193 B1
Portway La BA12 117 A8
Portwell 3 SN6 19 D7
Post Office La
Broad Hinton SN4 167 C7
Corsham SN13 77 A1
Post Office Rd RG17 177 F3
Poston Way BA15 99 D7
Pot La BA11 110 F8
Potley La SN13 84 E7
Potterdown Rd 3 SN2 35 C5
Potterne CE Prim Sch SN10 179 D5
Potterne Rd SN10 214 A1
Potters Way SP1 152 D8
Pottery La RG17 177 E3
Pottle St BA12 119 A6
Pottows Field SN11 166 B1
Poulsen Cl BA12 117 A5
Poulshot Rd SN10 179 A5
Poulton BA15 100 D5
Poulton Hill SN8 213 E4
Poulton La BA15 100 E5
Poulton St SN2 50 C8
Pound Cl Lyneham SN15 60 A3
Semington BA14 102 F6
Pound Hill
Melchet Park & Plaitford SO51 212 F7
St Paul Malmesbury Without SN16 43 A3
Pound La
Bradford-on-Avon BA15 100 C5
Damerham SP6 209 E3
Melchet Park & Plaitford SO51 212 F7
Semington BA14 102 E6
Shaftesbury SP7 202 D2
Swindon SN2 35 B2
Wilcot SN8 174 B2
Pound Mead SN13 84 F8
Pound Piece
Ashbury SN6 164 A8
5 Hungerford RG17 177 B7
Pound Pill SN13 77 A1
Pound Rd SN6 22 F7
Pound Row BA12 116 F6
Pound St
Ebbesborne Wake SP5 204 D3
Warminster BA12 116 F6
Pound The SN15 96 B7
Powell Rise SN16 28 B5
Powells Way GL8 13 B4
Power Rd SP4 197 E7
Pownall Rd SP4 198 A6
Poynder Pl SN11 166 A6
Poynder Rd SN13 76 E1
Poynings Way SN5 48 F4
Preshute La SN8 213 B2
Preshute Prim Sch SN8 213 A1
Prestbury Dr BA12 117 C5
Prestly Wood 3 SN13 76 B1
Preston La SN15 60 B1
Pretoria Rd 13 SP11 192 B5
Priddy Cl BA11 110 C7
Priestley CP Sch SN11 81 C2
Priestley Gr SN11 81 C2
Priestly Wood Rd 6 SN13 76 B1
Primrose Cl Calne SN11 81 B5
Swindon SN2 34 D5
Primrose Dr SN12 94 C4
Primrose Hill
Tockenham SN4 60 D6
Wilton SP2 144 D4
Primrose La
Manningford SN9 181 F6
Redlynch SP5 211 C7
Primrose Rd
24 Ludgershall SP11 192 A5
Salisbury SP2 145 C4
Primrose Way SN14 70 B2
Primrose Wlk 1 BA12 116 E7
Prince Charles Cl 14 SP11 192 A5
Prince Charles Dr SN11 81 C3
Princecroft CP Sch BA12 116 E6
Princecroft La 3 BA12 116 E6
Princes Cl SP5 211 D8
Princes Hill SP5 211 D8
Princes St 4 SN1 50 C5
Princess Anne Rd 9 BA11 110 A7
Princess Gdns
Trowbridge BA14 101 E4
Warminster BA12 117 D6
Princess Margaret Hospl
Liddington SN3 51 D1
Swindon SN1 50 A4
Princess Mary Gdns 19 SP11 192 A5
Prior Pk Sch SN6 19 E7
Prior's Hill SN4 64 B5
Priorsfield SN8 213 E2
Priory Ave RG17 177 B6
Priory Cl Alderbury SP5 153 F2
Bradford-on-Avon BA15 100 C7
5 Hungerford RG17 177 B6
5 Shrewton SP3 196 E6
Wilton SP2 144 C2
Priory Gn SN6 23 A6
Priory New Rd SN13 76 F2
Priory Pk BA15 100 D7
Priory Pl 1 RG17 177 B6
Priory Rd
Hungerford RG17 177 B6
Swindon SN3 51 A4
Priory Sq 5 SP2 146 A1
Priory St SN13 76 F2
Pritchard Cl SN2 35 F5
Private Rd BA11 123 C8
Privet La SP11 192 D2
Proby Pl BA14 102 A1
Professions Cnr SP5 206 D6
Prospect Box SN13 83 B4
Corsham SN13 85 A7
Prospect Hill SN1 50 C5
Prospect Pl
Bathford BA1 82 D2
Mere BA12 138 F5
Swindon SN1 50 C4
Trowbridge BA14 101 D1
Prospect Rd RG17 177 B7
Proud Cl SN5 33 B3
Providence La SN13 76 F1
Provis Mead SN15 79 A4
Provost St 23 SP6 210 D1
Pub La SN10 180 F8
Puck Well Nature Reserve* BA12 140 C4
Pucklands SN10 180 E5
Puddleslosh La SP6 210 C2
Pullman Dr SP2 145 B3
Pump La Bathford BA1 82 B1
Long Newnton GL8 13 C4
Purbeck Cl SN3 51 C7
Purbeck Pl SN11 81 D2
Purleigh Rd SN13 76 E1
Purley Ave SN3 51 B3
Purley Rd SN4 51 F1
Purley Way SO51 212 E6
Purlpit SN12 85 A1
Purlyn Acre SN8 213 D4
Purslane Cl SN2 34 C3
Purton Liby & Mus* SN5 33 C4
Purton Rd
Haydon Wick SN2 34 C3
Purton SN5 34 B2
Swindon SN2 34 D3
Purvis Cl 4 SP4 217 E3
Pyatts Cnr BA14 178 C4
Pye La SN4 167 A8

Q

Quadrangle The SN15 78 C6
Quakers Wlk SN11 73 F7
Quantock Cl
Melksham Without SN12 94 D4
5 Warminster BA12 117 A8
Quarr Barton SN11 81 B3
Quarries The SN1 50 C3
Quarry Cl BA2 99 D6
Quarry Cres SN6 22 F6
Quarry Fields Ind Est BA12 138 E5
Quarry Hill SN13 83 E6
Quarry La Colerne SN14 75 B3
Melbury Abbas SP7 206 A7
Quarry Mews SN1 50 C3
Quarry Rd SN1 50 C4
Quarrybrook Cl SN3 36 E5
Quarrydale Cl SN11 81 B2
Quartermaster Rd BA13 108 D6
Quarterway La BA14 101 E1
Quavey Rd SP5 211 D7
Quebec Rd SN4 168 E8
Queen Alexandra Rd SP2 145 D3
Queen Elizabeth Dr SN2 34 C4
Queen Manor Rd
Clarendon Park SP5 147 B1
Laverstock SP5 152 E8
Queen Mary Rd SP2 145 D3
Queen Oak* SN8 175 C4
Queen St Hale SP6 211 B5
Salisbury SP1 146 A1
Swindon SN1 50 B6
Wilton SP2 144 D4
Queen's Barrow* BA12 201 A7
Queen's Dr Swindon SN3 50 E6
Swindon SN1 50 E6
Queen's Rd
Devizes SN10 214 A2
Westbury BA13 108 E3
Wootton Bassett SN4 47 E2
Queenborough SN5 49 C4
Queens Ave
Corsham SN13 76 F3
Highworth SN6 23 A6
Queens Cl
27 Ludgershall SP11 192 A5
Sutton Benger SN15 57 D2
Queens Club Gdns BA14 105 A8
Queens Cres SN14 78 A6
Queens Cres Sch SN14 78 A6
Queens Dr SN3 51 B2
Queens Gdns
32 Fordingbridge SP6 210 D1
Trowbridge BA14 101 E4
Queens Gr BA9 137 C3
Queens Rd
Hannington SN6 21 F8
Mere BA12 139 B6
Salisbury SP1 146 B2
7 Tisbury SP3 203 E8
Trowbridge BA14 101 C2
Queens Sq SN15 78 F6
Queens Way SN8 213 F2
Queensberry Rd
Amesbury SP4 217 C4
Salisbury SP1 146 A3
Queensfield SN2 35 D5
Queensway
Melksham SN12 94 C4
2 Netheravon SP4 190 A3
Warminster BA12 117 D6
Queintin Rd SN1 50 D3
Quemerford Calne SN11 81 C1
Calne Without SN11 89 D8
Quidham St SP5 204 F2
Quilling Cl BA14 105 E7

R

Rabley Wood View SN8 213 E4
Radcliffe Rd SP2 152 A6
Radcot Cl SN5 34 A1
Radley Bottom RG17 177 F7
Radley Cl SN3 51 C7
Radnor Cl SN10 214 C2
Radnor Pk SN16 42 E4
Radnor Pl 3 SN12 94 A2
Radnor Rd SP1 146 A3
Radnor St SN1 50 A5
Radstock Ave SN3 51 B6
Radway Rd SN3 35 F3
Raffin La SN9 215 C4
Raggett St SN1 50 C5
Raglan Cl SN3 50 E2
Ragleth Gr BA14 101 E2
Railway Village Mus* SN1 50 B6
Rainer Cl SN3 36 B3
Raleigh Ave SN3 50 F6
Raleigh Cres SP4 217 E3
Rambler Cl BA14 105 A8
Ramblers Mead SP11 193 A2
Rambridge Cres SP2 145 B5
Ramleaze Dr
Salisbury SP2 145 C5
Swindon SN5 49 A7
Rampart Rd SP1 146 B1
Ramsbury Ave SN2 35 B6
Ramsbury Dr RG17 177 C7
Ramsbury Manor* SN8 169 F1
Ramsbury Sch SN8 170 B2
Ramsbury Terr RG17 177 C7
Ramsbury Wlk BA14 105 D6
Ramscliff SN10 187 F7
Ramsden Rd SN1 48 F3
Ramsthorn Cl SN2 34 D4
Randall Cres SN5 49 A8
Randall Ct SN13 76 D1
Randall's Croft Rd SP2 144 B2
Randolph Cl SN3 50 F5
Rank The BA14 105 C3
Rannoch Cl 4 SN5 34 B2
Ransome Cl SN5 49 B8
Raspberry La 8 SP7 202 B1
Ratcliff's Gdn 15 SP7 202 C1
Ratcoombe Rd SN5 34 A2
Ratfyn Barrow* SP4 217 B4
Ratfyn Rd SP4 217 B4
Raven Cl SP9 216 D6
Ravenglass Rd SN5 49 C6
Ravenhurst SN16 14 E6
Ravens Wlk SN4 48 A2
Ravenscroft
7 Salisbury SP2 152 A5
Swindon SN3 51 C8
Ravenscroft Gdns BA14 101 F1
Rawlence Rd
Salisbury SP2 145 B3
Wilton SP2 144 C2
Rawlings Cl SN3 36 E4
Rawlingswell La SN8 213 E3
Rawlins Rd SN9 215 C5
Rawlinson Rd SP4 198 E6
Rawston Cl SN3 51 C6
Ray Cl Chippenham SN15 78 F5
Swindon SN25 35 A4
Raybrook Cres SN2 49 E6
Rayfield Gr SN2 50 B8
Read St SN1 50 A5

Reading St 4 SN1 50 B6
Recreation Rd
10 Durrington/Bulford SP4 198 B7
Ludgershall SP11 192 A6
Rectory Cl Alton SN8 181 C8
Stanton St Quintin SN14 56 B4
11 Warminster BA12 117 A8
Rectory Hill SP5 155 F3
Rectory La
Alderbury SP5 153 E2
Breamore SP6 210 E5
Charlton Musgrove BA9 136 B1
Cricklade SN6 19 E8
Letcombe Bassett OX12 165 F8
Rectory Pl 4 SP11 192 F1
Rectory Rd
Alderbury SP5 153 E2
Salisbury SP2 151 F8
Sutton Mandeville SP3 204 C7
Rectory Wood 1 SN8 170 A6
Reculver Way 6 SP10 193 C2
Red Cross House* SN10 214 B4
Red La Mildenhall SN8 169 B2
Sixpenny Handley SP5 208 A3
Red Lion La SN6 19 E8
Red Pit BA13 112 A8
Red Post La SP11 192 F1
Red Way The BA12 115 F3
Redbridge Cl 1 SN1 49 F4
Redcliffe St SN2 49 F6
Redenham Dro SP11 192 E4
Redford Cl SP1 146 D3
Redhill Cl SN11 79 F2
Redhills SN4 62 B1
Redland SN14 78 B8
Redland CP Sch SN14 78 B8
Redland La BA13 108 F2
Redlands 3 BA13 186 B7
Redlands Cl SN6 23 A4
Redlynch CE Prim Sch SP5 211 E6
Redlynch Cl SN2 35 C5
Redman Rd SN11 81 C6
Redmans La SP7 206 A7
Redposts Dr SN1 49 E4
Redruth Cl SN3 51 B5
Redstocks La SN12 95 A2
Redwing Ave SN14 70 B2
Redwood Way SN14 75 A5
Reed Wlk 10 SP4 198 C7
Reeds SN6 19 C8
Reeds Farm Rd SN16 28 A4
Reeds Gd SN8 213 F3
Reeves Cl 2 SN3 51 C4
Reeves Rd SN10 214 D1
Regent Cir SN1 50 C5
Regent Cl
15 Hungerford RG17 177 B7
Swindon SN1 50 C6
Regent St 6 SN1 50 C5
Regents Pl BA15 100 D5
Regimental Mus* SP1 152 A8
Reid's Piece SN5 33 B3
Reith Way 2 SP10 193 B1
Rendall's Barn GL7 4 E5
Rendells Ct SN10 214 B3
Renoir Cl SN25 35 A8
Restrop Rd SN5 33 A3
Restrop View SN5 33 A4
Retingham Way SN2 36 A5
Reto Gr BA15 99 F3
Revell Cl SN2 35 E4
Reynolds Way SN25 35 A8
Rhine Cl SN1 49 F4
Rhuddlan SN5 49 B4
Ricardo Rd SN15 78 D8
Richard Jefferies Mus* SN3 51 B2
Richards Cl SN4 47 D1
Richards Way SP2 151 E7
Richborough Dr 3 SP10 193 C2
Richmond Cl 2 BA14 105 A7
Richmond Ct SN6 6 F1
Richmond Rd
Calne Without SN11 81 A4
2 Salisbury SP2 145 F2
Rickbarton 2 SN10 187 E7
Rickfield BA15 100 B6
Rickworth Pl BA12 195 A3
Ridge Gn SN5 49 B7
Ridge Nether Moor SN3 51 D2
Ridge The
Broad Blunsdon SN26 21 B2
Redlynch SP5 211 C7
Ridge Way SP7 202 C3
Ridgemead SN11 81 B4
Ridgeway SP3 201 A3
Ridgeway Cl SN2 34 F2
Ridgeway Hospl The SN4 64 C6
Ridgeway La SN15 44 E1
Ridgeway Rd
Salisbury SP1 146 B2
Swindon SN2 35 E5
Ridgeway Sch SN4 64 B7
Ridgeway The
Chiseldon SN4 65 D2
Crudwell SN16 14 E6
Liddington SN4 163 A2
Warminster BA12 117 B6
Ridgmount 6 SP4 198 B7
Ridings Mead SN14 70 C2
Ridings The SN14 70 A8
Rigsby's La SN16 16 F5
Ringsbury Camp* SN5 32 E2
Ringsbury Cl SN5 32 F3
Ringwood Ave 5 SP4 217 C3
Ringwood Cl SN3 51 B6
Ringwood Rd 27 SP6 210 D1
Rinsdale Cl SN5 34 B1
Ripley Rd SN1 50 C4
Ripon Cl SN14 78 A5
Ripple Field SN5 49 B4
Rise The SN11 89 C8
Risingham Mead SN5 49 C5
Rivar Rd SN8 176 F1
Rivenhall Rd SN5 49 C5
River Pk SN8 213 D2
River St SN9 215 C5
River Way
5 Durrington/Bulford SP4 198 C7
South Cerney GL7 6 F7
Trowbridge BA14 101 C1
Riverbourne Rd
Laverstock SP1 146 D1
Salisbury SP1 152 D8
Riverdale Cl
9 Fordingbridge SP6 210 D1
Swindon SN1 50 C2
Rivermead SP4 133 F8
Rivermead Dr SN5 49 C7
Rivermead Dr Ind Est SN5 49 C7
Rivers Reach 6 BA11 110 A4
Rivers Way SN6 22 F6
Riverside Calne SN11 89 D8
Wilton SP2 144 D3
Riverside Cl
Salisbury SP1 146 D2
South Newton SP2 130 A4
Riverside Dr
Chippenham SN15 79 A8
Melksham SN12 94 A6
Riverside Pk SN15 44 A2
Riverside Rd SP1 146 D2
Riverside Terr SP3 129 E8
Roach's La GL9 38 C1
Road Hill Box SN13 82 E8
Colerne SN14 74 D1
Robbers' Stone* SN10 187 E6
Robbins Ridge SP4 217 C2
Robert Franklin Way GL7 7 A7
Robert Le Kyng Sch SN1 50 A5
Roberts Cl SN4 64 B5
Roberts of Kandahar Rd BA12 113 F1
Roberts Rd
North Tidworth SP11 192 A5
Salisbury SP2 145 D3
Robin Cl BA12 117 C6
Robin Hill La SP4 217 C8
Robin Hood's Ball* SP4 189 C1
Robin Hood's Bower* BA12 117 B1
Robinia Cl SN9 215 D5
Robins Cl
Chippenham SN14 70 B2
Wootton Bassett SN4 48 A2
Robins Hill RG17 177 F3
Robinsgreen SN3 51 D7
Robinson Cl SN3 51 D6
Rochdale Ave SN11 81 B4
Roche Cl SN3 51 D4
Roche Ct* SP5 135 E1
Rochelle Ct 19 SN10 179 F1
Rocher Cl BA13 108 F3
Rochester Cl 5 SN5 49 B4
Rochford Cl SN5 49 A5
Rock La BA12 117 D6
Rock Rd BA14 105 B7
Rockbourne La SP6 209 F3
Rockbourne Mus* SP6 210 A3
Rockbourne Roman Villa* SP6 210 A4
Rockdown Ct SN2 35 D4
Rocker Bench SN6 163 E6
Rockfel Rd RG17 165 A1
Rockfield SN14 75 B3
Rockley Rd SN8 213 C7
Rockmoor La SP11 185 C5
Rodbourne Cheney CP Sch SN25 35 A3
Rodbourne House SN16 43 B4
Rodbourne Rd
St Paul Malmesbury Without SN16 42 F4
Swindon SN2 49 F7
Rodden Manor* BA11 110 D4
Rodden Rd BA11 110 A5
Roddenbury Cl BA11 110 B5
Roddenbury View BA12 115 A8
Rode Bridge* BA11 103 E1
Rode Hill BA11 103 F1
Rodsleigh BA14 104 F6
Rodway 13 SN4 163 A6
Rodwell Cl 3 SN3 51 A4
Rodwell Pk BA14 101 E2
Roebuck Cl SN4 47 F2
Roger Penny Way SP6 211 C3
Rogers Cl SN3 51 A7
Rogers Mdw SN8 213 D5
Rogers's La RG17 171 D7
Rolleston St 1 SN1 50 C5
Rollestone Rd SP3 196 E6
Rollestone St 1 SP1 146 B1
Roman Cres SN1 50 B3
Roman Mdw SP5 211 A8
Roman Rd SP2 145 D2
Roman Way
Andover SP10 193 E2
Chippenham SN15 79 B5
Highworth SN6 22 F5
Lechlade GL7 2 D5
13 Market Lavington SN10 179 F1
Roman Way Prim Sch SP10 193 E2
Romer Rd SP2 152 A6
Romney Way SN5 49 A6
Romsey Rd
Amesbury SP4 217 D2
Whiteparish SP5 162 B3
Romsey St SN2 49 F7
Ron Golding Cl SN16 28 A5
Rook St BA12 139 A4
Rookery La Ansty SP3 203 F6
Breamore SP6 210 D5
Swallowcliffe SP3 204 A6
Rookery Mdw SN8 174 A6
Rookery Pk SN11 89 C7
Rookes La SN10 179 D5
Rooks La BA11 110 E6
Rooks Nest Cl SN15 78 F4
Rookwood Gdns 9 SP6 210 C1
Rope Wlk SN12 94 B3
Rope Yd SN4 47 D1
Rosary The SN4 47 E2
Rose St SN2 49 F7
Rosebery St SN1 50 D7
Rosebrock Gdns SN12 94 C3
Rosedale Gdns BA14 101 A1
Rosedale Rd SN3 51 B4
Rosefield Way BA13 108 F4
Roseland Ave SN10 214 C3
Rosemary Cl Calne SN11 80 F4
Laverstock SP1 146 D1
Swindon SN2 34 D5
Rosemary La
Freshford BA2 99 B4
2 Salisbury SP1 152 A8
Rosenheim Rise 1 BA13 186 B7
Ross Gdns SN2 36 A4
Ross Rd SP4 197 E7
Rossett Gdns BA14 105 A8
Rothe Rise BA13 108 F1
Rother Cl SN25 34 F5
Rotherstone SN10 214 A4
Rotten Row SN4 163 A6
Rougemont Cl SP1 146 B1
Rough St SN13 84 F5
Roughmoor Way SN5 34 A1
Round Barrow Cl SN14 75 B3
Round Hill 25 SP6 210 D1
Round House SN11 81 D1
Roundaway La SP11 193 A5
Roundhills Mead SN6 23 B6
Roundpond SN12 93 F6
Roundstone St BA14 101 D1
Roundway Cl SN11 89 B1
Roundway Down SN5 49 B3
Roundway Gdns SN10 214 B6
Roundway Pk SN10 214 C5
Roundwood View SN15 58 A3
Roves La SN6 23 B1
Row La SN12 178 C7
Row The SP5 211 C8
Rowan Cl Colerne SN14 75 A5
5 Durrington/Bulford SP4 198 B7
Salisbury SP2 145 B4
Rowan Ct Frome BA11 110 B7
Melksham SN12 94 A3
Rowan Dr SN4 47 E1
Rowan Rd SN2 35 A3
Rowans The SN16 27 F4
Rowbarrow Cl SP2 152 B5
Rowde CE Prim Sch SN10 96 E2
Rowde Ct Rd SN10 96 D1
Rowdeford Sch SN10 96 D3
Rowden Hill SN15 78 C6
Rowden La
Bradford-on-Avon BA15 100 D4
Chippenham SN15 78 C5
Rowden Rd SN15 78 C6
Rowe Mead SN15 78 E5
Rowe's Hill BA12 119 C8
Rowland Hill Cl SN3 51 E4
Rowlands Cl BA1 82 B2
Rowley Medieval Village of* BA15 99 F1
Rowley Pl SN12 94 B4
Rowton Heath Way SN5 49 A4
Royal Cl SN15 78 D6
Royal Field Cl SN14 55 E8
Royce Cl 5 SP10 193 B1
Royston Rd SN3 51 A4
Rubens Cl SN25 34 F8
Ruckley Gdns SN3 36 B2
Rudge Hill BA11 107 D5
Rudge La
Beckington BA11 107 B6
Wilcot SN8 174 B1
Rudge Rd BA11 107 B2
Rumble Dene SN15 78 E5
Rune Dr 4 SP10 193 D2
Rushall CE Sch SN9 181 E3
Rushall Cl SN2 35 B5
Rushall Dro SN9 181 D1
Rushall Rd SN9 181 F3
Rushey La BA15 91 F3
Rushmead La SN14 66 A3
Rushmore Golf Club SP5 207 C5
Rushmore Pk* SP5 207 C5
Rushton Rd SN3 51 A3
Ruskin Ave
Melksham SN12 94 B4
Swindon SN2 35 F3
Ruskin Cty Jun Sch SN2 35 F4
Ruskin Dr
Warminster BA12 116 D6
Wootton Bassett SN4 47 F3
Russell Mill La SN10 179 D1
Russell Rd SP2 145 E2
Russell St SP2 144 D3
Russet Ct BA12 116 F7
Russley Cl SN5 33 F1
Russley Pk* SN8 164 A3
Rusty La SN12 178 E8
Rutland Cl SN12 94 C3
Rutland Cres BA14 105 C6
Rutts La 3 SN10 187 E7
Ruxley Cl SN4 47 D1
Ryan Ave SN14 78 A7
Ryan Cl SN5 34 B2
Rybury Camp (Hill Fort)* SN10 173 A2
Rycote Cl SN5 49 A6
Rydal Cl SN25 35 F5
Rye Cl SN5 49 A7
Ryeland Way BA14 105 E7
Ryeleaze SN10 179 D5
Rylands Way SN4 47 E2
Ryles La SN8 174 B6
Ryon Cl 11 SP10 193 E2

S

S Ugford Medieval Village of* SP2 144 A2
Sack Hill BA12 113 F1
Sackville Cl SN3 50 F7
Saddleback Cl SN11 81 C2
Saddleback La SN10 179 E5
Saddleback Rd SN5 49 A7
Saddlers Mead SP2 144 C3
Saddlers Way SN8 183 D7
Sadlers Mead SN15 78 E8
Sadlers Rd RG17 177 C3
Saffron Cl 2 Swindon SN2 34 E3
Wootton Bassett SN4 47 E4
Saffron Mdws SN11 80 F3
Sage Cl SN2 34 D5
St Albans Cl
Salisbury SP1 146 D5
Swindon SN2 49 E7
St Aldhelm Rd BA15 100 E5
St Aldhelms Rd SN16 27 F4
St Ambrose Cl SN3 51 D6
St Andrew's Cl
Wilton SP2 144 B2
Wooton Rivers SN8 174 F1
St Andrew's Rd
Melksham SN12 94 C5
Salisbury SP2 145 C2
South Newton SP2 130 B2
St Andrews SP1 146 D2
St Andrews Cl SN4 64 B7
St Andrews Gn SN3 51 E7
St Andrews Rd
Tidworth SP9 216 C6
Warminster BA12 116 D6
St Andrews Sch
Broad Blunsdon SN26 21 C1
Laverstock SP1 146 E3
St Ann Pl SP1 152 B8
St Ann St SP1 152 B8
St Annes Cl SP4 217 C4
St Arild's Rd GL9 24 B4
St Athan Cl BA14 178 B8
St Augustine's Rd 5 BA14 105 B8
St Augustines RC Sch BA14 105 B8
St Barnabas Sch SN10 179 F1
St Bartholomew's St SP7 203 B4
St Bartholomews CE Sch SN4 47 E2
St Bedes Cl 5 SP1 146 D5
St Birinus Rd 4 SP5 211 C7
St Catherines Cl SN11 81 C4
St Christophers Cl 4 SP1 146 D5
St Clair Rd SP2 152 B6
St Clements Way SP1 146 C5
St David's Way SN8 213 D3
St Davids Cl SP1 146 D5
St Dennis Rd 7 SN16 28 A3
St Dunstan Cl SN11 81 B5
St Edith's Cl SP2 144 C1
St Edith's Marsh SN15 96 D5
St Edmund's Church St 2 SP1 146 B1
St Edmunds Girls Sch SP1 146 E3
St Edmunds RC Prim Sch SN11 81 C5
St Edwards 12 SP7 202 C2
St Edwards Mdw SP4 133 B2
St Edwards Sch SO51 162 B1
St Francis Ave SN15 78 C6
St Francis Rd SP1 146 A4
St George's Cl
Ogbourne St George SN8 169 A5
Warminster BA12 117 E5
St George's Rd
Salisbury SP2 151 D7
Semington BA14 102 E5
11 Shaftesbury SP7 202 C1
St Georges Hospl BA14 102 E5
St Georges Prim Sch BA14 102 F6
St Georges RC Prim Sch BA12 117 E5
St Georges Rd
35 Fordingbridge SP6 210 D1
Tidworth SP9 216 C6
St Giles Cl SN16 29 A2
St Gregory's Ave SP2 145 D2
St Helens View SN1 49 F4
St James SN15 59 A7
St James Cl
Salisbury SP1 146 D5
Swindon SN2 35 D5
St James St
7 Ludgershall SP11 192 A5
Shaftesbury SP7 202 B1
St John Rd SN4 64 A6
St John's Cl
Donhead St Mary SP7 203 A1
Marlborough SN8 213 D4
2 Salisbury SP1 152 D8
St John's Cres BA14 104 F6
St John's Ct SP2 144 C3
St John's Hill 7 SP7 202 B1
St John's Rd
Frome BA11 110 B5
Warminster BA12 117 C5
St John's St
Devizes SN10 214 A3
Lechlade GL7 2 C4
Malmesbury SN16 28 B2
Salisbury SP1 152 B8
St Johns CE Prim Sch BA12 117 C6
St Johns Cl
Pewsey SN9 215 D5
19 Tisbury SP3 203 E8
St Johns RC Sch BA14 105 B8
St Johns Sch & Comminity Coll SN8 213 D1
St Johns Sch
Marlborough SN8 175 A8
Tisbury SP3 203 D8
St Joseph's Dr SN15 78 C6
St Josephs GM RC Lower Sch SN3 50 E7
St Josephs Sec Sch SP1 146 E3
St Judes Cl SP1 146 D4
St Just Cl SP4 199 B3
St Katharines Sch SN8 175 F3
St Katherine Gn 2 SN3 51 E7
St Katherines SN4 167 C6
St Laurence CE Sch GL7 2 D3
St Laurence Rd BA15 100 E5
St Laurence Sch BA15 100 B7
St Lawrence Cl SP1 145 E5
St Lawrence Cres 6 SP7 202 C2
St Lawrence Rd GL7 2 C4
St Lawrence Sq 8 RG17 177 B7
St Leonard's SN16 16 D3
St Leonard's Church* BA12 194 A4
St Leonard's Cl SP4 217 D8
St Leonards Cl SN16 16 D3
St Lukes Cl 8 SP1 146 D5
St Lukes Dr SN15 78 C6
St Lukes Sch SN2 35 D5
St Margaret's Cl 2 SP1 152 C8
St Margaret's Gdns SN12 94 C5
St Margaret's Gn 1 SN3 36 B2
St Margaret's Hill BA15 100 D6
St Margaret's Mead SN8 213 F2
St Margaret's Pl BA15 100 D6
St Margaret's Rd SN1 50 D3
St Margaret's St BA15 100 D6
St Margaret's Villas BA15 100 D6
St Margarets Ret Pk SN4 36 D1
St Margarets Cl SN11 81 A4
St Margarets Gdns SN15 78 C6
St Margarets Hospl SN3 36 B4
St Mark's Ave SP1 146 B3
St Mark's Rd SP1 146 B2
St Marks CE Jun Sch SP1 146 B3
St Martin's Chapel* SN8 176 C4
St Martin's Church St 5 SP1 152 B8
St Martin's Cl SP3 143 A4
St Martins SN8 213 E3
St Martins CE Inf Sch SP1 152 B8

St Martins CE Jun Sch SP1 152 C8
St Martins Cl SP3 143 A4
St Mary St SN15 78 E7
St Mary's BA14 178 A3
St Mary's Church (remains of)* SP7 206 A5
St Mary's Cl
Chitterne BA12 195 D6
Dinton SP3 201 E2
Kempsford GL7 10 E6
Lyneham SN15 59 C3
Potterne SN10 179 D5
Redlynch SP5 211 D7
Sixpenny Handley SP5 208 A4
Trowbridge BA14 101 E4
Wilton SP2 144 C1
Wylye BA12 201 E8
St Mary's Gdns BA14 101 E4
St Mary's Pl SN15 78 D8
St Mary's Rd
Dinton SP3 201 E2
Frome BA11 110 B5
12 Market Lavington SN10 179 F1
Salisbury SP2 151 F7
St Mary's St 1 SN16 28 A3
St Marys & St Johns Fst Sch SP3 200 B3
St Marys CE Inf Sch SN8 213 E2
St Marys CE Sch BA14 178 A3
St Marys Field GL7 1 A5
St Marys Gr SN2 35 B1
St Marys La
Dilton Marsh BA13 108 B1
2 Malmesbury SN16 28 A3
Westbury BA13 112 C8
St Marys RC Prim Sch SN2 35 A1
St Marys Sch
Calne SN11 81 B3
Chippenham SN15 78 C6
Donhead St Mary SP7 202 E1
Purton SN5 33 C3
St Mathews Cl SN10 96 D2
St Matthews Cl 6 SP1 146 D5
St Mellion Cl SN15 78 F7
St Michael's Ave SN6 22 E6
St Michael's C of E Sch SN8 170 A6
St Michael's Cl
8 Aldbourne SN8 170 A6
Brinkworth SN15 45 E6
3 Lambourn RG17 165 A1
Trowbridge BA14 102 A3
Wilton SP2 144 B1
St Michael's Rd
Melksham SN12 94 A3
Salisbury SP2 145 C4
St Michaels CE Prim Sch SN12 94 B4
St Michaels CE Sch SP4 190 B2
St Michaels Cl
Lyneham & Bradenstoke SN15 59 F4
Tidworth SP9 216 C5
St Nicholas CE Prim Sch SN8 164 B1
St Nicholas Cl
Calne SN11 81 C4
11 Ludgershall SP11 192 B5
Trowbridge BA14 105 D3
Wilton SP2 144 B1
Winsley BA15 99 D7
St Nicholas Sch SN14 70 C2
St Nicholas' Rd SP1 152 A7
St Osmonds Sch SP1 152 B7
St Osmund's Cl SP1 146 A5
St Patricks Ave SP9 216 B5
St Patricks RC Sch SN13 77 A1
St Paul St SN15 78 D8
St Paul's Dr SN3 51 E6
St Paul's Rd SP2 145 F1
St Paul's St SN2 35 C1
St Pauls Sch SN15 70 D2
St Peter's Church* SP3 127 D4
St Peter's Cl
Chippenham SN15 78 C6
Wilton SP2 144 B2
St Peter's Pump* BA12 123 C3
St Peters CE Jun Sch SN8 213 E3
St Peters Cl 5 SP9 199 D8
St Peters Rd SP1 146 C5
St Peters Sch SN14 78 A8
St Philip's Rd SN2 35 E3
St Rumbold's Rd 9 SP7 202 C1
St Sampsons Cty Infs Sch SN6 19 D8
St Stephen's Pl BA14 105 D8
St Teresa's Dr SN15 78 C7
St Teresas Cl 7 SP1 146 C5
St Thomas A'Becket CE Prim Sch SP3 188 B3
St Thomas Cl 14 SP10 193 D2
St Thomas Way SP1 146 C5
St Thomas' Rd BA14 101 D1
St Ursula's Cl 9 SP1 146 D5
Saintes Cl 1 SP1 146 D5
Salcombe Gr SN3 50 E5
Salisbury & S Wilts Golf Club SP2 151 A7
Salisbury & S Wiltshire Mus* SP1 152 A7
Salisbury Arts Ctr* SP1 146 B1
Salisbury Bsns Pk SP1 152 D7
Salisbury Cath* SP1 152 A8
Salisbury Cath Sch SP1 152 A7
Salisbury Cl 1 SN14 78 A6
Salisbury Coll of Tech SP1 152 B7
Salisbury District Hospl SP5 152 B3
Salisbury Hill SN8 213 E1
Salisbury Hollow BA13 186 D8
Salisbury Leisure Ctr SP1 145 F3
Salisbury Racecourse SP2 150 E5
Salisbury Rd
Amesbury SP4 217 B3
Breamore SP6 210 F5
Chilmark SP3 201 A4
Downton SP5 211 A8
Fordingbridge SP6 210 E1
Hungerford RG17 177 B6
Marlborough SN8 213 E2
Netheravon SP4 190 A3
Pewsey SN9 215 C3
Plaitford/Landford SO51 212 E6
14 Shaftesbury SP7 202 C1
Shaftesbury SP7 202 D1
Shipton Bellinger SP9 199 D7
9 Shrewton SP3 196 E6
South Tedworth SP9 216 C3
Steeple Langford SP3 128 C8
Wilton SP2 144 E3
Salisbury Sch of English SP1 152 B8
Salisbury St
Amesbury SP4 217 A3
Devizes SN10 179 D8
26 Fordingbridge SP6 210 D1
Mere BA12 139 A5
3 Shaftesbury SP7 202 C1
Swindon SN1 50 D7
Salisbury Sta SP2 145 F1
Salisbury Swimming Baths SP1 146 B2
Sally In the Wood BA1 90 C6
Sally Kings La 5 SP7 202 B2
Salt La Salisbury SP1 146 B1
Winterbourne SP4 133 C3
Salt Spring Dr SN4 47 C1
Saltersford La
Chippenham Without SN14 78 A5
Corsham SN14 78 A3
Saltram Cl SN3 51 C6
Salzgitter Dr SN25 35 A8
Sambourne Gdns BA12 117 A6
Sambourne Rd
Minety SN5 17 D2
Warminster BA12 117 A6
Sambre Rd SN4 65 D1
Sams La SN26 21 C1
Sanctuary The* SN8 173 D6
Sand Hole La BA13 112 E8
Sand St BA12 121 A6
Sand's La SN10 96 D2
Sandacre Rd
1 Swindon SN5 34 A1
3 Swindon SN5 48 F8
Sanden Cl RG17 177 B7
Sanders Rd BA14 101 C2
Sandes Cl SN15 78 C7
Sandfield
Littleton Panell SN10 187 E8
Sutton Veny BA12 194 A5
Sandford Pk BA14 104 F7
Sandgate SN3 36 B1
Sandhills Rd SP3 142 A4
Sandle Copse SP6 210 B1
Sandle Manor Sch SP6 210 C1
Sandlea Cl SN14 68 F5
Sandleaze SN10 179 C4
Sandleheath Rd SP6 210 A1
Sandown Ave SN3 50 E3
Sandown Ctr BA14 105 E4
Sandown Dr SN14 77 F6
Sandown Pl 7 SP2 145 F1
Sandpiper Bridge SN3 51 E7
Sandpit Hill SP3 141 A2
Sandpit Rd SN11 81 D4
Sandpits La
Sherston SN16 25 C1
Steeple Ashton BA14 106 E6
Sandridge Common SN12 94 D5
Sandridge Hill SN12 95 A6
Sandridge La SN15 95 C7
Sandridge Pk* SN12 95 B6
Sandridge Rd SN12 94 B5
Sandridge Sch SN12 94 E5
Sandringham Rd
Swindon SN3 50 F3
Trowbridge BA14 105 B5
Sandringhams The SP5 153 E1
Sandroyd Sch SP5 207 C5
Sands Cl SN10 96 D1
Sands The SN9 181 C7
Sands' La SP7 203 C3
Sandstone Rd SN25 34 F7
Sandwood Cl SN5 34 B2
Sandy La
Edington BA13 186 C7
Redlynch SP5 211 D8
Swindon SN1 50 B4
Sandy Lea Ave 5 SN13 76 B1
Sandy Leaze BA15 100 C6
Sandy Ridge SN11 81 C1
Sanford St 3 SN1 50 C6
Sangster Ave SN12 94 B4
Sarsen Cl SN1 49 F4
Sarson La SP11 192 E1
Sarum Ave SN12 94 B2
Sarum Cl Salisbury SP2 145 E3
Shipton Bellinger SP9 199 C8
Sarum Coll SP1 152 A8
Sarum Dr SN10 214 C2
Sarum Gdns BA13 109 A4
Sarum Rd SN14 78 A6
Sarum St Pauls CE Sch SP2 145 F2
Sarum Way Calne SN11 81 A3
2 Hungerford RG17 177 B6
Sassoon Cl BA12 116 D6
Saunders Gr SN13 76 D1
Saunders Mdw SN8 183 E1
Savernake Ave SN12 94 C6
Savernake Cl 4 BA12 117 A8
Savernake Cres SN8 213 F2
Savernake Ct SN8 213 E2
Savernake Hospl SN8 175 A7
Savernake Rd
Burbage SN8 175 D1
Corsham SN13 84 D8
Savernake St SN1 50 B5
Savill Cres SN4 63 F7
Sawpit Dr SN8 175 C5
Sawpit Hill BA12 140 B4
Sawyers Cl SN16 17 A2
Sawyers Hill SN16 17 A2
Saxby Rd SN15 70 E1
Saxifrage Bank SN12 94 C3
Saxon Cl Cricklade SN6 19 D7
14 Market Lavington SN10 179 F1
Westbury BA13 109 A4
Saxon Dr BA14 101 E4
Saxon Leas SP5 149 C6
Saxon Mdw SP5 211 A8
Saxon Mill SN4 65 D5
Saxon Rd SP2 151 F6
Saxon Rise SN8 183 E1
Saxon Spur 10 SP7 202 C2
Saxon St SN14 78 B8
Saxon Way
Andover SP10 193 D2
Winsley BA15 99 F7
Saxonhurst 4 SP5 211 B8
Saxons Acre BA12 116 D6
Scallows La SO51 212 F7
Scamell's Rd SP2 146 A2
Scarborough Rd SN2 49 F8
Scarlet Cl SN25 34 F7
Scholard's La 16 SN8 170 B2
School Cl
Chiseldown SN4 65 E4
Keevil BA14 178 B5
St Paul Malmesbury Without SN16 28 A1
Vernhams Dean SP11 185 C3
School Dr 25 SP4 198 B7
School Hill
Alderbury SP5 153 C2
Brinkworth SN15 45 E5
School La
All Cannings SN10 180 F8
1 Amesbury SP4 217 B3
Badminton GL9 38 E2
Castle Combe SN14 68 A7
Castle Eaton SN6 10 B4
East Garston RG17 171 E8
Grittleton SN14 54 E5
Hindon SP3 200 B3
Lea SN16 29 A2
Little Bedwyn SN8 176 C5
Marlborough SN8 213 A2
Meysey Hampton GL7 1 A4
South Cerney GL7 6 F7
Staverton BA14 101 D5
Westbury BA13 108 E1
Wroughton SN4 64 A6
School Rd
1 Durrington/Bulford SP4 198 C7
Kemble GL7 4 F7
Nomansland SP5 212 C4
Redlynch SP5 211 E6
Seend SN12 178 D8
School View SN9 215 B5
Science Mus Outstation* SN4 63 F3
Scotby Ave SN3 50 E2
Scotchel Gn SN9 215 D5
Scotland Hill SN15 57 A5
Scotland La
Beckington BA11 107 C4
Landford SP5 212 B8
Scotland Rd SN12 94 A6
Scotney Cres 2 SN25 34 F6
Scots La SP1 146 A1
Scott Cl SN8 183 C8
Scott's Hill SP7 203 C4
Scotts Cl SN11 89 B2
Scratchbury Camp* BA12 194 B7
Scrubbity Barrows* SP5 207 E4
Seaford Cl SN5 49 A6
Seagrim Rd SP2 144 C2
Seagry Hill SN15 57 D3
Seagry Rd
Hullavington SN14 56 D6
Sutton Benger SN15 57 D2
Seaton Cl SN25 34 F5
Second Broad Dr SP3 128 C2
Sedgebrook SN3 51 D2
Sedgefield Gdns SN10 214 B4
Sedgefield Way SN14 77 F6
Seend Hill SN12 178 F8
Seend Prim Sch SN12 178 E8
Selby Cres SN5 49 B4
Seldon Cl 4 SN3 50 E6
Selions Cl SN14 70 B2
Selwood Cres 1 BA11 110 A7
Selwood Mid Sch BA11 110 B6
Semington Rd
Berryfield SN12 94 A1
Melksham Without BA14 178 A8
Senior Dr SP2 152 A5
Seth Ward Dr SP1 146 D4
Seven Barrows*
Lambourn RG17 165 A5
South Tedworth SP9 191 B3
Seven Fields Jun & Inf Sch SN2 35 C4
Sevenfields SN6 23 A7
Severn Ave SN25 35 A4
Severn Rd SN12 94 A6
Seymour Ct BA14 101 C1
Seymour Rd
Chippenham SN15 78 F8
Swindon SN3 50 F6
Trowbridge BA14 101 C2
Seymours Ct* BA11 107 A6
Shady Bower SP1 152 C8
Shaftesbury Ave SN3 51 B4
Shaftesbury Fst Sch SP7 202 D1
Shaftesbury Mus* SP7 202 C1
Shaftesbury Rd
Barford St Martin SP3 143 B3
Mere BA12 139 B4
Motcombe SP7 202 A3
Wilton SP2 144 B3
Shaftesbury St 19 SP6 210 D1
Shaftesbury Upper Sch SP7 202 C1
Shails La
Melksham Without SN12 178 A8
Trowbridge BA14 101 C1
Shakespeare Ave SP10 193 C1
Shakespeare Dr SN8 213 C2
Shakespeare Path SN3 35 F3
Shakespeare Rd
Salisbury SP1 145 F4
Wootton Bassett SN4 47 F3
Shalbourne CE Sch SN8 176 F2
Shalbourne Cl RG17 177 A7
Shalford La BA9 136 A3
Shallow Wagon La BA13 108 F6
Shallowbrooks La SN14 39 F8
Shallows The SP6 210 F4
Shambles The BA15 100 D7
Shanklin Rd SN2 34 E4
Shaplands 4 SN3 36 A2
Shapwick Cl SN3 51 C7
Sharcott Dro SN9 215 A4
Share La SP3 203 C6
Sharp Cl SN5 49 B7
Sharpley Cl SP6 210 D2
Sharrat Ave 4 SP1 146 C5
Shaston Dro SP2 151 D5
Shave La BA10 122 A4
Shaw CE Sch SN12 93 D8
Shaw Hill
Collingbourne Ducis SN8 191 E7
Melksham Without SN12 93 D7
Shaw Rd SN5 49 B7
Shaw Ridge Leisure Pk* SN5 49 B6
Shaw Ridge Sch SN5 49 B7
Shaw Village* SN8 173 F4
Shawgrove SN8 176 B3
Shear Cross BA12 116 E1
Shearman St BA14 105 D7
Shearwater Way SN13 84 D7
Shearwood Rd SN5 34 A1
Sheasby Cl SP5 208 A3
Sheen Cl Salisbury SP2 145 B5
4 Swindon SN5 49 A4
Sheep Fair Way 13 RG17 165 A1
Sheep St Devizes SN10 214 B3
Highworth SN6 23 A6
Sheepbridge Rd SP4 198 E7
Sheepcote Barton 3 BA14 105 E7
Sheepdrove Rd RG17 165 B2
Sheepridge SN8 168 E3
Sheepscroft SN14 70 B2
Sheepwash La BA12 201 E8
Sheerwold Cl SN3 36 B3
Sheffield La SN13 84 D8
Shelburne Rd SN11 81 C1
Shelburne Way SN11 79 F2
Sheld Dr SN15 60 A1
Sheldon Manor* SN14 69 D1
Sheldon Rd SN14 78 B7
Sheldon Sch SN14 70 B1
Shelfinch SN5 49 D4
Shelley Ave 2 SN4 47 F3
Shelley Dr SP1 145 F4
Shelley Gdns SN12 94 B4
Shelley St SN1 50 B5
Shelley Way BA12 116 D6
Shenton Cl SN3 36 B3
Shepherd Spring Jun Sch SP10 193 E2
Shepherd's La
Donhead St Andrew SP7 203 B2
Selwood BA11 114 D6
Shepherds SN13 84 D6
Shepherds Breach 1 SN4 47 E2
Shepherds Cl
Coombe Bissett SP5 151 A1
Odstock SP5 152 A1
Shepherds Mead BA13 112 A8
Shepherds Rise SP11 185 C3
Shepherds Spring Cty Infs Sch SP10 193 E2
Sheppard Cl SN15 78 F5
Sheppard St SN1 50 B7
Sheppards Rise SN15 46 B7
Shepperton Way SN25 34 F6
Sherborne Rd BA14 100 F1
Sherborne St GL7 2 C4
Sherfield SP4 133 A2
Sherfield English La SO51 212 F7
Sherfield English Rd SP5 212 E6
Sherfields SN4 47 E1
Sherford Rd SN25 34 E4
Sheridan Dr SN4 47 F3
Sherrington La BA12 195 A2
Sherrington Mead SN15 79 B4
Sherston Ave SN2 35 C5
Sherston Rd
Brokenborough SN16 27 E4
Luckington SN14 39 E5
Sherston Vc Prim Sch SN16 40 C8
Sherwood Ave SN12 94 C6
Sherwood Cl 3 BA12 117 A8
Sherwood Rd SN3 51 B4
Shetland Gdns SN5 49 A7
Shipley Dr SN25 34 F6
Shipton Bellinger Cty Prim Sch SP9 199 C8
Shipton Gr SN3 50 E5
Shipton Hill 2 SN16 28 A4
Shiptons La SN15 43 F2
Shire Cl SN5 49 A7
Shire Ct 3 SN1 50 A5
Shire Hill SN14 66 A7
Shires Sh Ctr The BA14 105 C8
Shirley Cl SN3 50 F7
Shockerwick La BA1 82 D4
Shoddesden La SP11 192 B4
Shoemaker La SN15 45 F6
Shop La Badminton GL9 38 E2
Wingfield BA14 104 C6
Shore Pl BA14 100 F1
Shoreland Cl BA13 108 F3
Short Dro SN4 163 C6
Short La Andover SP11 193 B1
Barford St Martin SP3 143 A4
Short River Rd BA13 109 D2
Short St
Ludgershall SP11 192 A5
Melksham SN12 94 C6
Shortlands SP2 144 B3
Shorts Gn La SP7 202 A4
Shoscombe Gdns 3 BA11 110 C7
Showfield SN4 47 D3
Shrapnel Rd 1 SP4 197 E7
Shrewsbury Rd SN3 50 F6
Shrewton Cl BA14 105 D6
Shrewton Jun & Inf Sch SP3 196 F7
Shrewton Rd BA12 195 E6
Shrivenham Rd
Highworth SN6 23 B4
Swindon SN1 50 E7
Shropshire Cl
Salisbury SP2 145 C5
1 Swindon SN5 49 B7
Shurnhold SN12 93 F5
Shute End Rd SP5 153 B4
Shutts La SP5 151 A1
Sidbury Circular Rd SP9 216 B7
Sidbury Hill Ave SP9 216 C8
Sidings The 2 SP5 211 B8
Sidney Cl Swindon SN5 48 F4
3 Swindon SN3 50 E6
Sidney St SP2 145 F1
Sidney Wood Ct SN14 78 C7
Signal St SP4 198 E6
Signal Way SN1 50 D3
Silbury Cl BA13 108 F4
Silbury Hill* SN8 173 C7
Silbury Rd SN11 81 A3
Silchester Way SN5 49 C6
Sillen La SP6 209 B6
Sillington La SN10 179 B7
Silman Cl SN13 76 D1
Silton Rd SP8 137 F2
Silver Barrow* SP3 188 D2
Silver Birch Rd BA14 105 B5
Silver Cl SN16 17 B2
Silver La BA11 114 C6
Silver Mdws BA14 105 A5

Silver St Alderbury SP5 153 B2
Bradford-on-Avon BA15 100 D6
Calne SN11 81 B1
Calne Without SN11 89 B8
Colerne SN14 75 B3
Corsham SN13 85 C6
Kington Langley SN15 70 F7
Malmesbury SN16 28 A3
Minety SN16 17 B2
Potterne SN10 179 D5
Salisbury SP1 152 A8
Sherston SN16 40 C8
South Cerney GL7 6 F7
Steeple Ashton BA14 178 A3
Trowbridge BA14 105 D8
Warminster BA12 117 A7
Westbury BA13 112 C8
Wilton SP2 144 D3
Silver St La
Bromham SN15 87 D1
Trowbridge BA14 105 B5
Silver Wood SP5 153 C3
Silverless St SN8 213 D3
Silverton Rd SN3 51 B6
Silverwood Dr SP1 146 E2
Simmance Way SP4 217 C3
Simnel Cl SN5 48 F5
Simonds Rd 17 SP11 192 A5
Six Acre La
Shalbourne RG17 176 F3
West Knoyle BA12 140 A4
Sixpenny Handley Cty Fst Sch SP5 208 A4
Skew Bridge Cl SN4 47 C1
Skew Bridge Rd SP2 145 D2
Skew Rd SP2 145 B2
Skinner's Cl SN6 22 B7
Skye Cl SN6 22 F7
Slab La SP5 211 C7
Slade Dr SN3 36 B1
Slades The SN11 81 C3
Sladesbrook BA15 100 E8
Slag La BA13 108 F5
Slate Way SP5 148 B3
Slater Rd SN9 215 C5
Slaughterford Rd SN14 68 C1
Slay Barrow* SP4 189 A6
Sleight La SN10 179 F6
Sleight Rd SN10 214 E1
Slessor Rd
Lyneham SN15 60 A1
Lyneham & Bradenstoke SN15 166 A8
Sling Orch SP3 204 E7
Sling Rd SP4 198 E7
Slipper La SN4 65 D4
Slipway The BA14 101 D4
Slodbrook La SP8 138 D1
Slowgrove Cl BA14 105 F8
Small St SN10 180 F4
Smallbrook Gdns BA14 101 D5
Smallbrook La BA12 117 D5
Smallbrook Rd BA12 117 B5
Smannell Rd SP11 193 F2
Smay Down La SN8 184 E6
Smeaton Rd
1 Andover SP10 193 B1
Salisbury SP2 145 E1
Smitan Brook SN3 51 D6
Smith St SN14 67 A6
Smith's Hill OX12 165 F7
Smitham Bridge Rd RG17 177 B7
Smithfield St 2 SP4 217 B3
Smithy La SN9 181 C6
Smithys La SN8 183 C8
Smithywell Cl BA14 105 F8
Snail-Creep Hanging* SP3 200 E7
Snails' La SN10 214 A3
Snap Village* SN8 169 C7
Snappersnipes BA13 109 A3
Snapps Cl SN4 64 B5
Snarlton La SN12 94 D5
Snoddington Rd
Fyfield SP11 192 D1
Shipton Bellinger SP9 199 E7
Snow Hill Dinton SP3 201 F2
Hilmarton SN11 73 F5
Snowberry La SN12 94 C3
Snowdrop Cl SN25 34 D5
Snowshill Cl SN25 34 F5
Snowswick La SN7 12 E7
Snuff St SN10 214 A4
Sobers Sq SP11 193 F2
Sock's La BA10 122 A7
Sodom La SN15 59 C7
Soldier's Ring* SP6 209 D4
Solstice Rise SP4 217 B3
Somerdale Cl 6 SN5 49 C6
Somerford Cl SN2 35 C4
Somerford Lakes Reserve* GL7 5 D2
Somerset Cl 1 RG17 177 B7
Somerset Cres SN12 94 B3
Somerset Dr BA13 109 A5
Somerset Rd
Salisbury SP1 146 B3
Swindon SN2 34 F1
Somerset Way BA14 102 F6
Somerton Gdns BA11 110 C7
Somerville Rd SN3 50 F6
Somme Rd SP11 191 F4
Sopwith Pk 7 SP10 193 C1
Sopworth Rd SN14 39 E5
Sorley Cl SN8 213 B3
Sorrel Cl
Chippenham SN14 70 B3
Melksham SN12 94 B3
Trowbridge BA14 105 D5
Wootton Bassett SN4 47 E4
Sound Copse SN5 34 B2
South Alley 6 BA12 116 E5
South Bank SN8 174 F2
South Charford Dro SP6 210 D6
South Cliffe Rd 6 SN10 179 F1
South Cross La SN10 179 C3
South Dr SP9 216 C4
South La Downton SP5 211 A8
Nomansland SP5 212 C4
South Marston Pk Ind Est SN3 36 C7
South Mdw La SN5 19 F3
South Mill Cl SP4 217 B2
South Mill Rd SP4 217 B2
South Pk* SP11 192 B4
South Pl Calne SN11 81 B2
Corsham SN13 77 A1
South St
Aldbourne SN8 170 A6
Avebury SN8 173 B8
Broad Chalke SP5 205 B4
Corsham SN13 77 A1
Great Wishford SP2 130 A3
8 Salisbury SP2 145 F1
Swindon SN1 50 C4
Warminster BA12 116 E5
Wilton SP2 144 C1
South View RG17 177 B7
South View Ave SN3 50 E5
South View Pl SN8 213 E3
South Way
Alderbury SP5 153 E2
Trowbridge BA14 105 D7
South Western Rd SP2 145 F1
South Wilts Gram Sch For Girls SP1 146 A3
Southampton Rd
Alderbury SP5 153 D3
Fordingbridge SP6 210 E1
Salisbury SP1 152 C7
Southampton St SN1 50 D6
Southay BA13 186 B7
Southbank Gdns RG17 165 B1
Southbank Glen SN4 47 F2
Southbourne Way SP4 133 D6
Southbrook BA12 139 C4
Southbrook Gdns BA12 139 B4
Southbrook La BA13 178 B1
Southbrook Rd SN12 93 F6
Southbrook St SN2 35 B1
Southbroom Jun Sch SN10 214 C2
Southbroom Rd SN10 214 B3
Southcott Rd SN9 215 D4
Southcroft Dr BA13 111 D4
Southcroft Rd 1 SN13 76 B1
Southdown 3 SN4 163 A5
Southernwood Dr SN2 34 C4
Southerwicks SN13 84 F8
Southey Cl SN25 34 F8
Southfield
2 Aldbourne SN8 170 A6
Southwick BA14 104 F2
West Overton SN8 173 F6
Southfield Prim Sch SN6 23 A5
Southgate Cl SN10 214 B2
Southleigh BA15 100 C5
Southleigh View BA12 117 C5
Southmead SN14 78 B6
Southmill Hill SP4 217 B1
Southside
Laverstock SP4 146 D8
Shipton Moyne GL8 26 E7
Southview Rd BA14 105 D6
Southville Rd BA15 100 E5
Southward La SN8 170 A6
Southway SP4 134 B7
Southway Rd BA15 100 D4
Southwell Cl 2 SN14 78 A5
Southwick Ave SN2 35 B5
Southwick CE Prim Sch BA14 104 F3
Southwick Ctry Pk* BA14 104 F5
Southwick Rd BA14 105 C2
Southwood Rd BA14 105 F8
Spa Cl SN6 23 B6
Spa Ct SN12 94 B3
Spa Rd SN12 94 B3
Spackman La SN13 84 E8
Spanbourn Ave SN14 78 D7
Sparcells Dr SN5 34 B2
Speedwell Cl
Melksham SN12 94 C2
1 Swindon SN25 34 E5
3 Trowbridge BA14 105 D6
Spencer Cl
Melksham SN12 94 A6
Swindon SN5 48 F7
Spencers Orch
Bradford-on-Avon BA15 100 D5
Wroughton SN4 64 B6
Spenser Cl SN3 51 A7
Speresholt SN5 49 D4
Spiers Piece BA14 178 B3
Spin Hill SN10 179 E1
Spine Rd (East) GL7 7 C4
Spine Rd W GL7 6 A2
Spingfield Rd BA12 139 B5
Spinners Croft 5 BA14 105 D7
Spinners Way BA12 139 B6
Spinney Cl
Chippenham SN14 78 A6
3 Liddington SN4 163 A4
Spinney The
Lechlade GL7 2 C4
3 Littleton Panell SN10 187 E8
Spital La SN6 19 E7
Spitfire Rd SP4 146 D8
Spout La SN12 178 F8
Spouts La SO51 212 F7
Spracklands SP3 201 F2
Spratsgate La GL7 6 B4
Spray Leaze 10 SP11 192 B5
Spray Rd RG17 177 C2
Sprays 9 SN8 183 D8
Spread Eagle Hill SP7 206 B6
Spreckley Rd 1 SN11 166 A1
Spring Cl SN1 50 C6
Spring Gdns Lechlade GL7 2 C4
Swindon SN1 50 C6
Spring La SN13 84 C7
Spring Mdw SN8 191 D8
Spring Rd BA11 110 A6
Spring The SN10 187 E8
Springfield BA15 100 E6
Springfield Cl
Corsham SN13 84 A8
7 Shaftesbury SP7 202 C2
Trowbridge BA14 101 E2
Springfield Cres
11 Redlynch SP5 211 C7
Wootton Bassett SN4 47 D2
Springfield Dr SN11 81 A3
Springfield Gdns SN12 85 C1
Springfield Pk
18 Tisbury SP3 203 E8
Trowbridge BA14 101 E1
Springfield Rd
Rowde SN10 96 D1
Swindon SN1 50 C3
Westbury BA13 108 F2
Springfield Sports Ctr SN13 76 F1
Springfields Sch SN11 81 A3
Springhead BA12 194 A4
Springhill Cl 3 SN5 49 C5
Spur Way SN2 35 E3
Squalls La SP3 203 F6
Square The Calne SN11 81 B3
Mere BA12 139 A5
Pewsey SN9 215 C5
Squarey Cl SP5 211 A7
Squires Copse SN5 34 A1
Squires Hill Cl
4 Wootton Bassett SN4 47 F2
7 Wootton Bassett SN4 48 A2
Squirrel Cres 1 SN4 47 F2
Squirrel's Cnr BH21 208 D1
Stables Rd SP9 216 C4
Stacey's La SN4 163 B5
Stafford St SN1 50 B5
Stag Hill RG17 171 A1
Stainers Mead SP7 202 A5
Stainers Way SN14 70 B2
Stallard St BA14 105 C8
Stalls The BA12 114 F5
Stamford Cl SN5 49 B5
Stanbridge Pk 9 SN5 49 A7
Stanbury Rd SP11 192 C1
Stancomb Ave BA14 101 E1
Stancombe Pk 1 SN5 49 D5
Standen Way SN25 35 A7
Standings Cl 6 SN5 49 A8
Stanier Cl BA11 110 D6
Stanier Rd SN11 81 C6
Stanier St SN1 50 B5
Stanley Cl 9 SN4 163 B6
Stanley La SN15 79 D6
Stanley Little Rd SP2 145 B3
Stanley St SN1 50 C5
Stanmore St SN1 50 A5
Stansfield Cl 5 SN5 49 D4
Stanton Cl BA14 105 D5
Stanton La SN14 56 A1
Stanton St Quintin Prim Sch SN14 56 B4
Stanway Cl 5 SN3 51 A4
Stapleford Castle Ring & Bailey* SP3 129 D8
Stapleford Cl SN15 78 E4
Staples Hill BA2 99 C3
Stapleton Cl SN6 22 F5
Star La SN14 74 D8
Star The BA14 101 E7
Staring Cl 6 SN5 48 F8
Station App
4 Frome BA11 110 A4
Melksham SN12 94 A6
Minety SN16 17 C2
Swindon SN1 50 D3
Westbury BA13 108 E4
Station Hill SN15 78 D8
Station Rd
Ashbury SN6 164 A8
Badminton GL9 38 F1
Calne SN11 81 B2
Chiseldown SN4 65 D4
Christian Malford SN15 58 A2
Codford BA12 194 F3
Corsham SN13 77 A1
Devizes SN10 214 A3
East Garston RG17 171 E7
Great Wishford SP2 129 F3
Station Rd *continued*
Highworth SN6 22 F6
Holt BA14 92 E1
19 Hungerford RG17 177 B7
Kemble GL7 4 F7
10 Lambourn RG17 165 A1
Lechlade GL7 2 D5
Limpley Stoke BA2 99 C5
Minety SN16 17 C1
Purton SN5 33 C5
Sandleheath SP6 210 C1
Sedgehill & Semley SP7 202 D5
South Cerney GL7 7 B7
Swindon SN1 50 B7
Tidworth SP9 216 D5
Warminster BA12 117 B7
Westbury BA13 108 E5
Wootton Bassett SN4 47 D1
Station Terr 4 SP2 145 F1
Station Way BA14 105 C8
Staverton CE Sch BA14 101 D5
Staverton Way 2 SN2 35 C6
Stavordale Priory* BA9 136 D5
Steadings The
Salisbury SP4 146 D6
Wootton Bassett SN4 47 F1
Steam (Mus of Great Western Rly)* SN2 50 A6
Steel's La BA9 137 A3
Steele Cl SN10 214 D4
Steels Dro SP6 211 A4
Steels La SP6 209 F2
Steep Hollow SP3 201 E3
Steep St BA12 139 A6
Steepe Way SN8 175 C1
Steeple Langford CE Fst Sch SP3 128 C8
Stenbury Cl SN25 35 A7
Stenness Cl SN5 34 C2
Stephen Martin Gdns 7 SP6 210 D1
Stephens Cl 1 SP2 151 E7
Stephens Rd SN3 36 A1
Stephens Way BA12 116 F8
Stephenson Dr BA11 110 C6
Stephenson Rd
Salisbury SP2 145 E1
Swindon SN25 35 C7
Steplake La SO51 212 F8
Steplake Rd SO51 212 F8
Sterling Pk 1 SP10 193 C1
Stert Valley La SN10 180 A6
Stevenson Rd SN2 34 C5
Stewart Cl
Chippenham SN15 78 F4
Swindon SN25 35 B6
Steway La BA1 82 B6
Stibb Hill SN10 187 F7
Still Man Cl BA14 101 E8
Stirling Cl
3 Bower Hill SN12 178 B8
Wroughton SN4 64 A7
Stirling Rd
Market Lavington SN10 180 A1
South Marston Park SN3 36 C6
Stirling Way BA11 110 C6
Stobberts Pl 4 SN10 179 F1
Stobberts Rd 3 SN10 179 F1
Stock La
Aldbourne SN8 169 D4
Landford SP5 212 C7
Stock's Cross SO43 212 D2
Stockbridge Copse SN5 34 A2
Stockley Hollow SN11 89 C4
Stockley La SN11 89 C6
Stockley Rd SN11 89 C2
Stockport Rd SP4 217 D1
Stocks Bridge La SP5 151 A1
Stockton Earthworks* BA12 201 A6
Stockton House* BA12 195 B1
Stockton Rd SN2 35 C4
Stockwell Rd SN10 214 C4
Stockwood Cl SP1 146 C3
Stockwood Rd SN14 78 B6
Stoke Comm La SN5 19 A2
Stoke Mead BA2 98 F7
Stokes Rd SN13 85 A8
Stokes' Croft SN11 81 B4
Stokesay Dr SN5 49 C4
Stonar Sch SN12 92 B8
Stone (site of King's Elm)* SP3 142 B1
Stone Ave* SN8 173 C8
Stone Cl SP5 149 C6
Stone La
Lydiard Millicent SN5 33 E1
Ramsbury SN8 175 D8
Stonebridge Cl SN8 213 F3
Stonebridge Dr BA11 110 B7
Stonecrop Way SN25 34 E5
Stonefield Dr SN6 23 A5
Stonehenge* SP4 197 E5
Stonehenge Cursus* SP4 197 C6
Stonehenge Rd SP4 198 A4
Stonehenge Sch The SP4 217 B4
Stonehill Barn GL8 3 C6
Stonehill Gn SN5 49 D6
Stonehill La GL8 3 C6
Stonelea Cl SN14 78 B7
Stoneleigh Rise BA11 110 A6
Stoneover La
Lydiard Tregoze SN4 48 A3
Wootton Bassett SN4 47 F2
Stones La SN6 8 B1
Stoney Bridge BA12 140 D5
Stoney Cross 20 SP11 192 A5
Stony Gutter BA14 102 D1
Stony La
Damerham SP6 209 E2
Lambourn RG17 171 B6
Stonybeck Cl SN5 49 D6
Stop St SP3 200 C2
Stoppers Hill SN15 46 B7
Stops Hill SP3 200 B3
Stormore BA13 111 F8
Storridge Rd BA13 108 C6
Stour Cl 5 SO51 212 F6
Stour Wlk SN25 35 B4
Stourhead House & Gdns* BA12 123 F1
Stourton House Flower Gdn* BA12 123 F1
Stourton La BA12 123 E3
Stourton Pk BA14 102 B3
Stowell Pk* SN8 182 A8
Stradbrook BA13 186 B7
Straight La RG17 171 C6
Strand The Calne SN11 81 B3
Steeple Ashton BA14 178 A3
Stranks Cl SN6 23 A4
Stratford Cl SN5 49 D5
Stratford Rd SP1 146 A3
Stratford sub Castle CE Sch SP1 145 E5
Stratford Tony Rd SP5 150 E2
Stratton Orch 1 SN3 36 A2
Stratton Rd
Pewsey SN9 215 C4
Swindon SN1 50 F8
Strattons Wlk SN12 94 B4
Strawberry Hill SN10 187 E7
Strawberry La GL7 1 A4
Street La
Brewham BA10 122 A4
Sedgehill & Semley SP7 202 C6
Street The
All Cannings SN10 172 F1
Alvediston SP5 204 B2
Bishops Cannings SN10 172 B3
Brinkworth SN15 45 F6
Broughton Gifford SN12 93 B4
Castle Combe SN14 68 A7
Castle Eaton SN6 10 B4
Charlton SN16 29 B6
Cherhill SN11 166 B1
Chilmark SP3 201 A3
Chirton SN10 180 F4
Crudwell SN16 14 E5
Didmarton GL9 24 C3
East Knoyle SP3 141 C1
Holt BA14 101 D8
Hullavington SN14 41 F1
Kilmington BA12 123 F4
Latton SN6 8 C4
Lea SN16 28 F1
Liddington SN4 163 A4
Little Somerford SN15 44 C5
Luckington SN14 39 E4
Lydiard Millicent SN5 48 D8
Marden SN10 181 A4
Marston Maisey SN6 9 D6
Milton Lilbourne SN9 182 E7
Motcombe SP7 202 A5
Nettleton SN14 53 B4
Oaksey SN16 15 F8
Pitton & Farley SP5 154 E7
Shipton Moyne GL8 26 E8
Swindon SN25 34 E3
West Knoyle BA12 140 D5
Winterslow SP5 149 A5
Yatton Keynell SN14 68 F6
Stroma Way SN6 22 E7
Strongrove Hill RG17 177 A7
Strongs Cl BA14 178 C4
Stroud La SN10 179 F5
Stroud's Hill SN4 65 D4
Stuart Cl 2 Swindon SN3 50 F6
Trowbridge BA14 101 E4
Stuart Gn BA12 117 A6
Stubbs La SN14 70 A7
Stubhampton Bottom DT11 206 C3
Stubsmead SN3 51 C5
Stuckton Rd SP6 210 E1
Studland Cl SN3 51 B3
Studland Pk BA13 109 B2
Studley Castle* SP6 211 F3
Studley Gn Prim Sch BA14 105 A6
Studley Hill SN11 80 A4
Studley La SN11 80 A3
Studley Rise BA14 105 D6
Sturford La BA12 115 D6
Styles Ave BA11 110 C4
Styles Cl BA11 110 B4
Styles Hill BA11 110 B4
Styles Pk BA11 110 B4
Styles The SP5 205 F4
Sudeley Dr GL7 6 F6
Sudeley Way SN5 49 A5
Sudley Way SN5 48 F5
Suffolk Cl SN16 29 A7
Suffolk Pl GL7 8 D7
Suffolk Rd SP2 151 E6
Suffolk St SN2 50 C8
Summer Down Wlk BA14 105 C5

Summer La
Castle Combe SN14 53 F3
Monkton Combe BA2 98 D8
Summer Rd BA13 108 F4
Summerhouse Rd SN4 63 F7
Summerleaze BA14 105 A6
Summerlock App [2] SP2 146 A1
Summers La SN4 167 C7
Summers St SN2 49 F7
Sumsions Dr SN13 76 D1
Sun La BA13 108 E1
Sunderland Cl [14] SN12 178 B8
Sunningdale Cl SN15 78 F7
Sunningdale Rd SN25 35 C4
Sunnyhill SN8 191 D8
Sunnyhill La SN8 174 C1
Sunnyhill Rd SP1 146 A4
Sunnyside SN10 187 E8
Sunnyside Ave SN1 50 A4
Surrendell Cottage SN14 55 B8
Surrey Rd SN2 35 A1
Sussex Rd SP2 151 E6
Sutherland Cresent SN14 70 B3
Suthmere Dr SN8 183 D8
Sutton Benger CE Sch SN15 57 D2
Sutton Bottom SP3 141 B5
Sutton Hill
Sherrington BA12 195 A2
Sutton Mandeville SP3 204 C7
Sutton La
Langley Burrell Without SN15 71 C5
Sutton Benger SN15 57 D1
Sutton Pk SN26 21 C1
Sutton Rd Fovant SP3 204 D7
Kington Langley SN15 70 F7
Swindon SN3 51 C4
Sutton Veny CE Sch BA12 194 A4
Suvla La [6] SP4 198 E6
Swaddon St SN11 81 B4
Swallet House SN15 58 D5
Swallow Cl
Tidworth SP9 216 D6
[2] Warminster BA12 116 E5
Swallow Dr
Frome BA11 110 B6
[4] Trowbridge BA14 105 B8
Swallowdale SN3 51 D7
Swallowfield Ave SN3 50 F5
Swallowmead [1] SP2 152 A5
Swallows Mead [9] SN4 48 A2
Swan Barton SN16 40 C8
Swan Cl
[9] Durrington/Bulford SP4 198 C7
Lechlade GL7 2 C4
Salisbury SP2 152 A6
Swan Dr BA14 101 D5
Swan La SN6 17 F5
Swan Mdw SN9 215 D4
Swan Rd Corsham SN13 76 E1
Pewsey SN9 215 C4
Swan's Bottom [7] SN8 170 B2
Swan's Cl [9] SN8 170 B2
Swanborough Cl [6] SN15 78 F4
Swanborough Tump* SN9 181 F6
Swanbrook SN3 51 D8
Swangate RG17 177 B8
Swansfield GL7 2 D6
Swattons Cl SP4 217 E8
Swayne Cl [6] SN15 78 F5
Swayne Rd SP2 144 C2
Swaynes Cl [1] SP1 146 B2
Sweet Briar Rd SN12 94 C3
Sweetmans Rd SP7 202 C2
Swift Ave SN2 35 A7
Swift Mead BA12 116 E5
Swiftdown [5] SP2 152 A5
Swinburne Pl SN4 47 E3
Swindon & Cricklade Rly* SN25 33 F8
Swindon Arts Ctr* SN1 50 C4
Swindon Coll
Marlborough SN8 213 E1
Swindon SN2 50 B8
Swindon Coll of Further Ed SN8 213 D3
Swindon Greendown Sch SN5 48 F5
Swindon Mus & Art Gall* SN1 50 D4
Swindon Rd
Cricklade SN6 19 F7
Highworth SN6 22 F3
Hilmarton SN11 73 F3
Lydiard Tregoze SN4 48 C2
Swindon SN1 36 A1
Wootton Bassett SN4 47 F3
Wroughton SN4 64 C7
Swindon St SN6 23 A5
Swindon Sta SN2 50 B7
Swindon Town Football Club SN1 50 D7
Swinley Dr SN5 34 A1
Sword Gdns [5] SN1 49 F4
Swynford Cl GL7 10 D6
Sycamore Cl
Lyneham & Bradenstoke SN15 60 C2
North Tidworth SP9 216 E6
Sixpenny Handley SP5 208 A4
Sycamore Dr
[8] Frome BA11 110 B7
Salisbury SP1 146 C5
Sycamore Gr
Swindon SN2 35 C2
Trowbridge BA14 105 C5
Westbury BA13 108 F3
Sydnalls La BA12 115 D6
Symonds SN5 49 B3
Syon Cl Corsham SN13 84 E8
[4] Swindon SN25 34 F6
Sywell Rd SN3 51 C8

T

Tadpole La
Blunsdon St Andrew SN25 34 C8
Purton SN5 33 F8
Talavera Rd SN4 168 E8
Talbot Cl
Melksham SN12 94 D5
Salisbury SP1 146 C4
Talbot Rd BA14 105 A7
Talboys (Medieval Hall House)* BA14 178 B4
Tallow La [5] SN4 163 A6
Tamar Cl SN25 35 A4
Tamar Rd SN12 94 A6
Tamesis Dr GL7 4 F7
Tamworth Dr SN5 49 A7
Tan La SP8 138 A2
Tanarisk Cl SN11 81 C1
Tangmere Cl [13] SN12 178 B8
Tank La SP5 205 B4
Tankard La [15] SN8 170 B2
Tankey's Cl [5] BA11 110 A7
Tanner Cl SN15 78 F5
Tanners Cl
Winterbourne SP4 133 A1
Wootton Bassett SN4 47 D2
Tanners Field SP4 217 D3
Tanners Hill SN16 40 C8
Tanners La
Sandleheath SP6 210 A1
Shrewton SP3 196 E7
Winterbourne SP4 133 A1
Tansley Moor SN3 51 E3
Tanyard La [6] SP7 202 B1
Taramah Gdns [10] SP3 203 E8
Targetts Mead SP3 203 E8
Tarka Cl SN25 34 F7
Tarragon Cl SN2 34 C4
Tarrant's Hill [24] RG17 177 B7
Tarters The SN16 40 D8
Tascroft BA12 116 B5
Tasker Cl SN13 84 E8
Taskers La SN8 183 D8
Tattershall SN5 49 C3
Taunton Cl [2] SN14 77 F5
Taunton St SN1 50 A6
Tavinor Dr SN15 78 E4
Tavistock Rd SN3 51 B5
Tawny Owl Cl SN3 51 C8
Taylor Cres SN3 36 A4
Taylors Gn SN8 174 A7
Taylors La SN8 168 B1
Taylors View BA14 101 D1
Teal Ave SN15 60 A1
Teal Cl BA13 109 B4
Tealgate RG17 177 B8
Tealsbrook SN3 51 D7
Teapot St BA12 201 E8
Teasel Cl [28] SP11 192 A5
Teasels The BA12 116 F6
Technical Coll BA12 117 A7
Tedder Ave SN13 84 A8
Tees Cl SN25 35 A4
Teeswater Cl SN5 49 A6
Teffont Field Bldgs* SP3 201 D4
Teffont Manor* SP3 201 D2
Telford Rd SP2 151 E8
Tellcroft Cl SN13 84 F8
Tellings Orch SN16 16 D3
Tempest Rd [9] SP4 217 D3
Templar's Firs SN4 61 E8
Temple St SN1 50 C5
Ten Acres SP7 202 C2
Tenby Cl SN3 50 F3
Tennis Cnr Dro BA11 107 D2
Tennyson Cl BA12 116 E6
Tennyson Rd SN4 47 E3
Tennyson St SN1 50 B5
Tenzing Gdns SN25 35 C3
Tern Cl SN11 81 D2
Terncliff SN3 51 D7
Tetbury Hill SN16 27 F6
Tetbury La SN16 14 D6
Tetbury Rd SN16 25 D2
Tethering Dro SP6 211 C6
Tewkesbury Way
Lydiard Millicent SN5 48 E7
Swindon SN5 49 A6
Thackeray Cl SN3 51 D4
Thackeray Cres SN12 94 B4
Thames Ave SN25 34 E5
Thames Cl BA12 117 A5
Thames Cres SN12 94 A6
Thames La SN6 19 E8
Thames St GL7 2 C3
Thames View SN6 17 F8
Thamesdown Dr
Haydon Wick SN2 34 C4
Swindon SN25 35 A7
Theobald St SN1 50 B6
Thestfield Dr BA14 101 D4
Thetford Way SN25 34 C5
Thicketts Rd SN8 169 C1
Thickwood La SN14 75 C6
Thirsk Cl SN14 78 A5
Thistlebarrow Rd SP1 146 A4
Thistledown [6] SN4 163 A6
Thomas Byron Rd SN10 214 C1
Thomas Ct SN11 81 C1
Thomas Hardy Dr [8] SP7 202 D2
Thomas Mead SN15 78 E5
Thomas St SN2 49 F7
Thomas Wyatt Rd SN10 214 B1
Thompson Cl SP2 151 F5
Thompsons Hill SN16 40 C7
Thomson Way SN8 213 B2
Thornbank SN12 94 A3
Thornbridge Ave SN3 51 A4
Thornbury Rd BA13 108 F4
Thorne Cl SP5 150 F1
Thorne Rd
[2] Netheravon SP4 190 A4
Swindon SN3 51 C4
Thorneydown Rd SP4 133 E1
Thornford Dr SN5 49 C5
Thornhill Dr SN25 35 A8
Thornhill Rd BA12 116 D5
Thorns The SN8 213 D5
Threadgill Way [6] SP9 199 C8
Three Barrows* SN8 164 B3
Three Oak Hill Dr SN8 175 D4
Three Shire Stones* SN14 74 D1
Three Sisters Rd [1] SN4 163 B6
Thrushel Cl SN25 34 E4
Thruxton Motor Racing Circuit* SP11 192 C1
Thurlestone Rd SN3 50 E5
Thurlow Cl [10] SP4 217 E3
Tibb's Mdw SP11 192 D8
Tiberius Rd [24] SP10 193 E2
Tidcombe (Long Barrow)* SN8 184 D4
Tidling Cnr SN16 16 C5
Tidworth Cl [3] SN1 49 F4
Tidworth Coll SP9 216 D6
Tidworth Golf Club SP9 216 A4
Tidworth Leisure Ctr SP9 216 D6
Tidworth Oval* SP9 216 C5
Tidworth Rd
Bulford SP4 199 A7
Collingbourne Ducis SN8 191 D7
Ludgershall SP11 191 F5
Milston SP4 191 B1
Porton SP4 133 E7
Tile Hill BA10 122 A5
Tilley's La SN3 36 A2
Timandra Cl [1] SN25 35 A6
Timber St SN15 78 E7
Timberley La SP5 211 E7
Timbrell St BA14 101 D1
Timor Rd BA13 108 E2
Tin Pit SN8 213 E4
Tinhead Rd BA13 186 C8
Tinings The SN15 79 A8
Tinkers Field SN4 47 D2
Tinkers Mead SN9 215 D4
Tinneys Cl SP5 211 C6
Tintagel Cl
[18] Andover SP10 193 E2
Swindon SN5 49 B4
Tintern Rd SN10 214 B1
Tisbury & District Sports Ctr SP3 203 D8
Tisbury Cl [1] SN2 35 C6
Tisbury Rd SP3 204 D8
Tisbury Row SP3 203 F8
Tisbury Sta SP3 203 E7
Tismeads Cres SN1 50 C2
Titan Barrow BA1 82 C2
Titchfield Cl [5] SN5 48 F5
Tithe Barn Cres SN1 49 F3
Tittymouse La SP11 192 F1
Tiverton Rd SN2 35 C1
Tobruk Cl [5] SP11 193 E4
Tobruk Rd SP11 191 F3
Tobys Ct [25] SP7 202 C2
Tockenham Cnr SN4 60 D6
Toghill Cres SN13 76 B1
Tokes La SP7 202 E6
Toll Down Way SN14 53 A4
Tollard Cl SN3 51 C6
Tollgate Cl SP4 217 A5
Tollgate Pk SP7 202 C3
Tollgate Rd
Andover SP10 193 C1
Salisbury SP1 152 B8
Tombs Rd SP4 198 A6
Toothill Inf Sch SN5 49 C4
Top La
Atworth/Whitley SN12 85 C1
Stourton with Gasper BA12 137 D7
Top Rd GL7 10 C7
Top St SN15 44 A2
Toppers Cl SN25 35 A3
Tormarton Rd
Acton Turville GL9 52 E6
Marshfield SN14 66 A2
Tornio Cl SN10 214 D4
Torr Cl SN14 70 B2
Torridge Cl SN25 34 F4
Tottenham Ho* SN8 175 F2
Tottenham Pk* SN8 175 F3
Totterdown Cl [3] SN3 51 E7
Totts La SN14 75 B3
Touchorne La SP3 141 A4
Tournament Rd SP2 145 C3
Tout Hill SP7 202 B2
Tovey Rd SN2 35 B2
Tow Barrow (Long Barrow)* SN8 184 B4
Towcester Cl SN14 77 F5
Towcester Pl [1] SN14 77 F5
Towcester Rd
North Bradley BA14 105 E4
Swindon SN3 51 C8
Towell Rd [5] SP4 198 A6
Tower Cl Andover SP10 193 C2
Trowbridge BA14 105 A7
Tower Hill
Dilton Marsh BA13 112 D7
Iwerne Minster DT11 206 A1
Tower Mews SP1 146 B2
Tower Rd
Melksham SN12 94 C5
Stourton with Gasper BA10 122 F3
Swindon SN5 34 B2
Tower View SN10 96 D2
Town Bridge Bradford-on-Avon* BA15 100 C6
Town Cl SN14 69 F8
Town Farm Pl SP5 208 B4
Town Mill SN8 213 D2
Town Path SP2 151 E7
Townfield [10] SN8 170 B2
Townsend
Chitterne BA12 195 D7
Pitton & Farley SP5 148 C4
Townsend Cl BA12 138 F5
Townsend La SP6 209 A6
Townsend Pl SN14 77 F8
Towpath Rd BA14 101 D4
Tracy Cl SN25 35 A6
Trafalgar Ho* SP5 159 D4
Trajan Rd SN3 36 C1
Tregantle Wlk SN3 51 C6
Tregoze Prim Sch SN5 49 A6
Tregoze Way SN5 48 F6
Trenchard Ave
Box SN13 84 A8
Calne Without SN11 81 F1
[4] Corsham SN13 76 B1
Winterbourne SP4 133 C2
Trenchard Rd
Lyneham SN15 60 A1
Stanton Fitzwarren SN6 22 B2
Trent Cres SN12 94 A6
Trent Rd SN25 35 A4
Trentham Cl SN3 51 A4
Trevithick Cl [5] BA11 110 C6
Triangle The SP5 161 D4
Trimm's Dro SP6 211 A4
Trimnells SN14 75 B3
Trinity CE Sch GL9 53 A6
Trinity Cl SN3 51 A3
Trinity Pk SN11 81 C1
Trinity Rd SP3 196 F7
Trinity Rise SP11 193 A2
Trinity St SP1 152 B8
Tropenell Cl [2] SN13 76 E1
Tropical Bird Gdns* BA11 103 D2
Trout La SN13 84 B7
Trow La Brinkworth SN15 59 F8
Maiden Bradley with Yarnfield BA12 118 E4
Trowbridge Com Hospl BA14 101 D2
Trowbridge Mus* BA14 105 D8
Trowbridge Parochial Jun Sch BA14 101 E2
Trowbridge Rd
Bradford-on-Avon BA15 100 E5
Bratton BA13 186 A8
Seend SN12 178 C7
Trowbridge BA14 102 A2
Westbury BA13 109 B5
Trowbridge Sta BA14 105 C8
Trowle BA14 101 A2
Truman Cl SN3 51 C4
Truro Wlk SN14 77 F6
Tryhorn Dr SP1 146 C5
Tryon Cl SN3 51 D2
Tubbs Farm Cl [6] RG17 165 A1
Tucker Cl [6] SP4 217 C2
Tuckers La SN4 163 D6
Tuckwell Rd GL7 10 E6
Tudor Cl SN15 79 A4
Tudor Cres SN3 36 B1
Tudor Dr BA14 101 E4
Tudor Wlk SN3 50 F6
Tugela Rd SN15 70 E1
Tuggy's La BA2 98 E1
Tulip Tree Cl SN2 35 C2
Tulse Hill Zeale BA12 138 A4
Zennor BA12 137 F3
Tumlins SN10 180 F8
Tunball La SN8 184 F4
Tuners La SN16 14 E6
Tunnel Hill SP5 153 C2
Tupman Rd SN13 76 E2
Turf Ho La SN11 72 D1
Turin Ct [17] SP10 193 E2
Turl St SN1 50 C6
Turnball SN4 65 C4
Turnberry Cl SN15 78 F7
Turner Cl [2] SP2 151 E7
Turner St SN1 50 A5
Turnham Gn SN5 49 A4
Turnpike [4] SN8 170 A6
Turnpike Rd
Blunsdon St Andrew SN26 35 C8
Highworth SN6 23 A6
Turnpike The SP3 202 D8
Turpin Way SN14 77 F7
Tutton Hill SN14 75 B3
Twatley Cotts SN16 27 C4
Tweed Cl SN25 34 F4
Twickenham Way SN15 70 E1
Twineham Gdns SP5 153 F2
Twyford Cl SN3 51 A6
Twynham Cl SP5 211 A7
Twynnoy Cl SN16 28 A5
Tyburn Cl SN5 49 B5
Tydeman St SN2 35 D1
Tye Gdns SN5 48 F5
Tylers Cl SP2 151 D7
Tyndales Mdw SP3 201 F2
Tyneham Rd SN3 51 B6
Tyning Cl [1] BA14 105 A7
Tyning La [9] BA13 186 B7
Tyning Pk SN11 81 C1
Tyning Rd
Bathampton BA2 82 A2
Winsley BA15 99 E7
Tyning The BA2 99 B4
Tynings The
Biddestone SN14 76 D7
Westbury BA13 108 F2
Tynings Way BA15 99 F3
Tyrone Ave SP4 198 E7
Tytherington Rd BA12 194 C5
Tytherley Rd SP5 149 E6

U

Ullswater Cl SN3 51 E3
Umbers Hill [2] SP7 202 B1
Underdown Cl [12] SN4 163 A6
Underhill Mere BA12 138 F5
Pen Selwood BA9 137 B2
Underwood Dr SP4 217 D2
Union Rd
Chippenham SN15 78 D8
Tisbury SP3 203 E7
Union Row SN1 50 D4
Union St Melksham SN12 94 A4
Ramsbury SN8 170 B2
Swindon SN1 50 C5
Trowbridge BA14 101 D1
Unity St SN14 78 C7
Univ of Bath in Swindon SN3 51 A7
Up St BA12 194 E4
Upavon Airfield SN9 182 B1
Upavon Prim Sch SN9 182 A1
Upcott SN6 8 C4
Upfield SN3 51 D3
Upham Rd SN3 50 E5
Upham Village* SN8 169 C8
Upland Rise BA13 109 B2
Uplands [28] RG17 177 B7
Uplands Cl BA2 98 F7
Uplands The BA12 117 C7
Upnor Cl SP11 191 F4
Upper Avon Sch SP4 198 C7
Upper Backway SP3 196 F7
Upper Broad St BA14 101 C1
Upper Church Fields SN8 213 E1
Upper Dro SP10 193 C1
Upper Eddington RG17 177 C8
Upper Folly SP2 144 B1
Upper Garston La [8] BA13 186 B7
Upper Isbury SN8 213 E2
Upper La SN13 84 D7
Upper Lambourn Rd RG17 165 A2
Upper Ley SN13 83 D5
Upper Marsh La BA12 117 A5
Upper Marsh Rd BA12 117 A6
Upper N Rd SP5 207 C5
Upper Noremarsh SN4 47 F1
Upper Pavenhill SN5 32 F4
Upper Potley SN13 84 E7
Upper Regents Pk BA15 100 D6
Upper Seagry Sch SN15 57 D6
Upper St SP2 151 D7
Upper Wr St BA12 139 B5
Uppington La SP3 129 E8
Upton Cl [5] BA12 116 E7
Upton Great Barrow* BA12 194 F5
Urchfont Manor Coll SN10 180 B3
Urchfont Prim Sch SN10 180 B4
Utah Cl SN1 49 F4
Utterson View SN15 78 C7
Uxbridge Rd SN5 49 A3

V

Vale Leaze SN15 44 C5
Vale Rd Pewsey SN9 215 B5

Vale Rd *continued*
Redlynch SP5 .... 211 C7
Vale View SN4 .... 47 D1
Vale View Rd SP2 .... 130 B2
Valens Terr SN13 .... 83 C6
Valentia Ct SN12 .... 178 B8
Valiant Cl 9 SN12 .... 178 B8
Valletta Gdns SN14 .... 56 B5
Valley Cl SP5 .... 211 C7
Valley Rd SN13 .... 76 E1
Valley The SP2 .... 145 C5
Valley View SN11 .... 81 A2
Valley Way SN14 .... 75 C6
Valleyside SN1 .... 50 A4
Van Diemen's Cl SN8 .... 213 E2
Vanbrugh Gate SN3 .... 50 F1
Vanessa Ave SP1 .... 146 D1
Vastern Wharf SN4 .... 61 A7
Vasterne Cl SN5 .... 33 B5
Velley Hill
Corsham SN13 .... 85 C5
Corsham SN13 .... 85 C5
Venice Ct SP11 .... 193 F2
Venn The 11 SP7 .... 202 C2
Ventnor Cl SN2 .... 34 E4
Ventry Cl 3 SP1 .... 146 B2
Ventry The 4 SP1 .... 146 B2
Verden Way 19 SP10 .... 193 D2
Verney Cl SN3 .... 51 D6
Vernham Dean Sch SP11 .... 185 C3
Vernon Cl 2 SP4 .... 217 E3
Verona Rd SP1 .... 145 F4
Verulam Cl SN3 .... 51 D8
Verwood Cl SN3 .... 51 B4
Vespasian Cl SN3 .... 51 C8
Vespasian Rd 10 SP10 .... 193 E2
Vicarage Cl Calne SN11 .... 81 B3
Marlborough SN8 .... 213 E3
Vicarage Cotts SN15 .... 57 F6
Vicarage Gdns 3 SP4 .... 190 A3
Vicarage La
Charlton SN16 .... 29 B7
Colerne SN14 .... 75 C3
Easterton SN10 .... 179 F2
Hankerton SN16 .... 15 B1
Highworth SN6 .... 23 A6
Steeple Ashton BA14 .... 178 A3
Upavon SN9 .... 181 F2
Vicarage Pk 1 SP5 .... 211 C7
Vicarage Rd
Redlynch SP5 .... 211 E7
Swindon SN2 .... 34 F1
Tisbury SP3 .... 203 E8
Vicarage St BA12 .... 116 F7
Vice La SO51 .... 212 E2
Victoria Cl
Lyneham SN11 .... 73 E8
Wilton SP2 .... 144 C4
Victoria Cross Rd SN4 .... 63 F7
Victoria Ct SP1 .... 146 A3
Victoria Dr SN15 .... 60 B1
Victoria Gdns
14 Sandleheath SP6 .... 210 C1
Trowbridge BA14 .... 101 E2
Victoria Hospl SN1 .... 50 B4
Victoria Pk SN10 .... 187 B8
Victoria Rd
Devizes SN10 .... 214 B4
Frome BA11 .... 110 A4
Salisbury SP1 .... 146 A2
Sandleheath SP6 .... 210 C1
Swindon SN1 .... 50 C5
Trowbridge BA14 .... 101 E3
Warminster BA12 .... 116 C6
Wilton SP2 .... 144 C3
Victoria St 21 SP7 .... 202 C2
Victoria Terr SN11 .... 81 B3
Victory Rd BA13 .... 108 C6
Viking Cl SN25 .... 34 F7
Viking Way
Andover SP10 .... 193 E2
Salisbury SP2 .... 152 B5
Vilett St SN1 .... 50 B6
Village Mus The Castle Combe* SN14 .... 68 A7
Village St SN8 .... 173 D1
Villiers Cl
Chippenham SN15 .... 78 F7
Lydiard Tregoze SN5 .... 48 F7
Vimoutiers Ct 16 SP6 .... 210 D1
Vimy Cres 8 SP4 .... 198 E6
Vincent Cl SN12 .... 94 C4
Vincients Rd SN14 .... 69 F1
Viner's La GL9 .... 53 B5
Virginia Cl 1 SP4 .... 217 E3
Virginia Dr BA12 .... 116 E7
Viscount Way SN3 .... 36 C6
Vockins Cl SP9 .... 216 C8
Volpe Cl SN5 .... 48 F4
Volta Rd SN1 .... 50 C6
Vorda Rd SN6 .... 23 A7
Vowley View SN4 .... 47 F1

W

Wade Hill SN6 .... 22 F5
Wadswick La SN13 .... 84 B3
Wagtail Cl SN3 .... 51 C8
Waiblingen Way SN10 .... 214 A4
Wain-a-Long Rd SP1 .... 146 C1
Wains Way SP4 .... 190 A3
Wainwright Cl 4 SN3 .... 51 D4
Wainwright Dr 5 BA11 .... 110 C7
Waite Meads Cl SN5 .... 33 C4
Wakefield Cl
Kempsford GL7 .... 10 E6
Swindon SN5 .... 49 A4
Walbury Hill (Fort)* RG17 .... 185 F8
Walcot Rd SN3 .... 50 E5
Walden Lodge Cl SN10 .... 214 B2
Waldron Cl 3 SN3 .... 51 C4
Waleran Cl SP5 .... 153 E2
Walker Rd BA11 .... 110 A3
Walker's La 3 RG17 .... 165 A2
Wallbridge BA11 .... 110 B4
Wallbridge Ave 2 BA11 .... 110 A4
Wallbridge Gdns 1 BA11 .... 110 A4
Wallingford Cl SN5 .... 49 C3
Wallingtons Rd RG17 .... 177 F4
Wallis Dr SN25 .... 35 A8
Wallsworth Rd 4 SN3 .... 51 A4
Walmesley Chase BA14 .... 102 A1
Walnut Cl
3 Netheravon SP4 .... 190 A4
Pewsey SN9 .... 215 D5
Rowde SN10 .... 96 D1
Sutton Veny BA12 .... 121 F8
Walnut Dr SN14 .... 74 F6
Walnut Gr BA14 .... 105 B6
Walnut Tree Gdns SN5 .... 48 D8
Walnut Trees Hill SN6 .... 164 A8
Walnut Wlk 1 BA11 .... 110 B7
Walronds Cl SN8 .... 170 C8
Walsingham Rd SN3 .... 50 F6
Walter Cl SN5 .... 49 A6
Walter Powell Sch SN15 .... 44 B2
Walter Sutton Cl SN11 .... 80 F3
Walton Cl 5 SN3 .... 50 F4
Walwayne Field SN2 .... 36 A5
Wanborough Rd
Swindon SN3 .... 36 C1
Wanborough SN4 .... 51 F6
Wanborough Sch SN4 .... 163 A6
Wansdyke* SN11 .... 172 C5
Wansdyke Dr SN11 .... 81 A3
Wansdyke Rd SN8 .... 176 B4
Wansdyke Sch SN10 .... 214 B1
Wanshot Cl SN4 .... 64 C5
Wantage Rd RG17 .... 165 B2
War Meml Ave 13 RG17 .... 177 B6
Waram Cl RG17 .... 177 C8
Warbeck Gate 11 SN5 .... 48 F5
Warbler Cl 1 BA14 .... 105 B8
Wardley Cl SN3 .... 51 A4
Wardour Cl SN3 .... 50 E3
Wardour Pl 4 SN12 .... 94 A2
Wardour Prim Sch SP3 .... 203 C6
Wardour Rd 4 SN14 .... 78 A6
Wareham Cl SN5 .... 49 B5
Warleigh Dr BA1 .... 82 A3
Warleigh La BA1 .... 82 B1
Warmer's Inn La SN15 .... 27 D8
Warminster Ave 2 SN2 .... 35 C5
Warminster Com Hospl BA12 .... 117 A7
Warminster Prep Sch BA12 .... 116 F6
Warminster Rd
Claverton BA2 .... 90 B4
Frome BA11 .... 110 B4
Westbury BA13 .... 108 F1
Wilton SP2 .... 144 D5
Warminster Sch BA12 .... 116 F7
Warminster Sports Ctr BA12 .... 117 D6
Warminster Sta BA12 .... 117 B7
Warneage Gn 2 SN4 .... 163 A5
Warneford Cl 4 SN5 .... 49 D4
Warner Cl 2 SN3 .... 36 B3
Warren Cres SN11 .... 81 C4
Warrens La SP5 .... 159 A4
Warwick Cl
Chippenham SN14 .... 77 F5
Salisbury SP1 .... 145 F3
Warwick Cres SN12 .... 94 B3
Warwick Rd SN1 .... 50 C5
Washbourne Rd SN4 .... 47 E1
Washern Cl SP2 .... 144 C1
Washers Pit* DT11 .... 206 D3
Washington Rd BA13 .... 108 C6
Washmeres SN14 .... 75 B2
Washpool La GL7 .... 10 E8
Wason Rd 5 SP4 .... 197 E6
Wastfield SN13 .... 84 F8
Water Ditchampton SP2 .... 144 C4
Water Field SN5 .... 33 A3
Water Furlongs 2 SN6 .... 19 D7
Water La
Castle Combe SN14 .... 68 A7
Enford SN9 .... 190 B6
Horningsham BA12 .... 119 A8
Water St
Berwick St John SP7 .... 203 E1
Durrington/Bulford SP4 .... 217 D8
Mere BA12 .... 139 B5
Upton Lovell BA12 .... 194 E3
Watercrook Mews 2 SN5 .... 49 D5
Waterdown Cl 2 SN2 .... 34 C4
Watergate La SP4 .... 217 C7
Watergates SN14 .... 75 C3
Waterhouse La BA2 .... 98 F8
Waterloo Rd SP1 .... 152 C7
Watermead SN3 .... 36 C2
Watermeadow La BA12 .... 195 C1
Watermint Way SN11 .... 80 F4
Waters Bank Rd SN13 .... 84 B8
Waters Edge SN15 .... 78 E5
Waters Rd SP1 .... 146 A4
Watersmeet Rd SP2 .... 152 A6
Waterworks Rd BA14 .... 105 B7
Watery La
Donhead St Mary SP7 .... 203 A3
Shaftesbury SP7 .... 202 C1
Sutton Veny BA12 .... 117 F4
Watling Cl SN2 .... 49 E6
Watson Rd SP4 .... 197 E7
Watt Cl 4 SP10 .... 193 C1
Watt Rd SP2 .... 151 D8
Watt's Way 22 SN10 .... 179 F1
Watts La SN14 .... 41 F1
Wavell Rd
Salisbury SP2 .... 152 A6
Swindon SN2 .... 35 B2
Tidworth SP9 .... 216 B8
Waverley Cl
7 Fordingbridge SP6 .... 210 D2
Frome BA11 .... 110 C6
Waverley Gdns SN12 .... 94 A3
Waverley Rd
Fordingbridge SP6 .... 210 D2
Swindon SN3 .... 36 C1
Waylands Cricklade SN6 .... 19 E7
Devizes SN10 .... 214 D3
Wayne Cl SN25 .... 35 A5
Wayside Cl
Frome BA11 .... 110 C6
Kington Langley SN15 .... 70 E7
Swindon SN2 .... 49 E7
Weaveland Rd 2 SP3 .... 203 E8
Weavern Ct SN14 .... 78 A7
Weavern La SN13 .... 76 A5
Weavers Crofts SN12 .... 94 A5
Weavers Dr BA14 .... 105 D7
Weavers La RG17 .... 177 E3
Weavers Mead SN10 .... 179 C1
Weavers The SN3 .... 50 D4
Webb Cl SN15 .... 78 E5
Webbers Ct BA14 .... 105 A6
Webbington Rd SN15 .... 78 E5
Webbs Ct SN15 .... 60 A3
Webbs Way
Burbage SN8 .... 183 D8
Malmesbury SN16 .... 28 A5
Webbs Wood SN5 .... 34 A2
Wedgewood Cl SN2 .... 50 A7
Wedmore Ave SN15 .... 70 C1
Wedmore Cl BA11 .... 110 C7
Weedon Rd SN3 .... 51 B8
Weeke Cl 1 SP5 .... 210 F8
Weir Hayes Ave 7 SN13 .... 76 B1
Weir La SN14 .... 74 A8
Weir The BA13 .... 186 C8
Weirside Ave SN4 .... 64 B6
Welcombe Ave SN3 .... 51 A5
Welford Cl SN3 .... 51 C8
Well Cl SN4 .... 65 D4
Well House Cl SP6 .... 210 B6
Well La Godshill SP6 .... 211 A1
Hawkesbury GL9 .... 38 E5
4 Shaftesbury SP7 .... 202 B2
Welle Sley Cl 18 SN12 .... 178 B8
Weller Rd SN13 .... 76 F2
Wellhead Dro BA13 .... 109 A1
Wellhead La BA13 .... 109 A1
Wellington Dr
Bishops Cannings SN10 .... 214 F7
Bower Hill SN12 .... 94 C1
Wellington Pl SN14 .... 55 F8
Wellington Rd 5 SP4 .... 198 F7
Wellington Sq SN12 .... 94 C1
Wellington St SN1 .... 50 C7
Wellington Way SP2 .... 145 D3
Wellow Dr BA11 .... 110 C7
Wellow La BA2 .... 98 D1
Wellow Wood Rd SO51 .... 212 F8
Wells Cl
Chippenham SN14 .... 78 A5
Durrington SP4 .... 198 A6
Wells Rd SP4 .... 198 A6
Wells St SN1 .... 50 C6
Welsh Way GL7 .... 1 D8
Welton Rd SN5 .... 49 D6
Wembley St SN2 .... 49 F8
Wenhill Hts SN11 .... 81 B2
Wenhill La SN11 .... 81 A1
Wensleydale Cl SN5 .... 49 B6
Wentworth Cl SN15 .... 78 F7
Wentworth Pk 1 SN5 .... 49 A4
Were Cl 3 BA12 .... 116 E7
Werg SN8 .... 175 B8
Wesley Cl BA14 .... 104 E2
Wesley La BA14 .... 104 E2
Wesley Rd BA14 .... 105 C7
Wesley St SN1 .... 50 C4
Wessex Cl Calne SN11 .... 81 C3
2 Hungerford RG17 .... 177 B7
Melksham SN12 .... 94 B3
Semington BA14 .... 102 E5
Wessex Pl 29 RG17 .... 177 B7
Wessex Rd
Chippenham SN14 .... 78 B8
Salisbury SP1 .... 146 C1
Wilton SP2 .... 144 C1
Wessex Way SN6 .... 23 B7
Wessex Wlk BA13 .... 109 A4
Wessington Ave SN11 .... 81 C1
Wessington Pk SN11 .... 81 C1
West Ashton Prim Sch BA14 .... 106 B4
West Ashton Rd BA14 .... 105 E8
West Bourton Rd SP8 .... 137 D1
West Cepen Way
Chippenham SN14 .... 70 B3
Chippenham Without SN14 .... 77 F5
West Ditch La BA14 .... 106 E4
West End
Bishops Cannings SN10 .... 172 B3
Melksham SN12 .... 94 A3
Westbury BA13 .... 109 A3
West End La
Bishopstone SN6 .... 163 E6
Donhead St Andrew SP7 .... 203 B3
West End Rd SN3 .... 36 A1
West Ennox La SN13 .... 84 A6
West Hay Gr GL7 .... 4 F7
West Highland Rd SN25 .... 34 F7
West Hill
Broad Blunsdon SN26 .... 21 B2
Melksham Without SN12 .... 85 B1
West Kennett (Long Barrow)* SN8 .... 173 C6
West La Kemble GL7 .... 4 F7
Melbury Abbas SP7 .... 206 A7
West Manton SN8 .... 174 C7
West Mill La SN6 .... 8 C1
West Par BA12 .... 116 F6
West Park* SP6 .... 210 A3
West Pk SP11 .... 192 E3
West Pk Dr SP6 .... 209 F3
West Pk La SP6 .... 209 F3
West Pk Rd SN13 .... 76 E1
West Portway SP10 .... 193 C1
West St Aldbourne SN8 .... 170 A6
Barford St Martin SP3 .... 143 A4
Castle Combe SN14 .... 68 A7
22 Fordingbridge SP6 .... 210 D1
Great Somerford SN15 .... 43 F2
Great Wishford SP2 .... 129 F4
Lacock SN15 .... 86 D5
Malmesbury SN16 .... 27 F3
Salisbury SP2 .... 145 F1
Trowbridge BA14 .... 105 C8
Warminster BA12 .... 116 E6
Wilton SP2 .... 144 C3
West View SN8 .... 191 A8
West View Cres SN10 .... 214 A3
West View Rd BA1 .... 82 A3
West Way GL7 .... 2 C5
West Wilts Golf Club BA12 .... 113 B1
West Wilts Trading Est BA13 .... 108 D7
West Wlk SP1 .... 152 A7
Westbourne Cl SP1 .... 152 C8
Westbourne Gdns 6 BA14 .... 105 B8
Westbourne Rd
Trowbridge BA14 .... 105 B8
Westbury BA13 .... 109 A3
Westbrook Cl
Chippenham SN14 .... 78 A7
14 Hungerford RG17 .... 177 B7
Westbrook Gn SN15 .... 95 E8
Westbrook Rd
Bromham SN15 .... 88 A1
Swindon SN2 .... 35 A1
Westbury Com Hospl BA13 .... 109 A2
Westbury Infs Sch BA13 .... 108 F3
Westbury Jun Sch BA13 .... 108 E3
Westbury Leigh BA13 .... 108 E1
Westbury Leigh Prim Sch BA13 .... 108 E1
Westbury Pk SN4 .... 47 D1
Westbury Rd
Bratton BA13 .... 186 A7
Cheverell Magna SN10 .... 179 C1
Heywood BA13 .... 109 A8
North Bradley BA14 .... 105 E3
Swindon SN2 .... 35 B5
Warminster BA12 .... 113 A2
Westbury Sta BA13 .... 108 E5
Westbury View SN12 .... 94 C4
Westbury White Horse* BA13 .... 109 F3
Westcombe La BA12 .... 195 E1
Westcott Cl 9 BA11 .... 110 C6
Westcott Pl SN1 .... 50 A5
Westcott St SN1 .... 50 A5
Westcroft SN14 .... 78 A5
Westcroft St BA14 .... 101 C1
Westerham Wlk SN11 .... 81 C2
Westerleigh Cl SN14 .... 78 B6
Western Downland Prim Sch SP6 .... 209 F2
Western Downland Sch SP6 .... 210 A5
Western St SN1 .... 50 C5
Western Way
Melksham SN12 .... 93 F3
Salisbury SP2 .... 145 B3
Westfield BA15 .... 100 B7
Westfield Chase 18 SN8 .... 170 A6
Westfield Cl
15 Durrington/Bulford SP4 .... 198 B7
Laverstock SP1 .... 146 D2
Trowbridge BA14 .... 105 A6
Westfield Est BA12 .... 137 F4
Westfield Rd BA14 .... 105 A7
Westfield Way SN2 .... 34 D4
Westgrove 17 SP6 .... 210 D1
Westhill Cl SN6 .... 22 F5
Westlake Pl SN15 .... 57 D1
Westland Cl 3 SP4 .... 217 D3
Westlands 2 BA12 .... 194 C5
Westlands La SN12 .... 85 F2
Westlea CP Sch SN5 .... 49 C6
Westlea Dr SN5 .... 49 C5
Westlecot Rd SN1 .... 50 B3
Westmead Cres BA14 .... 105 B4
Westmead Dr SN5 .... 49 D7
Westmead Ind Est SN5 .... 49 D7
Westmead La SN15 .... 78 D7
Westminster Cl 1 SP7 .... 202 D2
Westminster Gdns SN14 .... 78 B7
Westminster Meml Hospl SP7 .... 202 B1
Westminster Rd
Salisbury SP2 .... 145 F2
Swindon SN5 .... 49 B4
Westmorland Rd SN1 .... 50 D5
Weston Ct 1 SP11 .... 193 E4
Weston La SP5 .... 149 B5
Westonbirt Arboretum* GL8 .... 25 B8
Westonbirt Sch GL8 .... 25 E8
Westrop SN6 .... 23 A6
Westrop Sch SN6 .... 22 F6
Westside SP4 .... 199 A2
Westside Cl SP4 .... 146 C8
Westview Orch BA2 .... 99 B5
Westwells SN13 .... 84 C6
Westwells Rd SN13 .... 84 B7
Westwood Manor House* BA15 .... 100 A3
Westwood Rd
Corsham SN13 .... 84 B8
Salisbury SP2 .... 145 B4
Swindon SN2 .... 35 C6
Wingfield BA15 .... 100 D2
Westwood St Thomas Sch SP2 .... 145 A4
Westwood With Iford Sch BA15 .... 99 F3
Westwoods BA1 .... 82 B3
Wet La BA12 .... 139 D2
Wet Pits La SN8 .... 168 E3
Wetherby Cl 1 SN14 .... 78 A5
Wexland Ave SP4 .... 189 F3
Wey Cl SN25 .... 35 A4
Weyhill Cl SN3 .... 51 B5
Weyhill Gdns 7 SP11 .... 192 F1
Weyhill Rd SP11 .... 193 A1
Weymouth St BA12 .... 117 A6
Whaddon La
Hilperton BA14 .... 102 B5
Trowbridge BA14 .... 102 A3
Whalley Cres SN4 .... 63 F6
Wharf Ct SN12 .... 94 B3
Wharf Ctr The* SN10 .... 214 A4
Wharf La Kempsford GL7 .... 10 D6
Lechlade GL7 .... 2 D3
Wharf Rd SN4 .... 49 C1
Wharf St SN10 .... 214 A4
Wharf The SN13 .... 83 D6
Wharfings The GL7 .... 10 D6
Whatcombe Brow SP3 .... 196 D8
Whatleys Cl SN10 .... 179 A4
Whatleys Orch SN6 .... 163 E6
Wheatlands SN25 .... 34 E4
Wheatstone Rd SN3 .... 51 E4
Wheeler Ave SN2 .... 35 D2
Wheelwright's Cl SP5 .... 208 A4
Whelford Rd GL7 .... 10 D7
Whilestone Way SN3 .... 36 C1
Whinyates Rd 2 SP4 .... 197 E7
Whistley Rd SN10 .... 179 C6
Whitbourne Ave SN3 .... 50 F5
Whitbred Cl 2 SN5 .... 49 B7
Whitbred Rd SP2 .... 145 C5
Whitby Gr SN2 .... 34 F1
Whitchers Mdw SP5 .... 153 D4
Whitcombe Cl SN15 .... 73 F8
White Barrow (Long Barrow)* SP3 .... 188 B1
White Castle SN5 .... 49 C3
White Cliff* BA13 .... 186 B6
White Edge Moor SN3 .... 51 D2
White Ennox La SN13 .... 83 F7
White Farm La SN8 .... 185 C7
White Hart La 12 SP7 .... 202 C1
White Hill
Bishopstone SN4 .... 163 D5
Pitton & Farley SP5 .... 148 C3
White Horse Cl BA14 .... 105 D6
White Horse Dr 8 BA11 .... 110 C6
White Horse Rd
Cricklade SN6 .... 19 D8
Winsley BA15 .... 99 E7
White Horse Sports Ctr SN11 .... 81 C1
White Horse Way
Calne SN11 .... 81 B1
Westbury BA13 .... 109 A4
White Lion Pk SN16 .... 27 E4
White Pit La SP7 .... 206 B6
White Rd Mere BA12 .... 139 B6
Savernake SN8 .... 175 A6
White Row Hill BA14 .... 105 A5
White Sheet Castle* BA12 .... 124 E1
White Sheet Hill Nature Reserve* BA12 .... 124 E2
White Sheet La BA12 .... 124 C3
White Shute RG17 .... 171 A8
White St
Easterton SN10 .... 180 A1

White St continued
Horningsham BA12 ... 119 B8
21 Market Lavington SN10 . 179 F1
White Way
Broad Town SN4 ... 167 A8
Pitton & Farley SP5 ... 148 C3
White's Hill SN8 ... 169 F2
Whitebridge Rd SP1 ... 146 D1
Whitecroft BA13 ... 112 C8
Whitefield Cl BA1 ... 82 B4
Whitefield Cres SN5 ... 34 A1
Whitefriars La SN6 ... 6 E3
Whitefriars Rd 1 SP1 ... 152 B7
Whitegates SN14 ... 68 A8
Whitehead St SN1 ... 50 B5
Whiteheads La BA15 ... 100 D7
Whitehill BA15 ... 100 D7
Whitehill Cl 11 SN8 ... 170 B2
Whitehill La SN4 ... 47 B2
Whitehill Way SN5 ... 48 F3
Whitehorn Cl SN4 ... 47 E4
Whitehorn Dr SP5 ... 212 C5
Whitehouse La GL8 ... 26 B8
Whitehouse Rd SN2 ... 50 B8
Whiteland Rise BA13 ... 109 B2
Whitelands Rd SN3 ... 36 A1
Whitelawn La BA14 ... 106 F4
Whitelocks Piece
RG17 ... 171 A1
Whiteman St SN2 ... 50 C8
Whitemarsh BA12 ... 139 B4
Whiterow Pk BA14 ... 105 A6
Whites Cnr SN12 ... 85 D1
Whitesbury Rd SP5 ... 152 B1
Whiteshoot SP5 ... 211 D6
Whiteshoot Hill SP5 ... 211 D6
Whitestone Rd BA11 ... 110 B6
Whitfield Cl BA12 ... 117 C7
Whitgift Cl SN5 ... 48 F6
Whitley Golf Club SN12 ... 93 E8
Whitley Rd 14 SN8 ... 170 A6
Whitlock Rise SP5 ... 205 F5
Whitmarsh Cl 7 SP4 ... 190 A4
Whitmore Cl SN5 ... 48 F6
Whitney St SN1 ... 50 C5
Whitsbury Rd SP6 ... 210 D2
Whittington Rd SN5 ... 49 C6
Whittle Ave SN11 ... 166 A1
Whittle Cl SN14 ... 78 A7
Whittle Rd
4 Andover SP10 ... 193 B1
Salisbury SP2 ... 145 D1
Whittonditch Rd SN8 ... 170 C2
Whitworth Rd SN25 ... 35 A3
Wichelstok Cl SN1 ... 50 C3
Wick Ball Camp*
SP3 ... 201 D3
Wick La Devizes SN10 ... 214 B1
Downton SP5 ... 210 E8
Lacock SN15 ... 85 F4
Manningford SN9 ... 181 F5
Wanborough SN4 ... 51 F6
Wick Rd SN16 ... 16 A8
Wickdown Ave SN25 ... 34 F3
Wicker Hill BA14 ... 101 C1
Wickfield SN10 ... 214 B2
Wicks Cl SN25 ... 34 E5
Wicks Dr SN15 ... 78 F5
Wickwater La GL7 ... 7 C4
Widbrook Mdw BA14 ... 105 A8
Widbrook View BA15 ... 100 E5
Widhill La SN26 ... 21 A1
Wigmore Ave SN3 ... 50 F3
Wilcot Ave SN2 ... 35 D5
Wilcot Cl
Amesbury SP4 ... 217 D2
Trowbridge BA14 ... 105 C6
Wilcot Rd SN9 ... 215 B5
Wilcox Cl SN2 ... 35 C2
Wild Acre 9 SN4 ... 163 A6
Wildern Sq SN3 ... 36 A4
Wilderness The BA15 ... 100 C7
Wildmoorway La GL7 ... 7 B7
Wiley Terr SP2 ... 144 D4
Wilkins Cl SN2 ... 35 F5
William Cl SP1 ... 146 D1
William Rd SN10 ... 214 D2
William St Calne SN11 ... 81 C4
Swindon SN1 ... 50 A5
Williams Gr SN13 ... 85 A8
Williamson Cl 3 SP11 ... 192 A5
Willis Cl
5 Chippenham SN15 ... 78 F4
Great Bedwyn SN8 ... 176 C3
Willis Way SN5 ... 33 B3
Willoughby Cl BA13 ... 108 E2
Willoughby Rd SP4 ... 197 E6
Willow Ave 5 SP6 ... 210 D1
Willow Cl
Laverstock SP1 ... 146 D2
Melksham SN12 ... 94 A3
Willow Cres
Broughton Gifford SN12 ... 93 A5
Warminster BA12 ... 117 C5
Willow Dr
Devizes SN10 ... 214 E5
4 Durrington SP4 ... 198 B7
Willow Gr
Chippenham SN15 ... 70 E2
Trowbridge BA14 ... 105 B5
Westbury BA13 ... 108 E3
Willow View BA14 ... 105 C3
Willow View Cl SN16 ... 27 F4
Willow Way SP7 ... 202 A4
Willow Wlk SN4 ... 64 B6
Willowbank SN14 ... 70 A2
Willowbrook SN5 ... 33 C4
Willowbrook End SN15 ... 57 D2
Willowherb Cl SN25 ... 34 E5
Willows Ave SN2 ... 35 C3
Willows The Calne SN11 ... 89 E8
Highworth SN6 ... 23 A5
Swindon SN5 ... 34 A2
Wills Ave SN1 ... 50 E8
Wilman Way SP2 ... 151 F5
Wilmot Cl SN5 ... 48 F6
Wilsford Group (Tumuli)*
SP4 ... 197 D2
Wilsford Rd SN9 ... 181 C5
Wilson Rd Larkhill SP4 ... 197 E6
Swindon SN25 ... 34 F6
Wilson Sq BA12 ... 117 C7
Wilton CE Mid Sch
SP2 ... 144 B4
Wilton Dr BA14 ... 105 D6
Wilton Fst Sch SP2 ... 144 B2
Wilton Ho* SP2 ... 144 D2
Wilton Mus* SP2 ... 144 D3
Wilton Pk* SP2 ... 144 D1
Wilton Rd
Barford St Martin SP3 ... 143 C3
East Grafton SN8 ... 184 A7
Quidhampton SP2 ... 144 F3
Wylye BA12 ... 201 F8
Wiltshire Ave SN2 ... 50 A8
Wiltshire Bassett Golf Club
SN4 ... 60 F7
Wiltshire Cl
Bulford SP4 ... 217 F8
3 Hungerford RG17 ... 177 B7
Wiltshire Coll BA14 ... 105 B6
Wiltshire Cres SN12 ... 94 C3
Wiltshire Dr 4 BA14 ... 105 D6
Wiltshire Heritage Mus*
SN10 ... 214 A3
Wiltshire Rd SP2 ... 151 E6
Wiltshire Way BA13 ... 109 A4
Wimpole Cl SN3 ... 51 B4
Win Gn View 7 SP7 ... 202 D2
Winchester Cl
Amesbury SP4 ... 217 D2
2 Chippenham SN14 ... 78 A6
North Bradley BA14 ... 105 C2
Swindon SN3 ... 36 B1
Winchester St SP1 ... 146 B1
Wincombe Bsns Pk
SP7 ... 202 C3
Wincombe La SP7 ... 202 D2
Wincombe Pk* SP7 ... 202 D3
Windbrook Mdw SN2 ... 36 A4
Windermere SN3 ... 51 D3
Windermere Rd BA14 ... 101 E2
Windflower Rd SN25 ... 34 E5
Winding Way SP2 ... 145 B3
Windlass Way SN15 ... 78 E5
Windlesham Rd SP1 ... 146 B4
Windmill Cl
3 Aldbourne SN8 ... 170 A7
Alderbury SP5 ... 153 E2
4 Shaftesbury SP7 ... 202 C2
Windmill Hill (Causewayed
Enclosure)* SN4 ... 167 A2
Windmill Hill Bsns Pk
SN5 ... 48 F3
Windmill Hill CP Sch
SN1 ... 49 A3
Windmill La
Hurstbourne Tarrant
SP11 ... 193 F8
Winterbourne SP4 ... 133 B4
Windmill Piece SN4 ... 65 D4
Windmill Rd GL7 ... 4 F8
Windmill Tump (Long
Barrow)* GL7 ... 3 A7
Windrush SN6 ... 22 E5
Windrush Rd SN25 ... 35 A3
Windsor Ave SN12 ... 94 B3
Windsor Cl
Chippenham SN14 ... 78 A6
Lydiard Tregoze SN4 ... 47 F6
Windsor Cres BA11 ... 110 A5
Windsor Dr
Devizes SN10 ... 214 D3
1 Trowbridge BA14 ... 105 B5
Westbury BA13 ... 109 B4
Windsor Mews 8 SP4 ... 198 B7
Windsor Rd
Calne Without SN11 ... 81 F1
9 Durrington/Bulford
SP4 ... 198 B7
North Bradley BA14 ... 105 E4
9 Salisbury SP2 ... 145 F1
Swindon SN3 ... 50 F2
Windsor St 10 SP2 ... 145 F1
Windwhistle Cnr SP7 ... 202 E2
Windwhistle La
Alderbury SP5 ... 160 B7
Grimstead SP5 ... 154 B1
Windwhistle Way SP5 ... 153 F2
Wine St
Bradford-on-Avon BA15 ... 100 C6
Devizes SN10 ... 214 B3
Wing Rd SP4 ... 198 E6
Wingate Par SN2 ... 35 A2
Wingfield SN2 ... 36 A5
Wingfield Ave SN2 ... 35 C6
Wingfield Prim Sch
BA14 ... 104 C6
Wingfield Rd BA14 ... 105 A7
Winifred St SN1 ... 50 D3
Winkelbury Hill (Hill Fort)*
SP7 ... 207 C8
Winkins La SN15 ... 44 A2
Winkworth Cottage
SN16 ... 29 C2
Winlaw Cl SN5 ... 49 C7
Winscombe Ct BA11 ... 110 B5
Winsley CE Sch BA15 ... 99 E7
Winsley Cl SN2 ... 35 C4
Winsley Hill BA2 ... 99 B6
Winsley Rd BA15 ... 100 B7
Winstanley Cl 8 SN5 ... 49 A4
Winston Rd SN12 ... 93 F1
Winter Gn SN11 ... 80 F3
Winterbourne Earls Sch
SP4 ... 133 A1
Winterbourne Stoke Group
(Tumuli)* SP4 ... 197 C4
Winterslow Prim Sch
SP5 ... 149 B6
Winterslow Rd
Idmiston SP4 ... 198 C1
Porton SP4 ... 133 D6
Swindon SN2 ... 35 B5
2 Trowbridge BA14 ... 105 B5
Winton Cl SP9 ... 216 D4
Winwick Rd SN5 ... 49 B4
Wirr The SP3 ... 128 D7
Wirral Way SN25 ... 34 F7
Wise La SP3 ... 141 A2
Wiseman Cl 2 SN3 ... 51 E6
Wishart Way SN15 ... 78 F5
Wishford Prim Sch
SP2 ... 130 A4
Wishford Rd SP2 ... 144 B5
Witan Cl 8 SP10 ... 193 E2
Witchcombe La SN10 ... 179 B1
Witchell La SN10 ... 180 B3
Witfield Cl SN5 ... 33 B5
Witham Way SN2 ... 35 F4
Witherington Rd
Alderbury SP5 ... 153 C2
Downton SP5 ... 159 C5
Witherington Ring (Field
System)* SP5 ... 159 D7
Witheys The 10 SN4 ... 163 A6
Withies The SN8 ... 175 D1
Withy Bed SN4 ... 61 C1
Withy Cl
Trowbridge BA14 ... 101 E3
Wootton Bassett SN4 ... 47 D3
Withybed La RG17 ... 177 F5
Withymead Rd SN14 ... 74 A8
Witt Rd SP5 ... 149 D5
Wittenham View 7 SP4 ... 217 C2
Wittensford La SO51 ... 212 F1
Witton Windmill*
SN8 ... 184 B8
Witts La SN5 ... 33 B5
Wivenhoe Ct 7 BA11 ... 110 C6
Woburn Cl
Swindon SN25 ... 34 F6
Trowbridge BA14 ... 105 A8
Wolferstan Dr SP1 ... 146 D5
Wolfhall Rd SN8 ... 183 D8
Wolsely Ave SN3 ... 51 A4
Wolverton Cl SN14 ... 77 F6
Wood H Dr SN2 ... 34 D3
Wood La
Brinkworth SN15 ... 46 D7
Chapmanslade BA13 ... 111 D4
Chippenham SN15 ... 78 E6
Fonthill Gifford SP3 ... 200 C2
Lydiard Millicent SN5 ... 32 A1
Nettleton SN14 ... 67 B8
Purton SN5 ... 31 E1
Sherston GL8 ... 25 B5
Wood Rd SP4 ... 198 A6
Wood St Calne SN11 ... 81 B3
Clyffe Pypard SN4 ... 61 D1
Swindon SN1 ... 50 D4
Wootton Bassett SN4 ... 47 D2
Woodborough CE Sch
SN9 ... 181 C6
Woodborough Cl
BA14 ... 105 D5
Woodborough Rd
Beechingstoke SN9 ... 181 B6
Corsham SN13 ... 85 B7
Pewsey SN9 ... 215 A5
Woodbury RG17 ... 165 B1
Woodbury Cl 2 SN5 ... 49 A8
Woodbury Gdns SP2 ... 152 A5
Woodchester SN5 ... 49 C5
Woodcock Cl SP9 ... 216 D6
Woodcock Gdns BA12 ... 117 C6
Woodcock Ind Est
BA12 ... 117 D7
Woodcock La BA12 ... 117 B7
Woodcock Rd BA12 ... 117 C6
Woodcombe SN12 ... 94 C6
Woodcote Rd SN8 ... 185 B8
Woodfern SP6 ... 210 F1
Woodfolds SN16 ... 15 F7
Woodford Cl 3 SN2 ... 35 C6
Woodford Prim Sch
SP4 ... 131 C5
Woodhayes Rd BA11 ... 110 C6
Woodhenge* SP4 ... 217 A7
Woodhill Ave SN11 ... 81 C3
Woodhill Pk* SN4 ... 166 E7
Woodhill Rise SN11 ... 81 C4
Woodhill Village*
SN4 ... 166 D8
Woodhouse Castle (rems
of)* BA12 ... 114 E1
Woodhouse Gdns
BA14 ... 102 B2
Woodland Dr SP5 ... 149 B6
Woodland Pk SN11 ... 81 B2
Woodland Rd
Patney SN10 ... 180 F5
2 Warminster BA12 ... 116 E6
Woodland View
Westbury BA13 ... 112 B8
Wroughton SN4 ... 50 B1
Woodland Way
Devizes SN10 ... 214 A1
Salisbury SP1 ... 146 E2
Woodlands SN13 ... 76 E2
Woodlands Cty Fst Sch
SP2 ... 145 B4
Woodlands La SP7 ... 203 E1
Woodlands Manor*
BA12 ... 139 A3
Woodlands Rd
Chippenham SN14 ... 78 C8
Mere BA12 ... 139 B2
Mildenhall SN8 ... 169 A1
Pewsey SN9 ... 215 D4
Woodlea SN14 ... 75 C6
Woodlea Grange SP5 ... 153 E2
Woodling Cres SP6 ... 210 F1
Woodman Mead 5
BA12 ... 116 F7
Woodmarsh BA14 ... 105 D4
Woodpecker Mews
SN14 ... 70 B2
Woodroffe Sq SN11 ... 81 C2
Woodrow SN12 ... 94 D7
Woodrow Rd SN12 ... 94 C6
Woods Cl SN16 ... 25 C1
Woods Hill BA2 ... 99 A6
Woods's La SP3 ... 200 F2
Woodsage Way SN11 ... 80 F3
Woodshaw Mead 8 SN4 ... 48 A2
Woodside Ave SN3 ... 50 E5
Woodside Rd
Salisbury SP2 ... 145 C3
South Marston Park SN3 ... 36 C7
Woodstock Gdns SN12 ... 94 B3
Woodstock Rd SP1 ... 146 B2
Woodvill Rd SP1 ... 146 D4
Woodway Cotts GL9 ... 24 E5
Woolands La 1 SP7 ... 202 B2
Woolcott La SP8 ... 137 D1
Wooley Dr BA15 ... 100 E7
Woolford Grange 2 SN4 . 48 A2
Woollaton Cl SN5 ... 49 A5
Woolley Cl BA15 ... 100 E7
Woolley Dr BA15 ... 100 E7
Woolley St BA15 ... 100 E6
Woolley Terr BA15 ... 100 E7
Woolmer Dro SN8 ... 168 F6
Woolpack Mdws BA14 ... 105 E7
Wootton Bassett Inf Sch
SN4 ... 47 C1
Wootton Bassett Mus*
SN4 ... 47 D1
Wootton Bassett Rd
SN5 ... 49 E5
Wootton Bassett Sch
SN4 ... 47 D2
Wor Barrow (Long Barrow)*
SP5 ... 208 C4
Worcester Lodge*
GL9 ... 24 A3
Wordsworth Cl 1 SN4 ... 47 F3
Wordsworth Rd SP1 ... 146 B2
Worlidge Dr SN5 ... 49 B8
Wormcliff La SN13 ... 83 A4
Worsley Rd SN5 ... 49 A4
Worsted Cl BA14 ... 105 E7
Wortheys Cl SN16 ... 28 A5
Worton & Marston Sch
SN10 ... 179 B4
Worton Rd SN10 ... 179 C4
Wouldham Cl SP11 ... 191 F4
Wren Cl Frome BA11 ... 110 B7
3 Warminster BA12 ... 116 E5
Wren Ct BA14 ... 105 B8
Wrenscroft 8 SP2 ... 152 A5
Wrenswood SN3 ... 51 D8
Wroughton Airfield
SN4 ... 63 F2
Wroughton Cty Inf Sch
SN4 ... 64 A6
Wroughton Cty Jun Sch
SN4 ... 64 A7
Wych Elm Rd BA11 ... 110 C6
Wychurch Rd 4 SN16 ... 28 A5
Wyck Village* SP3 ... 203 E7
Wycombe Cl SN11 ... 79 F2
Wycombe La SN10 ... 172 F1
Wyke Rd BA14 ... 101 E4
Wylye Cl Swindon SN25 ... 34 F4
Warminster BA12 ... 116 F5
Wylye Rd
Steeple Langford SP3 ... 128 B7
Tidworth SP9 ... 216 D7
Warminster BA12 ... 117 A5
Wylye BA12 ... 201 F8
Wyncies The SN6 ... 163 E6
Wynd The SN11 ... 81 B4
Wyndham Cl SN15 ... 79 A8
Wyndham La SP4 ... 199 A2
Wyndham Pk Sch SP1 ... 146 B3
Wyndham Rd
Salisbury SP1 ... 146 A2
Swindon SN2 ... 50 A7
Wyndham Terr SP1 ... 146 B2
Wynford Rd BA11 ... 110 B6
Wynndale Cl SN3 ... 36 A4
Wynsome St BA14 ... 104 F3
Wynwards Rd SN25 ... 35 A5
Wythburn Rd BA11 ... 110 C5
Wyvern Ave SN11 ... 81 C3
Wyvern Cl SN1 ... 50 C2
Wyvern Coll SP1 ... 146 E3
Wyvern Rd SP4 ... 198 E6
Wyvern Wlk BA13 ... 108 E3
Wyville Rd BA11 ... 110 C6

Y

Yard La SN15 ... 96 D7
Yard's La SN9 ... 181 C5
Yardley Cl SN2 ... 34 F2
Yarmley La SP5 ... 149 B6
Yarmouth Cl SN5 ... 49 B4
Yarnbrook Rd
Steeple Ashton BA14 ... 102 E1
West Ashton BA14 ... 105 F2
Yarnbury Castle (Fort)*
BA12 ... 196 B3
Yarnton Cl SN5 ... 49 A8
Yatton Rd SN14 ... 68 E1
Yeatmans Cl 6 SP7 ... 202 B2
Yeatmans La 3 SP7 ... 202 B2
Yeats Cl SN25 ... 35 A8
Yellow Way Rd BA11 ... 118 A5
Yeoman Cl
5 Market Lavington SN10 . 179 F1
Swindon SN5 ... 49 A7
Yeoman Way BA14 ... 105 C7
Yeovil Cl SN3 ... 51 B5
Yerbury St 1 BA14 ... 105 E8
Yew Tree Cl Calne SN11 ... 81 A3
Chirton SN10 ... 180 F4
The Common SP5 ... 149 B6
Yew Tree Gdns SN3 ... 36 E4
Yew Tree La SN4 ... 167 C7
Yews The BA12 ... 139 A6
Yewstock Cres W SN15 ... 70 C1
Yewtree Cl 8 SP4 ... 198 C7
Yiewsley Cres SN3 ... 36 B2
Yockney Cl SN13 ... 76 E1
Yonder Way 7 SN4 ... 163 A6
York Bldgs BA14 ... 101 D1
York Cl
Chippenham SN14 ... 78 A6
Corsham SN13 ... 76 F2
York Dro SP5 ... 212 C4
York La SN15 ... 46 A7
York Rd
7 Hungerford RG17 ... 177 B6
Lyneham SN15 ... 60 B2
Salisbury SP2 ... 145 F1
Stapleford SP3 ... 197 B1
Swindon SN1 ... 50 D6
Upavon Down SN9 ... 182 B1
Youngs Paddock SP5 ... 149 C6
Yule Hill SP3 ... 203 F6

Z

Zeals Fst Sch BA12 ... 138 A4
Zeals Gn Dr BA12 ... 138 A4
Zeals Rise BA12 ... 137 F4
Zig Zag Hill SP7 ... 206 C7
Zion Rd SP11 ... 199 F3
Zouch Ave SP9 ... 216 C7
Zouch Cl SP9 ... 216 C7
Zouch Farm Rd SP9 ... 216 C7
Zouch Prim Sch SP9 ... 216 B8

Notes

Using the Ordnance Survey National Grid

Any feature in this atlas can be given a unique reference to help you find the same feature on other Ordnance Survey maps of the area, or to help someone else locate you if they do not have a Street Atlas.

The grid squares in this atlas match the Ordnance Survey National Grid and are at 500 metre intervals. The small figures at the bottom and sides of every other grid line are the National Grid kilometre values (**00** to **99** km) and are repeated across the country every 100 km (see left).

To give a unique National Grid reference you need to locate where in the country you are. The country is divided into 100 km squares with each square given a unique two-letter reference. Use the administrative map to determine in which 100 km square a particular page of this atlas falls.

The bold letters and numbers between each grid line (**A** to **F**, **1** to **8**) are for use within a specific Street Atlas only, and when used with the page number, are a convenient way of referencing these grid squares.

***Example** The railway bridge over DARLEY GREEN RD in grid square B1*

Step 1: Identify the two-letter reference, in this example the page is in **SP**

Step 2: Identify the 1 km square in which the railway bridge falls. Use the figures in the southwest corner of this square: Eastings **17**, Northings **74**. This gives a unique reference: **SP 17 74**, accurate to 1 km.

Step 3: To give a more precise reference accurate to 100 m you need to estimate how many tenths along and how many tenths up this 1 km square the feature is (to help with this the 1 km square is divided into four 500 m squares). This makes the bridge about **8** tenths along and about **1** tenth up from the southwest corner.

This gives a unique reference: **SP 178 741**, accurate to 100 m.

Eastings (read from left to right along the bottom) come before Northings (read from bottom to top). If you have trouble remembering say to yourself "Along the hall, THEN up the stairs"!

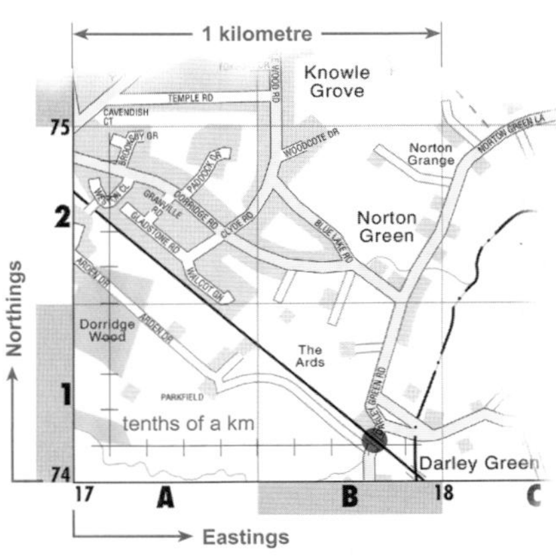

Addresses

Name and Address	Telephone	Page	Grid reference

Name and Address	Telephone	Page	Grid reference

Street Atlases from Philip's

Philip's publish an extensive range of regional and local street atlases which are ideal for motoring, business and leisure use. They are widely used by the emergency services and local authorities throughout Britain.

Key features include:

- **Superb county-wide mapping at an extra-large scale of 3½ inches to 1 mile, or 2½ inches to 1 mile in pocket editio**
- **Complete urban and rural coverage, detailing every named street in town and country**
- **Each atlas available in three handy formats – hardback, spiral, pocket paperback**

'The mapping is very clear... great in scope and value'

★★★★ BEST BUY AUTO EXPRESS

1 Bedfordshire
2 Berkshire
3 Birmingham and West Midlands
4 Bristol and Bath
5 Buckinghamshire
6 Cambridgeshire
7 Cardiff, Swansea and The Valleys
8 Cheshire
9 Derbyshire
10 Dorset
11 County Durham and Teesside
12 Edinburgh and East Central Scotland
13 North Essex
14 South Essex
15 Glasgow and Wes Central Scotland
16 Gloucestershire
17 North Hampshire
18 South Hampshire
19 Hertfordshire
20 East Kent
21 West Kent
22 Lancashire
23 Leicestershire and Rutland
24 London
25 Greater Manchest
26 Merseyside
27 Northamptonshire
28 Nottinghamshire
29 Oxfordshire
30 Staffordshire
31 Surrey
32 East Sussex
33 West Sussex
34 Tyne and Wear and Northumberland
35 Warwickshire
36 Wiltshire and Swindon
37 East Yorkshire and Northern Lincolnshi
38 North Yorkshire
39 South Yorkshire
40 West Yorkshire

How to order

The Philip's range of street atlases is available from good retailers or directly from the publisher by phoning 01903 828503